Overview

Contents

Acknowledgments

We would like to thank Greg Croy, Acquisitions Editor at Sams Publishing, for asking us to write this book.

Thanks also to Kitty Wilson, the production editor of this book, and Phil Paxton, the development editor of this book.

We would also like to thank Wayne Blankenbeckler and Keith Davenport, who helped in the creation of the CD of this book.

About the Authors

Ori Gurewich and **Nathan Gurewich** are the authors of several best-selling books in the area of Visual Basic for Windows, C/C++ programming, multimedia programming, communications, and database design and programming.

Ori Gurewich has an electrical engineering degree from Stony Brook University, New York. His background includes positions as senior software engineer and software consultant engineer for companies developing professional DOS, Windows, and Windows NT applications.

Nathan Gurewich has a master's degree in electrical engineering from Columbia University, New York, New York, and a bachelor's degree in electrical engineering from Hofstra University, Long Island, New York. Nathan has been involved in the design and implementation of commercial software packages for the PC. Nathan is an expert in the field of PC programming and PC software marketing.

Ori and Nathan can be contacted via CompuServe (CompuServe ID 72072,312).

1

Introduction: Developing Powerful Windows Applications with Visual Basic

1

Welcome to the fascinating world of Visual Basic. The word *Basic* in Visual Basic is misleading. You might think that to develop professional, powerful Windows applications you have to use a programming language such as C/C++. However, this is not the case at all. As you'll discover in this book, Visual Basic has a lot of programming power that enables you to design powerful, state-of-the-art Windows applications. The good news is that you can develop such Windows applications in a fraction of the time it takes to develop the same applications with programming languages such as C, Microsoft Visual C++, and Borland C++ 4.0.

So relax and prepare yourself for a very pleasant journey.

Does Visual Basic Have Enough Features?

The designers of Visual Basic predicted that during the development of your Visual Basic programs you'll need features that are not incorporated into the Visual Basic language. Visual Basic was designed as a highly modular object-oriented programming language that enables you to plug in other software modules with great ease. In particular, you can use dynamic linked libraries (DLLs) and VBX controls from within your Visual Basic programs. You can use VBX controls and DLLs designed by others, or you can write your own DLLs and VBX controls for Visual Basic. In this book you'll also learn how to write your own DLLs and VBX controls.

Granting Your PC the Power of Speech

This book assumes that you are already familiar with Visual Basic. However, if you feel that you need a quick tutorial that shows you how to use Visual Basic, start by reading Appendixes A, B, and C. The tutorial presented in these appendixes demonstrates how easy it is to write Windows programs with Visual Basic. In particular, the tutorial teaches you how to write a simple program called the ItsFun program. The ItsFun program is similar to the "standard" Hello World program that is presented at the beginning of many programming books. However, unlike the "regular" Hello World program that just displays the text `Hello World` on the screen, the ItsFun program also grants your PC the power of speech. The ItsFun program causes your PC to speak in human voice through the PC speaker. You don't need any sound card, and you don't need any software drivers.

> **NOTE**
>
> Even if you are familiar with Visual Basic, it is highly recommended that you browse through the tutorial presented in Appendixes A, B, and C. This tutorial contains information that is important for using this book, as well as conventions used in the book.

How This Book Is Organized

This book presents real-world applications. It shows how they work and how to implement them. The most desired Windows applications are covered in great detail in this book. Even if you are planning to write applications different from the ones in this book, by learning to write this book's applications, you'll learn how real-world Windows features are implemented with Visual Basic.

In Chapter 2, "Creating Animation Programs (Part I)," and Chapter 3, "Creating Animation Programs (Part II)," you'll learn to write the Just4Fun program. (See Figure 1.1.) This program shows you how to create synchronized animation.

Figure 1.1.
The main window of the Just4Fun program.

Through a sequence of pictures such as the ones shown in Figures 1.2 through 1.4, you'll see a man approach a woman and ask her to dance, and then through a sequence of another set of pictures, you'll see the couple dance to music.

1

Figure 1.2.
A picture used in the animation script of the Just4Fun program. A man approaching a woman.

Figure 1.3.
A picture used in the animation script of the Just4Fun program. A man asking a woman to dance.

Figure 1.4.
A picture used in the
animation script of the
Just4Fun program. A
woman getting up to dance
with a man.

In Chapter 4, "Creating Multimedia Programs (Part I)," and Chapter 5, "Creating Multimedia Programs (Part II)," you'll learn how to write the AllMedia application. As you know, Windows comes with the famous Media Player program (which usually resides inside the Accessories group of programs, as shown in Figure 1.5).

Figure 1.5.
The Accessories group of
programs with the Media
Player program in it.

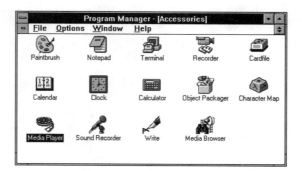

Figure 1.6 shows the main window of the Media Player program.

Figure 1.6.
The Media Player
program.

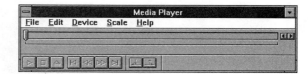

The Media Player program is a multimedia program that lets you play WAV and MIDI files through a sound card, play AVI video files, and play CD audio.

The AllMedia program that you'll develop yourself in Chapters 4 and 5 is similar in functionality to the AllMedia program. However, the AllMedia program is by far more powerful than the Media Player program. To begin with, like the Media Player program, the AllMedia program lets you play WAV and MIDI files through a sound card, it lets you play AVI video files, and it lets you play CD audio. However, unlike the Media Player program, the AllMedia program also lets you play WAV files through the PC speaker without any sound card and without any drivers. Also unlike the Media Player program, the AllMedia program lets you record WAV files with the sound card, and it lets you manipulate WAV files by providing you with a full WAV editor program. The WAV editor lets you perform operations such as Copy, Cut, and Paste.

Figure 1.7 shows the main window of the AllMedia program.

Figure 1.7.
The main window of the
AllMedia program.

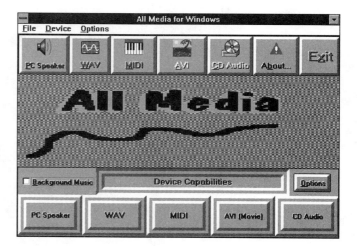

Figures 1.8 through 1.13 show some of the windows of the AllMedia application.

Figure 1.8.
The PC Speaker window.

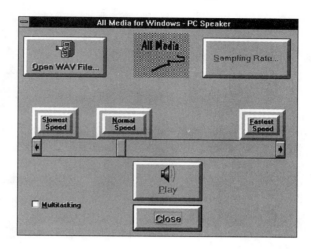

Figure 1.9.
The Wave Editor window.

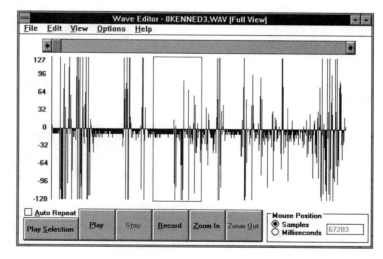

8

Figure 1.10.
The MIDI window.

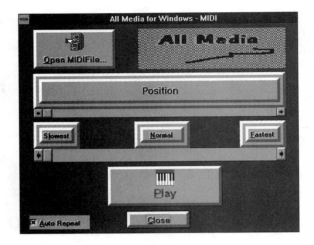

Figure 1.11.
The Movie window.

Figure 1.12.
Displaying movies with the
AllMedia application.

Figure 1.13.
The CD Player window.

In Chapter 6, "Creating a Multiple-Document Interface Text Editor Application (Part I)," and Chapter 7, "Creating a Multiple-Document Interface Text Editor Application (Part II)," you'll learn how to implement the Multipad application. Recall that Windows comes with the Notepad program (which usually resides inside the Accessories group of programs, as shown in Figure 1.14).

The main window of the Notepad program is shown in Figure 1.15.

Figure 1.14.
The Accessories group of
programs with the Notepad
program in it.

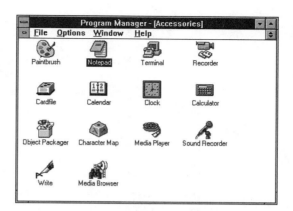

Figure 1.15.
The main window of the
Notepad program.

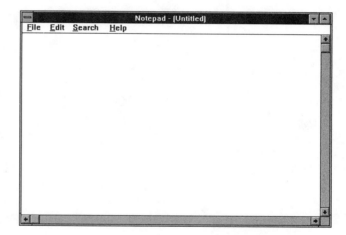

As you know, the Notepad program lets you open one file at a time. That is, the Notepad program is not a multiple-document interface (MDI) program.

The Multipad program that you'll write in Chapters 6 and 7 is a program similar to Notepad. However, the Multipad program is an MDI program, and has other features that do not exist in Notepad. The main window of the Multipad program is shown in Figure 1.16.

As you can see from Figures 1.17 and 1.18, the Multipad application lets you open several documents at once, and it behaves like a standard MDI program.

In Chapter 8, "Creating Database Applications (Part I)," and Chapter 9, "Creating Database Applications (Part II)," you'll learn how to write the TelBase application. (See Figure 1.19.)

The TelBase application lets you view data from a database. In particular, the TelBase application uses a database that contains phone numbers. In addition to letting you view the data of the database, the TelBase application lets you dial the phone numbers by using the modem. This type of application is commonly used by telemarketing businesses.

1

Figure 1.16.
The main window of the
Multipad application.

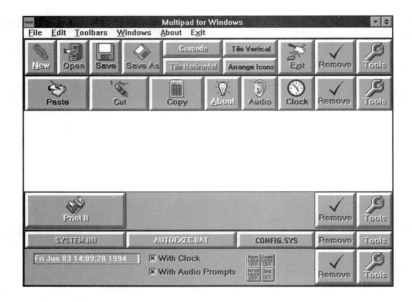

Figure 1.17.
Opening three documents
with the Multipad
program.

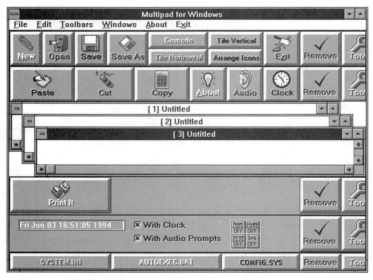

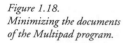
Figure 1.18.
Minimizing the documents
of the Multipad program.

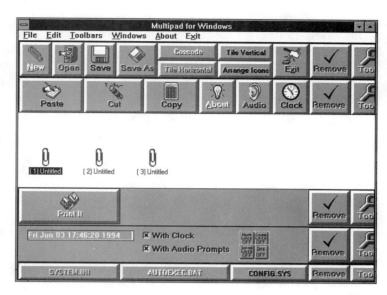

Figure 1.19.
The TelBase application.

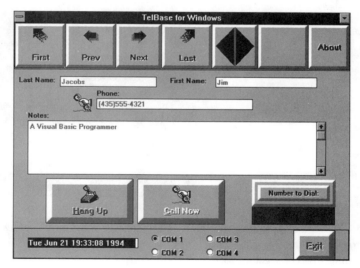

In Chapter 10, "Creating Card Game Programs (Part I)," and Chapter 11, "Creating Card Game Programs (Part II)," you'll learn how to implement a card game. (See Figures 1.20 and 1.21.)

1

Figure 1.20.
The 10 cards of the Cards
program, with the cards'
faces hidden.

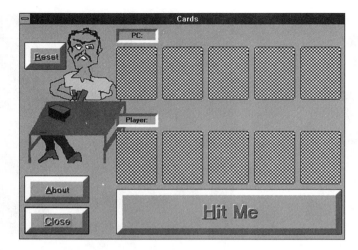

Figure 1.21.
The 10 dealt cards of the
Cards program.

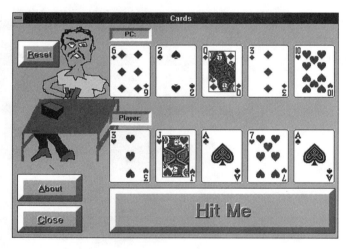

In Chapter 12, "Creating Dice Game Programs (Part I)," and Chapter 13, "Creating Dice Game Programs (Part II)," you'll learn how to create the Dice program. As implied by its name, this program lets you play games with dice. (See Figure 1.22.)

In Chapter 14, "Creating 3D Virtual Reality–Based Programs (Part I)," and Chapter 15, "Creating 3D Virtual Reality–Based Programs (Part II)," you'll learn how to implement 3D virtual reality–based programs. The Room program that you'll write demonstrates how you can let your users "travel" inside a 3D room. (See Figures 1.23 through 1.27.)

Figure 1.22.
Playing dice games with the
Dice program.

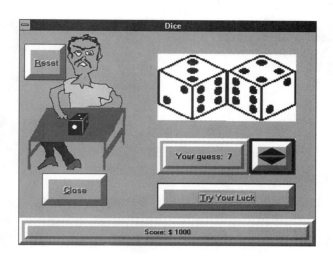

Figure 1.23.
Traveling inside a 3D
room (away from the
picture on the wall).

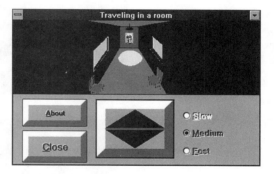

Figure 1.24.
Traveling inside a 3D
room (moving toward the
picture on the wall).

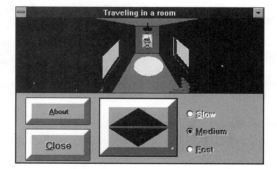

1

Figure 1.25.
Traveling inside a 3D
room (getting a bit closer to
the picture on the wall).

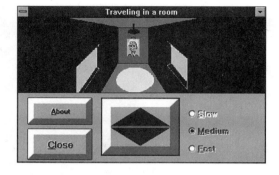

Figure 1.26.
Traveling inside a 3D
room (getting very close to
the picture on the wall).

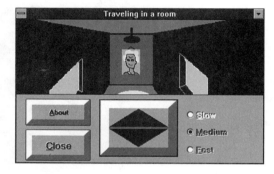

Figure 1.27.
Traveling inside a 3D
room (reaching the picture
on the wall).

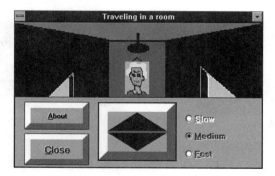

In Chapter 16, "Using the Joystick (Part I)," and Chapter 17, "Using the Joystick (Part II)," you'll
learn how to use the joystick from within your Visual Basic programs. (See Figures 1.28 and 1.29.)

Figure 1.28.
Shooting bullets with the
Joystick program.

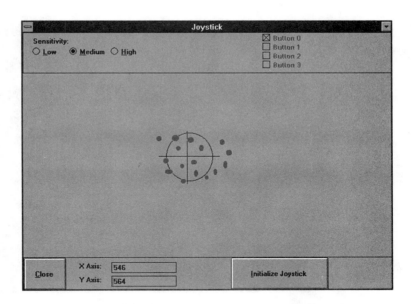

Figure 1.29.
Tearing apart the target
with the Joystick program.

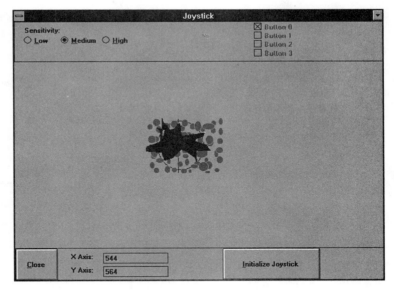

In Chapter 17 you'll also learn how to integrate all the game programs into one program. (See Figure 1.30.)

1

Figure 1.30.
Integrating all the game
programs.

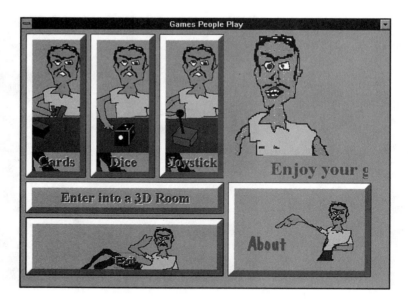

In Chapter 18, "Visual Basic Tools: Creating Dynamic Linked Libraries for Visual Basic," you'll learn how to write DLLs for Visual Basic. You'll write a DLL, and then you'll write a Visual Basic program that tests your DLL. (See Figure 1.31.)

Figure 1.31.
Writing a Visual Basic
program that tests your
DLL.

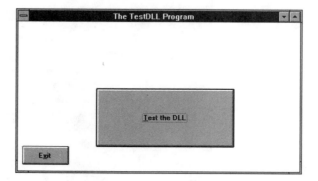

In Chapter 19, "Creating Your Own VBX Controls," you'll learn how to write custom controls (VBX files) for Visual Basic. As you'll see, once you write the custom controls, the custom controls will appear in the Tools window the same way as other controls. (See Figure 1.32.)

In Chapter 20, "Preparing Your Visual Basic Programs for Distribution and Preparing an Install Program," you'll learn how to prepare your application for distribution, and you'll also learn how to create distribution disks that include a sophisticated Install program.

As stated, Appendixes A, B, and C show you how to create a simple Visual Basic program that grants your PC the power of speech.

Figure 1.32.
Adding the custom control
(VBX) that you write in
Chapter 19 to the Tools
window of Visual Basic.

Appendix D contains a multimedia reference.

Appendix E explains in detail how to use and implement the Wave Editor program.

Appendix F explains how to install the AVI drivers (included on this book's CD). These drivers are needed for playing AVI video files on your PC.

Prototyping Your Visual Basic Programs

Visual Basic is a relatively easy programming language. One of the most important features of Visual Basic is its capability to show you how the application will look before writing a single line of code. That is, before writing the code of your application, you design the various windows of the application that you are implementing. This lets you add cosmetics to your application and fine-tune your application with great ease. In fact, as you'll see throughout this book, the applications that you'll design will consist of two parts. In the first part you'll design the prototype of the application, and in the second part you'll actually write the code of the application. For example, in Chapter 2 you'll write the prototype of the animation program, and in Chapter 3 you'll write the code of the animation program.

Using Third-Party Runtime Software Modules

One of the main advantages of using a modular object-oriented programming language such as Visual Basic lies in its ability to use software modules such as DLLs and VBX controls. This is a great advantage that can save you a lot of time: Instead of spending time developing DLLs and VBX controls yourself, you can spend your development time learning how to use off-the-shelf DLLs and VBX controls and using them from within your Visual Basic programs.

1

NOTE

Throughout this book, you'll use several DLLs and VBX controls that are included with this book's CD.

The sole purpose of providing these DLLs and VBX controls is so that you'll be able to execute the EXE programs that are included on the book's CD.

NOTE

If you own the VBX files that are needed by some of the programs of this book, you'll have to add the VBX control to your projects. That is, when creating a new project, you have to select New Project from the File menu, and then you add the required VBX control to your project as follows:

☐ Select Add File from the File menu.

Visual Basic responds by displaying the Add File dialog box.

☐ Select the VBX file that you want to add to your project. (Typically the VBX files reside inside the \Windows\System window.)

Visual Basic responds by adding the VBX control to the Tools window of the project.

Figures 1.33 through 1.46 show some of the VBX controls used in this book.

Figure 1.33.
The TegoMM.VBX control
(advanced multimedia
control for playing WAV
files, MIDI files, AVI video
files, CD audio, Joystick,
PC Speaker, and other
multimedia-related tasks).

Figure 1.34.
The MyClock.VBX control.
(You'll create this control in
Chapter 19.)

Figure 1.35.
The CMDIALOG.VBX control (the common dialog box control). This control comes with the standard Visual Basic Version 3.0 package.

Figure 1.36.
The MHCD200.VBX control (the cards control). This control comes with the Borland Visual Solution package.

Figure 1.37.
The MSCOMM.VBX control (the communication control). This control comes with the Visual Basic Version 3.0 Professional Edition package.

Figure 1.38.
The THREED.VBX control (the 3D command button control). This control comes with the Visual Basic Version 3.0 Professional Edition package.

Figure 1.39.
The SPIN.VBX control (the spin control). This control comes with the Visual Basic Version 3.0 Professional Edition package.

Figure 1.40.
The MHDC200.VBX control (the dice control). This control comes with the Borland Visual Solution package.

1

Figure 1.41.
The MHMQ200.VBX
control (the marquee
control). This control comes
with the Borland Visual
Solution package.

Figure 1.42.
The KEYSTAT.VBX
control (the keyboard status
control). This control comes
with the Visual Basic
Version 3.0 Professional
Edition package.

Figure 1.43.
The THREED.VBX
control (the 3D label
control). This control comes
with the Visual Basic
Version 3.0 Professional
Edition package.

Figure 1.44.
The THREED.VBX
control (the 3D checkbox
control). This control comes
with the Visual Basic
Version 3.0 Professional
Edition package.

Figure 1.45.
The THREED.VBX
control (the 3D option
button control). This
control comes with the
Visual Basic Version 3.0
Professional Edition
package.

Figure 1.46.
The THREED.VBX
control (the 3D frame
control). This control comes
with the Visual Basic
Version 3.0 Professional
Edition package.

All the other controls used by the applications that are discussed in this book come with the Standard Edition package of Visual Basic Version 3.0.

NOTE

Sometimes the lines of code in Visual Basic can be long. In fact, they can be too long to fit on a single line in this book. Therefore, the code continuation character, ➡, is used in this book to indicate that the code following this character must be typed on the previous line.

For example, the following code:

```
MyString = "This is
    ➡ My String.
    ➡ "
```

must be typed in Visual Basic on a single line, as follows:

```
MyString = "This is My String."
```

Installing the Book's CD

This book comes with a CD. The CD contains all the EXE files of the applications, source code of the applications, BMP picture files, Icon files, WAV files, MIDI files, AVI video files, and other files that are required for the execution of the EXE applications (for example, DLLs and VBX controls).

To install the book's CD do the following:

❑ Select Run from the File Manager of Windows and execute the X:\INSTALL.EXE program that resides on the CD. *X* represents the drive letter of your CD. For example, if your CD drive is installed as drive D, you have to execute the D:\INSTALL.EXE program, if your CD drive is installed as drive E, you execute the E:\INSTALL.EXE program, and so on.

Windows responds by executing the INSTALL.EXE program. The INSTALL.EXE program copies various files to your \Windows\System directory. The Install program also creates the C:\LearnVB directory and various subdirectories below the C:\LearnVB directory.

For example, the C:\LearnVB\WAV directory contains the WAV files, the C:\LearnVB\MIDI directory contains the MIDI files, and so on.

The Install program also creates the C:\LearnVB\Practice directory and the C:\LearnVB\Original directory.

1

The C:\LearnVB\Original directory contains the original files of the applications. For example, the C:\LearnVB\Original\AllMedia directory contains the original files of the AllMedia application, the C:\LearnVB\Original\MDI directory contains the original files of the Multipad application, and so on.

Throughout this book, you'll implement the book's applications inside the C:\Learn\Practice directory. For example, you'll implement the AllMedia application inside the C:\LearnVB\Practice\AllMedia directory, you'll implement the Multipad application inside the C:\LearnVB\Practice\MDI directory, and so on.

There is a lot of stuff to learn in this book. As you'll soon see, the book's applications are real-world applications for Windows. As you study each application, concentrate on the way a particular feature is implemented. For example, the Multipad program contains Save and Save As menu items. Once you understand the technique used, you can apply the technique for implementing this feature in your future Visual Basic projects.

As you know, there is practically no limit to the improvements and enhancements you can add to an application. Most of the chapters in this book include a section called "Further Enhancements—You Are on Your Own…" These sections contain some ideas about how you can further enhance and improve the applications by adding more features to them. Once you understand the applications, try to implement some of the enhancements suggested by the book (as well as some of your own ideas).

Finally, even if you are not planning to study and write the code of all the applications in this book, at least read the sections that explain how to execute the applications. This way, even if you currently don't need to write a similar application, you'll learn about the features that the application contains, and you'll get ideas regarding implementing your own Visual Basic projects.

2

Creating Animation Programs (Part I)

In this chapter you'll design the prototype of the Just4Fun program. This program performs animation.

Why Animation?

2

Animation is an important and an impressive feature that you can easily incorporate into your Visual Basic applications. Animation comes in handy in many applications. For example, you can incorporate animation into educational applications. You can also make your application (any type of application) more attractive by displaying an animated welcome message when your application starts or an animated good-bye message when your user terminates the application, or you can include an animated About dialog box, animated Help dialog box, animated icon, and so on.

The Specifications of the Just4Fun Program

Your objective now is to create a cartoon movie with Visual Basic. As always, you are not supposed to write a single line of code unless you have a complete set of specifications for the program.

Here are the specifications of the Just4Fun program:

- The name of the program is Just4Fun.EXE.
- This program displays a short cartoon movie.
- The script of the program is the following:

    Act I, Waiting, shows a woman sitting nervously on a bench, waiting for somebody to invite her to dance.

    Act II, Asking Her to Dance, shows a man approaching the woman and asking her to dance. The woman obliges, and they both go dancing.

    Act III, Dancing, shows the man and the woman dancing.

- When you start the program, Act I is displayed in an endless loop. The user can click the Exit button to terminate the program or click the Start Dance button to start the show. During the show, the user can click the Exit button to terminate the show or click the Stop button to stop the show.
- The program plays background music during the dance.
- The program displays the cartoon movie even on a PC that does not have a sound card.
- You should give users the ability to provide their own cartoon pictures for the movie. That is, users should be able to design their own cartoon movies.

Executing the Just4Fun.EXE Program

Before writing the Just4Fun program yourself, execute the copy of it that resides inside the C:\LearnVB\Original\Anim directory.

☐ Select Run from the File Manager, and execute the
C:\LearnVB\Original\Anim\Just4Fun.EXE program.

> *Windows responds by displaying the window shown in Figure 2.1. As you can see, Act I is displayed. This act is composed of four frames. The four frames of Act I are shown in Figures 2.2 through 2.5.*

Figure 2.1.
The main window of the
Just4Fun.EXE program
(Act I).

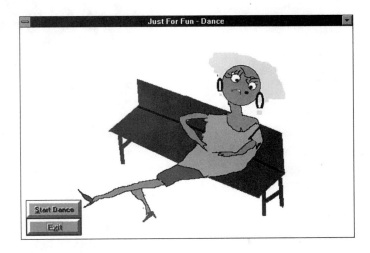

Figure 2.2.
Frame 1 of Act I
(Dance1.BMP).

2

Figure 2.3.
Frame 2 of Act I
(Dance2.BMP).

Figure 2.4.
Frame 3 of Act I
(Dance3.BMP).

Figure 2.5.
Frame 4 of Act I
(Dance4.BMP).

Note that Act I is played in an endless loop.

❑ Click the Start Dance button.

> *The Just4Fun program responds by displaying Act II. Act II is composed of three frames, which are shown in Figures 2.6 through 2.8.*

Figure 2.6.
Frame 1 of Act II
(Dance5.BMP).

2

Figure 2.7.
Frame 2 of Act II
(Dance6.BMP).

Figure 2.8.
Frame 3 of Act II
(Dance7.BMP).

The Just4Fun program then starts displaying Act III. Act III is composed of five frames. These five frames are shown in Figures 2.9 through 2.13.

Figure 2.9.
Frame 1 of Act III
(Dance8.BMP).

Figure 2.10.
Frame 2 of Act III
(Dance9.BMP).

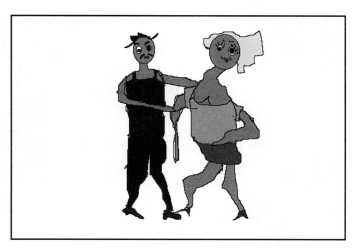

2

Figure 2.11.
Frame 3 of Act III
(Dance10.BMP).

Figure 2.12.
Frame 4 of Act III
(Dance11.BMP).

Figure 2.13.
Frame 5 of Act III
(Dance12.BMP).

Note that Act III is played in an endless loop. If you have a sound card, background music is played during the dance.

During the playback of the music, a picture of a man playing a horn is displayed whenever the music is played with a horn. The three BMP files that show the man playing his horn are shown in Figures 2.14 through 2.16.

Figure 2.14.
Frame 1 of a man playing
a horn (Horn1.BMP).

2

Figure 2.15.
Frame 2 of a man playing
a horn (Horn2.BMP).

Figure 2.16.
Frame 3 of a man playing
a horn (Horn3.BMP).

❑ Experiment with the Just4Fun program and then click its Exit button to terminate the program.

Building the Prototype of the Just4Fun Program

You'll now build the prototype of the Just4Fun program.

❑ Start Visual Basic.

❑ Select New Project from the File menu and save the new project as follows: Save the new form as DANCE.FRM in the C:\LearnVB\Practice\Anim directory. Save the new project as Just4Fun.MAK in the C:\LearnVB\Practice\Anim directory.

❑ Build the `frmDance` form according to the specifications in Table 2.1. When you finish building the form it should look like the one shown in Figure 2.17.

Table 2.1. The Properties table of the `frmDance` form.

Object: Form
Object Name: frmDance

BackColor	=	&H00FFFFFF&
BorderStyle	=	1 'Fixed Single

Comment: Setting the BorderStyle to Fixed Single prevents the user from changing the size of the form.

Caption	=	"Just For Fun - Dance"
ForeColor	=	&H00000000&
Height	=	6150
Icon	=	C:\LearnVB\Icons\Just4Fun.ICO
Left	=	465
MaxButton	=	0 'False

Comment: Setting the MaxButton to False prevents the user from maximizing the form.

ScaleHeight	=	5745
ScaleWidth	=	8685
Top	=	300
Width	=	8805

Object: 3D button
Object Name: cmdStartDance

Comment: This button serves as the Start Dance button and as the Stop button.

BevelWidth	=	5
Caption	=	"&Start Dance"
Font3D	=	2 'Raised w/heavy shading
ForeColor	=	&H00FF0000&
Height	=	495
Left	=	120
Top	=	4680
Width	=	1455

continues

Table 2.1. continued

2

Object: TegoMM.VBX (advanced multimedia control)
Object Name: TegommDance

Height	=	495
Left	=	2160
Top	=	4200
UpdateInterval	=	500

Comment: The timer of the control is set to 500 milliseconds.

Visible	=	0 'False
Width	=	3510

Object: 3D button
Object Name: cmdExit

Comment: This button serves as the Exit button.

BevelWidth	=	5
Caption	=	"E&xit"
Font3D	=	2 'Raised w/heavy shading
FontBold	=	-1 'True
FontName	=	"MS Sans Serif"
FontSize	=	9.75
ForeColor	=	&H000000FF&
Height	=	495
Left	=	120
Top	=	5160
Width	=	1455

Object: Image
Object Name: imgDance (array of images)

Comment: This is the image that is being displayed during the show.

Height	=	2295
Index	=	0

Comment: This is element imgDance(0).

Left	=	360
Stretch	=	-1 'True
Top	=	120
Width	=	6750

Object: Image
Object Name: imgDance

Comment: This image serves as Frame 1 of 4 in Act I.

BorderStyle   =   1 'Fixed Single

Comment: The border is set to Fixed Single so that during design time the object is identified easily.

Height   =   495

Index   =   1

Comment: This is element imgDance(1).

Left   =   3840

Stretch   =   -1 'True

Top   =   2640

Visible   =   0   'False

Width   =   510

Object: Image
Object Name: imgDance

Comment: This image serves as Frame 2 of 4 in Act I.

BorderStyle   =   1 'Fixed Single

Height   =   495

Index   =   2

Comment: This is element imgDance(2).

Left   =   4320

Stretch   =   -1 'True

Top   =   2640

Visible   =   0   'False

Width   =   510

Object: Image
Object Name: imgDance

Comment: This image serves as Frame 3 of 4 in Act I.

BorderStyle   =   1 'Fixed Single

Height   =   495

Index   =   3

Comment: This is element imgDance(3).

continues

2

Table 2.1. continued

Left	=	4800
Stretch	=	-1 'True
Top	=	2640
Visible	=	0 'False
Width	=	495

Object: Image
Object Name: imgDance

Comment: This image serves as Frame 4 of 4 in Act I.

BorderStyle	=	1 'Fixed Single
Height	=	495
Index	=	4

Comment: This is element imgDance(4).

Left	=	5280
Stretch	=	-1 'True
Top	=	2640
Visible	=	0 'False
Width	=	495

Object: Image
Object Name: imgDance

Comment: This image serves as Frame 1 of 3 in Act II.

BorderStyle	=	1 'Fixed Single
Height	=	495
Index	=	5

Comment: This is element imgDance(5).

Left	=	3840
Stretch	=	-1 'True
Top	=	3120
Visible	=	0 'False
Width	=	495

Object: Image
Object Name: imgDance

Comment: This image serves as Frame 2 of 3 in Act II.

BorderStyle	=	1 'Fixed Single
Height	=	495
Index	=	6

Comment: This is element imgDance(6).

Left	=	4320
Stretch	=	-1 'True
Top	=	3120
Visible	=	0 'False
Width	=	495

Object: Image
Object Name: imgDance

Comment: This image serves as Frame 3 of 3 in Act II.

BorderStyle	=	1 'Fixed Single
Height	=	495
Index	=	7

Comment: This is element imgDance(7).

Left	=	4800
Stretch	=	-1 'True
Top	=	3120
Visible	=	0 'False
Width	=	495

Object: Image
Object Name: imgDance

Comment: This image serves as Frame 1 of 5 in Act III.

BorderStyle	=	1 'Fixed Single
Height	=	495
Index	=	8

Comment: This is element imgDance(8).

Left	=	3840

continues

2

Table 2.1. continued

Stretch	= -1 'True
Top	= 3600
Visible	= 0 'False
Width	= 495

Object: Image
Object Name: imgDance

Comment: This image serves as Frame 2 of 5 in Act III.

BorderStyle	= 1 'Fixed Single
Height	= 495
Index	= 9

Comment: This is element imgDance(9).

Left	= 4320
Stretch	= -1 'True
Top	= 3600
Visible	= 0 'False
Width	= 495

Object: Image
Object Name: imgDance

Comment: This image serves as Frame 3 of 5 in Act III.

BorderStyle	= 1 'Fixed Single
Height	= 495
Index	= 10

Comment: This is element imgDance(10).

Left	= 4800
Stretch	= -1 'True
Top	= 3600
Visible	= 0 'False
Width	= 495

Object: Image
Object Name: imgDance

Comment: This image serves as Frame 4 of 5 in Act III.

BorderStyle	=	1 'Fixed Single
Height	=	495
Index	=	11

Comment: This is element imgDance(11).

Left	=	5280
Stretch	=	-1 'True
Top	=	3600
Visible	=	0 'False
Width	=	495

Object: Image
Object Name: imgDance

Comment: This image serves as Frame 5 of 5 in Act III.

BorderStyle	=	1 'Fixed Single
Height	=	495
Index	=	12

Comment: This is element imgDance(12).

Left	=	5760
Stretch	=	-1 'True
Top	=	3600
Visible	=	0 'False
Width	=	495

Object: Image
Object Name: imgHorn

Comment: imgHorn is an array of images. imgHorn(0) is the image that is being displayed during the playback of the horn.

Height	=	5535
Index	=	0

Comment: This is element imgHorn(0).

continues

2

Table 2.1. continued

Left	=	7080
Stretch	=	-1 'True
Top	=	120
Width	=	1575

Object: Image
Object Name: imgHorn

Comment: This image serves as Frame 1 of 3 in the man-playing-horn act.

BorderStyle	=	1 'Fixed Single
Height	=	495
Index	=	1

Comment: This is element imgHorn(1).

Left	=	2640
Top	=	4920
Visible	=	0 'False
Width	=	615

Object: Image
Object Name: imgHorn

Comment: This image serves as Frame 2 of 3 in the man-playing-horn act.

BorderStyle	=	1 'Fixed Single
Height	=	495
Index	=	2

Comment: This is element imgHorn(2).

Left	=	3240
Top	=	4920
Visible	=	0 'False
Width	=	615

Object: Image
Object Name: imgHorn

Comment: This image serves as Frame 3 of 3 in the man-playing-horn act.

BorderStyle	=	1 'Fixed Single
Height	=	495

Index   = 3
Comment: This is element imgHorn(3).
Left   = 3840
Top   = 4920
Visible   = 0   'False
Width   = 615

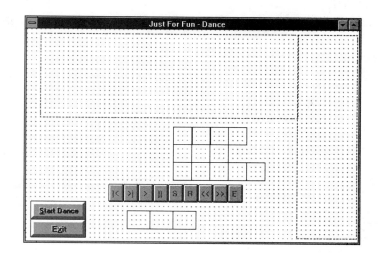

Figure 2.17.
The frmDance *form (in design mode).*

NOTE

Note that the Picture properties of the imgDance array of images and the Picture properties of the imgHorn array of images were not set to their corresponding BMP files in Table 2.1.

As you can guess, the Picture properties of these objects will be set from within the code at runtime. Why? There are 17 images in the form. If you set their Picture properties at design time, the Visual Basic program (during design time) is very slow! In fact, when the form contains many images it is almost impossible to work with the form at design time.

The "solution" is to load the BMP files into their corresponding Picture properties at runtime.

Attaching Code to the Click Event of the Exit Button

You'll now attach code to the Exit button of the frmDance form.

❑ Type the following code inside the cmdExit_Click() procedure of the frmDance form:

```
Sub cmdExit_Click ()

    End

End Sub
```

The code you entered terminates the Just4Fun program whenever the user clicks the Exit button.

Testing the Prototype

You have finished implementing the prototype. Now you can see how the program looks so far.

❑ Select Save Project from the File menu.

❑ Select Start from the Run menu.

Visual Basic responds by displaying the window shown in Figure 2.18.

Figure 2.18.
The initial window of the
Just4Fun program
(prototype).

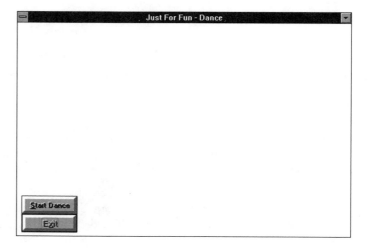

Of course, you can click the Start Dance button, but nothing will happen because you have not yet attached any code to this button.

❑ Click the Exit button to terminate the program.

Note that the prototype of the Just4Fun program does not contain any code (except the code inside the `cmdExit_Click()` procedure). Nevertheless, you can fine-tune the prototype by adjusting various cosmetic aspects of the program. For example, you can experiment with the BevelWidth property of the 3D buttons, with the Font3D property of the 3D button, and with other cosmetic properties.

In the next chapter you'll enter the code of the Just4Fun program.

3

Creating Animation Programs (Part II)

In this chapter you'll write the code of the Just4Fun program.

3 Loading the BMP Files and Performing Other Initialization Tasks

The Form_Load() procedure is executed when the user starts the program. Therefore, this is a good place to perform initialization tasks.

As discussed in Chapter 2, "Creating Animation Programs (Part I)," the Picture properties of the imgDance and imgHorn controls are loaded during runtime.

❏ Enter the following code inside the Form_Load() procedure of the frmDance form:

```
Sub Form_Load ()

    ' Show BMP file in its natural size.
    imgDance(0).Stretch = False


    ' Load the BMP files
    imgDance(1).Picture =
        ➥ LoadPicture("C:\LearnVB\BMP\Dance1.BMP")

    imgDance(1).Picture =
        ➥ LoadPicture("C:\LearnVB\BMP\Dance1.BMP")

    imgDance(2).Picture =
        ➥ LoadPicture("C:\LearnVB\BMP\Dance2.BMP")

    imgDance(3).Picture =
        ➥ LoadPicture("C:\LearnVB\BMP\Dance3.BMP")

    imgDance(4).Picture =
        ➥ LoadPicture("C:\LearnVB\BMP\Dance4.BMP")

    imgDance(5).Picture =
        ➥ LoadPicture("C:\LearnVB\BMP\Dance5.BMP")

    imgDance(6).Picture =
        ➥ LoadPicture("C:\LearnVB\BMP\Dance6.BMP")

    imgDance(7).Picture =
        ➥ LoadPicture("C:\LearnVB\BMP\Dance7.BMP")

    imgDance(8).Picture =
        ➥ LoadPicture("C:\LearnVB\BMP\Dance8.BMP")

    imgDance(9).Picture =
        ➥ LoadPicture("C:\LearnVB\BMP\Dance9.BMP")

    imgDance(10).Picture =
        ➥ LoadPicture("C:\LearnVB\BMP\Dance10.BMP")

    imgDance(11).Picture =
        ➥ LoadPicture("C:\LearnVB\BMP\Dance11.BMP")
```

```
imgDance(12).Picture =
    ➥ LoadPicture("C:\LearnVB\BMP\Dance12.BMP")

imgHorn(1).Picture =
    ➥ LoadPicture("C:\LearnVB\BMP\Horn1.BMP")

imgHorn(2).Picture =
    ➥ LoadPicture("C:\LearnVB\BMP\Horn2.BMP")

imgHorn(3).Picture =
    ➥ LoadPicture("C:\LearnVB\BMP\Horn3.BMP")

' Initially there is no dance in progress
gDanceInProgress = 0

' Set the multimedia device to the sound card
TegommDance.DeviceType = "WaveAudio"

' Set WAV path and file name
TegommDance.FileName = WAV_FILE_NAME


' Open the session
TegommDance.Command = "open"

' Prompt if WAV file cannot be opened
If TegommDance.Error > 0 Then
    MsgBox "Can't open " + WAV_FILE_NAME, 16, "Error"
End If

' Set time format to samples
TegommDance.TimeFormat = "Samples"
```

End Sub

The code you entered sets the Stretch property of imgDance(0) to False:

```
' Show BMP file in its natural size.
imgDance(0).Stretch = False
```

This means that the picture that the imgDance(0) control holds will be displayed in its natural size. That is, the imgDance(0) control will adjust its size to the dimension of the BMP picture that is assigned to the Picture property of the imgDance(0) control.

The next statements in the Form_Load() procedure load the BMP files into the Picture properties of the imgDance() and imgHorn() controls:

```
' Load the BMP files
imgDance(1).Picture =
    ➥ LoadPicture("C:\LearnVB\BMP\Dance1.BMP")

imgDance(1).Picture =
    ➥ LoadPicture("C:\LearnVB\BMP\Dance1.BMP")

. . . . . . . . . . . . .
. . . . . . . . . . . . .
. . . . . . . . . . . . .
```

```
imgDance(12).Picture =
     ➥ LoadPicture("C:\LearnVB\BMP\Dance12.BMP")


imgHorn(1).Picture =
     ➥ LoadPicture("C:\LearnVB\BMP\Horn1.BMP")

imgHorn(2).Picture =
     ➥ LoadPicture("C:\LearnVB\BMP\Horn2.BMP")

imgHorn(3).Picture =
     ➥ LoadPicture("C:\LearnVB\BMP\Horn3.BMP")
```

Note that so far you have not set the Picture properties of imgDance(0) and imgHorn(0). You will set the Picture properties of these images later in the program.

The next statement in Form_Load() sets the gDanceInProgress variable to 0:

```
' Initially there is no dance in progress
gDanceInProgress = 0
```

gDanceInProgress is a global variable that holds the status of the show. During Act I, gDanceInProgress is equal to 0. During Act II, gDanceInProgress is equal to 1. During Act III, gDanceInProgress is equal to 2. As you'll soon see, gDanceInProgress is declared inside the general declarations section of the frmDance form, and as such it is visible throughout the entire form. (It is accessible by any procedure of the frmDance form.)

Table 3.1 lists the frames of the show.

Table 3.1. The frames in the three acts of the show.

Act	imgDance()	BMP file	gDanceInProgress	gPictureIndex
I	imgDance(1)	Dance1.BMP	0	1
I	imgDance(2)	Dance2.BMP	0	2
I	imgDance(3)	Dance3.BMP	0	3
I	imgDance(4)	Dance4.BMP	0	4
II	imgDance(5)	Dance5.BMP	1	5
II	imgDance(6)	Dance6.BMP	1	6
II	imgDance(7)	Dance7.BMP	1	7
III	imgDance(8)	Dance8.BMP	2	8
III	imgDance(9)	Dance9.BMP	2	9
III	imgDance(10)	Dance10.BMP	2	10
III	imgDance(11)	Dance11.BMP	2	11
III	imgDance(12)	Dance12.BMP	2	12

The next statement in the Form_Load() procedure sets the DeviceType property of the TegommDance control to WaveAudio:

```
TegommDance.DeviceType = "WaveAudio"
```

This means that the multimedia control is set to play a WAV file through the sound card.

The FileName property of the TegommDance control is then set to WAV_FILE_NAME:

```
' Set WAV path and file name
TegommDance.FileName = WAV_FILE_NAME
```

WAV_FILE_NAME is a constant string that holds the pathname and filename of the WAV file that will be played during the dancing. Later you'll declare this constant inside the general declarations section of the frmDance form.

NOTE

Note that you can directly assign the pathname and filename of the WAV file to the FileName property of the TegommDance control. That is, you don't have to declare a constant in the general declarations section. Instead, you can use the following statement:

```
TegommDance.FileName =
        ➡ "C:\LearnVB\WAV\Bourb2M6.WAV"
```

However, it is a good practice to write the code in such a way that all the items that may be changed in the future are located in one place. For example, if in the future you'll decide to use another WAV file in the Just4Fun program, you'll know that such a change requires a single change inside the general declarations section. This way, if you decide to use a different WAV file, you will not have to search inside all the procedures of the form.

The next statement in the Form_Load() procedure uses the Open command to open the WAV file:

```
' Open the session
TegommDance.Command = "Open"
```

Naturally, you want to make sure that the WAV file was opened successfully. You accomplish that by examining the Error property of the TegommDance control:

```
' Prompt if WAV file cannot be opened
If TegommDance.Error > 0 Then
    MsgBox "Can't open " + WAV_FILE_NAME, 16, "Error"
End If
```

If the Error property is greater than 0, the WAV file was not opened (for example, there is no sound card in the system, or the specified WAV file was not found).

If the If condition is satisfied, a message box is displayed with the MsgBox statement.

3

> **NOTE**
>
> The Error property indicates whether an error occurred during the last command. Therefore, make sure to examine the Error property immediately after you issue the command you want to examine for errors. For example, in the preceding code you want to examine whether an error occurred during the execution of the Open command. Therefore, you examine the Error property immediately after you issue the Open command.

> **NOTE**
>
> Opening the WAV file does not cause the playback of the WAV file. To actually play the WAV file you need to issue the Play command. You'll issue the Play command later in the program.

The last statement in the Form_Load() procedure sets the TimeFormat property to Samples:

```
' Set time format to samples
TegommDance.TimeFormat = "Samples"
```

This means that from now on the Position property of the multimedia control will report the current playback position in units of samples. The Position property is later used for determining the current playback position during the animation show.

The General Declarations Section of the frmDance Form

You'll now enter the code of the general declarations section of the frmDance form.

❏ Type the following code in the general declarations section of the frmDance form:

```
Option Explicit

' WAV file used in the program
Const WAV_FILE_NAME = "C:\LearnVB\WAV\Bourb2M6.WAV"


' Frame to be displayed
Dim gPictureIndex As Integer

' Show Status
Dim gDanceInProgress As Integer

' Horn sections
Const START_HORN1 = 684000
Const END_HORN1 = 759000

Const START_HORN2 = 924600
Const END_HORN2 = 1149000
```

The first statement inside the general declarations section is

```
Option Explicit
```

This statement forces the declaration of all variables in the program. (See Appendix A.) This statement is automatically written for you by Visual Basic if you set Require Variable Declaration to Yes from the Environment item of the Options menu.

The next statement declares the WAV_FILE_NAME constant:

```
' WAV file used in the program
Const WAV_FILE_NAME = "C:\LearnVB\WAV\Bourb2M6.WAV"
```

As stated earlier, if in the future you want to use another WAV file, you'll have to change only this statement.

The next statement in the general declarations section of the frmDance form declares the gPictureIndex integer:

```
' Frame to be displayed
Dim gPictureIndex As Integer
```

As you'll soon see, you display the frames of the show by setting the Picture property of imgDance(0) to the Picture properties of the other elements of the imgDance() array. For example, to display Frame 2 of Act I, you use the following statement:

```
imgDance(0).Picture = imgDance(2).Picture
```

To display Frame 3 of Act I, you use the following statement:

```
imgDance(0).Picture = imgDance(3).Picture
```

However, because the current picture to be displayed is changing, you'll actually use the following statement:

```
imgDance(0).Picture = imgDance(gPictureIndex).Picture
```

In this case gPictureIndex holds an integer that indicates which picture should be displayed. For example, when gPictureIndex is equal to 2, Frame 2 of Act I is displayed, when gPictureIndex is equal to 3, Frame 3 of Act I is displayed, and so on. (See Table 3.1.)

The next statement inside the general declarations section declares the gDanceInProgress integer:

```
' Show Status
Dim gDanceInProgress As Integer
```

As discussed earlier, the gDanceInProgress integer holds the current status of the show, and this integer can hold the number 0 (Act I is in progress), the number 1 (Act II is in progress), or the number 2 (Act III is in progress).

The next statements inside the general declarations section declare four constants:

```
' Horn sections
Const START_HORN1 = 684000
Const END_HORN1 = 759000
```

3

```
Const START_HORN2 = 924600
Const END_HORN2 = 1149000
```

These constants define the audio sections where the horn is played during the playback of the WAV file. The first two statements declare the first audio section between sample 684,000 and sample 759,000. That is, a horn is played between these two coordinates. Similarly, a horn is played during the playback of samples 924,600 through 1,149,000.

NOTE

How do you know that a horn is played in the range specified by START_HORN1 to END_HORN1 and in the range specified by START_HORN2 to END_HORN2? You'll be able to determine this range by using the Wave Editor program of the AllMedia program. Later in the book you'll learn how to use the AllMedia program (and what is more exciting, you'll learn how to write the AllMedia program yourself!).

NOTE

Note that the "horn ranges" are specified in samples. This is necessary because you set the TimeFormat property of the TegommDance control to Samples (inside the Form_Load() procedure).

Starting and Stopping the Dance

Whenever the user clicks the Start Dance button, the cmdStartDance_Click() procedure is executed.

☐ Enter the following code inside the cmdStartDance_Click() procedure of the frmDance form:

```
Sub cmdStartDance_Click ()

    ''''''''''''''''''''''''''''''''''''''''''
    ' User clicked the Start Dance/Stop button
    ''''''''''''''''''''''''''''''''''''''''''

    If cmdStartDance.Caption = "&Start Dance" Then
        '''''''''''''''''''''''''''''''''''''''
        ' User clicked the Start Dance button
        '''''''''''''''''''''''''''''''''''''''
        gDanceInProgress = 1
        gPictureIndex = 5
        cmdStartDance.Caption = "&Stop"
    Else
        '''''''''''''''''''''''''''''''''''''''
        ' User clicked the Stop button
        '''''''''''''''''''''''''''''''''''''''
        gDanceInProgress = 0
```

```
        cmdStartDance.Caption = "&Start Dance"
        gPictureIndex = 0
        TegommDance.Command = "Stop"
    End If

End Sub
```

The Start Dance button serves as both the Start Dance button and the Stop button. The status of the button is determined by the value of its Caption property. If the Caption property of the button is equal to &Start Dance, the user clicked the Start Dance button to start the show. This means that the following If condition is satisfied:

```
If cmdStartDance.Caption = "&Start Dance" Then
    ''''''''''''''''''''''''''''''''''''''
    ' User clicked the Start Dance button
    ''''''''''''''''''''''''''''''''''''''
    gDanceInProgress = 1
    gPictureIndex = 5
    cmdStartDance.Caption = "&Stop"
Else
    ......
    ......
    ......
    End If
```

The code under the If statement sets the gDanceInProgress to 1 (because now the show should display Act II).

The code under the If statement sets gPictureIndex to 5, thus preparing gPictureIndex for Act II.

The last thing that the code under the If statement does is change the Caption property of the button to &Stop. This means that during the playback, the Caption property of the button is &Stop.

If the current Caption property of the button is &Stop, the user clicked the Stop button to stop the show. This means that the Else code is executed:

```
    If cmdStartDance.Caption = "&Start Dance" Then
        ......
        ......
        ......
    Else
        '''''''''''''''''''''''''''''''''''''
        ' User clicked the Stop button
        '''''''''''''''''''''''''''''''''''''
        gDanceInProgress = 0
        cmdStartDance.Caption = "&Start Dance"
        gPictureIndex = 0
        TegommDance.Command = "Stop"
    End If
```

The code under the Else statement sets gDanceInProgress to 0. Having gDanceInProgress equal to 0 causes the program to again display Act I.

The code under the Else sets the Caption property to &Start Dance, and the playback of the WAV file is stopped because the Stop command is issued to the TegommDance control:

```
TegommDance.Command = "Stop"
```

The Show

The code of the show is inside the `TegommDance_StatusUpdate()` procedure.

❑ Type the following code inside the `TegommDance_StatusUpdate()` procedure of the `frmDance` form:

```
Sub TegommDance_StatusUpdate ()


   ''''''''''''''''''''''''''''''''''''''
   ' This procedure is executed
   ' every UpdateInterval milliseconds
   ''''''''''''''''''''''''''''''''''''''

   If gDanceInProgress = 0 Then
      ''''''''''''''''''''''''''''''''''''''''''''''''''
      ' User did not yet click the Start Dance button
      ''''''''''''''''''''''''''''''''''''''''''''''''''

      ' Display current frame
      imgDance(0).Picture = imgDance(gPictureIndex).Picture

      ' Next frame
      gPictureIndex = gPictureIndex + 1

      ' Last frame was displayed?
      If gPictureIndex = 5 Then
         gPictureIndex = 0
      End If

   End If


   ' Man asks woman to dance
   If gDanceInProgress = 1 Then

      imgDance(0).Picture = imgDance(gPictureIndex).Picture

      gPictureIndex = gPictureIndex + 1
      If gPictureIndex = 8 Then
         gDanceInProgress = 2
         ' Rewind & Play WAV file
         TegommDance.Command = "Prev"
         TegommDance.Command = "Play"
         Exit Sub
      End If

   End If


   ' Dance starts
   If gDanceInProgress = 2 Then
      imgDance(0).Picture = imgDance(gPictureIndex).Picture

      gPictureIndex = gPictureIndex + 1
      If gPictureIndex = 13 Then
         gPictureIndex = 8
```

```
      End If
   End If
```

End Sub

Recall that the `TegommDance_StatusUpdate()` procedure is executed every 500 milliseconds (because you set the UpdateInterval property of the `TegommDance` control to 500 at design time).

If the user did not yet click the Start Dance button, `gDanceInProgress` is still equal to 0, and the following `If` condition is satisfied:

```
If gDanceInProgress = 0 Then
   ''''''''''''''''''''''''''''''''''''''''''''''''''
   ' User did not yet click the Start Dance button
   ''''''''''''''''''''''''''''''''''''''''''''''''''

   ' Display current frame
   imgDance(0).Picture = imgDance(gPictureIndex).Picture

   ' Next frame
   gPictureIndex = gPictureIndex + 1

   ' Last frame was displayed?
   If gPictureIndex = 5 Then
      gPictureIndex = 0
   End If

End If
```

This code assigns the Picture property of `imgDance(gPictureIndex)` to the Picture property of `imgDance(0)`:

```
' Display current frame
imgDance(0).Picture = imgDance(gPictureIndex).Picture
```

Initially `gPictureIndex` is equal to 0. This means that the Dance1.BMP picture is displayed. (See Table 3.1.)

Next, the `gPictureIndex` variable is increased by 1:

```
' Next frame
gPictureIndex = gPictureIndex + 1
```

So now `gPictureIndex` is equal to 2. Because none of the other `If` conditions in this procedure are satisfied, the procedure terminates.

After 500 milliseconds, the procedure is executed again. Now `gDanceInProgress` is again equal to 0, so the same `If` condition is again satisfied. However, now `gPictureIndex` is equal to 2. This means that now Dance2.BMP is displayed.

This process continues until `gPictureIndex` is equal to 5. When `gPictureIndex` is equal to 5, an `If` statement "catches" that, and `gPictureIndex` is set back to 0:

```
' Last frame was displayed?
If gPictureIndex = 5 Then
   gPictureIndex = 0
End If
```

3

If the user still has not clicked the Start Dance button, the procedure is again executed after 500 milliseconds, with gPictureIndex equal to 0. So as long as the user does not click the Start Dance button, gPictureIndex has the following values:

```
0
1
2
3
4
5
0
1
2
3
4
5
0
.
.
.
```

This corresponds to the display of the following BMP pictures:

```
Dance1.BMP
Dance2.BMP
Dance3.BMP
Dance4.BMP
Dance1.BMP
Dance2.BMP
Dance3.BMP
Dance4.BMP
Dance1.BMP
Dance2.BMP
Dance3.BMP
....
....
....
```

In other words, Act I is displayed in an endless loop.

When the user clicks the Start Dance button, gDanceInProgress is set to 1. (See the cmdStartDance_Click() procedure that was discussed earlier.)

As stated, the cmdTegommDance_StatusUpdate() procedure is executed every 500 milliseconds. So the next time this procedure is executed, the following If condition is satisfied:

```
' Man asks woman to dance
If gDanceInProgress = 1 Then

    imgDance(0).Picture = imgDance(gPictureIndex).Picture

    gPictureIndex = gPictureIndex + 1
    If gPictureIndex = 8 Then
       gDanceInProgress = 2
       ' Rewind & Play WAV file
       TegommDance.Command = "Prev"
       TegommDance.Command = "Play"
```

```
      Exit Sub
   End If

End If
```

The code under this `If` statement displays a picture:

```
imgDance(0).Picture = imgDance(gPictureIndex).Picture
```

Because the `cmdStartDance_Click()` procedure sets `gPictureIndex` to 5, Dance5.BMP is displayed. (See Table 3.1.)

Then `gPictureIndex` is incremented by 1:

```
gPictureIndex = gPictureIndex + 1
```

So now `gPictureIndex` is equal to 6.

An inner `If` statement is then executed to examine whether `gPictureIndex` is equal to 8:

```
If gPictureIndex = 8 Then
   ....
   ....
   ....
End If
```

Because currently `gPictureIndex` is equal to 6, the inner `If` is not satisfied, and because none of the other `If` statements in the procedure are satisfied, `cmdTegommDance_StatusUpdate()` is terminated.

After 500 milliseconds, the `cmdTegommDance_StatusUpdate()` procedure is again executed, and the same `If` condition that checks whether `gDanceInProgress` is equal to 1 is again satisfied.

Because now `gPictureIndex` is equal to 6, Dance6.BMP is displayed.

After 500 milliseconds, the `TegommDance_StatusUpdate()` procedure is executed again, and the Dance7.BMP picture is displayed.

So the following pictures are displayed:

```
Dance5.BMP
Dance6.BMP
Dance7.BMP
```

After Dance7.BMP is displayed, `gPictureIndex` is increased to 8, and the inner `If` condition is satisfied:

```
If gPictureIndex = 8 Then
   gDanceInProgress = 2
   ' Rewind & Play WAV file
   TegommDance.Command = "Prev"
   TegommDance.Command = "Play"
   Exit Sub
End If
```

The code inside the inner `If` sets `gDanceInProgress` to 2. The code also rewinds the WAV file, and the `Play` command is issued to start the playback:

```
' Rewind & Play WAV file
```

3

```
TegommDance.Command = "Prev"
TegommDance.Command = "Play"
```

After 500 milliseconds, the `TegommDance_Click()` procedure is again executed. However, because now gDanceInProgress is equal to 2, the following `If` statement is executed:

```
' Dance starts
If gDanceInProgress = 2 Then
   imgDance(0).Picture = imgDance(gPictureIndex).Picture

   gPictureIndex = gPictureIndex + 1
   If gPictureIndex = 13 Then
      gPictureIndex = 8
   End If
End If
```

This `If` statement causes the display of the following BMP pictures in an endless loop:

```
Dance8.BMP
Dance9.BMP
Dance10.BMP
Dance11.BMP
Dance12.BMP
Dance8.BMP
Dance9.BMP
Dance10.BMP
Dance11.BMP
Dance12.BMP
.....
.....
.....
```

This process continues until the user clicks the Stop button, which causes the execution of the `cmdStartDance_Click()` procedure. The `cmdStartDance_Click()` procedure sets gDanceInProgress to 0. This means that after 500 milliseconds, when the `TegommDance_StatusUpdate()` procedure is executed again, the first `If` condition is satisfied, which causes the display of Act I.

The `TegommDance_Done()` Procedure of the `frmDance` Form

The `TegommDance_Done()` procedure is automatically executed whenever the `TegommDance` control completes an operation. For example, whenever the playback reaches the end of the WAV file, the `TegommDance_Done()` procedure is automatically executed.

☐ Enter the following code inside the `TegommDance_Done()` procedure of the `frmDance` form:

```
Sub TegommDance_Done ()

   If TegommDance.Position = TegommDance.Length Then
      TegommDance.Command = "Prev"
      TegommDance.Command = "Play"
   End If

End Sub
```

The code that you entered uses an If statement to examine whether the playback position has reached the end of the WAV file. If the If statement is satisfied, the WAV file was played in its entirety, and the Prev command is issued to rewind the WAV file, followed by the Play command to start playing all over again.

So the playback of the WAV file continues in an endless loop (unless the user clicks the Stop button, which causes the playback to stop).

Although you have not yet finished writing the Just4Fun program, try to execute it:

❑ Select Save Project from the File menu.

❑ Select Start from the Run menu.

Verify that the Just4Fun program operates correctly. Note that you have not yet implemented the feature that displays the man playing the horn whenever the WAV file plays a horn. You will implement this feature in the next section.

❑ Experiment with the Just4Fun program and then click its Exit button to terminate it.

Synchronized Animation

You'll now add synchronized animation to the Just4Fun program. In particular, you'll synchronize the WAV playback with the animation, so that whenever the horn is played pictures of a man playing a horn are displayed.

❑ Add code to the end of the TegommDance_StatusUpdate() procedure. After you add the code your TegommDance_StatusUpdate() procedure should look like this:

```
Sub TegommDance_StatusUpdate ()

    Static sHornIndex As Integer

    ......
    ......
    ......
    ......

    If (TegommDance.Position > START_HORN1 And
        ➥ TegommDance.Position < END_HORN1) Or
        ➥ (TegommDance.Position > START_HORN2 And
        ➥ TegommDance.Position < END_HORN2) Then
        sHornIndex = sHornIndex + 1
        If sHornIndex = 4 Then
            sHornIndex = 0
        End If
        imgHorn(0).Picture = imgHorn(sHornIndex)
    Else
        imgHorn(0).Picture = LoadPicture("")
    End If

End Sub
```

3

The code that you implemented synchronizes the WAV playback with the display of the animation. The following explains how the synchronizing trick works.

An If statement checks whether the WAV playback is within certain ranges:

```
If (TegommDance.Position > START_HORN1 And
        ➥ TegommDance.Position < END_HORN1) Or
        ➥ (TegommDance.Position > START_HORN2 And
        ➥ TegommDance.Position < END_HORN2) Then
    .................................
    ...... Display the animation .......
    .................................

Else
    imgHorn(0).Picture = LoadPicture("")
End If
```

If indeed the playback is within these ranges, pictures of a man playing a horn are displayed:

```
        sHornIndex = sHornIndex + 1
        If sHornIndex = 4 Then
            sHornIndex = 0
        End If
        imgHorn(0).Picture = imgHorn(sHornIndex)
```

Recall that you declared sHornIndex as a Static variable inside the cmdTegommDance_StatusUpdate() procedure. When this variable is created its value is equal to 0. So in the first iteration, the picture Horn1.BMP is displayed.

After 500 milliseconds, the TegommDance_StatusUpdate() procedure is again executed. If the WAV file playback is still within the specified range, the If condition is satisfied, and because now sHornIndex is equal to 1, the Horn2.BMP picture is displayed. An inner If statement catches when sHornIndex is equal to 4, and returns its value to 0. So to summarize, sHornIndex has the following values:

```
0
1
2
3
4
0
1
2
3
4
.
.
.
```

This corresponds to the display of the following sequence of BMP pictures:

```
Horn1.BMP
Horn2.BMP
Horn3.BMP
```

```
Horn1.BMP
Horn2.BMP
Horn3.BMP
Horn1.BMP
....
....
....
```

A schematic diagram of the synchronized animation logic is shown in Figure 3.1.

Figure 3.1.
The synchronized
animation.

To see your code in action do the following:

☐ Select Save Project from the File menu.

☐ Select Start from the Run menu.

☐ Click the Start Dance button.

☐ Wait patiently until the WAV file plays the horn, and notice that a picture of a man playing a horn is displayed during the time when the horn is played.

☐ Experiment with the Just4Fun program and then click its Exit button to terminate the program.

☐ Select Make EXE File from the File menu.

☐ Save the program as Just4Fun.EXE in the C:\LearnVB\Practice\Anim directory.

You now have an EXE file. The complete application is composed of the following files:

```
Just4Fun.EXE
Tegomm.VBX
THREED.VBX
Dance1.BMP
Dance2.BMP
Dance3.BMP
Dance4.BMP
Dance5.BMP
Dance6.BMP
Dance7.BMP
```

3

```
Dance8.BMP
Dance9.BMP
Dance10.BMP
Dance11.BMP
Dance12.BMP
Horn1.BMP
Horn2.BMP
Horn3.BMP
Bourb2M6.WAV
```

NOTE

Don't forget that the Just4Fun program assumes that the Bourb2M6.WAV file resides inside the C:\LearnVB\WAV directory, and that the BMP files reside inside the C:\LearnVB\BMP directory.

Further Enhancements—You Are on Your Own . . .

You have finished implementing the Just4Fun program. However, you can continue enhancing the Just4Fun program by yourself.

You can alter the Just4Fun program so that the user is able to create his or her own cartoon shows.

Currently, the Just4Fun loads the Dance?.BMP files. You can let your user create his or her own cartoon movies by replacing the Dance?.BMP files.

Your C:\LearnVB\BMP directory contains the following files:

```
DD1.BMP
DD2.BMP
DD3.BMP
DD4.BMP
DD5.BMP
DD6.BMP
DD7.BMP
DD8.BMP
DD9.BMP
DD10.BMP
DD11.BMP
DD12.BMP
```

These files are shown in Figures 3.2 through 3.13.

Figure 3.2.
The DD1.BMP picture
(Frame 1 of Act I).

Figure 3.3.
The DD2.BMP picture
(Frame 2 of Act I).

Figure 3.4.
The DD3.BMP picture
(Frame 3 of Act I).

Figure 3.5.
The DD4.BMP picture
(Frame 4 of Act I).

Figure 3.6.
The DD5.BMP picture
(Frame 1 of Act II).

Figure 3.7.
The DD6.BMP picture
(Frame 2 of Act II).

3

Figure 3.8.
The DD7.BMP picture
(Frame 3 of Act II).

Figure 3.9.
The DD8.BMP picture
(Frame 1 of Act III).

Figure 3.10.
The DD9.BMP picture
(Frame 2 of Act III).

Figure 3.11.
The DD10.BMP picture
(Frame 3 of Act III).

Figure 3.12.
The DD11.BMP picture
(Frame 4 of Act III).

Figure 3.13.
The DD12.BMP picture
(Frame 5 of Act III).

Inside the C:\LearnVB\BMP directory you can see the DD2DANCE.BAT file. Here are the contents of the DD2DANCE.BAT file:

```
rem DD?.BMP to DANCE?.BMP
COPY C:\LEARNVB\BMP\DD1.BMP C:\LEARNVB\BMP\DANCE1.BMP
COPY C:\LEARNVB\BMP\DD2.BMP C:\LEARNVB\BMP\DANCE2.BMP
COPY C:\LEARNVB\BMP\DD3.BMP C:\LEARNVB\BMP\DANCE3.BMP
COPY C:\LEARNVB\BMP\DD4.BMP C:\LEARNVB\BMP\DANCE4.BMP
COPY C:\LEARNVB\BMP\DD5.BMP C:\LEARNVB\BMP\DANCE5.BMP
```

```
COPY C:\LEARNVB\BMP\DD6.BMP  C:\LEARNVB\BMP\DANCE6.BMP
COPY C:\LEARNVB\BMP\DD7.BMP  C:\LEARNVB\BMP\DANCE7.BMP
COPY C:\LEARNVB\BMP\DD8.BMP  C:\LEARNVB\BMP\DANCE8.BMP
COPY C:\LEARNVB\BMP\DD9.BMP  C:\LEARNVB\BMP\DANCE9.BMP
COPY C:\LEARNVB\BMP\DD10.BMP C:\LEARNVB\BMP\DANCE10.BMP
COPY C:\LEARNVB\BMP\DD11.BMP C:\LEARNVB\BMP\DANCE11.BMP
COPY C:\LEARNVB\BMP\DD12.BMP C:\LEARNVB\BMP\DANCE12.BMP
```

As you can see, this file copies the DD?.BMP files to DANCE?.BMP files.

❏ Double-click the MS-DOS icon (which is usually inside the Accessories group of icons).

Windows responds by executing a DOS shell.

❏ Log in to the C:\LearnVB\BMP directory.

❏ At the DOS prompt enter the following:

```
DD2DANCE  {Enter}
```

The DD2DANCE.BAT file copies the DD?.BMP files to the DANCE?.BMP files.

❏ At the DOS prompt enter the following:

```
EXIT  {Enter}
```

Windows responds by terminating the DOS shell and returning to Windows.

❏ Execute the Just4Fun.EXE program.

Windows responds by executing the Just4Fun program, and displaying the window shown in Figure 3.14.

Figure 3.14.
The Just4Fun program (with the DD?.BMP pictures).

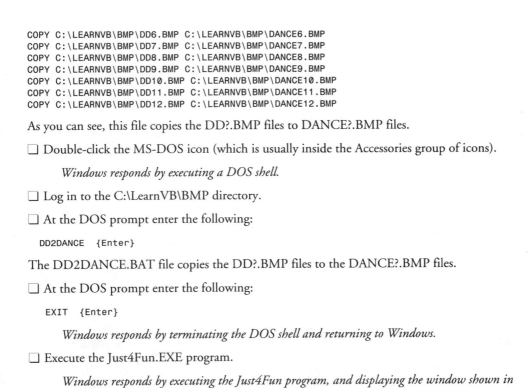
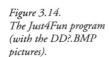

3

❑ Experiment with the Just4Fun program and then click its Exit button to terminate the program.

The C:\LearnVB\BMP directory also contains the D2DANCE.BAT file. Here are the contents of the D2DANCE.BAT file:

```
rem D?.BMP to DANCE?.BMP
COPY C:\LEARNVB\BMP\D1.BMP  C:\LEARNVB\BMP\DANCE1.BMP
COPY C:\LEARNVB\BMP\D2.BMP  C:\LEARNVB\BMP\DANCE2.BMP
COPY C:\LEARNVB\BMP\D3.BMP  C:\LEARNVB\BMP\DANCE3.BMP
COPY C:\LEARNVB\BMP\D4.BMP  C:\LEARNVB\BMP\DANCE4.BMP
COPY C:\LEARNVB\BMP\D5.BMP  C:\LEARNVB\BMP\DANCE5.BMP
COPY C:\LEARNVB\BMP\D6.BMP  C:\LEARNVB\BMP\DANCE6.BMP
COPY C:\LEARNVB\BMP\D7.BMP  C:\LEARNVB\BMP\DANCE7.BMP
COPY C:\LEARNVB\BMP\D8.BMP  C:\LEARNVB\BMP\DANCE8.BMP
COPY C:\LEARNVB\BMP\D9.BMP  C:\LEARNVB\BMP\DANCE9.BMP
COPY C:\LEARNVB\BMP\D10.BMP  C:\LEARNVB\BMP\DANCE10.BMP
COPY C:\LEARNVB\BMP\D11.BMP  C:\LEARNVB\BMP\DANCE11.BMP
COPY C:\LEARNVB\BMP\D12.BMP  C:\LEARNVB\BMP\DANCE12.BMP
```

The D2DANCE.BAP file copies the D?.BMP files to the DANCE?.BMP files. The D?.BMP files are the original DANCE?.BMP files. Therefore, you can switch back to the original animation by executing the D2DANCE.BAT file.

NOTE

Now that you know how to perform animation with Visual Basic, you can make the Just4Fun program as sophisticated as you want it to be. For example, you can add code to the program that further enhances the program, so that the number of frames in each act is programmable by the user. Also, you can enhance the program so that the user can program the number of acts.

Typically, you implement such a program by letting the user write a SCRIPT.TXT file. This TXT file contains information such as number of acts, the name of the WAV file(s), and the number of frames in each act. Upon loading the program (inside the Form_Load() procedure), the user can read the contents of the SCRIPT.TXT file, and according to the contents of the file, set the appropriate variables of the program.

Testing and Debugging the Just4Fun Program

One of the most challenging tasks in software development is testing and debugging the programs. It is difficult to test and debug a Windows program, because to completely test the program, you need to execute the program and experiment with all the possible actions that your users can take during the program's execution.

For example, the Just4Fun program currently has a small bug in it. Have you noticed it? Here it is:

❏ Execute the Just4Fun program.

❏ Click the Start Dance button.

❏ Wait until you hear the horn being played, and once the program displays the man playing the horn, click the Stop button.

> *The Just4Fun program stops the playback and returns to Act I. However, the program keeps displaying the man playing the horn! This is obviously a nasty bug.*

To fix this bug, examine the TegommDance_StatusUpdate() procedure. Why this procedure? This is the only place in the program where the man and the horn are displayed, so this procedure will be a good starting place to debug the program. Here is the code that is responsible for displaying the pictures during the horn playing:

```
Sub TegommDance_StatusUpdate ()

    Static sHornIndex As Integer

    ......
    ......
    ......
    ......

    If (TegommDance.Position > START_HORN1 And
        ➥ TegommDance.Position < END_HORN1) Or
        ➥ (TegommDance.Position > START_HORN2 And
        ➥ TegommDance.Position < END_HORN2) Then
        sHornIndex = sHornIndex + 1
        If sHornIndex = 4 Then
            sHornIndex = 0
        End If
        imgHorn(0).Picture = imgHorn(sHornIndex)
    Else
        imgHorn(0).Picture = LoadPicture("")
    End If

End Sub
```

Now suppose that the user clicks the Stop button during the playback of the horn. In that case, the cmdStartDance_Click() procedure is executed:

```
Sub cmdStartDance_Click ()

    ''''''''''''''''''''''''''''''''''''''''''''
    ' User clicked the Start Dance/Stop button
    ''''''''''''''''''''''''''''''''''''''''''''

    If cmdStartDance.Caption = "&Start Dance" Then
        ''''''''''''''''''''''''''''''''''''''''''
        ' User clicked the Start Dance button
        ''''''''''''''''''''''''''''''''''''''''''
        gDanceInProgress = 1
```

3

```
        gPictureIndex = 4
        cmdStartDance.Caption = "&Stop"
    Else
        ''''''''''''''''''''''''''''''''''''''
        ' User clicked the Stop button
        ''''''''''''''''''''''''''''''''''''''
        gDanceInProgress = 0
        cmdStartDance.Caption = "&Start Dance"
        gPictureIndex = 0
        TegommDance.Command = "Stop"
    End If

End Sub
```

So when the user clicks the Stop button (during the playback of the horn), gDanceInProgress is set to 0. After 500 milliseconds, the TegommDance_StatusUpdate() procedure is executed, and the If condition that causes the horn animation is still satisfied (because the position of the WAV file is still within the horn-playing range even though the WAV file is not played anymore).

The solution is to add code that causes the If condition not to be satisfied.

❏ Modify the cmdStartDance_Click() procedure so that it looks like this:

```
Sub cmdStartDance_Click ()

    ''''''''''''''''''''''''''''''''''''''''''''''
    ' User clicked the Start Dance/Stop button
    ''''''''''''''''''''''''''''''''''''''''''''''

    If cmdStartDance.Caption = "&Start Dance" Then
        ''''''''''''''''''''''''''''''''''''''''
        ' User clicked the Start Dance button
        ''''''''''''''''''''''''''''''''''''''''
        gDanceInProgress = 1
        gPictureIndex = 4
        cmdStartDance.Caption = "&Stop"
    Else
        ''''''''''''''''''''''''''''''''''''''''
        ' User clicked the Stop button
        ''''''''''''''''''''''''''''''''''''''''
        gDanceInProgress = 0
        cmdStartDance.Caption = "&Start Dance"
        gPictureIndex = 0

        TegommDance.Command = "Prev"

        TegommDance.Command = "Stop"
    End If

End Sub
```

The code you added issues the Prev command whenever the user clicks the Stop button. The If condition (which performs the synchronized animation) inside the TegommDance_StatusUpdate() procedure will not be satisfied anymore, because after issuing the Prev command, the WAV file is terminated and its position is at coordinate 0.

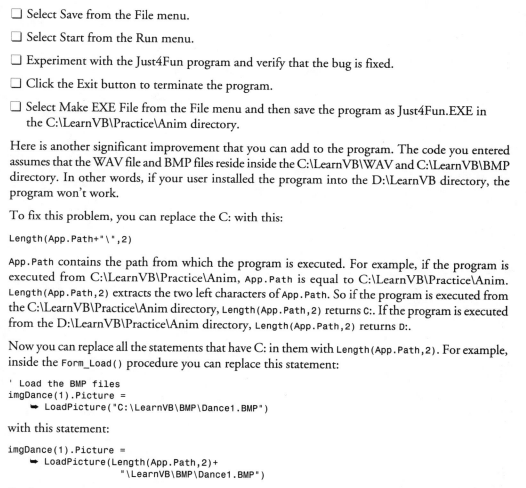

❑ Select Save from the File menu.

❑ Select Start from the Run menu.

❑ Experiment with the Just4Fun program and verify that the bug is fixed.

❑ Click the Exit button to terminate the program.

❑ Select Make EXE File from the File menu and then save the program as Just4Fun.EXE in the C:\LearnVB\Practice\Anim directory.

Here is another significant improvement that you can add to the program. The code you entered assumes that the WAV file and BMP files reside inside the C:\LearnVB\WAV and C:\LearnVB\BMP directory. In other words, if your user installed the program into the D:\LearnVB directory, the program won't work.

To fix this problem, you can replace the C: with this:

```
Length(App.Path+"\",2)
```

`App.Path` contains the path from which the program is executed. For example, if the program is executed from C:\LearnVB\Practice\Anim, `App.Path` is equal to C:\LearnVB\Practice\Anim. `Length(App.Path,2)` extracts the two left characters of `App.Path`. So if the program is executed from the C:\LearnVB\Practice\Anim directory, `Length(App.Path,2)` returns `C:`. If the program is executed from the D:\LearnVB\Practice\Anim directory, `Length(App.Path,2)` returns `D:`.

Now you can replace all the statements that have C: in them with `Length(App.Path,2)`. For example, inside the `Form_Load()` procedure you can replace this statement:

```
' Load the BMP files
imgDance(1).Picture =
    ➡ LoadPicture("C:\LearnVB\BMP\Dance1.BMP")
```

with this statement:

```
imgDance(1).Picture =
    ➡ LoadPicture(Length(App.Path,2)+
                "\LearnVB\BMP\Dance1.BMP")
```

Furthermore, you can change the `WAV_FILE_NAME` declaration as you did inside the general declarations section:

```
' WAV file used in the program
Const WAV_FILE_NAME = "\LearnVB\WAV\Bourb2M6.WAV"
```

When you specify the filename, use the following statement:

```
' Set WAV path and file name
TegommDance.FileName = Left(App.Path, 2) + WAV_FILE_NAME
```

4

Creating Multimedia Programs (Part I)

In this chapter you'll write the prototype of the AllMedia application.

The AllMedia application enables you to play all the possible multimedia devices that the PC can support. With the AllMedia application you'll be able to play WAV files through the sound card, play MIDI files through the sound card, play WAV files through the PC speaker (without any additional hardware or software drivers), play CD audio (music CDs that you can purchase at a record store), and play AVI video files.

NOTE

In order to be able to play AVI video files, you must first install the Microsoft AVI drivers. Therefore, be sure to read Appendix F of this book before executing the AllMedia application. Appendix F shows you how to determine whether your PC is already equipped with the required AVI drivers, and if your PC does not have the required drivers, Appendix F shows you how to install the required Microsoft AVI drivers.

Executing the AllMedia Application

Before writing the AllMedia application yourself, execute the copy of it that resides inside your C:\LearnVB\Original\AllMedia directory. This way you'll gain a better understanding of what the AllMedia program is supposed to do.

❏ Select Run from the File menu of the Program Manager and execute the C:\LearnVB\Original\AllMedia\AllMedia.EXE program.

> *Windows responds by executing the AllMedia.EXE program and displaying the window shown in Figure 4.1.*

Figure 4.1.
The main window of the
AllMedia application.

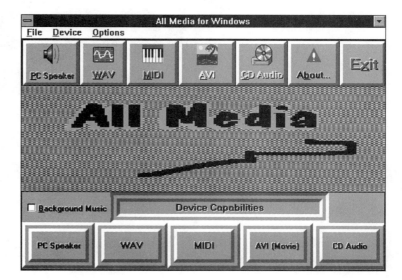

Animated Icon

The AllMedia application has an animated icon:

❏ Click the down-arrow icon of the AllMedia program that is located in the upper-right corner of the AllMedia window.

> *The AllMedia program minimizes itself, and an animated icon is displayed. As you can see, the animated icon builds the words* All *and* Media *in a continuous loop.*

Restore the original size of the AllMedia window:

❏ Click the animated icon.

> *Windows responds by displaying the system menu.*

❏ Select Restore from the system menu.

Playing Background Music and Animating the AllMedia Logo

The AllMedia program gives the user the option of displaying the AllMedia logo in an animated form and playing background music.

To see the animated logo and to hear the background music do the following:

❏ Place an X inside the Background Music checkbox that is located on the status bar of the AllMedia program.

> *AllMedia responds by playing background music in an endless loop and by displaying the AllMedia logo animated.*

To stop the animation of the AllMedia logo and the background music do the following:

❏ Remove the X from the Background Music checkbox that is located on the status bar of the AllMedia program.

> *AllMedia responds by stopping the background music and by displaying the AllMedia logo not animated.*

Inspecting the PC Multimedia Capabilities

The lower status bar of the AllMedia application displays five 3D labels:

> PC Speaker
> WAV
> MIDI
> AVI
> CD Audio

A PC that is capable of using all these multimedia devices displays these 3D labels enabled, as shown in Figure 4.1. Naturally, every PC has a PC speaker, and hence the PC Speaker label is always displayed, as shown in Figure 4.1. However, if your PC is not capable of playing MIDI files, the AllMedia application automatically detects that fact, and the lower status bar is displayed, as shown in Figure 4.2.

Figure 4.2.
The window of the
AllMedia program with its
lower status bar indicating
that MIDI files are not
supported by the PC.

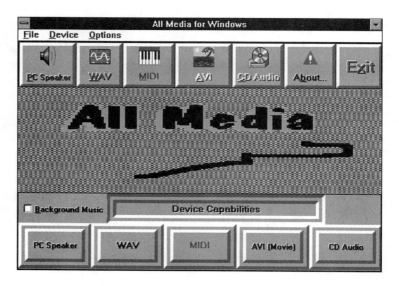

Similarly, the other 3D labels on the lower status bar indicate the PC capabilities regarding the other multimedia devices.

Playing Sound Through the PC Speaker

Playing sound through the PC speaker is an important feature for your Visual Basic programs because many businesses still consider the sound card to be a device used for games only (and not appropriate for PC work during business hours).

To use the AllMedia application for playing WAV files through the PC speaker do the following:

❑ Click the PC Speaker button that is located on the toolbar of the AllMedia window.

AllMedia responds by displaying the window shown in Figure 4.3.

To load a WAV file do this:

❑ Click the Open WAV File button.

AllMedia responds by displaying the Open dialog box, which is shown in Figure 4.4.

Figure 4.3.
The PC Speaker window.

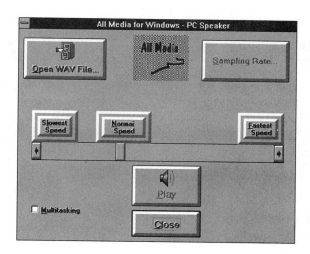

Figure 4.4.
The Open dialog box.

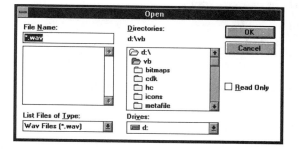

☐ Select the file C:\LearnVB\WAV\ItBeen1.WAV.

> *AllMedia responds by opening a WAV session for the ItsBeen1.WAV file and changing the*
> *caption of the PC Speaker window to* PC Speaker - (ITSBEEN1.WAV).

NOTE

As you'll see later in this chapter, the control that is used for playing the WAV files is the
advanced multimedia control, TegoMM.VBX. This control was supplied on the book's
CD and was installed to your \Windows\System directory during the installation of the
book's CD.

The provided TegoMM.VBX control is the limited edition. It displays a message whenever
you start a program that uses this control, and it lets you play through the PC speaker only
the limited number of WAV files that were supplied on the book's CD.

You can obtain the full version of the TegoMM.VBX control by sending a check or money order for $29.95 plus $5.00 for shipping and handling to this address:

TegoSoft Inc.
Box 389
Bellmore, NY 11710
Phone: (516)783-4824

When ordering, specify part number TegoMM.VBX-RWVB.

New York State residents should add appropriate sales tax.

❏ Click the Play button.

AllMedia responds by playing the ItsBeen1.WAV file through the PC speaker.

❏ Click the Slowest Speed label.

AllMedia Responds by moving the thumb tab of the speed scroll bar to the extreme left side of the scroll bar.

❏ Click the Play button.

AllMedia responds by playing the ItsBeen1.WAV file through the PC speaker at a slower speed.

❏ Click the Fastest Speed label.

AllMedia Responds by moving the thumb tab of the speed scroll bar to the extreme right side of the scroll bar.

❏ Click the Play button.

AllMedia responds by playing the ItsBeen1.WAV file through the PC speaker at a faster speed.

❏ Click the speed scroll bar to move the thumb tab of the scroll bar to various locations, click the Play button, and note that the WAV file is played at a speed proportional to the location of the thumb tab on the scroll bar.

❏ Click the Normal Speed label.

AllMedia Responds by placing the thumb tab of the speed scroll bar under the Normal Speed label.

❏ Click the Play button.

AllMedia responds by playing the ItsBeen1.WAV file through the PC speaker at a normal speed.

Note that during the playback the mouse cursor becomes an hourglass and you can't perform other tasks.

The AllMedia application lets you place the WAV playback in a multitasking mode:

❑ Place an X inside the Multitasking checkbox.

❑ Click the Play button.

> *AllMedia responds by playing the WAV file through the PC speaker. However, now the PC is in a multitasking mode, and while the playback is in progress you can move the mouse, perform other tasks, and even switch to other applications. Naturally, the quality of the playback is lower because the PC has to take care of many operations (playing the WAV file through the PC speaker as well as monitoring the mouse events and performing the tasks dictated by the mouse events).*

❑ Click the Sampling Rate button.

> *AllMedia responds by displaying a message box, telling you the sampling rate of the ItsBeen1.WAV file. (See Figure 4.5.)*

Figure 4.5.
The message box that
AllMedia displays after you
click the Sampling Rate
button of the PC Speaker
window.

As shown in Figure 4.5, the sampling rate of the ItsBeen1.WAV file is 22050 hertz.

❑ Experiment with the PC Speaker window and then click the Close button to return to the main window of the AllMedia application.

Playing WAV Files Through the Sound Card

Click the WAV button that is located on the toolbar of the AllMedia program's main window.

> *AllMedia responds by displaying the Wave Editor window. (See Figure 4.6.)*

The Wave Editor is a sophisticated program that lets you play WAV files, display the graphs of the WAV files, add recording to the WAV files, modify the contents of the WAV files, use Copy, Cut, and Paste on WAV samples, Zoom into a selected section of the WAV file, play selected sections of the WAV files, and perform a variety of other tasks. It is highly recommended that you now read the beginning of Appendix E, which explains how to use the Wave Editor.

❑ Read Appendix E to learn how to use the Wave Editor.

❑ Select Exit from the File menu to close the Wave Editor.

> *AllMedia responds by displaying its main window.*

Figure 4.6.
The main window of the
Wave Editor program.

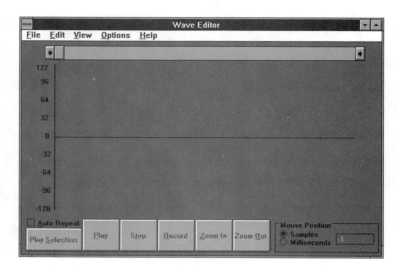

Playing MIDI Files with the AllMedia Application

AllMedia lets you play MIDI files through the sound card. To hear MIDI files do the following:

❑ Click the MIDI button that is located on the toolbar of the AllMedia window.

AllMedia responds by displaying the MIDI window, which is shown in Figure 4.7.

Figure 4.7.
The MIDI window of the
AllMedia application.

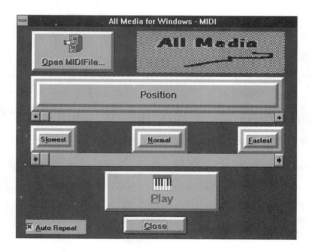

To select a MIDI file do the following:

❑ Click the Open MIDIFile button.

AllMedia responds by displaying the Open dialog box.

❏ Select the C:\LearnVB\MIDI\Pickin6.MID file.

❏ Click the Play button.

> *AllMedia responds by playing the Pickin6.MID file.*

Note that during the playback the Position scroll bar displays the position of the played file. When the thumb tab of the scroll bar is at the extreme left, the beginning of the MIDI file is played. When the thumb tab is at the extreme right side of the scroll bar, the end of the MIDI file is played.

You can play the MIDI file at various speeds.

❏ Experiment with the Slowest, Normal, and Fastest labels and the thumb tab of the Position scroll bar.

The MIDI window has an Auto Repeat checkbox. If the Auto Repeat checkbox is checked, the MIDI file will be played in an endless loop. If the Auto Repeat checkbox is not checked, the MIDI file will be played only once.

❏ Experiment with the MIDI window and then click the Close button to return to the main window of the AllMedia application.

Playing AVI Video Files with the AllMedia Application

The AllMedia application is capable of playing AVI video files. As stated at the beginning of this chapter, to play AVI files you must have installed the Microsoft AVI drivers. If you don't have the AVI drivers installed on your PC, read Appendix F.

❏ Click the AVI button that is located on the toolbar of the AllMedia program's window.

> *AllMedia responds by displaying the Movie window, as shown in Figure 4.8.*

Figure 4.8.
The Movie window of the
AllMedia application.

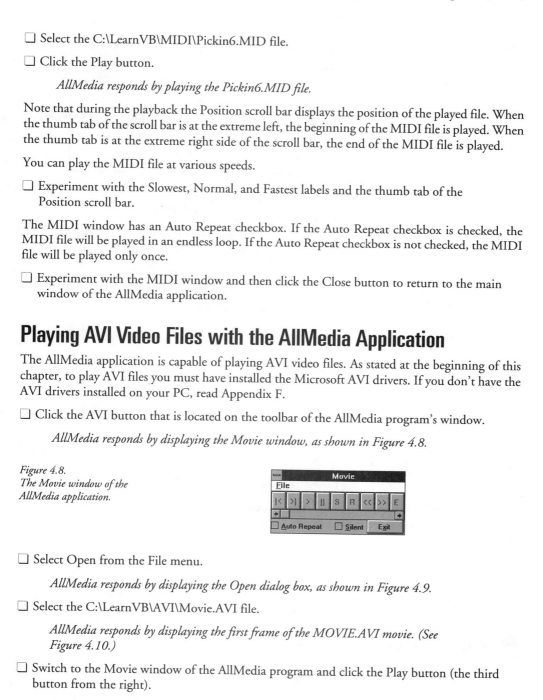

❏ Select Open from the File menu.

> *AllMedia responds by displaying the Open dialog box, as shown in Figure 4.9.*

❏ Select the C:\LearnVB\AVI\Movie.AVI file.

> *AllMedia responds by displaying the first frame of the MOVIE.AVI movie. (See Figure 4.10.)*

❏ Switch to the Movie window of the AllMedia program and click the Play button (the third button from the right).

> *AllMedia responds by playing the MOVIE.AVI movie.*

Figure 4.9.
The Open dialog box that
AllMedia displays after you
select Open from the File
menu of the Movie
window.

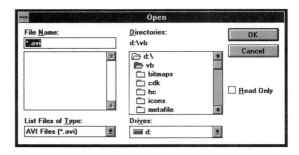

Figure 4.10.
The MOVIE.AVI window.

❑ Experiment with the other buttons of the TegoMM.VBX control.

The Movie window of AllMedia includes a Silence checkbox.

❑ Place an X inside the Silence checkbox, and then click the Play button.

AllMedia responds by playing the movie without sound.

The Movie window of AllMedia includes an Auto Repeat checkbox.

❑ Place an X inside the Auto Repeat checkbox, and then click the Play button.

AllMedia responds by playing the movie in an endless loop.

❑ While the movie is playing, minimize the window of the movie (by clicking the minus icon of the window where the movie is being displayed, and then select Minimize from the System menu that pops up).

AllMedia responds by playing the movie inside the minimized AllMedia window.

❑ Experiment with the Movie window, and then click the Exit button to return to the AllMedia program's main window.

Playing CD Audio

An audio CD is a CD that you can purchase at a record store. Here is how you play an audio CD with AllMedia:

❏ Click the CD Audio button on the toolbar of AllMedia's window.

   AllMedia responds by displaying the CD Player window. (See Figure 4.11.)

Figure 4.11.
The CD Player window.

❏ Insert an audio CD inside your CD drive, and experiment with the buttons of the CD Player window.

❏ Click the Exit button of the CD Player to return to the AllMedia program's main window.

❏ Click the About button on the toolbar of AllMedia

   AllMedia responds by displaying the About dialog box. (See Figure 4.12.)

Figure 4.12.
The About dialog box of
AllMedia.

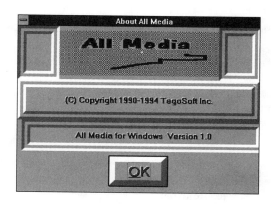

Click the OK button of the About dialog box to return to AllMedia's main window.

As stated, when the Background Music checkbox is checked, AllMedia plays music in the background.

❏ Place an X inside the Background Music checkbox.

   AllMedia responds by playing background music.

❏ Click the Exit button.

   AllMedia responds by playing Its been fun working with you.*, and then AllMedia terminates.*

The Prototype of the AllMedia Application

You'll now implement the prototype of the AllMedia application.

☐ Select New Project from the File menu and save the new project. Save the new form as AllMedia.FRM inside the C:\LearnVB\Practice\AllMedia directory. Save the new project as AllMedia.MAK inside the C:\LearnVB\Practice\AllMedia directory.

☐ Implement the frmAllMedia form according to the specifications in Table 4.1. When you finish implementing the form, it should look like the one shown in Figure 4.13. The Menu table of the frmAllMedia form is listed in Table 4.2. Figures 4.14, 4.15, and 4.16 show the menus of the frmAllMedia form.

Table 4.1. The Properties table of the frmAllMedia form.

Object: Form
Object Name: frmAllMedia

BorderStyle	=	1 'Fixed Single
Caption	=	"All Media for Windows"
Height	=	6150
Icon	=	C:\LearnVB\ICONS\AllMedia.ICO
Left	=	660
MaxButton	=	0 'False
Top	=	390
Width	=	8520

Object: Picture box
Object Name: picStatusBar

Align	=	2 'Align Bottom
BackColor	=	&H00C0C0C0&
Height	=	1860
Left	=	0
Top	=	3600
Width	=	8400

Object: TegoMM.VBX
Object Name: TegommFront

Comment: If your Tools window does not contain the TegoMM.VBX control, then add it by selecting Add File from the File menu, and then select the \Windows\System\TegoMM.VBX file. The TegoMM.VBX icon is shown in Figure 1.31.

Height	=	495
Left	=	1560
UpdateInterval	=	350
Visible	=	0 'False
Width	=	3510

Object: 3D checkbox
Object Name: chkBackMusic

Caption	=	"&Background Music"
Font3D	=	2 'Raised w/heavy shading
Height	=	495
Left	=	120
Top	=	120
Width	=	1935

Object: 3D label
Object Name: lblDeviceCap

BackColor	=	&H00C0C0C0&
BevelInner	=	1 'Inset
BevelOuter	=	1 'Inset
BevelWidth	=	5
BorderWidth	=	5
Caption	=	"Device Capabilities"
Font3D	=	4 'Inset w/heavy shading
FontSize	=	9.75
Height	=	735
Left	=	2040
Top	=	0
Width	=	5055

Object: 3D label
Object Name: lblCDAudio

BackColor	=	&H00C0C0C0&
BevelInner	=	2 'Raised
BevelWidth	=	5

continues

Table 4.1. continued

BorderWidth	=	5
Caption	=	"CD Audio"
Font3D	=	2 'Raised w/heavy shading
Height	=	1095
Left	=	6720
Top	=	720
Width	=	1695

Object: 3D label
Object Name: lblAVI

BackColor	=	&H00C0C0C0&
BevelInner	=	2 'Raised
BevelWidth	=	5
BorderWidth	=	5
Caption	=	"AVI (Movie)"
Font3D	=	2 'Raised w/heavy shading
Height	=	1095
Left	=	5040
Top	=	720
Width	=	1695

Object: 3D label
Object Name: lblMIDI

BackColor	=	&H00C0C0C0&
BevelInner	=	2 'Raised
BevelWidth	=	5
BorderWidth	=	5
Caption	=	"MIDI"
Font3D	=	2 'Raised w/heavy shading
FontSize	=	9.75
Height	=	1095
Left	=	3360
Top	=	720
Width	=	1695

Object: 3D label
Object Name: lblWAV

BackColor	=	&H00C0C0C0&
BevelInner	=	2 'Raised
BevelWidth	=	5
BorderWidth	=	5
Caption	=	"WAV"
Font3D	=	2 'Raised w/heavy shading
FontSize	=	9.75
Height	=	1095
Left	=	1680
Top	=	720
Width	=	1695

Object: 3D label
Object Name: lblPCSpeaker

BackColor	=	&H00C0C0C0&
BevelInner	=	2 'Raised
BevelWidth	=	5
BorderWidth	=	5
Caption	=	"PC Speaker"
Font3D	=	2 'Raised w/heavy shading
Height	=	1095
Left	=	0
Top	=	720
Width	=	1695

Object: Picture box
Object Name: picTopToolbar

Align	=	1 'Align Top
Height	=	1095
Left	=	0

continues

Table 4.1. continued

| Top | = 0 |
| Width | = 8400 |

Object: 3D command button
Object Name: cmdExit

BevelWidth	= 5
Caption	= "E&xit"
Font3D	= 2 'Raised w/heavy shading
FontSize	= 18
ForeColor	= &H000000FF&
Height	= 1095
Left	= 7320
Top	= 0
Width	= 1095

Object: 3D command button
Object Name: cmdAbout

BevelWidth	= 5
Caption	= "A&bout..."
Font3D	= 2 'Raised w/heavy shading
FontSize	= 9.75
ForeColor	= &H00000000&
Height	= 1095
Left	= 6120
Picture	= \VB\ICONS\MISC\MISC02.ICO
Top	= 0
Width	= 1215

Object: 3D command button
Object Name: cmdCD

| BevelWidth | = 5 |
| Caption | = "&CD Audio" |

Font3D	=	2 'Raised w/heavy shading
FontSize	=	9.75
ForeColor	=	&H00FFFF00&
Height	=	1095
Left	=	4920
Picture	=	Set an icon that shows a picture related to the CD-ROM, such as C:\LearnVB\Icons\CDICON.ICO or C:\LearnVB\Icons\CD-R.ICO.
Top	=	0
Width	=	1215

Object: 3D command button
Object Name: cmdAVI

BevelWidth	=	5
Caption	=	"&AVI"
Font3D	=	2 'Raised w/heavy shading
FontSize	=	9.75
ForeColor	=	&H0000FFFF&
Height	=	1095
Left	=	3600
Picture	=	\VB\ICONS\MISC\MISC42.ICO
Top	=	0
Width	=	1335

Object: 3D command button
Object Name: cmdMIDI

BevelWidth	=	5
Caption	=	"&MIDI"
Font3D	=	2 'Raised w/heavy shading
FontSize	=	9.75
ForeColor	=	&H00808080&
Height	=	1095
Left	=	2400
Picture	=	Set an icon that shows a picture related to music, such as C:\LearnVB\Icons\Note.ICO.

continues

Table 4.1. continued

Top	=	0
Width	=	1215

Object: 3D command button
Object Name: cmdWAV

BevelWidth	=	5
Caption	=	"&WAV"
Font3D	=	2 'Raised w/heavy shading
FontSize	=	9.75
ForeColor	=	&H00008000&
Height	=	1095
Left	=	1320
Picture	=	\VB\Icons\Industry\SINEWAVE.ICO
Top	=	0
Width	=	1095

Object: 3D command button
Object Name: cmdPCSpeaker

BevelWidth	=	5
Caption	=	"&PC Speaker"
Font3D	=	2 'Raised w/heavy shading
ForeColor	=	&H00FF0000&
Height	=	1095
Left	=	0
Picture	=	Set an icon that shows a picture related to playing music through the PC speaker, such as C:\LearnVB\Icons\PCSpeak.ICO.
Top	=	0
Width	=	1335

Object: Image
Object Name: imgFrontImage

Comment: Do not assign any picture to this image at design time. The Picture property of this image is set inside the Form_Load() procedure during runtime.

Height	=	975
Left	=	2880
Top	=	1680
Visible	=	0 'False
Width	=	1335

Object: Image
Object Name: imgFront

Comment: imgFront() is an array of images. This is element imgFront(0).

Height	=	1740
Index	=	0
Left	=	5280
Picture	=	C:\LearnVB\BMP\Media1.BMP
Top	=	1800
Visible	=	0 'False
Width	=	2295

Object: Image
Object Name: imgFront

Comment: imgFront() is an array of images. This is element imgFront(1).

Height	=	1740
Index	=	1
Left	=	5520
Picture	=	C:\LearnVB\BMP\Media2.BMP
Top	=	1680
Visible	=	0 'False
Width	=	2295

Object: Image
Object Name: imgFront

Comment: imgFront() is an array of images. This is element imgFront(2).

Height	=	1740
Index	=	2
Left	=	5760
Picture	=	C:\LearnVB\BMP\Media3.BMP

continues

4

Table 4.1. continued

Top	=	1440
Visible	=	0 'False
Width	=	2295

Object: Image
Object Name: imgFront

Comment: imgFront() is an array of images. This is element imgFront(3).

Height	=	1740
Index	=	3
Left	=	6000
Picture	=	C:\LearnVB\BMP\Media4.BMP
Top	=	1200
Visible	=	0 'False
Width	=	2295

Object: Image
Object Name: imgIcon

Comment: imgIcon() is an array of images. This is element imgIcon(0).

BorderStyle	=	1 'Fixed Single
Height	=	510
Index	=	0
Left	=	600
Picture	=	C:\LearnVB\Icons\Front0.ICO
Top	=	2760
Visible	=	0 'False
Width	=	510

Object: Image
Object Name: imgIcon

Comment: imgIcon() is an array of images. This is element imgIcon(1).

BorderStyle	=	1 'Fixed Single
Height	=	510

Index	= 1
Left	= 720
Picture	= C:\LearnVB\Icons\Front1.ICO
Top	= 2640
Visible	= 0 'False
Width	= 510

Object: Image
Object Name: imgIcon

Comment: imgIcon() is an array of images. This is element imgIcon(2).

BorderStyle	= 1 'Fixed Single
Height	= 510
Index	= 2
Left	= 840
Picture	= C:\LearnVB\Icons\Front2.ICO
Top	= 2520
Visible	= 0 'False
Width	= 510

Object: Image
Object Name: imgIcon

Comment: imgIcon() is an array of images. This is element imgIcon(3).

BorderStyle	= 1 'Fixed Single
Height	= 510
Index	= 3
Left	= 960
Picture	= C:\LearnVB\Icons\Front3.ICO
Top	= 2400
Visible	= 0 'False
Width	= 510

Object: Image
Object Name: imgIcon

Comment: imgIcon() is an array of images. This is element imgIcon(4).

BorderStyle	= 1 'Fixed Single

continues

Table 4.1. continued

Height	=	510
Index	=	4
Left	=	1080
Picture	=	C:\LearnVB\Icons\Front4.ICO
Top	=	2280
Visible	=	0 'False
Width	=	510

Object: Image
Object Name: imgIcon

Comment: imgIcon() is an array of images. This is element imgIcon(5).

BorderStyle	=	1 'Fixed Single
Height	=	510
Index	=	5
Left	=	1200
Picture	=	C:\LearnVB\Icons\Front5.ICO
Top	=	2160
Visible	=	0 'False
Width	=	510

Object: Image
Object Name: imgIcon

Comment: imgIcon() is an array of images. This is element imgIcon(6).

BorderStyle	=	1 'Fixed Single
Height	=	510
Index	=	6
Left	=	1320
Picture	=	C:\LearnVB\Icons\Front6.ICO
Top	=	2040
Visible	=	0 'False
Width	=	510

Object: Image
Object Name: imgIcon

Comment: imgIcon() is an array of images. This is element imgIcon(7).

BorderStyle	=	1 'Fixed Single
Height	=	510
Index	=	7
Left	=	1440
Picture	=	C:\LearnVB\Icons\Front7.ICO
Top	=	1920
Visible	=	0 'False
Width	=	510

Figure 4.13.
The frmAllMedia *form*
(in design mode).

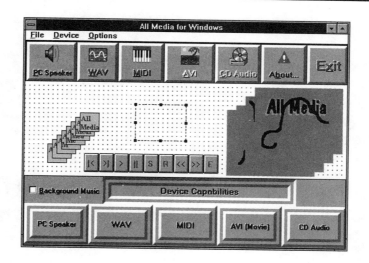

Table 4.2. The Menu table of the frmAllMedia **form.**

Menu Item	Menu Name	Shortcut
&File	mnuFile	
&About	mnuAbout	Ctrl+A
E&xit	mnuExit	Ctrl+X
&Device	mnuDevice	
&PC Speaker	mnuPCSpeaker	Ctrl+P

continues

Table 4.2. continued

Menu Item	Menu Name	Shortcut
&WAV	mnuWAV	Ctrl+W
&MIDI	mnuMIDI	Ctrl+M
A&VI (Movie)	mnuAVI	Ctrl+V
&CD Audio	mnuCD	Ctrl+C
&Options	mnuOptions	
&Background Music	mnuBackgroundMusic	Ctrl+B

Figure 4.14.
The File menu of the
frmAllMedia form.

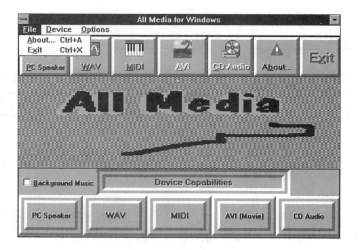

Figure 4.15.
The Device menu of the
frmAllMedia form.

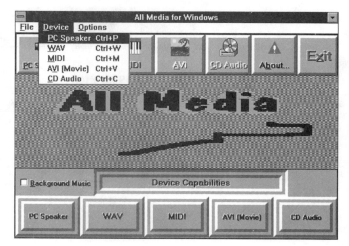

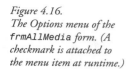

Figure 4.16.
The Options menu of the
`frmAllMedia` *form. (A*
checkmark is attached to
the menu item at runtime.)

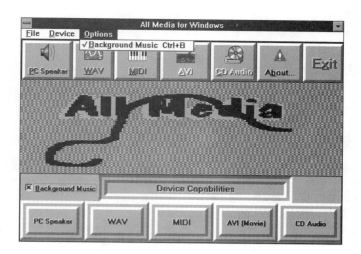

Implementing the Other Forms of the AllMedia Application

The AllMedia application is actually a collection of several programs. One program plays WAV files through the PC speaker, another program plays WAV files through the sound card, another program plays MIDI files, and so on.

In the following sections you'll implement the other forms of the AllMedia application.

Implementing the `frmPCSpeaker` Form

You'll now implement the `frmPCSpeaker` form of the AllMedia application.

❏ Select New Form from the File menu.

   Visual Basic responds by adding a new form to the project.

❏ Save the new form as SPEAKER.FRM inside the C:\LearnVB\Practice\AllMedia directory.

❏ Implement the `frmPCSpeaker` form according to the specifications in Table 4.3. When you finish implementing the form, it should look like the one shown in Figure 4.17.

Table 4.3. The Properties table of the `frmPCSpeaker` form.

Object: Form
Object Name: frmPCSpeaker

BackColor	=	&H00C0C0C0&
BorderStyle	=	1 'Fixed Single

continues

Table 4.3. continued

Caption	=	"All Media for Windows - PC Speaker"
Height	=	6060
Left	=	1275
MaxButton	=	0 'False
MinButton	=	0 'False
Top	=	120
Width	=	7395

Object: Common dialog control
Object Name: CMDialogPCSpeaker

CancelError	=	-1 'True
Left	=	5520
Top	=	4080

Object: TegoMM.VBX
Object Name: TegommPCSpeaker

Height	=	375
Left	=	2040
Top	=	1440
Visible	=	0 'False
Width	=	3510

Object: 3D command button
Object Name: cmdSamplingRate

BevelWidth	=	5
Caption	=	"&Sampling Rate..."
Enabled	=	0 'False
Font3D	=	2 'Raised w/heavy shading
FontSize	=	9.75
ForeColor	=	&H00FF0000&
Height	=	1095
Left	=	4800

| Top | = | 240 |
| Width | = | 2295 |

Object: 3D command button
Object Name: cmdPlay

BevelWidth	=	5
Caption	=	"&Play"
Font3D	=	2 'Raised w/heavy shading
FontSize	=	12
ForeColor	=	&H00FF0000&
Height	=	1095
Left	=	3000
Picture	=	Set the Picture property to the same picture that you set for the Picture property of the cmdPCSpeaker of the frmAllMedia form.
Top	=	3600
Width	=	1815

Object: 3D checkbox
Object Name: chkMultiTasking

Caption	=	"&Multitasking"
Font3D	=	2 'Raised w/heavy shading
Height	=	495
Left	=	360
Top	=	4560
Width	=	1455

Object: 3D label
Object Name: lblFastestSpeed

BackColor	=	&H00C0C0C0&
BevelInner	=	2 'Raised
BevelWidth	=	5
BorderWidth	=	5
Caption	=	"&Fastest Speed"
Font3D	=	2 'Raised w/heavy shading
Height	=	855

continues

4

Table 4.3. continued

Left	=	5760
Top	=	2160
Width	=	1215

Object: 3D label
Object Name: lblNormalSpeed

BackColor	=	&H00C0C0C0&
BevelInner	=	2 'Raised
BevelWidth	=	5
BorderWidth	=	5
Caption	=	"&Normal Speed"
Font3D	=	2 'Raised w/heavy shading
Height	=	855
Left	=	2040
Top	=	2160
Width	=	1455

Object: 3D label
Object Name: lblSlowestSpeed

BackColor	=	&H00C0C0C0&
BevelInner	=	2 'Raised
BevelWidth	=	5
BorderWidth	=	5
Caption	=	"S&lowest Speed"
Font3D	=	2 'Raised w/heavy shading
Height	=	855
Left	=	360
Top	=	2160
Width	=	1215

Object: Horizontal scroll bar
Object Name: hsbSpeed

Height	=	495
LargeChange	=	10

Left	=	360
Max	=	200
Min	=	50
Top	=	3000
Value	=	100
Width	=	6615

Object: 3D command button
Object Name: cmdOpen

BevelWidth	=	5
Caption	=	"&Open WAV File..."
Font3D	=	2 'Raised w/heavy shading
FontSize	=	9.75
ForeColor	=	&H00FF0000&
Height	=	1095
Left	=	120
Picture	=	\VB\ICONS\OFFIC\FILES04.ICO
Top	=	240
Width	=	2175

Object: 3D command button
Object Name: cmdClose

Comment: The Picture property of this button is not set. However, you may consider attaching your own picture to this button, or even a picture such as \VB\ICONS\COMM\NET11.ICO. This picture is usually used in communication programs and is attached to the button that terminates the communication. Nevertheless, this picture is also suitable for buttons that close forms.

BevelWidth	=	5
Caption	=	"&Close"
Font3D	=	2 'Raised w/heavy shading
FontSize	=	12
ForeColor	=	&H00FF0000&
Height	=	735
Left	=	3000

continues

Table 4.3. continued

Top	=	4800
Width	=	1815

Object: Image control
Object Name: imgPCSpeaker

Height	=	1215
Left	=	3000
Picture	=	C:\LearnVB\BMP\Media1.BMP
Stretch	=	-1 'True
Top	=	120
Width	=	1455

Figure 4.17.
The frmPCSpeaker *form*
(in design mode).

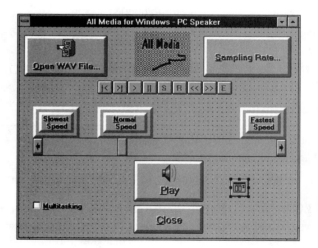

Implementing the Wave Editor Program

When the user presses the WAV button of the AllMedia program's toolbar, the Wave Editor program is executed.

The WEdit.FRM form is shown in Figure 4.18.

Figure 4.18.
The `frmWEdit` form (in
design mode).

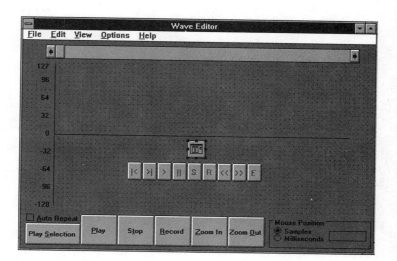

❏ Select New Form from the File menu.

> *Visual Basic responds by adding a new form to the project.*

❏ Save the new form as WEDIT.FRM inside the C:\LearnVB\Practice\AllMedia directory.

❏ Implement the `frmWEdit` form. The complete specifications for this form are outlined in Appendix E.

Implementing the `frmMIDI` Form

You'll now implement the `frmMIDI` form.

❏ Select New Form from the File menu.

> *Visual Basic responds by adding a new form to the project.*

❏ Save the new form as MIDI.FRM inside the C:\LearnVB\Practice\AllMedia directory.

❏ Implement the `frmMIDI` form according to the specifications in Table 4.4. When you finish implementing the form, it should look like the one shown in Figure 4.19.

Table 4.4. The Properties table of the `frmMIDI` form.

Object: Form
Object Name: frmMIDI

BackColor	=	&H00404000&
BorderStyle	=	1 'Fixed Single

continues

Table 4.4. continued

Caption	=	"All Media for Windows - MIDI"
Height	=	6045
Left	=	1125
MaxButton	=	0 'False
MinButton	=	0 'False
Top	=	75
Width	=	7410

Object: TegoMM.VBX control
Object Name: TegommMID

Height	=	330
Left	=	4680
Top	=	5040
Visible	=	0 'False
Width	=	3510

Object: 3D label
Object Name: Panel3D1

BackColor	=	&H00C0C0C0&
BevelInner	=	2 'Raised
BevelWidth	=	5
BorderWidth	=	5
Caption	=	"Position"
Font3D	=	2 'Raised w/heavy shading
FontSize	=	12
Height	=	975
Left	=	360
Top	=	1320
Width	=	6615

Object: Horizontal scroll bar
Object Name: hsbPosition

Height	=	255
Left	=	360

Top	=	2280
Width	=	6615

Object: 3D checkbox
Object Name: chkAutoRepeat

Caption	=	"&Auto Repeat"
Font3D	=	2 'Raised w/heavy shading
ForeColor	=	&H00000000&
Height	=	375
Left	=	240
Top	=	5160
Value	=	-1 'True
Width	=	1575

Object: 3D command button
Object Name: cmdPlay

BevelWidth	=	5
Caption	=	"&Play"
Font3D	=	2 'Raised w/heavy shading
FontSize	=	13.5
ForeColor	=	&H00FF0000&
Height	=	1095
Left	=	2280
Picture	=	Set the Picture property to the same picture to which you set the cmdMIDI button of the frmAllMedia form.
Top	=	3840
Width	=	3015

Object: Common dialog box control
Object Name: CMDialogMIDI

CancelError	=	-1 'True
Left	=	6600
Top	=	4320

continues

Table 4.4. continued

Object: 3D label
Object Name: lblFastestSpeed

BackColor	=	&H00C0C0C0&
BevelInner	=	2 'Raised
BevelWidth	=	5
BorderWidth	=	5
Caption	=	"&Fastest"
Font3D	=	2 'Raised w/heavy shading
Height	=	735
Left	=	5760
Top	=	2640
Width	=	1215

Object: 3D label
Object Name: lblNormalSpeed

BackColor	=	&H00C0C0C0&
BevelInner	=	2 'Raised
BevelWidth	=	5
BorderWidth	=	5
Caption	=	"&Normal"
Font3D	=	2 'Raised w/heavy shading
Height	=	735
Left	=	3000
Top	=	2640
Width	=	1455

Object: 3D label
Object Name: lblSlowestSpeed

BackColor	=	&H00C0C0C0&
BevelInner	=	2 'Raised
BevelWidth	=	5
BorderWidth	=	5
Caption	=	"S&lowest"
Font3D	=	2 'Raised w/heavy shading

Height	=	735
Left	=	360
Top	=	2640
Width	=	1215

Object: Horizontal scroll bar
Object Name: hsbTempo

Height	=	375
Left	=	360
Top	=	3360
Width	=	6615

Object: 3D button
Object Name: cmdOpen

BevelWidth	=	5
Caption	=	"&Open MIDI File..."
Font3D	=	2 'Raised w/heavy shading
FontSize	=	9.75
ForeColor	=	&H00FF0000&
Height	=	1095
Left	=	360
Picture	=	\VB\ICONS\OFFIC\FILES04.ICO
Top	=	120
Width	=	2175

Object: 3D button
Object Name: cmdClose

BevelWidth	=	5
Caption	=	"&Close"
Font3D	=	2 'Raised w/heavy shading
FontSize	=	9.75
ForeColor	=	&H00FF0000&
Height	=	495
Left	=	2760
Top	=	5040
Width	=	1695

continues

Table 4.4. continued

Object: Image
Object Name: imgMIDI

Height	=	1095
Left	=	3120
Picture	=	C:\LearnVB\BMP\Media1.BMP
Stretch	=	-1 'True
Top	=	120
Width	=	3855

Figure 4.19.
The frmMIDI *form (in design mode).*

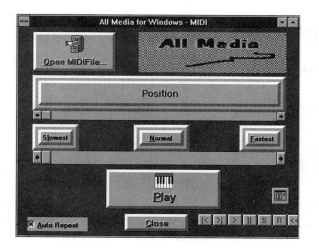

Implementing the frmMovie Form

You'll now implement the frmMovie form.

❑ Select New Form from the File menu.

Visual Basic responds by adding a new form to the project.

❑ Save the new form as MOVIE.FRM inside the C:\LearnVB\Practice\AllMedia directory.

❑ Implement the frmMovie form according to the specifications in Table 4.5. When you finish implementing the form, it should look like the one shown in Figure 4.20. The Menu table of the frmMovie form is listed in Table 4.6 and is shown in Figure 4.21.

Table 4.5. The Properties table of the `frmMovie` form.

Object: Form
Object Name: frmMovie

BackColor	=	&H00C0C0C0&
BorderStyle	=	1 'Fixed Single
Caption	=	"Movie"
Height	=	1800
Icon	=	C:\LearnVB\Icons\Movie.ICO
Left	=	1785
MaxButton	=	0 'False
Top	=	1260
Width	=	3630

Object: Common dialog box control
Object Name: CMDialogAVI

CancelError	=	-1 'True
Left	=	2280
Top	=	120

Object: Horizontal scroll bar
Object Name: hsbPosition

Height	=	255
Left	=	0
Top	=	480
Width	=	3510

Object: Command button
Object Name: cmdExit

Caption	=	"E&xit"
Height	=	375
Left	=	2520
Top	=	720
Width	=	975

continues

4

Table 4.5. continued

Object: Checkbox		
Object Name: chkSilent		
BackColor	=	&H00C0C0C0&
Caption	=	"&Silent"
Height	=	375
Left	=	1680
Top	=	720
Width	=	795

Object: Checkbox		
Object Name: chkAutoRepeat		
BackColor	=	&H00C0C0C0&
Caption	=	"&Auto Repeat"
Height	=	375
Left	=	0
Top	=	720
Width	=	1335

Object: TegoMM.VBX		
Object Name: TegommAvi		
Height	=	495
Left	=	0
Top	=	0
Width	=	3510

Table 4.6. The Menu table of the `frmMovie` form.

Menu Item	Menu Name
&File	mnuFile
&Open	mnuOpen
E&xit	mnuExit

Figure 4.20.
The frmMovie *form (in design mode).*

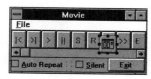

Figure 4.21.
The File menu of the frmMovie *form.*

Implementing the frmCdPlayer Form

❑ Select New Form from the File menu.

   Visual Basic responds by adding a new form to the project.

❑ Save the new form as CDPLAYER.FRM inside the C:\LearnVB\Practice\AllMedia directory.

❑ Implement the frmCdPlayer form according to the specifications in Table 4.7. When you finish implementing the form, it should look like the one shown in Figure 4.22.

Table 4.7. The Properties table of the frmCdPlayer form.

Object: Form
Object Name: frmCdPlayer

BackColor	=	&H000040C0&
Caption	=	"CD Player"
Height	=	2085
Icon	=	Set the Icon property to an icon that has some relevance to a CD player.
Left	=	465
MaxButton	=	0 'False
Top	=	2400
Width	=	8925

Object: Command button
Object Name: cmdExit

BackColor	=	&H000040C0&

continues

Table 4.7. continued

Caption	=	"E&xit"
Height	=	975
Left	=	7320
Top	=	360
Width	=	1335

Object: Command button
Object Name: cmdEject

BackColor	=	&H000040C0&
Caption	=	"&Eject"
Height	=	975
Left	=	5880
Top	=	360
Width	=	1335

Object: Command button
Object Name: cmdNext

BackColor	=	&H000040C0&
Caption	=	"&Next"
Height	=	975
Left	=	4440
Top	=	360
Width	=	1335

Object: Command button
Object Name: cmdPrev

BackColor	=	&H000040C0&
Caption	=	"P&revious"
Height	=	975
Left	=	3000
Top	=	360
Width	=	1335

Object: Command button
Object Name: cmdPlay

BackColor	=	&H000040C0&
Caption	=	"&Play"
Height	=	975
Left	=	1560
Top	=	360
Width	=	1335

Object: Command button
Object Name: cmdLoad

BackColor	=	&H000040C0&
Caption	=	"&Load"
Height	=	975
Left	=	120
Top	=	360
Width	=	1335

Object: TegoMM.VBX
Object Name: TegommCD

Height	=	330
Left	=	2640
Visible	=	0 'False
Width	=	3510

Figure 4.22.
The frmCdPlayer *form*
(in design mode).

Implementing the frmAbout Form

☐ Implement the frmAbout form according to the specifications in Table 4.8. When you
finish implementing the form, it should look like the one shown in Figure 4.23.

4

Table 4.8. The Properties table of the `frmAbout` form.

Object: Form
Object Name: frmAbout

BackColor	=	&H00C0C0C0&
BorderStyle	=	1 'Fixed Single
Caption	=	"About All Media"
Height	=	4890
Left	=	1035
MaxButton	=	0 'False
MinButton	=	0 'False
Top	=	1140
Width	=	6465

Object: 3D label
Object Name: Panel3D4

BackColor	=	&H00C0C0C0&
BevelInner	=	1 'Inset
BevelOuter	=	1 'Inset
BevelWidth	=	5
BorderWidth	=	5
Font3D	=	2 'Raised w/heavy shading
Height	=	1455
Left	=	5280
Top	=	0
Width	=	1095

Object: 3D label
Object Name: Panel3D3

BackColor	=	&H00C0C0C0&
BevelInner	=	1 'Inset
BevelOuter	=	1 'Inset
BevelWidth	=	5
BorderWidth	=	5
Font3D	=	2 'Raised w/heavy shading

Height	=	1455
Left	=	0
Top	=	0
Width	=	1095

Object: 3D label
Object Name: Panel3D2

BackColor	=	&H00C0C0C0&
BevelInner	=	1 'Inset
BevelOuter	=	1 'Inset
BevelWidth	=	5
BorderWidth	=	5
Caption	=	"All Media for Windows Version 1.0"
Font3D	=	2 'Raised w/heavy shading
FontSize	=	9.75
Height	=	855
Left	=	120
Top	=	2520
Width	=	6375

Object: 3D label
Object Name: Panel3D1

BackColor	=	&H00C0C0C0&
BevelInner	=	2 'Raised
BevelWidth	=	5
BorderWidth	=	5
Caption	=	"(C) Copyright 1990-1994 TegoSoft Inc."
Font3D	=	2 'Raised w/heavy shading
FontSize	=	9.75
Height	=	1095
Left	=	0
Top	=	1440
Width	=	6375

continues

Table 4.8. continued

Object: 3D command button
Object Name: cmdClose

BevelWidth	=	10
Caption	=	"&OK"
Font3D	=	2 'Raised w/heavy shading
FontSize	=	18
ForeColor	=	&H00FF0000&
Height	=	855
Left	=	2400
Top	=	3480
Width	=	1575

Object: Image control
Object Name: imgAbout

Height	=	1215
Left	=	1080
Picture	=	C:\LearnVB\BMP\Media1.BMP
Stretch	=	-1 'True
Top	=	120
Width	=	4215

Figure 4.23.
The frmAbout *form (in*
design mode).

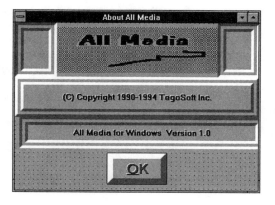

You have finished implementing all the forms used by the AllMedia application. In the next chapter you'll enter the code of the AllMedia application.

5

Creating Multimedia Programs (Part II)

In this chapter you'll write the code of the AllMedia application whose prototype you implemented in Chapter 4, "Creating Multimedia Programs (Part II)."

Attaching Code to the Load Event of the `frmAllMedia` Form

You'll now attach code to the `Form_Load()` procedure of the `frmAllMedia` form.

☐ Enter the following code inside the `Form_Load()` procedure of the `frmAllMedia` form:

```
Sub Form_Load ()

    ' Set the imgFrontImage image
    imgFrontImage.Picture = imgFront(0).Picture
    imgFrontImage.Top = picTopToolBar.Height
    imgFrontImage.Left = 0
    imgFrontImage.Stretch = True

    imgFrontImage.Height =
        ➥ frmAllMedia.ScaleHeight -
        ➥ picTopToolBar.Height -
        ➥ picStatusBar.Height

    imgFrontImage.Width = frmAllMedia.ScaleWidth
    imgFrontImage.Visible = True

    ' Update Status bar
    FindCapabilities


    ' Open the background music session
    TegommFront.DeviceType = "WaveAudio"
    TegommFront.FileName =
            ➥ Left(App.Path, 2) +
            ➥ "\LEARNVB\WAV\Bourb2M6.WAV"

    TegommFront.Command = "Open"

    ' Play the background music
    If chkBackMusic.Value = True Then
       TegommFront.Command = "Play"
    End If

End Sub
```

The code you entered is executed whenever the `frmAllMedia` form is loaded. Because `frmAllMedia` is the start-up form, the `Form_Load()` procedure of the `frmAllMedia` form is executed whenever you start the AllMedia application.

`imgFrontImage` is the image that appears inside the `frmAllMedia` form. The code you entered sets the Picture property of `imgFrontImage` to the Picture property of the first element of the `imgFront()` array of images:

```
imgFrontImage.Picture = imgFront(0).Picture
```

Recall that during design time, you set the Picture property of `imgFront(0)` to C:\LearnVB\BMP\Media1.BMP.

The `imgFrontImage` image is then placed inside the form so that the top of the image has the same height as the toolbar of the `frmAllMedia` form:

```
imgFrontImage.Top = picTopToolBar.Height
```

The left side of the `imgFrontImage` image is set to the left edge of the `frmAllMedia` form:

```
imgFrontImage.Left = 0
```

The Stretch property of the `imgFrontImage` image is then set to `True`:

```
imgFrontImage.Stretch = True
```

The Height property of `imgFrontImage` is set to the height of the `frmAllMedia` form minus the height of the toolbar and the status bar:

```
imgFrontImage.Height =
➥ frmAllMedia.ScaleHeight -
➥ picTopToolBar.Height -
➥ picStatusBar.Height
```

The width of the `imgFrontImage` image is set to the width of the `frmAllMedia` form:

```
imgFrontImage.Width = frmAllMedia.ScaleWidth
```

Finally, the Visible property of the `imgFrontImage` image is set to `True`:

```
imgFrontImage.Visible = True
```

So the Media1.BMP is placed inside the `frmAllMedia` form so that it covers the entire client area of the form. (The Media1.BMP picture will cover the entire area of the `frmAllMedia` form except the areas where the toolbar and status bar are.)

The code you entered then executes the `FindCapabilities` procedure:

```
' Update Status bar
FindCapabilities
```

The code of the `FindCapabilities` procedure is covered later in this chapter. For now, note that the `FindCapabilities` procedure sets the Enabled properties of the 3D labels that are located on the status bar of the `frmAllMedia` form to either `True` or `False`. The `FindCapabilities` procedure sets the Enabled property of the 3D labels based on the capabilities of the PC to play a particular multimedia device. For example, if the `FindCapabilities` procedure finds that the PC is capable of playing MIDI files, the Enabled property of the MIDI 3D label is set to `True`. If the `FindCapabilities` procedure determines that the PC is not capable of playing MIDI files, the Enabled property of the 3D MIDI label is set to `False`.

The `TegommFront` multimedia control is then set for playing WAV files through the sound card:

```
TegommFront.DeviceType = "WaveAudio"
```

Then the FileName property of the TegommFront control is set to the WAV file that will be played as the background music:

```
TegommFront.FileName =
            ➡ Left(App.Path, 2) +
            ➡ "\LEARNVB\WAV\Bourb2M6.WAV"
```

The Open command is issued:

```
TegommFront.Command = "Open"
```

If the chkBackMusic checkbox is checked, the Play command is issued to play the WAV file:

```
If chkBackMusic.Value = True Then
   TegommFront.Command = "Play"
End If
```

The FindCapabilities Procedure

As stated, the FindCapabilities procedure determines the multimedia capabilities of the PC and sets the Enabled properties of the status bar of the frmAllMedia form accordingly.

☐ Select New Procedure from the View menu, make sure the Sub option button is selected inside the New Procedure dialog box that pops up, type FindCapabilities inside the Name text box of the New Procedure dialog box, and then click the OK button of the New Procedure dialog box.

> *Visual Basic responds by creating the FindCapabilities procedure inside the general declarations section of the frmAllMedia form.*

☐ Enter the following code inside the FindCapabilities procedure:

```
Sub FindCapabilities ()

    TegommFront.DeviceType = "WaveAudio"
    TegommFront.Command = "open"
    If TegommFront.Error = 263 Then
       lblWAV.Enabled = False
       cmdWAV.Enabled = False
       mnuWAV.Enabled = False
    End If


    TegommFront.DeviceType = "Sequencer"
    TegommFront.Command = "open"
    If TegommFront.Error = 263 Then
       lblMIDI.Enabled = False
       cmdMIDI.Enabled = False
       mnuMIDI.Enabled = False
    End If

    TegommFront.DeviceType = "AVIVideo"
    TegommFront.Command = "open"
    If TegommFront.Error = 263 Then
       lblAVI.Enabled = False
```

```
        cmdAVI.Enabled = False
        mnuAVI.Enabled = False
    End If

    TegommFront.DeviceType = "CDAudio"
    TegommFront.Command = "open"
    If TegommFront.Error = 263 Then
        lblCDAudio.Enabled = False
        cmdCD.Enabled = False
        mnuCD.Enabled = False
    End If
```

End Sub

The code you entered sets the DeviceType property of the multimedia control to play WAV files through the sound card:

```
TegommFront.DeviceType = "WaveAudio"
```

Then the Open command is issued:

```
TegommFront.Command = "open"
```

An If statement is then executed to determine whether an error occurred due to the execution of the Open command:

```
    If TegommFront.Error = 263 Then
        lblWAV.Enabled = False
        cmdWAV.Enabled = False
        mnuWAV.Enabled = False
    End If
```

If the Error property is equal to 263, the PC is not capable of playing WAV files through the sound card, and the Enabled property of the 3D label lblWAV is set to False. In addition, the cmdWAV button on the toolbar and the mnuWAV menu item are disabled.

The next statement sets the DeviceType property of the multimedia control to play MIDI files:

```
    TegommFront.DeviceType = "Sequencer"
```

Then the Open command is issued:

```
    TegommFront.Command = "open"
```

An If statement is then executed to determine whether an error occurred during the execution of the last Open command:

```
    If TegommFront.Error = 263 Then
        lblMIDI.Enabled = False
        cmdMIDI.Enabled = False
        mnuMIDI.Enabled = False
    End If
```

If an error occurred, the Enabled property of the lblMIDI, cmdMIDI, and the MIDI menu items are set to False.

In a similar manner, the code you entered determines whether the PC is capable of playing AVI files:

```
TegommFront.DeviceType = "AVIVideo"
TegommFront.Command = "open"
If TegommFront.Error = 263 Then
   lblAVI.Enabled = False
   cmdAVI.Enabled = False
   mnuAVI.Enabled = False
End If
```

The following code determines whether the PC is capable of playing CD audio:

```
TegommFront.DeviceType = "CDAudio"
   TegommFront.Command = "open"
   If TegommFront.Error = 263 Then
      lblCDAudio.Enabled = False
      cmdCD.Enabled = False
      mnuCD.Enabled = False
   End If
```

Note that there is no need to check whether the PC is capable of playing WAV files through the PC speaker, because every PC has a speaker.

NOTE

It is important to understand that you determine the capabilities by examining various aspects of the multimedia device under investigation. For example, to determine whether the PC is capable of playing WAV files through the sound card, the TegoMM.VBX control seeks the presence of a sound card in the system, as well as all the Windows drivers that were supposed to be installed at the time the sound card was installed into the system.

The same method of determining capabilities is applied when determining whether the PC is capable of playing MIDI files, CD audio, and AVI video files.

As stated in Chapter 4, you can follow the directions listed in Appendix F to install the AVI video drivers that are needed by Windows to play AVI movie files.

Attaching Code to the Click Event of the Background Music Checkbox

You'll now attach code to the Click event of the Background Music checkbox.

❏ Enter the following code inside the chkBackMusic_Click() procedure of the frmAllMedia form:

```
Sub chkBackMusic_Click (Value As Integer)
```

```
    If Value = True Then
       TegommFront.Command = "Play"
       mnuBackgroundMusic.Checked = True
    Else
       TegommFront.Command = "Stop"
       mnuBackgroundMusic.Checked = False
    End If

End Sub
```

The code you entered uses an If…Else statement to play or stop the background music, and to toggle the state of the mnuBackgroundMusic menu item.

Recall that Value is the parameter of the chkBackMusic_Click() procedure:

```
Sub chkBackMusic_Click (Value As Integer)

    .....
    .....
    .....


End Sub
```

Value represents the state of the checkbox. If the checkbox is checked, the user placed an X inside the checkbox, and the If condition is satisfied:

```
    If Value = True Then
       TegommFront.Command = "Play"
       mnuBackgroundMusic.Checked = True
    Else
       .....
       .....
    End If
```

If the If condition is not satisfied, the user removed the X from the checkbox, and the statements under the Else are executed:

```
    If Value = True Then
       .....
       .....
    Else
       TegommFront.Command = "Stop"
       mnuBackgroundMusic.Checked = False
    End If
```

Note that the V mark to the left of the mnuBackgroundMusic menu item is checked or unchecked by setting the Checked property of this menu item to True or False.

Attaching Code to the Click Event of the cmdAbout Button of the Toolbar

You'll now attach code to the Click event of the cmdAbout button in the toolbar of the frmAllMedia form.

❑ Enter the following code inside the cmdAbout_Click() procedure of the frmAllAbout form:

```
Sub cmdAbout_Click ()

    If chkBackMusic.Value = True Then
        TegommFront.Command = "Stop"
    End If

    ' Minimize frmAllMedia
    frmAllMedia.WindowState = 1

    frmAbout.Show 1

    If chkBackMusic.Value = True Then
        TegommFront.Command = "Play"
    End If

End Sub
```

An If statement is used to determine whether the Background Music checkbox is checked:

```
    If chkBackMusic.Value = True Then
        TegommFront.Command = "Stop"
    End If
```

If the Background Music checkbox is checked, the statement under the If statement is satisfied, which issues the Stop command to stop the background music. This means that while the About dialog box is displayed, the background music is stopped.

The frmAllMedia form is then minimized:

```
frmAllMedia.WindowState = 1
```

Then the frmAbout form is displayed as a modal dialog box:

```
frmAbout.Show 1
```

Note that 1 is supplied as the parameter of the Show method. This means that the form is displayed as a modal dialog box (during the displaying of the About dialog box, the user can't switch to other windows of the AllMedia application).

Once the user closes the About dialog box, the next statement is executed:

```
    If chkBackMusic.Value = True Then
        TegommFront.Command = "Play"
    End If
```

This If statement checks whether the Background Music checkbox is checked, and if it is, a Play command is issued.

Attaching Code to the About Menu

You'll now attach code to the About menu of the frmAllMedia form.

❑ Enter the following code inside the mnuAbout_Click() procedure of the frmAllMedia form:

```
Sub mnuAbout_Click ()

    cmdAbout_Click

End Sub
```

The code you entered is executed whenever the user selects the About item from the File menu. This code executes the cmdAbout_Click() procedure. Therefore, selecting the About menu item has identical effects as clicking the About button on the toolbar.

Attaching Code to the Exit Button of the AllMedia Program's Toolbar

You'll now attach code to the Click event of the cmdExit button.

❑ Enter the following code inside the cmdExit_Click() procedure of the frmAllMedia form:

```
Sub cmdExit_Click ()

    Unload frmAllMedia

End Sub
```

The code you entered executes the Unload method on the frmAllMedia form. This causes the Form_Unload() procedure of the frmAllMedia form to be executed. The Form_Unload() procedure of the frmAllMedia form is discussed later in this chapter.

Attaching Code to the Exit Menu Item

You'll now attach code to the mnuExit menu item.

❑ Enter the following code inside the mnuExit_Click() procedure of the frmAllMedia form:

```
Sub mnuExit_Click ()

    cmdExit_Click

End Sub
```

The code you entered executes the cmdExit_Click() procedure whose code you typed already. Therefore, selecting the Exit menu has the same effect as clicking the Exit button on the toolbar.

Attaching Code to the Unload Event of the frmAllMedia Form

You'll now attach code to the Form_Unload() procedure of the frmAllMedia form. Recall that the Form_Unload() procedure is executed whenever the user clicks the Exit button, or when the user clicks the minus icon that is located on the upper-left corner of the frmAllMedia form, and then selects Close from the system menu that pops up.

☐ Enter the following code inside the `Form_Unload()` procedure of the `frmAllMedia` form:

```
Sub Form_Unload (Cancel As Integer)

    ' If playback is in progress, stop it
    If chkBackMusic.Value = True Then
        TegommFront.Command = "Stop"
    End If

    ' Open the ItsBeen1.WAV file
    TegommFront.DeviceType = "WaveAudio"
    TegommFront.FileName = Left(App.Path, 2) +
        ➥ "\LearnVB\WAV\ItsBeen1.WAV"

    TegommFront.Command = "Open"

    ' Play the ItsBeen1.WAV file
    If chkBackMusic.Value = True Then
        TegommFront.Wait = True
        TegommFront.Command = "Play"
    End If

End Sub
```

The code you entered checks whether background music is currently in progress, and if so, a `Stop` command is issued:

```
If chkBackMusic.Value = True Then
    TegommFront.Command = "Stop"
End If
```

Then the ItsBeen1.WAV file is opened:

```
TegommFront.DeviceType = "WaveAudio"
TegommFront.FileName = Left(App.Path, 2) +
    ➥ "\LearnVB\WAV\ItsBeen1.WAV"
TegommFront.Command = "Open"
```

If the Background Music checkbox is checked, the ItsBeen1.WAV file is played:

```
If chkBackMusic.Value = True Then
    TegommFront.Wait = True
    TegommFront.Command = "Play"
End If
```

Note that prior to issuing the `Play` command, the Wait property of the multimedia control is set to `True`. Therefore, the `Play` command will play the WAV file in its entirety and the application will resume only after the playback is done.

Attaching Code to the Click Event of the cmdPCSpeaker Button of the frmAllMedia Form

You'll now attach code to the Click event of the `cmdPCSpeaker` button of the toolbar of the `frmAllMedia` form.

❑ Enter the following code inside the `cmdPCSpeaker_Click()` procedure of the `frmAllMedia` form:

```
Sub cmdPCSpeaker_Click ()

    If chkBackMusic.Value = True Then
       TegommFront.Command = "Stop"
    End If


    ' Minimize frmAllMedia
    frmAllMedia.WindowState = 1

    frmPCSpeaker.Show 1

    If chkBackMusic.Value = True Then
       TegommFront.Command = "Play"
    End If

End Sub
```

The code you entered uses an `If` statement to determine whether the Background Music checkbox is checked, and if so, the background music is stopped:

```
If chkBackMusic.Value = True Then
   TegommFront.Command = "Stop"
End If
```

The `frmAllMedia` form is then minimized:

```
frmAllMedia.WindowState = 1
```

Then the `frmPCSpeaker` form is displayed as a modal dialog box:

```
frmPCSpeaker.Show 1
```

Eventually, the user will close the `frmPCSpeaker` form, and the next statements will be executed:

```
If chkBackMusic.Value = True Then
   TegommFront.Command = "Play"
End If
```

That is, if the `chkBackMusic` checkbox is checked, the `Play` command is issued, so that the background music will continue to play.

Attaching Code to the `mnuPCSpeaker` Menu Item

You'll now attach code to the `mnuPCSpeaker` menu item.

❑ Enter the following code inside the `mnuPCSpeaker_Click()` procedure of the `frmAllMedia` form:

```
Sub mnuPCSpeaker_Click ()

    cmdPCSpeaker_Click

End Sub
```

The code you entered executes the cmdPCSpeaker_Click() procedure, whose code you typed already. Therefore, selecting the PC Speaker menu has the same effect as clicking the PC Speaker button on the toolbar.

5

Attaching Code to the Click Event of the cmdWAV Button

You'll now attach code to the cmdWAV button of the frmAllMedia form.

☐ Enter the following code inside the cmdWAV_Click() procedure of the frmAllMedia form:

```
Sub cmdWAV_Click ()

    If chkBackMusic.Value = True Then
        TegommFront.Command = "Stop"
    End If

    ' Minimize frmAllMedia
    frmAllMedia.WindowState = 1

    frmWedit.Show 1

    If chkBackMusic.Value = True Then
        TegommFront.Command = "Play"
    End If

End Sub
```

The code you entered is executed whenever the user clicks the WAV button on the toolbar of the AllMedia program's window.

An If statement is used to determine whether the Background Music checkbox is checked, and if so, the code under the If statement stops the background music:

```
    If chkBackMusic.Value = True Then
        TegommFront.Command = "Stop"
    End If
```

The frmAllMedia form is minimized:

```
    frmAllMedia.WindowState = 1
```

Then the frmWEdit form is displayed as a modal dialog box:

```
    frmWEdit.Show 1
```

When the user closes the WEdit form, the next statements are executed:

```
    If chkBackMusic.Value = True Then
        TegommFront.Command = "Play"
    End If
```

The preceding statements use an If statement to determine whether the Background Music checkbox is checked, and if so, the Play command is issued.

Attaching Code to the mnuWAV Menu Item

You'll now attach code to the mnuWAV menu item.

☐ Enter the following code inside the mnuWAV_Click() procedure of the frmAllMedia form:

```
Sub mnuWAV_Click ()

    cmdWAV_Click

End Sub
```

The code you entered executes the cmdWAV_Click() procedure, whose code you typed already. Therefore, selecting the WAV menu has the same effect as clicking the WAV button on the toolbar.

Attaching Code to the Click Event of the cmdAVI Button of the frmAllMedia Form

You'll now attach code to the cmdAVI button of the toolbar of the frmAllMedia window.

☐ Enter the following code inside the cmdAVI_Click() procedure of the frmAllMedia form:

```
Sub cmdAVI_Click ()

    If chkBackMusic.Value = True Then
       TegommFront.Command = "Stop"
    End If

    ' Minimize frmAllMedia
    frmAllMedia.WindowState = 1

    frmMovie.Show 1

    If chkBackMusic.Value = True Then
       TegommFront.Command = "Play"
    End If

End Sub
```

The code you entered is similar to the code that you attached to the PC Speaker button and to the WAV button. However, in this procedure frmMovie is displayed.

Attaching Code to the mnuAVI Menu Item

You'll now attach code to the mnuAVI menu item.

☐ Enter the following code inside the mnuAVI_Click() procedure of the frmAllMedia form:

```
Sub mnuAVI_Click ()

    cmdAVI_Click

End Sub
```

The code you entered executes the cmdAVI_Click() procedure, whose code you typed already. Therefore, selecting the AVI menu has the same effect as clicking the AVI button on the toolbar.

Attaching Code to the Click Event of the CD Player Button of the frmAllMedia Form

You'll now attach code to the cmdCD button of the toolbar of the frmAllMedia window.

❑ Enter the following code inside the cmdCD_Click() procedure of the frmAllMedia form:

```
Sub cmdCD_Click ()

    If chkBackMusic.Value = True Then
       TegommFront.Command = "Stop"
    End If

    ' Minimize frmAllMedia
    frmAllMedia.WindowState = 1

    frmCDPlayer.Show 1

    If chkBackMusic.Value = True Then
       TegommFront.Command = "Play"
    End If

End Sub
```

The code you entered is similar to the code that you attached to the PC Speaker button, to the WAV button, and to the AVI Movie button. However, in this procedure the frmCDPlayer form is displayed.

Attaching Code to the CD Menu Item

You'll now attach code to the mnuCD menu item.

❑ Enter the following code inside the mnuCD_Click() procedure of the frmAllMedia form:

```
Sub mnuCD_Click ()

    cmdCD_Click

End Sub
```

The code you entered executes the cmdCD_Click() procedure, whose code you typed already. Therefore, selecting the CD menu has the same effect as clicking the CD button on the toolbar.

Attaching Code to the Click Event of the MIDI Button of the frmAllMedia Form

You'll now attach code to the cmdMIDI button of the toolbar of the frmAllMedia window.

❑ Enter the following code inside the cmdMIDI_Click() procedure of the frmAllMedia form:

```
Sub cmdMIDI_Click ()

    If chkBackMusic.Value = True Then
        TegommFront.Command = "Stop"
    End If

    ' Minimize frmAllMedia
    frmAllMedia.WindowState = 1

    frmMIDI.Show 1

    If chkBackMusic.Value = True Then
        TegommFront.Command = "Play"
    End If

End Sub
```

The code you entered is similar to the code that you attached to the PC Speaker button, to the WAV button, to the AVI Movie button, and to the CD Player button. However, in this procedure the frmMIDI form is displayed.

Attaching Code to the mnuMIDI Menu Item

You'll now attach code to the mnuMIDI menu item.

❑ Enter the following code inside the mnuMIDI_Click() procedure of the frmAllMedia form:

```
Sub mnuMIDI_Click ()

    cmdMIDI_Click

End Sub
```

The code you entered executes the cmdMIDI_Click() procedure, whose code you typed already. Therefore, selecting the MIDI menu has the same effect as clicking the MIDI button on the toolbar.

Attaching Code to the mnuBackgroundMusic Menu Item

You'll now attach code to the Background Music checkbox of the frmAllMedia form.

❑ Enter the following code inside the mnuBackgroundMusic_Click() procedure of the frmAllMedia form:

```
Sub mnuBackgroundMusic_Click ()
```

5

```
If chkBackMusic.Value = False Then
    chkBackMusic.Value = True
    mnuBackgroundMusic.Checked = True
Else
    chkBackMusic.Value = False
    mnuBackgroundMusic.Checked = False
End If
```

End Sub

The code you entered is executed whenever the user selects the Background Music menu item. This code toggles the V mark to the left of the Background Music menu item, and also toggles the state of the Background Music checkbox.

Attaching Code to the Done Event of the TegommFront Control

You'll now attach code to the Done event of the TegommFront control.

❑ Enter the following code inside the TegommFront_Done() procedure of the frmAllMedia form:

Sub TegommFront_Done ()

```
If TegommFront.Position = TegommFront.Length Then
    TegommFront.Command = "Prev"
    TegommFront.Command = "Play"
End If
```

End Sub

The code you entered is executed whenever the TegommFront control finishes performing an operation. An If statement is executed to determine whether the TegommFront_Done() procedure is executed because the Play command executed. This is accomplished by checking whether the Position property of the TegommFront control is equal to the Length property of the TegommFront control. If the If condition is satisfied, the Prev command is issued to rewind the WAV file, and then the Play command is issued to play the WAV file. So the background music is played all over again in an endless loop.

Attaching Code to the StatusUpdate Event of the TegommFront Control

Recall that at design time you set the UpdateInterval property of the TegommFront control to 350 milliseconds. This means that the TegommFront_StatusUpdate() procedure is automatically executed every 350 milliseconds.

❑ Enter the following code inside the TegommFront_StatusUpdate() procedure of the frmAllMedia form:

```
Sub TegommFront_StatusUpdate ()

    ' Variable used for the creation of the animated icon.
    Static sIconNumber

    ' Variable used for the creation of the
    ' animated front picture.
    Static sPictureNumber

' Display an animated front picture
If frmAllMedia.WindowState = 0 And
            ➥  TegommFront.Mode = 526 Then
    sPictureNumber = sPictureNumber + 1
    If sPictureNumber = 4 Then
        sPictureNumber = 0
    End If
    frmAllMedia.imgFrontImage =
            ➥  imgFront(sPictureNumber).Picture
End If



' Display an animated icon
If frmAllMedia.WindowState = 1 Then
    sIconNumber = sIconNumber + 1
    If sIconNumber = 8 Then
        sIconNumber = 0
    End If
    frmAllMedia.Icon = imgIcon(sIconNumber).Picture
End If

End Sub
```

The procedure starts by declaring a Static variable:

```
Static sIconNumber
```

Recall that a Static variable maintains its value throughout the life of the program. That is, a "regular" variable that is declared inside a procedure is created as a new variable every time the procedure is executed. For example, if you declare the variable MyVariable inside the procedure as follows:

```
Dim MyVariable As Integer
```

then upon executing the procedure, Visual Basic assigns the value 0 to the MyVariable variable. During the execution of the procedure, you can set the value of MyVariable to 5 in this way:

```
MyVariable = 5
```

When the procedure is terminated, MyVariable disappears! It does not exist anymore, and hence there is no trace of the fact that MyVariable was ever equal to 5. If you execute the procedure again, MyVariable is created all over. That is, it is created with the value 0.

Static variables, on the other hand, do not lose their values. When the procedure is executed again, the Static variable exists already, and its value is equal to the value that existed during the last execution of the procedure.

> **NOTE**
>
> As you can see, a `Static` variable maintains its value throughout the life of the program. This means that a `Static` variable utilizes memory, and that memory is dedicated to the variable throughout the life of the program.
>
> A "regular" variable, on the other hand, occupies memory only during the execution of the procedure. However, when the procedure is terminated, that memory is freed, and it can be used by other variables.

An `If` statement is then executed to display one frame of the animated logo:

```
If frmAllMedia.WindowState = 0 And
        ➥ TegommFront.Mode = 526 Then
   sPictureNumber = sPictureNumber + 1
   If sPictureNumber = 4 Then
      sPictureNumber = 0
   End If
   frmAllMedia.imgFrontImage =
          ➥ imgFront(sPictureNumber).Picture
End If
```

When the `Static` variable is created for the first time, `sPictureNumber` is set to 0.

The `If` statement is satisfied if the `frmAllMedia` form is at its normal size (`WindowState=0`).

The `Static` variable `sPictureNumber` is increased by 1:

```
sPictureNumber = sPictureNumber + 1
```

An inner `If` statement is executed to examine whether `sPictureNumber` reached its maximum value. If so, `sPictureNumber` is set back to 0:

```
If sPictureNumber = 4 Then
   sPictureNumber = 0
End If
```

The Picture property of the `imgFrontImage` image is then set to the Picture property of the `imgFront()` image:

```
frmAllMedia.imgFrontImage =
       ➥ imgFront(sPictureNumber).Picture
```

So when the `TegommFront_StatusUpdate()` procedure is executed for the first time, `sPictureNumber` is equal to 0. This means that the Picture property of the `imgFrontImage` image is set to the Picture property of the `imgFront(0)` image (which is Media1.BMP). After 350 milliseconds, the procedure is executed again. Now however, `sPictureNumber` is equal to 2, so the Picture property of the `imgFrontImage` image is set to the Picture property of the `imgFront(1)` image (which is Media2.BMP). This process repeats every 350 milliseconds. So the Picture property of the `imgFrontImage` image is set as follows:

```
Media1.BMP
Media2.BMP
Media3.BMP
Media4.BMP
Media1.BMP
Media2.BMP
Media3.BMP
Media4.BMP
....
....
....
```

In other words, the logo of AllMedia is shown animated.

> **NOTE**
>
> Note that the statement
>
> ```
> frmAllMedia.imgFrontImage =
>         ➥ imgFront(sPictureNumber).Picture
> ```
>
> has the same effect as the statement
>
> ```
> frmAllMedia.imgFrontImage.Picture =
>         ➥ imgFront(sPictureNumber).Picture
> ```
>
> That is, the default property of an image control is Picture.

In a similar manner, the `sIconNumber` variable that was declared as `Static` in this procedure is used to display the animated icon whenever the window of the `frmAllMedia` form is minimized:

```
If frmAllMedia.WindowState = 1 Then
    sIconNumber = sIconNumber + 1
    If sIconNumber = 8 Then
        sIconNumber = 0
    End If
    frmAllMedia.Icon = imgIcon(sIconNumber).Picture
End If
```

You have finished entering the code of the `frmAllMedia` form. In the following sections you'll enter the code of the `frmPCSpeaker` form.

The Code Inside the General Declarations Section of the `frmPCSpeaker` Form

You'll now declare several constants inside the general declarations section of the `frmPCSpeaker` form.

❑ Enter the following code inside the general declarations section of the `frmPCSpeaker` form:

```
Option Explicit
```

```
Const NORMAL_SPEED = 100
Const FASTEST_SPEED = 200
Const SLOWEST_SPEED = 50
```

Attaching Code to the Load Event of the frmPCSpeaker Form

You'll now attach code to the Load event of the frmPCSpeaker form.

❑ Enter the following code inside the Form_Load() procedure of the frmPCSpeaker form:

```
Sub Form_Load ()

    cmdPlay.Enabled = False

    TegommPCSpeaker.DeviceType = "PCSpeaker"

    hsbSpeed.Min = SLOWEST_SPEED
    hsbSpeed.Max = FASTEST_SPEED
    hsbSpeed.Value = NORMAL_SPEED

End Sub
```

The Enabled property of the cmdPlay button is set to False:

```
    cmdPlay.Enabled = False
```

This is done because when the form is loaded there is no WAV file opened, and therefore, the cmdPlay button should be disabled because there is no WAV file to play.

The multimedia control is then set for playback of WAV files through the PC speaker:

```
    TegommPCSpeaker.DeviceType = "PCSpeaker"
```

The hsbSpeed scroll bar is used for controlling the playback speed. The Min, Max, and Value properties of the scroll bar are set as follows:

```
    hsbSpeed.Min = SLOWEST_SPEED
    hsbSpeed.Max = FASTEST_SPEED
    hsbSpeed.Value = NORMAL_SPEED
```

This means that the current value of the scroll bar is NORMAL_SPEED, which was declared as 100 inside the general declarations section. Recall that FASTEST_SPEED and SLOWEST_SPEED were also declared inside the general declarations section of the frmPCSpeaker form.

Attaching Code to the Click Event of the Open Button of the frmPCSpeaker Form

You'll now attach code to the Click event of the cmdOpen button.

❑ Enter the following code inside the cmdOpen_Click() procedure of the frmPCSpeaker form:

```
Sub cmdOpen_Click ()
```

```
    On Error GoTo OpenPCSpeakerError

    ' Set the items of the File Type list box
    CMDialogPCSpeaker.Filter =
        ➥ "All Files (*.*) ¦*.* ¦Wav Files (*.wav)¦*.wav"


    ' Set the default File Type WAV Files (*.wav)
    CMDialogPCSpeaker.FilterIndex = 2


    ' Display the dialog box
    CMDialogPCSpeaker.Action = 1

    ' Remove the error trap
    On Error GoTo 0

    ' Open the selected WAV file
    TegommPCSpeaker.FileName = CMDialogPCSpeaker.Filename
    TegommPCSpeaker.Command = "Open"
    If TegommPCSpeaker.Error > 0 Then
        cmdPlay.Enabled = False
        cmdSamplingRate.Enabled = False
        frmPCSpeaker.Caption = "PC Speaker"

        MsgBox "Can't open " +
            ➥ CMDialogPCSpeaker.Filename, 16, "Error"

    Else
        frmPCSpeaker.Caption = "PC Speaker - ("
            ➥ + CMDialogPCSpeaker.Filetitle + ")"

        cmdPlay.Enabled = True
        cmdSamplingRate.Enabled = True
    End If


    ' Exit this procedure
    Exit Sub

OpenPCSpeakerError:
    ' The user pressed the Cancel key of
    ' the CMDialog1 control

    ' Exit this procedure
    Exit Sub

End Sub
```

The code you entered sets an error trap:

```
On Error GoTo OpenPCSpeakerError
```

That is, if during the execution an error occurs, the program will immediately jump to the OpenPCSpeaker label and will execute the statement following this label.

The Filter property of the common dialog control is set:

```
CMDialogPCSpeaker.Filter =
    ➡ "All Files (*.*) ¦*.* ¦Wav Files (*.wav)¦*.wav"
```

Therefore, when the common dialog box is displayed, the user will have the option of displaying only WAV files or all files.

The default setting of the common dialog box is such that it will display only WAV files:

```
CMDialogPCSpeaker.FilterIndex = 2
```

Then the common dialog box is displayed:

```
CMDialogPCSpeaker.Action = 1
```

When the common dialog box is displayed, the user can select a file or click the Cancel button of the dialog box to close it. Because the CancelError property of the common dialog control was set to True at design time, an error will occur if the user clicks the Cancel button of the dialog box. Because you set an error trap, the procedure will immediately execute the statements following the label that was specified with the On Error statement:

```
OpenPCSpeakerError:
    ' The user pressed the Cancel key of
    ' the CMDialog1 control

    ' Exit this procedure
    Exit Sub
```

This means that if the user clicks the Cancel button of the common dialog box, the procedure immediately terminates.

If the user did select a file, the path and filename are automatically stored inside the Filename property of the common dialog control.

The statement

```
On Error GoTo 0
```

removes the error trap.

The procedure opens the selected WAV file:

```
TegommPCSpeaker.FileName = CMDialogPCSpeaker.Filename
TegommPCSpeaker.Command = "Open"
```

Of course the user could have selected a TXT, DOC, or any other invalid WAV file. Therefore, there is a need to check whether the WAV session was opened successfully:

```
    If TegommPCSpeaker.Error > 0 Then
        .....
        .....
        .....
    Else
        .....
        .....
```

```
     .....
  End If
```

If an error occurred during the execution of the `Open` command, the statements under the `If` statement are executed:

```
If TegommPCSpeaker.Error > 0 Then
   cmdPlay.Enabled = False
   cmdSamplingRate.Enabled = False
   frmPCSpeaker.Caption = "PC Speaker"

   MsgBox "Can't open " +
      ➧ CMDialogPCSpeaker.Filename, 16, "Error"

Else
   ......
   ......
   ......
End If
```

That is, if the WAV session was not opened successfully, the `cmdPlay` button is disabled, the `cmdSamplingRate` button is disabled, and the Caption property of the `frmPCSpeaker` is set to `PC Speaker`. Then a message box is displayed, telling the user that the selected file can't be opened.

If the WAV file was opened successfully, the statements under the `Else` are executed:

```
If TegommPCSpeaker.Error > 0 Then
   .....
   .....
   .....
Else
   frmPCSpeaker.Caption = "PC Speaker - ("
      ➧ + CMDialogPCSpeaker.Filetitle + ")"

   cmdPlay.Enabled = True
   cmdSamplingRate.Enabled = True
End If
```

The Caption property of the `frmPCSpeaker` window is set to the FileTitle property of the common dialog control (so that the window's caption will display the name of the opened WAV file):

```
frmPCSpeaker.Caption = "PC Speaker - ("
      ➧ + CMDialogPCSpeaker.Filetitle + ")"
```

The `cmdPlay` button is enabled (so that the user will be able to play the WAV file):

```
cmdPlay.Enabled = True
```

The `cmdSamplingRate` button is enabled (so that the user will be able to examine the sampling rate of the opened WAV file):

```
cmdSamplingRate.Enabled = True
```

Finally, the procedure is terminated:

```
Exit Sub
```

Attaching Code to the Click Event of the cmdPlay **Button of the** frmPCSpeaker **Form**

You'll now attach code to the Click event of the cmdPlay button of the frmPCSpeaker form.

❏ Enter the following code inside the cmdPlay_Click() procedure of the frmPCSpeaker form:

```
Sub cmdPlay_Click ()

    cmdPlay.Caption = "Sto&p"
    frmPCSpeaker.Refresh
    TegommPCSpeaker.Command = "Play"

End Sub
```

The code you entered sets the Caption property of the cmdPlay button to Stop. Therefore, during the playback, the user will be able to stop the playback (provided that the user checked the Multitasking checkbox):

```
cmdPlay.Caption = "Sto&p"
```

The Refresh method is executed (so that the changes that you made to the Caption property of the cmdPlay button will be executed immediately):

```
frmPCSpeaker.Refresh
```

Finally, the Play command is issued:

```
TegommPCSpeaker.Command = "Play"
```

Attaching Code to the Click Event of the cmdSamplingRate **Button of the** frmPCSpeaker **Form**

You'll now attach code to the Click event of the cmdSamplingRate button of the frmPCSpeaker form.

❏ Enter the following code inside the cmdSamplingRate_Click() procedure of the frmPCSpeaker form:

```
Sub cmdSamplingRate_Click ()

    Dim SampRate As String

    SampRate = "Sampling Rate: "
    SampRate = SampRate + TegommPCSpeaker.SamplingRate

    MsgBox SampRate, 48, "Sampling Rate"

End Sub
```

The code you entered displays a message box that tells the user the sampling rate of the opened WAV file.

Note that the sampling rate is stored in the SamplingRate property of the multimedia control.

Attaching Code to the Change Event of the Speed Scroll Bar

You'll now attach code to the Change event of the speed scroll bar of the `frmPCSpeaker` form.

❏ Enter the following code inside the `hsbSpeed_Change()` procedure of the `frmPCSpeaker` form:

```
Sub hsbSpeed_Change ()

    ' Set the pcSpeed property to the current value
    ' of the hsbSpeed scroll bar.
    TegommPCSpeaker.pcSpeed = hsbSpeed.Value

End Sub
```

The code you entered is automatically executed whenever the user changes the speed scroll bar. This code sets the pcSpeed property of the multimedia control to the Value property of the speed scroll bar:

```
TegommPCSpeaker.pcSpeed = hsbSpeed.Value
```

From now on, the WAV file will be played at the speed set by the pcSpeed property of the multimedia control.

Attaching Code to the Click Event of the Fastest 3D Label

You'll now attach code to the Fastest 3D label.

❏ Enter the following code inside the `lblFastestSpeed_Click()` procedure of the `frmPCSpeaker` form:

```
Sub lblFastestSpeed_Click ()

    hsbSpeed.Value = FASTEST_SPEED
    TegommPCSpeaker.pcSpeed = hsbSpeed.Value

End Sub
```

The code you entered is executed whenever the user clicks the Fastest 3D label. This code sets the Value property of the speed scroll bar to FASTEST_SPEED and then the pcSpeed property of the multimedia control is set to the Value property of the speed scroll bar.

Attaching Code to the Click Event of the Normal 3D Label

You'll now attach code to the Normal 3D label.

❏ Enter the following code inside the `lblNormalSpeed_Click()` procedure of the `frmPCSpeaker` form:

```
Sub lblNormalSpeed_Click ()

    hsbSpeed.Value = NORMAL_SPEED
```

5

```
TegommPCSpeaker.pcSpeed = hsbSpeed.Value
```

End Sub

The code you entered is executed whenever the user clicks the Normal 3D label. This code sets the Value property of the speed scroll bar to NORMAL_SPEED and then the pcSpeed property of the multimedia control is set to the Value property of the speed scroll bar.

Attaching Code to the Click Event of the Slowest 3D Label

You'll now attach code to the Slowest 3D label.

❏ Enter the following code inside the lblSlowestSpeed_Click() procedure of the frmPCSpeaker form:

```
Sub lblSlowestSpeed_Click ()

    hsbSpeed.Value = SLOWEST_SPEED
    TegommPCSpeaker.pcSpeed = hsbSpeed.Value

End Sub
```

The code you entered is executed whenever the user clicks the Slowest 3D label. This code sets the Value property of the speed scroll bar to SLOWEST_SPEED and then the pcSpeed property of the multimedia control is set to the Value property of the speed scroll bar.

Attaching Code to the Done Event of the TegommPCSpeaker Multimedia Control

You'll now attach code to the Done event of the multimedia control. Recall that the Done event occurs whenever the multimedia control completes the execution of a command.

❏ Enter the following code inside the TegommPCSpeaker_Done() procedure of the frmPCSpeaker form:

```
Sub TegommPCSpeaker_Done ()

    ' Did playback position reach the end of the file?
    If TegommPCSpeaker.Position = TegommPCSpeaker.Length
                     ➥ Then

        ' Rewind the multimedia control.
        TegommPCSpeaker.Command = "Prev"

        ' Set the caption of the Play button to &Play
        cmdPlay.Caption = "&Play"


    End If

End Sub
```

An If statement is executed to determine whether the Done event occurred because the WAV file was played in its entirety:

```
If TegommPCSpeaker.Position = TegommPCSpeaker.Length
                      ➡ Then
   ......
   ......
   ......

End If
```

If this is the case, the WAV file is rewound:

```
TegommPCSpeaker.Command = "Prev"
```

The Caption of the cmdPlay button is set to Play:

```
cmdPlay.Caption = "&Play"
```

Attaching Code to the Click Event of the Multitasking Checkbox of the frmPCSpeaker Form

You'll now attach code to the Multitasking checkbox of the frmPCSpeaker form.

❑ Enter the following code inside the chkMultiTasking_Click() procedure of the frmPCSpeaker form:

```
Sub chkMultiTasking_Click (Value As Integer)

   ' Enable multitasking?
   If chkMultitasking.Value = True Then

      ' Set the multitask time slice to 400 milliseconds.
      TegommPCSpeaker.pcTaskInterval = 400

      ' Enable the mouse during playback
      TegommPCSpeaker.pcMouseEnabled = True

   Else

      ' No multitasking.
      TegommPCSpeaker.pcTaskInterval = 0

      ' Disable the mouse during playback.
      TegommPCSpeaker.pcMouseEnabled = False

      ' Set the caption of the cmdPlay button to "Play".
      cmdPlay.Caption = "&Play"

   End If

End Sub
```

5

If the Value property of the Multitasking checkbox is True, the If condition is satisfied and the statements under the If statement are executed.

These statements set the pcTaskInterval property to 400 milliseconds:

```
TegommPCSpeaker.pcTaskInterval = 400
```

Then pcMouseEnabled is set to True:

```
TegommPCSpeaker.pcMouseEnabled = True
```

If the Multitasking checkbox is not checked, the multitasking capability of the multimedia control is disabled:

```
TegommPCSpeaker.pcTaskInterval = 0
TegommPCSpeaker.pcMouseEnabled = False
```

Attaching Code to the Click Event of the cmdClose Button

You'll now attach code to the Click event of the cmdClose button of the frmPCSpeaker form.

❏ Enter the following code inside the cmdClose_Click() procedure of the frmPCSpeaker form:

```
Sub cmdClose_Click ()

    Unload frmPCSpeaker

End Sub
```

The code you entered is executed whenever the user clicks the Close button. This code causes the execution of the Form_Unload() procedure of the frmPCSpeaker form. The Form_Unload() procedure of the frmPCSpeaker form is covered in the following section.

Attaching Code to the Unload Event of the frmPCSpeaker Form

You'll now attach code to the Form_Unload() procedure of the frmPCSpeaker form. The Form_Unload() procedure is executed whenever the user clicks the Close button, or whenever the user clicks the minus icon that appears on the upper-left corner of the frmPCSpeaker form and then selects Close from the system menu that pops up.

❏ Enter the following code inside the Form_Unload() procedure of the frmPCSpeaker form:

```
Sub Form_Unload (Cancel As Integer)

    ' Restore size of frmAllMedia
    frmAllMedia.WindowState = 0

End Sub
```

The code you entered restores the frmAllMedia form to its normal size.

The Wave Editor Program

The code of the Wave Editor program is listed in detail in Appendix E.

☐ Enter the code of the Wave Editor program as outlined in Appendix E.

> **NOTE**
>
> Because the WEDIT.FRM form is long and complex, you might want to just copy the WEDIT.FRM file from the C:\LearnVB\Original\AllMedia directory to the C:\LearnVB\Practice\AllMedia directory, and study the code of WEDIT.FRM later.

The MIDI.FRM Form

You'll now enter the code of the MIDI.FRM form. The MIDI.FRM form is used for playing MIDI files.

The General Declarations Section of the `frmMIDI` Form

You'll now enter code inside the general declarations section of the `frmMIDI` form.

☐ Enter the following code inside the general declarations section of the `frmMIDI` form:

```
Option Explicit

Dim gNormalTempo
```

The `gNormalTempo` variable is declared inside the general declarations section, because as you'll soon see, it is being accessed from several procedures of the `frmMIDI` form.

Attaching Code to the Load Event of the `frmMIDI` Form

You'll now attach code to the Load event of the `frmMIDI` form.

☐ Enter the following code inside the `Form_Load()` procedure of the `frmMIDI` form:

```
Sub Form_Load ()

    cmdPlay.Enabled = False

    ' Set the multimedia control for playback of MIDI files.
    TegommMid.DeviceType = "Sequencer"

    ' Set the Min and Max of the hsbPosition scroll bar.
    hsbPosition.Min = 0
    hsbPosition.Max = 100

    ' Set the timer interval of the multimedia control
```

```
' to 100 milliseconds.
TegommMid.UpdateInterval = 100
```

End Sub

The code you entered is executed whenever the user clicks the MIDI button of the `frmAllMedia` form.

The code you entered inside the `Form_Load()` procedure of the `frmMIDI` form disables the `cmdPlay` button:

```
cmdPlay.Enabled = False
```

This makes sense because the MIDI form was just loaded, and therefore, currently there is no MIDI file to play.

The multimedia control is then set for playback of MIDI files:

```
TegommMid.DeviceType = "Sequencer"
```

The Min and Max properties of the position scroll bar are set:

```
hsbPosition.Min = 0
hsbPosition.Max = 100
```

The UpdateInterval property of the multimedia control is set to 100 milliseconds:

```
TegommMid.UpdateInterval = 100
```

This means that the `TegommMID_StatusUpdate()` procedure will be automatically executed every 100 milliseconds.

Attaching Code to the Click Event of the cmdOpen **Button of the** frmMIDI **Form**

You'll now attach code to the Click event of the `cmdOpen` button.

❏ Enter the following code inside the `cmdOpen_Click()` procedure of the `frmMIDI` form:

```
Sub cmdOpen_Click ()

    On Error GoTo OpenMIDIError

    ' Set the items of the File Type list box
    CMDialogMIDI.Filter =
        ➥ "All Files (*.*) ¦*.* ¦Midi Files (*.mid)¦*.mid"


    ' Set the default File Type MIDI Files (mid.*)
    CMDialogMIDI.FilterIndex = 2


    ' Display the dialog box
    CMDialogMIDI.Action = 1
```

```
' Remove the error trap
On Error GoTo 0

' Open the selected MIDI file
TegommMid.FileName = CMDialogMIDI.Filename
TegommMid.Command = "Open"
If TegommMid.Error > 0 Then

    cmdPlay.Enabled = False

    MsgBox "Can't open " +
        ➥ CMDialogMIDI.Filename, 16, "Error"

Else
    frmMIDI.Caption =
        ➥ "MIDI - (" + CMDialogMIDI.Filetitle + ")"
    cmdPlay.Caption = "&Play"
    cmdPlay.Enabled = True


    ' Store the normal tempo.
    gNormalTempo = TegommMid.Tempo

    ' Set the Min and Max of the hsbTempo scroll bar.
    hsbTempo.Min = gNormalTempo / 2
    hsbTempo.Max = gNormalTempo * 1.5

    ' Set the hsbTempo scroll bar to the normal tempo.
    hsbTempo.Value = gNormalTempo


End If


' Exit this procedure
Exit Sub

OpenMIDIError:
' The user pressed the Cancel key of
' the CMDialog1 control

' Exit this procedure
Exit Sub

End Sub
```

The code you entered inside the cmdOpen_Click() procedure is very similar to the code that you entered inside the cmdOpen_Click() procedure of the frmPCSpeaker form.

Of course, now you are opening a MIDI file, and therefore the Filter property of the common dialog box is set accordingly:

```
CMDialogMIDI.Filter =
    ➥ "All Files (*.*) ¦*.* ¦Midi Files (*.mid)¦*.mid"


CMDialogMIDI.FilterIndex = 2
```

Also, after the MIDI file is opened, the Tempo property of the multimedia control is assigned to the gNormalTempo variable:

```
gNormalTempo = TegommMid.Tempo
```

The Min and Max properties of the speed scroll bar are set to half the normal speed and one-and-a-half times the normal speed:

```
hsbTempo.Min = gNormalTempo / 2
hsbTempo.Max = gNormalTempo * 1.5
```

The Value property of the speed scroll bar is set to the value of gNormalTegmp:

```
hsbTempo.Value = gNormalTempo
```

Attaching Code to the Click Event of the cmdPlay Button of the frmMIDI Form

You'll now attach code to the Click event of the cmdPlay button of the frmMIDI form.

❑ Enter the following code inside the cmdPlay_Click() procedure of the frmMIDI form:

```
Sub cmdPlay_Click ()

    ' Play or Stop?
    If cmdPlay.Caption = "&Play" Then
       TegommMid.From =
          ➥ (hsbPosition.Value / 100) * TegommMid.Length
       TegommMid.Command = "Play"
       cmdPlay.Caption = "Sto&p"
    Else
       TegommMid.Command = "Stop"
       cmdPlay.Caption = "&Play"
    End If

End Sub
```

The code you entered uses an If statement to determine whether the clicking of the cmdPlay button should start the playback or stop the playback:

```
If cmdPlay.Caption = "&Play" Then
    ........
    ........
    ........
Else
    ........
    ........
    ........
End If
```

The statements under the `If` statement are executed if the user clicked the `cmdPlay` button while the caption of the `cmdPlay` button was Play. The statements under the `If` statements set the From property of the multimedia control to a location in the MIDI file that is proportional to the location of the thumb tab on the position scroll bar:

```
TegommMid.From =
    ➡ (hsbPosition.Value / 100) * TegommMid.Length
```

The `Play` command is issued:

```
TegommMid.Command = "Play"
```

Then the Caption property of the `cmdPlay` button is set to `"Stop&"`:

```
cmdPlay.Caption = "Sto&p"
```

Therefore, during the playback the caption of the `cmdPlay` button is set to Stop.

If the `cmdPlay` button was clicked while the playback was in progress, the statements under the `Else` statement are executed:

```
TegommMid.Command = "Stop"
cmdPlay.Caption = "&Play"
```

That is, the `Stop` command is issued, and the caption of the `cmdPlay` button is set to Play.

Attaching Code to the Change Event of the `hsbTempo` Scroll Bar of the `frmMIDI` Form

You'll now attach code to the Change event of the `hsbTempo` scroll bar of the `frmMIDI` form.

☐ Enter the following code inside the `hsbTempo_Change()` procedure of the `frmMIDI` form:

```
Sub hsbTempo_Change ()

    ' Set the Tempo property to the current value
    ' of the hsbTempo scroll bar.
    TegommMid.Tempo = hsbTempo.Value

End Sub
```

The code you entered is executed whenever the user changes the position of the tempo (speed) scroll bar.

The Tempo property of the multimedia control is set to the Value property of the scroll bar:

```
TegommMid.Tempo = hsbTempo.Value
```

So from now on, the MIDI file will be played at a speed proportional to the position of the thumb tab of the scroll bar.

Attaching Code to the Click Event of the Fastest 3D Label

You'll now attach code to the Click event of the Fastest 3D label.

❑ Enter the following code inside the lblFastestSpeed_Click() procedure of the frmMIDI form:

```
Sub lblFastestSpeed_Click ()

    hsbTempo.Value = hsbTempo.Max

End Sub
```

The code you entered sets the Value property of the scroll bar to the Max property of the scroll bar. Because the playback speed is proportional to the position of the thumb tab of the scroll bar, the MIDI file will be played at its fastest speed.

Attaching Code to the Click Event of the Normal 3D Label

You'll now attach code to the Click event of the Normal 3D label.

❑ Enter the following code inside the lblNormalSpeed_Click() procedure of the frmMIDI form:

```
Sub lblNormalSpeed_Click ()

    hsbTempo.Value = gNormalTempo

End Sub
```

The code you entered sets the Value property of the scroll bar to a number that represents the normal speed. Because the playback speed is proportional to the position of the thumb tab on the scroll bar, the MIDI file will be played at its normal speed.

Attaching Code to the Click Event of the Slowest 3D Label

You'll now attach code to the Click event of the Slowest 3D label.

❑ Enter the following code inside the lblSlowestSpeed_Click() procedure of the frmMIDI form:

```
Sub lblSlowestSpeed_Click ()

    hsbTempo.Value = hsbTempo.Min

End Sub
```

The code you entered sets the Value property of the scroll bar to the Min property of the scroll bar. Because the playback speed is proportional to the position of the thumb tab on the scroll bar, the MIDI file will be played at its minimum speed.

Attaching Code to the Done Event of the Multimedia Control

You'll now attach code to the Done event of the multimedia control.

☐ Enter the following code inside the `TegommMID_Done()` procedure:

```
Sub TegommMID_Done ()

    ' Did playback position reach the end of the file?
    If TegommMid.Position = TegommMid.Length Then
        If chkAutoRepeat = False Then
            cmdPlay.Caption = "&Play"
            TegommMid.Command = "Prev"
        Else
            TegommMid.Command = "Prev"
            TegommMid.Command = "Play"
        End If
    End If


    ' Set the hsbPosition scroll bar to the
    ' current playback position.
    hsbPosition.Value =
        ➥ (TegommMid.Position * 100) / TegommMid.Length

End Sub
```

The code you entered is executed automatically whenever the multimedia control finishes executing a command.

An `If` statement is used to determine whether the `Done` event was generated because the WAV file was played in its entirety:

```
If TegommMid.Position = TegommMid.Length Then
    .....
    .....
    .....
End If
```

An inner `If…Else` statement is executed to determine whether the `chkAutoRepeat` checkbox is checked:

```
    If chkAutoRepeat = False Then
        cmdPlay.Caption = "&Play"
        TegommMid.Command = "Prev"
    Else
        TegommMid.Command = "Prev"
        TegommMid.Command = "Play"
    End If
```

If the AutoRepeat checkbox is not checked, the `Prev` command is issued. If the AutoRepeat checkbox is checked, the `Prev` command is issued, followed by the `Play` command.

The position scroll bar is then updated to reflect the new position of the MIDI file:

```
hsbPosition.Value =
    ➥ (TegommMid.Position * 100) / TegommMid.Length
```

5

Attaching Code to the StatusUpdate Event of the Multimedia Control of the `frmMIDI` Form

You'll now attach code to the StatusUpdate event of the multimedia control of the `frmMIDI` form.

❑ Enter the following code inside the TegommMID_StatusUpdate() procedure of the `frmMIDI` form:

```
Sub TegommMID_StatusUpdate ()

    ' If currently playback is in progress,
    ' set the hsbPosition scroll bar to the
    ' current playback position.
    If TegommMid.Mode = 526 Then
       hsbPosition.Value =
          ➥ (TegommMid.Position / TegommMid.Length) * 100
    End If

End Sub
```

The code you entered is automatically executed every 100 milliseconds (because inside the Form_Load() procedure of the `frmMIDI` form you updated the UpdateInterval property of the multimedia control to 100).

An `If` statement is used to determine whether the playback is in progress:

```
If TegommMid.Mode = 526 Then
    .........
    .........
    .........
End If
```

If playback is in progress, the Value property of the position scroll bar is updated in accordance with the Position property of the multimedia control:

```
hsbPosition.Value =
        ➥ (TegommMid.Position / TegommMid.Length) * 100
```

So every 100 milliseconds the position scroll bar is updated with the new position of the MIDI file.

Attaching Code to the Click Event of the `cmdClose` Button of the `frmMIDI` Form

You'll now attach code to the Click event of the cmdClose button of the `frmMIDI` form.

❑ Enter the following code inside the cmdClose_Click() procedure of the `frmMIDI` form:

```
Sub cmdClose_Click ()

    Unload frmMIDI

End Sub
```

The code you entered is executed whenever the user clicks the Close button. This code executes the Unload method on the frmMIDI form. This causes the Form_Unload() procedure of the frmMIDI form to be executed.

Attaching Code to the Unload Event of the frmMIDI Form

You'll now attach code to the Unload event of the frmMIDI form.

❏ Enter the following code inside the Form_Unload() procedure of the frmMIDI form:

```
Sub Form_Unload (Cancel As Integer)

    ' Restore size of frmAllMedia
    frmAllMedia.WindowState = 0

End Sub
```

The code you entered is executed whenever the form is unloaded (for example, when the user closes the frmMIDI form by clicking the minus icon that appears on the upper-left corner of the frmMIDI form and then selecting Close from the system menu that pops up). Recall that when the user clicks the Close button, the cmdClose_Click() procedure of the frmMIDI form unloads the frmMIDI form.

The Code of the CDPLAYER.FRM Form

In the following sections you'll enter code inside the procedures of the frmCdPlayer form.

Attaching Code to the Load Event of the frmCdPlayer Form

You'll now attach code to the Load event of the frmCdPlayer form.

❏ Enter the following code inside the Form_Load() procedure of the frmCdPlayer form:

```
Sub Form_Load ()

    ' Make the multimedia control invisible.
    TegommCD.Visible = False

    ' Set the device type for playback of CD audio.
    TegommCD.DeviceType = "CDAudio"

    ' Issue an Open command.
    TegommCD.Command = "Open"

    ' Set the timer interval of the multimedia control
    ' to 500 milliseconds.
    TegommCD.UpdateInterval = 500

End Sub
```

The code you entered is executed whenever the user clicks the CD button of the frmAllMedia form.

The multimedia control is made invisible:

```
TegommCD.Visible = False
```

The multimedia control is set for playback of CD audio:

```
TegommCD.DeviceType = "CDAudio"
```

Then the Open command is issued:

```
TegommCD.Command = "Open"
```

Finally, the UpdateInterval property of the multimedia control is set to 500 milliseconds:

```
TegommCD.UpdateInterval = 500
```

This means that the TegommCD_StatusUpdate() procedure of the frmCdPlayer form will now automatically be executed every 500 milliseconds.

Attaching Code to the Click Event of the cmdLoad Button of the frmCdPlayer Form

You'll now attach code to the Click event of the cmdLoad button of the frmCdPlayer form.

☐ Enter the following code inside the cmdLoad_Click() procedure of the frmCdPlayer form:

```
Sub cmdLoad_Click ()

    ' Issue an Open command.
    TegommCD.Command = "Open"

    ' If Open command failed, display an error message.
    If TegommCD.Error <> 0 Then
        MsgBox "Cannot load the CD device.", 0, "ERROR"
    End If

End Sub
```

The code you entered is executed whenever the user clicks the Load button. The code issues the Open command, and then an If statement is executed to determine whether the Open command was executed without any errors:

```
TegommCD.Command = "Open"

If TegommCD.Error <> 0 Then
    MsgBox "Cannot load the CD device.", 0, "ERROR"
End If
```

If an error occurred during the execution of the Open command, a message box is displayed, telling the user that the CD cannot be loaded.

Attaching Code to the Click Event of the Play Button of the `frmCdPlayer` Form

You'll now attach code to the Click event of the Play button of the `frmCdPlayer` form.

☐ Enter the following code inside the `cmdPlay_Click()` procedure of the `frmCdPlayer` form:

```
Sub cmdPlay_Click ()

    ' Play or Stop?
    If TegommCD.Mode = 526 Then
        TegommCD.Command = "Stop"
    Else
        TegommCD.Command = "Play"
    End If

End Sub
```

The code you entered is executed whenever the user clicks the `cmdPlay` button.

An `If...Else` statement is executed to examine whether playback is in progress. If playback is in progress, the `Stop` command is issued:

```
    If TegommCD.Mode = 526 Then
        TegommCD.Command = "Stop"
    Else
        ......
    End If
```

If there is no playback in progress, the `Play` command is issued:

```
    If TegommCD.Mode = 526 Then
        .......
    Else
        TegommCD.Command = "Play"
    End If
```

Recall that the `cmdPlay` button serves as a Stop button if playback is in progress, and the same button serves as a Play button when there is no playback in progress.

Attaching Code to the Click Event of the `cmdNext` Button of the `frmCdPlayer` Form

You'll now attach code to the Click event of the `cmdNext` button of the `frmCdPlayer` form.

☐ Enter the following code inside the `cmdNext_Click()` procedure of the `frmCdPlayer` form:

```
Sub cmdNext_Click ()

    ' Issue a Next command.
    TegommCD.Command = "Next"

End Sub
```

The code you entered issues the Next command whenever the user clicks the Next button of the frmCdPlayer form. The Next command changes the playback position to the next track.

Attaching Code to the Click Event of the cmdPrev Button of the frmCdPlayer Form

You'll now attach code to the Click event of the cmdPrev button of the frmCdPlayer form.

☐ Enter the following code inside the cmdPrev_Click() procedure of the frmCdPlayer form:

```
Sub cmdPrev_Click ()

    ' Issue a Prev command.
    TegommCD.Command = "Prev"

End Sub
```

The code you entered issues the Prev command whenever the user clicks the cmdPrev button of the frmCdPlayer form. The Prev command changes the playback position to the previous track.

Attaching Code to the Click Event of the cmdEject Button of the frmCdPlayer Form

You'll now attach code to the Click event of the cmdEject button of the frmCdPlayer form.

☐ Enter the following code inside the cmdEject_Click() procedure of the frmCdPlayer form:

```
Sub cmdEject_Click ()

    ' If the door of the CD-ROM drive is currently open,
    ' then close it. Otherwise, open the door of the
    ' CD-ROM drive.
    If TegommCD.Mode = 530 Then
       TegommCD.Command = "CloseDoor"
    Else
       TegommCD.Command = "Eject"
    End If

End Sub
```

The code you entered is executed whenever the user clicks the Eject button. This code uses an If…Else statement to examine whether the CD drive's door is open, and the door is closed or opened accordingly. Note that some CD drives don't have the mechanism to accept commands from the PC for opening and closing the door of the CD drive.

> **NOTE**
>
> Issuing a `CloseDoor` command to the multimedia control, as in
>
> `TegommMyCD.Command = "Close Door",`
>
> closes the door of the CD-ROM drive (if the user's CD-ROM drive supports this feature).
>
> Issuing an `Eject` command to the multimedia control, as in
>
> `TegommMyCD.Command = "Eject",`
>
> opens the door of the CD-ROM drive (if the CD-ROM drive supports this feature).
>
> To determine whether the door of the CD-ROM drive is open, evaluate the Mode property of the multimedia control with an `If` statement. If the value of the Mode property is 530, the door of the CD-ROM drive is open.

Attaching Code to the StatusUpdate Event of the Multimedia Control

You'll now attach code to the StatusUpdate event of the multimedia control.

❏ Enter the following code inside the `TegommCD_StatusUpdate()` procedure of the `frmCdPlayer` form:

```
Sub TegommCD_StatusUpdate ()

    Static OldMode
    Static OldPosition

    ' Set the caption of the Play button according
    ' to the playback mode (only if mode has changed).
    If TegommCD.Mode <> OldMode Then
       If TegommCD.Mode = 526 Then
          cmdPlay.Caption = "Sto&p"
       Else
          cmdPlay.Caption = "&Play"
       End If
    End If

    ' If the CD-ROM drive is not ready, then
    ' disable the Play, Prev, and Next buttons, and
    ' terminate this procedure.
    If TegommCD.Mode = 524 Or
           ➥ TegommCD.Mode = 530 Or
           ➥ TegommCD.Mode = 0 Then
```

```
      cmdPlay.Enabled = False
      cmdPrev.Enabled = False
      cmdNext.Enabled = False
   Else
      cmdPlay.Enabled = True
      cmdPrev.Enabled = True
      cmdNext.Enabled = True
   End If

   ' Set the time format to Tracks.
   TegommCD.TimeFormat = "TMSF"

   ' If the position has changed (i.e. new track),
   ' then, update the caption of the form accordingly.
   If TegommCD.Position <> OldPosition Then
      frmCDPlayer.Caption = "CD Player - Track "
                   ➥ + TegommCD.Position
   End If

   ' Update the OldMode and OldPosition variables.
   OldMode = TegommCD.Mode
   OldPosition = TegommCD.Position

End Sub
```

The caption of the frmCdPlayer form (that is, the title of the program's main window) should display the current track number at all times. Furthermore, whenever the CD-ROM drive is not ready (for example, when the door of the CD-ROM drive is open), the Play, Previous, and Next buttons should be dimmed (that is, not available). The code you entered accomplishes all that.

Recall that the StatusUpdate event of the multimedia control occurs every X milliseconds, where X is the value of the UpdateInterval property. For example, if you set the UpdateInterval property of the multimedia control to 500, the StatusUpdate event will occur every 500 milliseconds.

The statement that you added to the Form_Load() procedure of the frmCdPlayer form

```
TegommCD.UpdateInterval = 500
```

sets the UpdateInterval property of the multimedia control to 500 milliseconds. Therefore, from now on, every 500 milliseconds (one-half second), a StatusUpdate event will occur.

The TegommCD_StatusUpdate() procedure starts by declaring two Static variables:

```
Static OldMode
Static OldPosition
```

These variables are declared as Static so that they will not lose their values when the procedure terminates.

The next group of statements updates the caption of the cmdPlay button according to the current playback mode:

```
' Set the caption of the Play button according
' to the playback mode (only if mode has changed).
If TegommCD.Mode <> OldMode Then
   If TegommCD.Mode = 526 Then
```

```
        cmdPlay.Caption = "Sto&p"
    Else
        cmdPlay.Caption = "&Play"
    End If
End If
```

Note that the caption of the cmdPlay button is updated only if the playback mode has changed since the last time the TegommCD_StatusUpdate() procedure was executed. To determine whether the playback mode has changed, an If statement is used:

```
If TegommCD.Mode <> OldMode Then
    ......
    ......
    ......
End If
```

If the Mode property has changed, the condition TegommCD.Mode <> OldMode will be satisfied (because the Static variable OldMode holds the old value of the Mode property), and the statements under the If will be executed:

```
If TegommCD.Mode = 526 Then
    cmdPlay.Caption = "Sto&p"
Else
    cmdPlay.Caption = "&Play"
End If
```

These statements update the caption of the cmdPlay button according to the current mode of the multimedia control. If the value of the Mode property is 526, playback is in progress, so the Caption property of the button is set to "Sto&p". Otherwise, the Caption property is set to "&Play".

NOTE

The code you entered inside the TegommCD_StatusUpdate() function updates the caption of the cmdPlay button only if the status of the multimedia control has changed since the last time the procedure was executed.

It is necessary to update the Play button's caption only when the status has changed, because if you update the button's caption continuously (whether or not the status has changed), the caption of the button will flicker.

The next statements enable or disable the Play, Previous, and Next buttons according to the current mode of the multimedia control:

```
If TegommCD.Mode = 524 Or TegommCD.Mode = 530
               ➥ Or TegommCD.Mode = 0 Then
    cmdPlay.Enabled = False
    cmdPrev.Enabled = False
    cmdNext.Enabled = False
Else
    cmdPlay.Enabled = True
    cmdPrev.Enabled = True
    cmdNext.Enabled = True
End If
```

If the mode of the multimedia control is 524 (not ready), or 530 (CD-ROM drive door is open), or 0 (an Open command was not issued successfully), the buttons are disabled. Otherwise, the buttons are enabled.

The next statement in the TegommCD_StatusUpdate() procedure

```
TegommCD.TimeFormat = "TMSF"
```

sets the TimeFormat property of the multimedia control to TMSF. After setting the TimeFormat property to TMSF, the Position property of the multimedia control reports the current playback position in units of tracks.

The next statement is an If statement that updates the Caption property of the frmCdPlayer form with the current playback position (track number):

```
If TegommCD.Position <> OldPosition Then
   frmCdPlayer.Caption = "CD Player - Track "
                         ➡ + TegommCD.Position
End If
```

Note that the caption of the form is updated only if the position has changed since the last time the TegommCD_StatusUpdate() procedure was executed (this is necessary to avoid flickering in the caption of the form).

The last two statements in the procedure are these:

```
OldMode = TegommCD.Mode
OldPosition = TegommCD.Position
```

These statements update the OldMode and OldPosition Static variables for the next time that the TegommCD_StatusUpdate() is executed.

So the TegommCD_StatusUpdate() procedure will be automatically executed every 500 milliseconds (because you set the UpdateInterval property to 500).

The code you wrote inside TegommCD_StatusUpdate() does two things:

- It updates the caption of the cmdPlay button according to the current mode of the multimedia control (only if the mode of the multimedia control has changed since the last time the procedure was executed).
- It updates the caption of the frmCdPlayer form with the current track number (only if the position [track number] has changed since the last time the procedure was executed).

Attaching Code to the Click Event of the Exit Button of the frmCdPlayer Form

You'll now attach code to the Click event of the Exit button of the frmCdPlayer form.

❏ Enter the following code inside the cmdExit_Click() procedure of the frmCdPlayer form:

```
Sub cmdExit_Click ()

    Unload frmCDPlayer

End Sub
```

The code you entered executes the Unload method on the frmCDPlayer form. This causes the Form_Unload() procedure of the frmCdPlayer form to be executed.

Attaching Code to the Unload Event of the frmCdPlayer Form

You'll now attach code to the Unload event of the frmCdPlayer form.

☐ Enter the following code inside the Form_Unload() procedure of the frmCdPlayer form:

```
Sub Form_Unload (Cancel As Integer)

    ' Restore size of frmAllMedia
    frmAllMedia.WindowState = 0

End Sub
```

The code you entered restores the frmAllMedia form to its normal size. Recall that the Form_Unload() procedure is executed whenever the form is unloaded (for example, when the user double-clicks the minus icon that appears in the upper-left corner of the frmCdPlayer form). The Form_Unload() procedure is also executed whenever the user clicks the Exit button of the frmCdPlayer form, because you used the Unload method inside the cmdExit_Click() procedure.

The Code of the MOVIE.FRM Form

In the following sections you'll enter code inside the procedures of the frmMovie form.

Attaching Code to the Load Event of the frmMovie Form

You'll now attach code to the Load event of the frmMovie form:

```
Sub Form_Load ()

    Dim AviFile

    ' Set the DeviceType for playback of AVI files.
    TegommAVI.DeviceType = "AVIVideo"

    ' Movie should play inside application's window.
    'TegommAVI.hWndDisplay = frmMovie.hWnd


    ' Set the timer interval of the multimedia control
    ' to 100 milliseconds.
    TegommAVI.UpdateInterval = 100

End Sub
```

5

The code you entered is executed whenever the frmMovie form is loaded.

The multimedia control is set for playback of AVI video files:

```
TegommAVI.DeviceType = "AVIVideo"
```

Then you entered a commented statement:

```
' Movie should play inside application's window.
'TegommAVI.hWndDisplay = frmMovie.hWnd
```

You commented this statement, because you want the movie to be displayed is its own window (not inside the frmMovie form).

However, if in the future you want to display the movie inside the frmMovie form, take out the comment character.

If you decide to display the movie inside the frmMovie window, then you have to increase the size of frmMovie, as shown in Figure 5.1.

Figure 5.1.
The frmMovie form (in design mode).

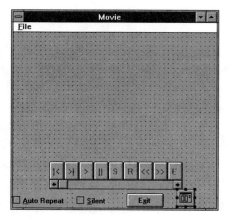

Later, when you execute the AllMedia program, the movie will be displayed inside the frmMovie form, as shown in Figure 5.2.

The last statement inside the Form_Load() procedure of the frmMovie form sets the UpdateInterval property of the multimedia control to 100 milliseconds:

```
TegommAVI.UpdateInterval = 100
```

This means that from now on the TegommAVI_StatusUpdate() procedure will be executed every 100 milliseconds.

Figure 5.2.
The movie displayed inside
the frmWindow *form*
(provided that you
increased the size of the
frmMovie *form and*
included the
TegommAVI.hWndDisplay
= frmMovie.hWnd
statement).

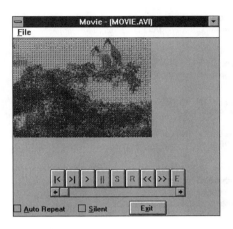

Attaching Code to the Open Menu Item of the frmMovie Form

You'll now attach code to the Open menu item of the frmMovie form.

❑ Enter the following code inside the mnuOpen_Click() procedure of the frmMovie form:

```
Sub mnuOpen_Click ()

    On Error GoTo OpenAVIError

    ' Set the items of the File Type list box
    CMDialogAVI.Filter =
        ➥ "All Files (*.*) ¦*.* ¦AVI Files (*.avi)¦*.avi"


    ' Set the default File Type AVI Files (avi.*)
    CMDialogAVI.FilterIndex = 2


    ' Display the dialog box
    CMDialogAVI.Action = 1

    ' Remove the error trap
    On Error GoTo 0


    ' Open the selected AVI file
    TegommAVI.FileName = CMDialogAVI.Filename
    TegommAVI.Command = "Open"
    If TegommAVI.Error > 0 Then

        frmMovie.Caption = "Movie"

        MsgBox "Can't open " +
               ➥ CMDialogAVI.Filename, 16, "Error"

    Else
```

5

```
frmMovie.Caption = "Movie - ("
    ➥ + CMDialogAVI.Filetitle + ")"

' Set the Time Format of the multimedia control
' to units of frames.
TegommAVI.TimeFormat = "frames"

' Set the minimum value of the scroll bar.
hsbPosition.Min = 0

' Set the maximum value of the scroll bar.
hsbPosition.Max = TegommAVI.Length

' Show the first frame of the movie
TegommAVI.From = 1
TegommAVI.To = 1
TegommAVI.Command = "Play"

End If


' Exit this procedure
Exit Sub

OpenAVIError:
' The user pressed the Cancel key of
' the CMDialogAVI control

' Exit this procedure
Exit Sub

End Sub
```

The code you entered is similar to the code you entered inside the cmdOpen_Click() procedure of the other forms of the AllMedia application.

An error trap is set:

```
On Error GoTo OpenAVIError
```

The common dialog box is set to display the list of AVI files:

```
CMDialogAVI.Filter =
    ➥ "All Files (*.*) ¦*.* ¦AVI Files (*.avi)¦*.avi"

CMDialogAVI.FilterIndex = 2

CMDialogAVI.Action = 1
```

Then the AVI file is opened with the Open command:

```
TegommAVI.FileName = CMDialogAVI.Filename
TegommAVI.Command = "Open"
```

If an error occurred during the execution of the Open command, the statements under the following If statement are executed:

```
If TegommAVI.Error > 0 Then

    frmMovie.Caption = "Movie"

    MsgBox "Can't open " +
           ➥ CMDialogAVI.Filename, 16, "Error"

Else
    .......
    .......
    .......
End If
```

If no errors occurred during the execution of the Open command, the statements under the Else statement are executed:

```
If TegommAVI.Error > 0 Then
    ......
    ......
    ......
Else
 frmMovie.Caption = "Movie - ("
       ➥ + CMDialogAVI.Filetitle + ")"

 ' Set the Time Format of the multimedia control
 ' to units of frames.
 TegommAVI.TimeFormat = "frames"

 ' Set the minimum value of the scroll bar.
 hsbPosition.Min = 0

 ' Set the maximum value of the scroll bar.
 hsbPosition.Max = TegommAVI.Length

 ' Show the first frame of the movie
 TegommAVI.From = 1
 TegommAVI.To = 1
 TegommAVI.Command = "Play"

End If
```

The statements under the Else statement set the Caption property of the AVI file that was opened successfully:

```
frmMovie.Caption = "Movie - ("
       ➥ + CMDialogAVI.Filetitle + ")"
```

The TimeFormat property of the multimedia control is set to frames:

```
TegommAVI.TimeFormat = "frames"
```

Then the Min and Max properties of the position scroll bar are set:

```
hsbPosition.Min = 0

hsbPosition.Max = TegommAVI.Length
```

Finally, the first frame of the AVI movie is displayed:

```
TegommAVI.From = 1
TegommAVI.To = 1
TegommAVI.Command = "Play"
```

Attaching Code to the Click Event of the Silent Checkbox

You'll now attach code to the Click event of the Silent checkbox of the frmMovie form.

☐ Enter the following code inside the chkSilent_Click() procedure of the frmMovie form:

```
Sub chkSilent_Click ()

    ' If the Silent checkbox is checked, make the movie
    ' a silent movie.
    If chkSilent.Value = 1 Then
        TegommAVI.Silent = True
    Else
        TegommAVI.Silent = False
    End If

End Sub
```

The code you entered sets the Silent property of the multimedia control to either True or False, according to the status of the chkSilent checkbox. When the Silent property of the multimedia control is set to True, the AVI movie is played without any audio.

Attaching Code to the Change Event of the Position Scroll Bar

You'll now attach code to the Change event of the position scroll bar of the frmMovie form.

☐ Enter the following code inside the hsbPosition_Change() procedure of the frmMovie form:

```
Sub hsbPosition_Change ()

    ' Change the playback position according to
    ' the scroll bar position, provided that the
    ' multimedia control is either stopped or paused.
    If TegommAVI.Mode = 525 Or TegommAVI.Mode = 529 Then
        TegommAVI.To = hsbPosition.Value
        TegommAVI.Command = "Seek"
    End If

End Sub
```

The code you entered uses an If statement to check whether the AVI movie is stopped or paused, and if so, the To property of the multimedia control is set to a place determined by the Value property of the scroll bar. Then the Seek command is issued to actually place the AVI file at the new location.

Attaching Code to the Scroll Event of the Position Scroll Bar

You'll now attach code to the Scroll event of the `hsbPosition` scroll bar of the `frmMovie` form.

❑ Enter the following code inside the `hsbPosition_Scroll()` procedure of the `frmMovie` form:

```
Sub hsbPosition_Scroll ()

    ' Call the hsbPosition_Change() procedure.
    hsbPosition_Change

End Sub
```

The code you entered executes the `hsbPosition_Change()` procedure, whose code you entered already.

Attaching Code to the StatusUpdate Event of the Multimedia Control

You'll now attach code to the StatusUpdate event of the multimedia control of the `frmMovie` form.

❑ Enter the following code inside the `TegommAvi_StatusUpdate()` procedure of the `frmMovie` form:

```
Sub TegommAvi_StatusUpdate ()

    ' Update the scroll bar with the current
    ' playback position.
    hsbPosition.Value = TegommAVI.Position

End Sub
```

The `TegommAvi_StatusUpdate()` procedure is automatically executed every X milliseconds, where X is the value of the UpdateInterval property of the `TegommAvi` control. The code you entered updates the Value property of the hsbPosition scroll bar according to the Position property of the `TegommAvi` control. So in other words, periodically the position scroll bar updates itself to reflect the position of the AVI file.

Attaching Code to the Done Event of the `TegommAvi` Control

You'll now attach code to the Done event of the `TegommAvi` control of the `frmMovie` form.

❑ Enter the following code inside the `TegommAvi_Done()` procedure of the `frmMovie` form:

```
Sub TegommAvi_Done ()

    ' Playback reached the end of the file?
    If TegommAVI.Position = TegommAVI.Length Then

        ' Rewind the playback position to start of file.
        TegommAVI.Command = "Prev"
```

5

```
        ' If Auto Repeat checkbox is checked, play again.
        If chkAutoRepeat.Value = 1 Then
            TegommAVI.Command = "Play"
        End If

    End If

End Sub
```

The Done event occurs whenever the multimedia control finishes executing a command. An `If` statement is executed to determine whether the Done event occurred because the `Play` command was executed and the AVI file was played in its entirety:

```
If TegommAVI.Position = TegommAVI.Length Then
    ......
    ......
    ......
End If
```

The code under the `If` statement rewinds the AVI file:

```
TegommAVI.Command = "Prev"
```

Then an inner `If` statement is executed to determine whether the Auto Repeat checkbox is checked:

```
' If Auto Repeat checkbox is checked, play again.
    If chkAutoRepeat.Value = 1 Then
        TegommAVI.Command = "Play"
    End If
```

If the Auto Repeat checkbox is checked, the `Play` command is issued.

Attaching Code to the Click Event of the Exit Button

You'll now attach code to the Click event of the Exit button of the frmMovie form.

☐ Enter the following code inside the cmdExit_Click() procedure of the frmMovie form:

```
Sub cmdExit_Click ()

    Unload frmMovie

End Sub
```

The code you entered executes the Unload method on the frmMovie form. This causes the Form_Unload() procedure of the frmMovie form to be executed.

Attaching Code to the Exit Menu Item of the frmMovie Form

You'll now attach code to the Exit menu item of the frmMovie form.

☐ Enter the following code inside the mnuExit_Click() procedure of the frmMovie form:

```
Sub mnuExit_Click ()

    cmdExit_Click

End Sub
```

The code you entered executes the `cmdExit_Click()` procedure of the `frmMovie` form. Therefore, clicking the Exit menu item has the same effect as clicking the Exit button.

Attaching Code to the Unload Event of the `frmMovie` Form

You'll now attach code to the Unload event of the `frmMovie` form.

☐ Enter the following code inside the `Form_Unload()` procedure of the `frmMovie` form:

```
Sub Form_Unload (Cancel As Integer)

    ' Restore size of frmAllMedia
    frmAllMedia.WindowState = 0

End Sub
```

The code you entered restores the `frmAllMedia` form to its normal size. Recall that the `Form_Unload()` procedure of the `frmMovie` form is executed whenever the form is unloaded (for example, when the user clicks the minus icon that appears on the upper-left corner of the `frmMovie` and then clicks the Close item from the system menu that pops up). Also, the `Form_Unload()` procedure is executed whenever the user clicks the Exit button or the Exit menu item (because the code that you attached to the Exit button unloads the `frmMovie` form).

6

Creating a Multiple-Document Interface Text Editor Application (Part I)

In this chapter you'll write the prototype of the Multipad program. The Multipad program is a multiple-document interface (MDI) version of the Notepad text editor program that comes with Windows.

6 Executing Notepad

Notepad is a single-document interface (SDI) program. This means that you can load only one document at any given time. To appreciate the Multipad program, you first need to execute the Notepad program.

❑ Double-click the program icon of the Notepad program that usually resides inside the Accessories group of icons. (See Figure 6.1.)

Windows responds by executing the Notepad program. (See Figure 6.2.)

Figure 6.1.
The program icon of the Notepad program.

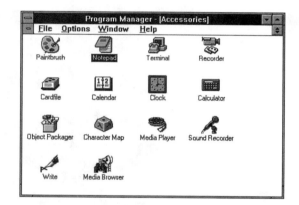

Figure 6.2.
The Notepad program.

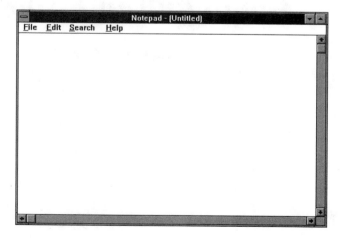

❏ Select Open from the File menu and load a text file. For example, Figure 6.3 shows the Notepad program with the AUTOEXEC.BAT file loaded.

Figure 6.3.
The Notepad program with the AUTOEXEC.BAT file loaded.

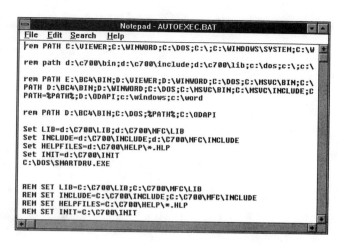

❏ Experiment with the Notepad program and then select Exit from the File menu to terminate the Notepad program.

Executing the Multipad Program

Now that you are familiar with Notepad, you should become familiar with the Multipad program.

❏ Select Run from the File menu of the Program Manager and execute the C:\LearnVB\Original\MDI\Multipad.EXE program.

Windows responds by executing the Multipad.EXE program and displaying the window shown in Figure 6.4.

As shown in Figure 6.4, Multipad has two toolbars and three status bars. You can remove all the toolbars and all the status bars by selecting Remove All Tools from the Toolbars menu.

❏ Select Remove All Tools from the Toolbars menu.

Multipad responds by removing all the tools. (See Figure 6.5.)

You can redisplay all the tools by selecting Show All Tools from the Toolbars menu.

❏ Select Show All Tools from the Toolbars menu.

Multipad responds by displaying all the toolbars and status bars.

You can remove individual toolbars or status bars by clicking the Remove buttons.

❏ Experiment with the Remove buttons.

6

Figure 6.4.
The window of the
Multipad.EXE program.

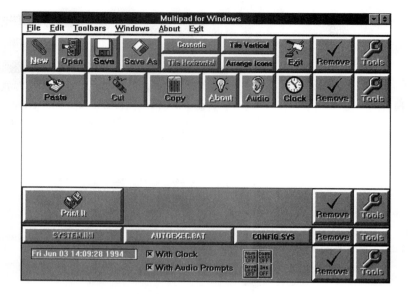

Figure 6.5.
The Multipad window
with no tool icons.

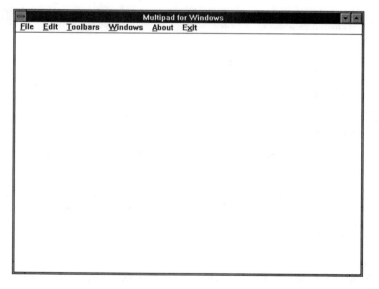

Figures 6.6 through 6.9 show the Multipad window with various toolbars and status bars removed.

Figure 6.6.
The Multipad window
without its status bars.

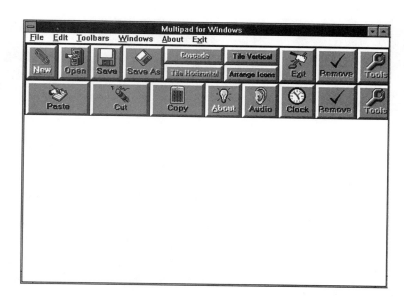

Figure 6.7.
The Multipad window
without its toolbars.

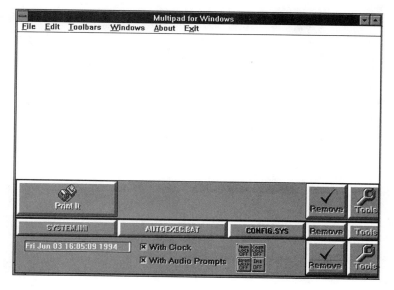

Figure 6.8.
The Multipad window
with one of its toolbars
removed.

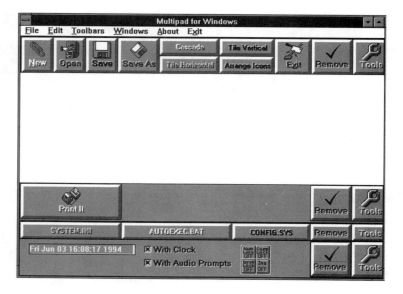

Figure 6.9.
The Multipad window
with one of its status bars
removed.

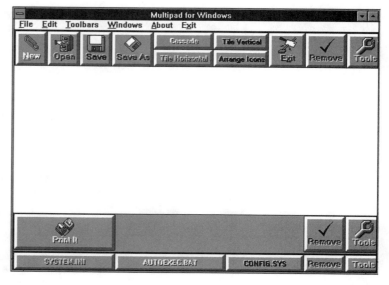

❏ Select Show All Tools from the Toolbars menu.

Multipad responds by displaying all the toolbars and status bars.

Each toolbar and each status bar has the Tools icon. Clicking the Tools icon causes Multipad to redisplay all the toolbars and status bars.

❏ Click the Remove tool of various toolbars and status bars, and then click any of the Tools icons.

> **NOTE**
>
> Note that because Multipad is a text editor program it needs a large client area—the user must be able to view a large portion of the text file without having to scroll the screen. This is the reason for having a Remove icon on every toolbar and status bar. Therefore, whenever you need a larger client area, you can easily make more room for the text by clicking a Remove icon. Similarly, if you need to perform a certain operation, you can click any of the Tools icons to redisplay all the toolbars and status bars.

❑ Experiment with the Audio button tool on the lower toolbar. Note that the X inside the With Audio Prompts checkbox is toggled whenever you click the Audio button tool.

Whenever the With Audio Prompts checkbox is checked, the Multipad program is capable of producing audio prompts. To see this in action do the following:

❑ Make sure that there is no X inside the With Audio Prompts checkbox.

❑ Click the Exit tool.

Multipad terminates itself, and there is no audio prompt.

❑ Start Multipad again by selecting Run from the File menu of the File Manager and select C:\LearnVB\Original\MDI\Multipad.EXE.

❑ Make sure that there is an X inside the With Audio Prompts checkbox.

❑ Click the Exit tool.

Multipad terminates itself and announces "It's been fun working with you." If you have a sound card, the audio prompt is announced through the installed sound card. If your PC does not have a sound card installed in it, the audio prompt is played through the PC speaker. (No drivers are needed for playing through the PC speaker.)

❑ Start Multipad again by selecting Run from the File menu of the File Manager and select C:\LearnVB\Original\MDI\Multipad.EXE.

The lower status bar displays the date and time. You can remove or display the time and date by clicking the Clock tool.

❑ Experiment with the Clock tool and note that the time and date are removed and redisplayed whenever you click the Clock tool.

❑ Click the About tool.

Multipad responds by displaying the About dialog box. (See Figure 6.10.)

Figure 6.10.
The About dialog box of
the Multipad program.

6

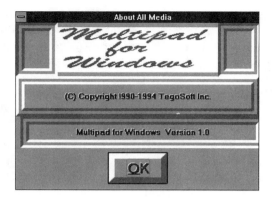

So far, you haven't seen the text editor capabilities of the Multipad program. To see them in action do the following:

☐ Click the New icon.

> *Multipad responds by opening a new document. (See Figure 6.11.)*

Figure 6.11.
The Multipad program
with a new document in its
window.

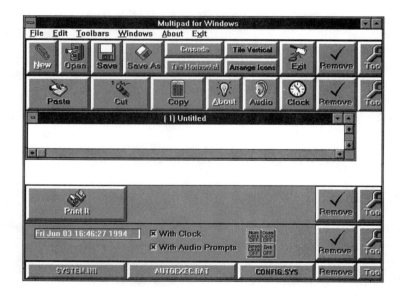

☐ Click the New icon twice more.

> *Multipad responds by opening two new documents. (See Figure 6.12.)*

The Windows menu in the Multipad program has the standard Arrange and Cascade menu items. (See Figure 6.13.)

Figure 6.12.
The Multipad program
with several new documents
in its window.

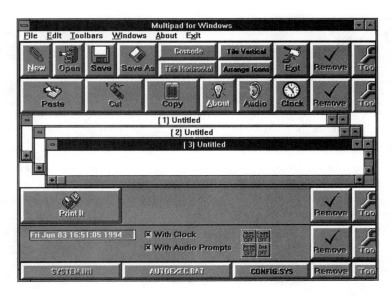

Figure 6.13.
The Windows menu of the
Multipad program.

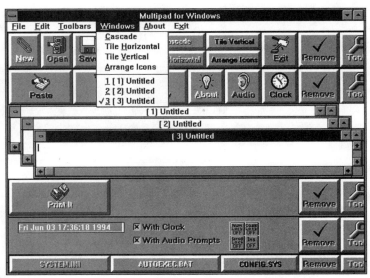

Note in Figure 6.13 that the (3) Untitled window is the active window (the window with its title highlighted). This explains why the (3) Untitled item in the Windows menu has a checkmark to its left. Also, there are three windows inside the Multipad window. All of these windows are listed in the Windows menu.

6

> ### NOTE
>
> The untitled windows shown in Figure 6.13 are called *child windows.* The child windows are contained within the *parent window* of the Multipad window.

❑ Minimize the child windows (by clicking the down-arrow icon that appears on the upper-right corner of each window).

   Multipad responds by minimizing the child windows. (See Figure 6.14.)

Figure 6.14.
The Multipad program
with its child windows
minimized.

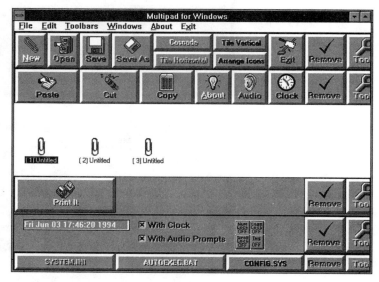

❑ Drag the icons of the child windows to different locations inside the parent window. (See Figure 6.15.)

❑ Click the Arrange Icons button (or select Arrange Icons from the Windows menu).

   Multipad responds by arranging the icons as shown in Figure 6.14.

❑ Click the icon of the (1) Untitled window and select Restore from the system menu that pops up.

   Multipad responds by restoring the (1) Untitled child window to its original size.

❑ Drag the (1) Untitled window so that you can access the icon of the (2) Untitled child window, click the icon of the (2) Untitled window, and select Restore from the system menu that pops up.

Figure 6.15.
Dragging the icons of the
child windows.

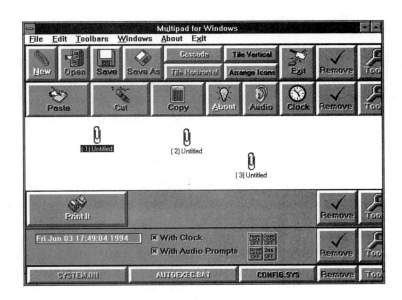

❑ Repeat this step to restore the size of the (3) Untitled window.

You can now arrange the child windows in a variety of ways.

❑ Select Tile Vertical (from the toolbar or from the Windows menu).

Multipad responds by tiling the child windows vertically, as shown in Figure 6.16.

Figure 6.16.
The child windows tiled
vertically.

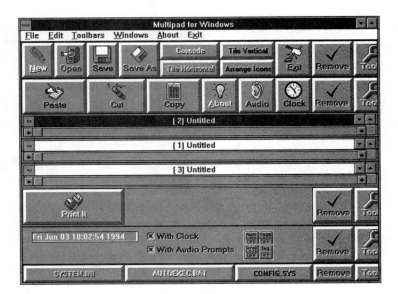

☐ Select Tile Horizontal (from the toolbar or from the Windows menu).

Multipad responds by tiling the child windows horizontally, as shown in Figure 6.17.

Figure 6.17.
The child windows tiled
horizontally.

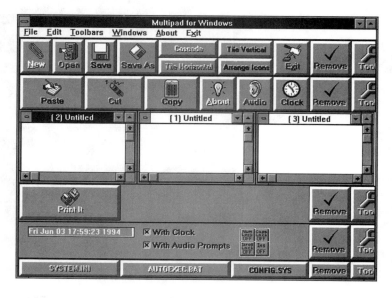

☐ Remove the upper status bars and then click the Tile Vertical tool.

Multipad responds by tiling the child windows vertically, as shown in Figure 6.18.

Figure 6.18.
The child windows tiled
vertically.

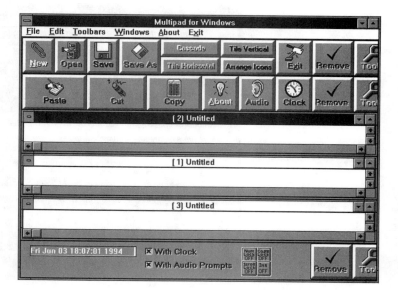

❏ Click the Cascade tool.

   Multipad responds by cascading the child windows, as shown in Figure 6.19.

Figure 6.19.
The child windows
cascaded.

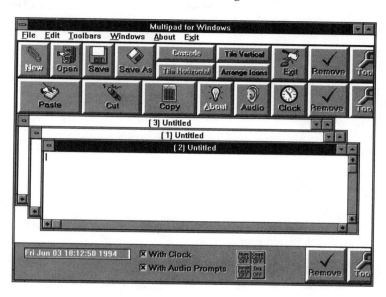

❏ Type something inside the child windows and then experiment with the Paste, Cut, and Copy tools. These features work the same way the Paste, Cut, and Copy features work in any standard Windows application.

NOTE

The Paste, Cut, and Copy operations are available from the Edit menu as well as from the toolbar. In addition, the Edit menu contains the Clear menu item.

The toolbar also contains the Open, Save, and Save As tools.

❏ Experiment with the Open, Save, and Save As features of the Multipad program. These features work the same way the Open, Save, and Save As features work in any standard Windows application.

NOTE

As stated, the parent window contains the child windows. Only one child window can be the *active window* at any given time. You can easily recognize which is the active window because the active window has its caption highlighted. To make a child window the active window, click inside the child window that you want to make active.

6

You can print the contents of the active window by clicking the Print It tool on the status bar.

❑ Make one of the child windows the active window, type something inside the active window, prepare your printer for printing, and then click the Print It tool.

   Multipad responds by printing the contents of the active window.

❑ Click one of the Tools icons to display all the toolbars and the status bars.

Note that one of the status bars has four small buttons in it:

   Caps Lock
   Num Lock
   Scroll Lock
   Ins

These buttons serve both as an indication of the corresponding status of the keys on the keyboard and as a way to change the status of the keys on the keyboard.

❑ Take a look at the LED lamp of the Caps Lock key on your keyboard. Now take a look at the Caps Lock button on the status bar. The Caps Lock button reflects the status of the Caps Lock key on your keyboard.

❑ Press the Caps Lock key on your keyboard to change the status of the Caps Lock button.

   Multipad responds by changing the caption of the Caps Lock button on the status bar.

This experiment demonstrates that the Caps Lock tool changes in accordance with the status of the Caps Lock key on your keyboard.

❑ Click on the Caps Lock button on the status bar.

   Multipad responds by changing the caption of the Caps Lock icon on the status bar, as well as the status of the Caps Lock key on your keyboard. In other words, you can turn on and off the LED lamp of the Caps Lock key by clicking the Caps Lock button on the status bar.

❑ Experiment with the other status key indicator buttons that appear on the status bar.

NOTE

Most keyboards contain LED lamps that indicate the status of the Caps Lock, Num Lock, and Scroll Lock keys. Typically, the Ins key does not have a corresponding LED lamp.

The Multipad program is a text editor program. As such, you'll probably use it for editing the AUTOEXEC.BAT and CONFIG.SYS files. The Multipad program contains the AUTOEXEC.BAT and CONFIG.SYS tools on one of its status bars. These icons serve as a shortcut mechanism for loading the AUTOEXEC.BAT and CONFIG.SYS files. In other words, clicking the AUTOEXEC.BAT tool has the same effect as clicking the Open tool and then selecting the AUTOEXEC.BAT file.

❏ Experiment with the AUTOEXEC.BAT and CONFIG.SYS buttons.

Another text file that is often loaded with a text editor is the \Windows\System.INI file. Clicking the SYSTEM.INI icon has the same result as clicking the Open icon and then selecting the \Windows\System.INI file.

NOTE

When developing programs that access important files such as AUTOEXEC.BAT, CONFIG.SYS, WIN.INI, and SYSTEM.INI files, it is always a good idea to first back up these files to a disk. If you accidentally corrupt these files you'll be able to boot up your system from a bootable disk, and then copy AUTOEXEC.BAT, CONFIG.SYS, WIN.INI, and SYSTEM.INI from the disk to your hard drive.

Backing up the files may take you less than a minute to do (and unfortunately, many programmers skip this safety step). However, consider the alternative: If you manage to corrupt these important files, you'll probably spend hours trying to return your system to its working condition, instead of spending hours developing Visual Basic programs.

❏ Keep experimenting with the Multipad application and then click the Exit icon to terminate the application. In particular, notice that if you try to exit the program after one of the child windows has been changed, the program prompts you, asking you if you want to save the changes.

The Visual Implementation of the Multipad Program's Prototype

You'll now visually implement the prototype of the Multipad program.

❏ Select New Project from the File menu.

❏ Select New MDI Form from the File menu.

❏ Save the MDI form as Multipad.FRM in the C:\LearnVB\Practice\MDI directory. (That is, make sure that the MDI form is highlighted, and select Save File As from the File menu.)

❏ Select Save Project As from the File menu and save the project as Multipad.MAK in the C:\LearnVB\Practice\MDI directory.

❏ Implement the `frmMultipad` form according to the specifications in Table 6.1. Before implementing the form, select Add File from the File menu, and add the TegoMM.VBX control and the MyClock.VBX control (which reside in the \Windows\System directory). When you finish implementing the form it should look like the one shown in Figure 6.20.

NOTE

The TegoMM.VBX file was copied to your \Windows\System directory when you installed the book's CD.

The MyClock.VBX file was copied to your \Windows\System directory when you installed the book's CD. (This file also resides in the C:\LearnVB\Original\Tools2 directory. In Chapter 19, "Creating Your Own VBX Controls," you'll learn how to implement the MyClock.VBX control yourself.

Table 6.1. The Properties table of the `frmMultipad` form.

Object: MDIForm
Object Name: frmMultipad

Comment: This is the parent form.

Caption	=	"Multipad for Windows"
Height	=	7140
Icon	=	\VB\ICONS\WRITING\NOTE18.ICO
Left	=	150
Top	=	180
Width	=	9150
WindowState	=	2 'Maximized

Comment: The window will appear maximized.

Object: Picture box
Object Name: picToolbar1

Comment: This is the top toolbar.

Align	=	1 'Align Top
BackColor	=	&H00C0C0C0&
Height	=	975
Left	=	0
Top	=	0
Width	=	9030

Object: 3D button
Object Name: cmdNew

Comment: This control is enclosed within the top toolbar. To place this control click the 3D button inside the Tools window, move the mouse inside the top toolbar, press down the left mouse button, and while the left mouse button is pressed down move the mouse. After you release the left mouse button, Visual Basic places the 3D button inside the picture control.

BevelWidth	=	5
Caption	=	"&New"
Font3D	=	2 'Raised w/heavy shading
FontName	=	"MS Sans Serif"
FontSize	=	9.75
ForeColor	=	&H00FFFFFF&
Height	=	975
Left	=	0
Icon	=	\VB\ICONS\OFFICE\CLIP02.ICO
Top	=	0
Width	=	855

Object: 3D button
Object Name: cmdOpen

Comment: This control is enclosed within the top toolbar.

BevelWidth	=	5
Caption	=	"Open"
Font3D	=	2 'Raised w/heavy shading
FontName	=	"MS Sans Serif"
FontSize	=	9.75
ForeColor	=	&H00FF00FF&
Height	=	975
Left	=	840
Icon	=	\VB\ICONS\OFFICE\FILES04.ICO
Top	=	0
Width	=	855

continues

6

Table 6.1. continued

Object: 3D button
Object Name: cmdSave

Comment: This control is enclosed within the top toolbar.

BevelWidth	=	5
Caption	=	"Save"
Font3D	=	2 'Raised w/heavy shading
FontName	=	"MS Sans Serif"
FontSize	=	9.75
ForeColor	=	&H00FF0000&
Height	=	975
Left	=	1680
Icon	=	\VB\ICONS\COMPUTER\DISK06.ICO
Top	=	0
Width	=	855

Object: 3D button
Object Name: cmdSaveAs

Comment: This control is enclosed within the top toolbar.

BevelWidth	=	5
Caption	=	"Save As"
Font3D	=	2 'Raised w/heavy shading
FontName	=	"MS Sans Serif"
FontSize	=	9.75
ForeColor	=	&H00808080&
Height	=	975
Left	=	2520
Icon	=	\VB\ICONS\COMPUTER\DISK12.ICO
Top	=	0
Width	=	1095

Object: 3D button
Object Name: cmdCascade

Comment: This control is enclosed within the top toolbar.

BevelWidth	=	5

Caption	=	"Cascade"
Font3D	=	2 'Raised w/heavy shading
Height	=	495
Left	=	3600
Top	=	0
Width	=	1575

Object: 3D button
Object Name: cmdTileVertical

Comment: This control is enclosed within the top toolbar.

BevelWidth	=	5
Caption	=	"Tile Vertical"
Font3D	=	2 'Raised w/heavy shading
ForeColor	=	&H00FF0000&
Height	=	495
Left	=	5160
Top	=	0
Width	=	1455

Object: 3D button
Object Name: cmdTileHorizontal

Comment: This control is enclosed within the top toolbar.

BevelWidth	=	5
Caption	=	"Tile Horizontal"
Font3D	=	2 'Raised w/heavy shading
ForeColor	=	&H0000C000&
Height	=	495
Left	=	3600
Top	=	480
Width	=	1575

Object: 3D button
Object Name: cmdArrangeIcons

Comment: This control is enclosed within the top toolbar.

continues

6

Table 6.1. continued

BevelWidth	=	5
Caption	=	"Arrange Icons"
Font3D	=	2 'Raised w/heavy shading
ForeColor	=	&H00000080&
Height	=	495
Left	=	5160
Top	=	480
Width	=	1455

Object: 3D button
Object Name: cmdExit

Comment: This control is enclosed within the top toolbar.

BevelWidth	=	5
Caption	=	"E&xit"
Font3D	=	2 'Raised w/heavy shading
FontName	=	"MS Sans Serif"
FontSize	=	9.75
ForeColor	=	&H000000FF&
Height	=	975
Left	=	6600
Picture	=	\VB\ICONS\COMM\NET11.ICO
Top	=	0
Width	=	975

Object: 3D button
Object Name: cmdRemove (array of 3D buttons)

Comment: This control is enclosed within the top toolbar.

BevelWidth	=	5
Caption	=	"Remove"
Font3D	=	4 'Inset w/heavy shading
FontName	=	"MS Sans Serif"
FontSize	=	9.75

ForeColor	=	&H000000FF&
Height	=	975
Index	=	0

Comment: This is Element 0 of the cmdRemove() array of 3D buttons.

Left	=	7560
Picture	=	\VB\ICONS\MISC\CHECKMRK.ICO
Top	=	0
Width	=	1095

Object: 3D button
Object Name: cmdTools (array of 3D buttons)

Comment: This control is enclosed within the top toolbar.

BevelWidth	=	5
Caption	=	"Tools"
Font3D	=	2 'Raised w/heavy shading
FontName	=	"MS Sans Serif"
FontSize	=	9.75
ForeColor	=	&H00FFFF00&
Height	=	975
Index	=	0

Comment: This is Element 0 of the cmdTool() array of 3D buttons.

Left	=	8640
Picture	=	\VB\ICONS\INDUSTRY\WRENCH.ICO
Top	=	0
Width	=	975

Object: Picture box
Object Name: picToolbar2

Comment: This control is enclosed within the lower toolbar.

Align	=	2 'Align Bottom
BackColor	=	&H00C0C0C0&
Height	=	960
Left	=	0

continues

Table 6.1. continued

Top	=	975
Width	=	9030

Object: 3D button
Object Name: cmdPaste

Comment: This control is enclosed within the lower toolbar. To place this control click the 3D button inside the Tools window, move the mouse inside the lower toolbar, press down the left mouse button, and while the left mouse button is pressed down move the mouse. After you release the left mouse button, Visual Basic places the 3D button inside the picture control.

BevelWidth	=	5
Caption	=	"Paste"
Font3D	=	2 'Raised w/heavy shading
FontName	=	"MS Sans Serif"
FontSize	=	9.75
ForeColor	=	&H00FF0000&
Height	=	975
Left	=	0
Picture	=	\VB\ICONS\WRITING\NOTE16.ICO
Top	=	0
Width	=	1695

Object: 3D button
Object Name: cmdCut

Comment: This control is enclosed within the lower toolbar.

BevelWidth	=	5
Caption	=	"Cut"
Font3D	=	2 'Raised w/heavy shading
FontName	=	"MS Sans Serif"
FontSize	=	9.75
ForeColor	=	&H000000FF&
Height	=	975

Left	=	1680
Picture	=	\VB\ICONS\WRITING\ERASE02.ICO
Top	=	0
Width	=	1575

Object: 3D button
Object Name: cmdCopy

Comment: This control is enclosed within the lower toolbar.

BevelWidth	=	5
Caption	=	"Copy"
Font3D	=	2 'Raised w/heavy shading
FontName	=	"MS Sans Serif"
FontSize	=	9.75
ForeColor	=	&H00000000&
Height	=	975
Left	=	3240
Picture	=	\VB\ICONS\MAIL\MAIL14.ICO
Top	=	0
Width	=	1455

Object: 3D button
Object Name: cmdAbout

Comment: This control is enclosed within the lower toolbar.

BevelWidth	=	5
Caption	=	"&About"
Font3D	=	2 'Raised w/heavy shading
FontName	=	"MS Sans Serif"
FontSize	=	9.75
ForeColor	=	&H0000FFFF&
Height	=	975
Left	=	4680
Picture	=	\VB\ICONS\MISC\LIGHTON.ICO
Top	=	0
Width	=	975

continues

Table 6.1. continued

Object: 3D button
Object Name: cmdAudio

Comment: This control is enclosed within the lower toolbar.

BevelWidth	=	5
Caption	=	"Audio"
Font3D	=	2 'Raised w/heavy shading
FontName	=	"MS Sans Serif"
FontSize	=	9.75
ForeColor	=	&H00808080&
Height	=	975
Left	=	5640
Picture	=	\VB\ICONS\MISC\EAR.ICO
Top	=	0
Width	=	975

Object: 3D button
Object Name: cmdClock

Comment: This control is enclosed within the lower toolbar.

BevelWidth	=	5
Caption	=	"Clock"
Font3D	=	2 'Raised w/heavy shading
FontName	=	"MS Sans Serif"
FontSize	=	9.75
ForeColor	=	&H00000000&
Height	=	975
Left	=	6600
Picture	=	\VB\ICONS\MISC\CLOCK02.ICO
Top	=	0
Width	=	975

Object: 3D button
Object Name: cmdRemove (array of 3D buttons)

Comment: This control is enclosed within the lower toolbar. To place this control click the 3D button inside the Tools window, move the mouse inside the lower toolbar, press down the left mouse button, and while the left mouse button is pressed down move the mouse. After you release the left mouse button, Visual Basic places the 3D button inside the picture control. Set the Name property of the 3D button control to cmdRemove, and when Visual Basic prompts you (with a dialog box) that a control with this name already exists, click the Yes button of the dialog box (because you want to create an array of 3D buttons).

BevelWidth	=	5
Caption	=	"Remove "
Font3D	=	4 'Inset w/heavy shading
FontName	=	"MS Sans Serif"
FontSize	=	9.75
ForeColor	=	&H000000FF&
Height	=	975
Index	=	1

Comment: This is Element 1 of the imgRemove() array of 3D buttons.

Left	=	7560
Picture	=	\VB\ICONS\MISC\CHECKMRK.ICO
Top	=	0
Width	=	1095

Object: 3D button
Object Name: cmdTools (array of 3D buttons)

Comment: This control is enclosed within the lower toolbar. To place this control click the 3D button inside the Tools window, move the mouse inside the lower toolbar, press down the left mouse button, and while the left mouse button is pressed down move the mouse. After you release the left mouse button, Visual Basic places the 3D button inside the picture control. Set the Name property of the 3D buttons to cmdTools, and when Visual Basic prompts you (with a dialog box) that a control with this name already exists, click the Yes button of the dialog box (because you want to create an array of 3D buttons).

BevelWidth	=	5
Caption	=	"Tools"
Font3D	=	2 'Raised w/heavy shading
FontName	=	"MS Sans Serif"
FontSize	=	9.75
ForeColor	=	&H00FFFF00&
Height	=	975

continues

Table 6.1. continued

Index	=	1

Comment: This is Element 1 of the imgTools() array of 3D buttons.

Left	=	8640
Picture	=	\VB\ICONS\INDUSTRY\WRENCH.ICO
Top	=	0
Width	=	975

Object: Picture box
Object Name: picStatusbar1

Comment: This control is enclosed within the lower status bar.

Align	=	2 'Align Bottom
BackColor	=	&H00C0C0C0&
Height	=	1005
Left	=	0
Top	=	5445
Width	=	9030

Object: MYCLOCK
Object Name: Myclock1

Comment: This control is enclosed within the lower status bar. To place this control, click the MYCLOCK icon inside the Tools window, move the mouse inside the lower status bar, press down the left mouse button, and while the left mouse button is pressed down move the mouse. After you release the left mouse button, Visual Basic places the MYCLOCK control inside the picture control.

BackColor	=	&H00C0C0C0&
ForeColor	=	&H00FFFFFF&
Height	=	285
Left	=	240
Top	=	120
UpdateInterval	=	1000

Comment: This control updates the time and date every second.

Width	=	2775

Object: Checkbox (3D checkbox)
Object Name: chkClock

Comment: This control is enclosed within the lower status bar.

Note: The Value property of a regular 2D checkbox can be 0, 1, or 2 (which correspond to not checked, checked, and dimmed). The Value property of a 3D checkbox can be True (checked) or False (not checked).

Caption	=	"With Clock"
Font3D	=	4 'Inset w/heavy shading
FontName	=	"MS Sans Serif"
FontSize	=	9.75
Height	=	255
Left	=	3240
Top	=	120
Value	=	-1 'True
Width	=	2295

Object: Checkbox (3D checkbox)
Object Name: chkWithAudio

Comment: This control is enclosed within the lower status bar.

Caption	=	"With Audio Prompts"
Font3D	=	4 'Inset w/heavy shading
FontName	=	"MS Sans Serif"
FontSize	=	9.75
Height	=	255
Left	=	3240
Top	=	480
Value	=	-1 'True
Width	=	2415

Object: KEYSTAT.VBX
Object Name: KeyStatCapsLock

Comment: This control is enclosed within the lower status bar.

Autosize	=	-1 'True
Height	=	420
Left	=	6120

continues

6

Table 6.1. continued

TimerInterval	=	250

Comment: This control checks the keyboard status every 250 milliseconds.

Top	=	120
Value	=	0 'False
Width	=	420

Object: KEYSTAT.VBX
Object Name: KeyStatNumLock

Comment: This control is enclosed within the lower status bar.

Height	=	420
Left	=	5760
Style	=	1 'Num Lock
TimerInterval	=	250

Comment: This control checks the keyboard status every 250 milliseconds.

Top	=	120
Value	=	0 'False
Width	=	420

Object: KEYSTAT.VBX
Object Name: KeyStatIns

Comment: This control is enclosed within the lower status bar.

Height	=	420
Left	=	6120
Style	=	2 'Insert State
TimerInterval	=	250

Comment: This control checks the keyboard status every 250 milliseconds.

Top	=	480
Value	=	0 'False
Width	=	420

Object: KEYSTAT.VBX
Object Name: KeyStatScroll

Comment: This control is enclosed within the lower status bar.

Height	= 420
Left	= 5760
Style	= 3 'Scroll Lock
TabIndex	= 7
TimerInterval	= 250

Comment: This control checks the keyboard status every 250 milliseconds.

Top	= 480
Value	= 0 'False
Width	= 420

Object: CMDIALOG.VBX (common dialog box)
Object Name: CMDialog1

Comment: This control is enclosed within the lower status bar.

CancelError	= -1 'True

Comment: Pressing the Cancel button of the common dialog box generates an error. This error is used to detect whether the user clicks the Cancel button of the common dialog box.

Left	= 4800
Top	= 0

Object: TEGOMM.VBX
Object Name: TegommFront

Comment: This control is enclosed within the lower status bar.

Height	= 330
Left	= 120
Top	= 480
Visible	= 0 'False
Width	= 3510

Object: 3D button
Object Name: cmdRemove (array of 3D buttons)

Comment: This control is enclosed within the lower status bar.

BevelWidth	= 5

continues

6

Table 6.1. continued

Caption	=	"Remove "
Font3D	=	4 'Inset w/heavy shading
FontName	=	"MS Sans Serif"
FontSize	=	9.75
ForeColor	=	&H000000FF&
Height	=	975
Index	=	2

Comment: This is Element 2 of the cmdRemove() array of 3D buttons.

Left	=	7560
Picture	=	\VB\ICONS\MISC\CHECKMRK.ICO
Top	=	0
Width	=	1095

Object: 3D button
Object Name: cmdTools (array of 3D buttons)

Comment: This control is enclosed within the lower status bar.

BevelWidth	=	5
Caption	=	"Tools"
Font3D	=	2 'Raised w/heavy shading
FontName	=	"MS Sans Serif"
FontSize	=	9.75
ForeColor	=	&H00FFFF00&
Height	=	975
Index	=	2

Comment: This is Element 2 of the imgTools() array of 3D buttons.

Left	=	8640
Picture	=	\VB\ICONS\INDUSTRIAL\WRENCH.ICO
Top	=	0
Width	=	975

Object: Picture box
Object Name: picStatusbar2

Comment: This picture box serves as the middle status bar.

Align	=	2 'Align Bottom
BackColor	=	&H00C0C0C0&
Height	=	480
Left	=	0
Top	=	4965
Width	=	9030

Object: 3D button
Object Name: cmdSYSTEM

Comment: This control is enclosed within the middle status bar. To place this control click the icon of the control inside the Tools window, move the mouse inside the lower status bar, press down the left mouse button, and while the left mouse button is pressed down move the mouse. After you release the left mouse button, Visual Basic places the control inside the picture control.

BevelWidth	=	5
Caption	=	"SYSTEM.INI"
Font3D	=	2 'Raised w/heavy shading
ForeColor	=	&H0000FF00&
Height	=	495
Left	=	0
Top	=	0
Width	=	2655

Object: 3D button
Object Name: cmdAUTOEXEC

Comment: This control is enclosed within the middle status bar.

BevelWidth	=	5
Caption	=	"AUTOEXEC.BAT"
Font3D	=	2 'Raised w/heavy shading
ForeColor	=	&H0000FFFF&
Height	=	495

continues

6

Table 6.1. continued

Left	=	2640
Top	=	0
Width	=	2895

Object: 3D button
Object Name: cmdCONFIG

Comment: This control is enclosed within the middle status bar.

BevelWidth	=	5
Caption	=	"CONFIG.SYS"
Font3D	=	2 'Raised w/heavy shading
ForeColor	=	&H00FF0000&
Height	=	495
Left	=	5520
Top	=	0
Width	=	2055

Object: 3D button
Object Name: cmdRemove (array of 3D buttons)

Comment: This control is enclosed within the middle status bar.

BevelWidth	=	5
Caption	=	"Remove"
Font3D	=	4 'Inset w/heavy shading
FontName	=	"MS Sans Serif"
FontSize	=	9.75
ForeColor	=	&H000000FF&
Height	=	495
Index	=	3

Comment: This is Element 3 of the cmdRemove() array of 3D buttons.

Left	=	7560
Top	=	0
Width	=	1095

Object: 3D button
Object Name: cmdTools (array of 3D buttons)

Comment: This control is enclosed within the middle status bar.

BevelWidth	=	5
Caption	=	"Tools"
Font3D	=	2 'Raised w/heavy shading
FontName	=	"MS Sans Serif"
FontSize	=	9.75
ForeColor	=	&H00FFFF00&
Height	=	495
Index	=	3

Comment: This is Element 3 of the cmdRemove() array of 3D buttons.

Left	=	8640
Top	=	0
Width	=	975

Object: Picture box
Object Name: picStatusbar3

Comment: This control is enclosed within the upper status bar.

Align	=	2 'Align Bottom
BackColor	=	&H00C0C0C0&
Height	=	1035
Left	=	0
Top	=	3930
Width	=	9030

Object: 3D button
Object Name: cmdPrint

Comment: This control is enclosed within the upper status bar. To place this control click the icon of the control inside the Tools window, move the mouse inside the upper status bar, press down the left mouse button, and while the left mouse button is pressed down move the mouse. After you release the left mouse button, Visual Basic places the control inside the picture control.

BevelWidth	=	5
Caption	=	"Print It"

continues

Table 6.1. continued

Font3D	=	2 'Raised w/heavy shading
FontName	=	"MS Sans Serif"
FontSize	=	9.75
ForeColor	=	&H0000FFFF&
Height	=	975
Left	=	0
Picture	=	\VB\ICONS\NET06.ICO
Top	=	0
Width	=	2655

Object: 3D button
Object Name: cmdRemove (array of 3D buttons)

Comment: This control is enclosed within the upper status bar.

BevelWidth	=	5
Caption	=	"Remove"
Font3D	=	4 'Inset w/heavy shading
FontName	=	"MS Sans Serif"
FontSize	=	9.75
ForeColor	=	&H000000FF&
Height	=	975
Index	=	3

Comment: This is Element 3 of the cmdRemove() array of 3D buttons.

Left	=	7560
Picture	=	\VB\ICONS\MISC\CHECKMRK.ICO
Top	=	0
Width	=	1095

Object: 3D button
Object Name: cmdTools (array of 3D buttons)

Comment: This control is enclosed within the upper status bar.

BevelWidth	=	5
Caption	=	"Tools"

Font3D		=	2 'Raised w/heavy shading
FontName		=	"MS Sans Serif"
FontSize		=	9.75
ForeColor		=	&H00FFFF00&
Height		=	975
Index		=	4

Comment: This is Element 4 of the cmdTools() array of 3D buttons.

Left		=	8640
Picture		=	\VB\ICONS\INDUSTRY\WRENCH.ICO
Top		=	0
Width		=	975

Figure 6.20.
The frmMultipad *form (in design mode).*

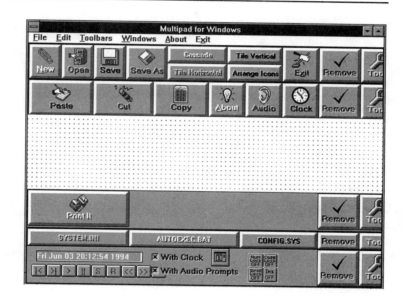

The Visual Implementation of the Menus

You'll now implement the menu of the frmMultipad form.

❏ Implement the menu of the frmMultipad form according to the specifications in Table 6.2. The menus of the frmMultipad form are shown in Figures 6.21 through 6.26.

Table 6.2. The Menu table of the `frmMultipad` form.

Caption	Name
&File	mnuFile
&New	mnuNew
&Open	mnuOpen
Save	mnuSave
Save As	mnuSaveAs
&Edit	mnuEdit
Paste	mnuPaste
	Shortcut = Ctrl+V
Copy	mnuCopy
	Shortcut = Ctrl+C
Cut	mnuCut
	Shortcut = Ctrl+X
Clear	mnuClear
&Toolbars	mnuToolbars
Show All Tools	mnuShowAllTools
Remove All Tools	mnuRemoveAllTools
&Windows	mnuWindows
	WindowList = -1 'True
&Cascade	mnuCascade
Tile &Horizontal	mnuTileHorizontal
Tile &Vertical	mnuTileVertical
&Arrange Icons	mnuArrangeIcons
&About	mnuAbout
E&xit	mnuExit
E&xit	mnuExitProgram

Figure 6.21.
The File menu of the
frmMultipad form.

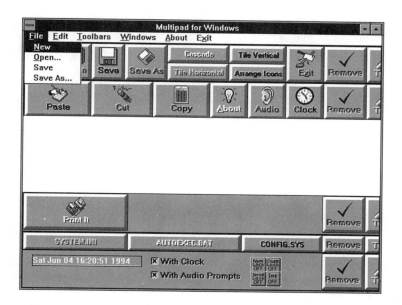

Figure 6.22.
The Edit menu of the
frmMultipad form.

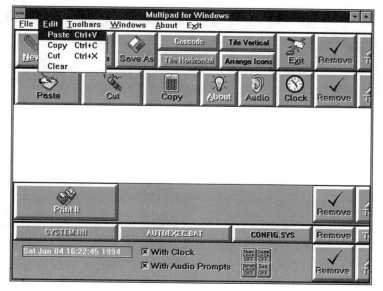

6

Figure 6.23.
The Toolbars menu of the
frmMultipad form.

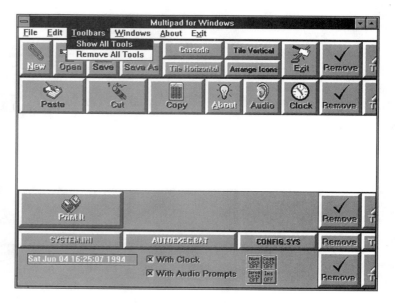

Figure 6.24.
The Windows menu of the
frmMultipad form.

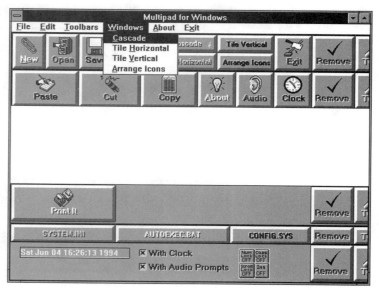

Figure 6.25.
The About menu of the
frmMultipad form.

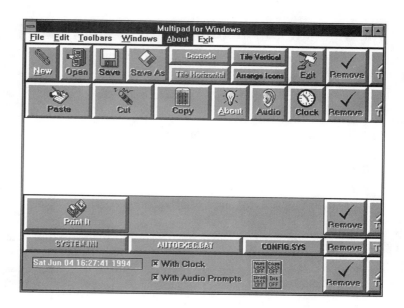

Figure 6.26.
The Exit menu of the
frmMultipad form.

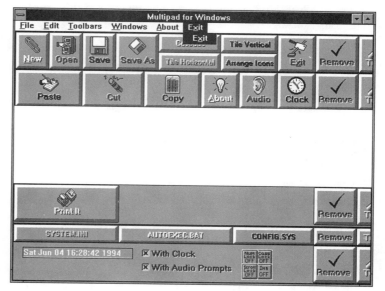

The Visual Implementation of the About Dialog Box

You'll now visually implement the frmAbout form of the Multipad program.

☐ Implement the frmAbout form according to the specifications in Table 6.3. When you finish implementing the form, it should look like the one shown in Figure 6.27.

Table 6.3. The Properties table of the frmAbout form.

Object: Form
Object Name: frmAbout

Comment: This is the About dialog box.

Note: When you created the Multipad.MAK project, Visual Basic automatically opened a new form called Form1. You can use the Form1 form as the frmAbout form. That is, set the properties of the form according to the specifications in Table 6.3 and save the form as ABOUT.FRM inside the C:\LearnVB\Practice\MDI directory. You save the form by highlighting the form and selecting Save File As from the File menu. If you deleted the Form1 form from the Project window, select New Form from the File menu, save the form as ABOUT.FRM, and then set the properties of the form according to the specifications in Table 6.3.

BackColor	=	&H00C0C0C0&
BorderStyle	=	1 'Fixed Single
Caption	=	"About All Media"
Height	=	4890
Left	=	1035
MaxButton	=	0 'False

Comment: No maximize (up-arrow) icon.

MinButton	=	0 'False

Comment: No minimize (down-arrow) icon.

Top	=	1140
Width	=	6465

Object: 3D label
Object Name: Panel3D1

BackColor	=	&H00C0C0C0&
BevelInner	=	2 'Raised
BevelWidth	=	5
BorderWidth	=	5

Caption	=	"Copyright 1990-1994"
Font3D	=	2 'Raised w/heavy shading
FontName	=	"MS Sans Serif"
FontSize	=	9.75
Height	=	1095
Left	=	0
Top	=	1440
Width	=	6375

Object: 3D label
Object Name: Panel3D2

BackColor	=	&H00C0C0C0&
BevelInner	=	1 'Inset
BevelOuter	=	1 'Inset
BevelWidth	=	5
BorderWidth	=	5
Caption	=	"Multipad for Windows Version 1.0"
Font3D	=	2 'Raised w/heavy shading
FontName	=	"MS Sans Serif"
FontSize	=	9.75
Height	=	855
Left	=	120
Top	=	2520
Width	=	6375

Object: 3D label
Object Name: Panel3D3

BackColor	=	&H00C0C0C0&
BevelInner	=	1 'Inset
BevelOuter	=	1 'Inset
BevelWidth	=	5
BorderWidth	=	5
Font3D	=	2 'Raised w/heavy shading

continues

Table 6.3. continued

Height	=	1455
Left	=	0
Text	=	(make it empty)
Top	=	0
Width	=	1095

Object: 3D label
Object Name: Panel3D4

BackColor	=	&H00C0C0C0&
BevelInner	=	1 'Inset
BevelOuter	=	1 'Inset
BevelWidth	=	5
BorderWidth	=	5
Font3D	=	2 'Raised w/heavy shading
Height	=	1455
Left	=	5280
Top	=	0
Width	=	1095

Object: 3D button
Object Name: cmdClose

BevelWidth	=	10
Caption	=	"&OK"
Font3D	=	2 'Raised w/heavy shading
FontName	=	"MS Sans Serif"
FontSize	=	18
ForeColor	=	&H00FF0000&
Height	=	855
Left	=	2400
Top	=	3480
Width	=	1575

Object: Image
Object Name: imgAbout

Height	=	1215
Left	=	1080
Picture	=	C:\LearnVB\BMP\Multipad.BMP
Stretch	=	-1 'True
Top	=	120
Width	=	4215

Figure 6.27.
The frmAbout *form (in design mode).*

The Code That Displays the About Dialog Box

You'll now write the code that displays the About dialog box.

☐ Enter the following code inside the cmdAbout_Click() procedure of the frmMultipad form:

```
Sub cmdAbout_Click ()

    frmAbout.Show 1

End Sub
```

The code you entered displays the About dialog box as a modal dialog box (because you supplied 1 as the parameter of the Show method). Recall that during the time that the About modal dialog box is displayed, the user cannot switch to the frmMultipad form.

So whenever the user clicks the About button, the About dialog box is displayed.

☐ Enter the following code inside the cmdClose_Click() procedure of the frmAbout form:

```
Sub cmdClose_Click ()

    Unload frmAbout

End Sub
```

The code you entered is executed whenever the user clicks the OK button of the About dialog box. This code closes the About dialog box.

The frmDocument Form

The Multipad program needs an additional form, the frmDocument form. This form appears whenever the user loads a text file or clicks the New button.

❑ Implement the frmDocument form according to the specifications in Table 6.4. When you finish implementing the form, it should look like the one shown in Figure 6.28.

Table 6.4. The Properties table of the frmDocument form.

Object: Form
Object Name: frmDocument

Comment: To create the frmDocument form, select New Form from the File menu, save the form as DOCUMENT.FRM inside the C:\LearnVB\Practice\MDI directory, and then set the properties of the form according to the specifications in Table 6.4.

Caption	=	"Form1"
Height	=	4425
Icon	=	\VB\ICONS\OFFICE\CLIP01.ICO
Left	=	1035
MDIChild	=	-1 'True

Comment: This form serves as a child form.

Top	=	1140
Width	=	7485

Object: Checkbox
Object Name: chkFileHasChanged

Comment: This control is invisible during runtime (that is, its Visible property is set to False). This control is placed inside the form for the purpose of storing data. When the checkbox is checked, the contents of the text file are changed, and therefore when the user closes the form (or exits the program), the program examines the Value property of the checkbox, and if it is equal to 1, the program displays a dialog box to the user, asking the user if he or she wants to save the changes.

Caption	=	"File has changed flag"
Height	=	495
Left	=	1080
Top	=	2280

| Visible | = | 0 'False |
| Width | = | 2655 |

Object: Text box
Object Name: txtDocument

Comment: This is the area where the contents of the text file are displayed. In the next chapter you'll write code that sizes this text box so that during runtime the text box covers the entire client area of the frmDocument form.

Height	=	495
Left	=	0
MultiLine	=	-1 'True
ScrollBars	=	3 'Both
Top	=	0
Width	=	1215

Object: Label
Object Name: lblFilename

Comment: This control is invisible during runtime (its Visible property is set to False). This control is placed inside the form for the purpose of storing data.

BorderStyle	=	1 'Fixed Single
Height	=	495
Left	=	4440
Top	=	2280
Visible	=	0 'False
Width	=	1215

Figure 6.28.
The frmDocument *form*
(in design mode).

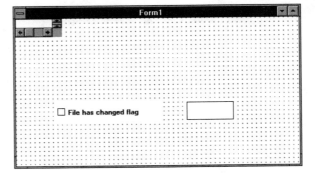

Testing the Prototype

You are now ready to test the prototype. Note that the Multipad.MAK project now contains three forms:

ABOUT.FRM, a regular form
DOCUMENT.FRM, a child form
MULTIPAD.FRM, a parent form

These names of forms are shown in the Project window of the Multipad.MAK project. (See Figure 6.29.)

Figure 6.29.
The Project window of the
Multipad.MAK project.

To save the project do the following:

❑ Select Save Project from the File menu.

To execute the prototype do the following:

❑ Select Start from the Run menu.

> *Visual Basic responds by executing the Multipad program.*

Of course, none of the Multipad program's tools (except the About button) have any functionality.

❑ Click the minus icon that appears on the upper-left corner of the Multipad program's window and select Close from the system menu that pops up.

In the next chapter you'll write the code of the Multipad program.

7

Creating a Multiple-Document Interface Text Editor Application (Part II)

In this chapter you'll write the code for the Multipad application.

The General Declarations Section of the frmMultipad Form

❑ Enter the following code inside the general declarations section of the frmMultipad form:

```
Option Explicit

Const WAV_FILE_NAME = "C:\LearnVB\WAV\ItsBeen1.WAV"
```

The Option Explicit statement instructs Visual Basic to generate a syntax error if your program uses a variable that has not yet been declared, and the WAV_FILE_NAME constant is the name of the WAV file that is played when the user terminates the program. Because WAV_FILE_NAME is declared inside the general declarations section, this constant is accessible from within any procedure of the frmMultipad form.

Attaching Code to the Clock Tool of the Toolbar

You'll now attach code to the Clock tool of the toolbar.

❑ Enter the following code inside the cmdClock_Click() procedure of the frmMultipad form:

```
Sub cmdClock_Click ()

    If MyClock1.Visible = True Then
        MyClock1.Visible = False
        chkClock.Value = False
    Else
        MyClock1.Visible = True
        chkClock.Value = True
    End If

End Sub
```

The cmdClock_Click() procedure is executed whenever the user clicks the Clock tool on the toolbar. Recall that when the user clicks the Clock tool the MyClock1 control should toggle its Visible property. Therefore, an If statement is used to check the current value of the Visible property of the MyClock1 control. If the MyClock1 control is visible, its Visible property is set to False:

```
MyClock1.Visible = False
```

The Value property of the chkClock checkbox is also set to False:

```
chkClock.Value = False
```

On the other hand, if the MyClock1 control is not visible, the Else is satisfied:

```
MyClock1.Visible = True
chkClock.Value = True
```

This causes the MyClock1 control to be visible, and an X is placed inside the chkClock checkbox.

> **NOTE**
>
> Note that you "remove" the MyClock1 control by setting its Visible property to False.
>
> This means that the clock is not displayed, but it is still functional (that is, it still updates the date and time every 1000 milliseconds). A better way to remove the clock is to set its Visible property to False and its UpdateInterval property to 0. This way, the MyClock1 control does not update itself every 1000 milliseconds (and the application works faster).

Attaching Code to the Clock Checkbox

The chkClock_Click() procedure is executed whenever the user clicks the chkClock checkbox.

☐ Enter the following code inside the chkClock_Click() procedure of the frmMultipad form:

```
Sub chkClock_Click (Value As Integer)

    If chkClock.Value = True Then
        MyClock1.Visible = True
    Else
        MyClock1.Visible = False
    End If

End Sub
```

The code you entered toggles the Visible property of the MyClock1 control. If the MyClock1 control is visible, the If statement is satisfied, and the MyClock1 control is made invisible. If the MyClock1 control is invisible, the Else is satisfied, and the MyClock1 control is made visible.

> **NOTE**
>
> The Multipad application has a lot of code in it. It is therefore a good idea to test the code from time to time as you enter it. Don't forget to save the project from time to time.
>
> To save the project do the following:
>
> ☐ Select Save Project from the File menu.
>
> To test the code you have entered so far do the following:
>
> ☐ Select Start from the Run menu (or press F5).

Attaching Code to the About Menu

In Chapter 6, "Creating a Multiple-Document Interface Text Editor Application (Part I)," you attached code to the About tool. (That is, you entered code inside the cmdAbout_Click() procedure of the frmMultipad form.) You'll now attach code to the About menu.

❑ Enter the following code inside the mnuAbout_Click() procedure of the frmMultipad form:

```
Sub mnuAbout_Click ()

    ' Display the About dialog box
    cmdAbout_Click

End Sub
```

The code you entered is executed whenever the user clicks the About menu. This code executes the cmdAbout_Click() procedure (which causes the About dialog box to appear).

Attaching Code to the Exit Tool

The cmdExit_Click() procedure is executed whenever the user clicks the Exit tool.

❑ Enter the following code inside the cmdExit_Click() procedure of the frmMultipad form:

```
Sub cmdExit_Click ()

    Unload frmMultipad

End Sub
```

The code you entered unloads the frmMultipad form, and the application terminates.

Attaching Code to the Exit Menu

Whenever the user selects Exit from the Exit menu, the Multipad application terminates.

❑ Enter the following code inside the mnuExitProgram_Click() procedure of the frmMultipad form:

```
Sub mnuExitProgram_Click ()

    cmdExit_Click

End Sub
```

The code you entered executes the cmdExit_Click() procedure (the code you already attached to the Exit tool).

Attaching Code to the New Tool

The cmdNew_Click() procedure is executed whenever the user clicks the New tool. This procedure displays a new child document inside the parent form.

❑ Enter the following code inside the cmdNew_Click() procedure of the frmMultipad form:

```
Sub cmdNew_Click ()

    Dim frmNewChild As New frmDocument
    Static DocNumber As Integer

    DocNumber = DocNumber + 1

    frmNewChild.Show

    frmMultipad.ActiveForm.Caption =
    ➥ "(" +
    ➥ Str(DocNumber) +
    ➥ ") Untitled"

    frmMultipad.ActiveForm.lblFilename =
    ➥ "Untitled.txt"

End Sub
```

The code you entered declares local variables:

```
Dim frmNewChild As New frmDocument

Static DocNumber As Integer
```

The frmNewChild variable is declared as New frmDocument. This means that when the user executes the cmdNew_Click() procedure, the program generates a new variable that is an exact replica of the frmDocument form you created in Chapter 6. The frmNewChild form is therefore a form with properties settings identical to those of the frmDocument form.

Note that DocNumber is declared as a Static variable. This means that when the cmdNew_Click() procedure is executed for the first time, Visual Basic sets the value of this integer to 0. During the execution of the cmdNew_Click() procedure, the value of DocNumber is increased by 1. So when the user exits the cmdNew_Click() procedure, the value of DocNumber is 1. If the user again clicks the New tool, the cmdNew_Click() procedure is again executed. Now, however, the value of DocNumber is 1 (because a Static variable retains its value).

The next statement increments DocNumber by 1:

```
    DocNumber = DocNumber + 1
```

As you'll soon see, DocNumber is used as part of the Caption property of the new child window that the cmdNew_Click() procedure generates.

The next statement actually displays the new child window:

```
    frmNewChild.Show
```

Then the Caption property of the new child window is set:

```
frmMultipad.ActiveForm.Caption =
  ➥ "(" +
  ➥ Str(DocNumber) +
  ➥ ") Untitled"
```

For example, if this is the first time that the cmdNew_Click() procedure is executed, the Caption property of the new child form is set to this:

```
(1) Untitled
```

If this is the second time the cmdNew_Click() procedure is executed, the Caption property of the new child form is set to this:

```
(2) Untitled
```

Note that the Caption property of the new child form is referenced as this:

```
frmMultipad.ActiveForm.Caption
```

ActiveForm is the name of the active form. When you display the new child form (with the Show method), the program displays the new child form, and the ActiveForm is this new child form.

The next statement updates the Caption property of the invisible lblFilename label:

```
frmMultipad.ActiveForm.lblFilename =
  ➥ "Untitled.txt"
```

As you'll see later, the Caption property of the lblFilename label is used for storing the name of the file that is displayed inside the child form. Because so far the file has not been saved, its name is set to Untitled.txt.

Note that the statement

```
frmMultipad.ActiveForm.lblFilename =
  ➥ "Untitled.txt"
```

is identical to the statement

```
frmMultipad.ActiveForm.lblFilename.Caption =
  ➥ "Untitled.txt"
```

because the default property of the label control is Caption.

Attaching Code to the New Item of the File Menu

You'll now attach code to the New item of the File menu.

❑ Enter the following code inside the mnuNew_Click() procedure of the frmMultipad form:

```
Sub mnuNew_Click ()

    cmdNew_Click

End Sub
```

The code you entered executes the cmdNew_Click() procedure. Therefore, clicking the New tool on the toolbar produces the same result as selecting New from the File menu.

Attaching Code to the Arrange Icons Button

Now that you have written code that implements the generation of the new child forms, you can write code that arranges the new child forms and their icons.

❑ Enter the following code inside the mnuArrangeIcons_Click() procedure of the frmMultipad form:

```
Sub mnuArrangeIcons_Click ()

    ' Arrange the icons of the child windows
    frmMultipad.Arrange ARRANGE_ICONS

End Sub
```

The code you entered executes the Arrange method with the ARRANGE_ICONS constant as a parameter of the Arrange method.

The ARRANGE_ICONS constant is declared inside the CONSTANT.TXT file. Therefore, you must add the CONSTANT.TXT file to the Multipad.MAK project:

❑ Select Add File from the File menu and add the file \VB\CONSTANT.TXT to the project.

After you add this file, the Project Window should contain the following files:

> ABOUT.FRM
> DOCUMENT.FRM
> MULTIPAD.FRM
> CONSTANT.TXT
> VBX files

If you examine the \VB\CONSTANT.TXT file, you'll see the following statements inside this file:

```
' Arrange Method
' for MDI Forms
Global Const CASCADE = 0
Global Const TILE_HORIZONTAL = 1
Global Const TILE_VERTICAL = 2
Global Const ARRANGE_ICONS = 3
```

This means that ARRANGE_ICONS is declared as 3. So the statement

```
frmMultipad.Arrange ARRANGE_ICONS
```

is identical to the statement

```
frmMultipad.Arrange 3
```

Attaching Code to the Arrange Icons Menu

You'll now write the code of the Arrange Icons menu.

☐ Enter the following code inside the cmdArrangeIcons_Click() procedure of the frmMultipad form:

```
Sub cmdArrangeIcons_Click ()

    mnuArrangeIcons_Click

End Sub
```

The code you entered executes the mnuArrangeIcons_Click() procedure. Therefore, selecting Arrange Icons from the Windows menu produces the same results as clicking the Arrange Icons tool on the toolbar.

Cascading the Child Windows

You'll now write the code that cascades the child windows.

☐ Enter the following code inside the mnuCascade_Click() procedure of the frmMultipad form:

```
Sub mnuCascade_Click ()

    ' Cascade the child windows
    frmMultipad.Arrange CASCADE

End Sub
```

The code you entered is executed whenever the user selects Cascade from the Windows menu. This code causes the child windows to be displayed cascaded.

This is accomplished by using the Arrange method with the constant CASCADE as the parameter of the Arrange method. (CASCADE is declared inside the CONSTANT.TXT file that you added to the Multipad.MAK project.)

Attaching Code to the Cascade Tool of the Toolbar

You'll now attach code to the Cascade tool of the toolbar.

☐ Enter the following code inside the cmdCascade_Click() procedure of the frmMultipad form:

```
Sub cmdCascade_Click ()

    mnuCascade_Click

End Sub
```

The code you entered executes the mnuCascade_Click() procedure. Therefore, selecting Cascade from the Windows menu produces the same results as clicking the Cascade tool on the toolbar.

Attaching Code to the Tile Horizontal Item of the Windows Menu

You'll now attach code to the Tile Horizontal item of the Windows menu.

☐ Enter the following code inside the `mnuTileHorizontal_Click()` procedure of the Windows menu:

```
Sub mnuTileHorizontal_Click ()

    frmMultipad.Arrange TILE_HORIZONTAL

End Sub
```

The code you entered uses the `Arrange` method with `TILE_HORIZONTAL` as its parameter. `TILE_HORIZONTAL` is declared inside the CONSTANT.TXT file that you added to the Multipad.MAK project.

Attaching Code to the Tile Horizontal Tool of the Toolbar

You'll now attach code to the Tile Horizontal tool of the toolbar.

☐ Enter the following code inside the `cmdTileHorizontal_Click()` procedure of the `frmMultipad` form:

```
Sub cmdTileHorizontal_Click ()

    mnuTileHorizontal_Click

End Sub
```

The code you entered executes the `mnuTileHorizontal_Click()` procedure. Therefore, clicking the Tile Horizontal tool produces the same results as selecting Tile Horizontal from the Windows menu.

Attaching Code to the Tile Vertical Item of the Windows Menu

You'll now attach code to the Tile Vertical item of the Windows menu.

☐ Enter the following code inside the `mnuTileVertical_Click()` procedure of the `frmMultipad` form:

```
Sub mnuTileVertical_Click ()

    frmMultipad.Arrange TILE_VERTICAL

End Sub
```

The code you entered executes the `Arrange` method with `TILE_VERTICAL` as the parameter. `TILE_VERTICAL` is declared inside the CONSTANT.TXT file that you added to the Multipad.MAK project.

Attaching Code to the Tile Vertical Tool of the Toolbar

You'll now attach code to the Tile Vertical tool of the toolbar.

☐ Enter the following code inside the cmdTileVertical_Click() procedure of the frmMultipad form:

```
Sub cmdTileVertical_Click ()

    mnuTileVertical_Click

End Sub
```

The code you entered executes the mnuTileVertical_Click() procedure. Therefore, clicking the Tile Vertical tool on the toolbar produces the same results as selecting Tile Vertical from the Windows menu.

Attaching Code to the Show All Tools Tool of the Toolbar

You'll now attach code to the Show All Tools tool of the Toolbars menu.

☐ Enter the following code inside the mnuShowAllTools_Click() procedure of the frmMultipad form:

```
Sub mnuShowAllTools_Click ()


    ' Show all toolbars and Status bars
    picToolbar1.Visible = True

    picToolbar2.Visible = True

    picStatusbar1.Visible = True

    picStatusbar2.Visible = True

    picStatusbar3.Visible = True

End Sub
```

The code you entered sets the Visible properties of the toolbars and status bars to True. This causes all the toolbars and status bars of the frmMultipad form to be displayed.

Attaching Code to the Remove All Tools Item of the Toolbars Menu

You'll now attach code to the Remove All Tools item of the Toolbars menu.

☐ Enter the following code inside the mnuRemoveAllTools_Click() procedure of the frmMultipad form:

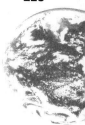

```
Sub mnuRemoveAllTools_Click ()

    ' Remove all toolbars and Status bars
    picToolbar1.Visible = False
    picToolbar2.Visible = False
    picStatusbar1.Visible = False
    picStatusbar2.Visible = False
    picStatusbar3.Visible = False

End Sub
```

The code you entered sets the Visible properties of the toolbars and status bars to False. This causes all the toolbars and status bars of the frmMultipad form to be invisible. Note that when the toolbars and status bars are made invisible, Visual Basic automatically increases the client area of the parent form.

Attaching Code to the Remove Tools of the Toolbars and Status Bars

You'll now attach code to the Remove tools that appear in each toolbar and status bar.

☐ Enter the following code inside the cmdRemove_Click() procedure of the frmMultipad form:

```
Sub cmdRemove_Click (Index As Integer)

    Select Case Index

    Case 0
        picToolbar1.Visible = False

    Case 1
        picToolbar2.Visible = False

    Case 2
        picStatusbar1.Visible = False

    Case 3
        picStatusbar2.Visible = False

    Case 4
        picStatusbar3.Visible = False


    End Select

End Sub
```

Recall that cmdRemove is an array of 3D buttons. cmdRemove(0) is the Remove tool that appears on the upper toolbar, cmdRemove(1) is the Remove tool that appears on the lower toolbar, cmdRemove(2) is the Remove tool that appears on the lower status bar, and so on.

The code you entered uses a Select Case statement to determine which Remove tool was clicked. The parameter of the cmdRemove_Click() procedure is Index:

```
Sub cmdRemove_Click (Index As Integer)

    . . .
    . . .
    . . .

End Sub
```

The value of Index indicates which Remove tool was clicked. For example, if the user clicks the Remove tool of the upper toolbar, the cmdRemove_Click() procedure is executed with Index equal to 0, when the user clicks the Remove tool on the lower toolbar, the cmdRemove_Click() procedure is executed with Index equal to 1, and so on.

If the user clicks the Remove tool on the upper toolbar, the Case 0 is satisfied:

```
Select Case Index

    Case 0
        picToolbar1.Visible = False

    ... Other cases ...
    ..................
    ..................
    ..................

End Select
```

This means that when the user clicks the Remove tool of the upper toolbar, the upper toolbar is made invisible.

Similarly, when the user clicks the Remove tool on the lower toolbar, the Case 1 is satisfied, and so on.

Attaching Code to the Tools Icons of the Toolbars and Status Bars

You'll now attach code to the Tools icons of the toolbars and status bars.

❑ Enter the following code inside the cmdTools_Click() procedure of the frmMultipad form:

```
Sub cmdTools_Click (Index As Integer)

    mnuShowAllTools_Click

End Sub
```

The code you entered executes the mnuShowAllTools_Click() procedure. Therefore, clicking any of the Tools icons produces the same results as selecting Show All Tools from the Toolbars menu.

Note that cmdTools is an array of 3D buttons. cmdTools(0) is the 3D button that appears on the upper toolbar, cmdTools(1) is the 3D button that appears on the lower toolbar, cmdTools(2) is the

3D button that appears on the lower status bar, and so on. This means that the `Index` parameter of the `cmdTools_Click()` procedure indicates which Tools button was clicked. However, you don't use the value of `Index`, because it does not matter which Tools button was clicked. Whenever any of the Tools buttons is clicked, the `cmdTools_Click()` procedure displays all the toolbars and all the status bars.

The Multipad.BAS Module

You'll now add a new module to the Multipad.MAK project.

❑ Select New Module from the File menu.

❑ Save the new module as Multipad.BAS inside the C:\LearnVB\Practice\MDI directory.

Your Project window now looks like the one shown in Figure 7.1.

Figure 7.1.
The Project window of the
Multipad.MAK project.

You'll now write code inside the general declarations section of the Multipad.BAS module.

❑ Enter the following code inside the general declarations section of the Multipad.BAS module. That is, highlight the MULTIPAD.BAS item inside the Project window, click the View Code button of the Project window, and then type the following code inside the general declarations section of the Multipad.BAS module:

```
Option Explicit

' Number of children
Global ggNumChildren As Integer
```

The code you entered declares a global integer called `ggNumChildren`. Because this integer is declared as `Global`, it is accessible from within any procedure of any form or module of the Multipad.MAK project. In other words, you can access this integer from within procedures of the `frmMultipad` form as well as from within procedures that reside inside the Multipad.BAS module. (Later you'll add procedures to the Multipad.BAS modules that need access to the `ggNumChildren` integer.)

_7_

Attaching Code to the `Form_Load()` Procedure of the `frmDocument` Form

You'll now attach code to the `Form_Load()` procedure of the `frmDocument` form. The `Form_Load()` procedure of the `frmDocument` form is executed whenever a new `frmDocument` form is loaded. You have already entered code that creates a new child window (of type `frmDocument`) inside the `cmdNew_Click()` procedure of the `frmMultipad` form. So whenever the user clicks the New tool, a new child form is created, and the `Form_Load()` procedure of the `frmDocument` form is executed.

❑ Enter the following code inside the `Form_Load()` procedure of the `frmDocument` form:

```
Sub Form_Load ()

    ggNumChildren = ggNumChildren + 1

End Sub
```

The code you entered increases the `ggNumChildren` integer by 1. You declared `ggNumChildren` as `Global` inside the Multipad.BAS module. As such, the `ggNumChildren` is accessible from within the procedures of the `frmDocument` form.

`ggNumChildren` represents the number of child windows that the parent form has. When the user starts the Multipad application, `ggNumChildren` is initialized to 0. Whenever the user generates a new child form (for example, by clicking the New tool), the `Form_Load()` procedure of the `frmDocument` form is executed, which increases the `ggNumChildren` variable by 1. Therefore, `ggNumChildren` represents the number of child forms inside the parent form.

Attaching Code to the Resize Event of the `frmDocument` Form

You'll now attach code to the `Resize` event of the `frmDocument` form.

❑ Enter the following code inside the `Form_Resize()` procedure of the `frmDocument` form:

```
Sub Form_Resize ()

    Me.txtDocument.Height = Me.ScaleHeight
    Me.txtDocument.Width = Me.ScaleWidth

End Sub
```

The code you entered sets the Height and Width properties of the text box to the ScaleHeight and ScaleWidth properties of the `frmDocument` form. This means that after this procedure is executed, the text box covers the entire client area of the `frmDocument` form.

The `Form_Resize()` procedure is executed whenever the user sizes the `frmDocument` form. Therefore, when the `frmDocument` form is loaded (for example, when the user clicks the New tool), the text box inside this form is sized so that the text box covers the entire client area of the `frmDocument` window. Furthermore, when the user changes the size of the `frmDocument` form with the mouse, the `Form_Resize()` procedure is executed.

Note that the `Form_Resize()` procedure uses the `Me` keyword. The `Me` variable is automatically up-dated by the program. This variable contains the name of the active form. Therefore, in the case of the `Form_Resize()` procedure, `Me` holds the name of the child form that is currently being sized.

Attaching Code to the Copy Tool of the Toolbar

You'll now attach code to the Copy tool of the toolbar. Recall that you use the Copy tool by first highlighting a section of text inside the child window, and then clicking the Copy tool. This causes the highlighted text to be copied into the Windows Clipboard.

❑ Enter the following code inside the `cmdCopy_Click()` procedure of the `frmMultipad` form:

```
Sub cmdCopy_Click ()

    If ggNumChildren > 0 Then
        If TypeOf ActiveForm.ActiveControl Is TextBox Then

            ' Clear the clipboard
            Clipboard.Clear

            ' Copy to the clipboard the currently
            ' selected text.
            Clipboard.SetText ActiveForm.txtDocument.SelText
        End If
    End If

End Sub
```

The code you entered uses an `If` statement to check the value of `ggNumChildren`:

```
If ggNumChildren > 0 Then
    .......
    .......
    .......
End If
```

If `ggNumChildren` is not greater than 0, the parent window does not have any child windows, and therefore it makes no sense to perform the Copy operation. However, if `ggNumChildren` is greater than 0, the `If` condition is satisfied and the code under the `If` statement is executed. This code contains an inner `If` statement:

```
If ggNumChildren > 0 Then

    If TypeOf ActiveForm.ActiveControl Is TextBox Then
        ......
        ......
        ......
    End If

End If
```

The inner `If` statement checks whether the active control of the active form is a text box. In other words, it makes sense to perform the Copy operation only if the active control is a text box. So if the active control is a button, it does not make sense to perform the Copy operation.

The code under the inner If statement clears the contents of the Clipboard:

```
Clipboard.Clear
```

Then the highlighted text is copied into the Clipboard:

```
Clipboard.SetText ActiveForm.txtDocument.SelText
```

Attaching Code to the Copy Item of the Edit Menu

You'll now attach code to the Copy item of the Edit menu.

❏ Enter the following code inside the mnuCopy_Click() procedure of the frmMultipad form:

```
Sub mnuCopy_Click ()

    cmdCopy_Click

End Sub
```

The code you entered executes the cmdCopy_Click() procedure. So selecting the Copy item from the Edit menu produces the same results as clicking the Copy tool.

Attaching Code to the Paste Tool of the Toolbar

You'll now attach code to the Paste tool of the toolbar.

❏ Enter the following code inside the cmdPaste_Click() procedure of the frmMultipad form:

```
Sub cmdPaste_Click ()

 ' Perform the Paste operation

 If ggNumChildren > 0 Then
    If TypeOf ActiveForm.ActiveControl Is TextBox Then
       ActiveForm.txtDocument.SelText = Clipboard.GetText()
    End If
 End If

End Sub
```

The code you entered checks whether there are any child windows inside the parent window and whether the active control is a text box. If these conditions are satisfied, the GetText method and the SelText methods are executed to perform the Paste operation:

```
ActiveForm.txtDocument.SelText = Clipboard.GetText()
```

Attaching Code to the Paste Item of the Edit Menu

You'll now attach code to the Paste item of the Edit menu.

❏ Enter the following code inside the mnuPaste_Click() procedure of the frmMultipad form:

```
Sub mnuPaste_Click ()

    cmdPaste_Click

End Sub
```

The code you entered executes the `cmdPaste_Click()` procedure. Therefore, clicking the Paste tool on the toolbar produces the same result as selecting Paste from the Edit menu.

Attaching Code to the Cut Tool of the Toolbar

You'll now attach code to the Cut tool of the toolbar.

❏ Enter the following code inside the `cmdCut_Click()` procedure of the `frmMultipad` form:

```
Sub cmdCut_Click ()

    If ggNumChildren > 0 Then

        If TypeOf ActiveForm.ActiveControl Is TextBox Then

            ' Clear the Clipboard
            Clipboard.Clear

            ' Copy to the Clipboard the currently
            ' selected text.
            Clipboard.SetText ActiveForm.txtDocument.SelText

            ' Replace the currently selected text
            ' with null.
            ActiveForm.txtDocument.SelText = ""

        End If

    End If

End Sub
```

The code you entered checks whether there are child windows inside the parent window (`If ggNumChildren>0`), and an inner `If` statement checks whether the active control is a text box. If both of the `If` conditions are satisfied, the Cut operation is performed. The contents of the Clipboard are cleared:

```
Clipboard.Clear
```

The contents of the text box are then copied to the Clipboard:

```
Clipboard.SetText ActiveForm.txtDocument.SelText
```

Finally, the highlighted text of the text box is cleared:

```
ActiveForm.txtDocument.SelText = ""
```

Attaching Code to the Cut Item of the Edit Menu

You'll now attach code to the Cut item of the Edit menu.

☐ Enter the following code inside the mnuCut_Click() procedure of the frmMultipad form:

```
Sub mnuCut_Click ()

    cmdCut_Click

End Sub
```

The code you entered executes the cmdCut_Click() procedure. Therefore, selecting Cut from the Edit menu produces the same result as clicking the Cut tool on the toolbar.

Attaching Code to the Clear Item of the Edit Menu

You'll now attach code to the Clear item of the Edit menu.

☐ Enter the following code inside the mnuClear_Click() procedure of the frmMultipad form:

```
Sub mnuClear_Click ()

    If ggNumChildren > 0 Then
       If TypeOf ActiveForm.ActiveControl Is TextBox Then

          ' Replace the currently selected text
          ' with null.
          ActiveForm.txtDocument.SelText = ""
       End If
    End If

End Sub
```

The code you entered checks whether there are any child windows in the parent window and whether the active control is a text box. If these conditions are satisfied, the highlighted text is cleared:

```
ActiveForm.txtDocument.SelText = ""
```

Attaching Code to the Change Event of the Text Box of the Child Form

You'll now attach code to the txtDocument_Change() procedure of the frmDocument form. This procedure is automatically executed whenever the user changes the contents of the txtDocument text box that is placed inside the frmDocument form.

```
Sub txtDocument_Change ()

  chkFileHasChanged.Value = 1

End Sub
```

The code you entered sets the Value property of the `chkFileHasChanged` checkbox to 1. Recall that you placed this checkbox inside the `frmDocument` form during design time and that you set the Visible property of this checkbox to `False`. This means that during runtime this checkbox is not displayed. The reason for using this checkbox is solely to store data in it. In particular, this checkbox is used to store information regarding the contents of the text box. If the user changes the contents of the text box, the Value property of the checkbox is set to 1. Later in the program, you'll check the Value property of `chkFileHasChanged` whenever the user wants to exit or close the child form. If the Value property of the `chkFileHasChanged` is equal to 1, the contents of the text box were changed, and the program will display a message box asking the user if the changes should be saved to the disk.

> **NOTE**
>
> The `txtDocument_Change()` procedure uses a control (a checkbox) to store data. Alternatively, you can declare a variable inside the general declarations section of the `frmDocument` form. In both cases, the data is accessible from within every procedure of the `frmDocument`. However, the data of the checkbox control is accessible also from other forms in the project.
>
> Note that a variable that is declared as `Global` in a separate module is also accessible throughout the project. However, it is more elegant to store such data inside a control.

Attaching Code to the Open Tool of the Toolbar

You'll now attach code to the Open tool of the toolbar.

❑ Enter the following code inside the `cmdOpen_Click()` procedure of the `frmMultipad` form:

```
Sub cmdOpen_Click ()

    Dim FileNum

    On Error GoTo OpenError

    ' Set the items of the File Type list box
    CMDialog1.Filter =
        ➡ "All Files (*.*) |*.* |
        ➡  Text Files (*.txt)|*.txt|
        ➡ DOS Batch Files (*.bat)|*.bat"

    ' Set the default File Type to All Files (*.*)
    CMDialog1.FilterIndex = 1


    ' Display the dialog box
    CMDialog1.Action = 1

    ' Create a new child form
```

7

```
cmdNew_Click

    ' Get a free file number
    FileNum = FreeFile

    ' Open the file
    Open CMDialog1.FileName For Input As FileNum

    ' Read all the contents of the file into the text box
    ActiveForm.txtDocument.Text =
        ➥ Input$(LOF(FileNum), FileNum)

    ' Close the file
    Close FileNum

    ActiveForm.Caption = CMDialog1.Filetitle
    ActiveForm.lblFilename.Caption = CMDialog1.FileName
    ActiveForm.chkFileHasChanged.Value = 0

    ' Exit this procedure
    Exit Sub

OpenError:
' The user pressed the Cancel key of the CMDialog1 control
' Exit this procedure
Exit Sub

End Sub
```

The code you entered is responsible for enabling the user to select a text file (in the common dialog box), creating a new child window, and displaying the contents of the text file inside the child window.

The procedure declares a local variable:

```
Dim FileNum
```

Then an error trap is set:

```
On Error GoTo OpenError
```

The error trap instructs the program to jump immediately to a label called OpenError when an error occurs. As you'll soon see, this is the mechanism by which you detect that the user clicked the Cancel button of the Open dialog box.

The Filter property of the common dialog box is set to the following string:

```
CMDialog1.Filter =
        ➥ "All Files (*.*) |*.* |
        ➥  Text Files (*.txt)|*.txt|
        ➥ DOS Batch Files (*.bat)|*.bat"
```

This means that the Open dialog box lets the user display all the files (*.*), the text files (*.txt), and the DOS batch files (*.bat). (See Figure 7.2.)

Figure 7.2.
The Open dialog box.

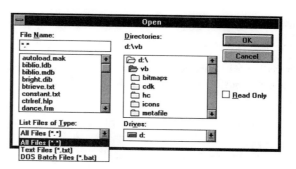

The FilterIndex property is then set to 0. This means that by default the Open dialog box displays all the files (*.*):

```
CMDialog1.FilterIndex = 0
```

Finally, you display the Open dialog box by setting its Action property to 1:

```
CMDialog1.Action = 1
```

When the Open dialog box is displayed, the user can select a file and click the OK button of the dialog box or click the Cancel button of the common dialog box. If the user clicks the Cancel button, an error is generated. This error is generated because during design time you set the CancelError property of the common dialog box control to True. Because you set an error trap, the procedure will immediately start executing the code, beginning at the OpenError label (which is located at the end of this procedure):

```
OpenError:
' The user pressed the Cancel key of the CMDialog1 control
' Exit this procedure
Exit Sub
```

The code under the OpenError label executes the Exit Sub statement to terminate the procedure.

If the user selects a file and then clicks the OK button of the Open dialog box, the procedure continues executing the rest of the statements.

You create a new child form by executing the cmdNew_Click() procedure:

```
cmdNew_Click
```

As you might recall, the cmdNew_Click() procedure creates a new child form. The next statements fill the newly created child form with the contents of the text file that the user selected in the Open dialog box.

The FileNum variable is updated with the FreeFile statement:

```
FileNum = FreeFile
```

Then the file is opened:

```
Open CMDialog1.FileName For Input As FileNum
```

In the preceding `Open` statement, note that the file to be opened is the value of the FileName property of the `CMDialog1` control, and `FileNum` is the file number that you extracted with the `FreeFile` statement.

The Text property of the text box is then filled with the contents of the file that you opened:

```
ActiveForm.txtDocument.Text =
      ➥ Input$(LOF(FileNum), FileNum)
```

Now that the text box is updated with the contents of the file, you can issue the `Close` statement to close the file:

```
Close FileNum
```

Note that in the preceding `Close` statement `FileNum` is used again (it is the same variable that was used to open the file).

The next statement sets the Caption property of the new child form:

```
ActiveForm.Caption = CMDialog1.Filetitle
```

Then the Caption property of the `lblFileName` control is set:

```
ActiveForm.lblFilename.Caption = CMDialog1.FileName
```

Recall that during design time you placed the `lblFileName` label inside the `frmDocument` form, and you set its Visible property to `False`. This label is used for storing data (for example, the filename of the selected file).

> **NOTE**
>
> The FileTitle property of the common dialog control contains the filename without its pathname. The FileName property of the common dialog box contains the pathname and filename of the file.

The Value property of `chkFileHasChanged` is set to 0 to indicate that contents of this file have not been changed (the file was only loaded):

```
ActiveForm.chkFileHasChanged.Value = 0
```

Finally, the `Exit Sub` statement is executed to cause the termination of the `cmdOpen_Click()` procedure:

```
Exit Sub
```

Attaching Code to the Open Item of the File Menu

You'll now attach code to the Open item of the File menu.

❏ Enter the following code inside the mnuOpen_Click() procedure of the frmMultipad form:

```
Sub mnuOpen_Click ()

    cmdOpen_Click

End Sub
```

The code you entered executes the cmdOpen_Click() procedure. This means that selecting Open from the File menu produces the same result as clicking the Open tool of the toolbar.

Attaching Code to the Save As Tool of the Toolbar

You'll now attach code to the Save As tool of the toolbar.

❏ Enter the following code inside the cmdSaveAs_Click() procedure of the frmMultipad form:

```
Sub cmdSaveAs_Click ()

    Dim Dummy

    Dummy = FileSaveAs()

End Sub
```

The code you entered declares a local variable called Dummy and then executes the FileSaveAs() function. You'll write the FileSaveAs() function in the next section. As implied by its name, the FileSaveAs() function opens a Save As dialog box and saves the file.

You must assign the returned value of the FileSaveAs() function to the Dummy variable, because in Visual Basic a function must return a value, and this value must be assigned to a variable (even if you are not using the returned value).

Writing the FileSaveAs() Function

In the preceding section you used the FileSaveAs() function. In this section you'll write the FileSaveAs() function.

The FileSaveAs() function is placed inside the Multipad.BAS module that you created. Here is how you prepare the FileSaveAs() function:

❏ Highlight the MULTIPAD.BAS item inside the Project window.

❏ Click the View Code button inside the Project window.

❏ Select New Procedure from the View menu.

7

Visual Basic responds by displaying the New Procedure dialog box.

❏ Make sure that the Function radio button inside the New Procedure dialog box is selected, and then type `FileSaveAs` inside the New Procedure dialog box text box.

❏ Click the OK button of the New Procedure dialog box.

Visual Basic responds by placing the `FileSaveAs()` function inside the Multipad.BAS module.

❏ Enter the following code inside the `FileSaveAs()` function that resides inside the Multipad.BAS module:

```
Function FileSaveAs ()

    Dim Msg, Answer

    FileSaveAs = True

    If ggNumChildren = 0 Then
        FileSaveAs = False
        Exit Function
    End If

    ' Set an error trap to detect the clicking
    ' of the Cancel key of the Save As dialog box.
    On Error GoTo SaveAsError

    ' Fill the items of the File Type list box of
    ' the Open dialog box.
    frmMultipad.CMDialog1.Filter =
        ➡ "All Files (*.*) |*.* |
        ➡ Text Files (*.txt)|*.txt|
        ➡ DOS Batch Files (*.bat)|*.bat"

    ' Set the default File Type to TXT files (*.txt).
    frmMultipad.CMDialog1.FilterIndex = 2

    ' Display the Save As dialog box.
    frmMultipad.CMDialog1.Action = 2

    ' Remove the error trap.
    On Error GoTo 0

    ' If the file specified by the user exists, and its
    ' size is not zero, ask the user if to overwrite it.
    If Dir(frmMultipad.CMDialog1.Filename) <> "" Then
        Msg = frmMultipad.CMDialog1.Filename + Chr(13)
        Msg =
            ➡ Msg +
            ➡ "This file already exists." +
            ➡ Chr(13) + Chr(13)

        Msg = Msg +
                ➡ "Replace existing file?"
```

```
      Answer = MsgBox(Msg, MB_ICONEXCLAMATION +
          ➥ MB_YESNO, "Multipad")

   If Answer = IDNO Then
      FileSaveAs = False
      Exit Function
   End If

End If

' Set mouse cursor to hourglass.
frmMultipad.ActiveForm.MousePointer = 11

' Change the FileName to the filename that
' the user selected, and issue a Save command.
frmMultipad.ActiveForm.lblFilename.Caption =
   ➥ frmMultipad.CMDialog1.Filename

SaveFile

' Set mouse cursor to default.
frmMultipad.ActiveForm.MousePointer = 0

' Reset the chkFileHasChanged flag.
frmMultipad.ActiveForm.chkFileHasChanged = False

' Set the title of the child window.
frmMultipad.ActiveForm.Caption =
   ➥ frmMultipad.CMDialog1.Filetitle


' Exit the procedure.
Exit Function

SaveAsError:
   ' The user clicked the Cancel button.
   FileSaveAs = False
   Exit Function
```

End Function

The code you entered declares two local variables:

```
Dim Msg, Answer
```

The `FileSaveAs` variable is the variable that is returned from the `FileSaveAs()` function. Initially `FileSaveAs` is set to `True`:

```
FileSaveAs = True
```

During the execution of the `FileSaveAs()` function the `FileSaveAs` variable might be set to `False`. (Note that there is no need to declare the `FileSaveAs` variable, because this variable is the returned value from the `FileSaveAs()` function.)

An `If` statement is then executed to determine whether there are child windows inside the parent window:

```
If ggNumChildren = 0 Then
   FileSaveAs = False
   Exit Function
End If
```

That is, if there are no child windows inside the parent window, there is no file to be saved. So the FileSaveAs() function is terminated with the Exit Function statement. Note that the FileSaveAs variable is set to False, which indicates to the procedure that calls the FileSaveAs() function that no file was saved.

If the preceding If statement is not satisfied, an error trap is set:

```
On Error GoTo SaveAsError
```

Recall that the CancelError property of the CMDialog1 control was set to True during design time. This means that if while the Save As dialog box is displayed the user clicks the Cancel button, an error occurs, and the program immediately branches to the SaveAsError label:

```
SaveAsError:
   ' The user clicked the Cancel button.
   FileSaveAs = False
   Exit Function
```

The code under the SaveAsError label sets the returned value of the function to False:

```
FileSaveAs = False
```

Then the Exit Function statement is executed:

```
Exit Function
```

The procedure sets the Filter property of the CMDialog1 control:

```
frmMultipad.CMDialog1.Filter =
   ➥ "All Files (*.*) |*.* |
   ➥ Text Files (*.txt)|*.txt|
   ➥ DOS Batch Files (*.bat)|*.bat"
```

and the default (FilterIndex) is set to 2:

```
' Set the default File Type to TXT files (*.txt).
frmMultipad.CMDialog1.FilterIndex = 2
```

Finally, the Save As dialog box is displayed:

```
' Display the Save As dialog box.
frmMultipad.CMDialog1.Action = 2
```

NOTE

Note that you display the Open dialog box by setting the Action property of the CMDialog1 control to 1. You display the Save As dialog box by setting the Action property to 2.

If no error was generated, the next statement, which removes the error trap, is executed:

```
' Remove the error trap.
On Error GoTo 0
```

The next statements check whether the file that the user specified exists already. If so, a message box is displayed:

```
' If the file specified by the user exists, and its
' size is not zero, ask the user if to overwrite it.
If Dir(frmMultipad.CMDialog1.Filename) <> "" Then
    Msg = frmMultipad.CMDialog1.Filename + Chr(13)
    Msg = Msg +
      ➥ "This file already exists." +
      ➥ Chr(13) + Chr(13)
    Msg = Msg + "Replace existing file?"

    Answer = MsgBox(Msg, MB_ICONEXCLAMATION +
          ➥ MB_YESNO, "Multipad")

    If Answer = IDNO Then
       FileSaveAs = False
       Exit Function
    End If

End If
```

Note that in the preceding code the following constants are used:

```
MB_ICONEXCLAMATION
MB_YESNO
IDNO
```

These constants are declared in the CONSTANT.TXT file that you added to the Multipad.MAK project. Also notice that if the user decides not to save the file, the returned value of the function (that is, the `FileSaveAs` variable) is set to `False`:

```
If Answer = IDNO Then
      FileSaveAs = False
      Exit Function
End If
```

If the user decides to save the file, the mouse cursor is set to the hourglass shape:

```
frmMultipad.ActiveForm.MousePointer = 11
```

The Caption property of the `lblFilename` label is set to the name of the file:

```
frmMultipad.ActiveForm.lblFilename.Caption =
      ➥ frmMultipad.CMDialog1.Filename
```

Recall that the `lblFilename` label is invisible, and its sole purpose is to store the filename in its Caption property.

You save the file by using the `SaveFile` procedure:

```
SaveFile
```

In the next section you'll write the `SaveFile` procedure.

Now that the file is saved, you can set the mouse cursor to its default shape:

```
frmMultipad.ActiveForm.MousePointer = 0
```

Because the file was just saved, you set the Value property of the `chkFileHasChanged` checkbox to `False`:

```
frmMultipad.ActiveForm.chkFileHasChanged = False
```

Note that because the default property of a checkbox is Value, you can omit Value. In other words, the following two statements are identical:

```
frmMultipad.ActiveForm.chkFileHasChanged = False
```

```
frmMultipad.ActiveForm.chkFileHasChanged.Value = False
```

The last thing the `FileSaveAs()` function does is to set the Caption property of the child window:

```
frmMultipad.ActiveForm.Caption =
    ➥ frmMultipad.CMDialog1.Filetitle
```

Then the `Exit Function` statement is executed:

```
Exit Function
```

Note that at the beginning of the `FileSaveAs()` function `FileSaveAs` was set to `True`. During the execution of the `FileSaveAs()` function, if the file is not saved, the `FileSaveAs` variable is set to `False` and the `Exit Function` statement is executed. If the file is saved, the `FileSaveAs` variable remains `True`. So the returned value of the `FileSaveAs()` function is `True` if the file is saved, and it is `False` if the file is not saved.

The SaveFile Procedure

The `FileSaveAs()` function that you wrote in the preceding section uses the `SaveFile` procedure. You'll now write the `SaveFile` procedure.

❑ Highlight the MULTIPAD.BAS item inside the Project window.

❑ Click the View Code button inside the Project window.

❑ Select New Procedure from the View menu.

   Visual Basic responds by displaying the New Procedure dialog box.

❑ Make sure that the `Sub` radio button inside the New Procedure is selected, and then enter `SaveFile` inside the text box of the New Procedure dialog box.

❑ Click the OK button of the New Procedure dialog box.

   Visual Basic responds by placing the `SaveFile` procedure inside the Multipad.BAS module.

☐ Enter the following code in the `SaveFile` procedure inside the Multipad.BAS module:

```
Sub SaveFile ()

    Dim FileNum

    If ggNumChildren = 0 Then
        Exit Sub
    End If

    ' Get a free file number
    FileNum = FreeFile

    ' Open the file
    Open frmMultipad.ActiveForm.lblFilename.Caption
    ➥ For Output As FileNum

    ' Write the contents of the text file into the file
    Print #FileNum, frmMultipad.ActiveForm.txtDocument.Text

    ' Close the file
    Close FileNum

    frmMultipad.ActiveForm.chkFileHasChanged.Value = 0

End Sub
```

An `If` statement checks whether there are any child windows:

```
If ggNumChildren = 0 Then
    Exit Sub
End If
```

If there are no child windows, there is nothing to save, and the procedure terminates.

The `FreeFile` statement is then executed:

```
FileNum = FreeFile
```

Then the file is opened:

```
Open frmMultipad.ActiveForm.lblFilename.Caption
        ➥ For Output As FileNum
```

Note that the filename is stored in the Caption property of the invisible `lblFilename` label.

The `Print` statement is then executed to store the contents of the text box into the file:

```
Print #FileNum, frmMultipad.ActiveForm.txtDocument.Text
```

Then the file is closed:

```
Close FileNum
```

Because you just saved the file, the Value property of `chkFileHasChanged` is set to 0:

```
frmMultipad.ActiveForm.chkFileHasChanged.Value = 0
```

Attaching Code to the Save Tool of the Toolbar

You'll now attach code to the Save tool of the toolbar.

7

❑ Enter the following code inside the cmdSave_Click() procedure of the frmMultipad form:

```
Sub cmdSave_Click ()

    If ggNumChildren = 0 Then
        Exit Sub
    End If

    If UCase(ActiveForm.lblFilename.Caption) =
            ➥ UCase("Untitled.txt") Then
        cmdSaveAs_Click
    Else
        SaveFile
    End If

End Sub
```

The cmdSave_Click() procedure checks whether there is anything to save:

```
If ggNumChildren = 0 Then
    Exit Sub
End If
```

If there is nothing to save, the If statement is satisfied, and the procedure terminates with the Exit Sub statement.

If there is a file to save, the procedure checks the Caption property of the invisible lblFilename label. If the Caption property of the label is Untitled.txt, the Save As operation has to be performed.

Recall that inside the cmdNew_Click() procedure you set the Caption property of the invisible lblFilename label to "Untitled.txt":

```
frmMultipad.ActiveForm.lblFilename = "Untitled.txt"
```

So now you can determine whether the file has ever been saved.

```
    If UCase(ActiveForm.lblFilename.Caption) =
                ➥ UCase("Untitled.txt") Then
        cmdSaveAs_Click
    Else
        SaveFile
    End If
```

If the file was never saved, the If condition is satisfied, and the cmdSaveAs_Click() procedure is executed. If the file was previously saved, the Else is satisfied, and the SaveFile procedure is executed.

Attaching Code to the Save Item of the File Menu

You'll now attach code to the Save item of the File menu.

☐ Enter the following code inside the `mnuSave_Click()` procedure of the `frmMultipad` form:

```
Sub mnuSave_Click ()

    cmdSave_Click

End Sub
```

The code you entered executes the `cmdSave_Click()` procedure. This means that selecting Save from the File menu produces the same result as clicking the Save tool of the toolbar.

Attaching Code to the Save As Item of the File Menu

You'll now attach code to the Save As item of the File menu.

☐ Enter the following code inside the `mnuSaveAs_Click()` procedure of the `frmMultipad` form:

```
Sub mnuSaveAs_Click ()

    cmdSaveAs_Click

End Sub
```

The code you entered executes the `cmdSaveAs_Click()` procedure. This means that selecting Save As from the File menu produces the same result as clicking the Save As tool of the toolbar. (You already wrote the code of the `cmdSaveAs_Click()` procedure.)

Attaching Code to the `Form_Unload()` Procedure of the `frmDocument` Form

You'll now attach code to the `Form_Unload()` procedure of the `frmDocument` form. The `Form_Unload()` procedure of the `frmDocument` form is executed whenever the user tries to close a child window. Therefore, you need to check whether there is a need to save the contents of the child window before you close the child window.

☐ Enter the following code inside the `Form_Unload()` procedure of the `frmDocument` form:

```
Sub Form_Unload (Cancel As Integer)

    Dim msg, Answer


    ' Before ending the program, check
    ' if the current file has changed, and if
    ' it has, give the user a chance to save it.
    If chkFileHasChanged.Value = 1 Then
        msg = lblFilename.Caption + Chr(13)
        msg = msg + "The file has changed." + Chr(13)
        msg = msg + "Do you want to save current changes?"
        Answer = MsgBox(msg, MB_ICONEXCLAMATION +
              ➥ MB_YESNOCANCEL, "Mulitpad")
        If Answer = IDYES Then
```

7

```
        If UCase(lblFilename.Caption) =
                    ➥ UCase("Untitled.txt") Then
            If FileSaveAs() = False Then
                Cancel = True
            End If
        Else
            SaveFile
        End If
    End If
    If Answer = IDCANCEL Then
        Cancel = True
    End If
End If


    ' User did not cancel the Close operation
    If Cancel = False Then
        ggNumChildren = ggNumChildren - 1
    End If
```

End Sub

The Value property of the invisible chkFileHasChanged checkbox indicates whether the file was changed since the last time it was saved. An If statement checks whether there is a need to save the file:

```
If chkFileHasChanged.Value = 1 Then
    .........
    .........
    .........
End If
```

If there is a need to save the file, a message box is displayed, asking the user if the file should be saved:

```
msg = lblFilename.Caption + Chr(13)
msg = msg + "The file has changed." + Chr(13)
msg = msg + "Do you want to save current changes?"
Answer = MsgBox(msg, MB_ICONEXCLAMATION +
            ➥ MB_YESNOCANCEL, "Mulitpad")
```

The returned value from the message box is Answer, which indicates the user's selection.

If Answer is equal to IDYES, the user clicked the Yes button of the message box (that is, yes, the user wants to save the file).

If the file has never been saved before, the Save As dialog box is displayed, and if the file was saved before, the SaveFile procedure is executed:

```
If UCase(lblFilename.Caption) =
            ➥ UCase("Untitled.txt") Then
    If FileSaveAs() = False Then
        Cancel = True
    End If
Else
    SaveFile
End If
```

In the preceding code the Caption property of the invisible lblFilename label is checked to determine if it is equal to Untitled.txt. If it is equal to Untitled.txt, this file has never been saved, and therefore the FileSaveAs() function is executed. Recall that the returned value of the FileSaveAs() function indicates whether the user actually saved the file. Therefore, the returned value from the FileSaveAs() function is checked. If this returned value is equal to False, the user has not saved the file from the Save As dialog box, and the Cancel variable is set to True.

NOTE

Note that the Form_Unload() procedure has a parameter called Cancel. By default, the Cancel variable is equal to False. Setting the Cancel variable to True has the same effect as canceling the close operation of the child window. In other words, when the Form_Unload() procedure is terminated, Visual Basic automatically checks the Cancel variable. If Cancel is equal to True, the child form is not closed. This Cancel operation may be summarized as follows:

- The user clicks the minus icon that appears on the upper-left corner of the child window and selects the Close item from the system menu that pops up.

- The Form_Unload() procedure checks whether the file has to be saved. If the file has to be saved, a dialog box is displayed, asking the user if the file should be saved.

- The user clicks the Yes button (that is, yes, the user wants to save the file).

- The Form_Unload() procedure further finds that the file has to be saved as (because the file has never been saved). The Save As dialog box is displayed.

- The user selects the Cancel button of the Save As dialog box.

- The Form_Unload() procedure sets the Cancel variable to True. This means that the child window will not be closed.

If the user clicked the Cancel button from the message box that asks the user to save the file, the following If condition is satisfied:

```
If Answer = IDCANCEL Then
   Cancel = True
End If
```

In this case, the Cancel variable is set to True, which means that the child window will not be closed.

Finally, the Cancel variable is checked:

```
If Cancel = False Then
   ggNumChildren = ggNumChildren - 1
End If
```

If the value of the Cancel variable is False, the child form will be closed, and therefore you need to subtract 1 from ggNumChildren (which indicates the number of child windows inside the parent window).

> **NOTE**
>
> When the user clicks the Exit tool, the program first unloads the child windows (if any). Therefore, the `Form_Unload()` procedure of the `frmDocument` form is executed when the user tries to exit the program, and the user is prompted with a message asking if child windows that have not been saved should be saved before the program terminates.

Attaching Code to the AUTOEXEC.BAT Tool of the Status Bar

You'll now attach code to the AUTOEXEC.BAT tool of the status bar.

❑ Enter the following code inside the `cmdAUTOEXEC_Click()` procedure of the `frmMultipad` form:

```
Sub cmdAUTOEXEC_Click ()

    ' User clicks the AUTOEXEC.BAT file
    Dim FileNum

    ' Create a new child form
    cmdNew_Click


    ' Get a free file number
    FileNum = FreeFile

    ' Open the file
    Open "C:\AUTOEXEC.BAT" For Input As FileNum


    ' Read all the contents of the file into the text box
    ActiveForm.txtDocument.Text =
            ➥ Input$(LOF(FileNum), FileNum)

    ' Close the file
    Close FileNum

    ActiveForm.lblFilename.Caption = "C:\AUTOEXEC.BAT"
    ActiveForm.Caption = "AUTOEXEC.BAT"
    ActiveForm.chkFileHasChanged = 0

End Sub
```

The code you entered creates a new child form by executing the `cmdNew_Click()` procedure:

```
cmdNew_Click
```

The `FreeFile` statement is executed:

```
FileNum = FreeFile
```

Then the AUTOEXEC.BAT file is opened:

```
Open "C:\AUTOEXEC.BAT" For Input As FileNum
```

The contents of the AUTOEXEC.BAT file are displayed inside the text box:

```
ActiveForm.txtDocument.Text =
         ➡ Input$(LOF(FileNum), FileNum)
```

Then the file is closed:

```
Close FileNum
```

The next statements update the Caption property of the child form, the Caption property of the invisible lblFilename label, and the invisible chkFileHasChanged checkbox:

```
ActiveForm.lblFilename.Caption = "C:\AUTOEXEC.BAT"
ActiveForm.Caption = "AUTOEXEC.BAT"
ActiveForm.chkFileHasChanged = 0
```

Attaching Code to the CONFIG.SYS Tool of the Status Bar

You'll now attach code to the CONFIG.SYS tool of the status bar.

❑ Enter the following code inside the cmdCONFIG_Click() procedure of the frmMultipad form:

```
Sub cmdCONFIG_Click ()

    ' User clicks the CONFIG.SYS file
    Dim FileNum

    ' Create a new child form
    cmdNew_Click


    ' Get a free file number
    FileNum = FreeFile

    ' Open the file
    Open "C:\CONFIG.SYS" For Input As FileNum


    ' Read all the contents of the file into the text box
    ActiveForm.txtDocument.Text =
            ➡ Input$(LOF(FileNum), FileNum)

    ' Close the file
    Close FileNum

    ActiveForm.lblFilename.Caption = "C:\CONFIG.SYS"
    ActiveForm.Caption = "CONFIG.SYS"
    ActiveForm.chkFileHasChanged = 0

End Sub
```

The code you entered creates a new child form:

```
cmdNew_Click
```

A file number is extracted:

```
FileNum = FreeFile
```

Then the CONFIG.SYS file is opened:

```
Open "C:\CONFIG.SYS" For Input As FileNum
```

The contents of the CONFIG.SYS file are read into the text box:

```
ActiveForm.txtDocument.Text =
        ➥ Input$(LOF(FileNum), FileNum)
```

Then the file is closed:

```
Close FileNum
```

Finally, the Caption property of the invisible lblFilename label, the Caption property of the child form, and the chkFileHasChanged checkbox are updated:

```
ActiveForm.lblFilename.Caption = "C:\CONFIG.SYS"
ActiveForm.Caption = "CONFIG.SYS"
ActiveForm.chkFileHasChanged = 0
```

Attaching Code to the SYSTEM.INI Tool of the Status Bar

You'll now attach code to the SYSTEM.INI tool of the status bar.

❑ Enter the following code inside the cmdSYSTEM_Click() procedure of the frmMultipad form:

```
Sub cmdSYSTEM_Click ()

    Dim FileNum

    ' Create a new child form
    cmdNew_Click


    ' Get a free file number
    FileNum = FreeFile

    ' Open the file
    Open TegommFront.WindowsDirectory + "\SYSTEM.INI"
            ➥ For Input As FileNum

    ' Read all the contents of the file into the text box
    ActiveForm.txtDocument.Text =
        ➥ Input$(LOF(FileNum), FileNum)

    ' Close the file
    Close FileNum

    ActiveForm.lblFilename.Caption =
      ➥ TegommFront.WindowsDirectory + "\SYSTEM.INI"
    ActiveForm.Caption = "SYSTEM.INI"
    ActiveForm.chkFileHasChanged = 0

End Sub
```

The code you entered is similar to the code you entered inside the `cmdAUTOEXEC_Click()` and `cmdCONFIG_Click()` procedures. However, unlike the AUTOEXEC.BAT and the CONFIG.SYS files that reside in the C:\ root directory, the SYSTEM.INI file resides in the \WINDOWS directory. The \WINDOWS directory can reside in the C: drive, the D: drive, or any other drive. This means that you must find the path of the \WINDOWS directory.

The `cmdSYSTEM_Click()` procedure creates a new child form:

```
cmdNew_Click
```

A file number is extracted:

```
FileNum = FreeFile
```

Then the SYSTEM.INI file is opened with the Open statement:

```
Open TegommFront.WindowsDirectory + "\SYSTEM.INI"
          ➥ For Input As FileNum
```

In the preceding `Open` statement, the name of the file is this:

```
TegommFront.WindowsDirectory + "\SYSTEM.INI"
```

That is, the WindowsDirectory property of the `TegommFront` control indicates the path of the Windows directory.

The file is then read into the text box:

```
ActiveForm.txtDocument.Text =
        ➥ Input$(LOF(FileNum), FileNum)
```

The file is closed:

```
Close FileNum
```

Finally, the Caption property of the invisible `lblFilename` label, the Caption property of the child form, and the `chkFileHasChanged` checkbox are updated:

```
ActiveForm.lblFilename.Caption =
      ➥ TegommFront.WindowsDirectory + "\SYSTEM.INI"
ActiveForm.Caption = "SYSTEM.INI"
ActiveForm.chkFileHasChanged = 0
```

Attaching Code to the Print It Tool of the Status Bar

You'll now attach code to the Print It tool of the status bar.

☐ Enter the following code inside the `cmdPrintIt_Click()` procedure of the `frmMultipad` form:

```
Sub cmdPrint_Click ()

    If ggNumChildren > 0 Then
       Printer.Print ActiveForm.txtDocument
```

7

```
        Printer.NewPage
        Printer.EndDoc
     End If

End Sub
```

The code you entered checks whether there are any child windows inside the parent window, and if there is a child window inside the parent window, the contents of the text box of the active child form are printed:

```
Printer.Print ActiveForm.txtDocument
```

After the contents of the text box are printed, the NewPage and EndDoc methods are executed on the Printer object:

```
Printer.NewPage
Printer.EndDoc
```

Attaching Code to the Audio Tool of the Toolbar

You'll now attach code to the Audio tool of the toolbar.

☐ Enter the following code inside the cmdAudio_Click() procedure of the frmMultipad form:

```
Sub cmdAudio_Click ()

    If chkWithAudio.Value = True Then
        chkWithAudio.Value = False
    Else
        chkWithAudio.Value = True
    End If

End Sub
```

The code you entered checks the Value property of the chkWithAudio checkbox. If the Value property is currently True, the If condition is satisfied and the Value property is set to False. If the Value property is currently equal to True, the Else is satisfied, and the Value property is set to True.

Attaching Code to the MDIForm_Load() Procedure of the frmMultipad Form

You'll now attach code to the MDIForm_Load() procedure of the frmMultipad form.

☐ Enter the following code inside the MDIForm_Load() procedure of the frmMultipad form:

```
Sub MDIForm_Load ()

    '''''''''''''''''''''''''''''''
    ' The Parent form is loaded
    '''''''''''''''''''''''''''''''

    ' Set the device to the sound card (WAV files)
    TegommFront.DeviceType = "Waveaudio"
```

```
' Set the WAV file name
TegommFront.FileName = WAV_FILE_NAME

' Open the session
TegommFront.Command = "Open"

If TegommFront.Error <> 0 Then
    ' Waveaudio was not opened, so prepare for
    ' playing through the PC Speaker

    TegommFront.DeviceType = "PCSpeaker"

    TegommFront.Command = "Open"
End If
```

End Sub

The code you entered is executed whenever the `frmMultipad` form is loaded (that is, upon start-up of the Multipad program).

The DeviceType property of the multimedia control is set to play WAV files through the sound card:

```
TegommFront.DeviceType = "Waveaudio"
```

Then the FileName property of the multimedia control is set:

```
TegommFront.FileName = WAV_FILE_NAME
```

The WAV session is then opened:

```
TegommFront.Command = "Open"
```

An `If` statement is executed to check whether the WAV session was opened successfully:

```
If TegommFront.Error <> 0 Then
    ' Waveaudio was not opened, so prepare for
    ' playing through the PC Speaker

    TegommFront.DeviceType = "PCSpeaker"

    TegommFront.Command = "Open"
End If
```

If an error occurred during the execution of the `Open` command, the Error property is not equal to 0, and the statements under the `If` statement are executed.

NOTE

Note that the Error property is checked immediately after the `Open` command is issued. The Error property reports the error that occurred (or did not occur) during the execution of the last command. This means that you must check the Error property *immediately* after issuing the `Open` command.

If an error occurred, the WAV session is opened for playback through the PC speaker:

```
TegommFront.DeviceType = "PCSpeaker"

TegommFront.Command = "Open"
```

So if the user does not have an installed sound card in the PC, the WAV file is opened for playback through the PC speaker.

Attaching Code to the `MDIForm_Unload()` Procedure of the `frmMultipad` Form

You'll now attach code to the Unload event of the `frmMultipad` form.

❑ Enter the following code inside the `MDIForm_Unload()` procedure of the `frmMultipad` form:

```
Sub MDIForm_Unload (Cancel As Integer)

    ''''''''''''''''''''''''''''''''
    ' The parent form is unloaded
    ''''''''''''''''''''''''''''''''

    ' Play only if the With Audio Prompts check box
    ' is checked
    If chkWithAudio = True Then
       TegommFront.Command = "Prev"
       TegommFront.Wait = True
       TegommFront.Command = "Play"
    End If

End Sub
```

The code you entered is executed whenever the use unloads the parent form (for example, when the user clicks the Exit tool).

This procedure examines the status of the `chkWithAudio` checkbox, and if this checkbox is checked, the WAV file is played:

```
TegommFront.Command = "Prev"
TegommFront.Wait = True
TegommFront.Command = "Play"
```

Note that the `Prev` command is issued to rewind the WAV file. The Wait property is set to `True`, and the `Play` command is issued.

It is important to set the Wait property to `True` because you want the WAV file to be played in its entirety. Only after the WAV file is played will the procedure continue its execution (which causes the termination of the Multipad program).

Further Enhancements—You Are on Your Own...

Although you have already implemented a lot in the Multipad program, you can further enhance it. This section contains some suggestions for further improvements and enhancements to the Multipad application.

A text editor is often used for preparing text files that you want to send via e-mail, using CompuServe and other e-mail services. These services charge you according to the size of the file. Therefore, it is a good idea to compress the files before sending them over the e-mail service. In addition to saving cost, you will spend less time transmitting if you send the files in a compressed form (and therefore you also save the time of the person who receives your files).

Inside the C:\LearnVB directory you can see the Yoshi subdirectory, which contains the Yoshi compression utility (copyright by Haruyasu Yoshizaki). This compression utility enables you to compress individual files as well as a group of files. The complete manual of this compression utility resides inside the C:\LearnVB\Yoshi directory.

To compress all the files inside the C:\TRY directory and its subdirectories, you can execute the MKYOSHI.BAT batch file that resides inside the C:\LearnVB\Yoshi directory.

Here are the contents of the MKYOSHI.BAT batch file:

```
@Echo off
cls
Echo To compress current directory and all its subdirectories:
pause
C:\yoshi\lha a /r2x1 %1 *.*
Echo The result of the above is %1.lzh
Echo ----------------------------------------
Echo To convert %1.lzh to a self extract:
pause
C:\yoshi\LHA s /r2x1 %1
ERASE %1.LZH
```

To use this file do the following:

❏ Exit to the DOS prompt (for example, double-click the MS-DOS program icon that is inside the Main group of icons).

❏ Log in to the directory that contains the files you want to compress. For example, if you want to compress all the files in the C:\TRY directory and its subdirectories, enter the following at the DOS prompt:

```
CD C:\TRY  {Enter}
```

❏ At the DOS prompt enter this:

```
MKYOSHI MELTME  {Enter}
```

The MKYOSHI.BAT file compresses all the files in the C:\TRY directory and in the subdirectory of C:\TRY and creates the file MELTME.LZH.

Then the MKYOSHI.BAT file creates a file called MELTME.EXE, and then the batch file deletes the MELTME.LZH file.

MELTME.EXE is a self-extract file that contains all the files in the C:\TRY directory and in the subdirectories of C:\TRY.

You can now send the MELTME.EXE file over your e-mail service. Whoever receives your MELTME.EXE file can create a C:\TRY directory, copy the MELTME.EXE file to the C:\TRY directory, log in to the C:\TRY directory, and then at the DOS prompt enter MELTME.

The MELTME.EXE file extracts itself, creates the subdirectories of C:\TRY if needed, and uncompresses the compressed files and copies them into the C:\TRY directory and its subdirectories (if any).

As you can see, the Yoshi compression utility is very powerful, and it compresses files very efficiently. In fact, its compression ratio is one of the best on the market. Note that your user does not need to have the Yoshi program on his or her PC, because you are sending your user a self-extract EXE file.

NOTE

Before using the Yoshi compression utility, read the manual, the license agreement, and all other information regarding this utility. This information is stored in the C:\LearnVB\Yoshi\LHA213.DOC file.

NOTE

You can use the Yoshi compression utility for compressing all types of files (for example, BMP files, WAV files, DOC files, or any other type of file).

As far as the Multipad program is concerned, you can add a Compress tool to the toolbar (or the status bar). When the user clicks the Compress tool, the program should let the user select a file (or a group of files), ask the user for the name of the resultant file, and compress the file with the Yoshi utility.

You can implement the actual compression by executing Visual Basic's Shell() function.

Another improvement that you can incorporate into the Multipad program is to implement a Search tool. When the user clicks on the Search tool, the Multipad program should display a Search message box asking the user to enter the text to be searched. When the user clicks the OK button of the Search dialog box, the Search feature should highlight inside the text box the found text. Implementing such a Search feature involves writing string manipulation code on the contents of the text box.

Another improvement that you could make to the Multipad application is to incorporate more audio prompts. Currently, the only audio prompt the Multipad program has is `It's been fun working with you`, which plays when the user exits the program. You can of course incorporate additional audio prompts. For example, you can incorporate the audio message `Save changes before closing file?`.

In the current version of Visual Basic, the text box control can contain a maximum of 64K characters. You should enhance the program so that it refuses to load files larger than 64K. You can check the size of the files by using the `FileLen()` function of Visual Basic. For example, here is how you check the size of the AUTOEXEC.BAT file:

```
' If file is too large exit.
If FileLen("C:\AUTOEXEC.BAT") > 64000 Then
    MsgBox
    ➡ "The AUTOEXEC.BAT file is too large for Multipad!",
    ➡ 48,
    ➡ "Use another text editor"
    Exit Sub
End If
```

The Multipad program assumes that the user installed the program into the C: drive. For example, the WAV file is declared inside the general declarations section in this way:

```
Const WAV_FILE_NAME = "C:\LearnVB\WAV\ItsBeen1.WAV"
```

You can improve the Multipad program by eliminating the hard-coded C:. That is, use the left two characters of the path from which the Multipad program was executed to extract the drive name.

Declare the WAV_FILE_NAME constant like this:

```
Const WAV_FILE_NAME = "\mvProg\WAV\ItsBeen1.WAV"
```

Then, when opening the WAV file, use the following statements:

```
' Extract the drive name where this program resides
DriveName = Left(App.Path, 2)

' Set the device to the sound card (WAV files)
TegommFront.DeviceType = "Waveaudio"

' Set the WAV filename
TegommFront.FileName = DriveName + WAV_FILE_NAME
```

Note that currently the Exit menu item has its own menu. (See Figure 6.26.) This does not conform to "standard" Windows applications, where the Exit menu is usually part of the File menu. Also, as shown in Figure 6.25, About has its own menu. Typically, you implement an About menu item inside a Help menu.

8

Creating Database Applications (Part I)

In this chapter you'll learn how to use database technologies from within your Visual Basic applications. The TelBase application that you'll write uses the modem to automatically dial phone numbers that appear in a database.

Executing the TelBase Program

Before writing the TelBase program yourself, execute the copy of it that resides inside your C:\LearnVB\Original\Database directory:

❑ Select Run from the File menu of the Program Manager and select the
  C:\LearnVB\Original\Database\TelBase.EXE program.

   *Windows responds by executing the TelBase.EXE program and displaying the window
   shown in Figure 8.1.*

Figure 8.1.
*The main window of the
TelBase program.*

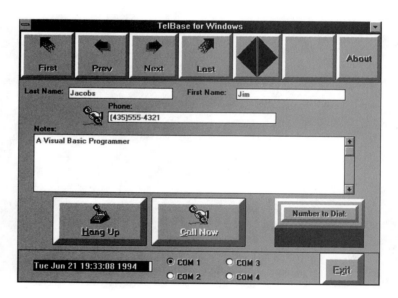

❑ Click the About button on the toolbar.

   The TelBase program responds by displaying the About dialog box. (See Figure 8.2.)

❑ Click the OK button of the About dialog box.

   *The TelBase program displays records from a database. When you start the program, the first
   record of the database is displayed.*

❑ Click the Next button on the toolbar.

   The TelBase program responds by displaying the contents of the second record.

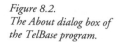

Figure 8.2.
The About dialog box of
the TelBase program.

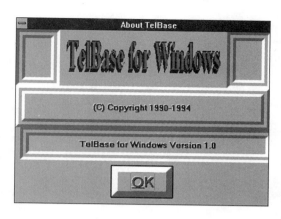

❏ Click the Next button again to advance to the next record. Note that when you reach the last record in the database TelBase beeps.

❏ Click the Prev button on the toolbar to display the contents of the previous record.

❏ Click the Prev button several more times. When there are no more previous records, the TelBase program beeps.

You can jump immediately to the first or last record of the database by clicking the First or the Last button on the toolbar.

❏ Click the First button on the toolbar.

   The TelBase program responds by displaying the first record of the database.

❏ Click the Last button on the toolbar.

   The TelBase program responds by displaying the last record of the database.

The toolbar also contains a spin control. You can display records by pressing the left and right arrows of the spin control.

❏ Press the arrows of the spin control, and note the results.

   The TelBase program lets you dial phone numbers through the modem.

The text box to the right of the Call Now button contains the phone number that the modem will dial.

❏ Double-click the Phone text box (which is located below the LastName text box).

   The TelBase program responds by copying the phone number to the Number to Dial text box.

You can also type a phone number directly inside the Number to Dial text box.

❏ Type a phone number inside the Number to Dial text box.

❑ Click the Call Now button to dial the phone number that appears inside the Number to Dial text box.

The TelBase program responds by dialing the phone number.

❑ Pick up the phone, and prepare to speak to the called party.

❑ Click the Hang Up button to terminate the phone call.

> **NOTE**
>
> Most modem cards have a provision for connecting two phone jacks. One phone jack is connected to the telephone line, and the other phone jack is connected to a phone. This way you can use the modem for dialing numbers, and then pick up the phone for accomplishing a voice session over the phone.
>
> This method is commonly used by marketing companies and other types of businesses that make a great number of phone calls.

The TelBase program has four option buttons on its status bar. These option buttons are marked COM 1, COM 2, COM 3, and COM 4. When the COM 1 option button is selected the TelBase program assumes that the modem is connected to COM 1 of the PC, when the COM 2 option button is selected the TelBase program assumes that the modem is connected to COM 2 of the PC, and so on.

❑ Experiment with the TelBase program and then click its Exit button to terminate the program.

Building a Database

The TelBase program extracts data from a database. In this chapter, the Microsoft Access database manager program is used as the database manager program for creating the database. If you do not own the Access program, use another database program manager (for example, dBASE, Paradox, FoxPro, or Btrieve).

The TelBase Database

The database that you'll create with Access (or another database manager program) is called TelBase.MDB, and it has a single table, called TelBase.

> **NOTE**
>
> A *database* is a collection of tables. Typically, the tables are linked to each other by referential integrity and other types of links. You'll be able to follow this chapter even if

you are not familiar with these database topics, because the database covered in this chapter consists of a single table.

The structure of the TelBase table is shown in Table 8.1.

Table 8.1. The structure of the TelBase table.

Field Name	Data Type
Last	Text
First	Text
Phone	Text
Notes	Text

The data in the records of the TelBase table are listed in Table 8.2.

Table 8.2. The records of the TelBase table.

First	Last	Phone	Notes
Jim	Jacobs	(435)555-4321	A Visual Basic Programmer
Jane	Taraz	(545)555-9898	Supplier of books
David	House	(676)555-1234	

If you do not own the Access program, build the TelBase table presented in Tables 8.1 and 8.2 by using FoxPro Version 2.0, FoxPro Version 2.5, dBASE III, dBASE IV, Btrieve, Paradox, or another program that is capable of producing a database file compatible with FoxPro 2.0 or 2.5, dBASE III or IV, Paradox, or Btrieve. When you finish building the TelBase table, skip to the section in this chapter called "Implementing the Prototype of the TelBase Program."

If you own the Microsoft Access program, follow these steps to create the TelBase table:

❏ Click the Microsoft Access icon from the Microsoft Access group of programs. (See Figure 8.3.)

   Access responds by displaying an opening window, which is shown in Figure 8.4.

Figure 8.3.
The Microsoft Access
program icon.

Figure 8.4.
The initial Microsoft Access
window.

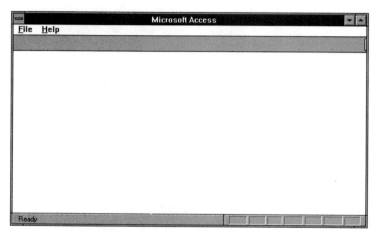

❑ Select New Database from the File menu.

Access responds by displaying the New Database dialog box. (See Figure 8.5.)

Figure 8.5.
The New Database dialog
box.

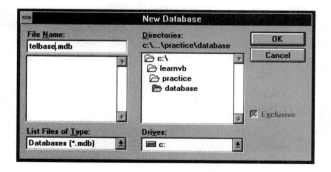

❑ Save the new database (the one that you are about to build) as TelBase.MDB in the
C:\LearnVB\Practice\Database directory.

Access responds by displaying the Database:TELBASE window. (See Figure 8.6.)

This window will contain all the tables of the TELBASE.MDB database. In this example, there is only one table—the TelBase table—in the TELBASE.MDB database.

Figure 8.6.
The Database:TELBASE
window.

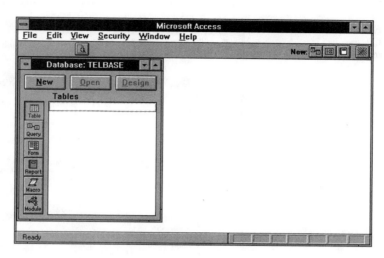

As shown in Figure 8.6, the Database:TELBASE window has several icons on its left side.

❏ Make sure that the Table icon is selected, and then click the New button in the Database:TELBASE window.

Access responds by displaying an empty table. The title of the empty table is Table:Table1. (See Figure 8.7.)

Figure 8.7.
The Table:Table1 window.

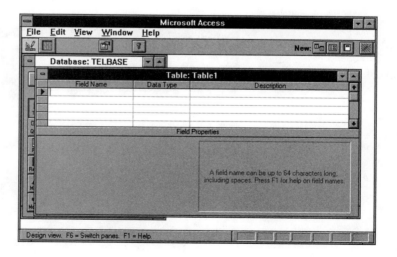

The left icon on the toolbar (the icon with the designer's triangle) is highlighted. This means that Access is in Design mode; it is ready for you to design your table.

❏ Build the table according to the specifications in Table 8.1.

When you finish building the table, it should look like the table in Figure 8.8.

Figure 8.8.
Constructing the fields of
the TelBase table.

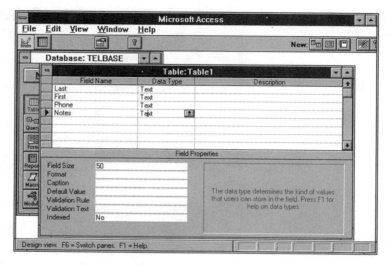

❏ Make sure that the cursor is in the Last field (or in any of the fields in the first row), and then click the key icon on the toolbar.

> *Access responds by placing a small key icon to the left of this row. (See Figure 8.9.) Placed here, the small key icon indicates that the Last field is the key field. (The records of the TelBase table are sorted by last name, so each last name must be unique.)*

Figure 8.9.
Making the Last field the
key field.

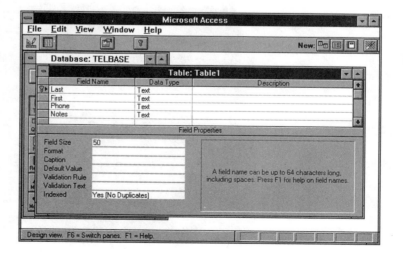

NOTE

When a table has a key field, the records of the table are sorted by the key field. Also, the key field must be unique. This means that in the TelBase program you cannot have two records with the same last name. Typically, a table that contains names should not have its last name field keyed, because it should be possible to have several records with an identical last name. The only reason for keying the last name field in the TelBase table is because during the execution of the TelBase program you'll be able to easily recognize the order of the records in the table.

☐ Select Save As from the File menu.

   Access responds by displaying the Save As dialog box.

☐ Type `TelBase` in the Table Name text box, and then click the OK button.

   Access responds by saving the table as TelBase.

Notice that the title of the window is now Table:TELBASE.

The TelBase table of the TELBASE.MDB database is now complete.

Entering Data into the TelBase Table

You'll now enter data into the TelBase table.

☐ Click the icon that appears to the right of the designer's triangle icon on the toolbar.

   Access responds by displaying the TelBase table, ready for you to enter data. (See Figure 8.10.)

Figure 8.10.
Entering data into the TelBase table.

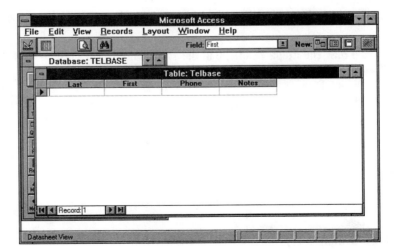

❏ Enter data into the TelBase table according to the specifications in Table 8.2. When you finish entering the data, the Table:TELBASE window should look like the one shown in Figure 8.11.

Figure 8.11.
The TelBase table with
data in it.

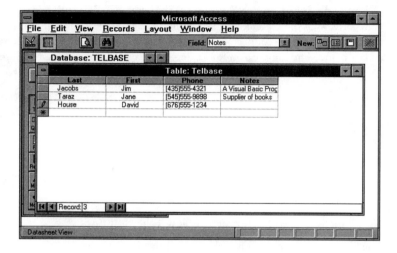

❏ Close the database by selecting Close Database from the File menu.

❏ Select Exit from the File menu to terminate Access.

Implementing the Prototype of the TelBase Program

You'll now implement the prototype of the TelBase program.

❏ Implement the frmTelBase form according to the specifications in Table 8.3. When you finish implementing the form, it should look like the one in Figure 8.12.

Table 8.3. The Properties table of the frmTelBase form.

Object: Form
Object Name: frmTelBase

BackColor	=	&H00C0C0C0&
BorderStyle	=	1 'Fixed Single
Caption	=	"TelBase for Windows"
Height	=	6750
Icon	=	C:\LearnVB\Icons\TelBase.ICO
Left	=	360
MaxButton	=	0 'False

Top	=	150
Width	=	8910

Object: 3D label
Object Name: Panel3D1

BackColor	=	&H00C0C0C0&
BevelInner	=	2 'Raised
BevelWidth	=	5
BorderWidth	=	5
Caption	=	"Number to Dial:"
Font3D	=	4 'Inset w/heavy shading
Height	=	735
Left	=	6240
Top	=	4200
Width	=	2190

Object: Text box
Object Name: txtDial

BackColor	=	&H00FF0000&
FontSize	=	12
ForeColor	=	&H00FFFFFF&
Height	=	495
Left	=	6240
MultiLine	=	-1 'True
Top	=	4920
Width	=	2175

Object: MSCOMM.VBX (communication control)
Object Name: Comm1

Interval	=	1000
Left	=	120
Top	=	4320

continues

8

Table 8.3. continued

Object: Data control
Object Name: Data1

Caption	=	"Data1"
Exclusive	=	0 'False
Height	=	270
Left	=	7080
Options	=	0
ReadOnly	=	0 'False
RecordSource	=	""
Top	=	1920
Visible	=	0 'False
Width	=	1215

Object: Text box
Object Name: txtFirst

DataSource	=	"Data1"
ForeColor	=	&H000000FF&
Height	=	285
Left	=	5280
Top	=	1440
Width	=	2655

Object: Text box
Object Name: txtNotes

DataSource	=	"Data1"
ForeColor	=	&H000000FF&
Height	=	1455
Left	=	360
MultiLine	=	-1 'True
ScrollBars	=	2 'Vertical
Top	=	2640
Width	=	7815

Object: Text box
Object Name: txtPhone

DataSource	=	"Data1"
ForeColor	=	&H000000FF&
Height	=	285
Left	=	2160
Top	=	2040
Width	=	4095

Object: Text box
Object Name: txtLast

DataSource	=	"Data1"
ForeColor	=	&H000000FF&
Height	=	285
Left	=	1200
Top	=	1440
Width	=	2535

Object: 3D button
Object Name: cmdHangUp

BevelWidth	=	10
Caption	=	"&Hang Up"
Font3D	=	2 'Raised w/heavy shading
FontSize	=	9.75
ForeColor	=	&H000000FF&
Height	=	1215
Left	=	840
Picture	=	\VB\ICONS\COMM\PHONE04.ICO
Top	=	4200
Width	=	2295

continues

Table 8.3. continued

Object: 3D button
Object Name: cmdCallNow

BevelWidth	=	10
Caption	=	"&Call Now"
Font3D	=	2 'Raised w/heavy shading
FontSize	=	9.75
ForeColor	=	&H0000FFFF&
Height	=	1215
Left	=	3240
Picture	=	\VB\ICONS\COMM\PHONE13.ICO
Top	=	4200
Width	=	2295

Object: Picture box
Object Name: picStatus

Comment: This picture box serves as the status bar.

Align	=	2 'Align Bottom
BackColor	=	&H00C0C0C0&
Height	=	810
Left	=	0
Top	=	5535
Width	=	8790

Object: 3D option button
Object Name: optCom

Comment: This is element 0 of the array of 3D option buttons.

Caption	=	"COM 1"
Font3D	=	2 'Raised w/heavy shading
Height	=	255
Index	=	0
Left	=	3600
Top	=	120
Value	=	-1 'True
Width	=	1215

Object: 3D option button
Object Name: optCom

Comment: This is element 1 of the array of 3D option buttons.

Caption	= "COM 2"
Font3D	= 2 'Raised w/heavy shading
Height	= 255
Index	= 1
Left	= 3600
Top	= 480
Width	= 1215

Object: 3D option button
Object Name: optCom

Comment: This is element 2 of the array of 3D option buttons.

Caption	= "COM 3"
Font3D	= 2 'Raised w/heavy shading
Height	= 255
Index	= 2
Left	= 5040
Top	= 120
Width	= 1335

Object: 3D option button
Object Name: optCom

Comment: This is element 3 of the array of 3D option buttons.

Caption	= "COM 4"
Font3D	= 2 'Raised w/heavy shading
Height	= 255
Index	= 3
Left	= 5040
Top	= 480
Width	= 1215

continues

Table 8.3. continued

Object: MyClock.VBX
Object Name: Myclock1

BackColor	=	&H00000000&
ForeColor	=	&H00FFFFFF&
Height	=	270
Left	=	360
Top	=	240
UpdateInterval	=	1000
Width	=	2895

Object: 3D button
Object Name: cmdExit

BevelWidth	=	10
Caption	=	"E&xit"
Font3D	=	4 'Inset w/heavy shading
FontSize	=	12
ForeColor	=	&H000000FF&
Height	=	855
Left	=	7320
Top	=	0
Width	=	1095

Object: Picture box
Object Name: picToolbar

Comment: This picture box serves as the toolbar.

Align	=	1 'Align Top
BackColor	=	&H00C0C0C0&
Height	=	1260
Left	=	0
Top	=	0
Width	=	8790

Object: 3D button
Object Name: Command3D1

Comment: This button is placed for cosmetic reasons only. This button does not have any code attached to it.

BevelWidth	=	5
Enabled	=	0 'False
Font3D	=	3 'Inset w/light shading
ForeColor	=	&H00000000&
Height	=	1215
Left	=	6360
Top	=	0
Width	=	1335

Object: 3D button
Object Name: cmdAbout

BevelWidth	=	5
Caption	=	"About"
Font3D	=	2 'Raised w/heavy shading
FontSize	=	9.75
ForeColor	=	&H00FF0000&
Height	=	1215
Left	=	7680
Top	=	0
Width	=	1095

Object: Spin control
Object Name: Spin1

Height	=	1215
Left	=	5160
ShadowBackColor	=	&H00C0C0C0&
SpinOrientation	=	1 'Horizontal
TdThickness	=	5
Top	=	0
Width	=	1215

continues

Table 8.3. continued

8

Object: 3D button
Object Name: cmdFirstRecord

BevelWidth	=	5
Caption	=	"First"
Font3D	=	4 'Inset w/heavy shading
FontSize	=	9.75
ForeColor	=	&H00000000&
Height	=	1215
Left	=	0
Picture	=	\VB\ICONS\ARROWS\ARW11NW.ICO
Top	=	0
Width	=	1335

Object: 3D button
Object Name: cmdLastRecord

BevelWidth	=	5
Caption	=	"Last"
Font3D	=	4 'Inset w/heavy shading
FontSize	=	9.75
ForeColor	=	&H00000000&
Height	=	1215
Left	=	3840
Picture	=	\VB\ICONS\ARROWS\ARW11NE.ICO
Top	=	0
Width	=	1335

Object: 3D button
Object Name: cmdPreviousRecord

BevelWidth	=	5
Caption	=	"Prev"
Font3D	=	4 'Inset w/heavy shading
FontSize	=	9.75
ForeColor	=	&H00000000&
Height	=	1215
Left	=	1320

Picture	=	\VB\ICONS\ARROWS\ARW07LT.ICO
Top	=	0
Width	=	1335

Object: 3D button
Object Name: cmdNextRecord

BevelWidth	=	5
Caption	=	"Next"
Font3D	=	3 'Inset w/light shading
FontSize	=	9.75
Height	=	1215
Left	=	2640
Picture	=	\VB\ICONS\ARROWS\ARW07RT.ICO
Top	=	0
Width	=	1215

Object: Image
Object Name: Image1

Height	=	480
Left	=	1560
Picture	=	\VB\ICONS\COMM\PHONE13.ICO
Top	=	1920
Width	=	480

Object: Label
Object Name: Label1

BackColor	=	&H00C0C0C0&
Caption	=	"Last Name:"
Height	=	255
Left	=	120
Top	=	1440
Width	=	975

continues

8

Table 8.3. continued

Object: Label
Object Name: Label2

BackColor	=	&H00C0C0C0&
Caption	=	"Phone:"
Height	=	255
Left	=	2160
Top	=	1800
Width	=	615

Object: Label
Object Name: Label3

BackColor	=	&H00C0C0C0&
Caption	=	"Notes:"
Height	=	255
Left	=	360
Top	=	2400
Width	=	615

Object: Label
Object Name: Label4

BackColor	=	&H00C0C0C0&
Caption	=	"First Name:"
Height	=	255
Left	=	4080
Top	=	1440
Width	=	1095

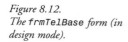

Figure 8.12.
The frmTelBase *form (in design mode).*

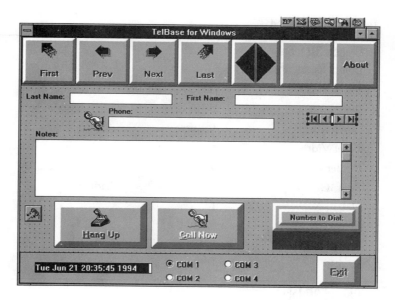

Implementing the About Dialog Box of the TelBase Program

You'll now implement the frmAbout form of the TelBase program.

☐ Implement the frmAbout form according to the specifications in Table 8.4. When you finish implementing the form it should look like the one shown in Figure 8.13.

Table 8.4. The Properties table of the frmAbout form.

Object: Form
Object Name: frmAbout

Property		Value
BackColor	=	&H00C0C0C0&
BorderStyle	=	1 'Fixed Single
Caption	=	"About TelBase"
Height	=	4890
Left	=	2055
MaxButton	=	0 'False
MinButton	=	0 'False
Top	=	1230
Width	=	6465

continues

8

Table 8.4. continued

Object: 3D label
Object Name: Panel3D4

BackColor	=	&H00C0C0C0&
BevelInner	=	1 'Inset
BevelOuter	=	1 'Inset
BevelWidth	=	5
BorderWidth	=	5
Font3D	=	2 'Raised w/heavy shading
Height	=	1455
Left	=	5280
Top	=	0
Width	=	1095

Object: 3D label
Object Name: Panel3D3

BackColor	=	&H00C0C0C0&
BevelInner	=	1 'Inset
BevelOuter	=	1 'Inset
BevelWidth	=	5
BorderWidth	=	5
Font3D	=	2 'Raised w/heavy shading
Height	=	1455
Left	=	0
Top	=	0
Width	=	1095

Object: 3D label
Object Name: Panel3D2

BackColor	=	&H00C0C0C0&
BevelInner	=	1 'Inset
BevelOuter	=	1 'Inset
BevelWidth	=	5
BorderWidth	=	5
Caption	=	"TelBase for Windows Version 1.0"

Font3D	=	2 'Raised w/heavy shading
FontSize	=	9.75
Height	=	855
Left	=	120
Top	=	2520
Width	=	6375

Object: 3D label
Object Name: Panel3D1

BackColor	=	&H00C0C0C0&
BevelInner	=	2 'Raised
BevelWidth	=	5
BorderWidth	=	5
Caption	=	"(C) Copyright 1990-1994 "
Font3D	=	2 'Raised w/heavy shading
FontSize	=	9.75
Height	=	1095
Left	=	0
Top	=	1440
Width	=	6375

Object: 3D button
Object Name: cmdClose

BevelWidth	=	10
Caption	=	"&OK"
Font3D	=	2 'Raised w/heavy shading
FontSize	=	18
ForeColor	=	&H00FF0000&
Height	=	855
Left	=	2400
Top	=	3480
Width	=	1575

continues

Table 8.4. continued

Object: Image
Object Name: imgAbout

Height	= 1215
Left	= 1200
Picture	= C:\LearnVB\BMP\About.BMP
Stretch	= -1 'True
Top	= 120
Width	= 3975

Figure 8.13.
The frmAbout *form (in design mode).*

In the next chapter you'll write the code of the TelBase program.

9

Creating Database Applications (Part II)

In this chapter you'll write the code of the TelBase program, whose prototype you implemented in Chapter 8, "Creating Database Applications (Part I)."

9 Attaching Code to the Load Event of the `frmTelBase` Form

You'll now attach code to the `Form_Load()` procedure of the `frmTelBase` form.

❑ Enter the following code inside the `Form_Load()` procedure of the `frmTelBase` form:

```
Sub Form_Load ()

    '''''''''''''''''''''''''''''''''''''''''''''''''
    ' Data1.Connect is left empty, because you are
    ' using the Microsoft Access database.
    ' If you are using another database, then you
    ' have to specify the Connect property of
    ' the Data1. control.
    '''''''''''''''''''''''''''''''''''''''''''''''''

    Data1.DatabaseName =
      ➥ Left(App.Path, 2) + "\LearnVB\MDB\TelBase.MDB"

    Data1.RecordSource = "Telbase"

    '''''''''''''''''''''''''''''''''''''''''''''''''''''''
    '''''''''''''''''''''''''''''''''''''''''''''''''''''''
    ' Note:
    ' The DataSource properties of the text boxes were set
    ' to Data1 during design time
    '''''''''''''''''''''''''''''''''''''''''''''''''''''''
    '''''''''''''''''''''''''''''''''''''''''''''''''''''''

    txtFirst.DataField = "First"
    txtLast.DataField = "Last"
    txtPhone.DataField = "Phone"
    txtNotes.DataField = "Notes"

    Comm1.CommPort = 1

    Comm1.Settings = "300,N,8,1"

End Sub
```

The `Form_Load()` procedure is executed when you start the TelBase program. The `Form_Load()` procedure sets the DatabaseName property of the data control:

```
Data1.DatabaseName =
  ➥ Left(App.Path, 2) + "\LearnVB\MDB\TelBase.MDB"
```

> **NOTE**
>
> The C:\LearnVB\MDB directory contains the TelBase.MDB database, which is supplied on the book's CD. To try the database that you implemented in Chapter 8, set the DatabaseName property of the data control as follows:
>
> ```
> Data1.DatabaseName =
>     ➥ Left(App.Path, 2) +
>     ➥ "\LearnVB\Practice\Database\TelBase.MDB"
> ```

The `Form_Load()` procedure then sets the RecordSource property of the data control with the name of the table:

```
Data1.RecordSource = "Telbase"
```

The next group of statements sets the DataField property of the text boxes that hold the data of the database's fields:

```
txtFirst.DataField = "First"
txtLast.DataField = "Last"
txtPhone.DataField = "Phone"
txtNotes.DataField = "Notes"
```

After you execute these statements, the `txtFirst` text box displays the contents of the First field of the database, the `txtLast` text box displays the contents of the Last field of the database, and so on.

Next, the CommPort property of the communication control is set to COM 1:

```
Comm1.CommPort = 1
```

Finally, the Settings property of the communication control is set to 300 baud, No parity, 8 bits, and 1 stop bit:

```
Comm1.Settings = "300,N,8,1"
```

> **NOTE**
>
> When using Access as the database program, you leave the Connect property of the data control empty. When using other database programs, you have to set the Connect property of the database as follows:
>
> For FoxPro Version 2.0 set the Connect property to this:
>
> ```
> FoxPro 2.0;
> ```

9

For FoxPro Version 2.5 set the Connect property to this:

```
FoxPro 2.5;
```

For dBASE III set the Connect property to this:

```
dBASE III;
```

For dBASE IV set the Connect property to this:

```
dBASE IV;
```

For Paradox set the Connect property to this:

```
Paradox 3.X;
```

For Btrieve set the Connect property to this:

```
btrieve;
```

Attaching Code to the Click Event of the Exit Button

You'll now attach code to the Click event of the Exit button.

❑ Enter the following code inside the cmdExit_Click() procedure of the frmTelBase form:

```
Sub cmdExit_Click ()

    End

End Sub
```

Attaching Code to the Click Event of the Next Button

You'll now attach code to the Click event of the Next button.

❑ Enter the following code inside the cmdNextRecord_Click() procedure of the frmTelBase form:

```
Sub cmdNextRecord_Click ()

    If Data1.Recordset.EOF = False Then
       Data1.Recordset.MoveNext
    End If

    If Data1.Recordset.EOF = True Then
       Beep
       Data1.Recordset.MovePrevious
    End If

End Sub
```

The code you entered is executed whenever the user clicks the Next button of the toolbar. An If statement is executed to determine whether the current record of the database is pointing to the end of the file (EOF):

```
If Data1.Recordset.EOF = False Then
    ' Move the current record to the next record
    Data1.Recordset.MoveNext
End If
```

If `Data1.Recordset.EOF` is `False`, the current record is not pointed to the EOF, and therefore it is okay to move the pointer to the next record.

If, however, the current record is at the EOF, the PC beeps, and the `MovePrevious` method is executed to move to the previous record:

```
If Data1.Recordset.EOF = True Then
    Beep
    Data1.Recordset.MovePrevious
End If
```

Attaching Code to the Click Event of the Prev Button

You'll now attach code to the Click event of the Prev button.

☐ Enter the following code inside the `cmdPreviousRecord_Click()` procedure of the `frmTelBase` form:

```
Sub cmdPreviousRecord_Click ()

    If Data1.Recordset.BOF = False Then
        Data1.Recordset.MovePrevious
    End If

    If Data1.Recordset.BOF = True Then
        Beep
        Data1.Recordset.MoveNext
    End If

End Sub
```

The `cmdPreviousRecord_Click()` procedure is very similar to the `cmdNextRecord_Click()` procedure. However, unlike the `cmdNextRecord_Click()` procedure, which moves to the next record, the `cmdPreviousRecord_Click()` procedure moves to the previous record.

It is possible to move to the previous record provided that `Data1.Recordset.BOF` is `False`. Therefore, an If statement is used to verify that the current record is not at the beginning of the file (BOF):

```
If Data1.Recordset.BOF = False Then
    Data1.Recordset.MovePrevious
End If
```

If the If condition is satisfied, the `MovePrevious` method is executed to move to the previous record.

9

If the current record is at the BOF, the PC beeps, and the MoveNext method is used to move to the next record:

```
If Data1.Recordset.BOF = True Then
    Beep
    Data1.Recordset.MoveNext
End If
```

Attaching Code to the Click Event of the First Button

You'll now attach code to the Click event of the First button.

❑ Enter the following code inside the cmdFirstRecord_Click() procedure of the frmTelBase form:

```
Sub cmdFirstRecord_Click ()

    Data1.Recordset.MoveFirst

End Sub
```

The code you entered executes the MoveFirst method to move to the first record of the database:

```
Data1.Recordset.MoveFirst
```

Attaching Code to the Click Event of the Last Button

You'll now attach code to the Click event of the Last button.

❑ Enter the following code inside the cmdLastRecord_Click() procedure of the frmTelBase form:

```
Sub cmdLastRecord_Click ()

    Data1.Recordset.MoveLast

End Sub
```

The code you entered executes the MoveLast method to move to the last record of the database:

```
Data1.Recordset.MoveLast
```

Attaching Code to the SpinDown Event of the Spin Control

Attach the following code to the SpinDown event of the spin control:

```
Sub Spin1_SpinDown ()

    cmdPreviousRecord_Click

End Sub
```

The code you entered is executed whenever the user presses the left arrow of the spin control. The `Spin1_SpinDown()` procedure executes the `cmdPreviousRecord_Click()` procedure, which you have already written.

Attaching Code to the SpinUp Event of the Spin Control

Attach the following code to the SpinUp event of the spin control:

```
Sub Spin1_SpinUp ()

    cmdNextRecord_Click

End Sub
```

The code you entered is executed whenever the user presses the right arrow of the spin control. The `Spin1_SpinUp()` procedure executes the `cmdNextRecord_Click()` procedure, which you have already written.

Attaching Code to the Array of Option Buttons

You'll now attach code to the Click event of the `optCom()` array of option buttons.

❑ Enter the following code inside the `optCom_Click()` procedure of the `frmTelBase` form:

```
Sub optCom_Click (Index As Integer, Value As Integer)

    Comm1.CommPort = Index + 1

End Sub
```

Recall that `optCom` is an array of option buttons. The first parameter of the `optCom_Click()` procedure is `Index`. This parameter indicates which option button was clicked. If the user clicked the COM 1 option button, `optCom_Click()` is executed with `Index` equal to 0, if the user clicked the COM 2 option button, `optCom_Click()` is executed with `Index` equal to 1, and so on.

The code you entered inside the `optCom_Click()` procedure sets the CommPort property of the communication control to `Index+1`:

```
Comm1.CommPort = Index + 1
```

So if the user clicked the COM 1 port, `Index` is equal to 0, and CommPort is set to 0+1+1 (which is the proper setting for COM 1). If the user clicked the COM 2 port, `Index` is equal to 1, and CommPort is set to 1+1+2, and so on.

Attaching Code to the Click Event of the Call Now Button

You'll now attach code to the Click event of the Call Now button.

☐ Enter the following code inside the `cmdCallNow_Click()` procedure of the `frmTelBase` form:

```
Sub cmdCallNow_Click ()

    On Error GoTo WrongPort
    Comm1.PortOpen = True

    ' Dial
    If txtDial.Text <> "" Then
        Comm1.Output = "ATDT" + txtDial.Text + Chr$(13)
    Else
        Comm1.PortOpen = False
        MsgBox "Dial where???"
    End If
    Exit Sub

WrongPort:
    MsgBox "Invalid port!"
    Exit Sub

End Sub
```

The code you entered causes the modem to call the number that appears inside the `txtDial` text box.

An error trap is set:

```
On Error GoTo WrongPort
```

This means that if an error occurs the program will immediately jump to the `WrongPort` label.

You open the communication session by setting the PortOpen property of the communication control to `True`:

```
Comm1.PortOpen = True
```

Then an `If` statement is executed to determine whether the `txtDial` text box contains text:

```
If txtDial.Text <> "" Then
    Comm1.Output = "ATDT" + txtDial.Text + Chr$(13)
Else
    Comm1.PortOpen = False
    MsgBox "Dial where???"
End If
```

If the `txtDial` text box is empty, the `Else` is satisfied. This causes the program to close the communication port by setting the PortOpen property of the communication control to `False`. The user is prompted with a message box, asking the user the sarcastic question `Dial where???`

> **NOTE**
>
> Typically, your program should not ask the user sarcastic questions. A more appropriate message instead of `Dial where???` is `Before clicking the Call Now button, type a number inside the Number to Dial text box.`

If the `txtDial` text box has text in it, the `If` statement is satisfied:

```
If txtDial.Text <> "" Then
    Comm1.Output = "ATDT" + txtDial.Text + Chr$(13)
Else
    ....
    ....
    ....
End If
```

The statement under the `If` statement causes the modem to dial the number that appears inside the `txtDial` text box.

```
Comm1.Output = "ATDT" + txtDial.Text + Chr$(13)
```

Note that the `ATDT` string precedes the number to be dialed (as required by Hayes-compatible modems).

Then the `Exit Sub` statement is executed to terminate the procedure:

```
Exit Sub
```

As stated, if an error has occurred, the procedure immediately jumps to the `WrongPort` label:

```
WrongPort:
    MsgBox "Invalid port!"
    Exit Sub
```

Because the error that occurred is probably due to the fact that the modem is not connected to the proper port, a message box is displayed, telling the user `Invalid port!`.

Attaching Code to the Click Event of the Hang Up Button

You'll now attach code to the Hang Up button of the `frmTelBase` form.

☐ Enter the following code inside the `cmdHangUp_Click()` procedure of the `frmTelBase` form:

```
Sub cmdHangUp_Click ()

    If Comm1.PortOpen = True Then
        Comm1.PortOpen = False
    End If

End Sub
```

9

The code you entered terminates the communication session. Note that an If statement is executed to verify that the PortOpen property is equal to True (which means that the communication session is currently open):

```
If Comm1.PortOpen = True Then
    Comm1.PortOpen = False
End If
```

Attaching Code to the Double-Click Event of the txtPhone Text Box

You'll now attach code to the Double-Click event of the txtPhone text box.

❑ Enter the following code inside the txtPhone_DblClick() procedure of the frmTelBase form:

```
Sub txtPhone_DblClick ()

    txtDial.Text = txtPhone.Text

End Sub
```

The code you entered is executed whenever the user double-clicks the txtPhone text box. Recall that the txtPhone text box contains the phone number as it appears in the Phone field of the current record. The code you entered sets the Text property of the txtDial text box to the Text property of the txtPhone text box:

```
txtDial.Text = txtPhone.Text
```

This means that the text that appears inside the txtPhone text box is transferred to the txtDial text box whenever the user double-clicks the txtPhone text box.

Attaching Code to the Click Event of the About Button

You'll now attach code to the Click event of the About button.

❑ Enter the following code inside the cmdAbout_Click() procedure of the frmTelBase form:

```
Sub cmdAbout_Click ()

    frmAbout.Show 1

End Sub
```

The code you entered displays the About dialog box as a modal dialog box (because the Show method is executed with its parameter equal to 1).

Attaching Code to the Click Event of the OK Button of the About Dialog Box

You'll now attach code to the Click event of the OK button of the About dialog box. Recall that the Name property of the OK button of the `frmAbout` form is `cmdClose`.

❑ Enter the following code inside the `cmdClose_Click()` procedure of the `frmAbout` form:

```
Sub cmdClose_Click ()

    Unload frmAbout

End Sub
```

The code you entered is executed whenever the user clicks the OK button of the About dialog box. This code closes the `frmAbout` form.

Further Enhancements—You Are on Your Own...

The following are some ideas for further improving and enhancing the TelBase program.

Inside the `cmdCallNow_Click()` procedure you assumed that an error occurred because the modem is not connected to the proper port. You can improve this procedure by prompting the user with a more informative message, such as `Select the option button in the status bar that represents the port of your modem`.

The TelBase program lets the user view the data of the TelBase database. You may enhance the TelBase program so that it lets the user extract data from other databases. You can accomplish this by incorporating the common dialog control into the program, and then letting the user select the database.

Recall that inside the `Form_Load()` procedure you entered the following two statements:

```
Data1.DatabaseName =
    ➥ Left(App.Path, 2) + "\LearnVB\MDB\TelBase.MDB"

Data1.RecordSource = "Telbase"
```

After the user selects the database, you'll have to replace the name of the database with the name of the file that the user selects.

The TelBase program is used only for viewing the data of the database. However, the Data control is a powerful control that lets you view the data of the database as well as manipulate the database in almost any conceivable way. You may enhance the TelBase program to include such capabilities as deleting records and adding new records.

10

Creating Card Game Programs (Part I)

In this chapter you'll learn how to create card game programs with Visual Basic.

10 | Executing the Cards Program

Before implementing the prototype of the Cards program yourself, execute the Cards.EXE program that resides inside your C:\LearnVB\Original\Cards directory:

❏ Select Run from the File menu of the Program Manager and execute the
C:\LearnVB\Original\Cards\Cards.EXE program.

> *Windows responds by executing the Cards.EXE program and displaying the window shown in Figure 10.1.*

Figure 10.1.
The main window of the Cards program. The design on the back of the cards is red checks.

The Cards program demonstrates how easy it is to implement a cards-based program with Visual Basic.

Do you like the design on the back of the cards shown in Figure 10.1? You can easily use a different deck of cards by clicking the Reset button:

❏ Click the Reset button.

> *The Cards program responds by changing the design of the pattern on the back of the cards. (See Figure 10.2.)*

❏ Click the Reset button several more times to see different designs for the backs of the cards. The different backs are shown in Figures 10.2 through 10.13.

Figure 10.2.
A deck of cards with a blue
checks design on the back of
the cards.

Figure 10.3.
A deck of cards with a red
hatch design on the back of
the cards.

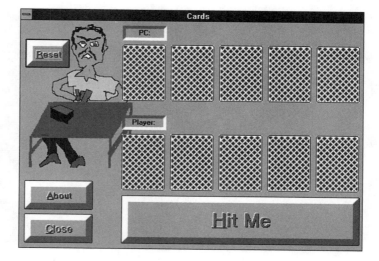

*Figure 10.4.
A deck of cards with a blue
hatch design on the back of
the cards.*

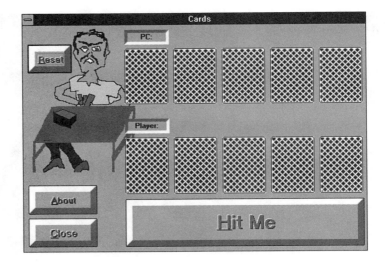

*Figure 10.5.
A deck of cards with a
robots design on the back of
the cards.*

Figure 10.6.
A deck of cards with a roses design on the back of the cards.

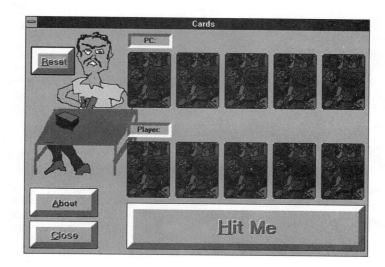

Figure 10.7.
A deck of cards with a leaves design on the back of the cards.

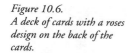

10

Figure 10.8.
A deck of cards with a
second leaves design on the
back of the cards.

Figure 10.9.
A deck of cards with a fish
design on the back of the
cards.

Figure 10.10.
A deck of cards with a
conch design on the back of
the cards.

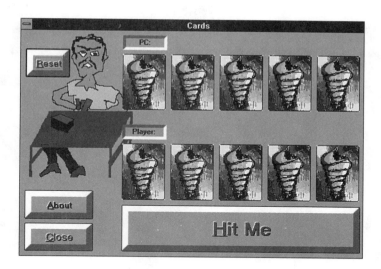

Figure 10.11.
A deck of cards with a
castle design on the back of
the cards.

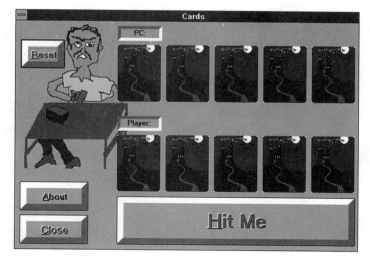

10

Figure 10.12.
A deck of cards with a
beach design on the back of
the cards.

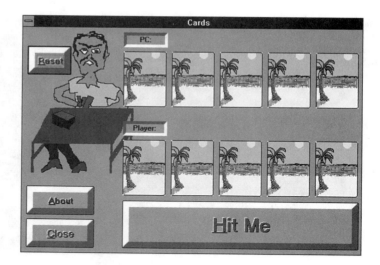

Figure 10.13.
A deck of cards with a
hand design on the back of
the cards.

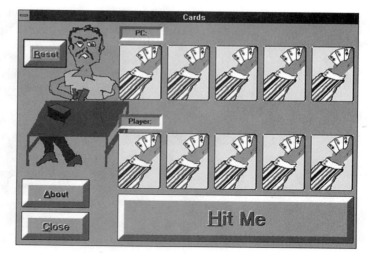

The cards in Figures 10.1 through 10.13 are shown with their faces hidden. To discover the value of any card, you have to double-click the card.

❑ Double-click one of the cards.

> *The Cards program shows the value of the card. (See Figure 10.14.) The value of the clicked card is a random value.*

❑ Double-click several more cards to display their random values.

Figure 10.14.
The Cards program after
you double-click one of its
cards.

To hide the face of a card you have to double-click it again:

❏ Double-click the cards to display and hide their values.

With the Cards program you can play straight poker against the PC. In this game the Cards program deals five cards to the PC and five cards to the user.

To deal cards do the following:

❏ Click the Hit Me button.

The Cards program deals five cards to the PC and five cards to the user. The cards are dealt one card after another with a 1 second delay after each card is dealt.

Note that while the program deals the cards, the caption of the Hit Me button is Now dealing cards…

After the 10 cards are dealt the caption of the Hit Me button is again Hit Me. (See Figure 10.15.)

❏ Experiment with the Hit Me button by dealing cards several more times.

The cards that are dealt by the Cards program to the PC and to the user are dealt randomly. However, you can place the Cards program in a "cheating mode." While in a cheating mode, the Cards program deals five winning cards to the PC and five random cards to the user. To place the Cards program in a cheating mode do the following:

❏ Double-click the picture of the deck of cards that is located on the table.

As shown in Figure 10.16, the Cards program responds by displaying a small line below the feet of the man in the picture.

Figure 10.15.
Dealing 10 cards.

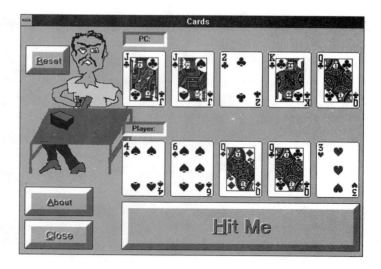

Figure 10.16.
The line below the man's feet, which indicates that the program is in a cheating mode.

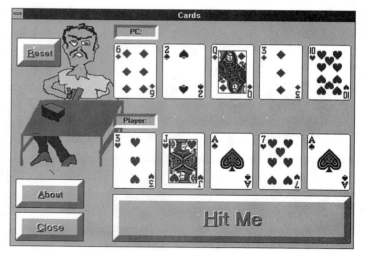

❏ Click the Hit Me button.

> *The Cards program responds by dealing cards to the PC and to the user. The five cards dealt to the PC are winning cards!*

❏ Experiment with the Hit Me button (while the Cards program is in a cheating mode) and notice that each click on the Hit Me button produces a winning combination for the PC.

To take the Cards program out of the cheating mode do this:

❏ Double-click the deck of cards that is placed on the table.

The Cards program cancels the cheating mode, and the small line below the man's feet disappears.

❏ Click the About button.

The Cards program responds by displaying the About dialog box. (See Figure 10.17.)

Figure 10.17.
The About dialog box of the
Cards program.

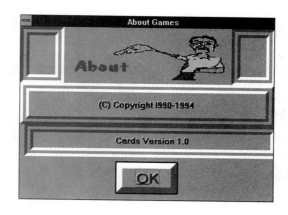

❏ Experiment with the Cards program, and then click the Close button to terminate the Cards program.

The Prototype of the Cards Program

You'll now implement the prototype of the Cards program.

❏ Select New Project from the File menu and save the new project: Save the new form as Cards.frm in the C:\LearnVB\Practice\Cards directory. Save the new project as Cards.mak in the C:\LearnVB\Practice\Cards directory.

❏ Implement the frmCards form according to the specifications in Table 10.1. When you finish implementing the form, it should look like the one shown in Figure 10.18.

Table 10.1. The Properties table of the frmCards form.

Object: Form
Object Name: frmCards

BackColor	=	&H00C0C0C0&
BorderStyle	=	1 'Fixed Single
Caption	=	"Cards"
Height	=	6180

continues

Table 10.1. continued

Icon	=	C:\LearnVB\ICONS\Cards.ICO
Left	=	885
MaxButton	=	0 'False
MinButton	=	0 'False
Picture	=	C:\LearnVB\BMP\CARDS01.BMP
Top	=	300
Width	=	8595

Object: 3D button
Object Name: cmdAbout

BevelWidth	=	10
Caption	=	"&About"
Font3D	=	2 'Raised w/heavy shading
FontSize	=	9.75
ForeColor	=	&H00FF0000&
Height	=	735
Left	=	120
Top	=	4080
Width	=	1695

Object: 3D button
Object Name: cmdReset

BevelWidth	=	10
Caption	=	"&Reset"
Font3D	=	2 'Raised w/heavy shading
FontSize	=	9.75
ForeColor	=	&H000000FF&
Height	=	735
Left	=	120
Top	=	480
Width	=	1095

Object: 3D button
Object Name: cmdHitMe

BevelWidth	=	10

Caption	=	"&Hit Me"
Font3D	=	2 'Raised w/heavy shading
FontName	=	"MS Sans Serif"
FontSize	=	24
ForeColor	=	&H000000FF&
Height	=	1215
Left	=	2520
Top	=	4440
Width	=	5895

Object: 3D button
Object Name: cmdClose

BevelWidth	=	10
Caption	=	"&Close"
Font3D	=	2 'Raised w/heavy shading
FontName	=	"MS Sans Serif"
FontSize	=	12
ForeColor	=	&H000000FF&
Height	=	735
Left	=	120
Top	=	4920
Width	=	1695

Object: 3D label
Object Name: lblPlayer

BackColor	=	&H00C0C0C0&
BevelOuter	=	1 'Inset
BevelWidth	=	5
Caption	=	"Player:"
Font3D	=	0 'None
Height	=	375
Left	=	2520
Top	=	2400
Width	=	1095

continues

10

Table 10.1. continued

Object: 3D label
Object Name: lblPC

BackColor	=	&H00C0C0C0&
BevelOuter	=	1 'Inset
BevelWidth	=	5
Caption	=	"PC:"
Font3D	=	0 'None
Height	=	375
Left	=	2520
Top	=	120
Width	=	1095

Object: Timer
Object Name: Timer1

Enabled	=	0 'False
Interval	=	1000
Left	=	4440
Top	=	2160

Object: Image
Object Name: imgBackDoorPC

Comment: There is no need to set the Picture property of this object.

Height	=	615
Left	=	720
Top	=	2040
Width	=	735

Object: Line
Object Name: LinePC

Comment: The Visible property of this object is set to True and False during runtime when the user double-clicks the imgBackDoorPC image.

Visible	=	0 'False
X1	=	960

X2	=	1080
Y1	=	3840
Y2	=	3960

Object: Cards
Object Name: Cards

Comment: This is an array of cards. This object is Cards(0).

AutoSize	=	-1 'True
Height	=	1425
Index	=	0
Left	=	2520
Top	=	600
Width	=	1065

Object: Cards (See Figure 1.36.)
Object Name: Cards

Comment: This object is Cards(1).

AutoSize	=	-1 'True
Height	=	1425
Index	=	1
Left	=	3720
Top	=	600
Width	=	1065

Object: Cards
Object Name: Cards

Comment: This object is Cards(2).

AutoSize	=	-1 'True
Height	=	1425
Index	=	2
Left	=	4920
Top	=	600
Width	=	1065

continues

10

Table 10.1. continued

Object: Cards
Object Name: Cards

Comment: This object is Cards(3).

AutoSize	=	-1 'True
Height	=	1425
Index	=	3
Left	=	6120
Top	=	600
Width	=	1065

Object: Cards
Object Name: Cards

Comment: This object is Cards(4).

AutoSize	=	-1 'True
Height	=	1425
Index	=	4
Left	=	7320
Top	=	600
Width	=	1065

Object: Cards
Object Name: Cards

Comment: This object is Cards(5).

AutoSize	=	-1 'True
Height	=	1425
Index	=	5
Left	=	2520
Top	=	2880
Width	=	1065

Object: Cards
Object Name: Cards

Comment: This object is Cards(6).

AutoSize	=	-1 'True

Height	=	1425
Index	=	6
Left	=	3720
Top	=	2880
Width	=	1065

Object: Cards
Object Name: Cards

Comment: This object is Cards(7).

AutoSize	=	-1 'True
Height	=	1425
Index	=	7
Left	=	4920
Top	=	2880
Width	=	1065

Object: Cards
Object Name: Cards

Comment: This object is Cards(8).

AutoSize	=	-1 'True
Height	=	1425
Index	=	8
Left	=	6120
Top	=	2880
Width	=	1065

Object: Cards
Object Name: Cards

Comment: This object is Cards(9).

AutoSize	=	-1 'True
Height	=	1425
Index	=	9
Left	=	7320
Top	=	2880
Width	=	1065

10

Figure 10.18.
The frmCards *form (in design mode).*

You'll now implement the frmAbout form (the About form of the Cards program).

☐ Implement the frmAbout form according to the specifications in Table 10.2. When you finish implementing the frmAbout form, it should look like the one shown in Figure 10.19.

Table 10.2. The Properties table of the frmAbout form.

Object: Form
Object Name: frmAbout

BackColor	=	&H00C0C0C0&
BorderStyle	=	1 'Fixed Single
Caption	=	"About Games"
Height	=	4890
Left	=	1035
MaxButton	=	0 'False
MinButton	=	0 'False
Top	=	1140
Width	=	6465

Object: 3D label
Object Name: Panel3D4

BackColor	=	&H00C0C0C0&
BevelInner	=	1 'Inset
BevelOuter	=	1 'Inset
BevelWidth	=	5
BorderWidth	=	5
Font3D	=	2 'Raised w/heavy shading
Height	=	1455
Left	=	5280
Top	=	0
Width	=	1095

Object: 3D label
Object Name: Panel3D3

BackColor	=	&H00C0C0C0&
BevelInner	=	1 'Inset
BevelOuter	=	1 'Inset
BevelWidth	=	5
BorderWidth	=	5
Font3D	=	2 'Raised w/heavy shading
Height	=	1455
Left	=	0
Top	=	0
Width	=	1095

Object: 3D label
Object Name: Panel3D2

BackColor	=	&H00C0C0C0&
BevelInner	=	1 'Inset
BevelOuter	=	1 'Inset
BevelWidth	=	5
BorderWidth	=	5

continues

10

Table 10.2. continued

Caption	=	"Cards Version 1.0"
Font3D	=	2 'Raised w/heavy shading
FontName	=	"MS Sans Serif"
FontSize	=	9.75
Height	=	855
Left	=	120
Top	=	2520
Width	=	6375

Object: 3D label
Object Name: Panel3D1

BackColor	=	&H00C0C0C0&
BevelInner	=	2 'Raised
BevelWidth	=	5
BorderWidth	=	5
Caption	=	"(C) Copyright 1990-1994 "
Font3D	=	2 'Raised w/heavy shading
FontName	=	"MS Sans Serif"
FontSize	=	9.75
Height	=	1095
Left	=	0
Top	=	1440
Width	=	6375

Object: 3D button
Object Name: cmdClose

BevelWidth	=	10
Caption	=	"&OK"
Font3D	=	2 'Raised w/heavy shading
FontName	=	"MS Sans Serif"
FontSize	=	18
ForeColor	=	&H00FF0000&
Height	=	855

Left	=	2400
Top	=	3480
Width	=	1575

Object: Image
Object Name: imgAbout

Height	=	1215
Left	=	1200
Picture	=	C:\LearnVB\BMP\GAMES05.BMP
Stretch	=	-1 'True
Top	=	120
Width	=	3975

Figure 10.19.
The frmAbout form (in
design mode).

Congratulations! You have finished designing the prototype of the Cards program. In Chapter 11, "Creating Card Game Programs (Part II)," you'll write the code for the Cards program.

11

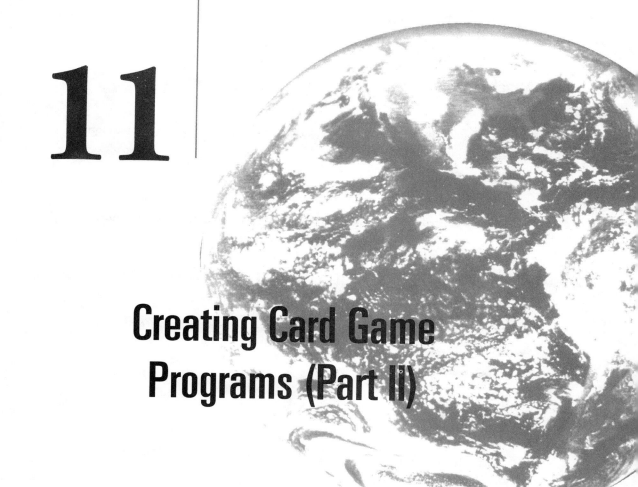

Creating Card Game
Programs (Part II)

In this chapter you'll write the code of the Cards program that was discussed in Chapter 10, "Creating Card Game Programs (Part I)."

11 | The Cards Program

You'll now enter the code of the Cards program.

Attaching Code to the Click Event of the About Button

You'll now attach code to the Click event of the About button.

☐ Enter the following code inside the cmdAbout_Click() procedure of the frmCards form:

```
Sub cmdAbout_Click ()

    frmAbout.Show 1

End Sub
```

The code you entered uses the Show method to display the About dialog box as a modal dialog box (the parameter of the Show method is equal to 1).

Attaching Code to the Close Button of the About Dialog Box

You'll now attach code to the Close button of the About dialog box.

☐ Enter the following code inside the cmdClose_Click() procedure of the frmAbout form:

```
Sub cmdClose_Click ()

    Unload frmAbout

End Sub
```

The code you entered unloads the frmAbout dialog box.

Attaching Code to the Click Event of the Close Button of the frmCards Form

You'll now attach code to the Click event of the Close button of the frmCards form.

☐ Enter the following code inside the cmdClose_Click() procedure of the frmCards form:

```
Sub cmdClose_Click ()

    Unload frmCards

End Sub
```

The code you entered terminates the Cards program.

Attaching Code to the Double-Click Event of the Cards Program

You'll now attach code to the Double-Click event of the card objects.

❑ Enter the following code inside the Cards_DblClick() procedure of the frmCards form:

```
Sub Cards_DblClick (Index As Integer)

    ' User double-clicked a card.

    If Cards(Index).Value = 0 Then
        ' Assign a random face to the clicked card
        Randomize
        Cards(Index).Value = Int(13 * Rnd + 1)
        Cards(Index).Suit = Int(4 * Rnd)
    Else
        ' Hide the face of the clicked card
        Cards(Index).Value = 0
    End If

End Sub
```

The code you entered is executed whenever the user double-clicks any of the cards.

Recall that the Cards() array is an array of 10 cards.

An If statement is used to determine which side of the double-clicked card is shown. The Value property of the card is 0 when the back of the card is shown.

Recall that the parameter of the Cards_DblClick() function is Index:

```
Sub Cards_DblClick (Index As Integer)

    .......
    .......
    .......

End Sub
```

Index indicates which card was double-clicked. For example, when Index is equal to 0, the Cards(0) card was double-clicked, when Index is equal to 1, Cards(1) was double-clicked, and so on.

The If statement checks whether the Value property of the double-clicked card is equal to 0:

```
    If Cards(Index).Value = 0 Then
        ' Assign a random face to the clicked card
        Randomize
        Cards(Index).Value = Int(13 * Rnd + 1)
        Cards(Index).Suit = Int(4 * Rnd)
    Else
        .......
        .......
        .......
    End If
```

If the double-clicked card is a card whose back is shown, the If is satisfied and the Value property of the double-clicked card is assigned with a random value.

11

The `Randomize` statement is used to generate a new seed number for Visual Basic's random number generator mechanism, and then the Value and the Suit properties of the card are set.

The Value property of the card is set in the following manner:

```
Cards(Index).Value = Int(13 * Rnd + 1)
```

Because the `Rnd` function returns a number equal to or greater than 0 but less than 1, the preceding statement assigns an integer to the Value property of the card with a value between 1 and 13.

The Value property determines the face value of the card in the following manner:

Value Setting	Description
0	Cover of the card is shown
1	Ace
2–10	Deuce through 10
11	Jack
12	Queen
13	King

Similarly, the Suit property of the card is set in the following manner:

```
Cards(Index).Suit = Int(4 * Rnd)
```

This means that the Suit property of the card is set to an integer with a value between 0 and 3.

The Suit property determines the suit of the card in the following manner:

Suit Setting	Description
0	Clubs
1	Diamonds
2	Hearts
3	Spades

If the face of the card that was double-clicked is displayed, the `Else` is satisfied, and the code under the `Else` statement is executed:

```
If Cards(Index).Value = 0 Then
    . . . .
    . . . .
    . . . .
Else
    ' Hide the face of the clicked card
    Cards(Index).Value = 0
End If
```

The code under the `Else` statement sets the Value property of the double-clicked card to 0, which causes the back of the card to be displayed.

Attaching Code to the Click Event of the Reset Button

You'll now attach code to the Click event of the Reset button of the frmCards form.

☐ Enter the following code inside the cmdReset_Click() procedure of the frmCards form:

```
Sub cmdReset_Click ()

    Dim Counter As Integer
    Static CardBackValue

    CardBackValue = CardBackValue + 1
    If CardBackValue = 13 Then
       CardBackValue = 0
    End If


    For Counter = 0 To 9 Step 1
    Cards(Counter).Value = 0
    Cards(Counter).CardBack = CardBackValue
    Next

End Sub
```

The cmdReset_Click() procedure is executed whenever the user clicks the Reset button.

Recall that whenever the user clicks the Reset button the program changes the design on the back of the cards.

The cmdReset_Click() procedure declares a local variable:

```
Dim Counter As Integer
```

It also declares a Static variable:

```
Static CardBackValue
```

When the cmdReset_Click() procedure is executed for the first time, Static CardBackValue is set to 0. The next statement increases the value of CardBackValue by 1:

```
CardBackValue = CardBackValue + 1
```

So if this is the first time the cmdReset_Click() procedure is executed, CardBackValue is equal to 0+1=1, if this is the second time the cmdReset_Click() procedure is executed, the value of CardBackValue is 1+1=2, and so on.

An If statement is then executed to check that CardBackValue does not exceed 12:

```
If CardBackValue = 13 Then
   CardBackValue = 0
End If
```

You must make sure that CardBackValue is a value between 0 and 12 because the CardBack property of the card control can have the value of an integer between 0 and 12.

A For loop is then executed, assigning the value of 0 to the Value property of the card control (so that the backs of the cards will be displayed), and the CardBack property is assigned with the value of the CardBackValue variable:

```
For Counter = 0 To 9 Step 1
    Cards(Counter).Value = 0
    Cards(Counter).CardBack = CardBackValue
Next
```

The For loop assigns 0 to the Value property of all 10 cards, and it assigns the value of the CardBackValue variable to the CardBack property of all 10 cards. The design on the back of the cards is determined according to the value of the CardBack property in the following manner:

Setting of the CardBack Property	Back Cover Design
0	Red checks
1	Blue checks
2	Red hatch
3	Blue hatch
4	Robot
5	Roses
6	Leaves 1
7	Leaves 2
8	Fish
9	Conch
10	Castle
11	Beach
12	Hand

For example, when the BackCard property of the card is set to 10, the design of the back cover is a picture of a castle.

Attaching Code to the Double-Click Event of the Back Door Image Control

You'll now attach code to the Double-Click event of the imgBackDoorPC image control. Recall that this image control serves as a "back door" mechanism that enables the PC to win.

☐ Enter the following code inside the imgBackDoorPC_DblClick() procedure of the frmCards form:

```
Sub imgBackDoorPC_DblClick ()

    If LinePC.Visible = True Then
        LinePC.Visible = False
    Else
        LinePC.Visible = True
```

```
        End If

End Sub
```

The code you entered uses an `If…Else` statement to toggle the value of the Visible property of the `LinePC` control. That is, if the image control is double-clicked while the `LinePC` control is visible, the `If` condition is satisfied and the line is made invisible. If the line is invisible when the image control is double-clicked, the code under the `Else` statement is executed and the line is made visible. As you'll soon see, the Visible property of the line control is later checked to determine whether the cards should be dealt honestly or in a crooked way.

Attaching Code to the Click Event of the Hit Me Button

You'll now attach code to the Click event of the Hit Me button.

❑ Enter the following code inside the `cmdHitMe_Click()` procedure of the `frmCards` form:

```
Sub cmdHitMe_Click ()

    Dim Counter As Integer

    imgBackDoorPC.Enabled = False

    For Counter = 0 To 9 Step 1
        Cards(Counter).Value = 0
    Next

    Timer1.Enabled = True
    cmdHitMe.Enabled = False
    cmdHitMe.Caption = "Now dealing cards..."

End Sub
```

The code you entered disables the image control:

```
imgBackDoorPC.Enabled = False
```

This code is necessary because when the user clicks the Hit Me button cards are dealt, and you want the image control to be disabled while the program deals cards (so that the user won't be able to switch to cheating mode after the program starts dealing the cards).

A `For` loop sets the Value property of all the cards to 0:

```
    For Counter = 0 To 9 Step 1
        Cards(Counter).Value = 0
    Next
```

So now all 10 cards are shown facedown.

Next, the timer is enabled:

```
Timer1.Enabled = True
```

As you'll soon see, the actual dealing of the cards is performed inside the Timer1_Timer() procedure. So by enabling the timer, you are actually starting the dealing of the 10 cards.

Finally, the Enabled property of the Hit Me button is set to False, and the Caption property of the Hit Me button is set to "Now dealing cards…":

```
cmdHitMe.Enabled = False
cmdHitMe.Caption = "Now dealing cards..."
```

The Hit Me button is disabled because you want to prevent the user from clicking the Hit Me button while the dealing of the cards is in progress.

Attaching Code to the Timer Event of the Timer

You'll now attach code to the Timer event of the timer.

☐ Enter the following code inside the Timer1_Timer() procedure of the frmCards form:

```
Sub Timer1_Timer ()

    Static Counter As Integer

    ' User clicked the Hit Me button while the
    ' line control is invisible (no cheating).
    ' 10 random cards are dealt.
    If LinePC.Visible = False Then

        Randomize
        Cards(Counter).Value = Int(13 * Rnd + 1)
        Cards(Counter).Suit = Int(4 * Rnd)

        Counter = Counter + 1

    End If


    ' User clicked the Hit Me button while the
    ' line control is visible.
    ' 5 sequential cards are dealt to the PC and
    ' 5 random cards are dealt to the player.
    If LinePC.Visible = True Then
        If Counter < 5 Then
            ' Deal sequential card to the PC
            Cards(Counter).Value = Counter + 9
            Cards(Counter).Suit = 2
            Counter = Counter + 1
            Exit Sub
        Else
            ' Deal a random card to the player.
            Randomize
            Cards(Counter).Value = Int(13 * Rnd + 1)
            Cards(Counter).Suit = Int(4 * Rnd)
            Counter = Counter + 1
        End If
    End If
```

```
' If 10 cards were dealt, disable the timer
If Counter = 10 Then
   cmdHitMe.Caption = "&Hit Me"
   cmdHitMe.Enabled = True
   Timer1.Enabled = False
   Counter = 0
   imgBackDoorPC.Enabled = True
End If
```

End Sub

As previously stated, the program deals the cards inside the `Timer1_Timer()` procedure. Recall that the `cmdHitMe_Click()` procedure enabled the `Timer1` control. So when the user clicks the Hit Me button, the `Timer1_Timer()` procedure is executed every 1000 milliseconds (because at design time you set the Interval property of the `Timer1` control to 1000 milliseconds).

The `Timer1_Timer()` procedure declares a `Static` variable:

```
Static Counter As Integer
```

The procedure then uses an `If` statement to check the Visible property of the line control. If the Visible property of the line control is equal to `False`, the code under the `If` statement is executed:

```
If LinePC.Visible = False Then
   ......
   ......
   ......
End If
```

This code randomly deals 10 cards:

```
Randomize
Cards(Counter).Value = Int(13 * Rnd + 1)
Cards(Counter).Suit = Int(4 * Rnd)

Counter = Counter + 1
```

The `Static` variable `Counter` is incremented by 1:

```
Counter = Counter + 1
```

The next `If` statement is not satisfied because the Visible property of the line control is `False`. So the procedure goes to the next `If` statement:

```
' If 10 cards were dealt, disable the timer
If Counter = 10 Then
   cmdHitMe.Caption = "&Hit Me"
   cmdHitMe.Enabled = True
   Timer1.Enabled = False
   Counter = 0
   imgBackDoorPC.Enabled = True
End If
```

The preceding `If` statement is used to determine whether 10 cards have already been dealt.

If 10 cards have already been dealt, the preceding `If` statement is satisfied. The Caption property of the Hit Me button is set back to `"&Hit Me"`, the Enabled property of the Hit Me button is set to

True, and the Enabled property of the `Timer1` control is set to `False`. Also, the `Counter` variable is set to 0 and the image control is enabled.

So if the Visible property of the line control is equal to `False` and the Hit Me button has been clicked, the `Timer1_Timer()` procedure is executed every 1 second. Each time the `Timer1_Timer()` procedure is executed another card is randomly dealt, until 10 cards are dealt.

The `Timer1_Timer()` procedure contains another `If` statement:

```
If LinePC.Visible = True Then
   .....
   .....
   .....
End If
```

This `If` statement is satisfied only if the Visible property of the line control is equal to `True`.

An `If…Else` statement is then executed to check which card should be dealt:

```
If Counter < 5 Then
   ' Deal sequential card to the PC
   Cards(Counter).Value = Counter + 9
   Cards(Counter).Suit = 2
   Counter = Counter + 1
   Exit Sub
Else
   ' Deal a random card to the player.
   Randomize
   Cards(Counter).Value = Int(13 * Rnd + 1)
   Cards(Counter).Suit = Int(4 * Rnd)
   Counter = Counter + 1
End If
End If
```

If the `Static` variable `Counter` is less than 5, the preceding `If` statement is satisfied, and the Value property of the card is set to `Counter+9`. So the first time the `Timer1_Timer()` procedure is executed (with the Visible property of the line control equal to `True`), the `Counter` variable is equal to 0, which means that the Value property of `Cards(0)` is assigned with the value of `Counter+9=0+9=9`. The Suit property of `Cards(0)` is assigned with the value 2.

The `Counter` variable is then increased by 1:

```
Counter = Counter + 1
```

Then the procedure is terminated:

```
Exit Sub
```

On the next execution of `Timer1_Timer()`, `Counter` is equal to 1, so the `Cards(1)` card is dealt. This time, however, the Value property of `Cards(1)` is set to `Counter+9=1+9=10`. This process continues until five cards are dealt. So the first five cards are 9, 10, 11, 12, and 13, and these five cards have their Suit property set to 2.

After five cards are dealt to the PC, the procedure executes the statements under the `Else` and randomly deals five cards to the player:

```
If Counter < 5 Then
     ......
     ......
     ......
Else
   ' Deal a random card to the player.
   Randomize
   Cards(Counter).Value = Int(13 * Rnd + 1)
   Cards(Counter).Suit = Int(4 * Rnd)
   Counter = Counter + 1
End If
```

If Counter is equal to 10, all 10 cards have already been dealt, and the last If statement in the procedure is executed.

Further Enhancements——You Are on Your Own. . .

You can further enhance and improve the Cards program. For example, you can add another image control and a line control that serve as a back door mechanism to deal five winning cards to the player.

As the Cards program now stands, it deals 10 cards from a deck that has an infinite number of cards in it. This means that the program does not take into account the fact that a particular card was dealt already (and therefore this card cannot be dealt again). This method is commonly used in electronic gambling machines, to prevent the user from "counting." That is, a user can enhance his or her chances of winning by taking note of which cards have already been dealt, and therefore the user can better predict what cards are left in the deck. This counting system gives the user a better chance when playing blackjack (commonly known as twenty-one). Of course, if the gambling program uses a deck with an infinite number of cards in it, the counting system will not work.

You can modify the Cards program yourself so that it deals cards from a deck with a finite number of cards. For example, you can build an array with 52 elements in it, where each element of the array contains a different card from a single deck. The value of the card is determined randomly. Your program should also maintain a counter variable that keeps track of how many cards have already been dealt, and when the last card is dealt, the program should inform the user that there are no more cards in the deck.

12

Creating Dice Game Programs (Part I)

In this and the next chapter you'll learn how to design dice game programs with Visual Basic.

Executing the Dice Program

Before writing the prototype of the Dice program yourself, execute the Dice.EXE program that resides inside your C:\LearnVB\Original\Dice directory:

❏ Select Run from the File menu of the Program Manager and execute the C:\LearnVB\Original\Dice\Dice.EXE program.

Windows responds by executing the Dice.EXE program and displaying the window shown in Figure 12.1.

Figure 12.1.
The main window of the Dice program.

Note that the window in Figure 12.1 contains a picture of a gambler rotating his eyes nervously. Below the picture of the gambler, the message Enjoy your game... is moving from right to left.

❏ Click the About button.

The Dice program responds by displaying the About dialog box. (See Figure 12.2.)

Note that while the About dialog box is displayed you can't switch to the main window of the Dice program (because the About dialog box is a modal dialog box).

❏ Click the OK button of the About dialog box.

The Dice program responds by closing the About dialog box and redisplaying the main window.

Figure 12.2.
The About dialog box of
the Dice program.

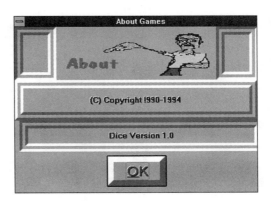

To play the game do the following:

❏ Click the Dice button.

> *The Dice program responds by playing a short WAV file through the sound card, and by*
> *displaying the Dice window shown in Figure 12.3.*

Figure 12.3.
The Dice window.

The Your guess label shown in Figure 12.3 contains the number 7. This means that you are gambling that in the next toss of the dice, the sum of the two numbers will be 7. Do you feel lucky?

❏ Click the Try Your Luck button.

> *The Dice program tosses the dice, and after a while displays the results.*

If the sum of the numbers on the dice is 7, the Dice program plays a siren sound through the sound card, and then displays the window shown in Figure 12.4.

Figure 12.4.
The Dice window after the
player wins.

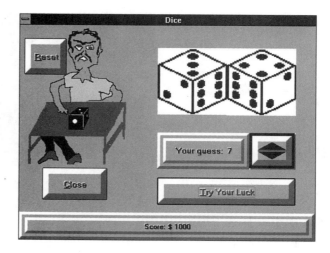

If the sum of the numbers on the dice is not 7, the Dice program plays through the sound card the sound of people laughing, and then displays the window shown in Figure 12.5.

Figure 12.5.
The Dice window
after the player loses.

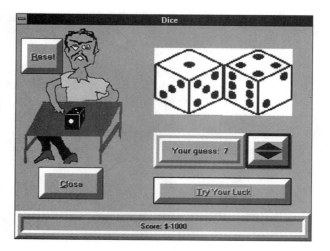

NOTE

The Dice program laughs whenever you lose! Typically, it is a bad practice to laugh at people who lose in gambling, so you might want to incorporate a different WAV file that plays whenever the player is losing.

Note that in Figure 12.3 the Score label is $0 (because you didn't lose and you didn't win). The Score label is displayed on the surface of the Dice window.

In Figure 12.4 the score is $1000 because the user won $1000, and the Score label is displayed "above" the surface of the Dice window.

In Figure 12.5 the score is $-1000 because the user lost $1000, and the Score label is displayed "embedded" in the surface of the Dice window.

❏ Press the spin control (the control that has two arrows on it).

If you press the up arrow of the spin control, the number displayed inside the Your guess label increases, and if you press the down arrow of the spin control, the number decreases. Because the minimum number that can be set is 2, the Dice program plays a bell sound through the sound card if you try to guess a number that's less than 2. Because the maximum number that can be set is 12, the Dice program also plays a bell sound through the sound card if you try to guess a number greater than 12.

❏ Click the Try Your Luck button.

The Dice program responds by tossing the dice, and after a while the dice stop and the score is calculated.

❏ Click the Reset button.

The Dice program sets the score back to $0.

The Dice program has a "back door" mechanism that lets you win on every toss. To see the back door in action do the following:

❏ Double-click the die that appears on the table.

The Dice program responds by displaying a small line. This small line indicates that the Dice program is in a cheating mode.

❏ Experiment with the Try Your Luck button and notice that now you are a winner every time.

❏ To take the Dice program out of cheating mode, double-click the die that appears on the table.

The Dice program responds by removing the small line and placing the Dice program in noncheating mode.

❏ Experiment with the Dice program, then click the Close button to return to the main window, and then click the Exit button of the main window to terminate the Dice program.

Implementing the Prototype of the Dice Program

You'll now implement the prototype of the Dice program.

❑ Select New Project from the File menu and save the new project: Save the new form as Front.FRM in the C:\LearnVB\Practice\Dice directory. Save the new project as Dice.MAK in the C:\LearnVB\Practice\Dice directory.

❑ Implement the frmFront form according to the specifications in Table 12.1. When you finish implementing the form, it should look like the one shown in Figure 12.6.

Table 12.1. The Properties table of the frmFront form.

Object Type: Form
Object Name: frmFront

BackColor	=	&H00C0C0C0&
BorderStyle	=	1 'Fixed Single
Caption	=	"Games People Play"
Height	=	7110
Icon	=	C:\LearnVB\Icons\Dice.ICO
Left	=	165
MaxButton	=	0 'False
Top	=	90
Width	=	9405
WindowState	=	2 'Maximized

Object Type: TegoMM (advanced multimedia control)
Object Name: TegommPrompt

Height	=	330
Left	=	600
Top	=	4080
Visible	=	0 'False
Width	=	3510

Object Type: 3D button
Object Name: cmdAbout

BevelWidth	=	10
Font3D	=	2 'Raised w/heavy shading
FontBold	=	-1 'True

FontSize	=	13.5
ForeColor	=	&H000000FF&
Height	=	2535
Left	=	5280
Picture	=	C:\LearnVB\BMP\GAMES05.BMP
Top	=	4200
Width	=	3735

Object Type: MhMarque (animation plus moving text; See Figure 1.41.)
Object Name: MhMarque1

BackColor	=	&H00C0C0C0&
BorderColor	=	&H00C0C0C0&
Caption	=	"Enjoy your game and good luck"
CaptionBottom	=	630
CaptionLeft	=	45
CaptionRight	=	30
CaptionTop	=	3210
FontName	=	"Times New Roman"
FontSize	=	24
FontStyle	=	4 'Lowered with more shading
FontTransParent	=	-1 'True
ForeColor	=	&H000000FF&
Height	=	4575
Interval	=	150
Left	=	5280
LightColor	=	&H00C0C0C0&
OuterFillColor	=	&H00C0C0C0&
Picture1	=	C:\LearnVB\BMP\Games01.BMP
Picture2	=	C:\LearnVB\BMP\Games02.BMP
Picture3	=	C:\LearnVB\BMP\Games03.BMP
PictureBottom	=	1350
PictureLeft	=	300
PictureRight	=	900
PictureTop	=	-240
ShadowColor	=	&H00C0C0C0&

continues

Table 12.1. continued

TextColor	=	&H000000FF&
TextFillColor	=	&H00C0C0C0&
Top	=	240
Width	=	3855

Object Type: 3D button
Object Name: cmdDice

BevelWidth	=	10
Caption	=	"&Dice"
Font3D	=	2 'Raised w/heavy shading
FontName	=	"Times New Roman"
FontSize	=	18
ForeColor	=	&H000000FF&
Height	=	3855
Left	=	2880
Picture	=	C:\LearnVB\BMP\DICE01.BMP
Top	=	120
Width	=	1695

Object Type: 3D button
Object Name: cmdExit

BevelWidth	=	10
Caption	=	"E&xit"
Font3D	=	2 'Raised w/heavy shading
FontName	=	"MS Sans Serif "
FontSize	=	13.5
ForeColor	=	&H000000FF&
Height	=	1575
Left	=	0
Picture	=	C:\LearnVB\BMP\GAMES04.BMP
Top	=	4560
Width	=	5175

Figure 12.6.
The `frmFront` *form (in design mode).*

Implementing the About Dialog Box

You'll now implement the About dialog box.

☐ Select New Form from the File menu and save the new form as About.FRM inside the C:\LearnVB\Practice\Dice directory.

☐ Implement the `frmAbout` form according to the specifications in Table 12.2. When you finish implementing the form, it should look like the one shown in Figure 12.7.

NOTE

If you implemented the About dialog box of the Cards program in Chapter 10, "Creating Card Game Programs (Part I)," you can use the same About dialog box:

☐ Copy the C:\LearnVB\Practice\Cards\About.FRM file to the C:\LearnVB\Practice\Dice directory.

☐ Select Add File from the File menu and select the C:\LearnVB\Practice\Dice\About.FRM file.

☐ Set the Caption property of the `Panel3D2` control to

`Dice Version 1.0`.

As you can see, the only difference between the About dialog box of the Cards program and the About dialog box of the Dice program is the Caption property of the `Panel3D2` control. To see this, compare Figure 10.17 with Figure 12.2.

12

Table 12.2. The Properties table of the frmAbout form.

Object Type: Form
Object Name: frmAbout

BackColor	=	&H00C0C0C0&
BorderStyle	=	1 'Fixed Single
Caption	=	"About Games"
Height	=	4890
Left	=	1035
MaxButton	=	0 'False
MinButton	=	0 'False
Top	=	1140
Width	=	6465

Object Type: 3D label
Object Name: Panel3D1

BackColor	=	&H00C0C0C0&
BevelInner	=	2 'Raised
BevelWidth	=	5
BorderWidth	=	5
Caption	=	" Copyright 1990-1994 "
Font3D	=	2 'Raised w/heavy shading
FontName	=	"MS Sans Serif"
FontSize	=	9.75
Height	=	1095
Left	=	0
Top	=	1440
Width	=	6375

Object Type: 3D label
Object Name: Panel3D2

BackColor	=	&H00C0C0C0&
BevelInner	=	1 'Inset
BevelOuter	=	1 'Inset
BevelWidth	=	5
BorderWidth	=	5

Caption	=	"Dice Version 1.0"
Font3D	=	2 'Raised w/heavy shading
FontName	=	"MS Sans Serif"
FontSize	=	9.75
Height	=	855
Left	=	120
Top	=	2520
Width	=	6375

Object Type: 3D label
Object Name: Panel3D3

BackColor	=	&H00C0C0C0&
BevelInner	=	1 'Inset
BevelOuter	=	1 'Inset
BevelWidth	=	5
BorderWidth	=	5
Font3D	=	2 'Raised w/heavy shading
Height	=	1455
Left	=	0
Top	=	0
Width	=	1095

Object Type: 3D label
Object Name: Panel3D4

BackColor	=	&H00C0C0C0&
BevelInner	=	1 'Inset
BevelOuter	=	1 'Inset
BevelWidth	=	5
BorderWidth	=	5
Font3D	=	2 'Raised w/heavy shading
Height	=	1455
Left	=	5280
Top	=	0
Width	=	1095

continues

Table 12.2. continued

Object Type: 3D button
Object Name: cmdClose

BevelWidth	=	10
Caption	=	"&OK"
Font3D	=	2 'Raised w/heavy shading
FontName	=	"MS Sans Serif"
FontSize	=	18
ForeColor	=	&H00FF0000&
Height	=	855
Left	=	2400
Top	=	3480
Width	=	1575

Object Type: Image
Object Name: imgMIDI

Height	=	1215
Left	=	1200
Picture	=	C:\LearnVB\BMP\GAMES05.BMP
Stretch	=	-1 'True
Top	=	120
Width	=	3975

Figure 12.7.
The frmAbout *form (in design mode).*

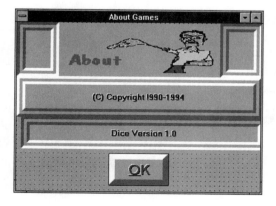

Implementing the Dice Window

You'll now implement the `frmDice` form.

☐ Implement the `frmDice` form according to the specifications in Table 12.3. When you finish implementing the form, it should look like the one shown in Figure 12.8.

Table 12.3. The Properties table of the `frmDice` form.

Object Type: Form
Object Name: frmDice

BackColor	=	&H00C0C0C0&
BorderStyle	=	1 'Fixed Single
Caption	=	"Dice"
Height	=	6165
Left	=	1020
MaxButton	=	0 'False
MinButton	=	0 'False
Picture	=	C:\LearnVB\BMP\DICE01.BMP
Top	=	795
Width	=	7845

Object Type: 3D button
Object Name: cmdReset

BevelWidth	=	10
Caption	=	"&Reset"
Font3D	=	2 'Raised w/heavy shading
FontName	=	"MS Sans Serif"
FontSize	=	9.75
ForeColor	=	&H000000FF&
Height	=	975
Left	=	120
Top	=	360
Width	=	1095

continues

12

Table 12.3. continued

Object Type: 3D label
Object Name: lblScore

Align	=	2 'Align Bottom
BackColor	=	&H00C0C0C0&
BevelOuter	=	0 'None
BevelWidth	=	5
BorderWidth	=	5
Caption	=	"Score: $"
Font3D	=	2 'Raised w/heavy shading
Height	=	735
Left	=	0
Top	=	5025
Width	=	7725

Object Type: Spin (See Figure 1.39.)
Object Name: Spin1

BorderThickness	=	5
Height	=	975
Left	=	6000
ShadowThickness	=	2
TdThickness	=	10
Top	=	2880
Width	=	1215

Object Type: 3D label
Object Name: lblGuess

BackColor	=	&H00C0C0C0&
BevelInner	=	2 'Raised
BevelWidth	=	5
BorderWidth	=	5
Caption	=	"Guess: "
Font3D	=	2 'Raised w/heavy shading
FontName	=	"MS Sans Serif"
FontSize	=	9.75

Height	=	975
Left	=	3600
Top	=	2880
Width	=	2415

Object Type: 3D button
Object Name: cmdTryYourLuck

BevelWidth	=	10
Caption	=	"&Try Your Luck"
Font3D	=	2 'Raised w/heavy shading
FontName	=	"MS Sans Serif"
FontSize	=	9.75
ForeColor	=	&H000000FF&
Height	=	735
Left	=	3600
Top	=	4080
Width	=	3615

Object Type: MhDice (dice; See Figure 1.40.)
Object Name: MhDice1

AutoSize	=	0 'False
FillColor	=	&H00FFFFFF&
Height	=	1800
Left	=	3600
LeftSideColor	=	&H00FFFFFF&
RightSideColor	=	&H00FFFFFF&
Top	=	600
TopSideColor	=	&H00FFFFFF&
Value	=	1
Width	=	1815

Object Type: MhDice (dice; See Figure 1.40.)
Object Name: MhDice2

AutoSize	=	0 'False
BackColor	=	&H00000000&

continues

12

Table 12.3. continued

FillColor	=	&H00FFFFFF&
Height	=	1815
Left	=	5400
LeftSideColor	=	&H00FFFFFF&
RightSideColor	=	&H00FFFFFF&
Top	=	600
TopSideColor	=	&H00FFFFFF&
Value	=	1
Width	=	1815

Object Type: 3D button
Object Name: cmdClose

BevelWidth	=	10
Caption	=	"&Close"
Font3D	=	2 'Raised w/heavy shading
FontName	=	"MS Sans Serif"
FontSize	=	9.75
ForeColor	=	&H000000FF&
Height	=	855
Left	=	600
Top	=	3840
Width	=	1695

Object Type: Image
Object Name: imgBackDoor

Comment: Leave the Picture property of this image empty. This image serves as the back door mechanism of the Dice program.

BorderStyle	=	1 'Fixed Single
Height	=	375
Left	=	1320
Top	=	2400
Width	=	375

Object Type: Line
Object Name: Line1

Visible	=	0	'False
X1	=	2880	
X2	=	3000	
Y1	=	3360	
Y2	=	3480	

Figure 12.8.
The frmDice form (in design mode).

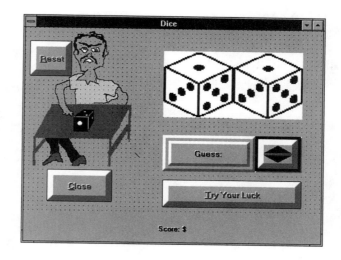

You have finished implementing all the forms that are used by the Dice program. In the next chapter you'll write the code of the Dice program.

13

Creating Dice Game Programs (Part II)

In this chapter you'll write the code of the Dice program whose prototype you implemented in Chapter 12, "Creating Dice Game Programs (Part II)."

Attaching Code to the Click Event of the Exit Button

You'll now attach code to the Click event of the Exit button of the frmFront form.

❑ Enter the following code inside the cmdExit_Click() procedure of the frmFront form:

```
Sub cmdExit_Click ()

    End

End Sub
```

The code you entered terminates the Dice program whenever the user clicks the Exit button.

Attaching Code to the About Button of the frmFront Form

You'll now attach code to the About button of the frmFront form.

❑ Enter the following code inside the cmdAbout_Click() procedure of the frmFront form:

```
Sub cmdAbout_Click ()

    ' Display frmAbout
    frmAbout.Show 1

End Sub
```

The code you entered is executed whenever the user clicks the About button. This code displays the About dialog box as a modal dialog box (because the parameter of the Show method is 1).

Attaching Code to the Load Event of the frmFront Form

You'll now attach code to the Load event of the frmFront form.

❑ Enter the following code inside the Form_Load() procedure of the frmFront form:

```
Sub Form_Load ()

    TegommPrompt.DeviceType = "WaveAudio"

End Sub
```

The code you entered is executed whenever the Dice program starts (because frmFront is the first form that is loaded). This code sets the DeviceType property of the multimedia control to the sound card device:

```
TegommPrompt.DeviceType = "WaveAudio"
```

Adding the DICE.BAS Module to the Project

You'll now attach a new module to the DICE.MAK project.

❑ Select New Module from the File menu and save the new module as DICE.BAS in the C:\LearnVB\Practice\Dice directory.

❑ Enter the following code inside the general declarations section of the DICE.BAS module:

```
Option Explicit

Global ggDiceGuess
Global ggDiceScore

Global Const ROBO_WAV_FILE_NAME =
    ➥ "\LearnVB\WAV\Roboarm1.WAV"

Global Const BELL1_WAV_FILE_NAME =
    ➥ "\LearnVB\WAV\DNRBell1.WAV"

Global Const SIREN1_WAV_FILE_NAME =
    ➥ "\LearnVB\WAV\Siren1.WAV"

Global Const LAUGH1_WAV_FILE_NAME =
    ➥ "\LearnVB\WAV\GrpLaff1.WAV"
```

The code you entered declares two global variables:

```
Global ggDiceGuess
Global ggDiceScore
```

`ggDiceGuess` is a variable that holds the number guessed by the player, and `ggDiceScore` is a variable that holds the score.

The rest of the statements you entered declare `Global Const` declarations. These declarations tell the pathnames and filenames of several WAV files.

NOTE

The pathnames and filenames of the WAV files are defined without drive names. That is, the pathname of the Roboarm1.WAV is declared as this:

```
Global Const ROBO_WAV_FILE_NAME =
    ➥ "\LearnVB\WAV\Roboarm1.WAV"
```

It is not declared as this:

```
Global Const ROBO_WAV_FILE_NAME =
    ➥ "C:\LearnVB\WAV\Roboarm1.WAV"
```

You will add the drive name to the pathname later in the program.

Attaching Code to the Click Event of the Dice Button

You'll now attach code to the Click event of the Dice button of the frmFront form.

❑ Enter the following code inside the cmdDice_Click() procedure of the frmFront form:

```
Sub cmdDice_Click ()

    ' Minimize frmFront
    frmFront.WindowState = 1

    ' Audio
    TegommPrompt.FileName =
        ➥ Left(App.Path, 2) + ROBO_WAV_FILE_NAME
    TegommPrompt.Command = "Open"
    TegommPrompt.Command = "Prev"
    TegommPrompt.Command = "Play"


    ' Display frmDice
    frmDice.Show 1

    ' Maximize frmFront
    frmFront.WindowState = 2

End Sub
```

The cmdDice_Click() procedure is executed whenever the user clicks the Dice button. The code inside this procedure minimizes the frmFront form:

```
' Minimize frmFront
frmFront.WindowState = 1
```

Then the Roboarm1.WAV file is played:

```
' Audio
TegommPrompt.FileName =
    ➥ Left(App.Path, 2) + ROBO_WAV_FILE_NAME
TegommPrompt.Command = "Open"
TegommPrompt.Command = "Prev"
TegommPrompt.Command = "Play"
```

The FileName property of the multimedia control is set in the following manner:

```
TegommPrompt.FileName =
        ➥ Left(App.Path, 2) + ROBO_WAV_FILE_NAME
```

App.Path is the pathname and filename of the Dice program. For example, if the Dice program resides inside the C:\LearnVB\Practice\Dice directory, App.Path is equal to C:\LearnVB\Practice\Dice\Dice.EXE.

The Left(App.Path, 2) statement returns the first two characters of App.Path. So if the Dice program resides inside the C:\LearnVB\Practice\Dice directory, Left(App.Path, 2) returns C:.

Because you declared ROBO_WAV_FILE_NAME as \LearnVB\WAV\Roboarm1.WAV, the statement

```
TegommPrompt.FileName =
        ➥ Left(App.Path, 2) + ROBO_WAV_FILE_NAME
```

means that if the Dice program resides inside the C: drive, the FileName property of the multimedia control is set to

```
C:\LearnVB\WAV\Roboarm1.WAV
```

If the Dice program resides inside the D: drive, the FileName property of the multimedia control is set to

```
D:\LearnVB\WAV\Roboarm1.WAV
```

The `cmdDice_Click()` procedure then displays the `frmDice` form as a modal dialog box:

```
' Display frmDice
frmDice.Show 1
```

Because the `frmDice` dialog box is displayed as a modal dialog box, the user can switch back to the `frmFront` window only by closing the `frmDice` form. After the `frmDice` form is closed, the `cmdDice_Click()` procedure continues with the execution of the next statement:

```
' Maximize frmFront
 frmFront.WindowState = 2
```

This statement maximizes the `frmFront` window.

Attaching Code to the Click Event of the `frmDice` Form's Close Button

You'll now attach code to the Click event of the `frmDice` form's Close button.

❑ Enter the following code inside the `cmdClose_Click()` procedure of the `frmDice` form:

```
Sub cmdClose_Click ()

    Unload frmDice

End Sub
```

The code you entered closes the `frmDice` form whenever the user clicks the `cmdClose` button of the Dice form.

Attaching Code to the Load Event of the `frmDice` Form

You'll now attach code to the Load event of the `frmDice` form.

❑ Enter the following code inside the `Form_Load()` procedure of the `frmDice` form:

```
Sub Form_Load ()

    ggDiceGuess = 7
    lblGuess.Caption = "Your guess: " + Str$(ggDiceGuess)
```

```
ggDiceScore = 0
lblScore.Caption = "Score: $" + Str$(ggDiceScore)
lblScore.BevelInner = 0
lblScore.BevelOuter = 0
```

End Sub

The code you entered sets the guessed number to 7:

```
ggDiceGuess = 7
lblGuess.Caption = "Your guess: " + Str$(ggDiceGuess)
```

Then it initializes the score:

```
ggDiceScore = 0
lblScore.Caption = "Score: $" + Str$(ggDiceScore)
```

Then the BevelInner and BevelOuter properties of the lblScore label are set to 0:

```
lblScore.BevelInner = 0
lblScore.BevelOuter = 0
```

These two statements cause the Score label to appear on the surface of the frmDice form.

Attaching Code to the SpinDown Event of the Spin Control

You'll now attach code to the SpinDown event of the spin control.

❑ Enter the following code inside the Spin1_SpinDown() procedure of the frmDice form:

Sub Spin1_SpinDown ()

```
    ggDiceGuess = ggDiceGuess - 1

    If ggDiceGuess = 1 Then
       ggDiceGuess = 2
       frmFront.TegommPrompt.FileName =
          ➥ Left(App.Path,2) + BELL1_WAV_FILE_NAME
       frmFront.TegommPrompt.Command = "Open"
       frmFront.TegommPrompt.Command = "Prev"
       frmFront.TegommPrompt.Command = "Play"
    End If

    lblGuess.Caption = "Your guess: " + Str$(ggDiceGuess)
```

End Sub

The Spin1_SpinDown() procedure is executed whenever the user presses the down arrow of the spin control.

Recall that pressing the down arrow of the spin control causes the guessed number to decrease. Therefore, the ggDiceGuess variable is decreased:

```
ggDiceGuess = ggDiceGuess - 1
```

Because the minimum guessed number is 2, an `If` statement is executed to check whether the user tries to decrease the guessed number by too much:

```
If ggDiceGuess = 1 Then
   ggDiceGuess = 2
   frmFront.TegommPrompt.FileName =
      ➥ Left(App.Path,2) + BELL1_WAV_FILE_NAME
   frmFront.TegommPrompt.Command = "Open"
   frmFront.TegommPrompt.Command = "Prev"
   frmFront.TegommPrompt.Command = "Play"
End If
```

If the `If` condition is satisfied, `ggDiceGuess` is set to 2 and a bell sound is played through the sound card.

Finally, the `lblGuess` label is updated:

```
lblGuess.Caption = "Your guess: " + Str$(ggDiceGuess)
```

Attaching Code to the SpinUp Event of the Spin Control

You'll now attach code to the SpinUp event of the spin control.

❑ Enter the following code inside the `Spin1_SpinUp()` procedure of the `frmDice` form:

```
Sub Spin1_SpinUp ()

    ggDiceGuess = ggDiceGuess + 1
    If ggDiceGuess = 13 Then
       ggDiceGuess = 12
       frmFront.TegommPrompt.FileName =
          ➥ Left(App.Path,2) + BELL1_WAV_FILE_NAME

       frmFront.TegommPrompt.Command = "Open"
       frmFront.TegommPrompt.Command = "Prev"
       frmFront.TegommPrompt.Command = "Play"
    End If

    lblGuess.Caption = "Your guess: " + Str$(ggDiceGuess)

End Sub
```

The `Spin1_SpinUp()` procedure is executed when the user presses the up arrow of the spin control.

Recall that pressing the up arrow of the spin control causes the guessed number to increase. Therefore, the `ggDiceGuess` variable is increased:

```
ggDiceGuess = ggDiceGuess + 1
```

Because the maximum guessed number is 12, an `If` statement is executed to check whether the user tries to increase the guessed number by too much:

```
If ggDiceGuess = 13 Then
   ggDiceGuess = 12
```

13

```
frmFront.TegommPrompt.FileName =
    ➥ Left(App.Path,2) + BELL1_WAV_FILE_NAME

frmFront.TegommPrompt.Command = "Open"
frmFront.TegommPrompt.Command = "Prev"
frmFront.TegommPrompt.Command = "Play"
End If
```

If the If condition is satisfied, ggDiceGuess is set to 13 and a bell sound is played through the sound card.

Finally, the lblGuess label is updated:

```
lblGuess.Caption = "Your guess: " + Str$(ggDiceGuess)
```

Attaching Code to the Click Event of the frmDice Form's Reset Button

You'll now attach code to the Click event of the Reset button of the frmDice form.

❑ Enter the following code inside the cmdReset_Click() procedure of the frmDice form:

```
Sub cmdReset_Click ()

    ggDiceGuess = 7
    lblGuess.Caption = "Your guess: " + Str$(ggDiceGuess)

    ggDiceScore = 0
    lblScore.Caption = "Score: $" + Str$(ggDiceScore)
    lblScore.BevelInner = 0
    lblScore.BevelOuter = 0

End Sub
```

The code you entered assigns the value 7 to the ggDiceGuess global variable:

```
ggDiceGuess = 7
```

Then the Caption property of the lblGuess label is set:

```
lblGuess.Caption = "Your guess: " + Str$(ggDiceGuess)
```

This means that when the user clicks the Reset button the program sets the guessed number to 7.

The cmdReset_Click() procedure then sets the score to 0:

```
ggDiceScore = 0
lblScore.Caption = "Score: $" + Str$(ggDiceScore)
```

Then the BevelInner and BevelOuter properties of the lblScore label are set to 0:

```
lblScore.BevelInner = 0
lblScore.BevelOuter = 0
```

The preceding two statements cause the Score label to appear on the surface of the frmDice form.

Attaching Code to the Click Event of the Try Your Luck Button

You'll now attach code to the Click event of the Try Your Luck button.

☐ Enter the following code inside the cmdTryYourLuck_Click() procedure of the frmDice form:

```
Sub cmdTryYourLuck_Click ()

    Dim Counter

    Randomize    ' Seed random number generator.

    For Counter = 1 To 20 Step 1
        MhDice1.Value = Int(6 * Rnd + 1)
        MhDice2.Value = Int(6 * Rnd + 1)
        frmDice.Refresh
    Next

    MhDice1.Value = Int(6 * Rnd + 1)
    MhDice2.Value = Int(6 * Rnd + 1)

    If Line1.Visible = True Then
        MhDice1.Value = Int(ggDiceGuess / 2)
        MhDice2.Value = ggDiceGuess - MhDice1.Value
    End If

    If (ggDiceGuess = MhDice1.Value + MhDice2.Value) Then
        frmFront.TegommPrompt.FileName = _
        ➥ Left(App.Path, 2) + SIREN1_WAV_FILE_NAME

        frmFront.TegommPrompt.Command = "Open"
        frmFront.TegommPrompt.Command = "Prev"
        frmFront.TegommPrompt.Command = "Play"

        ggDiceScore = ggDiceScore + 1000

    Else

        frmFront.TegommPrompt.FileName = _
        ➥ Left(App.Path, 2) + LAUGH1_WAV_FILE_NAME

        frmFront.TegommPrompt.Command = "Open"
        frmFront.TegommPrompt.Command = "Prev"
        frmFront.TegommPrompt.Command = "Play"

        ggDiceScore = ggDiceScore - 1000

    End If

    lblScore.Caption = "Score: $" + Str$(ggDiceScore)
    If ggDiceScore = 0 Then
        lblScore.BevelInner = 0
        lblScore.BevelOuter = 0
```

13

```
ElseIf ggDiceScore > 0 Then
    lblScore.BevelInner = 2
    lblScore.BevelOuter = 2
ElseIf ggDiceScore < 0 Then
    lblScore.BevelInner = 1
    lblScore.BevelOuter = 2
End If
```

End Sub

The cmdTryYourLuck_Click() procedure is executed whenever the user clicks the Try Your Luck button. The cmdTryYourLuck_Click() procedure is responsible for tossing the dice, determining whether the player guessed correctly, playing a WAV file that corresponds to the result (winning or losing), and updating the score.

The procedure declares a local variable:

```
Dim Counter
```

The Randomize statement is executed:

```
Randomize    ' Seed random number generator.
```

Then a For loop is executed:

```
For Counter = 1 To 20 Step 1
    MhDice1.Value = Int(6 * Rnd + 1)
    MhDice2.Value = Int(6 * Rnd + 1)
    frmDice.Refresh
Next
```

The preceding For loop is performed for cosmetic reasons only. The two dice are assigned with random numbers and the Refresh method is executed so that the user will be able to see the values of the dice immediately. The For loop is executed 20 times.

Finally, the dice are assigned their final values:

```
MhDice1.Value = Int(6 * Rnd + 1)
MhDice2.Value = Int(6 * Rnd + 1)
```

An If statement is then executed to examine the Visible property of the line control:

```
If Line1.Visible = True Then
    MhDice1.Value = Int(ggDiceGuess / 2)
    MhDice2.Value = ggDiceGuess - MhDice1.Value
End If
```

If the Visible property of the line control is True, the Value properties of the dice are set to match the value of the ggDiceGuess variable. For example, if ggDiceGuess is equal to 7, MhDice1.Value is set to Int(ggDiceGuess/2)=Int(7/2)=Int(3.5)=3 and MhDice2.Value is set to ggDiceGuess-MhDice1.Value=7-3=4. So indeed, MhDice1.Value+MhDice1.Value=3+4=7 is equal to 7.

An If…Else statement is then executed to check whether the player won or lost:

```
If (ggDiceGuess = MhDice1.Value + MhDice2.Value) Then
    frmFront.TegommPrompt.FileName =
        ➡ Left(App.Path, 2) + SIREN1_WAV_FILE_NAME
```

```
frmFront.TegommPrompt.Command = "Open"
frmFront.TegommPrompt.Command = "Prev"
frmFront.TegommPrompt.Command = "Play"

ggDiceScore = ggDiceScore + 1000

Else

frmFront.TegommPrompt.FileName =
    ➥ Left(App.Path, 2) + LAUGH1_WAV_FILE_NAME

frmFront.TegommPrompt.Command = "Open"
frmFront.TegommPrompt.Command = "Prev"
frmFront.TegommPrompt.Command = "Play"

ggDiceScore = ggDiceScore - 1000

End If
```

Finally, a series of If…ElseIf statements are executed to set the BevelInner and BevelOuter properties of the Score label according to the value of the `ggDiceScore` variable:

```
lblScore.Caption = "Score: $" + Str$(ggDiceScore)
If ggDiceScore = 0 Then
   lblScore.BevelInner = 0
   lblScore.BevelOuter = 0
ElseIf ggDiceScore > 0 Then
   lblScore.BevelInner = 2
   lblScore.BevelOuter = 2
ElseIf ggDiceScore < 0 Then
   lblScore.BevelInner = 1
   lblScore.BevelOuter = 2
End If
```

Attaching Code to the Double-Click Event of the Back Door Image

You'll now attach code to the Double-Click event of the `imgBackDoor` image.

❏ Enter the following code inside the `imgBackDoor_DblClick()` procedure of the `frmDice` form:

```
Sub imgBackDoor_DblClick ()

    If Line1.Visible = False Then
       Line1.Visible = True
    Else
       Line1.Visible = False
    End If

End Sub
```

The code you entered is executed whenever the user double-clicks the image control. This code toggles the Visible property of the line control so that it appears and disappears whenever the image is double-clicked.

> **NOTE**
>
> The preceding If...Else statement can be replaced with the following single statement:
>
> ```
> Line1.Visible = Not Line1.Visible
> ```

Attaching Code to the Click Event of the OK Button of the About Dialog Box

You'll now attach code to the Click event of the cmdClose button of the frmAbout form. Note that the Caption property of the cmdClose button is OK.

❑ Enter the following code inside the cmdClose_Click() procedure of the frmAbout form:

```
Sub cmdClose_Click ()

    Unload frmAbout

End Sub
```

The code you entered closes the About dialog box whenever the user clicks the OK button of the About dialog box.

Further Enhancements—You Are on Your Own...

The Dice program demonstrates how easy it is to implement dice programs with Visual Basic. However, as you can imagine, the Dice program is not a fair program. It is not a fair program not because of the back door implementation, but because the winnings are not proportional to the odds! For example, if you correctly guess the number 7, you win $1000. If you correctly guess the number 2, you also win $1000. This is obviously not fair, because the number 2 can come up only if both dice show 1. That is, there is only one combination that can result in the number 2. On the other hand, the number 7 can come up with the following combinations:

```
1+6
2+5
3+4
4+3
5+2
6+1
```

You have more chances to win if you guess the number 7 than if you guess the number 2. Therefore, you should win more money if you guess the number 2 (because you take more risk doing so).

You can improve the Dice program so that it will take into account the odds and pay the player accordingly.

Another possible improvement to the Dice program is the incorporation of a text box that lets the player select the betting amount. Recall that currently the Dice program assumes that you are betting $1000 dollars for each play. True, you are not losing any real money, but if you are trying to get the real feeling of how much you are going to lose in a casino, you better play with more realistic numbers (for example, $10 per bet is more appropriate for most people).

14

Creating 3D Virtual Reality—Based Programs (Part I)

In this chapter you'll learn how to create 3D virtual reality–based programs with Visual Basic.

What Is a 3D Virtual Reality–Based Application?

A virtual reality application is a combination of hardware and software that emulates real situations. To use it you attach sensors to the user. These sensors transmit signals to the computer, telling the computer the user's movements. For example, one sensor is attached to the user's head. As the user moves his or her head, the computer receives signals that tell the virtual reality program that the user moved his or her head. The program accordingly displays pictures that are viewed from the perspective of the user's eyes. In addition, you can attach sensors to the user's hands, legs, and fingers, and the program will react according to the user's actions. There are many ways to use virtual reality: as flight simulators, in games, for medical training, and more. As you can imagine, a virtual reality apparatus can be very costly. For example, an expensive flight simulator might include a cockpit apparatus that is connected to a computer. A pilot student can "fly" the virtual reality aircraft, and the virtual reality program sends signals to the cockpit instruments that make the student feel as though it is a real flight. The virtual reality program emulates various weather conditions, faulty instruments, and a variety of other conditions.

In recent years, virtual reality has found a new industry—the games industry. You can find virtual reality games in many amusement parks, where for a small fee sensors will be attached to your body and a set of goggles to your face. The goggles contain miniature displays that show you pictures of a room full of monsters and other bad creatures. The virtual reality apparatus is connected to a computer that detects your movements, and depending on the way you move and shoot, the virtual reality program either kills the monster or lets the monster kill you.

Basically, a virtual reality program is a program that progresses according to the user's input. In this chapter and Chapter 15, "Creating 3D Virtual Reality–Based Programs (Part II)," you'll implement the Room program, a program that lets you travel inside a 3D room.

Executing the Room.EXE Program

Before writing the prototype of the Room program yourself, execute the copy of it that resides inside the C:\LearnVB\Original\Room directory:

❑ Select Run from the File menu of the Program Manager and execute the
C:\LearnVB\Original\Room\Room.EXE program.

Windows responds by executing the Room.EXE program and displaying the window shown in Figure 14.1.

Figure 14.1.
The main window of the
Room.EXE program.

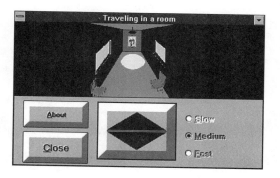

As you can see from Figure 14.1, the Room program displays a picture of a room.

You can move forward and backward inside the room by pressing the up and down arrows of the spin control.

❏ Press the up and down arrows of the spin control to move forward and backward inside the room.

The Room program responds by displaying the room according to your "movements." Several views of the room are shown in Figures 14.2 through 14.5.

Figure 14.2.
Traveling toward the
picture on the wall.

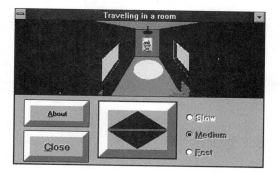

Figure 14.3.
Traveling toward the
picture on the wall (after
clicking the up arrow of the
spin control).

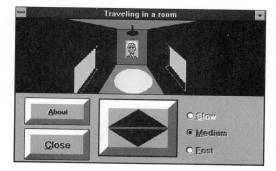

14

Figure 14.4.
Traveling toward the picture on the wall (getting a bit closer to the picture on the wall).

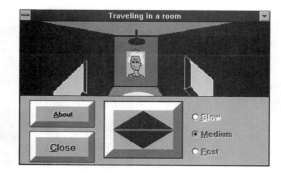

Figure 14.5.
Traveling toward the picture on the wall (reaching the wall).

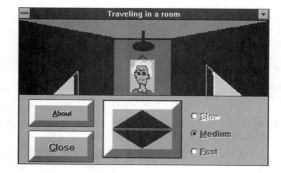

❏ Click the About button.

The Room program displays the About dialog box, as shown in Figure 14.6.

Figure 14.6.
The About dialog box of the Room program.

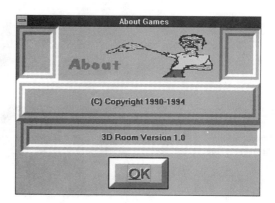

❑ Click the OK button of the About dialog box.

The Room program responds by closing the About dialog box.

The Room program contains Fast, Medium, and Slow radio buttons. These radio buttons enable you to travel at different speeds through the room.

❑ Experiment with the Room program and then click the Close button to terminate the Room program.

Implementing the Prototype of the Room Program

You'll now implement the prototype of the Room program.

❑ Select New Project from the File menu and save the new project: Save the new form as Room.FRM in the C:\LearnVB\Practice\Room directory. Save the new project file as Room.MAK in the C:\LearnVB\Practice\Room directory.

❑ Implement the frmRoom form according to the specifications in Table 14.1. When you finish implementing the form, it should look like the one shown in Figure 14.7.

Table 14.1. The Properties table of the frmRoom form.

Object: Form
Object Name: frmRoom

BackColor	= &H00000000&

Comment: This form has a black background.

BorderStyle	= 1 'Fixed Single
Caption	= "Traveling in a room"
Height	= 4305
Icon	= C:\LearnVB\Icons\GAMES.ICO
Left	= 1440
MaxButton	= 0 'False
Top	= 1335
Width	= 6585

Object: Image
Object Name: imgRoom

Comment: The Room.BMP picture is shown in Figure 14.8.

continues

Table 14.1. continued

Height	=	2295
Left	=	1920
Picture	=	C:\LearnVB\BMP\Room.BMP
Stretch	=	-1 'True
Top	=	0
Width	=	2295

Object: Picture
Object Name: picStatus

Comment: This picture control serves as the status bar.

Align	=	2 'Align Bottom
BackColor	=	&H00C0C0C0&
Height	=	1890
Left	=	0
Top	=	2010
Width	=	6465

Object: 3D button
Object Name: cmdAbout

Comment: This control is placed inside the status bar.

BevelWidth	=	10
Caption	=	"&About"
Font3D	=	2 'Raised w/heavy shading
ForeColor	=	&H00000000&
Height	=	735
Left	=	240
Top	=	120
Width	=	1695

Object: 3D radio button
Object Name: optSpeed

Comment: This is the first element of the optSpeed() array of option buttons. This control is placed inside the status bar.

Caption	=	"&Slow"
Font3D	=	4 'Inset w/heavy shading
FontName	=	"MS Sans Serif"
FontSize	=	9.75
ForeColor	=	&H0000FFFF&
Height	=	375
Index	=	0
Left	=	4440
Top	=	360
Width	=	1095

Object: 3D radio button
Object Name: optSpeed

Comment: This is the second element of the optSpeed() array of option buttons. This control is placed inside the status bar.

Caption	=	"&Medium"
Font3D	=	4 'Inset w/heavy shading
FontName	=	"MS Sans Serif"
FontSize	=	9.75
ForeColor	=	&H00FF0000&
Height	=	345
Index	=	1
Left	=	4440
Top	=	840
Value	=	-1 'True
Width	=	1335

Object: 3D radio button
Object Name: optSpeed

Comment: This is the third element of the optSpeed() array of option buttons. This control is placed inside the status bar.

Caption	=	"&Fast"
Font3D	=	4 'Inset w/heavy shading
FontName	=	"MS Sans Serif"
FontSize	=	9.75

continues

Table 14.1. continued

ForeColor	=	&H000000FF&
Height	=	330
Index	=	2
Left	=	4440
Top	=	1320
Width	=	975

Object: Spin (See Figure 1.39.)
Object Name: Spin1

Comment: This control is placed inside the status bar.

BackColor	=	&H00C0C0C0&
BorderThickness	=	2
Delay	=	50
Height	=	1575
Left	=	2160
ShadowBackColor	=	&H00C0C0C0&
TdThickness	=	15
Top	=	120
Width	=	2055
End		

Object: 3D button
Object Name: cmdClose

Comment: This control is placed inside the status bar.

BevelWidth	=	10
Caption	=	"&Close"
Font3D	=	2 'Raised w/heavy shading
FontName	=	"MS Sans Serif"
FontSize	=	12
ForeColor	=	&H00000000&
Height	=	855

Left	= 240
Top	= 960
Width	= 1695

Figure 14.7.
The frmRoom *form (in design mode).*

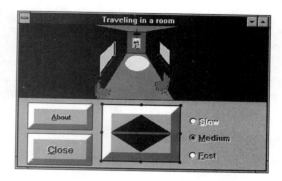

Figure 14.8.
The Room.BMP picture.

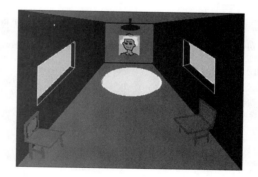

Implementing the About Dialog Box

You'll now implement the About dialog box of the Room program. When you finish implementing the About dialog box, it should look like the one shown in Figure 14.9.

The About dialog box of the Room program is almost identical to the About dialog box of the Cards program (which is covered in Chapter 10, "Creating Card Game Programs (Part I)," and Chapter 11, "Creating Card Game Programs (Part II)") and to the About dialog box of the Dice program (discussed in Chapter 12, "Creating Dice Game Programs (Part I)," and Chapter 13, "Creating Dice Game Programs (Part II)"). Therefore, you can quickly implement the About dialog box of the Room program in the following manner:

Figure 14.9.
The frmAbout form (in
design mode).

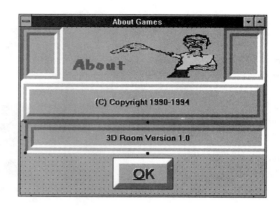

❏ Copy the About.FRM file from the C:\LearnVB\Practice\Cards directory to the
C:\LearnVB\Practice\Room directory.

❏ Select New Form from the File menu and select the
C:\LearnVB\Practice\Room\About.FRM file.

❏ Set the Caption property of the Panel3D2 control to 3D Room Version 1.0.

❏ Select Save Project from the File menu to save the project.

You have finished implementing the prototype of the Room program. In Chapter 15, "Creating
3D Virtual Reality–Based Programs (Part II)," you'll write the code of the Room program.

15

Creating 3D Virtual Reality—Based Programs (Part II)

In this chapter you'll write the code of the Room program, whose prototype you implemented in Chapter 14, "Creating 3D Virtual Reality–Based Programs (Part I)."

Declaring Variables Inside the General Declarations Section of the Room Form

You'll now declare variables inside the general declarations section of the frmRoom form.

❑ Enter the following code inside the general declarations section of the frmRoom form:

```
Option Explicit
Dim gMinRoomWidth
Dim gMinRoomHeight
Dim gMaxRoomWidth
Dim gMaxRoomHeight
Dim gRoomWidth
Dim gRoomHeight
Dim gInc
```

The code you entered declares variables. These variables are accessible from any procedure of the frmRoom form (because they are declared inside the general declarations section of the frmRoom form).

Attaching Code to the Click Event of the Close Button

You'll now attach code to the Click event of the Close button of the frmRoom form.

❑ Enter the following code inside the cmdClose_Click() procedure of the frmRoom form:

```
Sub cmdClose_Click ()

    Unload frmRoom

End Sub
```

The code you entered unloads the frmRoom form, and therefore the program terminates.

Attaching Code to the Click Event of the About Button

You'll now attach code to the Click event of the About button of the frmRoom form.

❑ Enter the following code inside the cmdAbout_Click() procedure of the frmRoom form:

```
Sub cmdAbout_Click ()

    frmAbout.Show 1

End Sub
```

The code you entered displays the About dialog box as a modal dialog box.

Attaching Code to the Load Event of the `frmRoom` Form

You'll now attach code to the `Form_Load()` procedure of the `frmRoom` form.

❑ Enter the following code inside the `Form_Load()` procedure of the `frmRoom` form:

```
Sub Form_Load ()

    gMinRoomWidth = imgRoom.Width
    gMinRoomHeight = imgRoom.Height
    gMaxRoomWidth = imgRoom.Width * 3
    gMaxRoomHeight = imgRoom.Height * 3
    gRoomWidth = imgRoom.Width
    gRoomHeight = imgRoom.Height
    gInc = 400

End Sub
```

The `Form_Load()` procedure is executed whenever the user starts the Room program.

The code you entered assigns the Width and Height properties of the image to the `gMinRoomWidth` and `gMinRoomHeight` global variables:

```
gMinRoomWidth = imgRoom.Width
gMinRoomHeight = imgRoom.Height
```

The `gMinRoomWidth` and `gMinRoomHeight` global variables hold the minimum width and height of the `imgRoom` image.

The code also assigns values to the `gMaxRoomWidth` and `gMaxRoomHeight` variables:

```
gMaxRoomWidth = imgRoom.Width * 3
gMaxRoomHeight = imgRoom.Height * 3
```

The initial width and height of the image are stored inside the `gRoomWidth` and `gRoomHeight` variables:

```
gRoomWidth = imgRoom.Width
gRoomHeight = imgRoom.Height
```

Finally, the `gInc` variable is assigned with a value:

```
gInc = 400
```

As you'll soon see, `gInc` represents the magnitude of the steps by which the image size is changing during the movements.

Attaching Code to the SpinUp Event of the Spin Control

You'll now attach code to the SpinUp event of the spin control.

❑ Enter the following code inside the `Spin1_SpinUp()` procedure of the `frmRoom` form:

```
Sub Spin1_SpinUp ()

    gRoomWidth = gRoomWidth + gInc
    gRoomHeight = gRoomHeight + gInc
    If gRoomWidth > gMaxRoomWidth Then
       gRoomWidth = gMaxRoomWidth
       gRoomHeight = gMaxRoomHeight
    End If
    imgRoom.Move
        ➥ Int((frmRoom.Width - imgRoom.Width) / 2),
        ➥ 0,
        ➥ gRoomWidth,
        ➥ gRoomHeight

End Sub
```

The code you entered is executed whenever the user presses the up arrow of the spin control.

The code you entered also updates the gRoomWidth and gRoomHeight variables:

```
gRoomWidth = gRoomWidth + gInc
gRoomHeight = gRoomHeight + gInc
```

The gRoomWidth and gRoomHeight variables hold the current Width and Height of the image control. Therefore, the preceding two statements increase by gInc the variables that hold the current width and height of the image.

An If statement is then executed to determine whether the maximum width has been reached:

```
If gRoomWidth > gMaxRoomWidth Then
   gRoomWidth = gMaxRoomWidth
   gRoomHeight = gMaxRoomHeight
End If
```

If the maximum width has been reached, the gRoomWidth and gRoomHeight variables are updated with the gMaxRoomWidth and gRoomHeight values.

Finally, the image is displayed using the Move method:

```
imgRoom.Move
    ➥ Int((frmRoom.Width - imgRoom.Width) / 2),
    ➥ 0,
    ➥ gRoomWidth,
    ➥ gRoomHeight
```

The first parameter of the Move method represents the coordinate of the left corner of the image. By setting the first parameter of the Move method to

```
Int((frmRoom.Width - imgRoom.Width) / 2),
```

you are moving the image so that its center appears at the center of the frmRoom form.

The second parameter of the Move method is 0. This means that the top coordinate of the image is at 0 (at the top of the form).

The third and fourth parameters of the Move method are the width and height of the image. These parameters are assigned with the gRoomWidth and gRoomHeight variables, which you already updated in this procedure.

So the image dimensions are increased, and then the image is moved. The `Move` method does two things:

- It moves the image to new coordinates (the first and second parameters of the `Move` method).
- It displays the image with new width and height (as supplied by the third and fourth parameters of the `Move` method).

Attaching Code to the SpinDown Event of the Spin Control

You'll now attach code to the SpinDown event of the spin control.

❑ Enter the following code inside the `Spin1_SpinDown()` procedure of the `frmRoom` form:

```
Sub Spin1_SpinDown ()

    gRoomWidth = gRoomWidth - gInc
    gRoomHeight = gRoomHeight - gInc
    If gRoomWidth < gMinRoomWidth Then
        gRoomWidth = gMinRoomWidth
        gRoomHeight = gMinRoomHeight
    End If

    imgRoom.Move
    ➥ Int((frmRoom.Width - imgRoom.Width) / 2),
    ➥ 0,
    ➥ gRoomWidth,
    ➥ gRoomHeight

End Sub
```

The code you entered is executed whenever the user presses the down arrow of the spin control.

Note that the code that you entered inside the `Spin1_SpinDown()` procedure is very similar to the code you entered inside the `Spin1_SpinUp()` procedure. The only difference between the two procedures is that the `Spin1_SpinUp()` procedure increases the size of the image and the `Spin1_SpinDown()` procedure decreases the size of the image control.

Attaching Code to the Option Buttons of the Room Form

You'll now attach code to the Click event of the option buttons of the `frmRoom` form.

❑ Enter the following code inside the `optSpeed_Click()` procedure of the `frmRoom` form:

```
Sub optSpeed_Click (Index As Integer,
                    Value As Integer)

    Select Case Index
        Case 0
            gInc = 50
        Case 1
            gInc = 400
```

```
        Case 2
                gInc = 1000
    End Select
```

End Sub

Recall that optSpeed() is an array of option buttons. Note that Index is the first parameter of the optSpeed_Click() procedure. If the user clicks the first option button of the optSpeed() array, Index is equal to 0, if the user clicks the second option button, Index is equal to 1, and so on.

The Select Case statement updates the gInc variable according to the value of Index. If the first option button was clicked, gInc is set to 50, if the second option button was clicked, gInc is set to 400, and so on. Recall that the size of the image is increased or decreased by gInc. (See the sections on the Spin1_SpinUp() and Spin1_SpinDown() procedures.)

Attaching Code to the Click Event of the OK Button of the About Dialog Box

You'll now attach code to the OK button (the cmdClose button) of the About dialog box.

❑ Enter the following code inside the cmdClose_Click() procedure of the frmAbout form:

Sub cmdClose_Click ()

```
    Unload frmAbout
```

End Sub

The code you entered unloads the frmAbout form.

You have now finished entering the code of the Room program.

❑ Select Save Project from the File menu to save the project.

❑ Execute the Room program and verify that it operates correctly.

Further Enhancements—You Are on Your Own . . .

You can improve and enhance the Room program in several ways. For example, instead of only enabling the user to move inside the 3D room by pressing the arrows of the spin control, you can alter the program so that the user can move in one of the following ways: using the mouse device, using the keyboard keys, or even through sensors attached to the user that send signals to the Room program via the parallel port, telling the Room program how the user moves. With any of these methods, the user's movements cause the picture of the 3D room to change accordingly.

The Room program demonstrates how to move only forward and backward. You can add additional BMP pictures that enable the user to move horizontally. For example, you can place another spin control inside the status bar and set its SpinOrientation property to Horizontal. The user will be able to move inside the room in the horizontal direction by supplying different values to the parameters of the Move method. After the user moves to the right or to the left, the program should display the room from a different view by showing a different BMP file. For example, after the user moves horizontally several times, you can have the program display a new BMP picture similar to the one shown in Figure 15.1. As you can see in Figure 15.1, the user now faces the room's window. The user can then move toward or away from the window, or he or she can use the horizontal spin control again to display the original view.

Figure 15.1.
The new BMP picture of
the room.

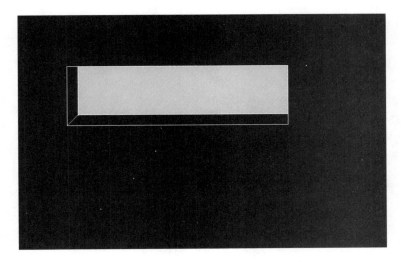

As you can imagine, you can design some impressive programs that enable your user to travel from one room to another. That is, when the user reaches a door at the end of the room, the user will have to open the door by pressing the space bar, for example, and then a new BMP file showing the next room is displayed.

Another improvement you can make to the Room program is to add background sounds (such as music or footsteps) during the movement.

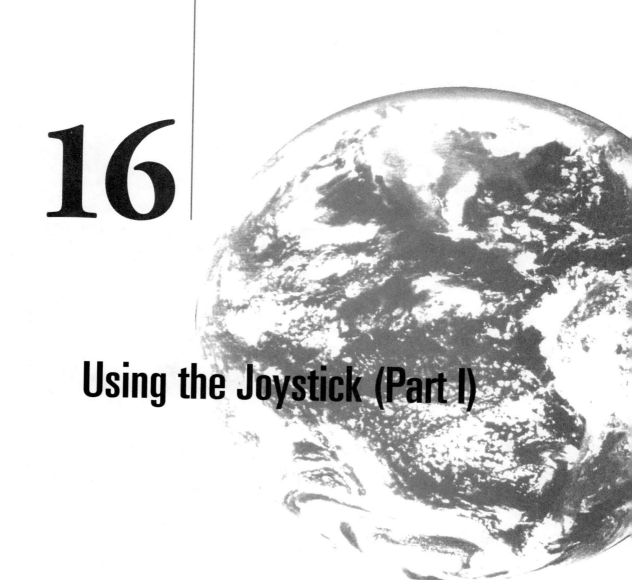

16

Using the Joystick (Part I)

In this chapter and Chapter 17, "Using the Joystick (Part II)," you'll learn how to incorporate a joystick into your Visual Basic programs.

Executing the Joystick.EXE Program

Before writing the Joystick program yourself, first execute the copy of it that resides inside your C:\LearnVB\Original\Joystick directory.

❏ Select Run from the File Manager of Windows and execute the C:\LearnVB\Original\Joystick\Joystick.EXE program.

> *Windows responds by executing the Joystick.EXE program and displaying the window shown in Figure 16.1.*

Figure 16.1.
The main window of the
Joystick.EXE program.

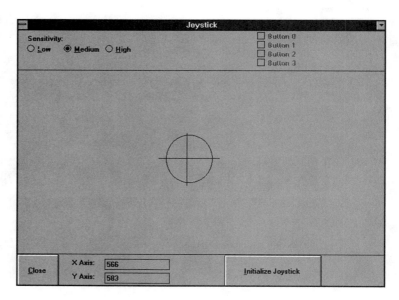

NOTE

If the Joystick.EXE program does not detect the presence of a joystick in the system, it displays a message telling the user that the joystick is not connected.

> **NOTE**
>
> To connect a joystick to your system, you need a game port. A game port card can be purchased as a card that you have to install into one of the slots of the PC. Alternatively, you can use a sound card that has a game port incorporated into it.

> **NOTE**
>
> You do not need any joystick driver software to use this program because TegoMM.VBX can handle the joystick without any drivers.

Calibrating the Joystick

Typically, you have to calibrate the joystick. This is accomplished by adjusting the two potentiometers of the joystick device (one is called the *X-axis trim control*, and the other is called the *Y-axis trim control*).

Here is how you calibrate the joystick:

❑ Leave the lever of the joystick in its natural position, turn the X-adjust potentiometer of the joystick clockwise until you cannot rotate it anymore, and note the number that is displayed in the X Axis text box of the Joystick program.

❑ Leave the lever of the joystick in its natural position, turn the X-adjust potentiometer of the joystick counterclockwise until you cannot rotate it anymore, and note the number that is displayed in the X Axis text box of the Joystick program.

❑ Leave the lever of the joystick in its natural position and turn the X-adjust potentiometer of the joystick until the number that is displayed in the X Axis text box of the Joystick program is equal to the average of the two numbers that you extracted in the preceding two steps. For example, if one number is 0 and the other number is 1600, you need to adjust the X-adjust potentiometer until you see the number (0+1600)/2=800 displayed inside the X Axis text box.

❑ Repeat the preceding three steps for the Y-adjust potentiometer.

❑ Click the Initialize Joystick button.

The joystick is now calibrated.

16

> **NOTE**
> _____
>
> Some joystick devices have a set of two joysticks (Joystick A and Joystick B).
>
> The Joystick program uses only Joystick A. So if your joystick device has two joysticks, you should calibrate Joystick A.
>
> In Chapter 17 you'll learn how to access from your program both Joystick A and Joystick B.

> **NOTE**
> _____
>
> As you can see, the joystick needs calibration. Typically, you will incorporate a Calibrate menu that lets the user calibrate the joystick. It is necessary to calibrate the joystick because the hardware of the joystick uses an RC technology, which depends on electronic components such as resistors and capacitors to implement timing circuitry.
>
> The Calibration process is a little annoying, but many users like to play games with the joystick, because unlike the keyboard and the mouse devices, the joystick gives the user a sense of having "power" in his or her hands.

Shooting Bullets with the Joystick

A typical joystick has two buttons.

❏ Press the buttons of the joystick.

As you press the buttons of the joystick, the Joystick program shoots bullets, and a machine gun noise is played through the sound card.

Figures 16.2 and 16.3 show the screen after the user has shot several bullets.

Note that the X Axis and Y Axis text boxes display the current coordinates of the joystick, and the Button 0 through Button 3 checkboxes (on the toolbar) display the button(s) that is currently pressed.

You can also change the sensitivity of the joystick by selecting the Low, Medium, or High option buttons.

❏ Experiment with the Joystick program and then click the Close button to exit the program.

Figure 16.2.
Shooting bullets with the
Joystick program.

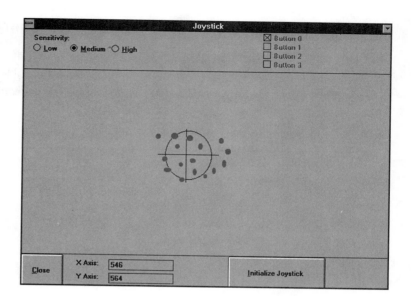

Figure 16.3.
Tearing up the target by
shooting more bullets at
the target.

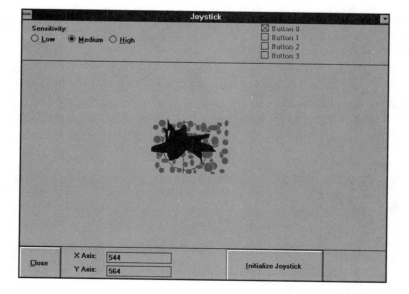

16

Implementing the Prototype of the Joystick Program

You'll now implement the prototype of the Joystick program.

☐ Implement the frmJoystick form according to the specifications in Table 16.1. When you finish implementing the form, it should look like the one shown in Figure 16.4.

Table 16.1. The Properties table of the frmJoystick form.

Object: Form
Object Name: frmJoystick

BackColor	=	&H00C0C0C0&
BorderStyle	=	1 'Fixed Single
Caption	=	"Joystick"
Height	=	6690
Icon	=	C:\LearnVB\ICONS\Joystick.ICO
Left	=	1140
MaxButton	=	0 'False
Top	=	150
Width	=	8025
WindowState	=	2 'Maximized

Object: Picture box
Object Name: picStatus

Comment: This picture box serves as a status bar.

Align	=	2 'Align Bottom
BackColor	=	&H00C0C0C0&
Height	=	885
Left	=	0
Top	=	5400
Width	=	7905

Object: Text box
Object Name: txtY

Alignment	=	2 'Center
BackColor	=	&H00C0C0C0&
Enabled	=	0 'False

Height	=	285
Left	=	2280
Top	=	480
Width	=	1695

Object: Text box
Object Name: txtX

Alignment	=	2 'Center
BackColor	=	&H00C0C0C0&
Enabled	=	0 'False
Height	=	285
Left	=	2280
Top	=	120
Width	=	1695

Object: Command button
Object Name: cmdClose

Caption	=	"&Close"
Height	=	855
Left	=	0
Top	=	0
Width	=	1095

Object: Command button
Object Name: cmdInitialize

BackColor	=	&H00FFFFFF&
Caption	=	"&Initialize Joystick"
Height	=	855
Left	=	5400
Top	=	0
Width	=	2535

Object: Label
Object Name: lblY

BackColor	=	&H00C0C0C0&
Caption	=	"Y Axis:"

continues

Table 16.1. continued

Height	=	255
Left	=	1440
Top	=	480
Width	=	855

Object: Label
Object Name: lblX

BackColor	=	&H00C0C0C0&
Caption	=	"X Axis:"
Height	=	255
Left	=	1440
Top	=	120
Width	=	855

Object: Advanced multimedia control
Object Name: TegommJoy

Height	=	330
Left	=	4080
Top	=	4800
Visible	=	0 'False
Width	=	3510

Object: Picture box
Object Name: picToolbar

Comment: This picture box serves as a toolbar.

Align	=	1 'Align Top
BackColor	=	&H00C0C0C0&
Height	=	1095
Left	=	0
Top	=	0
Width	=	7905

Object: Checkbox
Object Name: chkB0

BackColor	=	&H00C0C0C0&
Caption	=	"Button 0"
Enabled	=	0 'False
Height	=	255
Left	=	6240
Top	=	0
Width	=	1335

Object: Checkbox
Object Name: chkB1

BackColor	=	&H00C0C0C0&
Caption	=	"Button 1"
Enabled	=	0 'False
Height	=	255
Left	=	6240
Top	=	240
Width	=	1335

Object: Checkbox
Object Name: chkB2

BackColor	=	&H00C0C0C0&
Caption	=	"Button 2"
Enabled	=	0 'False
Height	=	255
Left	=	6240
Top	=	480
Width	=	1335

Object: Checkbox
Object Name: chkB3

BackColor	=	&H00C0C0C0&
Caption	=	"Button 3"
Enabled	=	0 'False

continues

16

Table 16.1. continued

Height	=	255
Left	=	6240
Top	=	720
Width	=	1335

Object: Option button
Object Name: optSensitivity

Comment: This is the first element of the optSensitivity() array of option buttons.

BackColor	=	&H00C0C0C0&
Caption	=	"&Low"
Height	=	255
Index	=	0
Left	=	240
Top	=	360
Width	=	855

Object: Option button
Object Name: optSensitivity

Comment: This is the second element of the optSensitivity() array of option buttons.

BackColor	=	&H00C0C0C0&
Caption	=	"&Medium"
Height	=	255
Index	=	1
Left	=	1200
Top	=	360
Value	=	-1 'True
Width	=	975

Object: Option button
Object Name: optSensitivity

Comment: This is the third element of the optSensitivity() array of option buttons.

BackColor	=	&H00C0C0C0&
Caption	=	"&High"

Height	=	255
Index	=	2
Left	=	2280
Top	=	360
Width	=	975

Object: Label
Object Name: Label1

Alignment	=	2 'Center
BackColor	=	&H00C0C0C0&
Caption	=	"Sensitivity:"
Height	=	255
Left	=	120
Top	=	120
Width	=	1215

Object: Image
Object Name: imgTarget

Comment: This is element 0 of the imgTarget() array of images.

Height	=	1500
Index	=	0
Left	=	2880
Picture	=	C:\LearnVB\BMP\Target01.BMP
Top	=	2280
Width	=	2040

Object: Image
Object Name: imgTarget

Comment: This is element 1 of the imgTarget() array of images.

Height	=	495
Index	=	1
Left	=	120
Picture	=	C:\LearnVB\BMP\Target01.BMP
Stretch	=	-1 'True
Top	=	4800

continues

Table 16.1. continued

Visible	= 0	'False
Width	= 495	

Object: Image
Object Name: imgTarget

Comment: This is element 2 of the imgTarget() array of images.

Height	= 495	
Index	= 2	
Left	= 720	
Picture	= C:\LearnVB\BMP\Target02.BMP	
Stretch	= -1	'True
Top	= 4800	
Visible	= 0	'False
Width	= 495	

Object: Image
Object Name: imgTarget

Comment: This is element 3 of the imgTarget() array of images.

Height	= 495	
Index	= 3	
Left	= 1320	
Picture	= C:\LearnVB\BMP\Target03.BMP	
Stretch	= -1	'True
Top	= 4800	
Visible	= 0	'False
Width	= 495	

Object: Image
Object Name: imgTarget

Comment: This is element 4 of the imgTarget() array of images.

Height	= 495	
Index	= 4	

Left	= 1920
Picture	= C:\LearnVB\BMP\Target04.BMP
Stretch	= -1 'True
Top	= 4800
Visible	= 0 'False
Width	= 495

Object: Image
Object Name: imgTarget

Comment: This is element 5 of the imgTarget() array of images.

Height	= 495
Index	= 5
Left	= 2520
Picture	= C:\LearnVB\BMP\Target05.BMP
Stretch	= -1 'True
Top	= 4800
Visible	= 0 'False
Width	= 495

Object: Image
Object Name: imgTarget

Comment: This is element 6 of the imgTarget() array of images.

Height	= 495
Index	= 6
Left	= 3120
Picture	= C:\LearnVB\BMP\Target06.BMP
Stretch	= -1 'True
Top	= 4800
Visible	= 0 'False
Width	= 495

Figure 16.4.
The frmJoystick form
(in design mode).

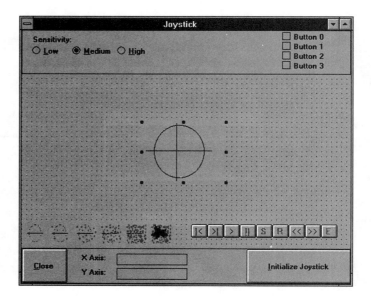

You have finished implementing the prototype of the Joystick program. In Chapter 17 you'll write the code of the program.

17

Using the
Joystick (Part II)

In this chapter you'll write the code of the Joystick program whose prototype you implemented in Chapter 16, "Using the Joystick (Part I)."

Declaring Variables Inside the General Declarations Section

You'll now declare variables and functions inside the general declarations section of the `frmJoystick` form.

❏ Enter the following code inside the general declarations section of the `frmJoystick` form:

```
Option Explicit
Dim gSensitivity As Integer
Dim gJoyNormalX, gJoyNormalY As Long
Dim gConnected As Integer

Declare Function tegScanJoyPos Lib "TegoMM.VBX" ()
    ➥ As Integer

Declare Function tegGetJoyPos Lib "TegoMM.VBX"
    ➥ (ByVal iAxis As Integer) As Long

Declare Function tegGetJoyButton Lib "TegoMM.VBX"
    ➥ (ByVal iButton As Integer) As Integer
```

The code you entered declares several variables. These variables are therefore accessible by any procedure inside the `frmJoystick` form.

The code that you entered also declares three functions from the TegoMM.VBX control.

Attaching Code to the Click Event of the Close Button

You'll now attach code to the Click event of the Close button.

❏ Enter the following code inside the `cmdClose_Click()` procedure of the `frmJoystick` form:

```
Sub cmdClose_Click ()

    End

End Sub
```

The code you entered terminates the Joystick program whenever the user clicks the Close button.

Attaching Code to the Load Event of the `frmJoystick` Form

You'll now attach code to the Load event of the `frmJoystick` form.

❏ Enter the following code inside the `Form_Load()` procedure of the `frmJoystick` form:

```
Sub Form_Load ()

    gSensitivity = 2
    TegommJoy.DeviceType = "WaveAudio"
```

```
TegommJoy.FileName =
   ➥ Left(App.Path, 2) +
   ➥ "\LearnVB\WAV\Gun.WAV"

TegommJoy.Command = "Open"
cmdInitialize_Click
TegommJoy.UpdateInterval = 50

End Sub
```

The code you entered is executed whenever the Joystick program starts.

The `gSensitivity` variable is set to 2:

```
gSensitivity = 2
```

As you'll see later, the `gSensitivity` variable is used to determine the sensitivity of the joystick. That is, the `gSensitivity` variable determines how much the image of the target moves in response to the joystick movements.

The DeviceType property of the multimedia control is set to play WAV files through the PC speaker:

```
TegommJoy.DeviceType = "WaveAudio"
```

The pathname and filename of the WAV file are set:

```
TegommJoy.FileName =
   ➥ Left(App.Path, 2) +
   ➥ "\LearnVB\WAV\Gun.WAV"
```

The `Open` command is issued:

```
TegommJoy.Command = "Open"
```

The `cmdInitialize_Click()` procedure is then executed:

```
cmdInitialize_Click
```

As you'll see in the next section, the `cmdInitialize_Click()` procedure performs initialization tasks.

Finally, the UpdateInterval property of the multimedia control is set to 50:

```
TegommJoy.UpdateInterval = 50
```

This means that from now on the `TegommJoy_StatusUpdate()` procedure is automatically executed every 50 milliseconds.

Attaching Code to the Click Event of the Initialize Button

You'll now attach code to the Click event of the Initialize button of the `frmJoystick` form.

❑ Enter the following code inside the `cmdInitialize_Click()` procedure of the `frmJoystick` form:

```
Sub cmdInitialize_Click ()
```

```
' Get the current X and Y coordinates of the joystick.
' Because the joystick is now assumed to be in its
' normal position, these X,Y coordinates are the
' joystick normal coordinates
gConnected = tegScanJoyPos()      ' Scan the joystick
gJoyNormalX = tegGetJoyPos(0)     ' Get X coordinate
gJoyNormalY = tegGetJoyPos(1)     ' Get Y coordinate

' If joystick is not connected, display "NC"
' inside the X and Y text boxes, and display
' an error message box.
If gConnected = False Then
   txtX.Text = "NC"
   txtY.Text = "NC"
   MsgBox "The joystick is not connected",
       ➥ 0,
       ➥ "Joystick Error"
End If
```

End Sub

The code you entered is executed whenever the user clicks the Initialize button.

The `tegScanJoyPos()` function (which you declared inside the general declarations section) is executed:

```
gConnected = tegScanJoyPos()      ' Scan the joystick
```

The returned value from the `tegScanJoyPos()` function indicates whether a joystick is detected. If gConnected is equal to 0, no joystick is present.

The `tegGetJoyPos()` function is then executed twice to determine the X and Y coordinates of the joystick:

```
gJoyNormalX = tegGetJoyPos(0)     ' Get X coordinate
gJoyNormalY = tegGetJoyPos(1)     ' Get Y coordinate
```

When you supply 0 as the parameter of the `tegGetJoyPos()` function, the `tegGetJoyPos()` function returns the X position, and when you supply 1 as the parameter of the `tegGetJoyPos()` function, the `tegGetJoyPos()` function returns the Y position.

So at this point gJoyNormalX and gJoyNormalY hold the X and Y coordinates of the joystick when the joystick lever is in its normal position. That is, you assume that when the `cmdInitialize_Click()` procedure is executed the user leaves the joystick lever in its normal position.

An If statement is then executed to determine whether the joystick is connected:

```
If gConnected = False Then
   txtX.Text = "NC"
   txtY.Text = "NC"
   MsgBox "The joystick is not connected",
       ➥ 0,
       ➥ "Joystick Error"
End If
```

If the joystick is not connected, the user is prompted with a message box telling the user that the joystick is not connected.

> **NOTE**
> _____
>
> You use the `tegScanJoyPos()` and `tegGetJoyPos()` functions to extract the current
> position of the joystick. You must call `tegScanJoyPos()` before calling `tegGetJoyPos()`. The
> parameters that you pass to `tegGetJoyPos()` determine which axis position is returned. The
> returned value of the `tegScanJoyPos()` determines whether the joystick is currently con-
> nected to the PC.
>
> If the joystick device has a set of two joysticks (Joystick A and Joystick B), you can use the
> following code to extract the X,Y coordinates of the two joysticks:
>
> ```
> ' Get the current position of joystick A
> ' and joystick B.
> gConnected = tegScanJoyPos() 'Scan the joystick
> XPosA = tegGetJoyPos(0) 'Get X coordinate of joystick A
> YPosA = tegGetJoyPos(1) 'Get Y coordinate of joystick A
> XPosB = tegGetJoyPos(2) 'Get X coordinate of joystick B
> XPosB = tegGetJoyPos(3) 'Get X coordinate of joystick B
> ' If the joystick device is not connected, beep.
> If gConnected = 0 Then Beep
> ```
>
> Note that if the joystick device does not have a second joystick (Joystick B), the statements
>
> ```
> XPosB = tegGetJoyPos(2)
> YPosB = tegGetJoyPos(3)
> ```
>
> will return -1.

Attaching Code to the Click Event of the `optSensitivity()` Array of Option Buttons

You'll now attach code to the Click event of the `optSensitivity` array of option buttons.

❏ Enter the following code inside the `optSensitivity_Click()` procedure of the `frmJoystick` form:

```
Sub optSensitivity_Click (Index As Integer)

    Select Case Index
        Case 0
            gSensitivity = 3 ' Low sensitivity
        Case 1
            gSensitivity = 2 ' Medium sensitivity
        Case 2
            gSensitivity = 1 ' High sensitivity
    End Select

End Sub
```

17

The code you entered sets the gSensitivity variable in accordance with the selected option button. Note that the parameter of the optSensitivity_Click() procedure is Index:

```
Sub optSensitivity_Click (Index As Integer)
    ....
    ....
    ....
End Sub
```

If the user clicked the first option button, Index is equal to 0, if the user clicked the second option button, Index is equal to 1, and so on.

Attaching Code to the StatusUpdate Event of the Multimedia Control

You'll now attach code to the StatusUpdate event of the multimedia control.

❑ Enter the following code inside the TegommJoy_StatusUpdate() procedure of the frmJoystick form:

```
Sub TegommJoy_StatusUpdate ()

    Dim XPos, YPos As Long
    Dim ImageX, ImageY As Integer
    Static PictureNumber

    ' If joystick is not connected terminate the procedure
    If gConnected = 0 Then Exit Sub

    ' Get the joystick current position
    gConnected = tegScanJoyPos()   ' Scan the joystick
    XPos = tegGetJoyPos(0)         ' Get the X coordinate
    YPos = tegGetJoyPos(1)         ' Get the Y coordinate

    ' If the the joystick is not connected, display "NC"
    ' inside the X and Y text boxes, and terminate this
    ' procedure
    If gConnected = 0 Then
       txtX.Text = "NC"
       txtY.Text = "NC"
       Exit Sub
    End If


    ' Display the X and Y coordinates of the joystick
    txtX.Text = XPos
    txtY.Text = YPos

    ' Move the image according to the current
    ' joystick position.
    ImageX = 240 + (XPos - gJoyNormalX) / gSensitivity
    ImageY = 184 + (YPos - gJoyNormalY) / gSensitivity
    imgTarget(0).Left = ImageX
    imgTarget(0).Top = ImageY
```

```
' If the joystick's button #0 or button #1 is pressed,
' play the GUN.WAV file.
If tegGetJoyButton(0) = True Or
        ➥ tegGetJoyButton(1) = True Then

    TegommJoy.Command = "Prev"
    TegommJoy.Command = "Play"
    PictureNumber = PictureNumber + 1
    If PictureNumber = 7 Then PictureNumber = 0
    imgTarget(0).Picture =
            ➥ imgTarget(PictureNumber).Picture
Else
    imgTarget(0).Picture = imgTarget(1).Picture
End If
' Is the joystick's button #0 pressed?
If tegGetJoyButton(0) = True Then
    chkB0.Value = 1
Else
    chkB0.Value = 0
End If

' Is the joystick's button #1 pressed?
If tegGetJoyButton(1) = True Then
    chkB1.Value = 1
Else
    chkB1.Value = 0
End If
' Is the joystick's button #2 pressed?
If tegGetJoyButton(2) = True Then
    chkB2.Value = 1
Else
    chkB2.Value = 0
End If
' Is the joystick's button #3 pressed?
If tegGetJoyButton(3) = True Then
    chkB3.Value = 1
Else
    chkB3.Value = 0
End If

End Sub
```

The code you entered is executed automatically every 50 milliseconds (because inside the `Form_Load()` procedure you set the UpdateInterval property of the multimedia control to 50).

The procedure declares local variables and a `Static` variable:

```
Dim XPos, YPos As Long
Dim ImageX, ImageY As Integer
Static PictureNumber
```

If `gConnected` is equal to 0, the joystick is not connected, and the procedure is terminated with the `Exit Sub` statement:

```
If gConnected = 0 Then Exit Sub
```

If the Joystick is connected, the tegScanJoyPos() and tegGetJoyPos() functions are executed to extract the X and Y coordinates of the current position of the joystick:

```
' Get the joystick current position
gConnected = tegScanJoyPos()   ' Scan the joystick
XPos = tegGetJoyPos(0)         ' Get the X coordinate
YPos = tegGetJoyPos(1)         ' Get the Y coordinate
```

An If statement is then executed to determine whether the joystick is still connected:

```
    ' If the joystick is not connected, display "NC"
    ' inside the X and Y text boxes, and terminate this
    ' procedure
    If gConnected = 0 Then
       txtX.Text = "NC"
       txtY.Text = "NC"
       Exit Sub
    End If
```

Don't forget that the TegommJoy_StatusUpdate() procedure is executed every 50 milliseconds, and therefore you need to ensure that the joystick is still connected to the system. In other words, it is possible that during the execution of the Form_Load() procedure the joystick was connected, and later the user removed the joystick from the system.

If the joystick is connected, the txtX and txtY text boxes are updated:

```
    ' Display the X and Y coordinates of the joystick
    txtX.Text = XPos
    txtY.Text = YPos
```

The image is then moved to a new position that is determined by the position of the joystick:

```
    ' Move according to the current
    ' joystick position.
    ImageX = 240 + (XPos - gJoyNormalX) / gSensitivity
    ImageY = 184 + (YPos - gJoyNormalY) / gSensitivity
    imgTarget(0).Left = ButtonX
    imgTarget(0).Top = ButtonY
```

If Button 0 or Button 1 is pressed, a machine-gun noise is played, and the Picture property of the image is set to the new sequential picture:

```
' If the joystick's button #0 or button #1 is pressed,
    ' play the GUN.WAV file.
    If tegGetJoyButton(0) = True Or
         ➥ tegGetJoyButton(1) = True Then

       TegommJoy.Command = "Prev"
       TegommJoy.Command = "Play"
       PictureNumber = PictureNumber + 1
       If PictureNumber = 7 Then PictureNumber = 0
       imgTarget(0).Picture =
              ➥ imgTarget(PictureNumber).Picture
    Else
       imgTarget(0).Picture = imgTarget(1).Picture
    End If
```

If Button 0 or Button 1 is not pressed, the statement under the `Else` is executed. The statement under the `Else` sets the Picture property of the `imgTarget(0)` image to the Picture property of the `imgTarget(1)` image:

```
imgTarget(0).Picture = imgTarget(1).Picture
```

Finally, a series of `If...Else` statements is executed to determine whether the buttons of the joystick are pressed, and to set the corresponding checkboxes accordingly:

```
' Is the joystick's button #0 pressed?
If tegGetJoyButton(0) = True Then
   chkB0.Value = 1
Else
   chkB0.Value = 0
End If
' Is the joystick's button #1 pressed?
If tegGetJoyButton(1) = True Then
   chkB1.Value = 1
Else
   chkB1.Value = 0
End If
' Is the joystick's button #2 pressed?
If tegGetJoyButton(2) = True Then
   chkB2.Value = 1
Else
   chkB2.Value = 0
End If
' Is the joystick's button #3 pressed?
If tegGetJoyButton(3) = True Then
   chkB3.Value = 1
Else
   chkB3.Value = 0
End If
```

As you can see, the `tegGetJoyButton()` function determines whether a joystick button is pressed.

❏ Select Save Project from the File menu.

❏ Select Start from the Run menu and verify that the program operates correctly.

Further Enhancements—You Are on Your Own . . .

The Joystick program demonstrates how easy it is to incorporate a joystick into your Visual Basic programs.

You can improve the Joystick program by displaying a moving image of a target on the screen and letting the user shoot at the target. If the user hits the target, your program will reward the user by giving the user points. You can detect whether the user hits or misses the moving target by comparing the coordinates of the moving target with the coordinates of the joystick at the time that the joystick's button is pressed.

Putting All the Games Together

Inside the C:\LearnVB\Original\Games directory you'll find the Games.EXE program with its source code. This program is the prototype of the Games program, a program that combines the Dice, Cards, Room, and Joystick programs. You may want to combine these games programs into a single program.

You can test the prototype of the Games program:

❏ Select Run from the File menu of the Program Manager and execute the C:\LearnVB\Original\Games\Games.EXE program.

> *Windows responds by executing the Games.EXE program and displaying the window shown in Figure 17.1.*

Figure 17.1.
The main window of the
Games.EXE program.

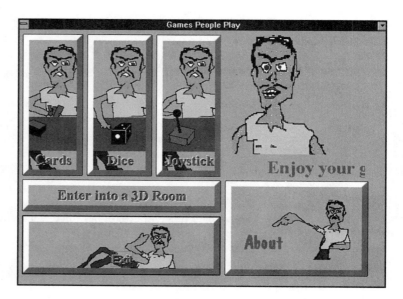

The actual games are not implemented in the Games.EXE program. However, it is easy to implement the games by using the code that you wrote already for the Cards, Dice, Room, and Joystick programs.

18

Visual Basic Tools: Creating Dynamic Linked Libraries for Visual Basic

Visual Basic is a highly modular programming language. This means that with Visual Basic you can "plug" external software modules into your project. These software modules can be dynamic linked libraries (DLLs) or VBX controls. In this chapter you will learn how to write your own DLLs.

18

Why Use DLLs?

Occasionally, you need a feature in your Visual Basic program that does not exist in the out-of-the-box Visual Basic package. In such cases, you have to "add" this feature to Visual Basic by using a DLL.

Windows contains many DLL functions that you can use from within your Visual Basic programs. For example, Windows contains DLL functions that enable you to determine the path of the \Windows\System directory, determine the amount of free space in the system, and do many other tasks. In fact, currently there are well over 400 documented DLL functions in Windows. Naturally, you don't need to use all of these Windows DLL functions, because the designers of Visual Basic incorporated most of the Windows DLL functions into Visual Basic. For example, one of the DLL functions of Windows causes the speaker to beep. However, it is much more convenient to use the Beep statement of Visual Basic than to use an external DLL function. Nevertheless, sometimes you'll find that you must use a feature that does not exist either in Visual Basic or in any of the Windows DLL functions. For example, in the appendixes of this book you learn how to use a DLL function that enables you to play WAV files through the PC speaker. This feature does not exist either in Visual Basic or in any of the Windows DLL functions. In such cases, you have to purchase a third-party DLL file that accomplishes your desired task.

You can also write your own DLL functions. However, to write a DLL function you need to know how to use the C programming language, and you need to use a C compiler. The rest of this chapter shows how you can use the Microsoft Visual C/C++ compiler to write your own DLL.

> **NOTE**
>
> You cannot write DLLs with Visual Basic. In this chapter, you'll write a DLL by using the C programming language and the Microsoft Visual C++ package.
>
> This chapter assumes that you are familiar with the C programming language and that you own the Microsoft Visual C++ package.

The Create Your Own DLL Tutorial

On the book's CD you'll find the directory \LearnVB\Tutor18. This tutorial includes a step-by-step explanation of how to create your own DLLs for Visual Basic.

The tutorial is supplied as a Word for Windows Version 6.0 document. This means that to read the tutorial you need to use the Microsoft Word for Windows Version 6.0 word processing program. The name of the DOC file is Tutor18.DOC.

If you don't have access to the Word for Windows word processing program, you can read the tutorial using your own word processing or text editor program, because the \LearnVB\Tutor18 directory of the CD also contains the text file (*.TXT) of this tutorial.

The tutorial shows you how to create your own DLL, and then it shows you how to test the DLL and how to use the DLL from within your programs.

19

Creating Your Own
VBX Controls

19

So far in this book you have written Visual Basic programs that use VBX controls created by other people. In this chapter you will create your own VBX control. The VBX control you'll create could be used by Visual Basic programs and by any other programming language that supports VBX controls (for example, Microsoft Visual C++ and Borland C++ 4.0). Therefore, after you finish implementing your VBX control, you could distribute it to Visual Basic programmers as well as to Microsoft Visual C++ and Borland C++ programmers.

> **NOTE**
>
> To create a VBX control you need to use a programming language that can create Windows DLLs.
>
> In this chapter you will use the C programming language to create a VBX control. Therefore, a prerequisite for this chapter is some knowledge of the C programming language.
>
> The tutorial in this chapter uses the Visual C++ compiler. If you have another C compiler that can create Windows DLLs, you'll still be able to follow the tutorial, but you will have to compile and link the source files in a different way (as required by your C compiler).

The MYCLOCK.VBX Control

The VBX control that you will create in this chapter is called MYCLOCK.VBX (MyClock). As implied by its name, this VBX control is used to display the current time. As always, before you start writing the code yourself, you will first see a copy of this control in action. This way you'll have a better understanding of what the control should do.

The Create Your Own VBX Tutorial

On the book's CD you'll find the directory \LearnVB\Tutor19. This tutorial includes a step-by-step explanation of how to create your own VBX custom control for Visual Basic.

The tutorial is supplied as a Word for Windows Version 6.0 document. This means that to read the tutorial you need to use the Microsoft Word for Windows Version 6.0 word processing program. The name of the DOC file is Tutor19.DOC.

If you don't have access to the Word for Windows word processing program, you can read the tutorial using your own word processing or text editor program, because the \LearnVB\Tutor19 directory of the CD also contains the text file (*.TXT) of this tutorial.

The tutorial shows you how to create your own VBX custom control, and then it shows you how to test the VBX and how to use the VBX control from within your programs.

20

Preparing Your Visual Basic Programs for Distribution and Preparing an Install Program

20

The word *Basic* in Visual Basic is misleading because it gives the impression that one cannot generate sophisticated Windows applications with Visual Basic. As demonstrated throughout this book, you can write professional, state-of-the-art Windows programs with Visual Basic. In this chapter you'll learn how to prepare the distribution disk(s) of your application.

Object-Oriented Programming Language

Visual Basic is a highly modular, object-oriented programming language. This means that it is possible to plug software modules into your Visual Basic programs. For example, you can incorporate dynamic linked libraries (DLLs) and VBX controls into your Visual Basic programs. This saves you a lot of time because you spend your development time learning and using third-party DLLs and VBX controls instead of developing the DLLs and the VBX controls yourself.

Distributing Third-Party Files

If you are planning to sell your Visual Basic programs, you should keep in mind that your distribution disk(s) should contain all the external files needed by your application. Of course, you must consult the software license agreements and make sure that you are complying with the software license agreements of the various files that you plan to distribute.

Distributing Your Applications

Imagine that you have finished writing a Visual Basic application, and now you want to distribute it. You'll now learn how to prepare your application for distribution.

Run-Module—Based Applications Versus Stand-Alone—Compiled Applications

If you write a program with the C or C++ programming language, the C/C++ compiler creates an EXE file.

For example, your source code file (the file that contains the code of your program) may be called MyApp.C. After you compile and link the MyApp.C program, a new file, MyApp.EXE, is created. When distributing your program to your users, you include MyApp.EXE on the distribution disk. Therefore, the EXE file that the C/C++ compiler generates is called a stand-alone EXE file, because this file does not need any additional files to run. Of course, if the MyApp program uses VBX files, DLL files, WAV files, or any other external files, you have to distribute these files together with the MyApp.EXE file.

As Appendix C demonstrates, Visual Basic enables you to create EXE files (by selecting Make EXE File from the File menu). However, your distribution disk must also include a run-module file called VBRUN300.DLL. If you ship your EXE file without the VBRUN300.DLL file and your user does

not have the VBRUN300.DLL file installed in his or her \Windows\System directory, the user will not be able to execute your EXE file. In other words, the EXE files that Visual Basic generates are not stand-alone EXE files, because they require the run-module file VBRUN300.DLL.

At first glance, this looks like a great limitation; however, this is not the case at all. After all, by nature the programs that you write with Visual Basic are composed of several VBX files. This means that in any case you'll have to include in your distribution disk the VBX files that your program utilizes. So think of the VBRUN300.DLL file as one additional file that must be distributed with your program.

NOTE

If you own Visual Basic Version 2.0, you have to distribute your programs with the VBRUN200.DLL file. If you own Visual Basic Version 3.0, you have to distribute your programs with the VBRUN300.DLL file, and so on.

Other Files That Must Be Distributed with Your Program

As stated, you must include the VBRUN300.DLL in your distribution disk. In addition, you have to include the following files:

The EXE file that you generated.
VBX file(s) that your program utilizes.
BMP file(s) that your program utilizes (provided that you wrote the programs in such a way that the BMP files are not an integral part of the EXE file).
WAV, MIDI, and AVI files used by your programs.
Any other external file that is needed by your program. For example, your program may need an external TXT file that is read during runtime.
A setup program that will install all the files.

Writing a Setup Program

The setup program that you have to include on your distribution disk must perform the following tasks:

Install the VBRUN300.DLL file into your user \Windows\System directory.
Install the VBX file(s) (if any) into your user \Windows\System directory.
Install the DLL file(s) (if any) into your user \Windows\System directory.
Install the EXE file(s) and all the other external files into your user PC.
Create a program group for your EXE files.

To save disk space, you should save the files to your distribution disk as compressed files. Your SETUP program should uncompress these files.

20

As you can see from these specifications, it could take a lot of time to write the SETUP program yourself.

Fortunately, Visual Basic comes with a utility that enables you to prepare your distribution disk and the SETUP program in a very short time. In the following section you'll learn how to use the Application Setup Wizard utility of Visual Basic.

Preparing the EXE File for Distribution

The program icon of the Application Setup Wizard utility of Visual Basic is shown in Figure 20.1.

Figure 20.1.
The program icon of the Application Setup Wizard utility in the Visual Basic group of icons.

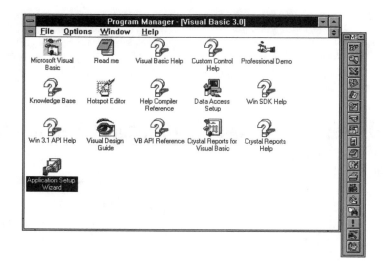

In the next sections you'll create a distribution disk for the Speaker.EXE program. The Speaker.EXE program resides inside your C:\LearnVB\Original\MySetUp directory.

Before making the distribution disk, you need to become familiar with the program. This way you'll make sure that you are properly preparing the Speaker.EXE program (and all its external files) for distribution.

❑ Select Run from the File menu of the Program Manager and execute the
   C:\LearnVB\Original\MySetUp\Speaker.EXE program.

   Windows responds by executing the Speaker.EXE program and displaying the window shown in Figure 20.2.

❑ Experiment with the Speaker.EXE program and take notes regarding the various external files that this program needs. The distribution disk of this program needs to include the WAV files that the Speaker.EXE program uses and the TegoMM.VBX file.

Figure 20.2.
The main window of the
Speaker.EXE program.

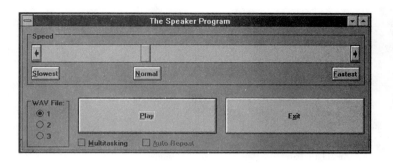

☐ Copy the files from the C:\LearnVB\ORIGINAL\SetUp directory to your
C:\LearnVB\PRACTICE\SetUp directory.

In the following steps you'll need to modify files. However, these files originally came from the CD
you got with this book. As such, the file attributes of these files are read-only. This means that you
will not be able to change these files. Therefore, change the file attributes of these files:

☐ Start the File Manager program.

☐ Select the C:\LearnVB\Original\MySetUp directory.

☐ Highlight the files in the C:\LearnVB\Original\MySetUp directory (by holding down the
Shift key and clicking on each of the files in this directory).

☐ Select Properties from the File menu of the File Manager.

The File Manager responds by displaying the Properties dialog box.

☐ Click the Read Only checkbox to remove the checkmark from this checkbox.

☐ Click the OK button.

Windows responds by removing the read-only attributes from the selected files.

☐ Start Visual Basic.

☐ Select Open Project from the File menu and load the
C:\LearnVB\PRACTICE\MySetUp\Speaker.MAK project.

Take a look at the Form_Load() procedure of the frmSpeaker form:

```
Sub Form_Load ()

    Dim WavFile

    ' Make the multimedia control invisible.
    TegommPC.Visible = False

    ' Set the DeviceType property for playback of
    ' WAV files through the PC speaker.
    TegommPC.DeviceType = "PCSpeaker"
```

```
' Set the FileName property.
WavFile = App.Path + "\BOURB1M1.WAV"
TegommPC.FileName = WavFile

' Issue an Open command.
TegommPC.Command = "Open"

' If Open command failed, display an error message.
If TegommPC.Error <> 0 Then
   MsgBox "Cannot open " + WavFile, 0, "ERROR"
End If

' Set the Min and Max of the hsbSpeed scroll bar.
hsbSpeed.Min = 50
hsbSpeed.Max = 200

' Set the hsbTempo scroll bar to the normal speed.
hsbSpeed.Value = 100
```

End Sub

In particular, note the statements that set the FileName property of the multimedia control:

```
' Set the FileName property.
WavFile = App.Path + "\BOURB1M1.WAV"
TegommPC.FileName = WavFile
```

App.Path is the name of the directory where the Speaker program resides. For example, if the Speaker program resides inside the C:\LearnVB\Practice\MySetUp directory, then App.Path is equal to C:\LearnVB\Practice\MySetUp.

The WavFile variable is set to App.Path+\BOURB1M1.WAV:

```
WavFile = App.Path + "\BOURB1M1.WAV"
```

If, for example, the Speaker program resides inside the C:\LearnVB\Practice\MySetUp directory, WavFile is set to C:\LearnVB\Practice\MySetUp\BOURB1M1.WAV.

So the Speaker program is written in such a way that the WAV file that the program uses must reside in the same directory where the Speaker program resides.

In addition to the Form_Load() procedure, the Speaker program sets the FileName property of the multimedia control in three other procedures: optWav1_Click(), optWav2_Click(), and optWav3_Click(). (These procedures are executed whenever the user clicks the option buttons of the Speaker program to set a new WAV file for the playback.) Note that in these three procedures the App.Path object is used again, and these procedures assume that the corresponding WAV file resides inside the App.Path directory:

Sub optWav1_Click ()

```
Dim WavFile

' Set the FileName property.
WavFile = App.Path + "\BOURB1M1.WAV"
TegommPC.FileName = WavFile
```

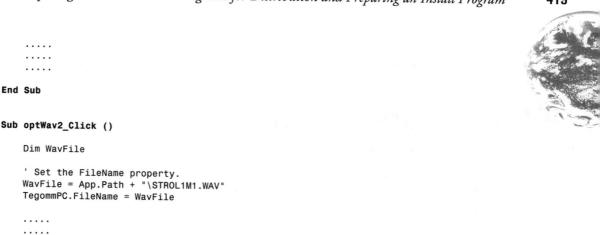

```
     . . . . .
     . . . . .
     . . . . .

End Sub


Sub optWav2_Click ()

    Dim WavFile

    ' Set the FileName property.
    WavFile = App.Path + "\STROL1M1.WAV"
    TegommPC.FileName = WavFile

     . . . . .
     . . . . .
     . . . . .

End Sub


Sub optWav3_Click ()

    Dim WavFile

    ' Set the FileName property.
    WavFile = App.Path + "\8KENNED3.WAV"
    TegommPC.FileName = WavFile


     . . . . .
     . . . . .
     . . . . .

End Sub
```

> **NOTE**
>
> The utility that you'll use in the next sections assumes that the project is saved as a text file (not as a binary file). As such, you must tell Visual Basic to save the project as a text file. To do that you select Environment from the Options menu, and then inside the Environment Options dialog box set the `Default Save As Format` item to `Text`.
>
> After you set the `Default Save As Format` to `Text`, save the project and the form of the program. Visual Basic will save these files as text files.

❏ Select Save Project from the File menu.

You'll now make an EXE file for the Speaker file:

❏ Select Make EXE File from the File menu and save the Speaker program as Speaker.EXE in the C:\LearnVB\PRACTICE\MySetUp directory.

The previous discussion is important because many of your Visual Basic programs will include external files (BMP files, WAV files, and other files). When preparing an EXE file for distribution, you have to consider the path of the external files.

20 Creating the SETUP Program

You'll now create the SETUP program and the distribution disk.

In the following steps you'll execute the Application Setup Wizard utility. This utility assumes that Visual Basic is not running. Therefore, you must terminate Visual Basic:

❑ Select Exit from the File menu of Visual Basic to terminate Visual Basic.

In the following steps you'll create a distribution disk. This means that you now have to prepare an empty, formatted disk:

❑ Prepare an empty, formatted disk and insert it into your a: or b: drive.

❑ Double-click the Application Setup Wizard program icon that resides inside the Visual Basic 3.0 Professional Edition group of icons. (See Figure 20.1.)

Windows responds by executing the Application Setup Wizard utility and displaying the window shown in Figure 20.3.

Figure 20.3.
The SetupWizard Step 1 of 6 window.

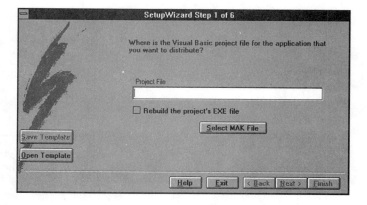

Note that the caption of the window in Figure 20.3 includes the text Step 1 of 6. Yes, as implied by the caption, it takes 6 easy steps to create your distribution disk.

In Step 1 you have to select the project:

❑ Click the Select MAK file button that appears inside the Step 1 of 6 window.

The SetupWizard program responds by displaying the Where is your VB application MAK file? window.

☐ Set the File Name to c:\learnvb\practice\mysetup\speaker.mak, as shown in Figure 20.4.

Figure 20.4.
Setting the MAK file.

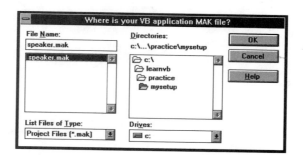

☐ Click the OK button of the Where is your VB application MAK file? window.

The SetupWizard utility closes the dialog box and displays the Step 1 of 6 window, as shown in Figure 20.5.

Figure 20.5.
The Step 1 of 6 window
with the MAK file selected.

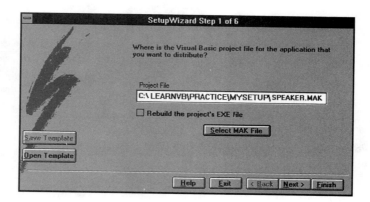

☐ Click the Next button to move to the next step.

The Setup Wizard utility responds by moving to the Step 2 of 6 window. (See Figure 20.6.)

As shown in Figure 20.6, you have to check the checkboxes that are relevant to the application you are now preparing. The Speaker.EXE program does not use the Data Access or any of the other options listed in the five checkboxes.

☐ Make sure that none of the checkboxes is checked, and move to Step 4 by clicking the Next button. (Note that Step 3 was skipped.)

The Setup Wizard utility responds by moving to the Step 4 of 6 window. (See Figure 20.7.)

As shown in Figure 20.7, you are required to set the disk type and the disk drive.

20

Figure 20.6.
The Step 2 of 6 window.

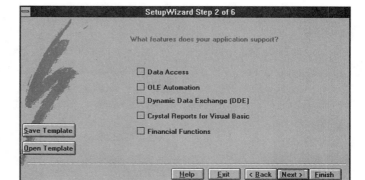

Figure 20.7.
The Step 4 of 6 window.

For example, if you are using a 1.44 MB disk in drive a:, set the Step 4 of 6 window as shown in Figure 20.8.

Figure 20.8.
Setting the distribution disk
to 1.44 MB and drive a:.

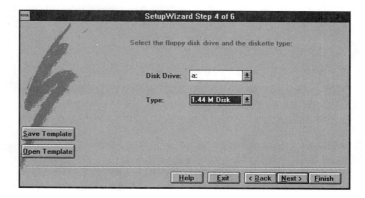

❑ Set the Disk Drive and Type list boxes to the drive and disk that you are using. (For example, if your distribution disk is in drive a: and it is a 1.4 MB disk, set the Disk Drive list box to a: and set the Type list box to 1.4 M disk.)

❑ Click the Next button on the Step 4 of 6 window to move to the Step 5 of 6 window. (See Figure 20.9.)

Figure 20.9.
The Step 5 of 6 window.

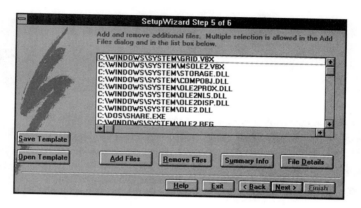

Look at all the files that appear in Figure 20.9! Every file that appears in the Step 5 of 6 window will be copied to your distribution disk! Naturally, you don't need to distribute all these files. Where did these files come from? Take a look at the Project window of the Speaker.MAK file. (See Figure 20.10.)

Figure 20.10.
The Project window of the
Speaker.MAK project.

As shown in Figure 20.10, the project contains many VBX files that are used in the project. Because you did not remove the unused VBX files from the project, the Setup Wizard assumes that you want to copy all the files that appear in the Project window to your distribution disk.

❑ Remove from the list of files that appears in the Step 5 of 6 window list the files that you don't want to copy to the distribution disk. To remove a file, highlight the files to be removed by holding down the Shift key, clicking on the files that you want to remove, and then clicking the Remove button.

Your Step 5 of 6 window should now look like the one shown in Figure 20.11.

20

Figure 20.11.
Removing the unused VBX
files from the list of files in
the Step 5 of 6 window.

Note that currently there are only two files in the Step 5 of 6 window: the Speaker.EXE file and the TegoMM.VBX file. You want these two files on your distribution disk. (You need the Speaker.EXE file because this is the program itself, and you need TegoMM.VBX because the Speaker.EXE program uses this VBX file.)

As you know, you also need to copy the three WAV files that the Speaker.EXE program uses:

❏ Click the Add Files button of the Step 5 of 6 window.

> *The Setup Wizard program responds by displaying the Select additional files dialog box. (See Figure 20.12.)*

Figure 20.12.
The Select additional files
dialog box.

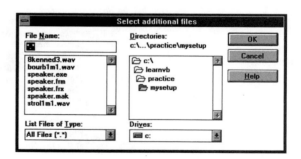

❏ Select the C:\LearnVB\PRACTICE\MySetUp\BOURB1M1.WAV file and then click the OK button.

> *The Setup Wizard program responds by adding the BOURB1M1.WAV file to the list of files that will be copied to the distribution disk.*

❏ Click the Add Files button again, select the C:\LearnVB\PRACTICE\MySetUp\STROL1M1.WAV file, and then click the OK button.

The Setup Wizard program responds by adding the STROL1M1.WAV file to the list of files that will be copied to the distribution disk.

❑ Click the Add Files button again, select the C:\LearnVB\PRACTICE\MySetUp\8KENNED3.WAV file, and then click the OK button.

The Setup Wizard program responds by adding the 8KENNED3.WAV file to the list of files that will be copied to the distribution disk.

Your Step 5 of 6 window should now look like the one shown in Figure 20.13.

Figure 20.13.
The Step 5 of 6 Window,
with the list of files that
will be copied to the
distribution disk.

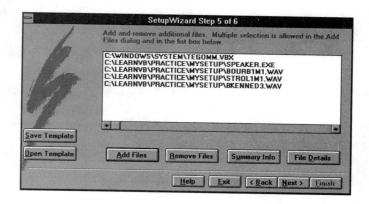

NOTE

Don't add VBRUN300.DLL to the list of files in the Step 5 of 6 window. SetupWizard knows already that this file should be copied to your distribution disk.

❑ Click the Next button of the Step 5 of 6 window to move to the final step.

The Setup Wizard program responds by switching to DOS, compressing all the files that should be compressed (a process that takes some time), switching back to Windows, starting Visual Basic, preparing the SETUP program (a program written with Visual Basic), and finally, displaying the dialog box shown in Figure 20.14.

❑ Make sure that your distribution disk (as you set it in the Step 4 of 6 window) is inserted, and click the OK button of the dialog box.

The Setup Wizard program responds by copying the files to your distribution disk. (If there is not enough space on the distribution disk, the Setup Wizard utility asks you to insert additional disks.) Finally, the Step 6 of 6 window is displayed. (See Figure 20.15.)

Congratulations! You now have a distribution disk.

20

Figure 20.14.
The dialog box that the
Setup Wizard program
displays after preparing the
files for distribution.

Figure 20.15.
The final window of the
Setup Wizard utility.

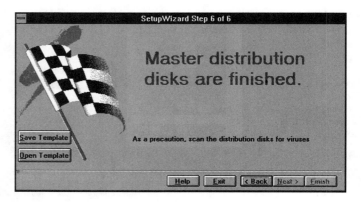

❑ Click the Exit button of the Step 6 of 6 window to terminate the SetupWizard utility.

Take a look at the distribution disk. It contains the following files:

```
TEGOMM.VB_
SPEAKER.EX_
BOURB1M1.WA_
STROL1M1.WA_
8KENNED3.WA_
SETUP.EXE
VER.DL_
SETUPKIT.DL_
VBRUN300.DL_
SETUP.LST
SETUP1.EX_
```

Every file that has an underscore as the last character in its file extension is a compressed file. Note that the SETUP.EXE file is not compressed (because this file will be executed by your user).

TEGOMM.VB_ is the compressed TEGOMM.VBX file.
SPEAKER.EX_ is the compressed SPEAKER.EXE file.
BOURB1M1.WA_ is the compressed BOURB1M1.WAV file.
STROL1M1.WA_ is the compressed STROL1M1.WAV file.
8KENNED3.WA_ is the compressed 8KENNED3.WAV file.
SETUP.EXE is the SETUP program.
VER.DL_ is a DLL that is used by the SETUP.EXE program to compare the
VBRUN300.DLL that came with your distribution disk with the VBRUN300.DLL that
may already exist on your user's PC. If the VBRUN300.DLL file that already exists on

your user's PC has a date and time earlier than the date and time of the VBRUN300.DLL that was shipped with your distribution disk, the SETUP program will prompt a message to your user. (Although the VER.DL_ file extension is DL_, this file is not compressed.) SETUPKIT.DL_ is the compressed SETUPKIT.DLL file. This DLL is used by the SETUP program.

VBRUN300.DL_ is the compressed VBRUN300.DLL file.

SETUP.LST is a text file used by the SETUP program.

SETUP1.EX_ is the compressed SETUP1.EXE file, a program that is used by the SETUP program.

NOTE

When making the distribution disk, make sure that you are complying with the software license agreement of the various files that you are distributing. For example, you can't distribute the VBX, WAV, MIDI, AVI, BMP, and other files that are supplied with this book's CD. The sole purpose of supplying these files is so you'll be able to execute the EXE files that are supplied with this book's CD.

Testing the Distribution Disk

Test the distribution disk that you prepared:

☐ Make sure the distribution disk is inserted in your A: or B: drive.

☐ Select Run from the File menu of the Program Manager and execute the SETUP.EXE program.

The SETUP program initializes itself and then displays the dialog box shown in Figure 20.16.

As shown in Figure 20.16, the SETUP program suggests to install the program in the C:\SPEAKER directory.

Figure 20.16.
The SPEAKER Setup dialog box.

☐ Click the Continue button.

The SETUP program responds by creating the C:\SPEAKER directory (if there is no such directory), and then the files are copied from the distribution disk to the hard drive. The

20

SETUP program copies the Speaker.EXE and the WAV files to the C:\SPEAKER directory, and it copies the VBRUN300.DLL and the TegoMM.VBX file to the \Windows\System directory. The SETUP program uncompresses the files back to their original sizes. The SETUP program displays a message that the program icon of the program is created (See Figure 20.17.), and then displays the final dialog box. (See Figure 20.18.)

Figure 20.17.
The message that the SETUP program displays when the program icon is created.

Figure 20.18.
The final dialog box of the SETUP program.

As shown in Figure 20.19, the SETUP program creates a new program group and places the icon of the Speaker.EXE program in it.

Figure 20.19.
The new program group with the icon of the Speaker.EXE program.

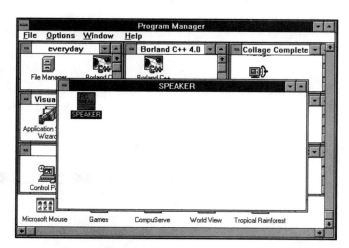

❑ Double-click the icon of the Speaker.EXE program and verify that the program operates correctly.

Doing It the Hard Way...

In the previous sections you used the Setup Wizard utility to make a distribution disk. As you saw, preparing a distribution disk with the Setup Wizard utility is very easy. Alternatively, you can pre-pare a distribution disk by manually doing all the things that the Setup Wizard utility does. This is a long process, but it lets you have full control of the process of making the distribution disk.

You'll now learn how to make a distribution disk by actually modifying the SETUP program ac-cording to your specifications.

One of the files that you'll copy to your distribution disk is a file called SETUP1.EXE. This pro-gram was written with Visual Basic. The name of the Visual Basic project is SETUP1.MAK, and it resides in the directory \VB\SETUPKIT\SETUP1.

To create the SETUP1.EXE file, you have to load the SETUP1.MAK project with Visual Basic and then make several changes to the SETUP1.FRM file (that is, you have to customize the file). These changes are covered later in this chapter. When you finish customizing the SETUP1.FRM file, you have to create an EXE file by selecting Make EXE File from the File menu, and save the file as SETUP1.EXE. You may save the EXE file by any name except SETUP.EXE. In this chapter it is assumed that you'll save the file as SETUP1.EXE.

As stated, besides copying SETUP1.EXE to your distribution disk, you need to copy to the diskette other files. In the next sections you'll examine each of these files.

Preparing the Distribution Diskette

❑ Format a diskette.

❑ Insert the diskette into your a: or b: drive.

This diskette will serve as the distribution diskette. In the following sections you'll be instructed to copy files to this diskette.

Preparing the Application to Be Distributed

The application that you are now preparing for distribution is the LOOP3 program.

❑ Copy the files of the LOOP3 program from the C:\LearnVB\ORIGINAL\LOOP directory to the C:\LearnVB\PRACTICE\LOOP directory.

❑ Start the File Manager program, select Properties from the File menu, and change the file attributes of the files so that they are not read-only. (Recall that files that were copied from this book's CD are read-only files. To be able to modify these files, you have to remove the read-only file attributes.)

❑ Start Visual Basic.

❑ Load the LOOP3.MAK project.

❑ Run the LOOP3 program and make sure it works properly.

❑ Terminate the LOOP3 program.

❑ Create an EXE file for the LOOP3 program by selecting Make EXE File from the File menu, and save the EXE file as LOOP3.EXE in the directory C:\LearnVB\ORIGINAL\LOOP.

❑ Select Run from the File menu of the Program Manager, and execute the C:\LearnVB\Original\LOOP\LOOP3.EXE program.

❑ Make sure the LOOP3.EXE program operates properly.

❑ Terminate the LOOP3.EXE program.

The SETUP.LST File

You must include the SETUP.LST file on your distribution diskette. The SETUP.LST file is a text file that contains a list of all the files that should be copied from the diskette to your user's \WINDOWS and \WINDOWS\SYSTEM directories.

The files in the list are listed line after line, with each file listed on a separate line. The very first line must contain the name of the Visual Basic installation program. For example, if the name of the installation program is SETUP1.EXE, the first line in the SETUP.LST file must be SETUP1.EX_.

To create the SETUP.LST file do the following:

❑ Start Notepad (which usually resides in the Accessories group) or any other editor that is capable of saving text files.

❑ Type the following lines:

```
SETUP1.EX_
VER.DL_
VBRUN300.DL_
SETUPKIT.DL_
```

❑ Save the file as SETUP.LST on your distribution diskette.

NOTE

The order of the files in the SETUP.LST is not important, except that the first line of the file must be SETUP1.EX_.

The SETUP.EXE File

SETUP.EXE is the program your user will execute to install your application. This pre-installation program is called the *bootstrap program*.

Don't be confused! There is a file called SETUP1.EXE, which is written in Visual Basic (and you have to customize this file), and there is another file called SETUP.EXE that comes with the Visual Basic package. The SETUP.EXE file resides in the directory \VB\SETUPKIT\KITFILES.

❑ Copy the file SETUP.EXE from the directory C:\VB\SETUPKIT\KITFILES to your distribution diskette. (You don't have to do any customization to this file.)

To install your application, your user will execute the SETUP.EXE program. The SETUP.EXE program will copy all the overhead files from your distribution diskette to your user's hard drive, and then will automatically execute the SETUP1.EXE program.

Compressing Files

To fit as many bytes as possible on the distribution diskette, you have to compress the files. To compress files, you have to use the COMPRESS.EXE utility that comes with Visual Basic Version 3.0. This utility resides in the directory C:\VB\SETUPKIT\KITFILES.

To use the COMPRESS utility, you must be at the DOS command line:

❑ Double-click the MS-DOS program icon that appears in the Main group of the Program Manager.

> *Windows responds by taking the PC to a DOS shell, where you see the DOS command line.*

❑ Log in to the directory C:\LearnVB\PRACTICE\Loop by typing the following at the DOS prompt:

```
CD C:\LearnVB\PRACTICE\Loop   {Enter}
```

Compress the LOOP3.EXE file:

❑ At the DOS prompt type this:

```
C:\VB\SETUPKIT\KITFILES\COMPRESS -r LOOP3.EXE {Enter}
```

> *The COMPRESS.EXE utility compresses the LOOP3.EXE to a file called LOOP3.EX_.*

❑ Copy the LOOP3.EX_ file to the distribution diskette:

```
Copy LOOP3.EX_  a:\  {Enter}
```

or if you are using the b: drive enter this:

```
Copy LOOP3.EX_  b:\  {Enter}
```

You now need to compress two more files. The first file to be compressed is the file VBRUN300.DLL that resides in the directory C:\WINDOWS\SYSTEM:

❑ Log in to the directory C:\WINDOWS\SYSTEM by typing this at the DOS prompt:

```
CD C:\WINDOWS\SYSTEM   {Enter}
```

20

To compress the VBRUN300.DLL file, at the DOS prompt type this:

```
C:\VB\SETUPKIT\KITFILES\COMPRESS -r VBRUN300.DLL {Enter}
```

The COMPRESS.EXE utility compresses the VBRUN300.DLL to a file called VBRUN300.DL_.

❏ Copy the VBRUN300.DL_ file to the distribution diskette:

```
Copy VBRUN300.DL_  a:\  {Enter}
```

or if you are using the b: drive enter this:

```
Copy VBRUN300.DL_  b:\  {Enter}
```

The second file to be compressed is the file SETUPKIT.DLL that resides in the directory C:\VB\SETUPKIT\KITFILES. Compress this file:

❏ Log in to the directory C:\VB\SETUPKIT\KITFILES by typing the following at the DOS prompt:

```
CD C:\VB\SETUPKIT\KITFILES   {Enter}
```

To compress the SETUPKIT.DLL file, at the DOS prompt type the following:

```
COMPRESS -r SETUPKIT.DLL {Enter}
```

The COMPRESS.EXE utility compresses the SETUPKIT.DLL to a file called SETUPKIT.DL_.

❏ Copy the SETUPKIT.DL_ file to the distribution diskette:

```
Copy SETUPKIT.DL_  a:\  {Enter}
```

or if you are using the b: drive enter this:

```
Copy SETUPKIT.DL_  b:\  {Enter}
```

NOTE

The files SETUP.LST and SETUP.EXE that you already copied to the distribution diskette are not compressed. These files must not be compressed.

As you can see from the list of files in the SETUP.LST file, you also need to copy the file VER.DL_ to the distribution disk. The name of the file is VER.DL_. However, do not compress this file (even though the file extension is DL_). You may find the file VER.DLL in the directory C:\WINDOWS\SYSTEM.

❏ Log in to the directory C:\WINDOWS\SYSTEM by typing the following at the DOS prompt:

```
CD C:\WINDOWS\SYSTEM  {Enter}
```

☐ Copy the file VER.DLL to the distribution diskette as VER.DL_ by typing the following at the DOS prompt:

```
COPY VER.DLL  a:\VER.DL_  {Enter}
```

or if you are using the b: drive enter this:

```
COPY VER.DLL  b:\VER.DL_  {Enter}
```

☐ To return to Windows, at the DOS prompt type the following:

```
EXIT {Enter}
```

Customizing the SETUP1 Project

You have finished copying all the necessary files into the distribution diskette except the file SETUP1.EX_. You'll now customize this file.

To customize the SETUP1.MAK project do the following:

☐ Start Visual Basic.

☐ Load the SETUP1.MAK file by selecting Open Project from the File menu, and select the file C:\VB\SETUPKIT\SETUP1\SETUP1.MAK.

Visual Basic responds by loading the SETUP1.MAK file.

You'll now customize the SETUP1.FRM file:

☐ Highlight SETUP1.FRM in the Project window.

☐ Click the View Code button that appears at the top-right corner of the Project window.

Visual Basic responds by displaying the Code window of the SETUP1.FRM file.

☐ Display the general declarations section of the SETUP1.FRM form, and note that the following constants appear:

```
Const APPNAME = "Loan Application"
Const APPDIR = "C:\LOAN"     ' The default install directory
Const fDataAccess% = False
Const fODBC% = False
Const fBtrieve% = False
Const fOLE2% = False

' Set the total uncompressed file sizes
' by adding the sizes of the files
Const WINSYSNEEDED = 40896  ' Files that go into WINDOWS and
                            ' SYSTEM directory
Const OTHERNEEDED = 12555   ' Files that don't go into the
                            ' WINDOWS or SYSTEM directory
```

Customizing the Constants

In the following steps you'll modify the SETUP1.FRM file, so it is a good idea to first save the original SETUP1.FRM file:

❑ Copy the SETUP1.FRM as SETUPORG.FRM.

If in the future you'll need to see the original SETUP1.FRM file, remember that it is saved as SETUPORG.FRM.

The first constant in the SETUP1.FRM file is this:

```
Const APPNAME = "Loan Application"
```

You have to change the constant:

❑ Change the APPNAME constant to this:

```
Const APPNAME = "The LOOP3 Application"
```

❑ Change the second constant to this:

```
Const APPDIR = "C:\LOOP3"   ' The default install directory
```

The SETUP program suggests to the user the C:\LOOP3 directory as the default directory in which the LOOP3 program be installed.

❑ The last two constants represent the number of bytes of the uncompressed files that will be copied from the distribution diskette to the hard drive.

The first constant, WINSYSNEEDED, contains the number of bytes in the uncompressed files that will be copied into the \WINDOWS directory and into the \WINDOWS\SYSTEM directory.

The second constant, OTHERNEEDED, contains the number of bytes in the files that will be copied to the directory where the LOOP3 program will be installed (that is, the size of the uncompressed LOOP3.EXE file).

Based on these two constants, the SETUP program will make a determination as to whether the user has sufficient hard-drive space to install the program.

❑ Leave the values of the WINSYSNEEDED and OTHERNEEDED constants at their current values (these values are good for the LOOP3 program).

Customizing the Form_Load( ) Procedure of the SETUP1.FRM Form

❑ Display the Form_Load() procedure of the SETUP1.FRM file.

❑ Select Find from the Edit menu, search for the string PromptForNextDisk, and then change the argument of the PromptForNextDisk() function:

```
If Not PromptForNextDisk(1, SourcePath$ + "LOOP3.EX_")
    ➥ Then GoTo ErrorSetup
```

During the installation, this statement checks whether the file LOOP3.EX_ exists on the diskette. If the file does not exist, the user has the wrong diskette in the drive, and the installation program prompts the user to insert the correct diskette. (Recall that the distribution disk will contain the file LOOP3.EX_.)

You'll now customize the argument of the CopyFile() function that appears several lines below the PromptForDisk() function:

❑ Change the argument of the CopyFile() function:

```
If Not CopyFile(SourcePath$, destPath$, "LOOP3.EX_",
        ➥ "LOOP3.EXE") Then GoTo ErrorSetup
```

This statement copies the LOOP3.EX_ file to the directory that the user will choose during the installation process.

In the case of the LOOP3 program, the LOOP3.EX_ file is the only file that has to be copied into this directory. However, if your application is such that there is a need to copy more files, include more CopyFile() statements. For example, if your application needs to copy the file ABC.BMP to the same directory where the LOOP3.EXE will reside, add the following statement:

```
If Not CopyFile(SourcePath$, destPath$, "ABC.BM_",
        ➥ "ABC.BMP") Then GoTo ErrorSetup
```

Don't forget to compress the file ABC.BMP to the file ABC.BM_ with the COMPRESS.EXE utility, and of course to copy ABC.BM_ to the distribution diskette.

You may repeat the process, adding more CopyFile() statements as necessary. For example, the following three statements copy the files LOOP3.EX_, ABC.BM_, and DEF.IC_ to the directory where the user selected to install the application:

```
If Not CopyFile(SourcePath$, destPath$, "LOOP3.EX_",
        ➥ "LOOP3.EXE") Then GoTo ErrorSetup

If Not CopyFile(SourcePath$, destPath$, "ABC.BM_",
        ➥ "ABC.BMP") Then GoTo ErrorSetup

If Not CopyFile(SourcePath$, destPath$, "DEF.IC_",
        ➥ "DEF.ICO") Then GoTo ErrorSetup
```

Again, if indeed your program uses these files, don't forget to compress these files (LOOP3.EXE to LOOP3.EX_, ABC.BMP to ABC.BM_, and DEF.ICO to DEF.IC_) and to copy these files to the distribution diskette.

The last argument in the CopyFile() function contains the name of the file after the installation program expands the file. LOOP3.EX_ will be expanded back to LOOP3.EXE, ABC.BM_ will be expanded back to ABC.BMP, and DEF.IC_ will be expanded back to DEF.ICO.

As stated, the distribution diskette of the LOOP3 program does not need a BMP file, an ICO file, or any other file.

20

The distribution disk of the LOOP3 program may be saved on a single diskette. However, some applications require more than one diskette. In these cases, you have to include more PromptForNextDisk() statements and CopyFile() statements. For example, suppose that the LOOP3 program requires three distribution diskettes. Assume that the three diskettes include the following files:

Disk Number 1	Comment
SETUP.EXE	Must reside in Disk #1
SETUP.LST	Must reside in Disk #1
VBRUN300.DL_	Must reside in Disk #1
SETUPKIT.DL_	Must reside in Disk #1
VER.DL_	Must reside in Disk #1
SETUP1.EX_	Must reside in Disk #1
LOOP3.EX_	Part of the application
FILE1.BM_	Part of the application
FILE2.DA_	Part of the application

Disk Number 2	Comment
FILE3.BM_	Part of the application
FILE4.BM_	Part of the application

Disk Number 3	Comment
FILE5.BM_	Part of the application
FILE6.BM_	Part of the application

The corresponding code in Form_Load() is the following:

```
' Is Disk #1 in the drive?
If Not PromptForNextDisk(1, SourcePath$ + "LOOP.EX_")
    ➡ Then GoTo ErrorSetup

' Copy the file LOOP3.EX_ from disk #1 to the directory
' where the user wants to install the program.
If Not CopyFile(SourcePath$, destPath$, "LOOP3.EX_",
    ➡ "LOOP3.EXE") Then GoTo ErrorSetup

' Copy the file FILE1.BM_ from disk #1 to the directory
' where the user wants to install the program.
If Not CopyFile(SourcePath$, destPath$, "FILE1.BM_",
    ➡ "FILE1.BMP") Then GoTo ErrorSetup


' Copy the file FILE2.DA_ from disk #1 to the directory
' where the user wants to install the program.
If Not CopyFile(SourcePath$, destPath$, "FILE2.DA_",
```

```
➥ "FILE2.DAT") Then GoTo ErrorSetup

' Is Disk #2 in the drive?
If Not PromptForNextDisk(2, SourcePath$ + "FILE3.BM_")
   ➥ Then GoTo ErrorSetup

' Copy the file FILE3.BM_ from disk #2 to the directory
' where the user wants to install the program.
If Not CopyFile(SourcePath$, destPath$, "FILE3.BM_",
   ➥ "FILE3.BMP") Then GoTo ErrorSetup

' Copy file FILE4.BM_from disk #2 to the directory
' where the user wants to install the program.
If Not CopyFile(SourcePath$, destPath$, "FILE4.BM_",
   ➥ "FILE4.BMP") Then GoTo ErrorSetup

' Is Disk #3 in the drive?
If Not PromptForNextDisk(3, SourcePath$ + "FILE5.BM_")
   ➥ Then GoTo ErrorSetup

' Copy the file FILE5.BM_ from disk #3 to the directory
' where the user wants to install the program.
If Not CopyFile(SourcePath$, destPath$, "FILE5.BM_",
   ➥ "FILE5.BMP") Then GoTo ErrorSetup

' Copy the file FILE6.BM_ from disk #3 to the directory
' where the user wants to install the program.
If Not CopyFile(SourcePath$, destPath$, "FILE6.BM_",
   ➥ "FILE6.BMP") Then GoTo ErrorSetup
```

This code causes the installation program to install the three diskettes. During the installation, the installation program will prompt the user to insert the proper diskette. The correct diskette is recognized by the `PromptForNextDisk()` function. The first argument of this function is the disk number (so the user will see the prompts `Insert Disk #1`, `Insert Disk #2`, and so on), and the third argument contains the name of one of the files that is included on the diskette. For example, the third argument of the `PromptForNextDisk()` function of Disk #2 is FILE3.BM_. Therefore, the installation program will make a determination as to whether the user inserted the correct diskette by looking for the file FILE3.BM_ on the diskette. If this file exists on the diskette, the program assumes that diskette Number 2 is in the drive. If the program does not find FILE3.BM_ on the diskette, it prompts the user with `Insert Disk #2`.

It is important to understand that all the overhead files (SETUP.LST, SETUP.EXE, SETUP1.EXE, VBRUN300.DL_, VER.DL_, and SETUPKIT.DL_) must be included in diskette Number 1, and you should not use the `CopyFile()` function to copy these files. This is because the SETUP.EXE program is responsible for copying these files.

The LOOP3 program does not require a VBX file. However, if your application requires a VBX file(s), add a `CopyFile()` statement for each of the VBX file(s). For example, if your application uses the GRID.VBX file, use the following statement:

```
If Not CopyFile(SourcePath$, WinSysDir$,
   ➥ "GRID.VB_", "GRID.VBX") Then GoTo ErrorSetup
```

The second argument of the CopyFile() function in this case is WinSysDir$. This causes the installation program to copy the file GRID.VB_ from the distribution diskette to the \WINDOWS\SYSTEM directory. As specified by the fourth argument of the CopyFile() function, this file will be expanded as GRID.VBX.

> **NOTE**
>
> Because the LOOP3 program does not need the GRID.VBX file, make sure to comment out the following statement:
>
> ```
> If Not CopyFile(SourcePath$, WinSysDir$,
>    ➥ "GRID.VB_", "GRID.VBX") Then GoTo ErrorSetup
> ```

Creating a Program Group in the Program Manager

The last thing you have to do in the customization process is to change the statements that are responsible for creating the program group in the Program Manager. You'll see the CreateProgManGroup() function and the CreateProgManItem() function in the SETUP1.FRM file, several lines below the CopyFile() statement. Change these statements in this way:

```
CreateProgManGroup Setup1, "The Loop3 Application",
     ➥ "LOOP3.GRP"

CreateProgManItem Setup1, destPath$ + "LOOP3.EXE",
     ➥ "The LOOP3 Application"
```

These two statements determine the title of the group and the title of the icon of the application that will appear in the group.

Making SETUP1.EXE and Copying It to the Distribution Diskette

☐ Save the project (Select Save Project from the File menu).

☐ Select Make EXE File from the File menu and save the file as SETUP1.EXE in the C:\LearnVB\PRACTICE\LOOP3 directory. (When making the SETUP1.EXE file, be sure to type LOOP3.EXE in the Application Title box of the Make EXE File dialog box. Later, when you execute the LOOP3.EXE program, if you select the Switch To item from the system menu of any window, the LOOP3 program will be listed with the same name that you set in the Application Title box when you created the LOOP3.EXE file.)

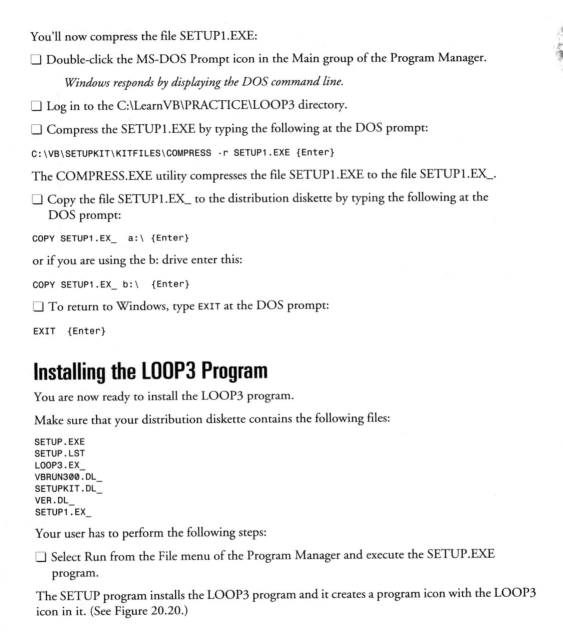

You'll now compress the file SETUP1.EXE:

☐ Double-click the MS-DOS Prompt icon in the Main group of the Program Manager.

   Windows responds by displaying the DOS command line.

☐ Log in to the C:\LearnVB\PRACTICE\LOOP3 directory.

☐ Compress the SETUP1.EXE by typing the following at the DOS prompt:

```
C:\VB\SETUPKIT\KITFILES\COMPRESS -r SETUP1.EXE {Enter}
```

The COMPRESS.EXE utility compresses the file SETUP1.EXE to the file SETUP1.EX_.

☐ Copy the file SETUP1.EX_ to the distribution diskette by typing the following at the DOS prompt:

```
COPY SETUP1.EX_  a:\ {Enter}
```

or if you are using the b: drive enter this:

```
COPY SETUP1.EX_  b:\  {Enter}
```

☐ To return to Windows, type EXIT at the DOS prompt:

```
EXIT  {Enter}
```

Installing the LOOP3 Program

You are now ready to install the LOOP3 program.

Make sure that your distribution diskette contains the following files:

```
SETUP.EXE
SETUP.LST
LOOP3.EX_
VBRUN300.DL_
SETUPKIT.DL_
VER.DL_
SETUP1.EX_
```

Your user has to perform the following steps:

☐ Select Run from the File menu of the Program Manager and execute the SETUP.EXE program.

The SETUP program installs the LOOP3 program and it creates a program icon with the LOOP3 icon in it. (See Figure 20.20.)

Figure 20.20.
The Program group
that the SETUP
program created.

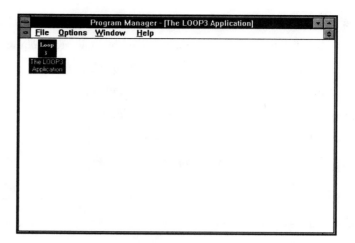

❑ Double-click the LOOP3 icon that was created by the SETUP program and verify that the
LOOP3.EXE program operates correctly.

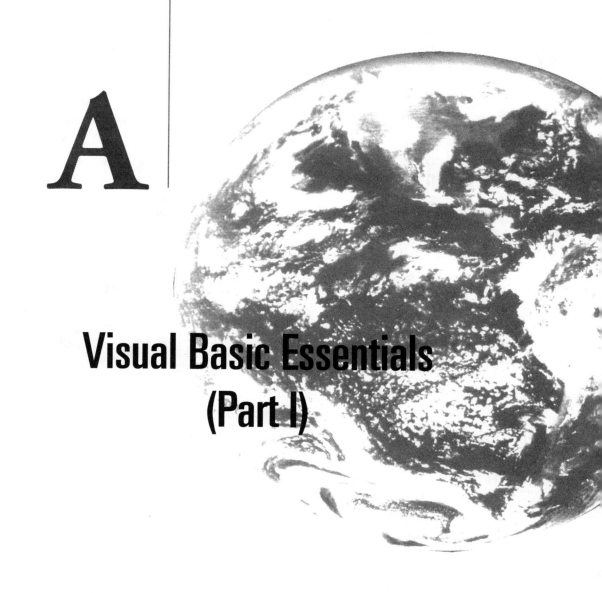

A

Visual Basic Essentials
(Part I)

A

Appendixes A, B, and C present a quick tutorial that teaches you how to use the Visual Basic for Windows package.

In these appendixes you'll write your first Windows application with Visual Basic. You'll learn how to apply the visual tools of Visual Basic and how to write code with Visual Basic. These appendixes assume that you have no previous experience with Visual Basic for Windows.

The program you'll write is called ItsFun. This program displays a message inside a text box, and it also causes the PC to speak in a human voice. Because the ItsFun program involves several topics, the implementation of the ItsFun program is spread over several appendixes (Appendixes A, B, and C).

The ItsFun Program

The ItsFun program is a very simple program that grants your PC the power of speech. It contains the Say Something button in its main window. (See Figure A.1.) When you click this button, the ItsFun program displays the message

```
It's been fun working with you.
```

Figure A.1.
The main window of the
ItsFun.EXE program.

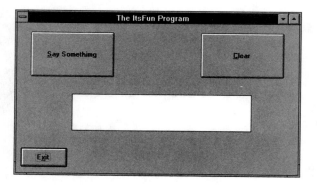

The ItsFun program also causes the PC to actually say these words through the PC speaker (you don't need a sound card, and you don't need any drivers).

Before writing the ItsFun program yourself, try executing it. This way, you'll gain a better understanding of what the program does. A copy of this program resides inside your C:\LearnVB\ORIGINAL\APPENDIX directory.

To execute the ItsFun.EXE program, do the following:

❑ Select Run from the File menu of the Program Manager program, and execute the ItsFun.EXE program that resides in your C:\LEARNVB\ORIGINAL\APPENDIX directory.

Windows responds by executing the program and displaying its main window. (See Figure A.1.)

❑ Click the Say Something button.

ItsFun responds by displaying a message inside the text box and by causing the PC to say the message through the PC speaker. (See Figure A.2.)

Figure A.2.
The message that appears after you click the Say Something button.

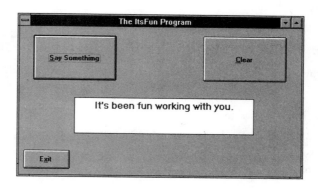

The main window of the ItsFun program also contains a Clear button.

❑ Click the Clear button.

ItsFun responds by clearing the message.

❑ Minimize all the windows that appear on the screen (that is, click the down-arrow icon that appears in the upper-right corner of each open window).

The desktop is shown with several minimized icons, as in Figure A.3. As you can see, the ItsFun program has its own icon.

Figure A.3.
The desktop, showing several icons, including the ItsFun icon.

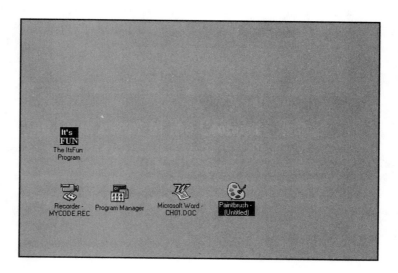

❑ Restore the windows to their original sizes (that is, click each program icon and then select Restore from the system menu that pops up).

❑ Experiment with the ItsFun program, and then terminate the ItsFun program by clicking the Exit button.

The Visual Implementation of the ItsFun Program

Writing Visual Basic programs involves the following two steps:

1. The visual design

2. The code design

During the visual design step, you design your Windows application visually. Before you write any code, you have to use the visual tools of Visual Basic to design the window of your application. Your objective now is to implement the window shown in Figure A.1.

NOTE

Throughout this book you'll be instructed to visually implement the form of the application. For example, you'll learn how to implement the form shown in Figure A.1.

The term *form* is used instead of the term *window*, because form is the term used by Visual Basic. In this book, window and form mean the same thing.

❑ Start Visual Basic. To start Visual Basic, you have to double-click the Visual Basic icon that appears in the Visual Basic group of icons, shown in Figure A.4. The icon that actually starts Visual Basic is the icon in the upper-left corner of the Visual Basic group of icons. However, your Visual Basic group may contain this icon in a different location inside this group of icons. The icon has been placed (by dragging the icon with the mouse) at the location shown in Figure A.4 because it is the icon most often used in this group of icons.

Windows responds by executing Visual Basic and displaying the windows of Visual Basic. (See Figure A.5.)

NOTE

Microsoft markets two separate Visual Basic packages:

Visual Basic for DOS
Visual Basic for Windows

As implied by their names, Visual Basic for DOS is designed to write DOS applications, and Visual Basic for Windows is designed to write Windows applications. This book teaches you how to write Windows applications by using the Visual Basic for Windows package. Therefore, unless otherwise specified, in this book the term *Visual Basic* means Visual Basic for Windows.

Figure A.4.
The Visual Basic group
of icons.

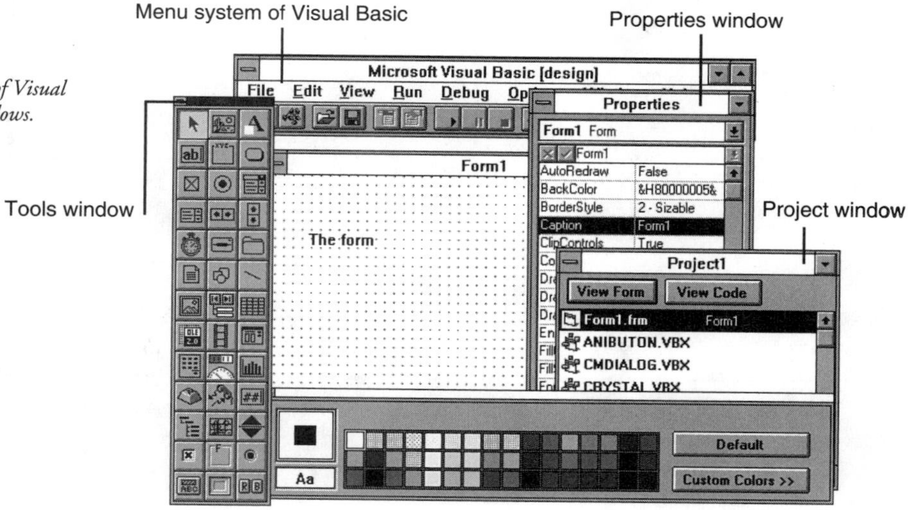

Figure A.5.
The windows of Visual
Basic for Windows.

Menu system of Visual Basic

Properties window

Tools window

Project window

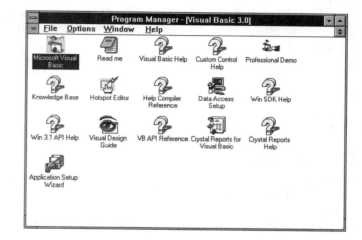

A

The screen that you see upon starting Visual Basic might look a little different from the screen shown in Figure A.5. The figure shows the windows positioned so that they all fit on a single page.

At first glance, the windows of Visual Basic may scare you. You might think that with all these windows it is difficult to use this software package. However, this is not the case. During the course of this appendix and the next two, you'll learn to use these windows.

> **NOTE**
>
> One of the windows in Figure A.5 is the Tools window. Depending on the particular version of Visual Basic that you are using, your Tools window might look a little different from the Tools window shown in Figure A.5.

The Form

The form shown in Figure A.5 is covered by all the other windows, so it is shown separately in Figure A.6. As you can see in Figure A.6, the form is empty (that is, it does not have buttons or any other objects in it). Your objective is to use the Tools window to make the empty form of Figure A.6 look like the one shown in Figure A.1.

Figure A.6.
The empty form.

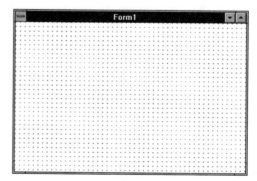

> **NOTE**
>
> Take a look at Figure A.6. It contains a picture of an empty form. Your objective is to transform this empty form into the form shown in Figure A.1.

Saving Your Project

You have not yet done any design work. That is, you have not yet started converting the empty form to the form shown in Figure A.1. Nevertheless, you should now assign a name to your project and save it.

Here is how you name and save your project:

❑ Select Save Project from the File menu of Visual Basic.

Visual Basic responds by displaying the Save File As dialog box. (See Figure A.7.)

Figure A.7.
The Save File As
dialog box.

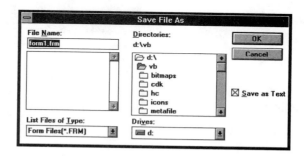

As shown in Figure A.7, Visual Basic suggests that you name the file form1.frm in the d:\vb directory. Do not click the OK button, because that's not what you want to name the file and that's not the directory to which you want to save the file.

When you save a project, Visual Basic saves two files:

- The FRM file. This file has the frm file extension. This file stores information regarding the form of the project.

- The MAK file. This file has the mak file extension. This file stores information regarding the project.

As you can see in Figure A.7, Visual Basic suggests that you use the name form1.frm for the file that stores information about the form, but this is not a good idea because you want the name of the frm file to be somehow related to the project that you are currently designing. A better name for the frm file is, for example, ItsFun.frm. You should save the file in the directory C:\LEARNVB\PRACTICE\APPENDIX:

❑ In the File Name box of the Save File As dialog box, enter the following:

```
C:\LEARNVB\PRACTICE\APPENDIX\ITSFUN.FRM
```

❑ Click the OK button.

Visual Basic responds by saving the empty form as ItsFun.frm in the directory C:\LEARNVB\PRACTICE\APPENDIX.

As stated, you must save the project (mak) file as well. After you click the OK button of the Save File As dialog box, Visual Basic immediately responds by displaying the Save Project As dialog box. (See Figure A.8.)

Figure A.8.
The Save Project As dialog box for saving the project (mak) file.

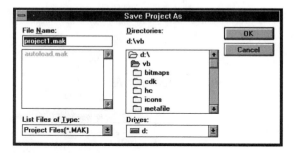

Figure A.8 shows that Visual Basic suggests that you save the project file as project1.mak in the directory d:\vb. Do not click the OK button, because you don't want to save the file as project1.mak, and you don't want to save the project file to the d:\vb directory.

❏ Enter C:\LEARNVB\PRACTICE\APPENDIX\ItsFun.mak inside the File Name box, and then click the OK button.

> *Visual Basic responds by saving the project file as ItsFun.mak in the directory C:\LEARNVB\PRACTICE\APPENDIX.*

If you examine your C:\LEARNVB\PRACTICE\APPENDIX directory, you'll see two files in it: ItsFun.frm and ItsFun.mak.

Designing the Form of the ItsFun Program

Again, your job is to make the empty form look like the form shown in Figure A.1.

Start by changing the caption of the form. In Figure A.6, the caption is Form1. In Figure A.1, the caption is The ItsFun Program. Now change the caption of the form:

❏ Click anywhere inside the form.

> *Visual Basic responds by making the form the active window. (You can recognize that the empty form is the active window because its caption is highlighted.)*

❏ Select Properties from the Window menu of Visual Basic.

> *Visual Basic responds by making the Properties window the active window.*

You set a new caption for the form by using the Properties window. Whenever you want to set a new property for the form, you use the Properties window.

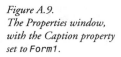

As shown in Figure A.9, the current setting of the Caption property is Form1. (If the Caption item in the list of properties is not highlighted, use the arrow keys to scroll the list and then highlight the Caption item.)

Figure A.9.
The Properties window,
with the Caption property
set to Form1.

Object box ⎯

List of properties ⎯

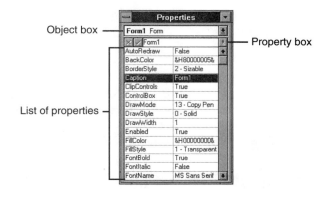

⎯ Property box

Note the three parts of the Properties window. The window contains a list of all the properties, a property box, and an object box. As shown in Figure A.9, the object box contains the Form object. This means that the Properties list lists the properties of the form. Furthermore, the Caption property is highlighted in the list. This means that the property box shows the value of the Caption property (which is currently Form1).

Change the Caption property to The ItsFun Program:

❑ Make sure that the Caption property is highlighted in the list of properties, click inside the property box, delete the text Form1, and enter The ItsFun Program inside the property box.

Your Properties window now looks like the one shown in Figure A.10.

Figure A.10.
The Properties window,
with the Caption property
set to The ItsFun
Program.

❑ Click in a free area of the form.

As shown in Figure A.11, the caption of the form is now The ItsFun Program.

Figure A.11.
The form with its new
caption.

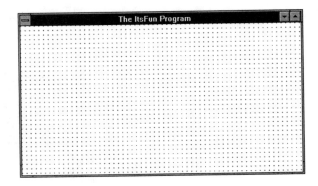

Congratulations! You now know how to set the Caption property of the form.

Changing the Background Color of the Form

Now try to set another property of the form.

☐ Select Properties from the Window menu of Visual Basic (or just press F4).

Visual Basic responds by making the Properties window the active window.

You want to change the background color of the form. Which property should you set? If you examine the list of properties, you'll see the BackColor property. This property determines the background color of the form.

☐ Use the arrow keys on your keyboard to highlight the BackColor property in the list of properties.

Your Properties window now looks like the one shown in Figure A.12.

Figure A.12.
The Properties window,
with the BackColor
property highlighted.

☐ Click the three dots that appear to the right of the property box.

Visual Basic responds by popping up a color palette. (See Figure A.13.)

Figure A.13.
Selecting a background
color for the form.

Select this color —

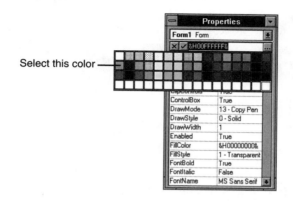

☐ Select the light gray area by clicking the light gray square.

Visual Basic responds by changing the background color of the form to light gray. (See Figure A.14.)

Figure A.14.
The form with its new
background color.

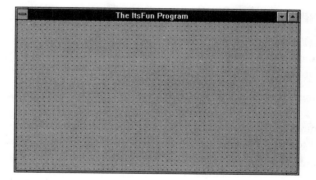

Executing the ItsFun Program

Do you want to execute the ItsFun program now? This is not a joke! Although you have not yet written a single line of code, you can execute the program and see your visual design in action. In fact, it is a very good idea to execute the program from time to time, to see your visual design in action.

Before you execute the program, you ought to save your project:

☐ Select Save Project from the File menu.

Visual Basic responds by saving all the changes that you have made so far to the ItsFun.frm and ItsFun.mak files.

A

To execute the ItsFun program, do the following:

❑ Select Start from the Run menu of Visual Basic (or press F5).

> *Visual Basic responds by executing the ItsFun program.*

As you can see, the main window of the ItsFun program appears exactly as you designed it; it has the caption The Its Fun Program, and its background color is light gray.

Now terminate the ItsFun program:

❑ Click the minus icon that appears on the upper-left corner of the window of the ItsFun program, and select Close from the system menu that pops up.

Changing the Name Property of the Form

As you can see, the form has many properties, and the Properties window lets you set these properties and see the effects of these properties immediately. For example, in the steps in the preceding section you set the Caption property and the BackColor property of the form.

Another property is the Name property. As you'll see later in this appendix, the code that you write will have to refer to the form. How will your code refer to the form? It will refer to its name. If you examine the Name property inside the properties list, you'll see that Visual Basic assigned the name Form1 to the Name property of the form. (See Figure A.15.) Therefore, your code will have to refer to the form as Form1.

Figure A.15.
The Name property of the form.

There is nothing wrong with the name Form1; however, a more friendly and informative name is frmItsFun. The first three characters are frm, to indicate that this is a name of a form, and the rest of the name is an indication that this is the form of the ItsFun program.

❑ Click anywhere inside a free area of the form, and press the F4 key.

Visual Basic responds by displaying the Properties window of the form.

❑ Change the Name property of the form to frmItsFun. (See Figure A.16.)

Figure A.16.
Changing the Name
property of the form to
frmItsFun.

From now on, the code you write will refer to the form as frmItsFun.

Placing a Button Inside the Form

As shown in Figure A.1, the form should contain three buttons.

NOTE

In Windows literature the button is called a pushbutton. In Visual Basic the button is called a command button. A command button and a pushbutton are the same thing.

Now place the Exit button inside the form:

❑ Make the Tools window the active window (that is, select Toolbox from the Window menu of Visual Basic).

Visual Basic responds by making the Toolbox the active window.

❑ Double-click the command button icon inside the Tools window. The icon of the command button is shown in Figure A.17. For clarity, the command button icon is also shown magnified.

Visual Basic responds by placing a command button inside the form. (See Figure A.18.)
This command button will serve as the Exit button.

Figure A.17.
The icon of the command
button in the Tools
window.

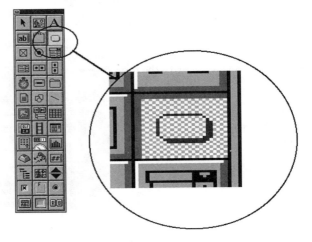

Figure A.18.
Placing a command button
inside the form.

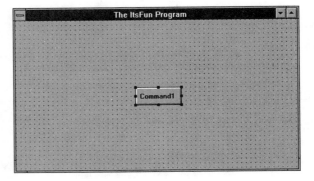

In Figure A.1, the Exit button is located on the lower-left corner of the window. Therefore, you
need to move the button to its proper location.

❑ Drag the button with the mouse. (With the mouse pointer in the Exit button, hold down
the left mouse button and move the mouse. As you can see, the command button moves
in accordance with the mouse movement.) Move the button to its new location, as shown
in Figure A.19.

As you moved the button, Visual Basic automatically changed the Top and Left properties of
the command button. The Top property holds a number that indicates the distance between
the upper-left corner of the command button and the top of the form, and the Left property of the
command button holds a number that indicates the distance between the upper-left corner of
the button and the left edge of the form.

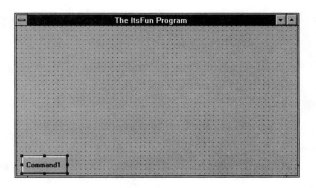

Instead of moving the command button by dragging it with the mouse, you can move the button by changing its Top and Left properties. Here is how you do that:

❑ Make sure that the command button is active (by clicking inside the button).

> *Visual Basic responds by enclosing the button with a rectangle. This rectangle serves as an indication that the button is the selected button. For example, in Figures A.18 and A.19 the command button is shown as selected.*

❑ Press F4 (to display the Properties window).

> *Visual Basic responds by displaying the Properties window of the command button. You can tell that indeed this is the Properties window of the command button by observing that the object box of the Properties window contains the text* Command1*.* Command1 *is the name that Visual Basic assigned to the Name property of the command button. If you place another command button, Visual Basic will assign the name* Command2 *to the Name property of the second command button.*

❑ Set the Top property of the command button to 100.

> *Visual Basic responds by placing the command button with its upper-left corner 100 units from the top edge of the form. (See Figure A.20.)*

Figure A.20.
Placing the command
button 100 units from the
top edge of the form.

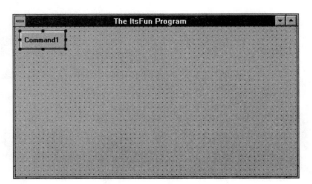

Now place the command button at its final location by setting its Top and Left properties:

❏ Set the Top property of the command property to 3360.

❏ Set the Left property of the command button to 120.

> **NOTE**
>
> The Properties window can display the properties of the form, the properties of the command button, and the properties of other controls that are placed inside the form.
>
> The Properties window displays the properties of the selected control. For example, if the selected control is the command button, pressing F4 will cause the Properties window of the command button to pop up. You can tell which control is described by the Properties window by looking at the object box of the Properties window. For example, in Figure A.16, the object box contains frmItsFun. This means that the Properties window lists the properties of the frmItsFun form.

In Figure A.1, the caption of the Exit button is Exit. Therefore, you must change the Caption property of the button from Command1 to Exit:

❏ Make sure that the command button is selected (by clicking inside it), press F4 to display the Properties window of the command button, and then set the Caption property to E&xit.

Visual Basic responds by changing the caption of the button to Exit. (See Figure A.21.)

Figure A.21.
The Caption property of the button set to E&xit.

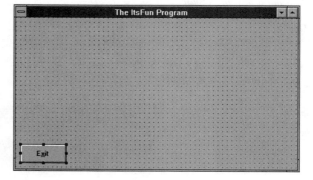

> **NOTE**
>
> The & character that precedes the x character in E&xit causes the x to appear underlined. (You can type the & character by pressing Shift+7.)

This means that during the execution of the program, pressing Alt+X has the same effect as clicking the Exit button.

Executing the ItsFun Program

Now look at your visual design in action:

❑ Select Save Project from the File menu.

❑ Select Start from the Run menu (or press F5).

> *Visual Basic responds by executing the ItsFun program. As you can see, the Exit button appears exactly as you visually designed it.*

❑ Click the Exit button.

Nothing happens! The ItsFun program does not terminate! Why? You have not yet attached any code to the Exit button to cause the ItsFun program to terminate.

To terminate the ItsFun program, do the following:

❑ Click the minus icon that appears in the upper-left corner of the window, and then select Close from the system menu that pops up.

Attaching Code to the Click Event of the Exit Button

When you clicked the Exit button the program did not terminate. This is because you have to write code that is executed whenever you click the Exit button.

Before attaching code to the Exit button, you need to review how Windows and the ItsFun program work together. When you execute the ItsFun program, Windows gives control to the ItsFun program, and the ItsFun program displays the main window. After ItsFun finishes displaying its main form, control is returned to Windows.

Now suppose that the user clicks the Exit button. Windows notices that the mouse is clicked on the Exit button of the ItsFun program, and it generates an event. The event is called the Click event. Windows sends a message to the ItsFun program. Basically, Windows tells the ItsFun program "The user clicked your Exit button."

Now it is up to the ItsFun program to do something about the fact that it received the Click event. You have not yet attached any code to the Exit button, so the ItsFun program does nothing when it receives a message from Windows that tells it that the Exit button was clicked.

In the following steps you'll attach code to the Exit button, so that whenever the user clicks the Exit button that code will be executed.

A

❑ Set the Name property of the Exit button to cmdExit. That is, make sure that the button is selected, and then use the Properties window to change the Name property of the button from Command1 to cmdExit. (See Figure A.22.)

Figure A.22.
Changing the Name
property of the Exit button
from Command1 to
cmdExit.

From now on, the ItsFun program will refer to the Exit button as cmdExit. Note that the first three characters of the name of the button are cmd, to emphasize that this is a command button. This naming convention is not a Visual Basic requirement, but as you'll see when you write the code of the program, it makes the code easier to read.

❑ Double-click the Exit button.

Visual Basic responds by displaying a new window. (See Figure A.23.)

Figure A.23.
The window that Visual
Basic displays when you
double-click the cmdExit
button.

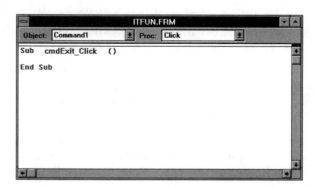

The text that appears inside the window of Figure A.23 is this:

```
Sub cmdExit_Click ()

End Sub
```

The text Sub that appears in the first line indicates that this is the beginning of a procedure. The text End Sub indicates that this is the last line of the procedure. The text cmdExit_Click () that appears in the first line is the name of the procedure.

When you double-click the Exit button, Visual Basic displays the window shown in Figure A.23. The code that appears inside that window shows the first line and the last line of a procedure called cmdExit_Click().

It is important to understand how Visual Basic constructed the name of the procedure. The procedure name is composed of two parts separated by the underscore character. The first part of the procedure name is cmdExit. This means that the procedure will be executed whenever an event that is related to the Exit button occurs. (Recall that you set the Name property of the Exit button to cmdExit.)

The second part of the procedure name is Click, which means that this procedure will be executed whenever the user clicks the object specified in the first part of the procedure name. In other words, the cmdExit_Click() procedure is automatically executed whenever the user clicks the Exit button.

Note that a procedure name ends with the () characters. Sometimes there is text inside the parentheses, but you don't have to worry about this, because it is the responsibility of Visual Basic to construct the name of the procedure, including the text that may appear inside the parentheses.

Visual Basic is kind enough to write for you the first and last lines of the procedure. However, Visual Basic does not write the actual code of the procedure. That is your responsibility.

What do you want to occur when the user clicks the Exit button? You want the ItsFun program to terminate. What if instead of terminating, you want the program to beep whenever the user clicks the Exit button. In this case you have to write code inside the cmdExit_Click() procedure that causes the PC to beep.

❑ Double-click the Exit button.

> *Visual Basic responds by displaying the window shown in Figure A.23. As shown in Figure A.23, Visual Basic prepared a procedure called* cmdExit_Click()*. This procedure is executed automatically whenever the user clicks the Exit button.*

You want the PC to beep whenever the Exit button is clicked, so you have to write code inside the cmdExit_Click() procedure that causes the beep to occur. In Visual Basic you tell the PC to beep by issuing the Beep statement.

❑ Enter the Beep statement inside the cmdExit_Click() procedure. After you enter the Beep statement, your cmdExit_Click() procedure looks like this (See Figure A.24.):

```
Sub cmdExit_Click ()

    Beep

End Sub
```

Note that as you enter the code inside the cmdExit_Click() procedure, you can press the Enter key a couple times to make spaces between the Beep statement and the first and last lines of the procedure. This is done for cosmetic reasons only (so that it is easy to read the procedure). Furthermore, you can type several spaces at the beginning of the line, before you type Beep. Again, this is done for cosmetic reasons only.

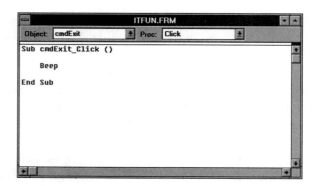

Figure A.24.
The Beep *statement inside the* cmdExit_Click() *procedure.*

Executing the ItsFun Program

❑ Select Save from the File menu of Visual Basic.

❑ Select Start from the Run menu of Visual Basic (or press F5).

> *Visual Basic responds by executing the ItsFun program.*

❑ Click the Exit button.

> *ItsFun responds by beeping every time you click the Exit button! This is because every time you click the Exit button, the* cmdExit_Click() *procedure is executed.*

❑ Experiment with the ItsFun program, and then click the minus icon that appears in the upper-left corner of the window of ItsFun, and select Close from the system menu that pops up.

Comments in Visual Basic

As you write the code of your programs, it is a good idea to add comments. A comment starts with the ' character. Visual Basic ignores all the text that appears to the right of the comment character. The comments that you add to your programs will help you (and others) understand your programs. For example, you can add a comment inside the cmdExit_Click() procedure that explains the purpose of the Beep statement.

❑ Add a comment inside the cmdExit_Click() procedure. That is, double-click the Exit button, and add text to the cmdExit_Click() procedure. After adding the comment, the cmdExit_Click() procedure looks like the following (See Figure A.25.):

```
Sub cmdExit_Click ()

    ' Make the PC beep
    Beep

End Sub
```

Figure A.25.
Adding a comment.

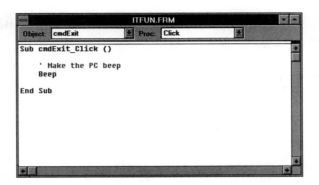

Whenever you click the Exit button the cmdExit_Click() procedure is executed.

You were instructed to type the Beep statement inside the cmdExit_Click() procedure only as an exercise. You don't really want the PC to beep whenever you click the Exit button. Instead, you want the ItsFun program to terminate when the Exit button is clicked. This means that you must remove the Beep statement and instead enter a statement that causes the ItsFun program to terminate. The statement that causes the ItsFun program to terminate is the End statement.

☐ Modify the code of the cmdExit_Click() procedure. (That is, double-click the Exit button, and modify the code inside the cmdExit_Click() procedure.) After modifying the code, your cmdExit_Click() procedure should look like this:

```
Sub cmdExit_Click ()

    ' Terminate the application
    End

End Sub
```

☐ Select Save Project from the File menu.

To execute the ItsFun program do the following:

☐ Select Start from the Run menu (or press F5).

Visual Basic responds by executing the ItsFun application.

☐ Click the Exit button.

ItsFun responds by terminating (because the code inside the cmdExit_Click() procedure was executed).

Placing the Other Controls of the ItsFun Program Inside the Form

As shown in Figure A.1, the ItsFun program should also contain a text box, a Say Something button, and a Clear button. Next you'll place the Say Something button inside the form.

A

Placing the Say Something Button Inside the Form

❑ Place a button inside the form by double-clicking the command button inside the Tools window, and set the properties of the command button according to the following specifications:

Property	Setting
Name	cmdSaySomething
Top	240
Left	360
Caption	&Say Something

Note that to view the form you have to select Project from the Window menu of Visual Basic and then click the View Form button that appears inside the Project window.

❑ Make sure that the button is selected and then use the mouse to make the button larger. You enlarge the button by dragging the small black squares that appear on the rectangle that surrounds the button.

After you place the Say Something button, the form looks like the one in Figure A.26.

Figure A.26.
The Say Something button
placed inside the form.

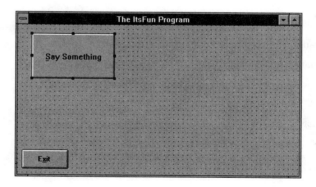

❑ Select Save Project from the File menu.

❑ Select Start from the Run menu.

Visual Basic responds by executing the ItsFun program.

❑ Click the Say Something button.

As you can see, nothing happens! This is because you have not yet attached any code to the Say Something button.

❑ Click the Exit button to terminate the ItsFun program.

Placing a Text Box Inside the Form

You'll now place a text box inside the form.

❑ Place a text box inside the form. The text box icon in the Tools window is shown in Figure A.27.

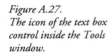

Figure A.27.
The icon of the text box
control inside the Tools
window.

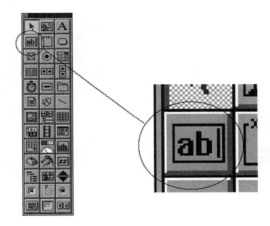

❑ Set the properties of the text box to be the following:

Property	Settings	Comment
Name	txtMyTextBox	
Text	(empty)	To empty the contents of the text box, delete the characters of the Text property.
Top	1920	The upper-left corner of the text box is 1920 units from the upper edge of the form.
Left	1320	The upper-left corner of the text box is 1320 units from the left edge of the form.
Width	4695	The width of the text box is 4695 units.
Height	975	The height of the text box is 975 units.

When you finish setting the properties, the form looks like the one shown in Figure A.28.

❑ Select Save Project from the File menu.

❑ Select Start from the Run menu.

Visual Basic responds by executing the ItsFun program.

❑ Click the Say Something button.

Figure A.28.
A text box added to the
frmItsFun form.

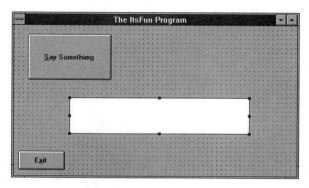

As you can see, nothing happens, because you have not yet attached any code to the Say Something button. Recall that when you click the Say Something button, the PC should talk in human voice.

❑ Click inside the text box and then type something in it.

You can type in the text box. However, you cannot type on multiple lines! You'll now fix this problem.

❑ Click the Exit button (or press Alt+X) to terminate the ItsFun program.

❑ To view the form, select Project from the Window menu, and then click the View Form button that appears inside the Project window.

❑ Select the text box control, and then press F4 to view the Properties window of the text box.

❑ Set the MultiLine property of the text box to True. You do that by highlighting the MultiLine property and then clicking the down-arrow icon that appears to the left of the property box and selecting True from the list that drops down.

❑ Select Save Project from the File menu.

To execute the ItsFun program, do the following:

❑ Press F5, or select Start from the Run menu, or click the Run icon. The Run icon is shown in Figure A.29.

> *Visual Basic responds by executing the ItsFun program.*

❑ Click inside the text box and type something.

❑ Press the Enter key to advance to the next line.

As you can see, now you can type on multiple lines (because you set the MultiLine property of the text box to True).

You can now click the Exit button of the ItsFun program to terminate the program. Alternatively, you can click the Stop icon to terminate the program. (See Figure A.30.) Note that during the execution of the ItsFun program, Visual Basic replaced the Run icon with the Stop icon. Similarly, after you click the Stop icon, Visual Basic replaces the Stop icon with the Run icon.

Figure A.29.
The Run icon.

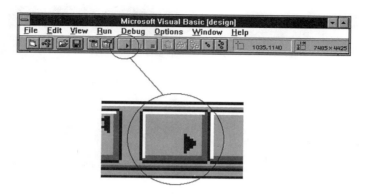

Figure A.30.
The Stop icon.

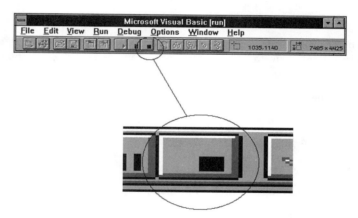

Note that the text box does not have a horizontal or vertical scroll bar. You can easily fix this.

❏ Set the ScrollBars property to 3—Both. That is, select the text box, press F4 to display the Properties window of the text box, highlight the ScrollBars property in the Properties window, click the down-arrow icon that appears to the left of the Property box, and select 3—Both.

Save the project and then execute the ItsFun program:

❏ Select Save Project from the File menu.

❏ Select Start from the Run menu.

Visual Basic responds by executing the ItsFun program. As shown in Figure A.31, now the text box contains horizontal and vertical scroll bars.

Figure A.31.
The text box with horizontal and vertical scroll bars.

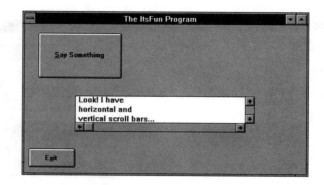

❏ Experiment with the ItsFun program and then click the Exit button to terminate the program.

The preceding steps were presented so that you can see how easy it is to manipulate controls in Visual Basic. However, the text box of the final ItsFun program should not have scroll bars and should not let the user type anything in it. Here is how you take off the scroll bars:

❏ Set the ScrollBars property of the text box to 0 – None.

Here is how you prevent the user from typing inside the text box:

❏ Set the Enabled property to False.

Save the project and then execute it:

❏ Select Save Project from the File menu.

❏ Select Start from the Run menu.

❏ Try to type inside the text box.

As you can see, the text box does not accept any characters (because you set its Enabled property to False).

❏ Terminate the ItsFun program.

Attaching Code to the Say Something Button

The code that you'll attach to the Say Something button will be executed automatically whenever the user clicks the Say Something button. This code will place text inside the text box. (The user is not able to place text inside the text box because the Enabled property of the text box is set to False. However, the code that you'll now add will place text inside the text box.)

❏ Double-click the Say Something button.

> *Visual Basic responds by displaying the* cmdSaySomething_Click() *procedure, which looks like this:*

```
Sub cmdSaySomething_Click ()

End Sub
```

❏ Enter code inside the cmdSaySomething_Click() procedure, so that the code looks like this:

```
Sub cmdSaySomething_Click ()

    txtMyTextBox.Text = "It's been fun working with you."

End Sub
```

The code you entered sets the Text property of the text box to It's been fun working with you.

Note how this statement is constructed. The text box is identified by its name, txtMyTextBox (because you set the Name property of this text box to txtMyTextBox). A period appears after the name of the object, followed by the name of the property:

```
txtMyTextBox.Text
```

The equals sign assigns the string It's been fun working with you. to the Text property of the txtMyTextBox text box:

```
txtMyTextBox.Text = "It's been fun working with you."
```

Figure A.32 illustrates this statement.

Figure A.32.
The structure of the statement that sets a property of an object.

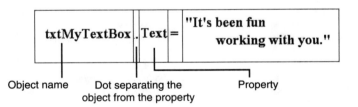

Object name   Dot separating the object from the property   Property

Save the project and then execute the ItsFun program:

❏ Select Save Project from the File menu.

❏ Select Start from the File menu.

> *Visual Basic responds by executing the ItsFun program.*

❏ Click the Say Something button.

> *ItsFun responds by placing the text* It's been fun working with you. *inside the text box. (See Figure A.33.)*

Figure A.33.
The text that appears inside
the text box after you click
the Say Something button.

A

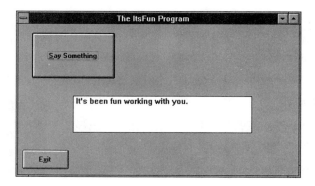

NOTE

In Visual Basic you must type a statement on a single line. For example, the statement

```
txtMyTextBox.Text = "It's been fun working with you."
```

must be typed on a single line.

In fact, if you spread this statement on two lines, Visual Basic will prompt you with a syntax error.

Therefore, you cannot type the statement this way:

```
txtMyTextBox.Text =
         "It's been fun working with you."
```

Note that the width of this book can accommodate only a certain number of characters on a single line. Unfortunately, sometimes Visual Basic's statements are long and cannot fit on a single line in this book!

To solve the problem, we use the ➥ character to denote a line continuation. When you see the ➥ character, make sure to type the line that follows the ➥ character on the previous line.

For example, if the book instructs you to type the line

```
txtMyTextBox.Text =
➥ "It's been fun"
```

you must type it as follows:

```
txtMyTextBox.Text = "It's been fun."
```

Sometimes, the code in the book is written like this:

```
MyString =
    ➥ String1 +
    ➥ String2 +
    ➥ String3
```

This statement must be typed as follows:

```
MyString = String1 + String2 + String3
```

Another example illustrates the very important ➡ notation. If you see the following:

```
MyProcedure (Para1,
    ➡    Para2, Para3,
    ➡    Para4,
    ➡    )
```

you must type the line like this:

```
MyProcedure (Para1, Para2, Para3, Para4 )
```

Aligning the Text Inside the Text Box

As shown in Figure A.33, the text inside the text box is left aligned. You can align the text in the center of the text box by setting the Alignment property of the text box in the Properties window.

❏ Set the Alignment property of the text box control to 2—Center.

Save your project and then execute the ItsFun program:

❏ Select Save Project from the File menu.

❏ Select Start from the Run menu.

❏ Execute the ItsFun program.

❏ Click the Say Something button.

> *The ItsFun program responds by placing the string at the center of the text box. (See Figure A.34.)*

Figure A.34.
The text box with its text centered.

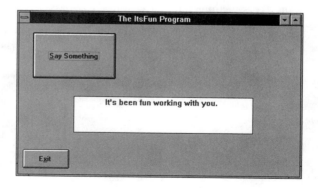

❏ Click the Exit button to terminate the ItsFun program.

Setting the FontSize Property from Within the Code

In the previous section, you set the Alignment property to 2—Center by using the Properties window. This is known as setting the property at design time. However, you can also set properties from within your code (just as you set the Text property from within the cmdSaySomething_Click() procedure). This is known as setting the property at runtime.

One of the properties of the text box is the FontSize property.

❏ Examine the FontSize property of the text box.

> *As you can see, Visual Basic set the default value of this property to 8.25 points.*

You can set this property to a different value at design time or at runtime. Try setting the value of this property to 12 points at runtime:

❏ Modify the cmdSaySomething_Click() procedure so that it looks like this:

```
Sub cmdSaySomething_Click ()

    ' Set the FontSize property of the text box
    ' to 12 points.
    txtMyTextBox.FontSize = 12


    txtMyTextBox.Text = "It's been fun working with you."

End Sub
```

Save the project and then execute the ItsFun program:

❏ Select Save Project from the File menu.

❏ Select Start from the Run menu.

> *Visual Basic responds by executing the ItsFun program.*

❏ Click the Say Something button.

> *ItsFun responds by displaying the message inside the text box with a 12-point font size. (See Figure A.35.)*

Figure A.35.
The text box with its
FontSize property set to
12 points.

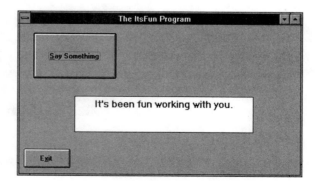

❑ Click the Exit button to terminate the ItsFun program.

Visually Designing and Writing the Code of the Clear Button

You'll now implement the Clear button in the ItsFun program.

First, you have to visually place a command button in the form so that it looks like the one in Figure A.1.

❑ Double-click the command button icon of the Tools window to place a command button inside the form.

> *Visual Basic responds by placing a command button in the center of the form.*

❑ Move and size the command button so that it looks like the one in Figure A.1.

Note that to size the button you can set its Width and Height properties. You can also size the button by using the mouse to drag the small squares that appear on the rectangle that surrounds the selected command button. (These solid squares are called *handles.*)

Set the properties of the Clear command button as follows:

> Name: cmdClear
> Caption: &Clear
> Top: 240
> Left: 4800
> Height: 1215
> Width: 2175

If you are new to Visual Basic, you probably want to see your visual design in action at this point.

Save the project and then execute the ItsFun program:

❑ Select Save Project from the File menu.

❑ Select Start from the Run menu.

> *The main window of ItsFun appears, as shown in Figure A.1.*

❑ Click the Say Something button.

> *ItsFun responds by displaying a message inside the text box.*

❑ Click the Clear button.

Of course nothing is cleared (because you have not yet attached any code to the Clear button).

❑ Click the Exit button to terminate the ItsFun program.

The Clear button looks fine. Now it's time to attach code to this button so that it will clear the text box:

❑ Add the following code inside the `cmdClear_Click()` procedure:

A

NOTE

To attach the code, double-click the Clear button. Visual Basic responds by opening the window that contains the `cmdClear_Click()` procedure.

```
Sub cmdClear_Click ()

    ' Clear the text box
    txtMyTextBox.Text = ""

End Sub
```

The code you entered consists of a single statement:

```
txtMyTextBox.Text = ""
```

This code assigns a null string (an empty string) to the Text property of the `txtMyTextBox` text box.

So when you click the Clear button, the Text property of the text box is assigned with the null string, which empties the contents of the text box.

Save your project and then execute the ItsFun program:

❏ Select Save Project from the File menu.

❏ Select Start from the Run menu.

   Visual Basic responds by executing the ItsFun program.

❏ Click the Say Something button.

   The ItsFun program responds by displaying a message box inside the text box.

❏ Click the Clear button.

   The ItsFun program responds by clearing the text box.

❏ Experiment with the ItsFun program.

❏ Click the Exit button to terminate the ItsFun program.

The ItsFun program is almost finished. As stated at the beginning of this chapter, you'll continue working on the ItsFun program in Appendixes B and C. As you read at the beginning of this chapter, the ItsFun program will also be able to speak in human voice.

B

Visual Basic Essentials
(Part II)

In this appendix you'll continue to implement the ItsFun program that you started in Appendix A.

Procedures, Functions, Variables, and All That...

In this appendix you'll learn about the main programming building blocks of Visual Basic. You'll learn about concepts such as procedures, functions, variables, and programming statements (for example, If, If...Else, and For loops).

Variables

In Appendix A you wrote (but did not complete) the ItsFun program. That program did not use any variables. Rather, the information was stored in the properties. For example, the contents of the text box are stored inside the Text property:

```
txtMyTextBox.Text = "Its been fun working with you"
```

Sometimes you need to store data, but there isn't any property designed to store that particular data. For example, suppose that the ItsFun program has to calculate the sum of all the integers from 1 to 5, and then display the result inside the text box.

In such a case, you could use a variable called Result and calculate the value of Result as follows:

```
Result = 1 + 2 + 3 + 4 + 5
```

Now add code that performs these calculations.

If your Visual Basic program is not running, complete the following steps to start Visual Basic and load the ItsFun.mak project:

☐ Double-click the icon of the Visual Basic program inside the Visual Basic group of icons.

Windows responds by executing Visual Basic.

☐ Select Open Project from the File menu.

Visual Basic responds by displaying the Open Project dialog box. (See Figure B.1.)

Figure B.1.
The Open Project
dialog box.

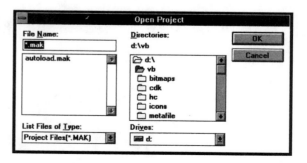

☐ Inside the File Name box, enter the following:

```
C:\LEARNVB\PRACTICE\Appendix\ItsFun.mak
```

Visual Basic responds by loading the ItsFun project, which you wrote in Appendix A.

☐ Double-click the command button tool inside the Tools window.

Visual Basic responds by placing a command button in the center of the form.

☐ Move the button so that it's between the Say Something and the Clear buttons. Recall that you can move a command button by dragging it.

☐ Set the Name property of the new button to cmdCalculate.

☐ Set the Caption property of the button to Ca&lculate.

Note that the *l* character in Ca&lculate is prefixed with the & character. This means that during the execution of the ItsFun program, pressing Alt+L has the same result as clicking the Calculate button. You don't want to prefix the *C* character of Calculate with the & character because the Clear button already has its *C* prefixed with the & character, and it does not make sense to have another button inside the form that can be clicked by pressing Alt+C.

Your form should now look like the one in Figure B.2.

Figure B.2.
The form with the
Calculate button.

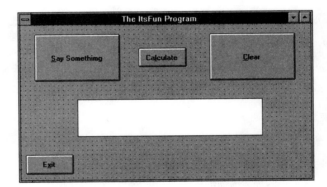

Attaching Code to the Click Event of the Calculate Button

You'll now attach code to the Click event of the Calculate button.

☐ Double-click the Calculate button.

Visual Basic responds by displaying the window that contains the cmdCalculate_Click() procedure.

B

❑ Add the following code inside the `cmdCalculate_Click()` procedure:

```
Sub cmdCalculate_Click ()

    Dim Result

    Result = 1 + 2 + 3 + 4 + 5

    txtMyTextBox.Text = Result

End Sub
```

The code you entered is executed whenever the user clicks the Calculate button.

The first line in the `cmdCalculate_Click()` procedure declares the `Result` variable:

```
Dim Result
```

`Dim` is a keyword in Visual Basic that is used for declaring variables. It means that the word following the `Dim` word is the name of a variable. Therefore, this statement declares a variable called `Result`.

The next statement calculates the sum of all the integers between 1 and 5, and assigns the result of the summation to the `Result` variable:

```
Result = 1 + 2 + 3 + 4 + 5
```

The last statement assigns the value of `Result` to the Text property of the text box:

```
txtMyTextBox.Text = Result
```

Because the `Result` variable is equal to 1+2+3+4+5=15, the text box is filled with 15.

Save your project:

❑ Select Save Project from the File menu.

Execute the ItsFun program:

❑ Select Start from the Run menu.

> *Visual Basic responds by executing the ItsFun program.*

❑ Click the Calculate button.

> *The ItsFun program responds by displaying the text 15 inside the text box. (See Figure B.3.)*

❑ Experiment with the ItsFun program and then click the Exit button to exit the program.

The `Option Explicit` Statement

If you know how to write programs using other programming languages, you probably know that in some programming languages you must declare a variable before using it. In the ItsFun program you did declare the variable. That is, you used the statement

```
Dim Result
```

Figure B.3.
The text box after the
Calculate button is clicked.

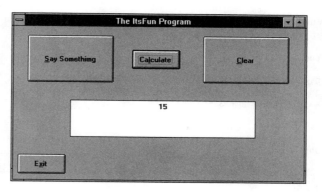

It is a good idea to declare variables because by doing so you can avoid serious bugs in your programs. To see how declaring a variable saves you from bugs, consider the following code:

```
Sub cmdCalculate_Click ()

    Result = 1 + 2 + 3 + 4 + 5

    txtMyTextBox.Text = Reslt

End Sub
```

This code omits the declaration of the Result variable, and also assigns the value of Reslt to the Text property of the text box. Note that the Text property was assigned the value of the Reslt variable (not the Result variable). Yes, it happens; sometimes you type a variable with an error! (In this case, the u character of Result was omitted.)

The text box will not display the value 15. Why? Result is equal to 15, but Reslt is equal to Null. That is, whenever Visual Basic creates a variable such as Result or Reslt, it initially sets the value of the variable to Null. Therefore, when Visual Basic first encounters the variable Result, it sets its value to Null. But it immediately changes the variable's value to 15 because of the statement

```
Result = 1 + 2 + 3 + 4 + 5
```

Then Visual Basic encounters the variable Reslt, and it automatically assigns to it the value Null.

Therefore, the statement

```
txtMyTextBox.Text = Reslt
```

tells Visual Basic to fill the Text property of the text box with Null!

Sometimes even a very experienced programmer can sit for hours trying to figure out why the text box displays Null instead of 15! This is particularly true in the case of long and complex programs.

To save you from yourself, the designers of Visual Basic introduced the Option Explicit statement.

The Option Explicit statement forces you to declare the variables before you can use them. If you use a variable that has not been declared, Visual Basic prompts you with an error message, telling you that the variable is not declared.

B

Now assume that you added the Option Explicit statement and then wrote the cmdCalculate_Click() function like this:

```
Sub cmdCalculate_Click ()

    Dim Result

    Result = 1 + 2 + 3 + 4 + 5

    txtMyTextBox.Text = Reslt

End Sub
```

This procedure includes the declaration of the Result variable. When Visual Basic encounters the statement

```
Result = 1 + 2 + 3 + 4 + 5
```

it has no problems with it, because Result had already been declared.

However, when Visual Basic encounters the statement

```
txtMyTextBox.Text = Reslt
```

it prompts you with an error message, because the statement Option Explicit tells Visual Basic that all variables must be declared, and the Reslt variable was not declared.

Now that you know that the Option Explicit statement is very important, attach this statement to your program.

❑ Double-click the Calculate button (or any other object inside the form).

Visual Basic responds by displaying the procedure window that corresponds to the object you double-clicked.

❑ Click the down-arrow icon that appears on the right side of the Object box at the top-left side of the Procedure window.

Visual Basic responds by dropping down a list of objects. (See Figure B.4.)

In Figure B.4, the list contains the cmdCalculate button, the cmdClear button, the cmdExit button, and so on.

Note that the first item in the list in Figure B.4 is (general), which is not a name of an object; it is just the name of a place in Visual Basic where you write special code.

❑ Click the (general) item in the list.

❑ Enter the following statement inside the general window:

```
Option Explicit
```

Your general window should look like the one in Figure B.5.

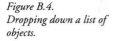
Figure B.4.
Dropping down a list of
objects.

Figure B.5.
Adding the Option
Explicit *statement inside*
the general declarations
section.

Note that the Proc text box is located to the left of the Object box. As shown in Figure B.5, the Proc box is filled with the text (declarations). You placed the Option Explicit statement inside the general declarations section.

NOTE

The Option Explicit statement tells Visual Basic that all variables must be declared.

Because the Option Explicit statement is so important, the designers of Visual Basic include a feature that automatically places this statement inside the general declarations section.

Here is how you tell Visual Basic to automatically place the Option Explicit statement inside the general declarations section:

❑ Select Environment from the Options menu of Visual Basic. (See Figure B.6.)

Visual Basic responds by displaying the Environment Options dialog box. (See Figure B.7.)

Figure B.6.
Selecting Environment
from the Options menu.

B

Figure B.7.
The Environment Options
dialog box.

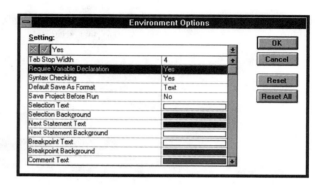

☐ Make sure that the Require Variable Declaration item is set to Yes. If it is set to No, double-click No.

> *Visual Basic responds by setting* Require Variable Declaration *to* Yes.

☐ Click the OK button of the Environment Options dialog box.

From now on, whenever you start a new project, the general declarations section will contain the Option Explicit statement.

Adding Strings

As shown in Figure B.3, when the user clicks the Calculate button the text box is filled with the text 15. To better show the meaning of the number that appears inside the text box, do the following:

☐ Modify the cmdCalculate_Click() procedure so that it looks like this:

```
Sub cmdCalculate_Click ()

    Dim Result

    Result = 1 + 2 + 3 + 4 + 5

    txtMyTextBox.Text =
        ➥ "The sum of the integers is:" +
        ➥ Result

End Sub
```

☐ Select Save Project from the File menu.

☐ Select Start from the Run menu.

> *Visual Basic responds by executing the ItsFun program.*

❑ Click the Calculate button.

> *The ItsFun program responds by displaying the string* The sum of the integers is:15 *inside the text box. (See Figure B.8.)*

Figure B.8.
The text that ItsFun
displays after the user clicks
the Calculate button.

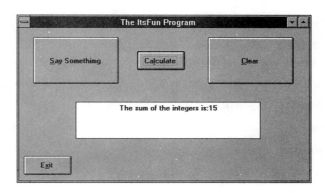

The Str$() Function

When you declared the Result variable, you used the following statement:

```
Dim Result
```

So what type of data can Result hold? Can it hold a string, an integer, or a date?

Because you did not specifically declare Result as any particular data type, Visual Basic assumes that it is a variant data type. A variant data type variable is a variable that can assume many types of data. For example, the Result variable is a variant data type (because you did not specify its data type), and in the cmdCalculate_Click() procedure you used a statement that treats the Result variable as an integer:

```
Result = 1 + 2 + 3 + 4 + 5
```

In this statement you add integers and assign the result (which is an integer) to the Result variable.

You treat the Result variable as a string when you use the statement

```
txtMyTextBox.Text = Result
```

In this statement you assign the value of Result to the Text property of the text box. The Text property expects a string. This means that Result is being treated as a string.

In the following statement also you treat Result as a string:

```
txtMyTextBox.Text =
        ➥ "The sum of the integers is:" +
        ➥ Result
```

B

The variant data type is convenient to use, but it could create bugs in your programs (because the conversion between the data types that the variant variable holds is performed automatically by Visual Basic). To avoid bugs, Visual Basic enables you to declare a variable as a specific data type. The following statement declares the Result variable as an integer:

```
Dim Result As Integer
```

From now on, if you try to use Result as data that is not an integer, Visual Basic will prompt you with an error message. To see this in action, try the following:

❑ Modify the cmdCalculate_Click() procedure so that it looks like this:

```
Sub cmdCalculate_Click ()

    Dim Result As Integer

    Result = 1 + 2 + 3 + 4 + 5

    ' This statement will cause an error!
    txtMyTextBox.Text =
            ➥ "The sum of the integers is:" +
            ➥ Result

End Sub
```

In this code you declare Result as an integer:

```
Dim Result As Integer
```

The statement

```
Result = 1 + 2 + 3 + 4 + 5
```

does not violate the declaration of the Result variable, but the following statement does violate the declaration:

```
txtMyTextBox.Text =
            ➥ "The sum of the integers is:" +
            ➥ Result
```

It violates the declaration of the Result variable because Result is declared as an integer, but the statement treats it as a string.

❑ Select Start from the Run menu.

> *Visual Basic responds by executing the ItsFun program. However, Visual Basic notices the error in the statement that violates the declaration of the* Result *variable, and it displays the dialog box shown in Figure B.9.*

Figure B.9.
The Type Mismatch
dialog box.

❑ Click the OK button of the Type Mismatch dialog box.

> *Visual Basic responds by terminating the ItsFun program and highlighting the piece of code that created the error.*

To fix the problem, you have to convert the integer `Result` to a string. You do that by using the `Str$()` function.

The `Str$()` function converts a numeric variable to a string. Inside the parentheses of the `Str$()` function you type the numeric value. For example, to convert the integer 3 to the string 3, use `Str$(3)`. The value that you enter inside the parentheses of the function is called the *parameter* of the function.

❑ Modify the `cmdCalculate_Click()` procedure so that it looks like this:

```
Sub cmdCalculate_Click ()

    Dim Result As Integer
    Dim StringResult As String


    Result = 1 + 2 + 3 + 4 + 5
    StringResult = Str$(Result)

    txtMyTextBox.Text =
            ➡ "The sum of the integers is:" +
            ➡ StringResult


End Sub
```

In this code you declare `Result` as an integer, and then declare `StringResult` as another variable of type `String`:

```
Dim Result As Integer
    Dim StringResult As String
```

You then assign an integer value to the `Result` variable:

```
    Result = 1 + 2 + 3 + 4 + 5
```

Then you convert the integer `Result` to a string:

```
    StringResult = Str$(Result)
```

In this statement, you supply `Result` as the parameter of the `Str$()` function and then assign the returned value of `Str$()` to the `StringResult` variable.

Finally, you add the two strings and assign their values to the Text property of the text box:

```
txtMyTextBox.Text =
            ➡ "The sum of the integers is:" +
            ➡ StringResult
```

❑ Select Start from the Run menu.

> *Visual Basic responds by executing the ItsFun program.*

❑ Click the Calculate button, and verify that the ItsFun program operates properly.

❑ Click the Exit button to terminate the ItsFun program.

Note that you can avoid the step of declaring the StringResult variable. For example, the following code does not declare the StringResult variable:

```
Sub cmdCalculate_Click ()

    Dim Result As Integer

    Result = 1 + 2 + 3 + 4 + 5

    txtMyTextBox.Text =
            ➨ "The sum of the integers is:" +
            ➨ Str$(Result)


End Sub
```

As you can see, Str$(Result) was used in the statement that assigns a value to the Text property:

```
txtMyTextBox.Text =
        ➨ "The sum of the integers is:" +
        ➨ Str$(Result)
```

This is the preferred way of writing the code, because the procedure is short and therefore easy to read.

The If Statement

A very important statement (in every programming language) is the If statement. The If statement checks to see whether certain conditions are satisfied.

Suppose that you want to add the integers from 1 to 5, and if the result is greater than 10, the program should display a message that tells you that the result is larger than 10. Here is how you accomplish that:

❑ Modify the cmdCalculate_Click() procedure so that it looks like this:

```
Sub cmdCalculate_Click ()

    Dim Result As Integer

    Result = 1 + 2 + 3 + 4 + 5

    If Result > 10 Then

        txtMyTextBox.Text = "Yes! Larger than 10."

    End If

End Sub
```

In this code you use the If statement to examine the value of Result:

```
If Result > 10 Then

    txtMyTextBox.Text = "Yes! Larger than 10."

End If
```

The first line of the If statement checks the value of Result. If Result is larger than 10, the code between the first line and the End If line is executed.

❑ Select Start from the Run menu.

❑ Click the Calculate button.

> *The ItsFun program responds by displaying the message* Yes! Larger than 10. *inside the text box. In other words, because* Result *is equal to 15, the* If *condition is satisfied and the code between the* If *line and the* End If *line is executed.*

❑ Click the Exit button to terminate the ItsFun program.

Note that if the If condition is not satisfied, the code between the If line and the End If line is skipped. You can verify this:

❑ Modify the cmdCalculate_Click() procedure so that it looks like this:

```
Sub cmdCalculate_Click ()

    Dim Result As Integer

    Result = 1 + 2 + 3 + 4 + 5

    If Result < 10 Then

        txtMyTextBox.Text = "Yes! Smaller than 10."

    End If

End Sub
```

In this code you modify the If condition, so now the If statement checks whether Result is less than 10:

```
If Result < 10 Then

    txtMyTextBox.Text = "Yes! Smaller than 10."

End If
```

If Result is less than 10, the string Yes! Smaller than 10. is assigned to the Text property:

```
txtMyTextBox.Text = "Yes! Smaller than 10."
```

❑ Select Start from the Run menu.

❑ Click the Calculate button.

As you can see, the contents of the text box do not change, because Result is not less than 10, and therefore the code inside the If block is not executed.

❏ Click the Exit button to terminate the ItsFun program.

The If...Else Statement

Suppose that you want to check the value of Result, and if its value is larger than 10, you want the program to display the Yes! Larger than 10. message inside the text box. However, if Result is less than 10, you want the program to display the Yes! Smaller than 10. message inside the text box.

One way of implementing this is the following:

```
Sub cmdCalculate_Click ()

    Dim Result As Integer

    Result = 1 + 2 + 3 + 4 + 5

    If Result > 10 Then

       txtMyTextBox.Text = "Yes! Larger than 10."

    End If


    If Result < 10 Then

       txtMyTextBox.Text = "Yes! Smaller than 10."

    End If

End Sub
```

In this code the first If statement checks whether the value of Result is larger than 10, and if so it displays the appropriate message.

Similarly, the second If block checks whether the value of Result is smaller than 10, and if so it displays the appropriate message.

There is nothing wrong with this implementation, except that there is a better way of accomplishing it.

❏ Modify the cmdCalculate_Click() procedure so that it looks like this:

```
Sub cmdCalculate_Click ()

    Dim Result As Integer

    Result = 1 + 2 + 3 + 4 + 5

    If Result < 10 Then
```

```
    txtMyTextBox.Text = "Yes! Smaller than 10."

Else

    txtMyTextBox.Text = "Yes! Larger than 10."

End If
```

End Sub

In this code you use the If...Else statement. The program checks the If condition, and if the condition is satisfied, the code between the If and the Else is executed. The program then skips the code between the Else and the End If lines.

If the condition is not satisfied, the program does not execute the code between the If and the Else, but it executes the code between the Else and the End If.

❑ Select Start from the Run menu.

❑ Click the Calculate button, and verify that the ItsFun program operates properly.

❑ Click the Exit button to terminate the ItsFun program.

The For Loop

Another important programming building block is the For loop.

When you calculate the sum of integers between 1 and 5, you use the statement

```
Result = 1 + 2 + 3 + 4 + 5
```

What will you do if you have to calculate the sum of integers between 1 and 100? In this case, you should use the For loop statement.

❑ Modify the cmdCalculate_Click() procedure so that it looks like this:

```
Sub cmdCalculate_Click ()

    Dim Result, I

    For I = 1 To 5 Step 1

        Result = Result + I

    Next I

    txtMyTextBox.Text = Result

End Sub
```

In this code you declare two variables, Result and I:

```
Dim Result, I
```

In other words, instead of using two separate Dim statements, as in

```
Dim Result
Dim I
```

you use a single Dim statement to declare both variables. The only reason for doing so is to save typing.

Then a For loop is executed:

```
For I = 1 To 5 Step 1

    Result = Result + I

Next I
```

When the program encounters the For loop, it sets I to 1 (as indicated on the first line of the For loop). It then checks to see whether I is equal to 5 (because the To 5 appears on the first line of the For loop). Because I is currently not equal to 5, the program executes the code between the first line of the For loop and the Next I line.

As stated, I is equal to 1, and therefore the code inside the For loop is executed:

```
Result = Result + I
```

Because Result is currently equal to 0, this statement means the following:

```
Result = 0 + 1
```

Therefore, Result is assigned with the value of 1.

The program then encounters the Next I statement. This statement causes the program to return to the first line of the For loop. The program then increases the value of I by 1. Why by 1? The first line of the For loop includes the text Step 1.

So now I is increased from 1 to 2. Because I is equal to 2 (which is less than 5), the statement

```
Result = Result + I
```

is executed again. Now Result is equal to 1, and I is equal to 2.

Therefore, this statement means the following:

```
Result = 1 + 2
```

After this statement executes, Result is equal to 3. The program then encounters the Next I statement, and the whole process repeats.

Eventually I is equal to 5. At that point, the program executes the code of the For loop, and then the For loop is terminated. The loop is terminated because the condition of the loop is For I =1 To 5.

The program executes the code inside the For loop five times, which amounts to the following:

```
Result =  0 + 1 = 1
Result =  1 + 2 = 3
Result =  3 + 3 = 6
Result =  6 + 4 = 10
Result = 10 + 5 = 15
```

❑ Select Start from the Run menu.

❑ Click the Calculate button, and verify that Result is equal to 15.

❑ Click the Exit button to terminate the ItsFun program.

As an exercise, write a For loop that calculates the following sum:

```
Result = 1 + 3 + 5 + 7 = 16
```

❑ Modify the cmdCalculate_Click() procedure so that it looks like this:

```
Sub cmdCalculate_Click ()

    Dim Result, I

    For I = 1 To 7 Step 2

        Result = Result + I

    Next I

    txtMyTextBox.Text = Result

End Sub
```

This loop starts by setting I to 1, and then Result is calculated like this:

```
Result = 0 + 1
```

On the next iteration, I is equal to 3. This is because the first line of the For loop includes the text Step 2. So now I equals I = 1 + 2 = 3. Because 3 is not greater than 7, the following statement is executed again:

```
Result = Result + I
```

This means the following:

```
Result = 1 + 3
```

The program continues executing the For loop until eventually I is equal to 7. When I is equal to 7, the code inside the For loop is executed for the first time.

❑ Select Start from the Run menu.

❑ Click the Calculate button, and verify the proper operation of the ItsFun program.

❑ Click the Exit button to terminate the ItsFun program.

The MsgBox **Statement**

Sometimes you will need to display a message to your users. As you already saw, one way of accomplishing this is by placing a text box inside the form and filling the Text property of the text box with the message you want to display.

Alternatively, you can use the MsgBox statement.

❏ Modify the cmdCalculate_Click() procedure so that it looks like this:

```
Sub cmdCalculate_Click ()

    Dim Result, I

    For I = 1 To 100 Step 1

        Result = Result + I

    Next I


    MsgBox "Result =" + Result

End Sub
```

The code you entered uses a For loop to calculate the sum of all the integers from 1 to 100:

```
    For I = 1 To 100 Step 1

        Result = Result + I

    Next I
```

Then the MsgBox statement is executed:

```
MsgBox "Result =" + Result
```

The MsgBox statement displays a dialog box. The dialog box contains this:

```
"Result =" + Result
```

❏ Select Start from the Run menu.

❏ Click the Calculate button.

The ItsFun program responds by displaying the dialog box shown in Figure B.10.

Figure B.10.
The dialog box that the
MsgBox statement displays.

As shown in Figure B.10, the MsgBox statement displays Result =5050.

❑ Click the OK button of the dialog box to close it.

❑ Click the Exit button to terminate the ItsFun program.

Other Parameters of the MsgBox Statement

As you saw in the previous section, you have to write the text that you want to be displayed inside the dialog box after MsgBox, as in the following:

```
MsgBox  "Displaying this string"
```

So in this statement "Displaying this string" serves as the parameter of the MsgBox statement, and in the statement

```
MsgBox "Result =" + Result
```

"Result =" + Result serves as the parameter of the MsgBox statement.

As it turns out, you can enter other optional parameters to the MsgBox statement. That is, the first parameter is the string that is displayed inside the dialog box, which is not optional; you must supply this parameter. However, the MsgBox statement has other parameters that are optional:

❑ Double-click the word MsgBox inside the cmdCalculate_Click() procedure.

Visual Basic responds by highlighting the word MsgBox. *(See Figure B.11.)*

Figure B.11.
Highlighting the word
MsgBox.

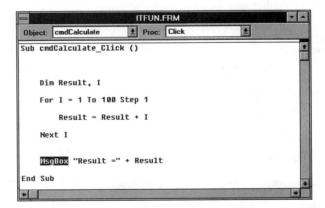

❑ Press the F1 key on your keyboard.

Visual Basic responds by displaying the Help window for the highlighted word. In this case Visual Basic displays the Help window of MsgBox. *(See Figure B.12.)*

Figure B.12.
The Help window of
MsgBox.

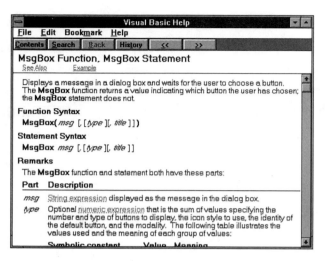

As shown in the Help window of MsgBox, Visual Basic supports a MsgBox statement and a MsgBox() function. This section covers the topic of the MsgBox statement, and the next section covers the topic of the MsgBox() function.

As indicated in the Help window of MsgBox, the syntax of the MsgBox statement is this:

```
MsgBox msg [,[type][,title]]
```

The Help window also indicates the following:

```
msg    String expression displays as the message in the dialog box.
```

This tells you that msg is the first parameter of the MsgBox statement, and that msg should be a string that is to be displayed in the dialog box.

So in the statement

```
MsgBox  "Displaying this string"
```

the first parameter is "Displaying this string", and in the message

```
MsgBox "Result =" + Result
```

the first parameter is "Result =" + Result.

The first parameter that is shown in the statement syntax of the MsgBox statement is not inside square brackets. This means that this parameter is not optional. You must supply this parameter.

The next two parameters are enclosed in square brackets. This means that these parameters are optional.

Now take a look at the second parameter of the MsgBox statement:

The second parameter is Type. The Help window explains that Type could have a value of 0, 1, 4, and so on. By supplying this parameter, you are telling the MsgBox statement to insert an icon inside the dialog box. For example, the dialog box shown in Figure B.10 does not have an icon in it, because you did not supply a second parameter to the MsgBox statement.

To close the Help window, do the following:

❑ Click the minus icon that appears in the upper-left corner of the Help window, and select Close from the system menu that pops up.

❑ Modify the cmdCalculate_Click() procedure so that it looks like this:

```
Sub cmdCalculate_Click ()

    Dim Result, I

    For I = 1 To 100 Step 1

        Result = Result + I

    Next I


    MsgBox "Result =" + Result, 16

End Sub
```

With this code you added a second parameter to the MsgBox statement. As indicated in the Help window of the MsgBox statement, when you supply 16 as the second parameter of the MsgBox statement, a Stop icon is drawn inside the dialog box. The purpose of the Stop icon is cosmetic only.

❑ Select Save from the File menu.

❑ Select Start from the Run menu.

❑ Click the Calculate button.

> *Visual Basic responds by displaying the dialog box shown in Figure B.13. As shown, the dialog box contains the Stop icon.*

Figure B.13.
The dialog box with the Stop icon in it.

❑ Click the OK button in the dialog box.

Visual Basic responds by closing the dialog box.

❑ Click the Exit button to terminate the ItsFun program.

The MsgBox() Function

As indicated in the Help menu of MsgBox, there is also a function called MsgBox(). A statement (such as MsgBox, End, Beep) does not return any value.

A function, on the other hand, does return a value. For example, the Str$() function returns a value. It converts the numeric parameter that is supplied to it to a string, and the function returns the string.

Similarly, the MsgBox() function returns a value. What value does the MsgBox() function return? The following example illustrates the value that is returned from the MsgBox() function.

❑ Modify the cmdCalculate_Click() procedure so that it looks like this:

```
Sub cmdCalculate_Click ()

    Dim Result, I, WhoWasPressed

    For I = 1 To 100 Step 1

        Result = Result + I

    Next I


    WhoWasPressed = MsgBox("Result =" + Result, 1)

    If WhoWasPressed = 1 Then
       txtMyTextBox.Text = "OK was pressed"
    End If


    If WhoWasPressed = 2 Then
       txtMyTextBox.Text = "Cancel was pressed"
    End If

End Sub
```

The code you entered declares the WhoWasPressed variable:

```
Dim Result, I, WhoWasPressed
```

Then a For loop is executed to calculate the sum of all the integers from 1 to 100:

```
    For I = 1 To 100 Step 1

        Result = Result + I

    Next I
```

Then the `MsgBox()` function is executed to display the dialog box:

```
WhoWasPressed = MsgBox("Result =" + Result, 1)
```

Note that the first parameter of the `MsgBox()` function is `"Result ="` + `Result`, and the second parameter is 1. When you supply 1 as the second parameter of the `MsgBox()` function, the dialog box appears with an OK button and a Cancel button. (How do you know that? The Help window of the `MsgBox` indicates it.)

`MsgBox()` is a function, and it therefore returns a value. The returned value from the `MsgBox()` function is assigned to the `WhoWasPressed` variable. What does the returned value represent? If the user clicks the OK button of the dialog box, the returned value is 1, and if the user clicks the Cancel button of the dialog box, the returned value is 2.

The rest of the code you entered consists of two `If` blocks that display messages inside the text box. The first `If` block is the following:

```
If WhoWasPressed = 1 Then
    txtMyTextBox.Text = "OK was pressed"
End If
```

This `If` block displays the message `OK was pressed` if the returned value from the `MsgBox()` function is 1.

The second `If` block checks the value of the returned value from the `MsgBox()` function, and if it is equal to 2, the `Cancel was pressed` message is displayed inside the text box:

```
If WhoWasPressed = 2 Then
    txtMyTextBox.Text = "Cancel was pressed"
End If
```

❑ Select Save Project from the File menu.

❑ Select Start from the Run menu.

❑ Click the Calculate button.

The ItsFun program responds by displaying the dialog box shown in Figure B.14. As shown, the dialog box contains the OK button and the Cancel button (because you supplied 1 as its second parameter).

Figure B.14.
The dialog box with its OK and Cancel buttons.

❑ Click the OK button.

> *The ItsFun program responds by displaying a message inside the text box, telling you that you clicked the OK button.*

❏ Click the Calculate button.

The ItsFun program responds by displaying the dialog box.

❏ Click the Cancel button of the dialog box.

The ItsFun program responds by displaying a message inside the text box, telling you that you clicked the Cancel button.

❏ Experiment with the ItsFun program, and then click the Exit button to terminate the program.

Is There More Visual Basic Stuff to Learn?

In this chapter you have learned about declaring variables in Visual Basic, about the Option Explicit statement, about the Str$() function, about the If, If…Else, and For statements, about the MsgBox statement and function, and how to get help from Visual Basic. These are the most important things that you should know. You'll use these statements and features extensively throughout this book. But is there anything else you should know about Visual Basic? Yes. These additional topics are covered on a need-to-know basis. That is, rather than being flooded with more information at this point, you'll learn about the other goodies of Visual Basic when a program needs to use them.

In Appendix C you'll finally finish the ItsFun program. As promised, you'll add code to it that grants your PC the power of speech.

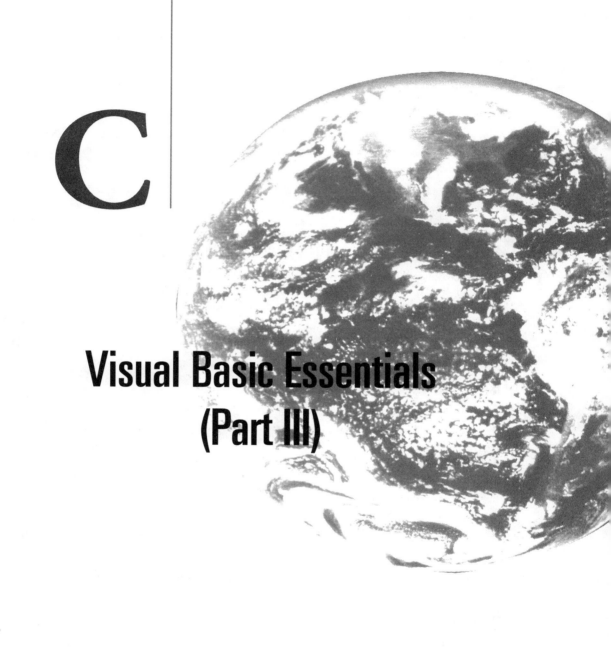

C

Visual Basic Essentials
(Part III)

In this appendix you'll finish writing the ItsFun program.

Using Dynamic Linked Libraries

At the beginning of Appendix A you executed a copy of the final version of the ItsFun program, and whenever you clicked the Say Something button, the ItsFun program displayed a message inside the text box, as well as saying the message through the PC speaker.

You'll now implement the speaking feature. The bad news is that Visual Basic does not come with such capability! That is, there isn't any Visual Basic statement or function that enables you to play a human voice through the PC speaker.

The good news is that the designers of Visual Basic anticipated that you'd need features that are not included in the out-of-the-box Visual Basic package, so they designed Visual Basic with means to extend its capabilities. If you need a certain feature that is not included in Visual Basic, you can always "add" that feature to Visual Basic by using dynamic linked libraries (DLLs) or VBX controls. DLLs are libraries that extend the capability of Visual Basic.

How do you obtain these DLLs? You can purchase them from a third-party vendor or you can develop them yourself. To develop a DLL yourself, you typically use a C/C++ compiler such as Microsoft Visual C++ or Borland C/C++, and you need to know how to write C/C++ programs.

An additional source of DLL functions is installed already in your \WINDOWS\SYSTEM directory. That is, Windows came with some powerful DLLs.

Using the TegoSND.DLL Library

The library that enables you to play any sound through the PC speaker is called TegoSND.DLL. This file was saved into your \Windows\System directory when you installed the book's CD. This library enables you to play sound through the PC speaker as well as perform animation (moving text and graphics) simultaneously and in synchronization with the playback of background sound through the PC.

The files that contain sound are called WAV files. The file extension of these files is WAV, as in MySong.WAV and MySpeech.WAV.

When you installed the book's CD, several WAV files were copied into your C:\LEARNVB\WAV directory.

The WAV file that says It's been fun working with you. is called ItsBeen1.WAV.

Declaring the DLL

When your program uses an external DLL, you must tell Visual Basic that your program is using that DLL. You do that inside the general declarations section.

Here is how you tell Visual Basic that the ItsFun program uses the TegoSND.DLL:

❏ Double-click the Clear button (or any other control inside the form).

> *Visual Basic responds by displaying the procedure of the control that you double-clicked.*

❏ Click the arrow icon that appears on the right side of the Object box at the top of the procedure window.

> *Visual Basic responds by dropping down a list of all the procedures.*

As stated in the previous appendix, general is not a procedure. It is a special place where you write all types of general things. One of the things that you write inside the general declarations section is the information about the DLL that your program uses.

❏ Select the (general) item from the list.

> *Visual Basic responds by displaying the window of the general declarations section. (See Figure C.1.)*

Figure C.1.
The general declarations window.

The window shown in Figure C.1 has only one statement in it (the Option Explicit statement). You'll now add additional code inside the general declarations section:

❏ Enter the following code inside the general declarations section (When typing the code remember that the ➡ character means that the text that follows it should be typed on the previous line.):

```
' All variables must be declared before using them.
Option Explicit

' Declare a variable that will hold the session number.
Dim gSessionNumber

' Declare constants
Const SP_START_OF_FILE = -1
Const SP_END_OF_FILE = -2

' Declare the sp_OpenSession() function from
' the TegoSND.DLL library.
```

C

```
Declare Function
    ➡ sp_OpenSession Lib
    ➡ "TegoSND.DLL"
    ➡ (ByVal lpstrFileName As String)
    ➡ As Integer

' Declare the sp_PlaySnd() function from
' the TegoSND.DLL library.
Declare Function
    ➡ sp_PlaySnd Lib
    ➡ "TegoSND.DLL"
    ➡ (ByVal iSessionHandler As Integer,
    ➡ ByVal lStartPoint As Long,
    ➡ ByVal lEndPoint As Long)
    ➡ As Long

' Declare the sp_CloseSession() function from
' the TegoSND.DLL library.
Declare Function
    ➡ sp_CloseSession Lib
    ➡ "TegoSND.DLL"
    ➡ (ByVal iSessionHandler As Integer)
    ➡ As Integer
```

The first line of code in the general declarations section is this:

```
Option Explicit
```

As discussed in Appendix B, this statement tells Visual Basic that all variables must be declared.

The next statement is this:

```
Dim gSessionNumber
```

This statement declares a variable called `gSessionNumber`.

As you'll see later, the ItsFun program needs to use this variable in several procedures. So why do you type the declaration of the `gSessionNumber` variable inside the general declarations section? If you declare this variable inside the general declarations section, it is accessible throughout all the other procedures. (This is known as making the variable a global or public variable.)

NOTE

When you declare a variable inside the general declarations section, this variable is accessible throughout the procedures of the form.

The variable `Result` was declared inside the `cmdCalculate_Click()` procedure of the ItsFun program. This means that `Result` can be used anywhere inside the `cmdCalculate_Click()` procedure.

However, if you attempt to use the variable `Result` from within the `cmdSaySomething_Click()` procedure, Visual Basic prompts you with the `Unknown Variable` error message because the variable `Result` is unknown inside the `cmdSaySomething_Click()` procedure.

On the other hand, if you declare the `Result` variable inside the general declarations section, you can use the `Result` variable in any procedure in the form.

NOTE

A variable that is declared inside the general declarations section is called a *public variable* or a *global variable* to the form.

Try to minimize the number of global variables in your programs. For example, the `Result` variable is used inside the `cmdCalculate_Click()` procedure, and it is not used by any other procedure. Therefore, it is best to declare this variable inside the `cmdCalculate_Click()` procedure.

If you declare a variable inside the general declarations section (for example, the `gSessionNumber` variable) be careful because any procedure inside the form has the right to change the value of this variable.

To make the program easier to read, precede the name of the global variable with the character g (as in `gSessionNumber`). This way you'll recognize immediately that the variable is global.

Declaring Constants

The next two statements that you typed inside the general declarations section are these:

```
Const SP_START_OF_FILE = -1
Const SP_END_OF_FILE = -2
```

The keyword `Const` means that the text that follows the `Const` keyword defines a constant. The first constant is `SP_START_OF_FILE`. This constant is defined as -1. So from now on, whenever you need to type -1 in the program, you can type -1 or `SP_START_OF_FILE`.

Similarly, `SP_END_OF_FILE` is defined as -2. So from now on, whenever you have to use -2 in the program, you can either type -2 or `SP_END_OF_FILE`.

Declaring Functions from the DLL

What is this strange code that you typed after the constant declarations? This code tells Visual Basic to use functions from TegoSND.DLL. This is the same as telling Visual Basic to add three more statements to its programming vocabulary. You already know about the End statement, the Beep statement, the MsgBox statement, the Str$() function, and the MsgBox() function. You can think of the code that declares the functions from TegoSND.DLL as three more statements added to Visual Basic. Later in this appendix you'll read about the syntax of the three statements that declare the functions from the TegoSND.DLL library.

Opening a WAV Session

Before playing a WAV file, the very first thing you have to do is open a WAV session. This must be done before playing the WAV file.

You have to open the WAV session only once during the life of the program. Therefore, a good place to type the statement that opens a WAV file is at a place that is executed when the program starts.

☐ Double-click inside a free area of the form (a free area is an area inside the form where there are no objects).

> **NOTE**
>
> To display the form, select Project from the Window menu, highlight the frmItsFun item inside the Project window, and then click the View Form button that appears at the top of the Project window.

Visual Basic responds by displaying the Form_Load() procedure:

```
Sub Form_Load ()

End Sub
```

The Form_Load() procedure is a very important procedure. It is executed whenever the form of your program is loaded. In other words, when the ItsFun program starts, the very first thing it does is load and display the form of the program. You don't have to write any code that loads and displays the form. However, after the form is loaded, the Form_Load() procedure is executed automatically. This is your opportunity to execute any code that you want to execute at the beginning of your program.

As stated, the Form_Load() procedure of the ItsFun program is executed only once during the life of the program. Because you want to open a WAV session only once during the life of the program, it makes sense to place the statement that opens a WAV session inside the Form_Load() procedure.

☐ Add the following code inside the `Form_Load()` procedure:

```
Sub Form_Load ()

    Dim DriveName As String
    Dim WavFileName As String

    ' Extract the drive name where this program resides
    DriveName = Left(App.Path, 2)

    ' Open a WAV session
    WavFileName = DriveName + "\LearnVB\WAV\ITSBEEN1.WAV"
    gSessionNumber = sp_OpenSession(WavFileName)

End Sub
```

`sp_OpenSession()` is the name of a function. This function is part of the TegoSND.DLL library, and it was declared inside the general declarations section.

The `sp_OpenSession()` function opens a WAV session. But what is the name of the WAV file that the `sp_OpenSession()` function opens? The name of the WAV file is mentioned as its parameter. You typed `WavFileName` inside the parentheses of the `sp_OpenSession()` function, so the `sp_OpenSession()` function opens a WAV session for that WAV file that this variable holds.

The value of `WavFileName` is assigned in the following manner:

First, the `DriveName` variable is extracted:

```
' Extract the drive name where this program resides
DriveName = Left(App.Path, 2)
```

`App.Path` is the path of the directory where the ItsFun program resides. For example, if the ItsFun program resides inside the C:\LearnVB\Practice\Appendix directory, `App.Path` is equal to C:\LearnVB\Practice\Appendix.

`Left()` is a function that enables you to extract characters from a string.

The first parameter of the `Left()` function is the string, and the second parameter of the `Left()` function is an integer that indicates how many characters should be extracted (starting from the left character of the string). For example, `Left("ABCDEF",3)` returns `ABC`, which is the first three characters of the `ABCDEF` string.

In the `Form_Load()` procedure you entered the statement

```
DriveName = Left(App.Path, 2)
```

So if `App.Path` is equal to C:\LearnVB\PRACTICE, the `Left(App.Path, 2)` function returns `C:`.

So `DriveName` is equal to `C:`.

Finally, the `WavFileName` variable is set:

```
' Open a WAV session
WavFileName = DriveName + "\LearnVB\WAV\ITSBEEN1.WAV"
```

This means that if the ItsFun program resides inside the C: drive, the WAV file is C:\LearnVB\WAV\ITSBEEN1.WAV.

> **NOTE**
>
> In the preceding code, you could open the WAV session in this manner:
>
> ```
> gSessionNumber = sp_OpenSession("C:\LearnVB\WAV\ITSBEEN1.WAV")
> ```
>
> However, the method that involves extracting the drive name is better, because this way you do not hard-code the drive name inside your code. That is, if the user installs the book's CD into the D:\LearnVB directory, the ItsFun program will still work, because the ItsFun program resides inside the D:\LearnVB\Practice\Appendix directory, and the ItsBeen1.WAV file resides inside the D:\LearnVB\WAV directory.

Again, the purpose of the `sp_OpenSession()` function is to open a WAV session. The name of the WAV file that will be opened is the name of the file that you supplied as the parameter of this function. After the `sp_OpenSession()` is executed, it returns a number. That number is assigned to the `gSessionNumber` variable. The `gSessionNumber` variable serves as the identification of the WAV file. That is, as you'll soon see, you'll have to write more code that refers to the C:\LEARNVB\WAV\ITSBEEN1.WAV file. So instead of referring to this WAV file by its real filename, you'll refer to it by its ID number, `gSessionNumber`.

The Syntax Used for Declaring the `sp_OpenSession()` Function

Now take a look at the statement that declares the `sp_OpenSession()` function. Recall that you declared this function inside the general declarations section:

```
Declare Function
    ➥ sp_OpenSession Lib
    ➥ "TegoSND.DLL"
    ➥ (ByVal lpstrFileName As String)
    ➥  As Integer
```

This declaration was supplied by the vendor of the DLL. Writing the declaration of a function from a DLL is actually very easy, because it is the responsibility of the vendor of the DLL to supply the syntax of the declaration.

Generally, the statements that declare functions from DLLs look very strange and complicated, so make sure to type the declarations exactly as supplied by the vendors of the DLLs.

The declaration of the `sp_OpenSession()` function starts with the words `Declare Function`:

```
Declare Function
    ➥ ....
    ➥ ....
```

> ....
> ....

This means that the text that follows these words declares a function.

The next words in the declaration are the name of the function followed by the keyword `Lib`. In this case, the `sp_OpenSession()` function is being declared.

So far the declaration looks like this:

```
Declare Function
    ➥ sp_OpenSession Lib
    ➥ ....
    ➥ ....
    ➥ ....
```

The next word in the declaration is the name of the DLL, so the declarations look like this:

```
Declare Function
    ➥ sp_OpenSession Lib
    ➥ "TegoSND.DLL"
    ➥ ....
    ➥ ....
```

The next thing that appears in the declaration is the parameter(s) of the function. The `sp_OpenSession()` function has a single parameter. This parameter holds the filename of the WAV file. So now the declaration looks like this:

```
Declare Function
    ➥ sp_OpenSession Lib
    ➥ "TegoSND.DLL"
    ➥ (ByVal lpstrFileName As String)
    ➥  .....
```

As you can see, the parameter is defined as a string. The strange word `lpstrFileName` is not important. That is, you can supply any other name instead. The important thing to note is that the `sp_OpenSession()` function takes one parameter, and that parameter is a string.

The last thing that is mentioned in the declaration is the type of data that the function returns:

```
Declare Function
    ➥ sp_OpenSession Lib
    ➥ "TegoSND.DLL"
    ➥ (ByVal lpstrFileName As String)
    ➥  As Integer
```

As you can see, the function returns an integer.

To summarize, the `sp_OpenSession()` function has one parameter, which is a string, and it returns an integer. This explains how to use the function from within your Visual Basic programs.

As you saw, that's the way you used the `sp_OpenSession()` function in the `Form_Load()` function:

```
gSessionNumber =
    ➥ sp_OpenSession("C:\LEARNVB\WAV\ITSBEEN1.WAV")
```

You have not yet finished writing the ItsFun program, but look at what you've accomplished so far:

❑ Save the project (select Save Project from the File menu).

Execute the ItsFun program:

❏ Select Start from the Run menu (or click the Run icon).

> *Visual Basic responds by executing the ItsFun program. As you can see, an hourglass appears for a while, and then the main form of the program appears. The hourglass appears while the* sp_OpenSession() *function is executing.*

❏ Click the Say Something button.

> *The ItsFun program responds by displaying the message inside the text box, but no sound is played through the PC speaker. This is because you have not yet written code that causes the PC to speak.*

Playing the WAV File

When you click the Say Something button, you want the ItsFun program to display a message inside the text box, and to cause the PC to speak. Therefore, you need to add to the cmdSaySomething_Click() procedure the code that causes the PC to speak.

❏ Double-click the Say Something button and add code to the SaySomething_Click() procedure. After you add the code, your SaySomething_Click() procedure looks like this:

```
Sub cmdSayHello_Click ()

    Dim Dummy

    ' Set the FontSize property of the text
    ' box to 12 points.
    txtMyTextBox.FontSize = 12

    txtMyTextBox.Text = "It's been fun working with you."

    ' Play the WAV file through the PC speaker
    Dummy = sp_PlaySnd ( gSessionNumber,
                    ➥ SP_START_OF_FILE,
                    ➥ SP_END_OF_FILE )

End Sub
```

The first line that appears in the procedure (before the statement that sets the FontSize property) is this:

```
Dim Dummy
```

This statement declares a variable called Dummy.

After you set the FontSize to 12 and displayed the string inside the text box, you entered the following statement:

```
Dummy = sp_PlaySnd ( gSessionNumber,
                ➥ SP_START_OF_FILE,
                ➥ SP_END_OF_FILE )
```

This statement uses another function from TegoSND.DLL. The name of the function is sp_PlaySnd(). Unlike the sp_OpenSession() function that takes only one parameter, this function takes three parameters.

The first parameter indicates which WAV file to play. As you can see, you supplied the variable gSessionNumber as the first parameter. Recall that gSessionNumber represents the ID of the WAV file, and you updated the gSessionNumber variable inside the Form_Load() function with the ID of the ItsBeen1.WAV file.

The variable gSessionNumber is not declared inside the cmdSaySomething_Click() procedure. So will the cmdSaySomthing_Click() procedure know the value of gSessionNumber? Yes, because gSessionNumber was declared inside the general declarations section.

The second parameter that you typed is SP_START_OF_FILE. Recall that you declared SP_START_OF_FILE as -1 inside the general declarations section. This means that you simply supplied -1 as the second parameter of sp_PlaySnd(). In fact, the following two statements are identical to one another:

```
Dummy = sp_PlaySnd ( gSessionNumber,
                 ➦ SP_START_OF_FILE,
                 ➦ SP_END_OF_FILE )


Dummy = sp_PlaySnd ( gSessionNumber,
                 ➦ -1,
                 ➦ SP_END_OF_FILE )
```

When you supply -1 as the second parameter of sp_PlaySnd(), the sp_PlaySnd() function plays from the beginning of the file.

The third parameter that you supplied to the sp_PlaySnd() function is SP_END_OF_FILE. Recall that you declared SP_END_OF_FILE as a constant with the value -2. This means that you supplied -2 as the third parameter of sp_PlaySnd(). When you supply -2 as the third parameter of sp_PlaySnd(), the sp_PlaySnd() function plays until the end of the file.

NOTE

The sp_PlaySnd() function plays the WAV file. Here are the things that you have to remember when using the sp_PlaySnd() function:

- Before you play the WAV file, you must open the WAV session with the sp_OpenSession() function. Usually, you use the sp_OpenSession() function from within the Form_Load() function.

- The sp_PlaySnd() function has three parameters:

  The first parameter is the ID of the WAV file. The value that you supply as the ID of the WAV session is the value that was returned from the sp_OpenSession() function.

C

The second parameter that you supply to the sp_PlaySnd() function is the starting point (in byte coordinates) of the WAV file. If you supply -1 or 0 as the second parameter of sp_PlaySnd(), the WAV file is played from the beginning of the file.

The third parameter that you supply to the sp_PlaySnd() function is the end point (in byte coordinates) of the WAV file. If you supply -2 as the third parameter of sp_PlaySnd(), the WAV file is played until the end of the file.

To play the entire WAV file, use the following statement:

```
Dummy = sp_PlaySnd ( gSessionNumber,
            ➡ -1,
            ➡ -2 )
```

Or use this statement:

```
Dummy = sp_PlaySnd ( gSessionNumber,
            ➡ SP_START_OF_FILE,
            ➡ SP_END_OF_FILE )
```

Or use this statement:

```
Dummy = sp_PlaySnd ( gSessionNumber,
            ➡ 0,
            ➡ SP_END_OF_FILE )
```

As another example, to play from byte coordinate 1000 to byte coordinate 20000, use the following statement:

```
Dummy = sp_PlaySnd ( gSessionNumber,
            ➡ 1000,
            ➡ 20000 )
```

The sp_PlaySnd() function returns a value. The value that sp_PlaySnd() returns is not important in the ItsFun program. (It is important in programs that perform animation.) In any case, because Visual Basic requires that you assign the returned value of a function to a variable, you assigned the returned value of sp_PlaySnd() to the Dummy variable.

You'll never use this returned value in the ItsFun program (hence, the name of the variable is Dummy). It is important to understand that even though you'll never use the value of Dummy, you must assign the returned value of sp_PlaySnd() to a variable, because that's the way functions are used in Visual Basic.

Save the ItsFun program:

❏ Select Save from the File menu.

Execute the ItsFun program:

❑ Select Start from the Run menu.

Visual Basic responds by displaying the hourglass icon for a while (that is, the `sp_OpenSession()` function is executed), and then displaying the main window of the ItsFun program.

❑ Click the Say Something button.

The ItsFun program responds by displaying a message inside the text box, and then the PC says the message through the PC speaker.

❑ Experiment with the ItsFun program, and then click the Exit button to terminate it.

Note that the way you have used the `sp_PlaySnd()` function agrees with the way you declared it in the general declarations section. (If it didn't agree, Visual Basic would prompt you with an error message, telling you that you did not use the function in accordance with its declaration.)

You entered the declaration of the `sp_PlaySnd()` function:

```
Declare Function
➥ sp_PlaySnd Lib
➥ "TegoSND.DLL"
➥ (ByVal iSessionHandler As Integer,
➥  ByVal lStartPoint As Long,
➥  ByVal lEndPoint As Long)
➥  As Long
```

This declaration was supplied by the vendor of the DLL. As you can see, the function takes three parameters.

The first parameter is an `Integer`, and the second and third parameters are `Long`. (A data type `Long` is a variable that holds long integers. It uses 4 bytes to store the data, whereas an `Integer` variable uses 2 bytes to store the data.)

The returned value from the `sp_PlaySnd()` function is `Long`.

Indeed, that's the way you use the `sp_PlaySnd()` function in the `cmdSaySomething_Click()` function; you assign the returned value to a variable.

Closing the WAV Session

It looks as if you have finished writing the ItsFun program. However, there is one more thing to do. You loaded the WAV file with the `sp_OpenSession()` function, but you never closed the WAV session. If you don't close the session, the PC will not release the memory that was used by the `sp_OpenSession()` function, even after you terminate the ItsFun program.

To release the memory, you have to use the `sp_CloseSession()` function. But where will you execute the `sp_CloseSession()` function? A good point in the program to close the WAV session is at the point where the ItsFun program terminates. This means that you want to execute the `sp_CloseSession()` function from within the `cmdExit_Click()` function.

C

❏ Double-click the Exit button and add code to it. After adding the code, your `cmdExit_Click()` function should look like this:

```
Sub cmdExit_Click ()

    Dim Dummy

    Dummy = sp_CloseSession(gSessionNumber)


    ' Terminate the application
    End

End Sub
```

The code you added declares a variable called `Dummy`:

```
Dim Dummy
```

Then the `sp_CloseSession()` function is executed:

```
Dummy = sp_CloseSession(gSessionNumber)
```

The `sp_CloseSession()` function takes one parameter. The value of the parameter that you supply to the `sp_CloseSession()` function is the ID of the WAV session that you want to close. This is the reason for supplying `gSessionNumber` as the parameter.

Recall that you declared the `sp_CloseSession()` function inside the general declarations section:

```
Declare Function
      ➥ sp_CloseSession Lib
      ➥ "TegoSND.DLL"
      ➥ (ByVal iSessionHandler As Integer)
      ➥  As Integer
```

This means that the function takes one parameter (an integer), and it returns an integer. Indeed, you supplied `gSessionNumber` as the parameter of the `sp_CloseSession()` function, and you assigned the returned value of the function to the `Dummy` variable. You'll never use the returned value from the `sp_CloseSession()` function, but because it returns an integer, you must assign the returned value to a variable.

You closed the WAV session inside the `cmdExit_Click()` procedure because whenever the user clicks the Exit button the program terminates. However, there is another way to terminate the program. The user can terminate the program by clicking the minus icon that appears on the upper-left corner of the window and then selecting Close from the system menu that pops up. In this case, the `Form_Unload()` procedure is executed. Therefore, you also have to close the WAV session inside the `Form_Unload()` procedure.

❏ Double-click inside a free area of the form and enter the following code inside the `Form_Unload()` procedure. After you add the code, your `Form_Unload()` function looks like this:

```
Sub Form_Unload (Cancel As Integer)
```

```
Dim Dummy
Dummy = sp_CloseSession(gSessionNumber)
```

End Sub

> **NOTE**
>
> The TegoSND.DLL file that comes with the book's CD is a limited version. This means that you'll be able to play only some of the WAV files that were supplied with the book's CD. You can obtain the full version of TegoSND.DLL by sending a check or money order for $29.95, plus $5.00 for shipping and handling, to this address:
>
> TegoSoft Inc.
> Box 389
> Attn: TegoSND.DLL
> Bellmore, NY 11710
> Phone: (516)783-4824

Removing the Calculate Button

The Calculate button that you added to the ItsFun program in Appendix B was added for the sake of illustrating various topics. However, this button is not needed in the program.

Here is how you remove it from the program:

❑ Make sure that the Calculate button is selected (that is, click inside the button).

Visual Basic responds by enclosing the Calculate button in a rectangle.

❑ Press the Delete button.

Visual Basic responds by deleting the Calculate button from the form.

But wait a minute! In Appendix B you added code to the cmdCalculate_Click() button. Where did this code go? Visual Basic moved the code to the general declarations section. To see the code of the old Calculate button do the following:

❑ Double-click any of the buttons that are inside the form.

Visual Basic responds by displaying the code of the procedure that corresponds to the button that you double-clicked.

❑ Click the down-arrow icon that appears on the right side of the object box and select the (general) item from the list that Visual Basic drops down.

Visual Basic responds by displaying the general declarations section window.

❑ Click the down-arrow icon that appears to the right of the Proc box.

Visual Basic responds by dropping down a list, as shown in Figure C.2.

C

Figure C.2.
The list that Visual Basic
drops down when you click
the down-arrow icon of the
Proc box.

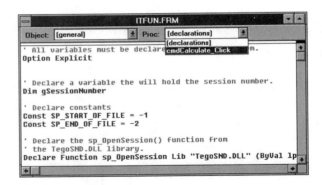

As shown in Figure C.2, the list contains two items:

```
(declarations)
cmdCalculate_Click
```

The declarations section is a place inside the `general` area where you typed the `Option Explicit` statement and the declarations of the `sp_` functions. The `cmdCalculate_Click` item is a place inside the `general` area, where the `cmdCalculate_Click()` procedure is now residing. In other words, Visual Basic noticed that you deleted the Calculate button, and it therefore moved the `cmdCalculate_Click()` procedure into the `general` area.

Because you do not need the code of the `cmdCalculate_Click()` procedure anymore, you can delete this code:

☐ Click the `cmdCalculate_Click()` item in the list. (See Figure C.2.)

Visual Basic responds by displaying the `cmdCalculate_Click()` *procedure of the* `general` *area.*

☐ Highlight the text of the `cmdCalculate_Click()` procedure, and then press the Delete button on your keyboard. You have to delete the whole procedure, including its first and last lines.

That's it! You have completely removed the Calculate button and its code from the ItsFun program.

☐ Select Save Project from the File menu to save your project.

Making an Executable File

The ItsFun program is now complete. So can you write a program such as the ItsFun program and send it to your friend? If your friend owns the Visual Basic package, you can send your friend the FRM file and the MAK file of the program that you wrote, and your friend will be able to load the project and execute it. This is not an elegant way of sending programs for the following reasons:

• It is unreasonable to assume that everyone who receives your program owns Visual Basic.

- The FRM and MAK files of the program that you write are the source code of your program. If you send these, the person who receives them might accidentally (or not accidentally) mess up your source code.
- People expect a program to be an EXE file, which they can execute from the File Manager, or from the File menu of the Program Manager.

To make an EXE file for the ItsFun program do the following:

❑ Select Make EXE File from the File menu.

> *Visual Basic responds by displaying the Make EXE File dialog box. (See Figure C.3.)*

Figure C.3.
The Make EXE File
dialog box.

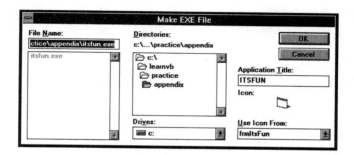

❑ Select the directory C:\LEARNVB\PRACTICE\APPENDIX and type ITSFUN.EXE inside the File Name box.

❑ Click the OK button.

> *Visual Basic responds by creating the ITSFUN.EXE file and saving it in the C:\LEARNVB\PRACTICE\APPENDIX directory.*

Verify that indeed Visual Basic created the ItsFun.EXE file:

❑ Select Exit from the File menu.

If Visual Basic notices that you have not saved the project, it will prompt you with a dialog box, asking if you want to save the project before exiting.

❑ Select Run from the File menu of the Program Manager, and execute the ItsFun.EXE program that resides inside the C:\LEARNVB\PRACTICE\APPENDIX directory.

> *Windows responds by executing the ItsFun.EXE program.*

❑ Experiment with the ItsFun.EXE program and then click the Exit button to exit.

So can you send to your friend the EXE file of the program? Well, you can, but you have to send your friend another file as well. The other file that must accompany your EXE program is a file called VBRUN300.DLL, which resides in your \WINDOWS\SYSTEM directory. If you examine the VBRUN300.DLL file, you'll see that the size of the VBRUN300.DLL file is approximately 400,000 bytes!

C

NOTE

If you are using Visual Basic Version 2.0, in your \WINDOWS\SYSTEM directory you'll see the file VBRUN200.DLL and not the file VBRUN300.DLL.

While we are on the subject of file sizes, take a look at the size of the ItsFun.EXE file. It is about 7000 bytes! As you may realize, it takes more than 7000 bytes to create a program such as the ItsFun.EXE program. This is the reason for having to supply the VBRUN300.DLL file together with your EXE file.

If your program also plays WAV files through the PC speaker, you also have to supply the TegoSND.DLL file.

Don't confuse the reasons for supplying the VBRUN300.DLL and the TegoSND.DLL files. You must supply the VBRUN300.DLL file and install this file in your user's \WINDOWS\SYSTEM directory with every EXE file that is generated with Visual Basic. You have to supply the TegoSND.DLL file and install it in your user's \WINDOWS\SYSTEM directory only if your program plays WAV files through the PC speaker.

NOTE

If your program uses WAV files, of course you also have to supply your WAV files to your users.

NOTE

The ItsFun.EXE program searches for the TegoSND.DLL in the \Windows\System directory. However, the program also searches for the DLL in the directories mentioned in the DOS path. So, for example, if your DOS path includes the \Windows directory, the program will search for the DLL in the \Windows directory. If for some reason you have an older version of the TegoSND.DLL file in your \Windows directory, you have to delete this file from the \Windows directory.

Attaching an Icon to the ItsFun Program

As you saw in Appendix A, the ItsFun program has its own icon. This means that when you minimize the window of the ItsFun program the icon of the program is displayed, as shown in Figure A.3 in Appendix A.

Before attaching the icon of the ItsFun program, look at what happens when you minimize the window of the ItsFun program at this point:

❏ Select Start from the Run menu.

❏ Minimize all the windows that are currently on the desktop of Windows.

As shown in Figure C.4, one of the icons is the icon of the ItsFun.EXE program. This icon is the default icon that Visual Basic attached to the ItsFun.EXE program.

Figure C.4.
Minimizing the windows
on the desktop of Windows.

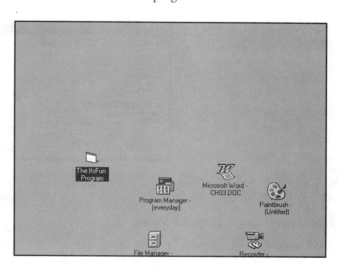

There is nothing wrong with the icon that Visual Basic attached to your ItsFun program. However, by default every EXE file that you generate with Visual Basic will be given the same program icon. As you know, a program icon is supposed to contain a picture that somehow helps the user to identify the program easily.

To attach a more appropriate icon to the ItsFun.EXE program do the following:

❏ Start Visual Basic.

❏ Select Open Project from the File menu, and load the
C:\LEARNVB\PRACTICE\APPENDIX\Itsfun.MAK file.

Visual Basic responds by loading the ItsFun project.

❏ Click inside a free area inside the form of the ItsFun program, and press F4.

Visual Basic responds by displaying the Properties window of the form.

❏ Highlight the Icon property, then click the three dots that appear on the right side of the Property box.

> *Visual Basic responds by displaying the Load Icon dialog box.*

❏ Select the File C:\LEARNVB\ICONS\SAY.ICO. Your Load Icon dialog box now looks like the one shown in Figure C.5.

❏ Click the OK button of the Load Icon dialog box.

Figure C.5.
The Load Icon dialog box.

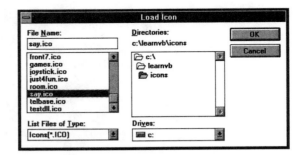

In the preceding steps you set the Icon property of the form to the SAY.ICO icon that resides inside the C:\LEARNVB\ICONS directory. To see this icon in action do the following:

❏ Select Save Project from the File menu.

❏ Select Make EXE File from the File menu.

> *Visual Basic responds by displaying the Make EXE File dialog box. (See Figure C.6.) As shown in Figure C.6, the icon that will be attached to the EXE file is the icon shown on the right side of the Make EXE File dialog box. This icon is shown magnified in Figure C.7.*

Figure C.6.
The Make EXE File dialog box (with the SAY.ICO icon).

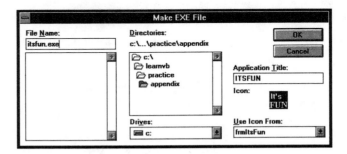

Figure C.7.
The Say.ICO icon.

❑ Click the OK button in the Make EXE File dialog box.

> *Visual Basic responds by warning you that there is already an ItsFun.EXE file.*

❑ Click the Yes button of the warning dialog box that tells Visual Basic to overwrite the old ItsFun.EXE file.

> *Visual Basic responds by saving the new ItsFun.EXE file.*

❑ Select Exit from the File menu to terminate Visual Basic.

❑ Use the Run item from the File menu of the Program Manager to execute the ItsFun.EXE program that resides in the C:\LEARNVB\PRACTICE\APPENDIX\ITSFUN directory.

❑ Experiment with the ItsFun.EXE program and notice that when you minimize its window, its icon appears, as shown in Figure C.7.

❑ Click the Exit button to terminate the ItsFun program.

Creating a Program Group and a Program Icon for the ItsFun Program

The icon in Figure C.7 is also the default icon that is assigned to the ItsFun program when you create a program icon. To see this in action do the following:

❑ Select New from the File menu of the Program Manger.

> *Windows responds by displaying the New Program Object dialog box. (See Figure C.8.)*

C

Figure C.8.
The New Program Object
dialog box.

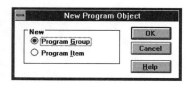

❑ Make sure that the Program Group radio button inside the New Program Object dialog box is selected (because you are about to create a new group).

❑ Click the OK button of the New Program Object dialog box.

Windows responds by displaying the Program Group Properties dialog box. (See Figure C.9.)

Figure C.9.
The Program Group
Properties dialog box.

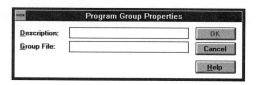

❑ Inside the Description box of the Program Group Properties dialog box type the name of the group. For example, in Figure C.10, the name of the group is `Visual Basic Apps by Gurewich`.

Figure C.10.
Assigning a name to the
group.

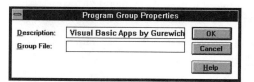

❑ Click the OK button of the Program Group Properties dialog box. (There is no need to fill the Group File box.)

Windows responds by creating a new group. (See Figure C.11.)

You now have to place the ItsFun.EXE program inside the new group that you created.

❑ Select New from the File menu of the Program Manger.

Windows responds by displaying the New Program Object dialog box. (See Figure C.8.)

❑ Make sure that the Program Item radio button is selected (because you are about to create a new program icon).

Windows responds by displaying the Program Item Properties dialog box. (See Figure C.12.)

Figure C.11.
The new group that
Windows creates.

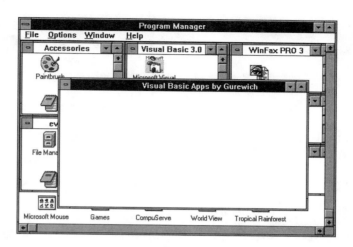

Figure C.12.
The Program Item
Properties dialog box.

☐ Type The ItsFun Program in the Description box of the Program Item Properties dialog box.

☐ Type C:\LearnVB\practice\Appendix\Itsfun.exe inside the Command Line box.

Your Program Item Properties dialog box now looks like the one shown in Figure C.13.

Figure C.13.
Filling the Description and
Command Line boxes of
the Program Item
Properties dialog box.

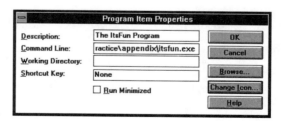

☐ Click the Change Icon button of the Program Item Properties dialog box.

> *Windows responds by displaying the Change Icon dialog box. (See Figure C.14.) As shown in Figure C.14, Windows notices that the SAY.ICO icon is attached to the ItsFun.EXE program, and it therefore displays its icon.*

C

Figure C.14.
The Change Icon
dialog box.

☐ Click the OK button of the Change Icon dialog box.

Windows responds by displaying the Program Item Properties dialog box.

☐ Click the OK button of the Program Item Properties dialog box.

Windows responds by adding the ItsFun program to the new program group that you
created. (See Figure C.15.)

Figure C.15.
The ItsFun program icon
inside the new program
group.

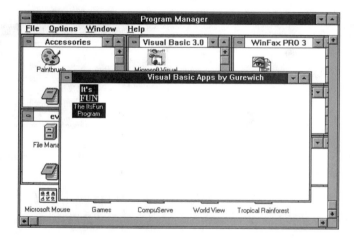

You can now execute the ItsFun.EXE program as you would any other true Windows program:

☐ Double-click the ItsFun icon, experiment with the ItsFun program, and then terminate it.

Congratulations! You have finished writing the ItsFun program from beginning to end, created a
new program group, and placed the program icon of the ItsFun program inside the new group.

The Application Title

Take a look at Figure C.6. It also contains the Application Title box. As you can see, the Application Title box contains the text ITSFUN. This is the default application title that Visual Basic assigned to the ItsFun.EXE program.

To see the application title in action do the following:

❏ Double-click the ItsFun program icon in the new group of programs that you created.

Windows responds by executing the ItsFun.EXE program.

❏ Press Ctrl+Esc to display the Task List dialog box.

Windows responds by displaying the Task List dialog box. (See Figure C.16.)

As you can see, one of the applications that is listed is the ITSFUN program.

Figure C.16.
The Task List dialog box.

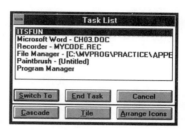

❏ Make sure that the ITSFUN item is selected, and then click the Switch To button.

Windows responds by making the ItsFun program the active window.

❏ You can now click the Exit button to terminate the ItsFun program.

The Properties Table

As you saw, it took a lot of steps and a lot of explanation to instruct you on how to place controls inside the form. As you become more familiar with Visual Basic, you'll find these detailed steps more annoying than helpful.

Therefore, during the course of the book, you'll be instructed to visually implement the forms of the programs by consulting figures and tables.

For example, to visually implement the form of the ItsFun program, you'll have to consult Figure C.17 and build the form according to the specifications in Table C.1.

Figure C.17.
The form of the ItsFun
program (in design mode).

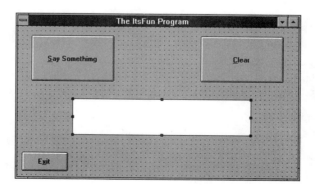

C

Table C.1. The Properties table of the form.

Object: Form
Object Name: frmItsFun

BackColor	&H00C0C0C0&

Comment: The background color is light gray.

Caption	"The ItsFun Program"
Height	4425
Icon	C:\LEARNVB\ICONS\SAY.ICO
Left	1035
Top	1140
Width	7485

Object: Command button
Object Name: cmdClear

Caption	"&Clear"
Height	1215
Left	4800
Top	240
Width	2175

Object: Text box
Object Name: txtMyTextBox

Alignment	2 'Center
Enabled	0 'False
Height	975
Left	1440
MultiLine	-1 'True
Top	1920
Width	4695

Object: Command button
Object Name: cmdSaySomething

Caption	"&Say Somethimg"
Height	1215
Left	360

| Top | 240 |
| Width | 2175 |

Object: Command button
Object Name: cmdExit

Caption	"E&xit"
Height	510
Left	120
Top	3360
Width	1215

The Properties table lists only those properties that are different from the default properties. So to implement the form, you have to place the controls mentioned in the table, and then set their properties to the specifications in the table.

Obtaining a Printout of Your Visual Design and Code Design

As stated in the previous section, a figure and a Properties table are all you need to implement a form visually. You can obtain a printout of your work in the following manner:

❑ Start Visual Basic.

❑ Select Open Project from the File menu and load the
C:\LEARNVB\PRACTICE\APPENDIX\ITSFUN.MAK file.

❑ Select Environment from the Options menu.

Visual Basic responds by displaying the Environment Options dialog box. (See Figure C.18.)

Figure C.18.
Setting the Default Save As
Format item to `Text`.

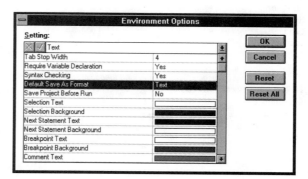

C

☐ Set the Default Save As Format item to Text. If this item is set to Binary, double-click the word Binary so it changes to Text.

☐ Click the OK button of the Environment Options dialog box.

☐ Select Save Project from the File menu.

☐ Select Exit from the File menu to terminate Visual Basic.

In the preceding steps you told Visual Basic to save the ItsFun.frm file as a text file. Now take a look at the ItsFun.frm file:

☐ Use an editor program (such as the Notepad program that is shipped with Windows) to load the ItsFun.frm file that resides in the C:\LEARNVB\PRACTICE\APPENDIX directory.

Listing C.1 shows the contents of the ItsFun.frm file.

Listing C.1. The contents of the ItsFun.frm file.

```
VERSION 2.00
Begin Form frmItsFun
   BackColor       =   &H00C0C0C0&
   Caption         =   "The ItsFun Program"
   ClientHeight    =   4020
   ClientLeft      =   1095
   ClientTop       =   1485
   ClientWidth     =   7365
   Height          =   4425
   Icon            =   ITFUN.FRX:0000
   Left            =   1035
   LinkTopic       =   "Form1"
   ScaleHeight     =   4020
   ScaleWidth      =   7365
   Top             =   1140
   Width           =   7485
   Begin CommandButton cmdClear
      Caption      =   "&Clear"
      Height       =   1215
      Left         =   4800
      TabIndex     =   3
      Top          =   240
      Width        =   2175
   End
   Begin TextBox txtMyTextBox
      Alignment    =   2    'Center
      Enabled      =   0    'False
      Height       =   975
      Left         =   1440
      MultiLine    =   -1   'True
      TabIndex     =   2
      Top          =   1920
      Width        =   4695
   End
```

```
        Begin CommandButton cmdSaySomething
            Caption         =   "&Say Somethimg"
            Height          =   1215
            Left            =   360
            TabIndex        =   1
            Top             =   240
            Width           =   2175
        End
        Begin CommandButton cmdExit
            Caption         =   "E&xit"
            Height          =   510
            Left            =   120
            TabIndex        =   0
            Top             =   3360
            Width           =   1215
        End
End
' All variables must be declared before using them.
Option Explicit


' Declare a variable the will hold the session number.
Dim gSessionNumber

' Declare constants
Const SP_START_OF_FILE = -1
Const SP_END_OF_FILE = -2

' Declare the sp_OpenSession() function from
' the TegoSND.DLL library.
Declare Function sp_OpenSession Lib "TegoSND.DLL" (ByVal
➥ lpstrFileName As String) As Integer

' Declare the sp_PlaySnd() function from
' the TegoSND.DLL library.
Declare Function sp_PlaySnd Lib "TegoSND.DLL"
➥ (ByVal iSessionHandler As Integer,
➥ ByVal lStartPoint As Long, ByVal
➥ lEndPoint As Long) As Long

' Declare the sp_CloseSession() function from
' the TegoSND.DLL library.
Declare Function sp_CloseSession Lib "TegoSND.DLL" (ByVal
➥ iSessionHandler As Integer) As Integer

Sub cmdClear_Click ()

    ' Clear the text box
    txtMyTextBox.Text = ""

End Sub

Sub cmdExit_Click ()

    Dim Dummy

    Dummy = sp_CloseSession(gSessionNumber)
```

continues

Listing C.1. continued

```
    ' Terminate the application
    End

End Sub

Sub cmdSaySomething_Click ()

    Dim Dummy

    ' Set the FontSize property of the text box to 12
➡ points.
    txtMyTextBox.FontSize = 12

    txtMyTextBox.Text = "It's been fun working with you."

    ' Play the WAV file through the PC speaker
    Dummy = sp_PlaySnd(gSessionNumber, SP_START_OF_FILE,
➡ SP_END_OF_FILE)


End Sub

Sub Form_Load ()

    Dim DriveName As String
    Dim WavFileName As String

    ' Extract the drive name where this program resides
    DriveName = Left(App.Path, 2)

    ' Open a WAV session
    WavFileName = DriveName + "\LearnVB\WAV\ITSBEEN1.WAV"

    gSessionNumber = sp_OpenSession(WavFileName)

End Sub

Sub Form_Unload (Cancel As Integer)

    Dim Dummy

    Dummy = sp_CloseSession(gSessionNumber)

End Sub
```

As you can see from Listing C.1, the ItsFun.frm file lists all the properties (including the default properties) and the code that you attached to the events.

D

Multimedia Reference

This appendix describes the properties, commands, events, and functions of the TegoMM.VBX advanced multimedia control.

Each command, event, and function includes three short samples of code that illustrate how to use it in Visual Basic, Visual C++, and Borland C++. All the commands, events, and functions are listed in one alphabetically sorted list.

The Properties, Commands, Events, and Functions of the TegoMM.VBX Control

The following sections describe all the properties, commands, events, and functions of the TegoMM.VBX multimedia control. The sections are listed in alphabetical order.

The icon of the TegoMM.VBX control in the Tools window of Visual Basic is shown in Figure D.1.

Figure D.1.
The icon of the
TegoMM.VBX control
in the Tools window of
Visual Basic.

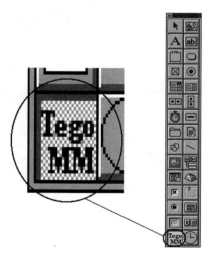

Back **Command**

This command steps backward *X* frames, where *X* is specified by the Frames property. This command is applicable only with devices that have frames (for example, AVIVideo).

In addition to the required Frames property, the Back command also uses the following optional properties:

- Notify (The default is FALSE.)
- Wait (The default is TRUE.)

```
' Visual Basic Example.
' Step backward 10 frames.
tegomm1.Frames = 10
tegomm1.Command = "Back"

// Visual C++ Example.
// Step backward 10 frames.
tegomm1->SetNumProperty("Frames", 10);
tegomm1->SetStrProperty("Command", "Back");

// Borland C++ Example.
// Step backward 10 frames.
tegomm1->SetProp("Frames", 10);
tegomm1->SetProp("Command", "Back");
```

BitsPerSample Property

Data Type: Integer

This property is available only at runtime.

This property is read-only.

Description: This property returns the number of bits per sample of the currently open WAV file. For example, if the WAV file is a 16-bit WAV file, the BitsPerSample property will return 16.

```
' Visual Basic Example
BitsPerSample = tegomm1.BitsPerSample

// Visual C++ Example
int BitsPerSample;
BitsPerSample = tegomm1->GetNumProperty("BitsPerSample");

// Borland C++ Example
int BitsPerSample;
tegomm1->GetProp("BitsPerSample", (int &)BitsPerSample);
```

CanEject Property

Data Type: Integer (Boolean)

This property is available only at runtime.

This property is read-only.

Description: This property enables you to determine whether the open multimedia device can eject its media. For example, a CD-ROM drive (CD Audio) can eject its media, but a WAV file cannot eject its media.

Value	Description
FALSE	The currently open device cannot eject its media.
TRUE	The currently open device can eject its media.

```
' Visual Basic Example
If tegomm1.CanEject Then
   MsgBox "Can eject!"
Else
   MsgBox "Cannot eject"
End If

// Visual C++ Example
if (tegomm1->GetNumProperty("CanEject"))
   ::MessageBox(NULL, "Can eject!", "MESSAGE", MB_OK);
else
   ::MessageBox(NULL, "Cannot eject!", "MESSAGE", MB_OK);

// Borland C++ Example
BOOL CanEject;
tegomm1->GetProp("CanEject", (BOOL &)CanEject);
if (CanEject)
   ::MessageBox(NULL, "Can eject!", "MESSAGE", MB_OK);
else
   ::MessageBox(NULL, "Cannot eject!", "MESSAGE", MB_OK);
```

CanPlay Property

Data Type: Integer (Boolean)

This property is available only at runtime.

This property is read-only.

Description: This property enables you to determine whether the currently open multimedia device can play.

Value	Description
FALSE	The currently open device cannot play.
TRUE	The currently open device can play.

```
' Visual Basic Example
If tegomm1.CanPlay Then
   MsgBox "Can play!"
Else
```

```
    MsgBox "Cannot play"
End If

// Visual C++ Example
if (tegomm1->GetNumProperty("CanPlay"))
    ::MessageBox(NULL, "Can play!", "MESSAGE", MB_OK);
else
    ::MessageBox(NULL, "Cannot play!", "MESSAGE", MB_OK);

// Borland C++ Example
BOOL CanPlay;
tegomm1->GetProp("CanPlay", (BOOL &)CanPlay);
if (CanEject)
    ::MessageBox(NULL, "Can play!", "MESSAGE", MB_OK);
else
    ::MessageBox(NULL, "Cannot play!", "MESSAGE", MB_OK);
```

CanRecord Property

Data Type: Integer (Boolean)

This property is available only at runtime.

This property is read-only.

Description: This property enables you to determine whether the currently open multimedia device can record.

Value	Description
FALSE	The currently open device cannot record.
TRUE	The currently open device can record.

```
' Visual Basic Example
If tegomm1.CanRecord Then
    MsgBox "Can record!"
Else
    MsgBox "Cannot record"
End If

// Visual C++ Example
if (tegomm1->GetNumProperty("CanRecord"))
    ::MessageBox(NULL, "Can record!", "MESSAGE", MB_OK);
else
    ::MessageBox(NULL, "Cannot record!", "MESSAGE", MB_OK);

// Borland C++ Example
BOOL CanRecord;
tegomm1->GetProp("CanRecord", (BOOL &)CanRecord);
if (CanRecord)
    ::MessageBox(NULL, "Can record!", "MESSAGE", MB_OK);
else
    ::MessageBox(NULL, "Cannot record!", "MESSAGE", MB_OK);
```

CanStep Property

Data Type: Integer (Boolean)

This property is available only at runtime.

This property is read-only.

Description: This property enables you to determine whether the currently open multimedia device can step forward or backward to the next or previous frame. For example, AVI video files can step a frame forward or backward, but a WAV file cannot (because WAV files don't have frames).

Value	Description
FALSE	The currently open device cannot step.
TRUE	The currently open device can step.

```
' Visual Basic Example
If tegomm1.CanStep Then
   MsgBox "Can step!"
Else
   MsgBox "Cannot step!"
End If

// Visual C++ Example
if (tegomm1->GetNumProperty("CanStep"))
   ::MessageBox(NULL, "Can step!", "MESSAGE", MB_OK);
else
   ::MessageBox(NULL, "Cannot step!", "MESSAGE", MB_OK);

// Borland C++ Example
BOOL CanStep;
tegomm1->GetProp("CanStep", (BOOL &)CanStep);
if (CanStep)
   ::MessageBox(NULL, "Can step!", "MESSAGE", MB_OK);
else
   ::MessageBox(NULL, "Cannot step!", "MESSAGE", MB_OK);
```

Channels Property

Data Type: Integer

This property is available only at runtime.

This property is read-only.

Description: This property returns the number of channels of the currently open WAV file. (A stereo WAV file has two channels, and a mono WAV file has one channel.)

```
' Visual Basic Example
If tegomm1.Channels = 2 Then
   MsgBox "This WAV file is a stereo WAV file!"
End If
```

```
// Visual C++ Example
if (tegomm1->GetNumProperty("Channels")==2)
    {
    ::MessageBox(NULL,
                "This WAV file is a stereo WAV file!",
                "MESSAGE",
                MB_OK);
    }

// Borland C++ Example
int NumChannels;
tegomm1->GetProp("Channels", (int &)NumChannels);
if (NumChannels==2)
    {
    ::MessageBox(NULL,
                "This WAV file is a stereo WAV file!",
                "MESSAGE",
                MB_OK);
    }
```

Close **Command**

This command closes the currently open device.

The Close command uses the following optional properties:

- Notify (The default is FALSE.)
- Wait (The default is TRUE.)

```
' Visual Basic Example
tegomm1.Command = "Close"

// Visual C++ Example
tegomm1->SetStrProperty("Command", "Close");

// Borland C++ Example
tegomm1->SetProp("Command", "Close");
```

CloseDoor **Command**

This command closes the door of the currently open device. It is applicable for devices that have doors (for example, CDAudio).

The CloseDoor command uses the following optional properties:

- Notify (The default is FALSE.)
- Wait (The default is TRUE.)

```
' Visual Basic Example.
tegomm1.Command = "CloseDoor"

// Visual C++ Example.
```

```
tegomm1->SetStrProperty("Command", "CloseDoor");

// Borland C++ Example.
tegomm1->SetProp("Command", "CloseDoor");
```

D

Command Property

Data Type: String

This property is available only at runtime.

Description: This property enables you to issue a command to the multimedia control. To see how to issue and use a command, look under the heading of a particular command. For example, to see how to use the Open command look under the "Open Command" heading.

Copy Command

Copy a section of a WAV file to the Clipboard. The section to be copied is specified with the From and To properties. For this command, the From and To properties are always in units of samples regardless of the TimeFormat property.

This command is applicable only for the WaveAudio device.

This command uses the Wave Buffer. Therefore, programs that use this command should issue an UpdateWaveBuffer command immediately after opening the WAV file and whenever the WAV file is changed (for example, after the user performs recording).

```
' Visual Basic Example.
' Copy samples 5000 through 10000 to the Clipboard.
tegomm1.From = 5000
tegomm1.To   = 10000
tegomm1.Command = "Copy"

// Visual C++ Example.
// Copy samples 5000 through 10000 to the Clipboard.
tegomm1->SetNumProperty("From", 5000);
trgomm1->SetNumProperty("To", 10000);
tegomm1->SetStrProperty("Command", "Copy");

// Borland C++ Example.
// Copy samples 5000 through 10000 to the Clipboard.
tegomm1->SetProp("From", 5000);
tegomm1->SetProp("To", 10000);
tegomm1->SetProp("Command", "Copy");
```

Delete Command

This command deletes a section of a WAV file. The section to be deleted is specified with the From and To properties. The units of the From and To properties are specified with the TimeFormat property.

The `Delete` command uses the following optional properties:

- From (The default is the current playback position.)
- To (The default is the end of the file.)
- Notify (The default is FALSE.)
- Wait (The default is TRUE.)

```
' Visual Basic Example.
' Delete samples 5000 through 10000.
tegomm1.TimeFormat = "Samples"
tegomm1.From = 5000
tegomm1.To   = 10000
tegomm1.Command = "Delete"
```

```
// Visual C++ Example.
// Delete samples 5000 through 10000.
tegomm1->SetStrProperty("TimeFormat", "Samples");
tegomm1->SetNumProperty("From", 5000);
trgomm1->SetNumProperty("To", 10000);
tegomm1->SetStrProperty("Command", "Delete");
```

```
// Borland C++ Example.
// Delete samples 5000 through 10000.
tegomm1->SetProp("TimeFormat", "Samples");
tegomm1->SetProp("From", 5000);
tegomm1->SetProp("To", 10000);
tegomm1->SetProp("Command", "Delete");
```

DeviceId Property

Data Type: Integer

This property is available only at runtime.

This property is read-only.

Description: This property returns a unique ID for the currently open device.

```
' Visual Basic Example
dev_id = tegomm1.DeviceId
```

```
// Visual C++ Example
int dev_id;
dev_id = tegomm1->GetNumProperty("DeviceId");
```

```
// Borland C++ Example
int dev_id;
tegomm1->GetProp("DeviceId", (int &)dev_id);
```

DeviceType Property

Data Type: String

Description: You use this property to specify the device type to be opened.

The most commonly used device types are the following:

- WaveAudio (for playing/recording WAV files through a sound card)
- PCSpeaker (for playing 8-bit mono WAV files through the PC speaker)
- AVIVideo (for playing AVI video files)
- CDAudio (for playing CD audio through a CD-ROM drive)
- Sequencer (for playing MIDI files)

```
' Visual Basic Example
' Open the WAV file MyMusic.WAV
tegomm1.DeviceType = "WaveAudio"
tegomm1.FileName = "MyMusic.WAV"
tegomm1.Command = "Open"

// Visual C++ Example
// Open the WAV file MyMusic.WAV
tegomm1->SetStrProperty("DeviceType", "WaveAudio");
tegomm1->SetStrProperty("FileName", "MyMusic.WAV");
tegomm1->SetStrProperty("Command", "Open");

// Borland C++ Example
// Open the WAV file MyMusic.WAV
tegomm1->SetProp("DeviceType", "WaveAudio");
tegomm1->SetProp("FileName", "MyMusic.WAV");
tegomm1->SetProp("Command", "Open");
```

Done Event

The Done event occurs when a command that was issued with the Notify property set to TRUE finishes. For example, the default value of the Notify property for the Play command is TRUE. Therefore, after issuing a Play command, a Done event occurs when the playback is over.

When the Done event occurs, the NotifyValue property is automatically filled with one of the following values:

Value	Meaning
1	Command completed successfully
2	Command was superseded by another command
4	Command was aborted
8	Command failed

DragDrop Event

The DragDrop event is a standard Visual Basic event. It can be used only by Visual Basic programs. This event occurs when a drag-and-drop operation is completed.

DragIcon Property

Data Type: Integer

Description: This property is a standard Visual Basic property. It can be used only by Visual Basic programs.

```
' Visual Basic Example
tegomm1.DragIcon = LoadPicture("MyIcon.ICO")
```

DragMode Property

Data Type: Integer (Enumerated)

Description: This property is a standard Visual Basic property. It can be used only by Visual Basic programs.

```
' Visual Basic Example
tegomm1.DragMode = 1
```

DragOver Event

The DragOver event is a standard Visual Basic event. It can be used only by Visual Basic programs. This event occurs when a drag-and-drop operation is in progress.

Eject Command

This command opens the door of the currently open device. It is applicable for devices that have doors (for example, CD audio).

The Eject command uses the following optional Properties:

- Notify (The default is FALSE.)
- Wait (The default is TRUE.)

```
' Visual Basic Example.
tegomm1.Command = "Eject"

// Visual C++ Example.
tegomm1->SetStrProperty("Command", "Eject");

// Borland C++ Example.
tegomm1->SetProp("Command", "Eject");
```

Enabled Property

Data Type: Integer (Boolean)

Description: You use this property to enable or to disable the multimedia control.

Value	Description
FALSE	Enable the multimedia control.
TRUE	Disable the multimedia control.

```
' Visual Basic Example.
' Disable the multimedia control.
tegomm1.Enabled = False

// Visual C++ Example
// Disable the multimedia control.
tegomm1->SetNumProperty("Enabled", FALSE);

// Borland C++ Example
// Disable the multimedia control.
tegomm1->SetProp("Enabled", FALSE);
```

Error Property

Data Type: Integer

This property is available only at runtime.

This property is read-only.

Description: This property returns an error code from the last issued command. If the last issued command was successful, the Error property will be 0. If the last issued command caused an error, the Error property will report an error code.

Value	Meaning
0	Last command was issued successfully
261	Unrecognized command
262	Hardware error
263	Invalid device name
264	Out of memory
265	Device open
266	Cannot load driver
272	Internal driver error
274	Unsupported function
275	File not found
276	Device not ready
277	Internal error
282	Invalid range
286	File not saved
287	Device type required
291	Must use shareable

292	Missing device name
293	Bad time format
296	Invalid file
304	Filename required
306	Device not installed
513	Unknown error
514	No open sound session
515	Invalid range
516	Too many open sound sessions
517	Cannot open the file
518	Cannot determine file size
519	Not enough memory
520	Cannot allocate memory
521	Cannot lock memory
522	Cannot read the file
523	Limited version can be used only with the supplied files
524	Cannot create swap file for WAV buffer
525	No WAV buffer
526	Cannot access the Clipboard
527	Clipboard is empty

```
' Visual Basic Example
' Open the WAV file MyMusic.WAV and display
' an error message if Open command fails.
tegomm1.DeviceType = "WaveAudio"
tegomm1.FileName = "MyMusic.WAV"
tegomm1.Command = "Open"
If tegomm1.Error<>0 Then
   MsgBox "Cannot open the WAV file!"
End If
```

```
// Visual C++ Example
// Open the WAV file MyMusic.WAV and display
// an error message if Open command fails.
tegomm1->SetStrProperty("DeviceType", "WaveAudio");
tegomm1->SetStrProperty("FileName", "MyMusic.WAV");
tegomm1->SetStrProperty("Command", "Open");
if ( tegomm1->GetNumProperty("Error") != 0 )
   ::MessageBox(NULL,"Cannot open file!","ERROR", MB_OK);
```

```
// Borland C++ Example
// Open the WAV file MyMusic.WAV and display
// an error message if Open command fails.
tegomm1->SetProp("DeviceType", "WaveAudio");
tegomm1->SetProp("FileName", "MyMusic.WAV");
tegomm1->SetProp("Command", "Open");
int error;
tegomm1->GetProp("Error", (int &)error);
if (error!=0)
   ::MessageBox(NULL, "Cannot open file!", "ERROR", MB_OK);
```

ErrorMessage Property

Data Type: String

This property is available only at runtime.

This property is read-only.

Description: This property returns an error string message from the last issued command. The string message corresponds to the error code that is reported by the Error property. For example, when the Error property is 0 (that is, no error), the ErrorMessage property contains the string The specified command was carried out. The ErrorMessage property is typically used for debugging purposes. When you debug your program you can display message boxes that display the contents of the ErrorMessage property.

```
' Visual Basic Example
MsgBox tegomm1.ErrorMessage
```

```
// Visual C++ Example
::MessageBox(NULL,
             tegomm1->GetStrProperty("ErrorMessage"),
             "MESSAGE",
             MB_OK);
```

```
// Borland C++ Example
string msg;
tegomm1->GetProp("ErrorMessage", (string &)msg);
::MessageBox(NULL,
             msg.c_str(),
             "MESSAGE",
             MB_OK);
```

FileName Property

Data Type: String

Description: You use this property to specify the file to be opened with the Open command or the file to be saved with the Save command.

```
' Visual Basic Example
' Open the WAV file MyMusic.WAV
tegomm1.DeviceType = "WaveAudio"
tegomm1.FileName = "MyMusic.WAV"
tegomm1.Command = "Open"
```

```
// Visual C++ Example
// Open the WAV file MyMusic.WAV
tegomm1->SetStrProperty("DeviceType", "WaveAudio");
tegomm1->SetStrProperty("FileName", "MyMusic.WAV");
tegomm1->SetStrProperty("Command", "Open");
```

```
// Borland C++ Example
// Open the WAV file MyMusic.WAV
tegomm1->SetProp("DeviceType", "WaveAudio");
tegomm1->SetProp("FileName", "MyMusic.WAV");
tegomm1->SetProp("Command", "Open");
```

Frames Property

Data Type: Long

Description: You use this property to specify the number of frames the Step command will step forward or the Back command will step backward. The Step and Back commands are applicable only with devices that use frames (for example, AVIVideo).

```
' Visual Basic Example.
' Step forward 10 frames.
tegomm1.Frames = 10
tegomm1.Command = "Step"

// Visual C++ Example.
// Step forward 10 frames.
tegomm1->SetNumProperty("Frames", 10);
tegomm1->SetStrProperty("Command", "Step");

// Borland C++ Example.
// Step forward 10 frames.
tegomm1->SetProp("Frames", 10);
tegomm1->SetProp("Command", "Step");
```

From Property

Data Type: Long

This property is available only at runtime.

Description: You use this property to specify the starting point of various commands (for example, Play, Record, Delete, Copy, Paste). Setting a value for the From property before issuing these commands is optional. If you issue these commands without first setting the From property, the starting point will be the current playback position. The units of the From property are specified by the TimeFormat property.

```
' Visual Basic Example.
' Delete samples 5000 through 10000.
tegomm1.TimeFormat = "Samples"
tegomm1.From = 5000
tegomm1.To   = 10000
tegomm1.Command = "Delete"

// Visual C++ Example.
// Delete samples 5000 through 10000.
tegomm1->SetStrProperty("TimeFormat", "Samples");
tegomm1->SetNumProperty("From", 5000);
trgomm1->SetNumProperty("To", 10000);
tegomm1->SetStrProperty("Command", "Delete");

// Borland C++ Example.
// Delete samples 5000 through 10000.
tegomm1->SetProp("TimeFormat", "Samples");
tegomm1->SetProp("From", 5000);
tegomm1->SetProp("To", 10000);
tegomm1->SetProp("Command", "Delete");
```

hCtl Property

Data Type: Long

This property is available only at runtime.

This property is read-only.

Description: This property returns the control handle (hCtl) of the multimedia control. You need the control handle when you use some of the functions of the multimedia control (because the first parameter of these functions is the control handle).

```
' Visual Basic Example
hCtl = tegomm1.hCtl

// Visual C++ Example
long hCtl;
hCtl = tegomm1->GetNumProperty("hctl");

// Borland C++ Example
long hCtl;
tegomm1->GetProp("hctl", (long &)hCtl);
```

Height Property

You use this property to specify the height of the multimedia control.

```
' Visual Basic Example.
Tegomm1.Height = 25

// Visual C++ Example.
tegomm1->SetNumProperty("Height", 25);

// Borland C++ Example.
tegomm1->SetProp("Height", 25);
```

hWnd Property

Data Type: Integer

This property is available only at runtime.

This property is read-only.

Description: This property returns the window handle of the multimedia control.

```
' Visual Basic Example
hWnd = tegomm1.hWnd

// Visual C++ Example
int hWnd;
hWnd = tegomm1->GetNumProperty("hWnd");

// Borland C++ Example
int hWnd;
tegomm1->GetProp("hWnd", (int &)hWnd);
```

hWndDisplay Property

Data Type: Integer

This property is available only at runtime.

Description: You use this property to specify the output window where the show will be displayed. This property is applicable only with devices that display a show (for example, AVIVideo).

```
' Visual Basic Example.
' Movie should play inside the program's main window.
' (Form1 is the name of the main form of the program).
Tegomm1.hWndDisplay = Form1.hWnd

// Visual C++ Example.
// (hWnd = the handle of the window where the movie will be
// displayed).
tegomm1->SetNumProperty("hWndDisplay", hWnd);

// Borland C++ Example.
// (hWnd = the handle of the window where the movie will be
// displayed).
tegomm1->SetProp("hWndDisplay", hWnd);
```

Index Property

Data Type: Integer

Description: This property is a standard Visual Basic property. It can be used only by Visual Basic programs. This property specifies the element number of the multimedia control (if the control is part of a control array).

Left Property

You use this property to specify the X coordinate of the top-left corner of the control.

```
' Visual Basic Example.
Tegomm1.Left = 10

// Visual C++ Example.
tegomm1->SetNumProperty("Left", 10);

// Borland C++ Example.
tegomm1->SetProp("Left", 10);
```

Length Property

Data Type: Long

This property is available only at runtime.

This property is read-only.

Description: This property returns the total length of the currently open file. The units of the Length property are specified by the TimeFormat property. For example, if the TimeFormat property is set to Milliseconds, the Length property reports the length of the file in units of milliseconds.

```
' Visual Basic Example
TotalLength = tegomm1.Length

// Visual C++ Example
long TotalLength;
TotalLength = tegomm1->GetNumProperty("Length");

// Borland C++ Example
long TotalLength;
tegomm1->GetProp("Length", (long &)TotalLength);
```

Mode Property

Data Type: Long

This property is available only at runtime.

This property is read-only.

Description: This property returns a code that represents the current playback mode of the multimedia control.

Value	Meaning
0	Device is not open. An Open command failed or was never issued.
524	Device is not ready.
525	Stopped. No playback in progress.
526	Playing. There is playback in progress.
527	Recording. Recording is currently in progress.
528	Seeking. The device is in the process of seeking a new position.
529	Paused. The device is currently paused.
530	Door open. Applicable for devices that have doors (for example, CD audio).

```
' Visual Basic Example
If tegomm1.Mode=526 Then
   MsgBox "There is currently playback in progress."
End If

// Visual C++ Example
if ( tegomm1->GetNumProperty("Mode") == 526 )
   {
   ::MessageBox(NULL,
               "There is currently playback in progress.",
               "MESSAGE",
               MB_OK);
   }
```

```
// Borland C++ Example
long mode;
tegomm1->GetProp("Mode", (long &)mode);
if ( mode == 526 )
    {
    ::MessageBox(NULL,
                "There is currently playback in progress.",
                "MESSAGE",
                MB_OK);
    }
```

MousePointer Property

Data Type: Integer

Description: You use this property to specify the type of mouse pointer that is displayed when the mouse is over the multimedia control.

Value	Description of Displayed Mouse Pointer
0	Default
1	Arrow
2	Cross
3	I-beam
4	Icon (small square within a square)
5	Size (four-pointed arrow pointing north, south, east, west)
6	Size NE SW (double arrow pointing northeast and southwest)
7	Size N S (double arrow pointing north and south)
8	Size NW SE (double arrow pointing northwest and southeast)
9	Size W E (double arrow pointing west and east)
10	Up arrow
11	Hourglass
12	No drop

```
' Visual Basic Example.
' Set the mouse pointer to an Up Arrow.
tegomm1.MousePointer = 10

// Visual C++ Example
// Set the mouse pointer to an Up Arrow.
tegomm1->SetNumProperty("MousePointer", 10);

// Borland C++ Example
// Set the mouse pointer to an Up Arrow.
tegomm1->SetProp("MousePointer", 10);
```

Next **Command**

This command changes the playback position to the end of the open file. (If the open device is CDAudio, the Next command changes the playback position to the next track.)

The Next command uses the following optional properties:

- Notify (The default is FALSE.)
- Wait (The default is TRUE.)

```
' Visual Basic Example.
tegomm1.Command = "Next"

// Visual C++ Example.
tegomm1->SetStrProperty("Command", "Next");

// Borland C++ Example.
tegomm1->SetProp("Command", "Next");
```

Notify **Property**

Data Type: Integer (Boolean)

This property is available only at runtime.

Description: You use this property to specify whether a Done event should occur when the next issued command is completed. Normally you don't have to set the Notify property because all commands that use the Notify property have a default value for the Notify property. For example, if prior to issuing a Play command you don't specify any value for the Notify property, the Play command assumes that the value of the Notify property is TRUE, and once the Play command is completed, a Done event occurs. Similarly, if prior to issuing a Stop command you don't specify any value for the Notify property, the Stop command assumes that the value of the Notify property is FALSE, and once the Stop command is completed, a Done event does not occur. To see what is the default value of the Notify property for other commands (for example, Record, Delete, Copy) see the descriptions of these commands.

Value	Description
FALSE	A Done event will not occur when the next command is completed.
TRUE	A Done event will occur when the next command is completed.

```
' Visual Basic Example.
' Issue a Play command without a Done event.
' (i.e. once playback is completed a Done event will not
' occur).
tegomm1.Notify = False
tegomm1.Command = "Play"

// Visual C++ Example.
// Issue a Play command without a Done event.
```

```
// (i.e. once playback is completed a Done event will not
// occur).
tegomm1->SetNumProperty("Notify", FALSE);
tegomm1->SetStrProperty("Command", "Play");

// Borland C++ Example.
// Issue a Play command without a Done event.
// (i.e. once playback is completed a Done event will not occur).
tegomm1->SetProp("Notify", FALSE);
tegomm1->SetProp("Command", "Play");
```

NotifyMessage Property

Data Type: String

This property is available only at runtime.

This property is read-only.

Description: When the Done event occurs, the NotifyMessage property is automatically filled with one of the following strings:

> Command was completed successfully.
> Command was superseded by another command.
> Command was aborted.
> Command failed.

For example, if the command that caused the Done event was completed successfully, the NotifyMessage property is filled with the string Command completed successfully.

The NotifyMessage property is typically used for debugging purposes. When you debug your program you can attach code to the Done event that displays the contents of the NotifyMessage property.

If you want to process the result of the last issued command for purposes other than debugging, you should use the NotifyValue property. The NotifyValue property is numeric.

```
' Visual Basic Example
MsgBox tegomm1.NotifyMessage

// Visual C++ Example
::MessageBox(NULL,
            tegomm1->GetStrProperty("NotifyMessage"),
            "MESSAGE",
            MB_OK);

// Borland C++ Example
string msg;
tegomm1->GetProp("NotifyMessage", (string &)msg);
::MessageBox(NULL,
            msg.c_str(),
            "MESSAGE",
            MB_OK);
```

NotifyValue Property

Data Type: Integer

This property is available only at runtime.

This property is read-only.

Description: When the Done event occurs, the NotifyValue property is automatically filled with one of the following values:

Value	Meaning
1	Command was completed successfully
2	Command was superseded by another command
4	Command was aborted
8	Command failed

For example, if the command that caused the Done event was completed successfully, the NotifyValue property is filled with 1.

Typically, you attach the code that evaluates the NotifyValue property to the Done event.

```
' Visual Basic Example
If tegomm1.NotifyValue = 1 Then
   MsgBox "Command completed successfully"
End If

// Visual C++ Example
if (tegomm1->NotifyValue == 1)
   {
   ::MessageBox(NULL,
                "Command completed successfully",
                "MESSAGE",
                MB_OK);
   }

// Borland C++ Example
int value;
tegomm1->GetProp("NotifyValue", (int &)value);
if (value == 1)
   {
   ::MessageBox(NULL,
                "Command completed successfully",
                "MESSAGE",
                MB_OK);
   }
```

Open Command

You open the file or device as specified by the DeviceType and FileName properties. Some devices don't use the FileName property for the Open command because they don't use files (for example, CDAudio). The Open command also uses the Shareable property. If Shareable is set to TRUE, the

device is opened in "shared" mode. That is, several applications can use the same device simultaneously. Note that some devices do not support "shared" mode.

In addition to the required properties (DeviceType, FileName, and Shareable), the Open command also uses the following optional properties:

- Notify (The default is FALSE.)
- Wait (The default is TRUE.)

```
' Visual Basic Example
' Open the WAV file MyMusic.WAV
tegomm1.DeviceType = "WaveAudio"
tegomm1.FileName = "MyMusic.WAV"
tegomm1.Command = "Open"
```

```
// Visual C++ Example
// Open the WAV file MyMusic.WAV
tegomm1->SetStrProperty("DeviceType", "WaveAudio");
tegomm1->SetStrProperty("FileName", "MyMusic.WAV");
tegomm1->SetStrProperty("Command", "Open");
```

```
// Borland C++ Example
// Open the WAV file MyMusic.WAV
tegomm1->SetProp("DeviceType", "WaveAudio");
tegomm1->SetProp("FileName", "MyMusic.WAV");
tegomm1->SetProp("Command", "Open");
```

Paste **Command**

This command pastes the sound section that is currently stored in the Clipboard to the currently open WAV file. The Paste command performs two tasks:

- It deletes the samples of the currently open WAV file that are in the range specified by the From and To properties.
- It inserts the Clipboard contents to the currently open WAV file at the point specified by the From property.

For example, if the From property is set to 1000 and the To property is set to 2000, then samples 1000 through 2000 of the currently open WAV file are deleted and the Clipboard contents are inserted to the currently open WAV file, starting at sample number 1000.

If you want to insert the Clipboard at a certain point without deleting any samples in the WAV file, set the From and To properties to the same value. For example, if you set both the From property and the To property to 5000 and then issue a Paste command, the Clipboard contents will be inserted to the currently open WAV file, starting at sample number 5000, without deleting any samples in the WAV file.

For this command, the From and To properties are always in units of samples regardless of the TimeFormat property.

This command is applicable only for the WaveAudio device.

This command uses the Wave Buffer. Therefore, programs that use this command should issue an UpdateWaveBuffer command immediately after the WAV file is opened and whenever the WAV file is changed (for example, after the user performs recording).

To copy samples into the Clipboard, use the Copy command.

```
' Visual Basic Example.
' Delete samples 5000 through 10000 and insert the Clipboard
' contents starting at sample 5000.
tegomm1.From = 5000
tegomm1.To   = 10000
tegomm1.Command = "Paste"

// Visual C++ Example.
// Delete samples 5000 through 10000 and insert the
// Clipboard contents starting at sample 5000.
tegomm1->SetNumProperty("From", 5000);
trgomm1->SetNumProperty("To", 10000);
tegomm1->SetStrProperty("Command", "Paste");

// Borland C++ Example.
// Delete samples 5000 through 10000 and insert the
// Clipboard contents starting at sample 5000.
tegomm1->SetProp("From", 5000);
tegomm1->SetProp("To", 10000);
tegomm1->SetProp("Command", "Copy");
```

Pause Command

This command pauses the playback or the recording.

The Pause command uses the following optional properties:

- Notify (The default is FALSE.)
- Wait (The default is TRUE.)

```
' Visual Basic Example
tegomm1.Command = "Pause"

// Visual C++ Example
tegomm1->SetStrProperty("Command", "Pause");

// Borland C++ Example
tegomm1->SetProp("Command", "Pause");
```

pcMouseEnabled Property

Data Type: Integer (Boolean)

This property is available only at runtime.

Description: You use this property to specify whether the mouse should be enabled while the multimedia control plays through the PC speaker. The pcMouseEnabled property is applicable only

for the PCSpeaker device. When the pcMouseEnabled property is set to TRUE, the mouse is enabled during playback. When the pcMouseEnabled property is set to FALSE, the mouse is not available during playback.

The playback quality of the PC speaker is best when the pcMouseEnabled property is set to FALSE and the pcTaskInterval property is set to 0.

```
' Visual Basic Example.
' Mouse will be available when the PC speaker plays.
tegomm1.pcMouseEnabled = True

// Visual C++ Example.
// Mouse will be available when the PC speaker plays.
tegomm1->SetNumProperty("pcMouseEnabled", TRUE);

// Borland C++ Example.
// Mouse will be available when the PC speaker plays.
tegomm1->SetProp("pcMouseEnabled", TRUE);
```

pcSpeed Property

Data Type: Integer

Description: This property determines the speed at which the PC speaker plays WAV files. The playback speed is set in this way:

```
[Playback speed] = [pcSpeed Property]% X [Natural Speed]
```

Typical examples are the following:

- When the pcSpeed property is set to 100, the PC speaker will play the WAV file at the natural speed (that is, 100% of the natural speed).

- When the pcSpeed property is set to 50, the PC speaker will play the WAV file at half the natural speed (that is, 50% of the natural speed).

- When the pcSpeed property is set to 200, the PC speaker will play the WAV file at twice the natural speed (that is, 200% of the natural speed).

```
' Visual Basic Example.
' Set the PC speaker playback speed to twice the natural
' speed.
tegomm1.pcSpeed = 200

// Visual C++ Example.
// Set the PC speaker playback speed to twice the natural
// speed.
tegomm1->SetNumProperty("pcSpeed", 200);

// Borland C++ Example.
// Set the PC speaker playback speed to twice the natural
// speed.
tegomm1->SetProp("pcSpeed", 200);
```

pcTaskInterval Property

Data Type: Long

Description: This property determines the time slice (in milliseconds) that is allocated to the task that plays through the PC speaker. If you set a non-zero value for this property, the user will be able to switch to other applications while the PC speaker keeps on playing in the background. If the pcTaskInterval property is set to 0, the user will not be able to perform other tasks while the PC speaker plays.

The playback quality of the PC speaker is best when the pcMouseEnabled property is set to FALSE and the pcTaskInterval property is set to 0.

```
' Visual Basic Example.
' Mouse will be available when the PC speaker plays
' and the user will be able to switch to other tasks.
tegomm1.pcMouseEnabled = True
tegomm1.pcTaskInterval = 400

// Visual C++ Example.
// Mouse will be available when the PC speaker plays
// and the user will be able to switch to other tasks.
tegomm1->SetNumProperty("pcMouseEnabled", TRUE);
tegomm1->SetNumProperty("pcTaskInterval", 400);

// Borland C++ Example.
// Mouse will be available when the PC speaker plays.
// and the user will be able to switch to other tasks.
tegomm1->SetProp("pcMouseEnabled", TRUE);
tegomm1->SetProp("pcTaskInterval", 400);
```

Play Command

This command starts the playback of the currently open device.

The Play command uses the following optional properties:

- From (The default is the current playback position.)
- To (The default is the end of the file.)
- Notify (The default is TRUE.)
- Wait (The default is FALSE.)

```
' Visual Basic Example
tegomm1.Command = "Play"

// Visual C++ Example
tegomm1->SetStrProperty("Command", "Play");

// Borland C++ Example
tegomm1->SetProp("Command", "Play");
```

Position Property

Data Type: Long

This property is available only at runtime.

This property is read-only.

Description: This property returns the current playback position. The units of the Position property are specified by the TimeFormat property. For example, if the TimeFormat property is set to Milliseconds, the Position property reports the current playback position in units of milliseconds.

```
' Visual Basic Example
CurrentPosition = tegomm1.Position

// Visual C++ Example
long CurrentPosition;
CurrentPosition = tegomm1->GetNumProperty("Position");

// Borland C++ Example
long CurrentPosition;
tegomm1->GetProp("Position", (long &)CurrentPosition);
```

Prev Command

This command changes the playback position to the beginning of the open file. (If the open device is CDAudio, the Prev command changes the playback position to the previous track.)

The Prev command uses the following optional properties:

- Notify (The default is FALSE.)
- Wait (The default is TRUE.)

```
' Visual Basic Example.
tegomm1.Command = "Prev"

// Visual C++ Example.
tegomm1->SetStrProperty("Command", "Prev");

// Borland C++ Example.
tegomm1->SetProp("Command", "Prev");
```

Record Command

This command starts recording.

The Record command uses the following optional properties:

- From (The default is the current playback position.)
- To (The default is no limit.)
- Notify (The default is TRUE.)
- Wait (The default is FALSE.)
- RecordMode (The default is 0, or Insert mode.)

```
' Visual Basic Example
tegomm1.Command = "Record"

// Visual C++ Example
tegomm1->SetStrProperty("Command", "Record");

// Borland C++ Example
tegomm1->SetProp("Command", "Record");
```

RecordMode Property

Data Type: Integer (Enumerated)

Description: You use this property to specify the recording mode—either Insert mode or Overwrite mode. In Insert mode, the recording is inserted to the file without deleting the original file contents. In Overwrite mode the recording overwrites the original file contents. The RecordMode property is applicable only for devices that support recording. To check whether a device supports recording you can use the CanRecord property. Note that some devices support only Insert mode or only Overwrite mode. Other devices support both Insert mode and Overwrite mode. To check whether the device supports a particular recording mode, set the RecordMode property to the desired value, then issue a `Record` command and check the Error property. If the Error property is non-zero (that is, the `Record` command failed), change the value of the RecordMode property to the other mode and issue another `Record` command.

Value	Meaning
0	Insert mode
1	Overwrite mode

```
' Visual Basic Example.
tegomm1.InsertMode = 0

// Visual C++ Example.
tegomm1->SetNumProperty("InsertMode", 0);

// Borland C++ Example.
tegomm1->SetProp("InsertMode", 0);
```

Repaint Command

This command repaints the current frame. It is applicable only for devices that use frames (for example, AVI video).

```
' Visual Basic Example.
tegomm1.Command = "Repaint"

// Visual C++ Example.
tegomm1->SetStrProperty("Command", "Repaint");

// Borland C++ Example.
tegomm1->SetProp("Command", "Repaint");
```

SampleNumber Property

Data Type: Long

This property is available only at runtime.

Description: This property is used by the SampleValue1 property and by the SampleValue2 property. For example, if you want to extract the value of sample number 1000 in Channel 1 of a WAV file, you need to first set the SampleNumber property to 1000, and then extract the value of the SampleValue1 property.

> **NOTE**
>
> To access samples of a WAV file efficiently, use the functions `tegSetByte()`, `tegGetByte()`, `tegSetWord()`, and `tegGetWord()`.

```
' Visual Basic Example
' Extract the value of sample number 1000 in channel 1.
tegomm1.SampleNumber = 1000
Value = tegomm1.SampleValue1

// Visual C++ Example
// Extract the value of sample number 1000 in channel 1.
int Value;
tegomm1->SetNumProperty("SampleNumber", 1000);
Value = tegomm1->GetNumProperty("SampleValue1");

// Borland C++ Example
// Extract the value of sample number 1000 in channel 1.
int Value;
tegomm1->SetProp("SampleNumber", 1000);
tegomm1->GetProp("SampleValue1", (int &)Value);
```

SampleValue1 Property

Data Type: Integer

This property is available only at runtime.

Description: Use the SampleValue1 property to read or to set the value of the sample that is specified by the SampleNumber property. If the currently open WAV file is a stereo WAV file (that is, it has two channels), the sample that is being read (or set) is in the first channel (left channel). To access the second channel (right channel), use the SampleValue2 property.

> **NOTE**
>
> To access samples of a WAV file efficiently, use the functions `tegSetByte()`, `tegGetByte()`, `tegSetWord()`, and `tegGetWord()`.

```
' Visual Basic Example
' Extract the value of sample number 1000 in channel 1.
tegomm1.SampleNumber = 1000
Value = tegomm1.SampleValue1
...
...
...
' Set sample number 500 in channel 1 to a value of 128.
tegomm1.SampleNumber = 500
tegomm1.SampleValue1 = 128


// Visual C++ Example
// Extract the value of sample number 1000 in channel 1.
int Value;
tegomm1->SetNumProperty("SampleNumber", 1000);
Value = tegomm1->GetNumProperty("SampleValue1");
...
...
...
// Set sample number 500 in channel 1 to a value of 128.
tegomm1->SetNumProperty("SampleNumber", 500);
tegomm1->SetNumProperty("SampleValue1", 128);

// Borland C++ Example
// Extract the value of sample number 1000 in channel 1.
int Value;
tegomm1->SetProp("SampleNumber", 1000);
tegomm1->GetProp("SampleValue1", (int &)Value);
...
...
...
// Set sample number 500 in channel 1 to a value of 128.
tegomm1->SetProp("SampleNumber", 500);
tegomm1->SetProp("SampleValue1", 128);
```

SampleValue2 Property

Data Type: Integer

This property is available only at runtime.

Description: You use the SampleValue2 property to read or to set the value of the sample that is specified by the SampleNumber property. If the currently open WAV file is a stereo WAV file (that is, it has two channels), the sample that is being read (or set) is in the second channel (right channel). To access the first channel (left channel), use the SampleValue1 property.

NOTE

To access samples of a WAV file efficiently, use the functions tegSetByte(), tegGetByte(), tegSetWord(), and tegGetWord().

```
' Visual Basic Example
' Extract the value of sample number 1000 in channel 2.
tegomm1.SampleNumber = 1000
Value = tegomm1.SampleValue2
...
...
...
' Set sample number 500 in channel 2 to a value of 128.
tegomm1.SampleNumber = 500
tegomm1.SampleValue2 = 128


// Visual C++ Example
// Extract the value of sample number 1000 in channel 2.
int Value;
tegomm1->SetNumProperty("SampleNumber", 1000);
Value = tegomm1->GetNumProperty("SampleValue2");
...
...
...
// Set sample number 500 in channel 2 to a value of 128.
tegomm1->SetNumProperty("SampleNumber", 500);
tegomm1->SetNumProperty("SampleValue2", 128);

// Borland C++ Example
// Extract the value of sample number 1000 in channel 2.
int Value;
tegomm1->SetProp("SampleNumber", 1000);
tegomm1->GetProp("SampleValue2", (int &)Value);
...
...
...
// Set sample number 500 in channel 2 to a value of 128.
tegomm1->SetProp("SampleNumber", 500);
tegomm1->SetProp("SampleValue2", 128);
```

SamplingRate Property

Data Type: Long

This property is available only at runtime.

This property is read-only.

Description: This property returns the sampling rate of the currently open file. The SamplingRate property is applicable only with devices that have sampling rates (for example, WaveAudio, PCSpeaker).

```
' Visual Basic Example
SamplingRate = tegomm1.SamplingRate

// Visual C++ Example
long SamplingRate;
SamplingRate = tegomm1->GetNumProperty("SamplingRate");
```

```
// Borland C++ Example
long SamplingRate;
tegomm1->GetProp("SamplingRate", (long &)SamplingRate);
```

Save **Command**

This command saves the open file to the disk. The file is saved under the name specified by the FileName property.

In addition to the required FileName property, the Save command also uses the following optional properties:

- Notify (The default is FALSE.)
- Wait (The default is TRUE.)

```
' Visual Basic Example
tegomm1.Command = "Save"

// Visual C++ Example
tegomm1->SetStrProperty("Command", "Save");

// Borland C++ Example
tegomm1->SetProp("Command", "Save");
```

Seek **Command**

This command changes the playback position to the position specified by the To property. The units of the To property are specified by the TimeFormat property. If the open device is PCSpeaker, the units of the To property are always bytes, regardless of the TimeFormat property.

In addition to the To property, the Seek command also uses the following optional properties:

- Notify (The default is FALSE.)
- Wait (The default is TRUE.)

```
' Visual Basic Example.
' Seek to position 500 milliseconds.
tegomm1.TimeFormat = "Milliseconds"
tegomm1.To = 500
tegomm1.Command = "Seek"

// Visual C++ Example.
// Seek to position 500 milliseconds.
tegomm1->SetStrProperty("TimeFormat", "Milliseconds");
tegomm1->SetNumProperty("To", 500);
tegomm1->SetStrProperty("Command", "Seek");

// Borland C++ Example.
tegomm1->SetProp("TimeFormat", "Milliseconds");
tegomm1->SetProp("To", 500);
tegomm1->SetProp("Command", "Seek");
```

Shareable Property

Data Type: Integer (Boolean)

Description: The Shareable property is used by the Open command. If the Shareable property is set to TRUE, the Open command will open the device in shared mode. That is, several applications can use the same device simultaneously. Note that some devices do not support shared mode.

Value	Meaning
FALSE	The device cannot be accessed by other controls or programs.
TRUE	The device can be accessed by other controls or programs.

```
' Visual Basic Example.
tegomm1.Shareable = True

// Visual C++ Example.
tegomm1->SetNumProperty("Shareable", TRUE);

// Borland C++ Example.
tegomm1->SetProp("Shareable", TRUE);
```

Silent Property

Data Type: Integer (Boolean)

Description: You use this property to turn the sound of the currently open device either on or off. When the Silent property is set to TRUE, the sound is turned off. For example, if the currently open device is AVIVideo, setting the Silent property to TRUE will turn the sound of the video off (that is, silent movie).

Value	Meaning
FALSE	Sound is turned on.
TRUE	Sound is turned off.

```
' Visual Basic Example.
tegomm1.Silent = True

// Visual C++ Example.
trgomm1->SetNumProperty("Silent", TRUE);

// Borland C++ Example.
tegomm1->SetProp("Silent", TRUE);
```

Sound Command

This command plays the sound of the WAV file specified by the FileName property. To have more control over the playback you should use the Play command. (Most programs use the Play command.)

In addition to the FileName property, the Sound command also uses the following optional properties:

- Notify (The default is FALSE.)
- Wait (The default is FALSE.)

```
' Visual Basic Example
tegomm1.FileName = "MySound.WAV"
tegomm1.Command = "Sound"

// Visual C++ Example
tegomm1->SetStrProperty("FileName", "MySound.WAV");
tegomm1->SetStrProperty("Command", "Sound");

// Borland C++ Example
tegomm1->SetProp("FileName", "MySound.WAV");
tegomm1->SetProp("Command", "Sound");
```

Start Property

Data Type: Long

This property is available only at runtime.

This property is read-only.

Description: This property returns the starting position of the media. The units of the Start property are specified by the TimeFormat property. For example, if the TimeFormat property is set to Milliseconds, the Start property reports the start position in units of milliseconds.

```
' Visual Basic Example
StartPosition = tegomm1.Start

// Visual C++ Example
long StartPosition;
StartPosition = tegomm1->GetNumProperty("Start");

// Borland C++ Example
long StartPosition;
tegomm1->GetProp("Start", (long &)StartPosition);
```

StatusUpdate Event

The StatusUpdate event is a timer event that occurs every X milliseconds, where X is the value of the UpdateInterval property. For example, if you set the UpdateInterval property to a value of 1000, a StatusUpdate event will occur every 1000 milliseconds. When the UpdateInterval property is set to a value of 0, the StatusUpdate event does not occur.

Step Command

This command steps forward X frames, where X is specified by the Frames property. This command is applicable only with devices that have frames (for example, AVIVideo).

In addition to the required Frames property, the `Step` command also uses the following optional properties:

- Notify (The default is FALSE.)
- Wait (The default is TRUE.)

```
' Visual Basic Example.
' Step forward 10 frames.
tegomm1.Frames = 10
tegomm1.Command = "Step"

// Visual C++ Example.
// Step forward 10 frames.
tegomm1->SetNumProperty("Frames", 10);
tegomm1->SetStrProperty("Command", "Step");

// Borland C++ Example.
// Step forward 10 frames.
tegomm1->SetProp("Frames", 10);
tegomm1->SetProp("Command", "Step");
```

Stop **Command**

This command stops the playback or the recording.

The `Stop` command uses the following optional properties:

- Notify (The default is FALSE.)
- Wait (The default is TRUE.)

```
' Visual Basic Example
tegomm1.Command = "Stop"

// Visual C++ Example
tegomm1->SetStrProperty("Command", "Stop");

// Borland C++ Example
tegomm1->SetProp("Command", "Stop");
```

Tag Property

Data Type: String

Description: You use this property to store a string. The value that you assign to the Tag property has no effect on the multimedia control. You can use the Tag property to assign a unique string to the multimedia control that identifies the control.

```
' Visual Basic Example
tegomm1.Tag = "My Control"

// Visual C++ Example
tegomm1->SetStrProperty("Tag", "My Control");
```

```
// Borland C++ Example
tegomm1->SetProp("Tag", "My Control");
```

tegGetByte() **Function**

C/C++ prototype:

```
int  FAR PASCAL _export tegGetByte ( long lhctl,
                                     long ByteNumber );
```

Visual Basic declaration:

```
Declare Function tegGetByte Lib "tegomm.vbx"
➥ (ByVal lhctl As Long, ByVal lByteNumber As Long)
➥ As Integer
```

The tegGetByte() function enables you to read the value of any byte in the currently open WAV file. The tegGetByte() function uses the Wave Buffer. Therefore, any program that uses the tegGetByte() function needs to issue an UpdateWaveBuffer command immediately after opening the WAV file and whenever the WAV file is changed (for example, after the user performs recording). The UpdateWaveBuffer command fills the Wave Buffer (in memory) with the current contents of the WAV file.

The tegGetByte() function takes two parameters:

- The handle of the multimedia control
- The byte number of the byte whose value you want to get

The tegGetByte() function returns the value of the specified byte.

Use the tegGetByte() function to extract values of samples of 8-bit mono and 8-bit stereo WAV files.

In an 8-bit mono WAV file...

> Byte number 0 is sample number 0
> Byte number 1 is sample number 1
> Byte number 2 is sample number 2
> Byte number 3 is sample number 3
> ...
> ...
> ...

In an 8-bit stereo WAV file...

> Byte number 0 is sample number 0 of Channel 1
> Byte number 1 is sample number 0 of Channel 2
> Byte number 2 is sample number 1 of Channel 1
> Byte number 3 is sample number 1 of Channel 2
> Byte number 4 is sample number 2 of Channel 1
> Byte number 5 is sample number 2 of Channel 2

Byte number 6 is sample number 3 of Channel 1
Byte number 7 is sample number 3 of Channel 2
...
...
...

To detect whether the currently open WAV file is mono or stereo use the Channels property.

> **NOTE**
>
> To get samples of 16-bit WAV files use the `tegGetWord()` function.

```
' Visual Basic example.
' Get the value of byte number 500.
hctl = tegomm1.hctl
Value = tegGetByte(hctl, 500)

// Visual C++ example.
// Get the value of byte number 500.
long hctl;
int Value;
hctl = tegomm1->GetNumProperty("hctl");
Value = tegGetByte(hctl, 500);

// Borland C++ example.
// Get the value of byte number 500.
long hctl;
int Value;
tegomm1->GetProp("hctl", (long &)hctl);
Value = tegGetByte(hctl, 500);
```

`tegGetJoyButton()` Function

C/C++ prototype:

```
int  FAR PASCAL _export tegGetJoyButton ( int iButton );
```

Visual Basic declaration:

```
Declare Function tegGetJoyButton Lib "tegomm.vbx"
➥ (ByVal iButton As Integer) As Integer
```

Use the `tegGetJoyButton()` function to get the current status of any of the joystick's buttons.

The `tegGetJoyButton()` function takes one parameter, `iButton`. This parameter identifies the joystick button whose status you want to extract. If the joystick button is pressed, then `tegGetJoyButton()` returns `-1`. Otherwise, `tegGetJoyButton()` returns `0`.

A joystick device can have a maximum of four buttons. The value of the `tegGetJoybutton()` parameter (`iButton`) can be 0, 1, 2, or 3:

iButton	Returned Value
0	The status of button 0
1	The status of button 1
2	The status of button 2
3	The status of button 3

```
' Visual Basic example.
' If button #0 of the joystick is pressed, beep.
If tegGetJoyButton(0)=-1 Then Beep

// Visual C++ example.
// If button #0 of the joystick is pressed, beep.
if (tegGetJoyButton(0)==-1)
   ::MessageBeep(-1);

// Borland C++ example.
// If button #0 of the joystick is pressed, beep.
if (tegGetJoyButton(0)==-1)
   ::MessageBeep(-1);
```

tegGetJoyPos() Function

C/C++ prototype:

```
long FAR PASCAL  _export tegGetJoyPos( int iAxis );
```

Visual Basic declaration:

```
Declare Function tegGetJoyPos Lib "tegomm.vbx"
➥ (ByVal iAxis As Integer) As Long
```

The tegGetJoyPos() function extracts the current position of the joystick.

The tegGetJoyPos() function takes one parameter, iAxis. This parameter indicates the joystick axis whose position you want to extract.

In a joystick device that has only two axes (X and Y), the value of the iAxis parameter can be 0 or 1:

iAxis	Returned Value
0	The joystick's X-axis position
1	The joystick's Y-axis position

In a joystick device that has three axes (X, Y, and Z), the value of the iAxis parameter can be 0, 1, or 2:

iAxis	Returned Value
0	The joystick's X-axis position
1	The joystick's Y-axis position
2	The joystick's Z-axis position

In a joystick device that has a set of two joysticks (Joystick A and Joystick B), the value of the iAxis parameter can be 0, 1, 2, or 3:

iAxis	Returned Value
0	The X-axis position of Joystick A
1	The Y-axis position of Joystick A
2	The X-axis position of Joystick B
3	The Y-axis position of Joystick B

Before calling the tegGetJoyPos() function you must first call the tegScanJoyPos() function. The tegScanJoyPos() function scans the current joystick position.

```
' Visual Basic example.
' Get the current X and Y coordinates
' of the joystick position.
Connected = tegScanJoyPos() ' Scan the joystick.
JoystickX = tegGetJoyPos(0) ' Get the joystick X coordinate.
JoystickY = tegGetJoyPos(1) ' Get the joystick Y coordinate.
' If the joystick is not connected, beep.
If Connected=0 Then Beep

// Visual C++ example.
// Get the current X and Y coordinates
// of the joystick position.
int Connected;
long JoystickX, JoystickY;
Connected=tegScanJoyPos(); // Scan the joystick.
JoystickX=tegGetJoyPos(0); // Get the joystick X coordinate.
JoystickY=tegGetJoyPos(1); // Get the joystick Y coordinate.
// If joystick is not connected, beep.
if (Connected==0)
   ::MessageBeep(-1);

// Borland C++ example.
int Connected;
long JoystickX, JoystickY;
Connected=tegScanJoyPos(); // Scan the joystick.
JoystickX=tegGetJoyPos(0); // Get the joystick X coordinate.
JoystickY=tegGetJoyPos(1); // Get the joystick Y coordinate.
// If joystick is not connected, beep.
if (Connected==0)
   ::MessageBeep(-1);
```

tegGetWord() Function

C/C++ prototype:

```
int  FAR PASCAL _export tegGetWord ( long lhctl,
                                     long WordNumber );
```

Visual Basic declaration:

```
Declare Function tegGetWord Lib "tegomm.vbx"
➥ ByVal lhctl As Long, ByVal lWordNumber As Long)
➥ As Integer
```

The `tegGetWord()` function enables you to read the value of any word in the currently open WAV file. The `tegGetWord()` function uses the Wave Buffer. Therefore, any program that uses the `tegGetWord()` function needs to issue an `UpdateWaveBuffer` command immediately after opening the WAV file and whenever the WAV file is changed (for example, after the user performs recording). The `UpdateWaveBuffer` command fills the Wave Buffer (in memory) with the current contents of the WAV file.

The `tegGetWord()` function takes two parameters:

- The handle of the multimedia control
- The word number of the word whose value you want to get

The `tegGetWord()` function returns the value of the specified word.

Use the `tegGetWord()` function to extract values of samples of 16-bit mono and 16-bit stereo WAV files.

In a 16-bit mono WAV file...

Word number 0 is sample number 0
Word number 1 is sample number 1
Word number 2 is sample number 2
Word number 3 is sample number 3
...
...
...

In a 16-bit stereo WAV file...

Word number 0 is sample number 0 of Channel 1
Word number 1 is sample number 0 of Channel 2
Word number 2 is sample number 1 of Channel 1
Word number 3 is sample number 1 of Channel 2
Word number 4 is sample number 2 of Channel 1
Word number 5 is sample number 2 of Channel 2
Word number 6 is sample number 3 of Channel 1
Word number 7 is sample number 3 of Channel 2
...
...
...

To determine whether the currently open WAV file is mono or stereo use the Channels property.

NOTE

To read the samples of 8-bit WAV files use the `tegGetByte()` function.

```
' Visual Basic example.
' Get the value of word number 500.
hctl = tegomm1.hctl
Value = tegGetWord(hctl, 500)

// Visual C++ example.
// Get the value of word number 500.
long hctl;
int Value;
hctl = tegomm1->GetNumProperty("hctl");
Value = tegGetWord(hctl, 500);

// Borland C++ example.
// Get the value of word number 500.
long hctl;
int Value;
tegomm1->GetProp("hctl", (long &)hctl);
Value = tegGetWord(hctl, 500);
```

tegScanJoyPos() Function

C/C++ prototype:

```
int FAR PASCAL  _export tegScanJoyPos( void );
```

Visual Basic declaration:

```
Declare Function tegScanJoyPos Lib "tegomm.vbx" ()
➥ As Integer
```

The tegScanJoyPos() function scans the current position of the joystick. You must call this function prior to calling the tegGetJoyPos() function.

The tegScanJoyPos() function takes no parameters. You can use the returned value of tegScanJoyPos() to determine whether a joystick is currently connected to the PC. If the returned value is 0, a joystick is not connected. If the returned value is -1, a joystick is connected.

```
' Visual Basic example.
' Get the current X and Y coordinates
' of the joystick position.
Connected = tegScanJoyPos() ' Scan the joystick.
JoystickX = tegGetJoyPos(0) ' Get the joystick X coordinate.
JoystickY = tegGetJoyPos(1) ' Get the joystick Y coordinate.
' If the joystick is not connected, beep.
If Connected=0 Then Beep

// Visual C++ example.
// Get the current X and Y coordinates
// of the joystick position.
int Connected;
long JoystickX, JoystickY;
Connected=tegScanJoyPos(); // Scan the joystick.
JoystickX=tegGetJoyPos(0); // Get the joystick X coordinate.
JoystickY=tegGetJoyPos(1); // Get the joystick Y coordinate.
// If joystick is not connected, beep.
if (Connected==0)
   ::MessageBeep(-1);
```

```
// Borland C++ example.
int Connected;
long JoystickX, JoystickY;
Connected=tegScanJoyPos(); // Scan the joystick.
JoystickX=tegGetJoyPos(0); // Get the joystick X coordinate.
JoystickY=tegGetJoyPos(1); // Get the joystick Y coordinate.
// If joystick is not connected, beep.
if (Connected==0)
   ::MessageBeep(-1);
```

tegSetByte() Function

C/C++ prototype:

```
int  FAR PASCAL _export tegSetByte ( long lhctl,
                                     long ByteNumber,
                                     short value );
```

Visual Basic declaration:

```
Declare Function tegSetByte Lib "tegomm.vbx"
➡ (ByVal lhctl As Long, ByVal lByteNumber As Long,
➡ ByVal iValue As Integer) As Integer
```

The tegSetByte() function enables you to set the value of any byte in the currently open WAV file. The tegSetByte() function uses the Wave Buffer. Therefore, any program that uses the tegSetByte() function needs to issue an UpdateWaveBuffer command immediately after opening the WAV file and whenever the WAV file is changed (for example, after the user performs recording).

After using the tegSetByte() function you need to validate the Wave Buffer by issuing a ValidateWaveBuffer command. Typically, you use the tegSetByte() function in a loop that sets a range of samples (for example, samples 1000 through 2000) in the Wave Buffer. When you finish the loop, you validate the Wave Buffer by issuing a ValidateWaveBuffer command.

The tegSetByte() function takes three parameters:

- The handle of the multimedia control
- The byte number of the byte whose value you want to set
- The value that you want to set

The returned value of the tegSetByte() function is not used.

Use the tegSetByte() function to set values of samples of 8-bit mono and 8-bit stereo WAV files.

In an 8-bit mono WAV file...

> Byte number 0 is sample number 0
> Byte number 1 is sample number 1
> Byte number 2 is sample number 2
> Byte number 3 is sample number 3
> ...
> ...
> ...

In an 8-bit stereo WAV file...

> Byte number 0 is sample number 0 of Channel 1
> Byte number 1 is sample number 0 of Channel 2
> Byte number 2 is sample number 1 of Channel 1
> Byte number 3 is sample number 1 of Channel 2
> Byte number 4 is sample number 2 of Channel 1
> Byte number 5 is sample number 2 of Channel 2
> Byte number 6 is sample number 3 of Channel 1
> Byte number 7 is sample number 3 of Channel 2
> ...
> ...
> ...

To determine whether the currently open WAV file is mono or stereo use the Channels property.

NOTE

To set samples of 16-bit WAV files use the `tegSetWord()` function.

```
' Visual Basic example.
' Set bytes 1000 through 2000 to a value of 128.
hctl = tegomm1.hctl
For I = 1000 To 2000
    Dummy = tegSetByte(hctl, I, 128)
Next I
tegomm1.Command = "ValidateWaveBuffer"
```

```
// Visual C++ example.
// Set bytes 1000 through 2000 to a value of 128.
long hctl;
int i;
hctl = tegomm1->GetNumProperty("hctl");
for (i=1000; i<2001; i++)
    tegSetByte(hctl, i, 128);
tegomm1->SetStrProperty("Command", "ValidateWaveBuffer");
```

```
// Borland C++ example.
// Set bytes 1000 through 2000 to a value of 128.
long hctl;
int i;
tegomm1->GetProp("hctl", (long &)hctl);
for (i=1000; i<2001; i++)
    tegSetByte(hctl, i, 128);
tegomm1->SetProp("Command", "ValidateWaveBuffer");
```

tegSetWord() **Function**

C/C++ prototype:

```
int  FAR PASCAL _export tegSetWord ( long lhctl,
                                     long WordNumber,
                                     short value );
```

Visual Basic declaration:

```
Declare Function tegSetWord Lib "tegomm.vbx"
➥ (ByVal lhctl As Long, ByVal lWordNumber As Long,
➥ ByVal iValue As Integer) As Integer
```

The tegSetWord() function enables you to set the value of any word in the open WAV file. The tegSetWord() function uses the Wave Buffer. Therefore, any program that uses the tegSetWord() function needs to issue an UpdateWaveBuffer command immediately after the WAV file is opened and whenever the WAV file is changed (for example, after the user performs recording).

After using the tegSetWord() function you need to validate the Wave Buffer by issuing a ValidateWaveBuffer command. Typically, you use the tegSetWord() function in a loop that sets a range of samples (for example, samples 1000 through 2000) in the Wave Buffer. When you finish the loop, you validate the Wave Buffer by issuing a ValidateWaveBuffer command.

The tegSetWord() function takes three parameters:

- The handle of the multimedia control
- The word number of the word whose value you want to set
- The value that you want to set

The returned value of the tegSetWord() function is not used.

Use the tegSetWord() function to set values of samples of 16-bit mono and 16-bit stereo WAV files.

In a 16-bit mono WAV file...

> Word number 0 is sample number 0
> Word number 1 is sample number 1
> Word number 2 is sample number 2
> Word number 3 is sample number 3
> ...
> ...
> ...

In a 16-bit stereo WAV file...

> Word number 0 is sample number 0 of Channel 1
> Word number 1 is sample number 0 of Channel 2
> Word number 2 is sample number 1 of Channel 1
> Word number 3 is sample number 1 of Channel 2
> Word number 4 is sample number 2 of Channel 1
> Word number 5 is sample number 2 of Channel 2

Word number 6 is sample number 3 of Channel 1
Word number 7 is sample number 3 of Channel 2
...
...
...

To determine whether the currently open WAV file is mono or stereo use the Channels property.

> **NOTE**
>
> To set samples of 8-bit WAV files use the `tegSetByte()` function.

```
' Visual Basic example.
' Set words 1000 through 2000 to a value of 0.
hctl = tegomm1.hctl
For I = 1000 To 2000
    Dummy = tegSetWord(hctl, I, 0)
Next I
tegomm1.Command = "ValidateWaveBuffer"
```

```
// Visual C++ example.
// Set bytes 1000 through 2000 to a value of 0.
long hctl;
int i;
hctl = tegomm1->GetNumProperty("hctl");
for (i=1000; i<2001; i++)
    tegSetWord(hctl, i, 0);
tegomm1->SetStrProperty("Command", "ValidateWaveBuffer");
```

```
// Borland C++ example.
// Set bytes 1000 through 2000 to a value of 128.
long hctl;
int i;
tegomm1->GetProp("hctl", (long &)hctl);
for (i=1000; i<2001; i++)
    tegSetWord(hctl, i, 128);
tegomm1->SetProp("Command", "ValidateWaveBuffer");
```

Tempo Property

Data Type: Long

Description: You use this property to set the playback tempo. This property is applicable only for some devices (for example, Sequencer). The higher the value of the Tempo property, the faster the playback tempo is. To extract the normal tempo value, you can store the value of the Tempo property immediately after issuing an Open command in a global variable.

```
' Visual Basic Example
' Open the MyMusic.Mid MIDI file, and store the normal
' playback tempo in the global variable gNormalTempo.
tegomm1.DeviceType = "Sequencer"
```

```
tegomm1.FileName = "MyMusic.Mid"
tegomm1.Command = "Open"
gNormalTempo = tegomm1.Tempo
...
...
...
' Set the playback tempo to twice the normal tempo.
tegomm1.Tempo = gNormalTempo * 2

// Visual C++ Example
// Open the MyMusic.Mid MIDI file, and store the normal
// playback tempo in the global variable gNormalTempo.
tegomm1->SetStrProperty("DeviceType", "Sequencer");
tegomm1->SetStrProperty("FileName", "MyMusic.Mid");
tegomm1->SetStrProperty("Command", "Open");
gNormalTempo = tegomm1->GetNumProperty("Tempo");
...
...
...
// Set the playback tempo to twice the normal tempo.
tegomm1->SetNumProperty("Tempo", gNormalTempo*2);

// Borland C++ Example
// Open the MyMusic.Mid MIDI file, and store the normal
// playback tempo in the global variable gNormalTempo.
tegomm1->SetProp("DeviceType", "Sequencer");
tegomm1->SetProp("FileName", "MyMusic.Mid");
tegomm1->SetProp("Command", "Open");
tegomm1->GetProp("Tempo", (long &)gNormalTempo);
...
...
...
// Set the playback tempo to twice the normal tempo.
tegomm1->SetProp("Tempo", gNormalTempo*2);
```

TimeFormat Property

Data Type: String

This property is available only at runtime.

Description: You use this property to specify the units of the position properties. Position properties are properties such as From, To, Position, and Length. For example, if you set the TimeFormat property to Milliseconds, the Length property will report the length of the currently open file in units of milliseconds. You can set the TimeFormat property to any of the following strings:

- Bytes. Position properties will report in units of bytes.
- Frames. Position properties will report in units of frames.
- Milliseconds. Position properties will report in units of milliseconds.
- MS. Same as Milliseconds.
- TMSF. Position properties will report in units of tracks.

Note that some time formats are not applicable for all device types. For example, TMSF is applicable only for devices that have tracks (for example, CDAudio).

```
' Visual Basic Example
tegomm1.TimeFormat = "Milliseconds"

// Visual C++ Example
tegomm1->SetStrProperty("TimeFormat", "Milliseconds");

// Borland C++ Example
tegomm1->SetProp("TimeFormat", "Milliseconds");
```

To Property

Data Type: Long

This property is available only at runtime.

Description: You use this property to specify the ending point of various commands (for example, Play, Record, Delete, Copy, Paste, Seek). Setting a value for the To property before issuing these commands is optional. If you issue these commands without first setting the To property, the ending point will be the end position of the file. The units of the To property are specified by the TimeFormat property.

```
' Visual Basic Example.
' Delete samples 5000 through 10000.
tegomm1.TimeFormat = "Samples"
tegomm1.From = 5000
tegomm1.To   = 10000
tegomm1.Command = "Delete"

// Visual C++ Example.
// Delete samples 5000 through 10000.
tegomm1->SetStrProperty("TimeFormat", "Samples");
tegomm1->SetNumProperty("From", 5000);
tegomm1->SetNumProperty("To", 10000);
tegomm1->SetStrProperty("Command", "Delete");

// Borland C++ Example.
// Delete samples 5000 through 10000.
tegomm1->SetProp("TimeFormat", "Samples");
tegomm1->SetProp("From", 5000);
tegomm1->SetProp("To", 10000);
tegomm1->SetProp("Command", "Delete");
```

Top Property

Use this property to specify the Y coordinate of the top-left corner of the control.

```
' Visual Basic Example.
tegomm1.Top = 10

// Visual C++ Example.
tegomm1->SetNumProperty("Top", 10);

// Borland C++ Example.
tegomm1->SetProp("Top", 10);
```

Track Property

Data Type: Long

This property is available only at runtime.

Description: This property is used by the TrackLength property and by the TrackPosition property. For example, if you want to extract the length of track 1, you need to first set the Track property to 1, and then extract the value of the TrackLength property. This property is applicable only for devices that use tracks (for example, CDAudio).

```
' Visual Basic Example
tegomm1.Track = 1
LengthOfTrack1 = tegomm1.TrackLength

// Visual C++ Example
long LengthOfTrack1;
tegomm1->SetNumProperty("Track", 1);
LengthOfTrack1 = tegomm1->GetNumProperty("TrackLength");

// Borland C++ Example
long LengthOfTrack1;
tegomm1->SetProp("Track", 1);
tegomm1->GetProp("TrackLength", (long &)LengthOfTrack1);
```

TrackLength Property

Data Type: Long

This property is available only at runtime.

This property is read-only.

Description: The TrackLength property reports the length of the track that is specified by the Track property. This property is applicable only for devices that use tracks (for example, CDAudio).

```
' Visual Basic Example
tegomm1.Track = 1
LengthOfTrack1 = tegomm1.TrackLength

// Visual C++ Example
long LengthOfTrack1;
tegomm1->SetNumProperty("Track", 1);
LengthOfTrack1 = tegomm1->GetNumProperty("TrackLength");

// Borland C++ Example
long LengthOfTrack1;
tegomm1->SetProp("Track", 1);
tegomm1->GetProp("TrackLength", (long &)LengthOfTrack1);
```

TrackPosition Property

Data Type: Long

This property is available only at runtime.

This property is read-only.

Description: The TrackPosition property reports the starting position of the track that is specified by the Track property. This property is applicable only for devices that use tracks (for example, CDAudio).

```
' Visual Basic Example
tegomm1.Track = 2
StartPosOfTrack2 = tegomm1.TrackPosition

// Visual C++ Example
long StartPosOfTrack2;
tegomm1->SetNumProperty("Track", 2);
StartPosOfTrack2 = tegomm1->GetNumProperty("TrackPosition");

// Borland C++ Example
long StartPosOfTrack2;
tegomm1->SetProp("Track", 2);
tegomm1->GetProp("TrackPosition", (long &)StartPosOfTrack2);
```

Tracks Property

Data Type: Long

This property is available only at runtime.

This property is read-only.

Description: The Tracks property reports the total number of tracks in the currently open device. This property is applicable only for devices that use tracks (for example, CDAudio).

```
' Visual Basic Example
TotalNumOfTracks = tegomm1.Tracks

// Visual C++ Example
long TotalNumOfTracks;
TotalNumOfTracks = tegomm1->GetNumProperty("Tracks");

// Borland C++ Example
long TotalNumOfTracks;
tegomm1->GetProp("Tracks", (long &)TotalNumOfTracks);
```

UpdateInterval Property

Data Type: Long

Description: The multimedia control has a timer event called StatusUpdate that occurs every *X* milliseconds, where *X* is the value of the UpdateInterval property. For example, after you set the UpdateInterval property to 1000, a StatusUpdate event will occur every 1000 milliseconds. To disable the StatusUpdate event, set the UpdateInterval property to 0.

```
' Visual Basic Example
' From now on, a StatusUpdate event will occur every 500
' milliseconds.
tegomm1.UpdateInterval = 500

// Visual C++ Example
// From now on, a StatusUpdate event will occur every 500
// milliseconds.
tegomm1->SetNumProperty("UpdateInterval", 500);

// Borland C++ Example
// From now on, a StatusUpdate event will occur every 500
// milliseconds.
tegomm1->SetProp("UpdateInterval", 500);
```

UpdateWaveBuffer Command

Any program that uses any of the following properties, commands, or functions needs to use the UpdateWaveBuffer command:

- Copy command
- Paste command
- SampleValue1 property
- SampleValue2 property
- tegGetByte() function
- tegSetByte() function
- tegGetWord() function
- tegSetWord() function

Any program that uses any of these commands, properties, or functions needs to issue an UpdateWaveBuffer command immediately after opening the WAV file and whenever the WAV file is changed (for example, after the user performs recording). The UpdateWaveBuffer command fills a Wave Buffer (in memory) with the current contents of the WAV file.

```
' Visual Basic Example.
tegomm1.Command = "UpdateWaveBuffer"

// Visual C++ Example.
tegomm1->SetStrProperty("Command", "UpdateWaveBuffer");

// Borland C++ Example.
tegomm1->SetProp("Command", "UpdateWaveBuffer");
```

UsesWindows Property

Data Type: Integer (Boolean)

This property is available only at runtime.

This property is read-only.

Description: You use this property to determine whether the currently open device uses a window for output. For example, the AVIVideo device uses a window to display video files. If the currently open device uses a window for output, the UsesWindows property returns TRUE; otherwise it returns FALSE.

```
' Visual Basic Example
If tegomm1.UsesWindows Then
   MsgBox "The open device uses a window!"
End If
```

```
// Visual C++ Example
if (tegomm1->GetNumProperty("UsesWindows"))
   {
   ::MessageBox(NULL,
               "The open device uses a window!",
               "MESSAGE",
               MB_OK);
   }
```

```
// Borland C++ Example
BOOL UsesWindows;
tegomm1->GetProp("UsesWindows", (BOOL &)UsesWindows);
if (UsesWindows)
   {
   ::MessageBox(NULL,
               "The open device uses a window!",
               "MESSAGE",
               MB_OK);
   }
```

ValidateWaveBuffer Command

Any program that uses the tegSetByte() function or the tegSetWord() function needs to use the ValidateWaveBuffer command.

The ValidateWaveBuffer command validates the Wave Buffer. The tegSetByte() and tegSetWord() functions let you change the values of the samples of a WAV file. Typically, you use the tegSetByte() function or the tegSetWord() function in a loop that sets a range of samples (for example, samples 1000 through 7000) in the Wave Buffer. When you finish the loop, you need to validate the Wave Buffer by issuing a ValidateWaveBuffer command.

```
' Visual Basic Example.
tegomm1.Command = "ValidateWaveBuffer"
```

```
// Visual C++ Example.
tegomm1->SetStrProperty("Command", "ValidateWaveBuffer");
```

```
// Borland C++ Example.
tegomm1->SetProp("Command", "ValidateWaveBuffer");
```

Visible Property

Data Type: Integer (Boolean)

Description: You use this property to make the multimedia control either visible or invisible. To hide the multimedia control from view, set the Visible property to FALSE. To make the multimedia control visible, set the Visible property to TRUE.

```
' Visual Basic Example.
' Hide the multimedia control.
tegomm1.Visible = False
```

```
// Visual C++ Example.
// Hide the multimedia control.
trgomm1->SetNumProperty("Visible", FALSE);
```

```
// Borland C++ Example.
// Hide the multimedia control.
tegomm1->SetProp("Visible", FALSE);
```

Wait Property

Data Type: Integer (Boolean)

This property is available only at runtime.

Description: You use this property to specify whether the multimedia control should wait for the next issued command to complete before returning control to the program. For example, if you set the Wait property to TRUE prior to issuing a Play command, the multimedia control will perform the Play command and wait until the playback is done. Once the playback is done, the program will resume. Normally you don't have to set the Wait property because all commands that use the Wait property have a default value for the Wait property. For example, if prior to issuing a Play command you don't specify any value for the Wait property, the Play command assumes that the value of the Wait property is FALSE, and the program resumes while the playback is in progress in the background. To see what is the default value of the Wait property for other commands (for example, Stop, Record, Delete, Copy), see the description of these commands.

```
' Visual Basic Example.
' Issue a Play command and wait until playback is done.
tegomm1.Wait = True
tegomm1.Command = "Play"
```

```
// Visual C++ Example.
// Issue a Play command and wait until playback is done.
trgomm1->SetNumProperty("Wait", TRUE);
tegomm1->SetStrProperty("Command", "Play");
```

```
// Borland C++ Example.
// Issue a Play command and wait until playback is done.
tegomm1->SetProp("Wait", TRUE);
tegomm1->SetProp("Command", "Play");
```

Width Property

You use this property to specify the width of the multimedia control.

```
' Visual Basic Example.
tegomm1.Width = 300

// Visual C++ Example.
tegomm1->SetNumProperty("Width", 300);

// Borland C++ Example.
tegomm1->SetProp("Width", 300);
```

E

Writing a Complete Wave Editor Program Application

In this appendix you learn how to implement a complete Wave Editor program. You learn how to perform WAV file editing tasks, such as accessing samples from the WAV file, displaying the samples of the WAV file in a graph format, selecting a section of samples from the WAV file, copying a section of the WAV file (or the whole WAV file) to the Clipboard, pasting from the Clipboard to any point in the WAV file, deleting sections of the WAV file, cutting any section in the WAV file, recording sound into the WAV file, determining the type of WAV file (such as mono, stereo, 8 bits, 16 bits), extracting the sampling rate of the WAV file, and completing other advanced WAV file editing tasks.

The topics covered in this appendix are relevant for tasks other than writing a Wave Editor program. Knowing how to access samples of the WAV file is important in any application in which you need to analyze the sound of the WAV file. For example, if you need to write a speech recognition program, you'll have to analyze the samples of the recorded sound to detect various words.

The AllMedia program that is discussed in Chapter 4, "Creating Multimedia Programs (Part I)," and Chapter 5, "Creating Multimedia Programs (Part II)," and is included with this book's CD provides the source code files of a Wave Editor program. In this appendix you learn how to implement a Wave Editor program by reviewing the code of the WEdit.FRM form of the AllMedia program. Feel free to add your own code to the WEdit.FRM form to add more features to it.

This appendix is divided into two parts:

- Using the Wave Editor program
- How the Wave Editor program works

In the first part you'll learn how to use the Wave Editor program of the AllMedia program from a user's point of view. The second part is a detailed walk-through of the code of the WEdit.FRM form.

NOTE

To test the code presented in this appendix, your computer must have a Windows-compatible sound card that supports playback of WAV files.

Using the Wave Editor Program

The AllMedia program that was presented in Chapters 4 and 5 includes a Wave Editor program. In this first part of the appendix, you'll experiment with all the features of the Wave Editor program of the AllMedia program. In the second part of the appendix, the source code of the Wave Editor program is covered in detail.

Start the Wave Editor program:

❑ Select Run from the File menu of the Program Manager and execute the AllMedia program (C:\LEARNVB\ORIGINAL\ALLMEDIA\ALLMEDIA.EXE).

> *Windows responds by executing the AllMedia program.*

Run the Wave Editor program of the AllMedia program:

❑ Click the WAV button inside the toolbar of the AllMedia program.

> *The main window of the Wave Editor program appears, as shown in Figure E.1.*

Figure E.1.
The main window of the
Wave Editor program.

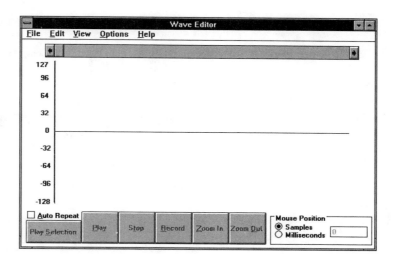

As you can see, the main window of the Wave Editor program includes an empty graph area as well as various controls. Notice that the buttons at the bottom of the window are disabled because no WAV file is currently open.

In the following sections you'll open a WAV file and explore all the features of the Wave Editor program.

Opening a WAV File

To open a WAV file do the following:

❑ Select Open from the File menu. (See Figure E.2.) (Notice that the Open and Exit menu items are the only items currently available in the File menu because no WAV file is open.)

> *The Wave Editor program responds by displaying an Open File dialog box. (See Figure E.3.)*

Figure E.2.
The File menu of the Wave
Editor program.

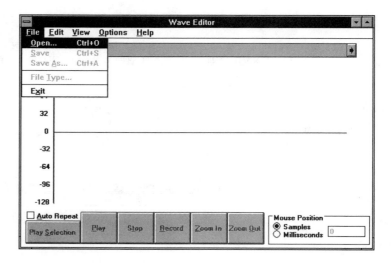

Figure E.3.
The Open File dialog box
that is displayed after you
select Open from the File
menu.

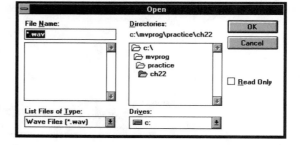

☐ Use the Open File dialog box to select the file C:\LEARNVB\WAV\8KENNED3.WAV.
(This WAV file was copied to your hard drive when you installed the CD provided with
this book.)

> *The Wave Editor program responds by opening the 8KENNED3.WAV file. The graph that*
> *represents the samples of 8KENNED3.WAV is displayed. (See Figure E.4.)*

Notice that the title of the window is now

```
Wave Editor - 8KENNED3.WAV [Full View]
```

This title indicates that you are currently viewing the graph of the 8KENNED3.WAV file, and you
are viewing the WAV file in Full View mode. What does *Full View mode* mean? It means that the
graph that is currently being displayed represents the entire WAV file. That is, the extreme left bar
of the graph represents the first sample of the WAV file, and the extreme right bar of the graph
represents the last sample of the WAV file. As you will soon see, it is also possible to view the graph
of the WAV file in Zooming mode. When you view the graph in Zooming mode, the graph area
represents a portion of the WAV file (not the entire WAV file).

Figure E.4.
The graph displayed when
the 8KENNED3.WAV file
is open.

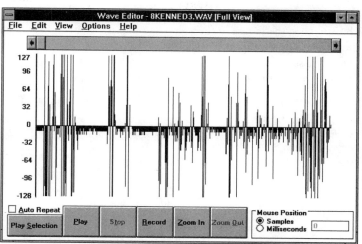

Starting the Playback

To start the playback of the 8KENNED3.WAV file do the following:

❏ Click the Play button.

> *The Wave Editor program responds by playing the 8KENNED3.WAV file through the*
> *sound card.*

Notice that during the playback, the thumb tab of the horizontal scroll bar (at the top of the window) changes its position in accordance with the playback position. This scroll bar represents the current playback position. You cannot change this scroll bar while playback is in progress, but when there is no playback, you can use this scroll bar to navigate to any point in the WAV file.

Experiment with the horizontal scroll bar:

❏ Stop the playback of the WAV file by clicking the Stop button.

❏ Drag the thumb tab of the scroll bar to any desired point and then click the Play button.

> *The Wave Editor program responds by playing the WAV file from the position indicated by*
> *the scroll bar.*

❏ Stop the playback by clicking the Stop button.

Playing a Section of the WAV File

The Wave Editor program lets you play any desired section of the WAV file. To play a section, you need to select the desired section with the mouse, and then click the Play Selection button. Here is how you play a section:

☐ Click the mouse at any point inside the graph area. While holding down the mouse button, drag the mouse to the right or to the left. As you drag the mouse, a thin red rectangle is drawn around the graph area in accordance with the mouse movement. This rectangle specifies the section that you are selecting. When you finish selecting the desired section, release the mouse button.

Figure E.5 shows the selection rectangle enclosing a small section in the middle of the graph.

Figure E.5.
Selecting a section of the
WAV file.

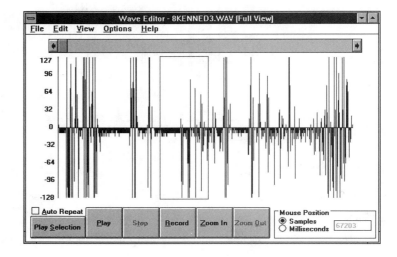

To play the selected section do the following:

☐ Click the Play Selection button. (The Play Selection button is to the left of the Play button.)

> *The Wave Editor program responds by playing the section that you selected.*

You can play the selected section in a continuous loop. Here is how you do that:

☐ Use the mouse to select any desired section.

☐ Click the Auto Repeat box to place an X in it. (The Auto Repeat checkbox is above the Play Selection button.)

☐ Click the Play Selection button.

> *The Wave Editor program responds by playing the selected section again and again. The selected section keeps on playing until you click the Stop button.*

Notice that while the playback of the selected section is in progress you can use the mouse to select a different playback section. The Wave Editor program will play the newly selected section. To see (or rather hear) this feature of the Wave Editor program do the following:

☐ Make sure the Auto Repeat checkbox is checked.

❑ Use the mouse to select any small section of the WAV file.

❑ Click the Play Selection button.

❑ While the playback is in progress, use the mouse to select other small sections of the WAV file.

As you can hear, after the Wave Editor program finishes playing the current sound section, it starts playing the new sound section that you selected (you don't have to click the Play Selection button again). This feature is very useful when you want to isolate a sound section within the WAV file.

❑ Use the mouse and the Play Selection button to play various sections of the WAV file. Notice that sections of the graph showing large positive values (or large negative values) represent parts of the WAV file that have high volumes. The sections of the graph showing values close to zero represent parts of the WAV file that have low volumes.

❑ Stop the playback of the WAV file by clicking the Stop button.

The Mouse Position Indicator

After you isolate a particular section of the WAV file, you can determine the coordinates of the section by using the Mouse Position indicator. The Mouse Position indicator is located at the bottom-right corner of the window.

The Mouse Position indicator includes two radio buttons (Samples and Milliseconds) and a text box that displays the current mouse position. If you select the Samples radio button, the mouse position is reported in units of samples. If you select the Milliseconds radio button, the mouse position is reported in units of milliseconds.

The Mouse Position indicator does not report the current position of the selected section; it reports the mouse position. Therefore, if you want to find the coordinates of the currently selected sound section you need to do the following:

1. Place the mouse cursor over the left edge of the selection rectangle and observe the Mouse Position indicator. This gives you the starting coordinate of the selected section.

2. Place the mouse cursor over the right edge of the selection rectangle and observe the Mouse Position indicator. This gives you the ending coordinate of the selected section.

Note that if the selected section is very small, it's difficult to point the mouse cursor accurately on the edges of the selection rectangle. As you will soon discover, however, the Wave Editor program lets you zoom in to a section. After you zoom in to a sound section, the sound section is displayed over the entire width of the graph.

Zooming In to a Sound Section

To see the Zoom feature of the Sound Editor program in action, perform the following exercise.

As you heard in the preceding steps, the 8KENNED3.WAV file contains a portion of a famous speech by former President John F. Kennedy:

588

```
So my fellow Americans
ask not
what your country can do for you
ask what you can do for your country.
```

Suppose that you want to zoom in to the sound section containing the audio of the words ask not. Here is how you do that:

❑ Make sure the Mouse Position indicator is set to units of samples (that is, make sure that the Samples radio button in the Mouse Position indicator is selected).

❑ Select the audio section 29610 through 43514. That is, move the mouse over the graph until the Mouse Position indicator reports 29610. Then drag the mouse to the right until the Mouse Position indicator reports 43514. Then release the mouse button.

Your graph should now look like the one shown in Figure E.6.

Figure E.6.
Selecting the sound section
29610 through 43514.

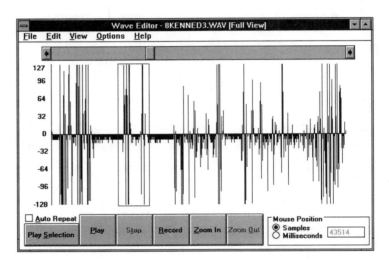

To verify that the audio section you selected indeed contains the words ask not do the following:

❑ Click the Play Selection button.

The Wave Editor program responds by playing the audio section ask not through the sound card. (If the Auto Repeat checkbox is checked, the audio section will play again and again until you click the Stop button).

Now that you are sure that the selected sound section contains the desired audio prompt, you can zoom in to this section:

❑ Click the Zoom In button.

The Wave Editor program responds by zooming in to the selected sound section. (See Figure E.7.) Notice that the title of the window is now

```
Wave Editor - 8KENNED3.WAV [Zooming]
```

You are no longer in Full View mode; instead you are in Zooming mode.

Figure E.7.
Zooming in to a sound
section.

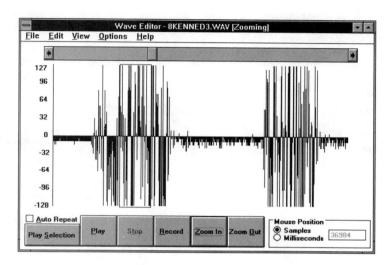

So at this point the entire graph area displays the sound section that you selected (samples 29610 through 43514). The extreme left bar of the graph represents sample number 29610, and the extreme right bar of the graph represents sample number 43514. You can verify this in the following way:

❑ Move the mouse cursor to the extreme left point of the graph and observe the Mouse Position indicator. It should read 29610.

❑ Similarly, move the mouse cursor to the extreme right point of the graph and observe the Mouse Position indicator. It should read 43514.

As you can see from Figure E.7, it is very easy to visually approximate where the two words ask and not of the audio prompt ask not begin and end. By trial and error you can determine that the range for the word ask includes samples 31487 through 36167. To verify this do the following:

❑ Use the mouse to select the audio section 31487 through 36167. (See Figure E.8.)

❑ Click the Play Selection button.

> *The Wave Editor program responds by playing the sound section that contains the audio phrase* ask.

The Wave Editor program enables you to further zoom in to smaller and smaller sections with no limitations. In fact, you can keep on zooming until the graph finally displays only one sample. To see this unlimited zooming feature of the Wave Editor program, zoom in to the sound section that contains the word ask:

E

☐ Leave the selection rectangle as it is now. That is, in the previous step you selected the sound section that contains the word ask (sample number 31487 through 36167), and because you now want to zoom in to the sound section that contains the word ask you don't have to change the current state of the selection rectangle.

☐ Click the Zoom In button.

The Wave Editor program responds by zooming in to the sound section that contains the word ask. *(See Figure E.9.)*

Figure E.8.
Selecting samples 31487 through 36167 (the word ask*).*

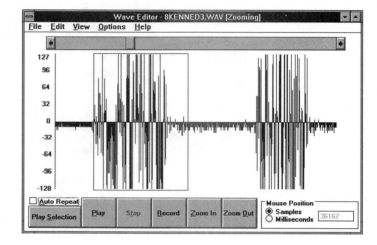

Figure E.9.
Zooming in to the sound section that contains the word ask (samples 31487 through 36167).

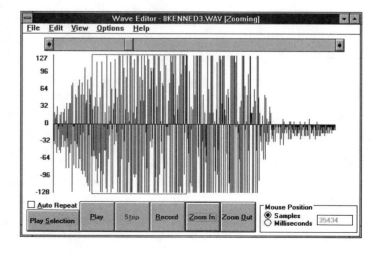

So at this point the entire graph area displays the sound section that you zoomed in to (samples 31487 through 36167). The extreme left bar of the graph represents sample number 31487, and the extreme right bar of the graph represents sample number 36167. You can verify this in the following way:

☐ Move the mouse cursor to the extreme left point of the graph and observe the Mouse Position indicator. It should read 31487.

☐ Similarly, move the mouse cursor to the extreme right point of the graph and observe the Mouse Position indicator. It should read 36167.

You can now keep zooming in on smaller and smaller sound sections. Figures E.10 through E.18 show how the graph looks when you zoom in on various sound sections.

Figure E.10.
Zooming in to samples
32119 through 33694
(1576 samples).

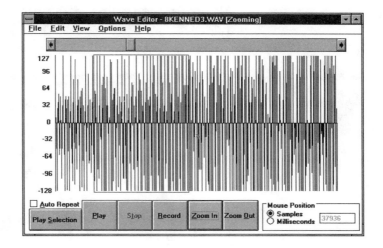

Figure E.11.
Zooming in to samples
32332 through 32862
(531 samples).

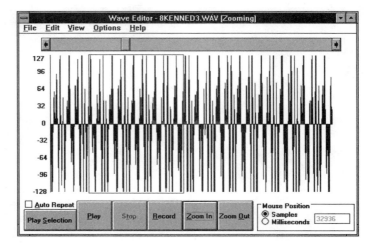

Figure E.12.
Zooming in to samples
32404 through 32582
(178 samples).

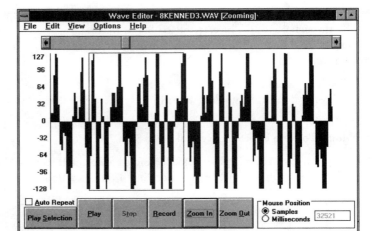

Figure E.13.
Zooming in to samples
32428 through 32488
(61 samples).

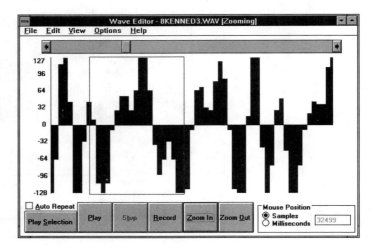

Figure E.14.
Zooming in to samples
32436 through 32456
(21 samples).

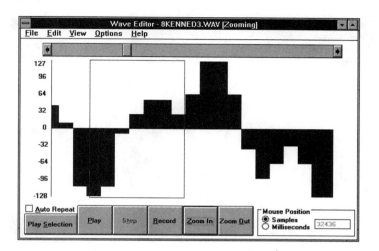

Figure E.15.
Zooming in to samples
32439 through 32445
(7 samples).

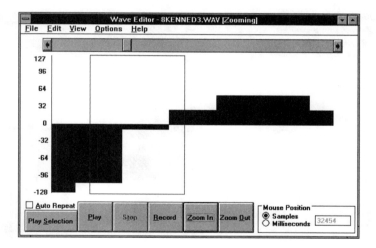

Figure E.16.
Zooming in to samples
32440 through 32442
(3 samples).

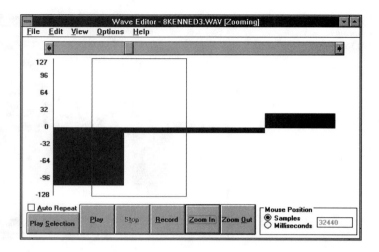

Figure E.17.
Zooming in to samples
32440 and 32441
(2 samples).

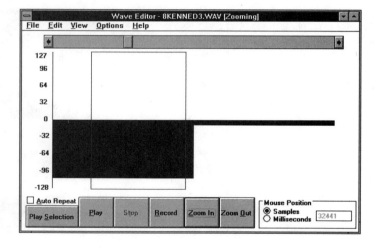

Figure E.18.
Zooming in to sample
32440 (1 sample!).

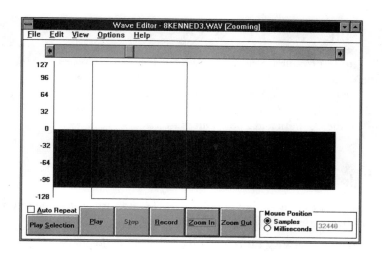

As you can see, you can zoom in on very small groups of sound samples. Figure E.17 shows the graph after you zoom in to samples 32440 and 32441 (only 2 samples). The first half of the graph represents sample number 32440 and the second half of the graph represents sample number 32441. Consequently, when the user moves the mouse over the first half of the X-axis, the Mouse Position indicator displays 32440, and when the user moves the mouse over the second half of the X-axis, the Mouse Position indicator displays 32441.

Figure E.18 shows the ultimate zoom! In this figure, only 1 sample is displayed (sample number 32440).

To zoom back out to Full View, you need to click the Zoom Out button:

❏ Click the Zoom Out button.

The Wave Editor program responds by zooming out and by changing the title of the window back to Wave Editor - 8KENNED3.WAV [Full View].

The window of your Wave Editor program now looks like the one shown in Figure E.4. That is, now the graph represents the entire WAV file (in Full View).

E

> **NOTE**
>
> In the preceding steps, you used the Zoom In and Zoom Out buttons to zoom in to sound sections and then to zoom out again to Full View. In addition to the Zoom In and Zoom Out buttons, the Wave Editor program's View menu has two menu items (also called Zoom In and Zoom Out). The Zoom In and Zoom Out menu items work the same way as the Zoom In and Zoom Out buttons.

Deleting Sound Sections

You can use the Wave Editor program to delete a particular sound section from the WAV file. For practice, perform the following experiment.

Currently, the WAV file contains the following audio phrase:

```
So my fellow Americans
ask not
what your country can do for you
ask what you can do for your country.
```

Now delete the word not from the WAV file so that the WAV file contains the audio phrase:

```
So my fellow Americans
ask
what your country can do for you
ask what you can do for your country.
```

(Don't worry, you are not going to save this version of the WAV file, so you won't be permanently changing this famous speech.)

Follow these steps to delete the word not:

❑ Use the mouse to select the audio section 38880 through 43514. (See Figure E.19.)

❑ Click the Delete key on your keyboard (or select Delete from the Edit menu).

The Wave Editor program responds by deleting the selected section and by updating the graph of the WAV file. (See Figure E.20.)

Figure E.19.
Selecting samples 38880
through 43514 (the word
not).

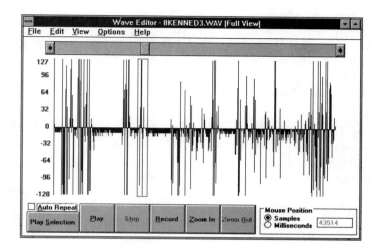

Figure E.20.
The graph of the
8KENNED3.WAV file
after the word not is
deleted.

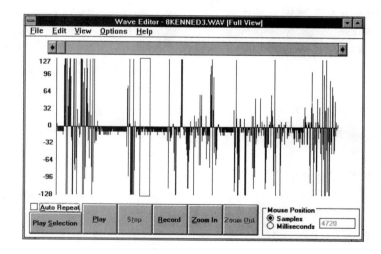

To verify that the word *not* is removed do the following:

☐ Drag the thumb tab of the horizontal scroll bar to the extreme left position and then click the Play button.

The Wave Editor program responds by playing the WAV file from the beginning. As you can hear, the word not is no longer in the WAV file. The speech now contains these words:

```
So my fellow Americans
ask
what your country can do for you
ask what you can do for your country.
```

NOTE

In the preceding step, you were instructed to play the WAV file from beginning to end by dragging the thumb tab of the horizontal scroll bar to the extreme left position and then clicking the Play button. Alternatively, you can use the mouse to select the entire graph area and then click the Play Selection button.

Using the Wave Editor Program to Perform Your Own Recording

You can perform your own recording and insert it at any desired point in the WAV file. For practice, insert at the beginning of the WAV file the audio recording of the word HELLO:

❏ Drag the thumb tab of the horizontal scroll bar to the extreme left position so that you can insert your recording at the beginning of the WAV file.

❏ Prepare the microphone of your sound card to record.

❏ Click the Record button and speak the word HELLO into the microphone of your sound card.

❏ Click the Stop button to stop the recording.

> *The Wave Editor program responds by displaying the updated graph of the WAV file, which includes your recording. (See Figure E.22.) Your graph, of course, will not look exactly like the one shown in Figure E.22.*

NOTE

You probably noticed when you were recording that the title in the Wave Editor program's main window changed to RECORDING. (See Figure E.21.)

To attract the user's attention, the title "blinks" at regular intervals by changing between RECORDING and R E C O R D I N G.

Figure E.21.
The window of the Wave
Editor program while
recording is in progress.

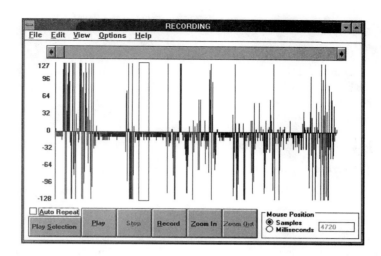

Figure E.22.
The graph of the
8KENNED3.WAV file
after you have inserted a
recording of the word
hello at the beginning
of the file.

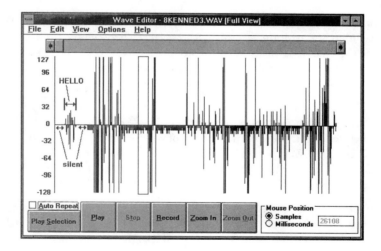

NOTE

In the preceding steps, you inserted your recording at the beginning of the WAV file by dragging the thumb tab of the horizontal scroll bar to the extreme left position and then clicking the Record button.

> If you want to insert your recording at another point in the WAV file, move the thumb tab of the scroll bar to the desired point and then click the Record button. Alternatively, you can use the Play button to play the WAV file and listen until you come to the section where you want to insert your recording. Click the Stop button and then click the Record button.

Now listen to your recording:

❑ Click the Play button.

> *The Wave Editor program responds by playing your recording of the word HELLO, followed by the original recording of the WAV file.*

❑ Stop the playback by clicking the Stop button.

Notice that in Figure E.22 the samples of the recording that you inserted in the WAV file are divided into three parts.

In the first part of the recording, all the samples are zero (silent samples). Why is that? When the recording was performed, a small delay occurred between the time the Record button was pressed and the time you actually spoke the word HELLO. During this time, the microphone did not pick up any sound, so the graph shows samples with zero values.

The second part of the recording is where you actually spoke the word HELLO. Notice that the values of the samples of the HELLO recording are smaller than the values of the samples in the rest of the WAV file. They are smaller because the original 8KENNED3.WAV file contains a recording with a high volume. If you want the samples of your recording to be as high as the original samples of the 8KENNED3.WAV file, you need to raise your voice when you speak into the microphone. Alternatively, you can select the HELLO audio section with the mouse, and then use the Increase Volume menu item from the Edit menu.

In the third part of the recording, the samples are zero again (silent samples). Why? After you finished saying the word HELLO, it took a moment for you to click the Stop button. During this time, the microphone did not pick up any sound, so the graph shows samples with zero values.

You can zoom in to the word HELLO and view it in more detail:

❑ Use the mouse to select the sound section of your recording of the word HELLO. Then click the Zoom In button.

> *The Wave Editor program responds by zooming in on the samples of your HELLO recording. (See Figure E.23.)*

Figure E.23.
Zooming in to the HELLO
recording.

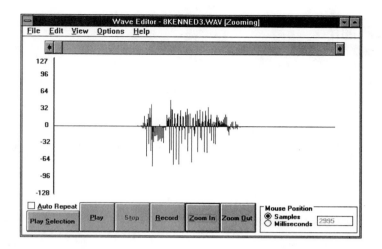

In the preceding steps, you inserted your recording into the original 8KENNED3.WAV file. If you want, you can delete the entire contents of the WAV file and start your own recording from scratch:

❑ Change back to Full View mode. (Click the Zoom Out button to zoom out from the samples of the HELLO recording.)

Your graph now looks like the one shown in Figure E.22.

❑ Use the mouse to select the entire graph area. (See Figure E.24.)

Figure E.24.
Selecting the entire graph
area.

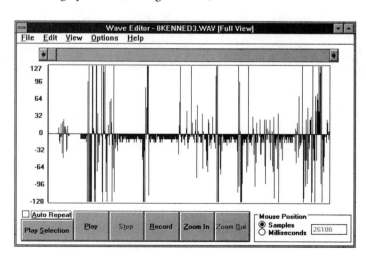

NOTE

In the preceding step, you were instructed to use the mouse to select the entire graph area. Another way to select the entire graph area is to use the Select All menu item of the Edit menu. Using Select All from the Edit menu has the same effect as using the mouse to select the entire graph area.

The Select All menu item of the Edit menu selects all the samples that are represented by the currently displayed graph. When the graph is in Full View mode (that is, when you are not zooming), selecting Select All from the Edit menu selects all the samples of the WAV file.

❑ Press the Delete key on your keyboard (or select Delete from the Edit menu).

> *The Wave Editor program responds by deleting all the samples that are currently selected (that is, all the samples of the WAV file).*

You can now perform your own recording. When you finish recording, you can save your recording under a different name:

❑ Prepare the microphone of your sound card to record.

❑ Click the Record button and speak the words ONE, TWO, THREE into the microphone.

❑ Click the Stop button to stop the recording.

> *The Wave Editor program responds by displaying the updated graph of the WAV file, which includes your recording. (See Figure E.25.)*

Figure E.25.
The graph of the WAV file after you record the words ONE, TWO, THREE.

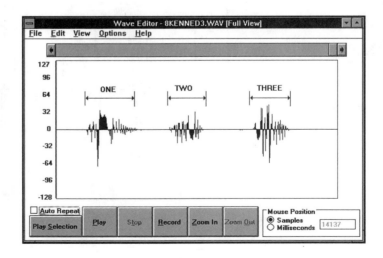

You can now save your recording under a different filename so that you don't overwrite the original 8KENNED3.WAV file. Here is how you save the file:

☐ Select Save As from the File menu.

> *The Wave Editor program responds by displaying the Save As dialog box, which is shown in Figure E.26.*

Figure E.26.
The Save As dialog box of the Wave Editor program.

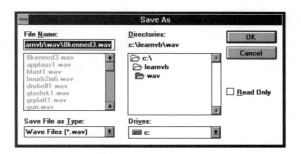

☐ Use the Save As dialog box to save the file as C:\LEARNVB\WAV\TRY.WAV.

> *The Wave Editor program responds by saving your recording into the file TRY.WAV. Notice in Figure E.27 that the Wave Editor program window now displays* TRY.WAV *in the title.*

Figure E.27.
The window of the Wave Editor program after you save the WAV file as TRY.WAV.

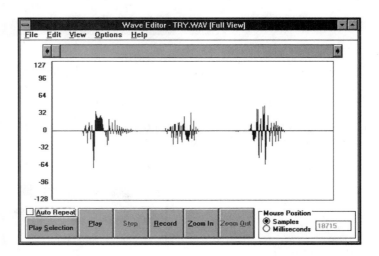

The Maximum Recording Length Feature

The Wave Editor program has a maximum recording length feature, which is a safety mechanism that prevents the user from accidentally recording a huge WAV file. Suppose that the user clicks the Record button to perform a recording and then is interrupted by a phone call. If the user forgets to click the Stop button, the recording continues without any limitation and may waste the user's entire hard drive capacity. (Although the recording is not saved to a WAV file, the recording process uses the hard drive for swap files.)

To avoid such a scenario, the Wave Editor program includes a maximum recording length feature. The user can specify the maximum recording length by using the Maximum Recording menu item from the Options menu.

When the user selects Maximum Recording Length, a submenu appears, as shown in Figure E.28.

Figure E.28.
Selecting the maximum
recording length.

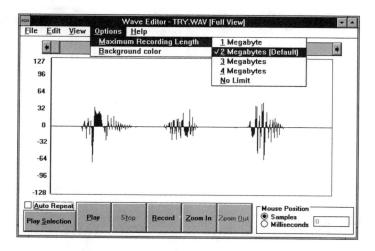

The user can use this menu to select the maximum recording length. For example, when the maximum recording length is set to 2 Megabytes, the user can record a maximum of 2,000,000 bytes. When the recording length reaches 2,000,000 bytes, the recording stops automatically.

If the user wishes to make recordings that have no length limitations, the user can select the No Limit option. If the user selects the No Limit option, the warning message shown in Figure E.29 appears.

Figure E.29
The warning message
displayed by the Wave
Editor program when the
user selects No Limit from
the Maximum Recording
Length submenu.

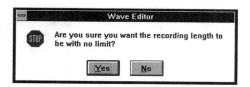

The Copy, Paste, Cut, Silence, and Volume Features

You have already experimented with the Delete option of the Edit menu. The Edit menu has other very useful menu items that enable you to copy, paste, and cut sound sections from or to the WAV file and change the volume of any sound section in the WAV file.

The Copy, Paste, and Cut options of the Edit menu work in the same way as the Copy, Paste, and Cut options of a word processing program.

When you select Copy, the current selection is copied to the Clipboard.

When you select Paste, the current selection is deleted, and the contents of the Clipboard are inserted at the position of the current selection. If nothing is currently selected (that is, the selection rectangle is only one vertical line), the contents of the Clipboard are inserted and nothing is deleted.

When you select Cut, the current selection is deleted and copied to the Clipboard.

❏ Experiment with the Copy, Paste, and Cut menu items of the Edit menu. For example, you can use these menu items to rearrange the TRY.WAV file that you saved earlier so that instead of saying ONE, TWO, THREE, the WAV file says THREE, TWO, ONE.

> **NOTE**
>
> You can use the Copy, Paste, and Cut options of the Edit menu to copy sound sections from one WAV file to another. You can run two (or more) instances of the AllMedia program, open a different WAV file in each instance, and then use the Copy, Paste, and Cut options to copy sound sections from one WAV file to another.

The Silence, Increase Volume, and Decrease Volume options of the Edit menu let you change the volume of any sound section in the WAV file.

As implied by its name, the Silence menu option lets you silence a sound section. To silence a sound section use the mouse to select the desired sound section and then select Silence from the Edit menu.

The Increase Volume menu option lets you increase the volume of a sound section by 25%. To increase the volume of a sound section (by 25%) use the mouse to select the desired sound section and then select Increase Volume from the Edit menu. You can select the Increase Volume option several times until the selected section has the desired volume.

The Decrease Volume menu option lets you decrease the volume of a sound section by 25%. To decrease the volume of a sound section (by 25%) use the mouse to select the desired sound section and then select Decrease Volume from the Edit menu. You can select the Decrease Volume option several times until the selected section has the desired volume.

8-bit, 16-bit, Mono, and Stereo WAV Files

The Wave Editor program supports only 8-bit mono WAV files. If you try to open a 16-bit or a stereo WAV file, the message box shown in Figure E.30 appears.

Figure E.30.
The message box that the
Wave Editor program
displays when you try to
open a 16-bit or a stereo
WAV file.

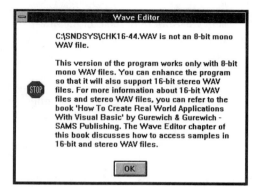

You can add code to the Wave Editor program so that 16-bit and stereo WAV files are also supported. You will learn how to do this later in this appendix.

Other Features of the Wave Editor Program

You have already used the Save As menu item of the Wave Editor program. The File menu also offers a Save option. The Save option saves the current changes to the WAV file and is available only after you make changes to the WAV file. If you don't make any changes to the WAV file, the Save option appears dimmed.

If you try to exit the Wave Editor program (or open a new WAV file) without first saving changes that you made to the current WAV file, the Wave Editor program prompts you with the warning message shown in Figure E.31.

Figure E.31.
The message box that the
Wave Editor program
displays when you try to
exit the program or open a
new WAV file without first
saving the current WAV
file.

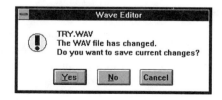

The File menu also offers a File Type option. When you select File Type from the File menu, the Wave Editor program displays a message box with information about the currently open WAV file. (See Figure E.32.)

Figure E.32.
The File Type message box.

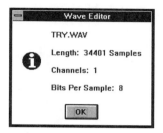

The Wave Editor program's Options menu offers a Background Color menu item that lets you change the background color of the Wave Editor program's window, as shown in Figure E.33.

Figure E.33.
Changing the background
color.

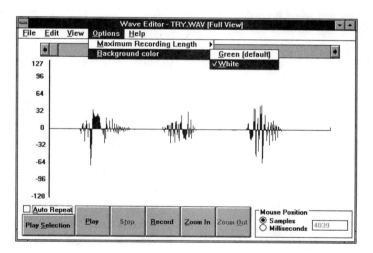

As Figure E.33 shows, you can select either green or white for the background color.

The Wave Editor program's Help menu has two options, Info and About, as shown in Figure E.34.

Figure E.34.
The Help menu of the
Wave Editor program.

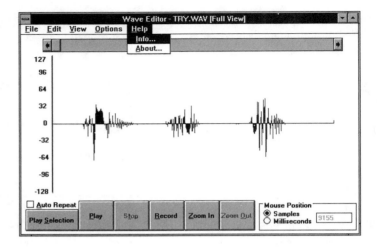

When you select Info, the dialog box shown in Figure E.35 appears; when you select About, the dialog box shown in Figure E.36 appears.

Figure E.35.
The Wave Editor program's
Information dialog box.

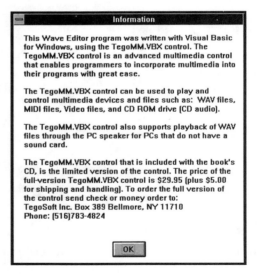

That's it! You have tested all the features, menu items, and buttons of the Wave Editor program. Now that you know what the Wave Editor program does, you can read the rest of this appendix, which covers in detail the Wave Editor program's source code.

❑ Terminate the Wave Editor program by selecting Exit from the File menu.

Figure E.36.
The Wave Editor program's
About dialog box.

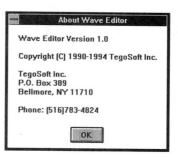

How the Wave Editor Program Works

This part of the appendix discusses the source code of the Wave Editor program. All the source code of the Wave Editor program is attached to the WEdit.FRM form of the AllMedia program. The WEdit.FRM file resides in your C:\LEARNVB\ORIGINAL\ALLMEDIA directory.

The code of the Wave Editor program is longer than any of the code of other programs covered so far in this book. Therefore, you are not asked to type the code. Rather, the code of the program is explained in detail, procedure by procedure. While you read this appendix, you can load the C:\LEARNVB\ORIGINAL\ALLMEDIA\ALLMEDIA.MAK project and view the source code of the WEdit.FRM form on your PC.

The Visual Implementation of the Main Form of the Wave Editor Program

Before you begin reviewing the code of the form of the Wave Editor program, look at the form's properties, which are shown in Table E.1. Figure E.37 shows how the form looks in design mode after it has been completed.

Table E.1. The form of the Wave Editor program.

Object	Property	Setting
Form	**Name**	**frmWEdit**
	BackColor	&H00008000&
	Caption	"Wave Editor program"
	Height	6315
	Icon	C:\LEARNVB\ICONS\WEDIT.ICO
	Left	150

continues

Table E.1. continued

Object	Property	Setting
	ScaleMode	3 'Pixel
	Top	450
	Width	9315
Command button	**Name**	**cmdZoomOut**
	Caption	"Zoom &Out"
	Enabled	0 'False
	Height	855
	Left	5400
	Top	4680
	Width	975
Command button	**Name**	**cmdZoomIn**
	Caption	"&Zoom In"
	Enabled	0 'False
	Height	855
	Left	4440
	Top	4680
	Width	975
Checkbox	**Name**	**chkAutoRepeat**
	BackColor	&H00008000&
	Caption	"&Auto Repeat"
	Height	270
	Left	150
	Top	4650
	Width	1350
Command button	**Name**	**cmdRecord**
	Caption	"&Record"
	Enabled	0 'False
	Height	855
	Left	3480
	Top	4680
	Width	975

E

Object	Property	Setting
Command button	**Name**	**cmdStop**
	Caption	"S&top"
	Enabled	0 'False
	Height	855
	Left	2520
	Top	4680
	Width	975
Command button	**Name**	**cmdPlaySelection**
	Caption	"Play &Selection"
	Enabled	0 'False
	Height	615
	Left	120
	Top	4920
	Width	1455
Command button	**Name**	**cmdPlay**
	Caption	"&Play"
	Enabled	0 'False
	Height	855
	Left	1560
	Top	4680
	Width	975
Text box	**Name**	**txtMousePosition**
	BackColor	&H00008000&
	Enabled	0 'False
	Height	285
	Left	8040
	Top	5040
	Width	975
Option button	**Name**	**optMilliseconds**
	BackColor	&H00008000&
	Caption	"Milliseconds"
	Height	195
	Left	6600

continues

E

Table E.1. continued

Object	Property	Setting
	Top	5160
	Width	1335
Option button	**Name**	**optSamples**
	BackColor	&H00008000&
	Caption	"Samples"
	Height	255
	Left	6600
	Top	4920
	Value	-1 'True
	Width	1215
Frame	**Name**	**Frame1**
	BackColor	&H00008000&
	Caption	"Mouse Position"
	Height	855
	Left	6480
	Top	4680
	Width	2655
Horizontal scroll bar	**Name**	**hsbPosition**
	Height	375
	LargeChange	10
	Left	600
	Top	120
	Width	8175
Multimedia control	**Name**	**TegommWav**
	Height	495
	Left	2760
	Top	3240
	UpdateInterval	500
	Visible	0 'False
	Width	3510

Object	Property	Setting
Common dialog	**Name**	**CMDialog1**
	CancelError	-1 'True
	Left	4320
	Top	2640
Label	**Name**	**Label9**
	BackColor	&H00008000&
	Caption	"-96"
	Height	255
	Left	480
	Top	3840
	Width	270
Label	**Name**	**Label8**
	BackColor	&H00008000&
	Caption	"-64"
	Height	255
	Left	480
	Top	3360
	Width	270
Label	**Name**	**Label7**
	BackColor	&H00008000&
	Caption	"-32"
	Height	255
	Left	480
	Top	2880
	Width	270
Label	**Name**	**Label6**
	BackColor	&H00008000&
	Caption	"-128"
	Height	255
	Left	360
	Top	4320
	Width	375

continues

Table E.1. continued

Object	Property	Setting
Label	**Name**	**Label5**
	BackColor	&H00008000&
	Caption	"96"
	Height	255
	Left	480
	Top	960
	Width	255
Label	**Name**	**Label4**
	BackColor	&H00008000&
	Caption	"32"
	Height	255
	Left	480
	Top	1920
	Width	255
Label	**Name**	**Label3**
	BackColor	&H00008000&
	Caption	"64"
	Height	255
	Left	480
	Top	1440
	Width	255
Label	**Name**	**Label2**
	BackColor	&H00008000&
	Caption	"127"
	Height	255
	Left	360
	Top	600
	Width	375
Label	**Name**	**Label1**
	BackColor	&H00008000&
	Caption	"0"

E

Object	Property	Setting
	Height	255
	Left	600
	Top	2400
	Width	135
Line	**Name**	**linY**
	X1	56
	X2	56
	Y1	40
	Y2	296
Line	**Name**	**linX**
	X1	57
	X2	568
	Y1	168
	Y2	168

Menu (See Table E.2.)

Figure E.37.
The form of the Wave
Editor program (in design
mode).

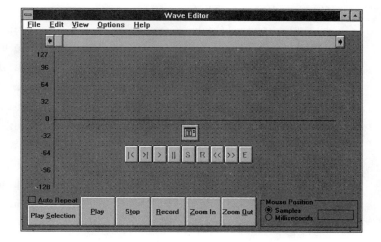

Table E.2. The Menu table of the `frmWEdit` form.

Caption	Shortcut	Name
&File		mnuFile
&Open	Ctrl+O	mnuOpen
&Save	Ctrl+S	mnuSave
Save &As	Ctrl+A	mnuSaveAs
-		mnuSep1
File &Type		mnuFileType
-		mnuSep2
E&xit		mnuExit
&Edit		mnuEdit
Cu&t	Ctrl+X	mnuCut
&Copy	Ctrl+C	mnuCopy
&Paste	Ctrl+V	mnuPaste
&Delete	Del	mnuDelete
-		mnuSep3
&Silence		mnuSilence
&Increase Volume (25%)		mnuIncreaseVolume
Dec&rease Volume (25%)		mnuDecreaseVolume
-		mnuSep4
Select A&ll	Ctrl+L	mnuSelectAll
&View		mnuView
&Zoom In		mnuZoomIn
Zoom &Out		mnuZoomOut
&Options		mnuOptions
&Maximum Recording Length		mnuMaxRecordLength
&1 Megabyte		mnuMaxRecLen1
&2 Megabytes (default)		mnuMaxRecLen2
&3 Megabytes		mnuMaxRecLen3
&4 Megabytes		mnuMaxRecLen4
No Limit		mnuMaxRecLenNoLimit
&Background Color		mnuBackColor

E

Caption	Shortcut	Name
&Green (default)		mnuGreen
White		mnuWhite
&Help		mnuHelp
&Info		mnuInfo
&About		mnuAbout

The General Declarations Section of the `frmWEdit` Form

The general declarations section of the `frmWEdit` form includes declarations of constants and variables that must be visible in all the procedures of the form. The general declarations section also includes declarations of two functions from the TegoMM.VBX control (`tegSetByte()` and `tegGetByte()`) that are used by the program.

Here is the code in the general declarations section:

```
Option Explicit

' Define constants
Const MB_YESNOCANCEL = 3
Const MB_YESNO = 4
Const MB_ICONSTOP = 16
Const MB_ICONEXCLAMATION = 48
Const MB_ICONINFORMATION = 64
Const IDYES = 6
Const IDNO = 7
Const IDCANCEL = 2

' Functions for accessing WAV samples in an 8-bit WAV file.
Declare Function tegSetByte Lib "tegomm.vbx" (ByVal lhctl As Long,
                             ➥ ByVal lSampleNumber As Long,
                             ➥ ByVal iValue As Integer)
                             ➥ As Integer

Declare Function tegGetByte Lib "tegomm.vbx" (ByVal lhctl As Long,
                             ➥ ByVal lSampleNumber As Long)
                             ➥ As Integer


' Flag that signals whether the selection rectangle
' is being drawn now.
Dim gDrawRectNow

' The name of the WAV file without the path.
Dim gWavNameNoPath

' The starting X position of the selection rectangle.
Dim gX1
```

```
' The ending X position of the selection rectangle.
Dim gX2

' The starting sample number of the graph.
Dim gGraphSampNum1

' The ending sample number of the graph.
Dim gGraphSampNum2

' The Zooming flag.
Dim gZooming

' Recording flag.
Dim gRecording

' Playing flag.
Dim gPlaying

' Playing selection flag.
Dim gPlayingSelection

' The maximum recording length.
Dim gMaxRecordLength

' The background color.
Dim gBackgroundColor

' WAV file has changed flag.
Dim gWavFileHasChanged
```

The Form_Load() Procedure

The Form_Load() procedure of the frmWEdit form is executed when you start the program. This procedure initializes various controls and variables of the program:

```
Sub Form_Load ()

    ' Set the multimedia control for playback of WAV files.
    TegommWav.DeviceType = "WaveAudio"

    ' Initialize the gX1 and gX2 variables.
    gX1 = linX.X1
    gX2 = linX.X1

    ' Initialize the maximum recording length.
    gMaxRecordLength = 2000000
    mnuMaxRecLen2.Checked = True

    ' Initialize the background color variable to green.
    gBackgroundColor = 2
    mnuGreen.Checked = True

    ' Set the background color of all the controls
    ' (per gBackgroundColor).
    SetBackgroundColor

    ' Upon starting the program, controls should be
```

```
' disabled.
DisableAllControls

End Sub
```

The first statement

```
TegommWav.DeviceType = "WaveAudio"
```

initializes the multimedia control for playback of WAV files through the sound card.

The next two statements

```
gX1 = linX.X1
gX2 = linX.X1
```

initialize the gX1 and gX2 variables. These two variables are visible in all the procedures of the frmWEdit form because they were declared inside the general declarations section of the form.

What is the purpose of the gX1 and gX2 variables? These variables indicate the boundaries of the selection rectangle. Recall that the Wave Editor program lets the user select a section of the graph by using the mouse. When the user makes a selection, a red rectangle is drawn in accordance with the mouse movement. The gX1 and gX2 variables hold the X coordinates (horizontal coordinates) of the selection rectangle. In the Form_Load() procedure, gX1 and gX2 are both initialized to the value of the X1 property of the linX line:

```
gX1 = linX.X1
gX2 = linX.X1
```

The linX line is the X-axis of the graph (it was created at design time). The X1 property is the X coordinate of the starting point of the line. Therefore, when you start the program, the left edge of the selection rectangle and the right edge of the selection rectangle are at the extreme left point on the linX line. That is, when you start the program, the selection rectangle is a single vertical line at the extreme left point of the X-axis of the graph.

The next two statements in the Form_Load() procedure are these:

```
gMaxRecordLength = 2000000
mnuMaxRecLen2.Checked = True
```

These statements initialize the gMaxRecordLength variable to 2000000 and place a checkmark next to the mnuMaxRecLen2 menu item. Recall that the Wave Editor program includes a safety feature that enables the user to select the maximum allowed recording length. (See Figure E.28.) The gMaxRecordLength variable is used to store the current setting of the maximum recording length. When you start the program, Form_Load() initializes gmaxRecordLength to 2,000,000 bytes and places a checkmark next to the 2 Megabytes menu item.

The next two statements in the Form_Load() procedure are these:

```
gBackgroundColor = 2
mnuGreen.Checked = True
```

These statements initialize the gBackgroundColor variable to 2, and place a checkmark next to the mnuGreen menu item. Recall that the Wave Editor program includes a Background Color menu that enables the user to select the background color of the program's window. (See Figure E.33.) The gBackgroundColor variable is used to store the current setting of the background color. When you start the program, Form_Load() initializes gBackgroundColor to 2 (green) and places a checkmark next to the Green menu item.

The next statement

```
SetBackgroundColor
```

calls the SetBackgroundColor() procedure. This procedure sets the background color of the program's main window (that is, the background color of the frmWEdit form) to the color specified by the gBackgroundColor variable. Because gBackgroundColor is now 2, the SetBackgroundColor() procedure sets the background color to green. (The code of the SetBackgroundColor() procedure is covered in the next section.)

The last statement in the Form_Load() procedure

```
DisableAllControls
```

calls the DisableAllControls() procedure. As its name implies, the DisableAllControls() procedure disables controls, such as push buttons and menu items. Form_Load() calls DisableAllControls() because when the program starts, no WAV file is open, and controls such as the Zoom In and Zoom Out buttons are disabled. (The code of the DisableAllControls() procedure is discussed shortly.)

The SetBackgroundColor() Procedure

The SetBackgroundColor() procedure sets the background color of the frmWEdit form (and all the controls inside it) to the color specified by the variable gBackgroundColor:

```
Sub SetbackgroundColor ()

    Dim NewColor

    ' Get the value of the new color.
    NewColor = QBColor(gBackgroundColor)

    ' Set the background color of the form and the
    ' controls to the new color.
    frmWEdit.BackColor = NewColor
    Label1.BackColor = NewColor
    Label2.BackColor = NewColor
    Label3.BackColor = NewColor
    Label4.BackColor = NewColor
    Label5.BackColor = NewColor
    Label6.BackColor = NewColor
    Label7.BackColor = NewColor
    Label8.BackColor = NewColor
    Label9.BackColor = NewColor
    Frame1.BackColor = NewColor
    chkAutoRepeat.BackColor = NewColor
    optSamples.BackColor = NewColor
    optMilliseconds.BackColor = NewColor
    txtMousePosition.BackColor = NewColor

End Sub
```

The `DisableAllControls()` Procedure

The `DisableAllControls()` procedure sets the Enabled property of controls inside the `frmWEdit` form to False:

```
Sub DisableAllControls ()

    ' Disable all the controls.
    mnuZoomIn.Enabled = False
    mnuZoomOut.Enabled = False
    mnuSave.Enabled = False
    mnuSaveAs.Enabled = False
    mnuFileType.Enabled = False
    mnuCopy.Enabled = False
    mnuPaste.Enabled = False
    mnuDelete.Enabled = False
    mnuCut.Enabled = False
    mnuSelectAll.Enabled = False
    cmdZoomIn.Enabled = False
    cmdPlay.Enabled = False
    cmdPlaySelection.Enabled = False
    cmdRecord.Enabled = False

End Sub
```

The `DisableAllControls()` procedure is called whenever no WAV file is open, such as when the program first starts. Some controls, such as the Open and Exit menu items, are not disabled. The user should always be able to exit the program or open a new WAV file, so these controls should never be disabled.

The `EnableAllControls()` Procedure

The `EnableAllControls()` procedure sets the Enabled property of controls inside the `frmWEdit` form to True:

```
Sub EnableAllControls ()

    ' Enable all the controls.
    mnuZoomIn.Enabled = True
    mnuZoomOut.Enabled = True
    mnuSave.Enabled = True
    mnuSaveAs.Enabled = True
    mnuFileType.Enabled = True
    mnuCopy.Enabled = True
    mnuPaste.Enabled = True
    mnuDelete.Enabled = True
    mnuCut.Enabled = True
    mnuSelectAll.Enabled = True
    cmdZoomIn.Enabled = True
    cmdPlay.Enabled = True
    cmdPlaySelection.Enabled = True
    cmdRecord.Enabled = True

    ' The Stop button is the only button that is
    ' being disabled.
    cmdStop.Enabled = False

End Sub
```

The `EnableAllControls()` procedure is called whenever a new WAV file is opened. The Stop button is the only button that is not enabled. Instead, it is disabled. Why? The Stop button should be enabled only during playback or recording. As you'll see later, the Stop button is enabled in the `cmdPlay_Click()` procedure and in the `cmdRecord_Click()` procedure.

Opening a WAV File

Whenever the user selects Open from the File menu, the `mnuOpen_Click()` procedure is executed automatically. This procedure lets the user select a WAV file from the Open File dialog box. (See Figure E.3.) The `mnuOpen_Click()` procedure opens the WAV file that the user selects and displays the graph of the WAV file.

Here is the code of the `mnuOpen_Click()` procedure:

```
Sub mnuOpen_Click ()

Dim Msg, Answer

' Before displaying an Open File dialog box, check
' if the current WAV file has changed, and if
' it has, give the user a chance to save it.
If gWavFileHasChanged = True Then
   Msg = gWavNameNoPath + Chr(13)
   Msg = Msg + "The WAV file has changed." + Chr(13)
   Msg = Msg + "Do you want to save current changes?"
   Answer = MsgBox(Msg, MB_ICONEXCLAMATION +
                  ➥ MB_YESNOCANCEL, "Wave Editor")
   If Answer = IDYES Then
      mnuSave_Click
   End If
   If Answer = IDCANCEL Then
      Exit Sub
   End If
End If

' Set an error trap to detect the clicking
' of the Cancel key of the Open dialog box.
On Error GoTo OpenError

' Fill the items of the File Type list box of
' the Open dialog box.
CMDialog1.Filter = "All Files (*.*)¦*.*¦Wave Files
                  ➥ (*.wav)¦*.wav"

' Set the default File Type to Wave Files (*.wav).
CMDialog1.FilterIndex = 2

' Display the Open dialog box.
CMDialog1.Action = 1

' Remove the error trap.
On Error GoTo 0

' Open the WAV file that the user selected.
TegommWav.FileName = CMDialog1.Filename
```

```
TegommWav.Command = "Open"

' If Open command failed, abort this procedure.
If TegommWav.Error <> 0 Then
   MsgBox "Cannot open " + TegommWav.FileName, 0, "ERROR"
   CloseWavFile
   Exit Sub
End If


' Make sure that the WAV file is 8-bits mono.
' (This version of the program works only with 8 bit/Mono).
If TegommWav.BitsPerSample <> 8 Or TegommWav.Channels <> 1
   ➡ Then

   ' Display a message box.
   Msg = TegommWav.FileName + " is not an 8-bit mono WAV "
   Msg = Msg + "file." + Chr(13) + Chr(13)
   Msg = Msg + "This version of the program works with "
   Msg = Msg + "8-bit mono WAV files. You can enhance "
   Msg = Msg + "the program so that it will also support "
   Msg = Msg + "16-bit stereo WAV files. For more "
   Msg = Msg + "information about 16-bit WAV files and "
   Msg = Msg + "stereo WAV files, you can refer to the "
   Msg = Msg + "book 'How To Create Real World Application With "
   Msg = Msg + "Visual Basic' by Gurewich & "
   Msg = Msg + "Gurewich - SAMS Publishing. The Wave "
   Msg = Msg + "Editor chapter of this book discusses "
   Msg = Msg + "how to access samples in 16-bit and "
   Msg = Msg + "stereo WAV files."
   MsgBox Msg, MB_ICONSTOP, "Wave Editor"

   ' Close the WAV file and exit this procedure.
   CloseWavFile
   Exit Sub

End If

' Get the name of the WAV file (without the path).
gWavNameNoPath = CMDialog1.Filetitle

' Set the Position units to Samples.
TegommWav.TimeFormat = "Samples"

' Initialize the hsbPosition scroll bar.
hsbPosition.Min = 0
hsbPosition.Max = 1000
hsbPosition.Value = 0

' Update the Wave buffer.
TegommWav.Command = "UpdateWaveBuffer"

' Zoom out to Full-View mode.
cmdZoomOut_Click

' Enable all the controls.
EnableAllControls

' Reset the gWavFileHasChanged flag.
gWavFileHasChanged = False
```

```
' Exit the procedure.
Exit Sub

OpenError:
' The user clicked the Cancel button.
Exit Sub

End Sub
```

The `mnuOpen_Click()` procedure starts with an `If` statement:

```
If gWavFileHasChanged = True Then
   Msg = gWavNameNoPath + Chr(13)
   Msg = Msg + "The WAV file has changed." + Chr(13)
   Msg = Msg + "Do you want to save current changes?"
   Answer = MsgBox(Msg, MB_ICONEXCLAMATION +
                         ➥ MB_YESNOCANCEL, "Wave Editor")
   If Answer = IDYES Then
      mnuSave_Click
   End If
   If Answer = IDCANCEL Then
      Exit Sub
   End If
End If
```

This `If` statement checks whether the currently open WAV file has been changed by examining the value of the `gWavFileHasChanged` variable. This variable serves as a flag to indicate whether the currently open WAV file has been changed. When `gWavFileHasChanged` is `TRUE`, it indicates that the user modified the currently open WAV file (for example, by deleting samples or performing a recording). If the WAV file has been modified, the statements under the `If` are executed:

```
Msg = gWavNameNoPath + Chr(13)
Msg = Msg + "The WAV file has changed." + Chr(13)
Msg = Msg + "Do you want to save current changes?"
Answer = MsgBox(Msg, MB_ICONEXCLAMATION +
                      ➥ MB_YESNOCANCEL, "Wave Editor")
If Answer = IDYES Then
   mnuSave_Click
End If
If Answer = IDCANCEL Then
   Exit Sub
End If
```

These statements cause a message box to be displayed that asks the user whether the currently open WAV file should be saved. (See Figure E.38.)

Figure E.38.
The message box that is displayed if the currently open WAV file has been changed.

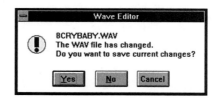

If the user clicks the Yes button of the message box, the statement

```
mnuSave_Click
```

is executed and it saves the currently open WAV file by calling the `mnuSave_Click()` procedure. (The code of the `mnuSave_Click()` procedure is discussed later in this appendix.)

If the user clicks the Cancel button, the statement

```
Exit Sub
```

terminates the procedure.

So if the current WAV file has been modified by the user, a message box is displayed. If the user selects Cancel, the procedure is terminated. If the user selects Yes, the current WAV file is saved and the procedure resumes. If the user selects No, the procedure resumes without saving the current WAV file.

The next four statements in the procedure

```
On Error GoTo OpenError
CMDialog1.Filter = "All Files (*.*)¦*.*¦Wave Files
              ➥ (*.wav)¦*.wav"
CMDialog1.FilterIndex = 2
CMDialog1.Action = 1
```

are responsible for displaying an Open File dialog box, as shown in Figure E.39.

Figure E.39.
The Open File dialog box
that is displayed after the
user selects Open from the
File menu.

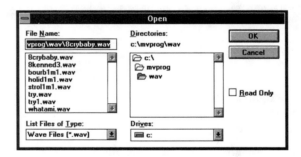

Notice that because of the statement

```
On Error GoTo OpenError
```

if the user cancels the Open File dialog box, the code following the `OpenError` label is executed. The `OpenError` label is at the end of the procedure, and the code following it simply terminates the procedure:

```
OpenError:
 ' The user clicked the Cancel button.
 Exit Sub
```

However, if the user does not cancel the Open File dialog box, the procedure resumes.

> **NOTE**
>
> The statement
>
> ```
> On Error GoTo OpenError
> ```
>
> sets an error trap. If the user cancels the Open File dialog box, an error occurs. The code under the OpenError label is then executed. The error occurs because the CancelError property of the CMDialog1 object was set (at design time) to True. (See Table E.1.)

The next statement in the procedure

```
On Error GoTo 0
```

removes the error trap.

Then the next two statements

```
TegommWav.FileName = CMDialog1.Filename
TegommWav.Command = "Open"
```

open the WAV file that the user selected in the Open File dialog box.

The next statement is an If statement that checks whether the Open command failed:

```
If TegommWav.Error <> 0 Then
   MsgBox "Cannot open " + TegommWav.FileName, 0, "ERROR"
   CloseWavFile
   Exit Sub
End If
```

If the Open command failed, the statements under the If display an error message box and call the CloseWavFile() procedure to close the current WAV file. (The code of the CloseWavFile() procedure is discussed later in this appendix.)

The next statement in the procedure is another If statement:

```
If TegommWav.BitsPerSample <> 8 Or TegommWav.Channels <> 1
   ➥ Then

   ' Display a message box.
   Msg = TegommWav.FileName + " is not an 8-bit mono WAV "
   Msg = Msg + "file." + Chr(13) + Chr(13)
   Msg = Msg + "This version of the program works with "
   Msg = Msg + "8-bit mono WAV files. You can enhance "
   Msg = Msg + "the program so that it will also support "
   Msg = Msg + "16-bit stereo WAV files. For more "
   Msg = Msg + "information about 16-bit WAV files and "
   Msg = Msg + "stereo WAV files, you can refer to the "
   Msg = Msg + "book 'Master Visual Basic' by Gurewich & "
   Msg = Msg + "Gurewich - SAMS Publishing. The Wave "
   Msg = Msg + "Editor chapter of this book discusses "
```

```
Msg = Msg + "how to access samples in 16-bit and "
Msg = Msg + "stereo WAV files."
MsgBox Msg, MB_ICONSTOP, "Wave Editor"

' Close the WAV file and exit this procedure.
CloseWavFile
Exit Sub
```

End If

The purpose of this If statement is to ensure that the WAV file the user selected is an 8-bit mono WAV file. If the WAV file is not an 8-bit mono WAV file, an error message box is displayed (See Figure E.30.), the CloseWavFile() procedure is called, and the procedure is terminated.

NOTE

The preceding code determines whether the WAV file is 8-bit mono by examining the BitsPerSample and Channels properties of the multimedia control. If the BitsPerSample property of the multimedia control returns 8, the WAV file is an 8-bit WAV file. If the Channels property of the multimedia control returns 1, the WAV file is a mono WAV file.

NOTE

The current version of the Wave Editor program supports only 8-bit mono WAV files. Later in this appendix you will learn how to enhance the Wave Editor program so that it also supports 16-bit and stereo WAV files.

If the WAV file is of the 16-bit stereo type, the BitsPerSample property of the multimedia control returns 16, and the Channels property returns 2.

The next statement in the procedure

```
gWavNameNoPath = CMDialog1.Filetitle
```

updates the gWavNameNoPath variable with the name of the WAV file, without the path. This variable is used later when the title of the program's window is set.

Then the statement

```
TegommWav.TimeFormat = "Samples"
```

sets the TimeFormat property of the multimedia control to "Samples". So from this point on the Position and Length properties of the multimedia control report values in units of samples.

The next three statements in the procedure

```
hsbPosition.Min = 0
hsbPosition.Max = 1000
```

`hsbPosition.Value = 0`

initialize the `hsbPosition` scroll bar.

Then the statement

`TegommWav.Command = "UpdateWaveBuffer"`

issues an `UpdateWaveBuffer` command to the multimedia control. As its name implies, the `UpdateWaveBuffer` command updates a buffer (in RAM) that contains all the samples of the open WAV file. When an `UpdateWaveBuffer` command is issued, all the samples of the WAV file are copied to a buffer in memory. Subsequent commands can then access the buffer to read the samples of the WAV file. Because the buffer is in memory, the samples can be accessed very quickly.

> **NOTE**
>
> The `UpdateWaveBuffer` command of the multimedia control fills a buffer in memory with all the samples of the currently open WAV file.
>
> You need to use the `UpdateWaveBuffer` command only in programs in which you have to access samples of the WAV file.
>
> Typically, you issue the `UpdateWaveBuffer` command immediately after you open the WAV file and whenever the WAV file is changed (such as after the user performs a recording, deletes samples, and pastes samples).

The next statement in the procedure

`cmdZoomOut_Click`

calls the `cmdZoomOut_Click()` procedure, which draws a graph that corresponds to all the samples of the WAV file. As you'll see later in this appendix, the `cmdZoomOut_Click()` procedure displays the samples of the WAV file by accessing the samples in the Wave Buffer (which is why earlier you issued an `UpdateWaveBuffer` command).

The next statement

`EnableAllControls`

calls the `EnableAllControls()` procedure. A WAV file was just opened, so controls such as the Zoom In and Zoom Out buttons are enabled.

The next statement in the procedure

`gWavFileHasChanged = False`

resets the `gWavFileHasChanged` variable to `False`. As mentioned earlier, the `gWavFileHasChanged` variable serves as a flag to indicate whether the user has changed the WAV file. Because the WAV file has just been opened, this flag is set to `False`.

The next statement in the procedure

```
Exit Sub
```

terminates the procedure.

The remaining lines of the `mnuOpen_Click()` procedure

```
OpenError:
  Exit Sub
```

were covered earlier. (As previously mentioned, the program branches to the `OpenError` label only if the user cancels the Open File dialog box.)

Displaying the Samples of the WAV File in a Graph Format

As you have seen, the code of the `mnuOpen_Click()` procedure calls the `cmdZoomOut_Click()` procedure. The `cmdZoomOut_Click()` procedure is also executed automatically whenever the user clicks the Zoom Out button.

The purpose of the `cmdZoomOut_Click()` procedure is to display a graph that represents all the samples of the WAV file. Whenever the user clicks the Zoom Out button, the graph of the WAV file should correspond to all the samples of the WAV file.

Here is the code of the `cmdZoomOut_Click()` procedure:

```
Sub cmdZoomOut_Click ()

    ' Disable the Zoom Out button and menu item.
    cmdZoomOut.Enabled = False
    mnuZoomOut.Enabled = False

    ' Display entire WAV file.
    gGraphSampNum1 = 0
    gGraphSampNum2 = TegommWav.Length - 1
    UpdateGraph

    ' Update the gZooming flag.
    gZooming = False

    ' Update the window title.
    SetWindowTitle

End Sub
```

The first two statements in the procedure

```
cmdZoomOut.Enabled = False
mnuZoomOut.Enabled = False
```

disable the Zoom Out button and the Zoom Out menu item. These items are disabled because the user is zooming out to Full View mode. After the graph is displayed in Full View mode, it makes no sense to zoom out again.

The next three statements in the procedure are

```
gGraphSampNum1 = 0
gGraphSampNum2 = TegommWav.Length - 1
UpdateGraph
```

These statements display the graph that corresponds to the entire WAV file. The gGraphSampNum1 variable specifies the first sample that the graph should display, and the gGraphSampNum2 variable specifies the last sample that the graph should display. The procedure UpdateGraph() displays the samples of the graph in accordance with the values of gGraphSampNum1 and gGraphSampNum2. (The code of the UpdateGraph() procedure is discussed later in the appendix.)

The next statement

```
gZooming = False
```

sets the gZooming variable to False. The gZooming variable serves as a flag that indicates the current view mode. When gZooming is True, the graph is currently in Zooming mode; when gZooming is False, the graph is currently in Full View mode.

The last statement in the procedure

```
SetWindowTitle
```

calls the SetWindowTitle() procedure. The SetWindowTitle() procedure updates the title of the program's main window. The cmdZoomOut_Click() procedure has to update the title of the main window because, as you may recall, the main window's title specifies whether the graph is currently in Zooming mode or in Full View mode.

As you have just seen, the cmdZoomOut_Click() procedure updates the gGraphSampNum1 and gGraphSampNum2 variables and then calls the UpdateGraph() procedure. It is the UpdateGraph() procedure that actually displays the graph. Here is the code of the UpdateGraph() procedure:

```
Sub UpdateGraph ()

 Dim I
 Dim Sample

 ' Clear the current graph.
 Cls

 ' Validate gGraphSampNum1 and gGraphSampNum2
 If gGraphSampNum1 < 0 Then gGraphSampNum1 = 0
 If gGraphSampNum2 > TegommWav.Length - 1 Then
    gGraphSampNum2 = TegommWav.Length - 1
 End If

' Display the bars of the graph.
For I = linX.X1 To linX.X2 Step 1
    TegommWav.SampleNumber = X2SampleNumber(I)
    Sample = TegommWav.SampleValue1 - 128
    Line (I, linX.Y1)-(I, linX.Y1 - Sample)
Next I

 ' Draw the selection rectangle.
```

```
Line (gX1, linY.Y1 - 1)-(gX2, linY.Y2 + 1), QBColor(4), B
```

```
End Sub
```

The first statement of the UpdateGraph() procedure

```
Cls
```

clears the current graph.

The next two statements are If statements that validate the values of the variables gGraphSampNum1 and gGraphSampNum2:

```
If gGraphSampNum1 < 0 Then gGraphSampNum1 = 0
If gGraphSampNum2 > TegommWav.Length - 1 Then
    gGraphSampNum2 = TegommWav.Length - 1
End If
```

These two If statements ensure that the gGraphSampNum1 and gGraphSampNum2 variables specify a valid range within the WAV file.

The UpdateGraph() procedure then actually draws the vertical bars of the graph using a For loop:

```
For I = linX.X1 To linX.X2 Step 1
    TegommWav.SampleNumber = X2SampleNumber(I)
    Sample = TegommWav.SampleValue1 - 128
    Line (I, linX.Y1)-(I, linX.Y1 - Sample)
Next I
```

This For loop displays one vertical bar after another, across the linX line. (Recall that the linX line is the X-axis of the graph.)

The For loop counter, I, starts with a value of linX.X1 (the extreme left coordinate of the X-axis) and increments in steps of 1 for each iteration of the loop. The loop terminates after the value I reaches linX.X2, which is the extreme right coordinate of the X-axis.

The first statement inside the For loop

```
TegommWav.SampleNumber = X2SampleNumber(I)
```

uses the X2SampleNumber() function to convert the X-coordinate specified by I to a sample number. Each X-coordinate of the graph corresponds to a certain sample in the WAV file, and X2SampleNumber() returns the corresponding sample number of the X-coordinate that is passed to it. The code of the X2SampleNumber() function is covered later in this appendix.

Notice that in the preceding statement the returned value of the X2Samplenumber() function is assigned to the SampleNumber property of the multimedia control. So at this point the SampleNumber property of the multimedia control holds the number of the sample (not the sample value) whose value you want to display.

The next statement

```
Sample = TegommWav.SampleValue1 - 128
```

uses the SampleValue1 property of the multimedia control to extract the value of the sample number that is pointed by the SampleNumber property of the multimedia control.

NOTE

The multimedia control has three properties that let you read the value of a sample within the WAV file:

    SampleNumber
    SampleValue1
    SampleValue2

The SampleNumber property specifies which sample within the WAV file you want to get.

The SampleValue1 property reports the value of the sample in Channel 1 of the WAV file.

The SampleValue2 property reports the value of the sample in Channel 2 of the WAV file. This property is applicable to stereo WAV files only.

The SampleValue1 and SampleValue2 properties extract the values of samples from the Wave file buffer. Therefore, before you can use these properties, you must use the UpdateWaveBuffer command to update the Wave buffer. In the Wave Editor program, for example, an UpdateWaveBuffer command is issued in the mnuOpen_Click() procedure.

Here's an example: To get the value of sample number 50 in a mono WAV file, use these statements:

```
TegommWav.SampleNumber = 50

Sample = TegommWav.SampleValue1
```

Here's another example: To get the value of sample number 75 in Channel 1 of a stereo WAV file, use these statements:

```
TegommWav.SampleNumber = 75

Sample = TegommWav.SampleValue1
```

Here's another example: To get the value of sample number 75 in Channel 2 of a stereo WAV file, use these statements:

```
TegommWav.SampleNumber = 75
Sample = TegommWav.SampleValue2
```

NOTE

You can use the SampleValue1 and SampleValue2 properties to access any sample of a WAV file. However, a much more efficient way to access the samples of WAV files is to use the sample access functions of the TegoMM.VBX control: `tegGetByte()`, `tegSetByte()`, `tegGetWord()`, and `tegSetWord()`. These functions are discussed later in this appendix.

As you can see, the statement that extracts the sample value (inside the `For` loop)

```
Sample = TegommWav.SampleValue1 - 128
```

subtracts 128 from the SampleValue1 property of the multimedia control. Why is this necessary? It is necessary because 8-bit WAV files store the sample values in the following format:

> The minimum value of a sample is 0.
> The midpoint value of a sample is 128.
> The maximum value of a sample is 255.

In the graph, you want to display samples with midpoint values as 0, so you subtract 128 from the sample value. A sample whose value is 128 (a midpoint value), therefore, is displayed as 128-128=0. A sample whose value is 0 (the minimum value) is displayed as 0-128=-128. A sample whose value is 255 (the maximum value) is displayed as 255-128=127. Any sample value greater than 128 is displayed as a positive value (above the X-axis); any sample value less than 128 is displayed as a negative value (below the X-axis).

The next statement inside the `For` loop

```
Line (I, linX.Y1)-(I, linX.Y1 - Sample)
```

uses the `Line` method to draw a vertical line that corresponds to the value of `Sample`. In each iteration of the loop, another vertical line (that is, another bar of the graph) is drawn.

The last statement in the `UpdateGraph()` procedure (after the `For` loop)

```
Line (gX1, linY.Y1 - 1)-(gX2, linY.Y2 + 1), QBColor(4), B
```

draws the selection rectangle as specified by the gX1 and gX2 variables. Recall that the gX1 and gX2 variables specify the coordinates of the left and right edges of the selection rectangle. Note that the top edge of the rectangle is drawn at coordinate `linY.Y1-1`, and the bottom edge of the rectangle is drawn at coordinate `linY.Y2+1`. The `linY` line is the Y-axis of the graph. (See Table E.1.) The selection rectangle is drawn red (`QBColor(4)`).

> **NOTE**
>
> As discussed earlier, the beginning code of the UpdateGraph() procedure validates the gGraphSampNum1 and gGraphSampNum2 variables to ensure that they specify a valid range within the WAV file. The remaining code of the UpdateGraph() procedure, however, does not use these variables. So why are these variables validated? They are validated because, as you will soon see, the X2SampleNumber() function uses the gGraphSampNum1 and gGraphSampNum2 variables, and X2SampleNumber() is called from the For loop of UpdateGraph().

The X2SampleNumber() Function

As you have just seen, the code of the UpdateGraph() procedure uses the X2SampleNumber() function to convert an X coordinate to its corresponding sample number in the WAV file. Here is the code of the X2SampleNumber() function:

```
Function X2SampleNumber (x As Variant)

Dim NumberOfSamples
Dim NumberOfPixels
Dim PixelNumber

' Total number of samples in the graph.
NumberOfSamples = gGraphSampNum2 - gGraphSampNum1 + 1

' Total number of pixel on the X axis.
NumberOfPixels = linX.X2 - linX.X1 + 1

' The pixel number at point X.
PixelNumber = x - linX.X1

' Return the Sample number that corresponds to
' PixelNumber.
X2SampleNumber = RoundNumber
            ➥ (
            ➥ gGraphSampNum1 +
            ➥ (PixelNumber * (NumberOfSamples - 1)) /
            ➥ (NumberOfPixels - 1)
            ➥ )

End Function
```

The first statement in the X2SampleNumber() function

```
NumberOfSamples = gGraphSampNum2 - gGraphSampNum1 + 1
```

calculates the total number of samples that the graph represents, based on the gGraphSampNum1 and gGraphSampNum2 variables. (Recall that these variables specify the sample numbers of the first and last samples that the graph displays.)

The next statement in the function

```
NumberOfPixels = linX.X2 - linX.X1 + 1
```

calculates the total number of pixels (points) on the X-axis of the graph.

Then the statement

```
PixelNumber = x - linX.X1
```

calculates the pixel number (point number) to which the x coordinate (the parameter of the function) corresponds.

Finally, the last statement of the function returns the sample number that corresponds to the pixel number:

```
X2SampleNumber = RoundNumber
            ➥ (
            ➥ gGraphSampNum1 +
            ➥ (PixelNumber * (NumberOfSamples - 1)) /
            ➥ (NumberOfPixels - 1)
            ➥ )
```

For example, if the graph has 100 points and the WAV file has 1000 samples, and the first sample of the graph (gGraphSampNum1) is sample number 0, and the pixel number whose corresponding sample number you want to find is pixel number 49, then the formula will yield the following:

```
X2SampleNumber = RoundNumber(0+(49*(1000-1))/(100-1)) =
               = RoundNumber ( 494.45 ) = 494
```

That is, point number 49 in the graph corresponds to sample number 494 of the WAV file.

Similarly, point number 0 yields sample number 0, and point number 99 yields sample number 999.

The RoundNumber() Function

As you have just seen, the X2SampleNumber() function uses the RoundNumber() function to round the resultant number of the calculation. Here is the code of the RoundNumber() function:

```
Function RoundNumber (Number)

If Number - Int(Number) >= .5 Then
   RoundNumber = Int(Number) + 1
Else
   RoundNumber = Int(Number)
End If

End Function
```

The RoundNumber() function simply rounds to the nearest integer the number that is passed to it. For example, 8.4 is converted to 8, 8.8 is converted to 9, 7.1 is converted to 7, 7.5 is converted to 8, and so on.

The Selection Rectangle

You may recall that the selection rectangle enables the user to select any section in the graph. When the user drags the mouse over the graph area, a red rectangle is drawn over the graph, in accordance with the mouse movement.

The code that is responsible for drawing the selection rectangle is written in the following three procedures:

```
Form_MouseDown()
Form_MouseMove()
Form_MouseUp()
```

The code of these procedures is discussed in the following sections.

The `Form_MouseDown()` Procedure

The `FormMouseDown()` procedure is automatically executed whenever the user presses the mouse button over the form. Here is the code of the `FormMouseDown()` procedure:

```
Sub Form_MouseDown (Button As Integer, Shift As Integer,
                ➥ X As Single, Y As Single)

    Dim Sample

    ' Was the mouse button pressed in the graph area?
    If Y < linY.Y1 Or Y > linY.Y2 Then
        Exit Sub
    End If

    ' Make sure X is within the X axis boundaries.
    If X < linX.X1 Then X = linX.X1
    If X > linX.X2 Then X = linX.X2

    ' Clear the previous rectangle.
    Line (gX1, linY.Y1 - 1)-(gX2, linY.Y2 + 1),
        ➥ QBColor(gBackgroundColor), B

    ' Repaint the linX line.
    Line (linX.X1, linX.Y1)-(linX.X2, linX.Y2)

    ' Redraw the two samples that were erased by
    ' the rectangle edges.
    TegommWav.SampleNumber = X2SampleNumber(gX1)
    Sample = TegommWav.SampleValue1 - 128
    Line (gX1, linX.Y1)-(gX1, linX.Y1 - Sample)
    TegommWav.SampleNumber = X2SampleNumber(gX2)
    Sample = TegommWav.SampleValue1 - 128
    Line (gX2, linX.Y1)-(gX2, linX.Y1 - Sample)

    ' Update gX1 and gX2.
    gX1 = X
    gX2 = X

    ' Draw the selection rectangle.
    Line (gX1, linY.Y1 - 1)-(gX2, linY.Y2 + 1), QBColor(4), B
```

```
' Signal that the selection rectangle should be
' drawn now (when the mouse moves).
gDrawRectNow = True

End Sub
```

The first statement in the `Form_MouseDown()` procedure checks whether the mouse button was pressed outside the graph area:

```
If Y < linY.Y1 Or Y > linY.Y2 Then
    Exit Sub
End If
```

If the mouse button was pressed outside the graph area, the procedure is terminated. Note that a point is considered to be outside the graph area if it is below the endpoint of the Y-axis or above the starting point of the Y-axis.

The next two statements

```
If X < linX.X1 Then X = linX.X1
If X > linX.X2 Then X = linX.X2
```

validate the X parameter. These statements ensure that X points to a coordinate on the X-axis.

The next statement

```
Line (gX1, linY.Y1 - 1)-(gX2, linY.Y2 + 1),
    ➥ QBColor(gBackgroundColor), B
```

clears the previous selection rectangle because before a new selection rectangle is drawn, the old rectangle must be erased. Note that the rectangle is erased because the Line method specifies the color `QBColor(gBackgroundColor)`. Recall that `gBackgroundColor` holds the background color of the form.

The next statement

```
Line (linX.X1, linX.Y1)-(linX.X2, linX.Y2)
```

redraws the `linX` line (the X-axis). It is necessary to redraw the `linX` line because when the old selection rectangle was erased, the two edges of the rectangle erased two pixels on the `linX` line.

The next six statements

```
TegommWav.SampleNumber = X2SampleNumber(gX1)
Sample = TegommWav.SampleValue1 - 128
Line (gX1, linX.Y1)-(gX1, linX.Y1 - Sample)
TegommWav.SampleNumber = X2SampleNumber(gX2)
Sample = TegommWav.SampleValue1 - 128
Line (gX2, linX.Y1)-(gX2, linX.Y1 - Sample)
```

redraw the two samples that were erased by the old rectangle edges. That is, the two edges of the old selection rectangle covered two graph bars, and these bars must be redrawn.

Then these three statements

```
gX1 = X
```

```
gX2 = X
Line (gX1, linY.Y1 - 1)-(gX2, linY.Y2 + 1), QBColor(4), B
```

update the gX1 and gX2 variables with the current X coordinate of the mouse and draw the corresponding selection rectangle. Because gX1 is now equal to gX2, the new selection rectangle is currently one pixel wide (that is, it has only one edge).

The last statement in the Form_MouseDown() procedure

```
gDrawRectNow = True
```

raises the gDrawRectNow flag. The gDrawRectNow variable serves as a flag to indicate that the mouse is currently down and the Form_MouseMove() procedure should draw the selection rectangle as the user moves the mouse.

To summarize, when the user presses the mouse button, the old selection rectangle is erased and a 1-pixel-wide selection rectangle is drawn at the point where the user pressed the mouse button. In addition, the gDrawRectNow flag is raised so that the Form_MouseMove() procedure is alerted to draw the selection rectangle.

The Form_MouseMove() Procedure

The Form_MouseMove() procedure is automatically executed whenever the user moves the mouse over the form. Here is the code of the Form_MouseMove() procedure:

```
Sub Form_MouseMove (Button As Integer, Shift As Integer, x
                ➥ As Single, y As Single)

Dim NumPoints, Increment, Sample

' Was the mouse moved in the graph area?
If y < linY.Y1 Or y > linY.Y2 Then
   Exit Sub
End If

If x < linX.X1 Then x = linX.X1
If x > linX.X2 Then x = linX.X2

' Draw the selection rectangle now?
If gDrawRectNow Then

   ' Clear the previous rectangle.
   Line (gX1, linY.Y1 - 1)-(gX2, linY.Y2 + 1),
      ➥ QBColor(gBackgroundColor), B

   ' Repaint the linX line.
   Line (linX.X1, linX.Y1)-(linX.X2, linX.Y2)

   ' Redraw the two samples that were erased by the
   ' the rectangle edges.
   TegommWav.SampleNumber = X2SampleNumber(gX1)
   Sample = TegommWav.SampleValue1 - 128
   Line (gX1, linX.Y1)-(gX1, linX.Y1 - Sample)
   TegommWav.SampleNumber = X2SampleNumber(gX2)
```

```
    Sample = TegommWav.SampleValue1 - 128
    Line (gX2, linX.Y1)-(gX2, linX.Y1 - Sample)

    ' Update the gX2 variable.
    gX2 = x

    ' Draw the selection rectangle.
    Line (gX1, linY.Y1 - 1)-(gX2, linY.Y2 + 1),QBColor(4),B

End If

' Update the txtMousePosition text box.
If optSamples Then
    txtMousePosition = Int(X2SampleNumber(x))
Else
    If TegommWav.SamplingRate > 0 Then
        txtMousePosition = Int((X2SampleNumber(x) /
                       ↪ TegommWav.SamplingRate) * 1000)
    End If
End If

End Sub
```

The `Form_MouseMove()` procedure is similar to the `Form_MouseDown()` procedure. However, the `Form_MouseMove()` procedure draws the selection rectangle only if the `gDrawRectNow` flag is raised:

```
If gDrawRectNow = True Then
    ...................................
    ... Draw the selection rectangle ...
    ...................................
End If
```

That is, if `gDrawRectNow` is `True`, the user is moving the mouse while the mouse button is pressed down. In other words, the user is dragging the mouse. The code that draws the selection rectangle is similar to the code that draws the selection rectangle in the `Form_MouseDown()` procedure. The only difference is that now only the `gX2` variable is updated with the current X coordinate of the mouse. The value of `gX1` (the left edge of the rectangle) is not changed. It still holds the X coordinate for the point at which the mouse button was first pressed.

The remaining code of the `Form_MouseMove()` procedure updates the `txtMousePosition` text box:

```
' Update the txtMousePosition text box.
If optSamples Then
    txtMousePosition = Int(X2SampleNumber(x))
Else
    If TegommWav.SamplingRate > 0 Then
        txtMousePosition = Int((X2SampleNumber(x) /
                       ↪ TegommWav.SamplingRate) * 1000)
    End If
End If
```

Recall that the `txtMousePosition` text box holds the current mouse position, within the graph area, in units of samples or in units of milliseconds, depending on the `optSamples` option button. If the `optSamples` option button is selected, the statement

```
txtMousePosition = Int(X2SampleNumber(x))
```

fills the text box with the sample number that corresponds to the current X coordinate of the mouse. However, if the optSamples option button is not selected, the statement

```
txtMousePosition = Int((X2SampleNumber(x) /
                 ➥ TegommWav.SamplingRate) * 1000)
```

fills the text box with the time position, in units of milliseconds, that corresponds to the current X coordinate of the mouse. The conversion between sample number and milliseconds is performed by using the formula

```
[Milliseconds] = 1000 * [Sample Number] / [Sampling Rate]
```

The sampling rate of the WAV file is reported by the SamplingRate property of the multimedia control.

The Form_MouseUp() Procedure

The Form_MouseUp() procedure is automatically executed whenever the user releases the mouse button. Here is the code of the Form_MouseUp() procedure:

```
Sub Form_MouseUp (Button As Integer, Shift As Integer, x As
               ➥ Single, y As Single)

    ' Signal that the selection rectangle should not be
    ' drawn anymore.
    gDrawRectNow = False

End Sub
```

As you can see, the code of the Form_MouseUp() procedure simply resets the gDrawRectNow flag:

```
gDrawRectNow = False
```

So if the user now moves the mouse, the Form_MouseMove() procedure will not draw the selection rectangle.

The cmdPlay_Click() Procedure

The cmdPlay_Click() procedure is automatically executed whenever the user clicks the Play button. Here is the code of the cmdPlay_Click() procedure:

```
Sub cmdPlay_Click ()

  ' Play from the position specified by the
  ' hsbPosition scroll bar.
  TegommWav.From = hsbPosition.Value * TegommWav.Length / 1000

  ' Make sure From is not greater than Length.
  If TegommWav.From > TegommWav.Length Then
     TegommWav.From = TegommWav.Length
  End If

  ' Set the Playing flag.
  gPlaying = True
```

```
' Issue a Play command.
TegommWav.Command = "Play"

' Disable the Play and Record buttons.
cmdPlay.Enabled = False
cmdPlaySelection.Enabled = False
cmdRecord.Enabled = False

' Enable the Stop button.
cmdStop.Enabled = True

End Sub
```

The first statement in the `cmdPlay_Click()` procedure

```
TegommWav.From = hsbPosition.Value * TegommWav.Length / 1000
```

sets the From property of the multimedia control in accordance with the current value of the `hsbPosition` scroll bar. The From property determines the position from which the next `Play` command starts the playback. The From property is also used by other commands, such as `Record`.

NOTE

The From property of the multimedia control determines the position from which the next Play command plays the WAV file. The position is specified in the units of the current time format. For example, in the Wave Editor program, the TimeFormat property of the multimedia control was set to Samples. (See the `mnuOpen_Click()` procedure in the section "Opening a WAV File.") Therefore, the statements

```
TegommWav.From = 1000
TegommWav.Command = "Play"
```

will play the WAV file from sample number 1000.

The value you assign to the From property is used only in the next command. Subsequent commands ignore the From property. Consider the following code:

```
TegommWav.From = 1000
TegommWav.Command = "Play"
...
...
...
TegommWav.Command = "Play"
```

In this code the first `Play` command plays the WAV file from position 1000. The second `Play` command, however, ignores the From property, and the playback starts from the current playback position.

The next statement in the procedure

```
If TegommWav.From > TegommWav.Length Then
    TegommWav.From = TegommWav.Length
End If
```

validates the value that was assigned to the From property. If the value is greater than the total length of the WAV file, the From property is set to the length of the WAV file.

The next statement

```
gPlaying = True
```

sets the gPlaying variable to True. This variable is used as a flag to indicate that the Play button has been clicked.

Then the statement

```
TegommWav.Command = "Play"
```

starts the playback by issuing a Play command.

The remaining statements in the cmdPlay_Click() procedure are the following:

```
cmdPlay.Enabled = False
cmdPlaySelection.Enabled = False
cmdRecord.Enabled = False
cmdStop.Enabled = True
```

These statements disable the Play buttons (remember that there are two Play buttons), disable the Record button, and enable the Stop button. During playback, the user should not be permitted to click the Play and Record buttons and should be permitted to click the Stop button.

The cmdPlaySelection_Click() Procedure

The cmdPlaySelection_Click() procedure is executed automatically whenever the user clicks the Play Selection button. Here is the code of the cmdPlaySelection_Click() procedure:

```
Sub cmdPlaySelection_Click ()

    Dim StartPos, EndPos
    Dim Temp

    ' Play from the section specified by the
    ' selection rectangle.
    StartPos = X2SampleNumber(gX1)
    EndPos = X2SampleNumber(gX2)
    If StartPos > EndPos Then
        Temp = EndPos
        EndPos = StartPos
        StartPos = Temp
    End If
    If StartPos > TegommWav.Length Then
        StartPos = TegommWav.Length
    End If
    If EndPos > TegommWav.Length Then
```

```
      EndPos = TegommWav.Length
   End If
   TegommWav.From = StartPos
   TegommWav.To = EndPos
   gPlayingSelection = True
   TegommWav.Command = "Play"

   ' Disable the Play and Record buttons.
   cmdPlay.Enabled = False
   cmdPlaySelection.Enabled = False
   cmdRecord.Enabled = False

   ' Enable the Stop button.
   cmdStop.Enabled = True

End Sub
```

The `cmdPlaySelection()` procedure plays a section from the WAV file as specified by `gX1` and `gX2` (the boundaries of the selection rectangle).

The first two statements

```
StartPos = X2SampleNumber(gX1)
EndPos = X2SampleNumber(gX2)
```

set the `StartPos` and `EndPos` (local) variables with the corresponding sample numbers of the selection rectangle boundaries.

Then three `If` statements are used to validate `StartPos` and `EndPos`. The first `If` statement

```
If StartPos > EndPos Then
   Temp = EndPos
   EndPos = StartPos
   StartPos = Temp
End If
```

ensures that `StartPos` is not greater than `EndPos`. If `StartPos` is greater than `EndPos`, the values of `StartPos` and `EndPos` are swapped.

> **NOTE**
>
> It is necessary to ensure that `StartPos` is not greater than `EndPos` because if the user selects a section of the WAV file by dragging the mouse from right to left, `gX1` will be greater than `gX2`. As a result, `EndPos` will be smaller than `StartPos`. `StartPos` and `EndPos` are used for specifying the playback range, so `EndPos` must be larger than `StartPos`.

The second and third `If` statements

```
If StartPos > TegommWav.Length Then
   StartPos = TegommWav.Length
End If
If EndPos > TegommWav.Length Then
   EndPos = TegommWav.Length
```

644

```
End If
```

ensure that `StartPos` and `EndPos` are not larger than the length of the WAV file.

Then the statements

```
TegommWav.From = StartPos
TegommWav.To = EndPos
```

set the From and To properties of the multimedia control with the values of `StartPos` and `EndPos`.

> **NOTE**
>
> Just as the From property specifies the starting position of the next Play command, the To property specifies the ending position of the next Play command. For example, the statements
>
> ```
> TegommWav.From = 10000
> TegommWav.To   = 20000
> TegommWav.Command = "Play"
> ```
>
> play the WAV file from position 10000 through 20000.
>
> The From and To properties are also used by other commands, such as Record.

The next statement

```
gPlayingSelection = True
```

sets the `gPlayingSelection` variable to `True`. This variable is used as a flag to indicate that the Play Selection button was clicked.

The next command

```
TegommWav.Command = "Play"
```

starts the playback by issuing a Play command.

The remaining statements in the `cmdPlaySelection_Click()` procedure are the following:

```
cmdPlay.Enabled = False
cmdPlaySelection.Enabled = False
cmdRecord.Enabled = False
cmdStop.Enabled = True
```

These statements disable the two Play buttons (both Play and Play Selection), disable the Record button, and enable the Stop button. During playback, the user should not be permitted to click the Play and Record buttons and should be permitted to click the Stop button.

The cmdRecord_Click() **Procedure**

The cmdRecord_Click() procedure is automatically executed whenever the user clicks the Record button. Here is the code of the cmdRecord_Click() procedure:

```
Sub cmdRecord_Click ()

 ' Raise the recording flag.
 gRecording = True

 ' Recording should be inserted to position
 ' specified by the hsbPosition scroll bar.
 TegommWav.From=hsbPosition.Value * TegommWav.Length / 1000

 ' Make sure From is not greater than Length.
 If TegommWav.From > TegommWav.Length Then
    TegommWav.From = TegommWav.Length
 End If

 ' Issue a Record command.
 If gMaxRecordLength = 0 Then
    TegommWav.Command = "Record"
 Else
    TegommWav.To = TegommWav.From + gMaxRecordLength
    TegommWav.Command = "Record"
 End If

 ' Enable the Stop button.
 cmdStop.Enabled = True

 ' Disable the Record and Play buttons.
 cmdRecord.Enabled = False
 cmdPlay.Enabled = False
 cmdPlaySelection.Enabled = False

 ' Raise the gWavFileHasChanged flag.
 gWavFileHasChanged = True

End Sub
```

The first statement in the cmdRecord_Click() procedure

```
gRecording = True
```

sets the gRecording variable to True. This variable is used as a flag to indicate that the Record button was clicked.

The next command

```
TegommWav.From=hsbPosition.Value * TegommWav.Length / 1000
```

sets the From property of the multimedia control in accordance with the current value of the hsbPosition scroll bar. This is done because the recording should be inserted at the position specified by the hsbPosition scroll bar.

> **NOTE**
>
> Just as the From property specifies the starting position of the next Play command, it also specifies the starting position of the next Record command. For example, the statements
>
> ```
> TegommWav.From = 15000
> TegommWav.Command = "Record"
> ```
>
> start the recording and insert the recording at position 15000.

The next statement

```
If TegommWav.From > TegommWav.Length Then
   TegommWav.From = TegommWav.Length
End If
```

ensures that the value of the From property is not greater than the total length of the WAV file.

The next statement starts the recording by issuing a Record command:

```
If gMaxRecordLength = 0 Then
   TegommWav.Command = "Record"
 Else
   TegommWav.To = TegommWav.From + gMaxRecordLength
   TegommWav.Command = "Record"
End If
```

Depending on the value of the variable gMaxRecordLength, the Record command is issued either with or without specifying a value for the To property of the multimedia control. If gMaxRecordLength is 0, the user requested no limit on the recording length. That is, the user selected No Limit from the Maximum Recording Length menu. (See Figure E.28.) If gMaxRecordLength is 0 the statement under the If is executed:

```
TegommWav.Command = "Record"
```

This statement issues a Record command without first setting the To property of the multimedia control. When the To property is not set before a Record command is issued, the recording is performed without any limitations. In other words, the recording continues until a Stop command is issued.

However, if the user did not select No Limit from the Maximum Recording Length menu, gMaxRecordLength is not set to 0, and the two statements under the Else are executed:

```
TegommWav.To = TegommWav.From + gMaxRecordLength
TegommWav.Command = "Record"
```

In these statements, the To property is set to the value of the From property plus the value of gMaxRecordLength. Consequently, if the user does not stop the recording, the recording stops automatically after gMaxRecordLength bytes have been recorded.

> **NOTE**
>
> If you issue a Record command without first setting the To property, the recording continues indefinitely until a Stop command is issued. For example, the statements
>
> ```
> TegommWav.From = 10000
> TegommWav.Command = "Record"
> ```
>
> insert the user's recording at position 10000, and the recording continues until the user stops the recording.
>
> On the other hand, if the To property is specified before the Record command is issued, the recording stops when the recording position reaches the value of the To property. For example, the statements
>
> ```
> TegommWav.From = 10000
> TegommWav.To   = 20000
> TegommWav.Command = "Record"
> ```
>
> insert the user's recording at position 10000, and the recording continues until the user stops the recording or until the recording position reaches 20000.

The next four statements in the cmdRecord_Click() procedure are the following:

```
cmdStop.Enabled = True
cmdRecord.Enabled = False
cmdPlay.Enabled = False
cmdPlaySelection.Enabled = False
```

These statements enable the Stop button and disable the Record and Play buttons. This is done because during recording, the user should not be permitted to click the Record and Play buttons and should be permitted to click the Stop button.

The last statement in the procedure

```
gWavFileHasChanged = True
```

sets the gWavFileHasChanged variable to True. Recall that the gWavFileHasChanged variable is used as a flag to indicate that the currently open WAV file has changed. Because the user is now recording sound into the WAV file, the gWavFileHasChanged flag is raised.

The cmdStop_Click() Procedure

The cmdStop_Click() procedure is automatically executed whenever the user clicks the Stop button. Here is the code of the cmdStop_Click() procedure:

```
Sub cmdStop_Click ()
```

```
' Reset the gPlaying and gPlayingSelection flags.
gPlaying = False
gPlayingSelection = False

' Issue a Stop command.
TegommWav.Command = "Stop"

' Disable/Enable buttons.
cmdStop.Enabled = False
cmdPlay.Enabled = True
cmdPlaySelection.Enabled = True
cmdRecord.Enabled = True

End Sub
```

The first two statements in the `cmdStop_Click()` procedure

```
gPlaying = False
gPlayingSelection = False
```

reset the `gPlaying` and `gPlayingSelection` flags. Recall that the `gPlaying` flag is used to indicate that the Play button was clicked, and the `gPlayingSelection` flag is used to indicate that the Play Selection button was clicked. Because the Stop button was clicked, these flags are set to `False`. Note that the `gRecording` flag is not set to `False`. As you'll see later, the Done event procedure of the multimedia control (`TegommWav_Done()`) still has to know that recording has stopped.

The next statement

```
TegommWav.Command = "Stop"
```

issues a Stop command. This causes any playback or recording to end.

The last four statements in the procedure are the following:

```
cmdStop.Enabled = False
cmdPlay.Enabled = True
cmdPlaySelection.Enabled = True
cmdRecord.Enabled = True
```

These statements disable the Stop button and enable the Play and Record buttons. No playback or recording is currently in progress, so the user should not be permitted to click the Stop button and should be permitted to click the Play and Record buttons.

The `TegommWav_Done()` Procedure

The `TegommWav_Done()` procedure is executed whenever playback or recording is stopped. Here is the code of the `TegommWav_Done()` procedure:

```
Sub TegommWav_Done ()

' Has Recording just stopped?
If gRecording = True Then
   gRecording = False
   TegommWav.Command = "UpdateWaveBuffer"
   cmdZoomOut_Click
```

```
      cmdStop_Click
   End If

   ' Has Playback just stopped?
   If gPlaying = True Then
      gPlaying = False
      If TegommWav.Position = TegommWav.Length Then
         TegommWav.Command = "Prev"
         hsbPosition.Value = 0
         If chkAutoRepeat = 1 Then
            cmdPlay_Click
         Else
            cmdStop_Click
         End If
      End If
   End If

   ' Has Playback of selection just stopped?
   If gPlayingSelection = True Then
      gPlayingSelection = False
      If TegommWav.Position = TegommWav.To Then
         If chkAutoRepeat = 1 Then
            cmdPlaySelection_Click
         Else
            cmdStop_Click
         End If
      End If
   End If

End Sub
```

As you can see, the `TegommWav_Done()` procedure consists of three `If` statements:

```
' Has Recording just stopped?
If gRecording = True Then
   ...
   ...
   ...
End If

' Has Playback just stopped?
If gPlaying = True Then
   ...
   ...
   ...
End If

' Has Playback of selection just stopped?
If gPlayingSelection = True Then
   ...
   ...
   ...
End If
```

If the condition of the first `If` is satisfied (`gRecording=True`), recording has just stopped. The recording stopped either because the recording range reached the maximum recording length or because the user clicked the Stop button. The statements under the first `If` are the following:

```
gRecording = False
TegommWav.Command = "UpdateWaveBuffer"
cmdZoomOut_Click
cmdStop_Click
```

 The first statement

```
gRecording = False
```

resets the gRecording flag to False because recording is no longer in progress.

The second statement

```
TegommWav.Command = "UpdateWaveBuffer"
```

issues an UpdateWaveBuffer command to the multimedia control. As discussed earlier, the UpdateWaveBuffer command fills a Wave buffer (in memory) with all the samples of the WAV file. It is the programmer's responsibility to update the WAV buffer when the WAV file is first opened (See the code of the mnuOpen_Click() procedure.) and whenever the WAV file is changed, such as after the user performs a recording. The UpdateWaveBuffer command should be used only in programs in which you need to access samples of the WAV files, such as the Wave Editor program. For programs in which you don't need to access the samples of the WAV file, you do not have to issue an UpdateWaveBuffer command.

The next statement

```
cmdZoomOut_Click
```

calls the cmdZoomOut_Click() procedure. Remember that the cmdZoomOut_Click() procedure displays the graph of the WAV file in Full View mode. So whenever recording ends, the WAV file is displayed in Full View mode.

The last statement under the first If is this:

```
cmdStop_Click
```

This statement calls the cmdStop_Click() procedure to simulate a clicking of the Stop button. Why call the cmdStop_Click() procedure if the recording has already stopped? The only reason for calling this procedure is to ensure that the Play, Record, and Stop buttons are enabled or disabled appropriately. Remember that the cmdStop_Click() procedure enables the Play and Record buttons and disables the Stop button.

The code under the second If statement in the TegommWav_Done() procedure

```
' Has Playback just stopped?
If gPlaying = True Then
   ...
   ...
   ...
End If
```

is executed if playback has just stopped. If playback has stopped as a result of the user clicking the Stop button, the If condition gPlaying=True is not satisfied because the code of the cmdStop_Click()

procedure has reset the gPlaying flag to False. The condition gPlaying=True is satisfied only if playback has stopped because of an error or because the playback position has reached the end of the WAV file.

The statements under the second If statement are the following:

```
gPlaying = False
If TegommWav.Position = TegommWav.Length Then
   TegommWav.Command = "Prev"
   hsbPosition.Value = 0
   If chkAutoRepeat = 1 Then
      cmdPlay_Click
   Else
      cmdStop_Click
   End If
End If
```

These statements perform the following tasks:

The gPlaying flag is set to False because playback is no longer in progress.

If the playback position has reached the end of the WAV file, a Prev command is issued to rewind the playback position to the beginning of the WAV file, and the hsbPosition scroll bar is set to 0.

If the playback position has reached the end of the WAV file and the Auto Repeat checkbox is checked, the cmdPlay_Click() procedure is called so that the playback starts again.

The code under the third If statement in the TegommWav_Done() procedure

```
' Has Playback of selection just stopped?
If gPlayingSelection = True Then
   ...
   ...
   ...
End If
```

is executed if playback of a section has just stopped. Remember that playback of a section is started when the user clicks the Play Selection button. The condition gPlayingSelection=True is satisfied only if playback has stopped because of an error or because the playback position has reached the end of the selected section.

The statements under the third If statement are the following:

```
gPlayingSelection = False
If TegommWav.Position = TegommWav.To Then
   If chkAutoRepeat = 1 Then
      cmdPlaySelection_Click
   Else
      cmdStop_Click
   End If
End If
```

These statements perform the following tasks:

- The gPlayingSelection flag is set to False because playback of a selection is no longer in progress.

- If the playback position has reached the end of the selection and the Auto Repeat checkbox is checked, the cmdPlaySelection() procedure is called so that the selection is played again.
- If the playback position has reached the end of the selection but the Auto Repeat checkbox is not checked, the cmdStop_Click() procedure is called so that the Play, Record, and Stop buttons are disabled or enabled as they should be when no playback or recording is in progress.

The TegommWav_StatusUpdate() Procedure

The TegommWav_StatusUpdate() procedure is executed every *X* milliseconds, where *X* is the value of the UpdateInterval property. In the Wave Editor program, the UpdateInterval property of the multimedia control was set to 500 at design time. (See Table E.1.) Consequently, in the Wave Editor program, the TegommWav_StatusUpdate() procedure is executed every 500 milliseconds (every half second). Here is the code of the TegommWav_StatusUpdate() procedure:

```
Sub TegommWav_StatusUpdate ()

' Update the hsbPosition scroll bar.
' (Only if currently playing).
If TegommWav.Mode = 526 Then
   If TegommWav.Length > 0 Then
      hsbPosition.Value = 1000 * TegommWav.Position /
                     ➥ TegommWav.Length
   Else
      hsbPosition.Value = 0
   End If
End If

' Display a blinking "RECORDING" - "R E C O R D I N G"
' in the program's window title.
' (Only if currently recording).
If TegommWav.Mode = 527 Then
   SetWindowTitle
End If

End Sub
```

As you can see, the TegommWav_StatusUpdate() procedure is responsible for updating the hsbPosition scroll bar during playback, and for displaying the blinking RECORDING message in the program's window title during recording.

The hsbPosition scroll bar is updated with these statements:

```
If TegommWav.Mode = 526 Then
   If TegommWav.Length > 0 Then
      hsbPosition.Value = 1000 * TegommWav.Position /
                     ➥ TegommWav.Length
   Else
      hsbPosition.Value = 0
   End If
End If
```

The condition `TegommWav.Mode=526` is satisfied only if playback is currently in progress. As long as playback is in progress, the `hsbPosition` scroll bar is updated every 500 milliseconds, and the thumb tab of the scroll bar moves in accordance with the current playback position.

The following statements set the program's window title to a blinking `RECORDING` during recording time:

```
If TegommWav.Mode = 527 Then
    SetWindowTitle
End If
```

The condition `TegommWav.Mode=527` is satisfied only if a recording is currently in progress. As long as a recording is in progress, the `SetWindowTitle()` procedure is called every 500 milliseconds, and `SetWindowTitle()` sets the program's window title one time to

`RECORDING`

and the next time to

`R E C O R D I N G.`

The `SetWindowTitle()` Procedure

The `SetWindowTitle()` procedure is called from various points in the program whenever it is necessary to update the program's window title. Here is the code of the `SetWindowTitle()` procedure:

```
Sub SetWindowTitle ()

Dim Status
Static Toggle

' If currently recording, set the program's window
' title to "RECORDING" or to "R E C O R D I N G"
' depending on the value of Toggle.
If gRecording = True Then
   If Toggle = True Then
      Toggle = False
      frmWEdit.Caption = "R E C O R D I N G"
   Else
      Toggle = True
      frmWEdit.Caption = "RECORDING"
   End If
   Exit Sub
End If

' Zooming mode or Full View mode?
If gZooming = True Then
   Status = "[Zooming]"
Else
   Status = "[Full View]"
End If

' Set the window's title.
frmWEdit.Caption = "Wave Editor - " + gWavNameNoPath + " "
                ➡ + Status

End Sub
```

The procedure first checks whether recording is currently in progress:

```
If gRecording = True Then
    If Toggle = True Then
        Toggle = False
        frmWEdit.Caption = "R E C O R D I N G"
    Else
        Toggle = True
        frmWEdit.Caption = "RECORDING"
    End If
    Exit Sub
End If
```

If recording is currently in progress (that is, gRecording=True) the title of the program's main window is set to either RECORDING or R E C O R D I N G, depending on the current value of the static variable Toggle. As you can see, in each iteration of the procedure (when recording is in progress), Toggle is inverted. One time it is set to True and the next time it is set to False.

The remaining code of the SetWindowTitle() procedure is executed only if no recording is in progress (because the last statement under the If gRecording = True statement exits the procedure).

The If statement

```
If gZooming = True Then
    Status = "[Zooming]"
Else
    Status = "[Full View]"
End If
```

sets the Status variable either with "[Zooming]" or with "[Full View]", depending on the value of the gZooming flag.

The last statement in the procedure

```
frmWEdit.Caption = "Wave Editor - " + gWavNameNoPath + " "
                ➥ + Status
```

sets the program's window title with the string

```
"Wave Editor - " + gWavNameNoPath + " " + Status
```

Recall that the gWavNameNoPath variable contains the name of the currently open WAV file, without the path.

The CloseWavFile() Procedure

The CloseWavFile() procedure is called from various points in the program whenever it is necessary to close the WAV file. Here is the code of the CloseWavFile() procedure:

```
Sub CloseWavFile ()

' Issue a Close command.
TegommWav.Command = "Close"
```

```
' Disable the controls.
DisableAllControls

' Update the program's window title.
frmWEdit.Caption = "Wave Editor"

' Update the graph.
UpdateGraph

End Sub
```

As you can see, the CloseWavFile() procedure closes the WAV file, disables the controls, updates the program's window title, and updates the graph.

The cmdZoomIn_Click() Procedure

The cmdZoomIn_Click() procedure is automatically executed whenever the user clicks the Zoom In button. This procedure lets the user zoom in to the current selection and display it on the entire graph area. Here is the code of the cmdZoomIn_Click() procedure:

```
Sub cmdZoomIn_Click ()

Dim Temp
Dim newGraphSampNum1, newGraphSampNum2

' Enable the Zoom Out button and Zoom Out menu item.
cmdZoomOut.Enabled = True
mnuZoomOut.Enabled = True

' Find the new boundaries of the graph.
newGraphSampNum1 = X2SampleNumber(gX1)
newGraphSampNum2 = X2SampleNumber(gX2)

' Set the boundaries of the graph.
gGraphSampNum1 = newGraphSampNum1
gGraphSampNum2 = newGraphSampNum2

' Make sure that gGraphSampNum1 is not less than
' gGraphSampNum2
If gGraphSampNum2 < gGraphSampNum1 Then
   Temp = gGraphSampNum2
   gGraphSampNum2 = gGraphSampNum1
   gGraphSampNum1 = Temp
End If

' Update the graph.
UpdateGraph

' Update the gZooming flag.
gZooming = True

' Update the window title.
SetWindowTitle

End Sub
```

The first two statements of the procedure

```
cmdZoomOut.Enabled = True
mnuZoomOut.Enabled = True
```

enable the Zoom Out button and the Zoom Out menu item. These items are enabled because the graph is now going to be displayed in Zooming mode. The user, therefore, should be able to go back to Full View mode by clicking the Zoom Out button or by selecting the Zoom Out menu item. Note that the Zoom In button and the Zoom In menu item are not disabled because the user is allowed to zoom in to still smaller sound sections.

The next two statements

```
newGraphSampNum1 = X2SampleNumber(gX1)
newGraphSampNum2 = X2SampleNumber(gX2)
```

calculate the new boundaries of the graph, based on the boundaries of the current selection. The results are stored in the local variables newGraphSampNum1 and newGraphSampNum2.

Then the statements

```
gGraphSampNum1 = newGraphSampNum1
gGraphSampNum2 = newGraphSampNum2
```

set the gGraphSampNum1 and gGraphSampNum2 variables with the new boundaries of the graph.

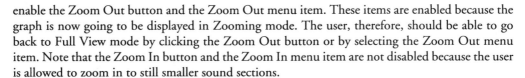

NOTE

The gGraphSampNum1 and gGraphSampNum2 variables are set indirectly with the new boundaries of the graph, as follows:

```
newGraphSampNum1 = X2SampleNumber(gX1)
newGraphSampNum2 = X2SampleNumber(gX2)
gGraphSampNum1 = newGraphSampNum1
gGraphSampNum2 = newGraphSampNum2
```

rather than directly, as follows:

```
gGraphSampNum1 = X2SampleNumber(gX1)
gGraphSampNum2 = X2SampleNumber(gX2)
```

because the X2SampleNumber() function is using the current values of gGraphSampNum1 and gGraphSampNum2.

The next statement in the procedure

```
If gGraphSampNum2 < gGraphSampNum1 Then
    Temp = gGraphSampNum2
    gGraphSampNum2 = gGraphSampNum1
    gGraphSampNum1 = Temp
End If
```

ensures that `gGraphSampNum2` is not less than `gGraphSampNum1`. If `gGraphSampNum2` is less than `gGraphSampNum1`, the values of `gGraphSampNum1` and `gGraphSampNum2` are swapped.

The next statement

`UpdateGraph`

calls the `UpdateGraph()` procedure to display the new graph. Remember that the `UpdateGraph()` procedure displays the graph based on the values of `gGraphSampNum1` and `gGraphSampNum2`. The extreme left bar of the graph represents sample number `gGraphSampNum1`, and the extreme right bar of the graph represents sample number `gGraphSampNum2`.

The next statement

`gZooming = True`

raises the `gZooming` flag. That is, the graph is now displayed in Zooming mode, so `gZooming` is `True`.

The last statement in the procedure

`SetWindowTitle`

calls the `SetWindowTitle()` procedure to update the program's window. This is necessary because the graph is now displayed in Zooming mode, and the window's title should specify this mode.

The `mnuCopy_Click()` Procedure

The `mnuCopy_Click()` procedure is automatically executed whenever the user selects Copy from the Edit menu. This procedure copies the current selection into the Clipboard. Here is the code of the `mnuCopy_Click()` procedure:

```
Sub mnuCopy_Click ()

    Dim StartPos, EndPos
    Dim Temp

    ' Convert the selection rectangle boundaries
    ' from X coordinates to Sample coordinates.
    StartPos = X2SampleNumber(gX1)
    EndPos = X2SampleNumber(gX2)

    ' Validate the selection range.
    If StartPos > EndPos Then
       Temp = EndPos
       EndPos = StartPos
       StartPos = Temp
    End If
    If StartPos > TegommWav.Length Then
       StartPos = TegommWav.Length
    End If
    If EndPos > TegommWav.Length Then
       EndPos = TegommWav.Length
    End If
```

```
' Copy the selected sound section to the Clipboard.
TegommWav.From = StartPos
TegommWav.To = EndPos
TegommWav.Command = "Copy"

End Sub
```

The first two statements in the `mnuCopy_Click()` procedure

```
StartPos = X2SampleNumber(gX1)
EndPos = X2SampleNumber(gX2)
```

convert the boundaries of the selection rectangle (`gX1` and `gX2`) from X coordinates to Samples co-ordinates. The results of the conversion are stored in `StartPos` and `EndPos` (two local variables).

Three `If` statements are used to validate the values of `StartPos` and `EndPos`. The first `If` statement

```
If StartPos > EndPos Then
   Temp = EndPos
   EndPos = StartPos
   StartPos = Temp
End If
```

ensures that `StartPos` is not greater than `EndPos`. If it is greater, the values of `StartPos` and `EndPos` are swapped.

The other two `If` statements ensure that `StartPos` and `EndPos` are not larger than the total length of the WAV file:

```
If StartPos > TegommWav.Length Then
   StartPos = TegommWav.Length
End If
If EndPos > TegommWav.Length Then
   EndPos = TegommWav.Length
End If
```

Finally, the last three statements of the procedure

```
TegommWav.From = StartPos
TegommWav.To = EndPos
TegommWav.Command = "Copy"
```

issue a Copy command to the multimedia control. As you can see, the From and To properties specify the range of samples to be copied to the Clipboard.

NOTE

To copy a range of samples to the Clipboard, you have to specify a sample range with the From and To properties of the multimedia control, and then you have to issue a Copy command. For example, the statements

```
TegommWav.From = 10000
TegommWav.To   = 20000
TegommWav.Command = "Copy"
```

copy the samples in the range 10000 through 20000 of the WAV file into the Clipboard. Note that the From and To properties for the Copy command are always in units of samples. No matter what the current setting of the TimeFormat property, the units for specifying the range for the Copy command are always in units of samples.

The Copy command uses the Wave Buffer. Therefore, before you issue a Copy command, the Wave Buffer must be updated. The Wave Buffer is always updated in the Wave Editor program because whenever the user changes the WAV file, such as after a recording, the Wave Editor program issues an UpdateWaveBuffer command. Recall that the Wave Editor program also issues an UpdateWaveBuffer command upon opening the WAV file (in the mnuOpen_Click() procedure).

The mnuPaste_Click() Procedure

The mnuPaste_Click() procedure is automatically executed whenever the user selects Paste from the Edit menu. This procedure pastes the current contents of the Clipboard into the currently selected section of the WAV file. Here is the code of the mnuPaste_Click() procedure:

```
Sub mnuPaste_Click ()

Dim StartPos, EndPos
Dim Temp

' Convert the selection rectangle boundaries
' from X coordinates to Sample coordinates.
StartPos = X2SampleNumber(gX1)
EndPos = X2SampleNumber(gX2)

' Validate the selection range.
If StartPos > EndPos Then
   Temp = EndPos
   EndPos = StartPos
   StartPos = Temp
End If
If StartPos > TegommWav.Length Then
   StartPos = TegommWav.Length
End If
If EndPos > TegommWav.Length Then
   EndPos = TegommWav.Length
End If

' Paste the Clipboard contents onto the current
' selection in the WAV file.
TegommWav.From = StartPos
TegommWav.To = EndPos
TegommWav.Command = "Paste"

' Update the Wave buffer.
TegommWav.Command = "UpdateWaveBuffer"
```

```
' If currently in Full View mode, update gGraphSampNum2.
' (Because the length of the WAV file has been changed).
If gZooming = False Then
   gGraphSampNum1 = 0
   gGraphSampNum2 = TegommWav.Length - 1
End If

' Update the graph.
UpdateGraph

' Raise the gWavFileHasChanged flag.
gWavFileHasChanged = True

' Simulate a click of the Stop button.
cmdStop_Click

End Sub
```

The first two statements in the mnuPaste_Click() procedure

```
StartPos = X2SampleNumber(gX1)
EndPos = X2SampleNumber(gX2)
```

convert the boundaries of the selection rectangle (gX1 and gX2) from X coordinates to Samples coordinates. The results of the conversion are stored in StartPos and EndPos (two local variables).

Then three If statements are used to validate the values of StartPos and EndPos. The first If statement

```
If StartPos > EndPos Then
   Temp = EndPos
   EndPos = StartPos
   StartPos = Temp
End If
```

ensures that StartPos is not greater than EndPos. If it is greater, the values of StartPos and EndPos are swapped.

The other two If statements ensure that StartPos and EndPos are not larger than the total length of the WAV file:

```
If StartPos > TegommWav.Length Then
   StartPos = TegommWav.Length
End If
If EndPos > TegommWav.Length Then
   EndPos = TegommWav.Length
End If
```

The next three statements

```
TegommWav.From = StartPos
TegommWav.To = EndPos
TegommWav.Command = "Paste"
```

paste the Clipboard contents into the WAV file.

> **NOTE**
>
> To paste the Clipboard contents into the WAV file, you have to specify a samples range within the WAV file and then issue a Paste command. The Paste command causes the specified range in the WAV file to be replaced with the Clipboard contents.
>
> Here's an example: The statements
>
> ```
> TegommWav.From = 10000
> TegommWav.To   = 20000
> TegommWav.Command = "Paste"
> ```
>
> delete samples 10000 through 20000 in the WAV file and then insert the Clipboard contents into the WAV file at byte position 10000.
>
> Here's another example: The statements
>
> ```
> TegommWav.From = 10000
> TegommWav.To   = 10000
> TegommWav.Command = "Paste"
> ```
>
> insert the Clipboard contents into the WAV file at byte position 10000. Nothing is deleted because the From property is equal to the To property.
>
> Note that the From and To properties for the Paste command are always in units of samples. No matter what the current setting of the TimeFormat property, the units for specifying the range for the Paste command are always samples.
>
> The Paste command uses the Wave Buffer. Therefore, before you issue a Paste command, the Wave Buffer must be updated. The Wave Buffer is always updated in the Wave Editor program because whenever the user changes the WAV file, such as after a recording, the Wave Editor program issues an `UpdateWaveBuffer` command. Recall that the Wave Editor program also issues an `UpdateWaveBuffer` command upon opening the WAV file (in the `mnuOpen_Click()` procedure).

The next statement

```
TegommWav.Command = "UpdateWaveBuffer"
```

issues an `UpdateWaveBuffer` command. This action is necessary because the user just changed the WAV file by pasting the contents of the Clipboard into the WAV file. As discussed earlier, whenever the user changes the WAV file, the program has to update the Wave Buffer.

The next statement in the procedure is an `If` statement:

```
If gZooming = False Then
    gGraphSampNum1 = 0
    gGraphSampNum2 = TegommWav.Length - 1
End If
```

This If statement checks whether the user is currently in Full View mode. If the user is in Full View mode, the gGraphSampNum2 variable is updated with TegommWav.Length-1. This action is necessary because the Paste command has changed the length of the WAV file, and if the user is currently in Full View mode, gGraphSampNum2 must be updated with the new length of the WAV file. Full View mode means displaying the entire WAV file (gGraphSampNum1 is 0 and gGraphSampNum2 is TegommWav.Length-1).

The next statement

```
UpdateGraph
```

calls the UpdateGraph() procedure. Remember that the UpdateGraph() procedure displays the graph in accordance with the values of gGraphSampNum1 and gGraphSampNum2.

The next statement

```
gWavFileHasChanged = True
```

raises the gWavFileHasChanged flag. This flag is raised because the user has just changed the WAV file by pasting the contents of the Clipboard into the WAV file.

The last statement in the procedure

```
cmdStop_Click
```

calls the cmdStop_Click() procedure. This procedure is called because if the user selects Paste from the Edit menu while playback is in progress, the multimedia control stops the playback. Calling cmdStop_Click() ensures that the Play, Record, and Stop buttons are disabled or enabled as they should be when no playback is in progress.

The mnuDelete_Click() Procedure

The mnuDelete_Click() procedure is automatically executed whenever the user selects Delete from the Edit menu or presses the Delete key on the keyboard. This procedure deletes the current selection from the WAV file. Here is the code of the mnuDelete_Click() procedure:

```
Sub mnuDelete_Click ()

Dim StartPos, EndPos
Dim Temp

' Convert the selection rectangle boundaries
' from X coordinates to Sample coordinates.
StartPos = X2SampleNumber(gX1)
EndPos = X2SampleNumber(gX2)

' If the user is trying to delete the last sample
' in the WAV file, display a message box and terminate
' this procedure.
If TegommWav.Length = 1 Then
   MsgBox "WAV file must have at least one sample.",
       ➥ MB_ICONEXCLAMATION, "Wave Editor"
   Exit Sub
```

```
    End If

    ' Validate the selection range.
    If StartPos > EndPos Then
        Temp = EndPos
        EndPos = StartPos
        StartPos = Temp
    End If
    If StartPos > TegommWav.Length - 1 Then
        StartPos = TegommWav.Length - 1
    End If
    If EndPos > TegommWav.Length - 1 Then
        EndPos = TegommWav.Length - 1
    End If

    ' Make sure that at least one sample is left in the
    ' WAV file.
    If StartPos = 0 And EndPos = TegommWav.Length - 1 Then
        StartPos = 1
    End If

    ' Perform the deletion.
    TegommWav.From = StartPos
    TegommWav.To = EndPos + 1
    TegommWav.Command = "Delete"

    ' Update the Wave buffer.
    TegommWav.Command = "UpdateWaveBuffer"

    ' If currently in Full View mode, update gGraphSampNum2.
    ' (Because the length of the WAV file has been changed).
    If gZooming = False Then
        gGraphSampNum1 = 0
        gGraphSampNum2 = TegommWav.Length - 1
    End If

    ' Update the graph.
    UpdateGraph

    ' Raise the gWavFileHasChanged flag.
    gWavFileHasChanged = True

    ' Simulate a click of the Stop button.
    cmdStop_Click

End Sub
```

The first two statements in the `mnuDelete_Click()` procedure

```
StartPos = X2SampleNumber(gX1)
EndPos = X2SampleNumber(gX2)
```

convert the boundaries of the selection rectangle (`gX1` and `gX2`) from X coordinates to Samples co-ordinates. The results of the conversion are stored in `StartPos` and `EndPos` (two local variables).

E

Then an `If` statement is used to make sure that the user is not trying to delete the last sample in the WAV file:

```
If TegommWav.Length = 1 Then
    MsgBox "WAV file must have at least one sample.",
        ➥ MB_ICONEXCLAMATION, "Wave Editor"
    Exit Sub
End If
```

This `If` statement checks whether the current length of the WAV file is only one sample. If the WAV file currently has only one sample, a message box is displayed and the procedure is terminated. The reason the user is not permitted to delete the last sample in the WAV file is that some commands require the WAV file to be at least 1 sample long.

Three `If` statements are then used to validate the values of `StartPos` and `EndPos`. The first `If` statement

```
If StartPos > EndPos Then
    Temp = EndPos
    EndPos = StartPos
    StartPos = Temp
End If
```

ensures that `StartPos` is not greater than `EndPos`. If it is greater, the values of `StartPos` and `EndPos` are swapped.

The other two `If` statements ensure that `StartPos` and `EndPos` are not larger than the total length of the WAV file:

```
If StartPos > TegommWav.Length - 1 Then
    StartPos = TegommWav.Length - 1
End If
If EndPos > TegommWav.Length - 1 Then
    EndPos = TegommWav.Length - 1
End If
```

The next statement is another `If` statement:

```
If StartPos = 0 And EndPos = TegommWav.Length - 1 Then
    StartPos = 1
End If
```

This `If` statement ensures that the user is not trying to delete the entire WAV file. If the user is trying to delete the entire WAV file (that is, `StartPos` is 0 and `EndPos` is `TegommWav.Length-1`), `StartPos` is set to 1 so that one sample remains in the WAV file after the deletion. As mentioned earlier, at least one sample should remain because some commands won't work when the WAV file is completely empty.

The next three statements perform the deletion:

```
TegommWav.From = StartPos
TegommWav.To = EndPos + 1
TegommWav.Command = "Delete"
```

> **NOTE**
>
> To delete a section of the WAV file, you have to specify with the From and To properties the range to be deleted and then issue a Delete command. The range is specified in the units of the current time format. For example, in the Wave Editor program, the TimeFormat property of the multimedia control was set to Samples. (See the mnuOpen_Click() procedure.) Therefore, the statements
>
> ```
> TegommWav.From = 1000
> TegommWav.To = 2000 + 1
> TegommWav.Command = "Delete"
> ```
>
> delete samples 1000 through 2000. Notice that the To property is set to 2000+1 (not to 2000) because the last sample in the specified range is not deleted. For example, the statements
>
> ```
> TegommWav.From = 0
> TegommWav.To = 2
> TegommWav.Command = "Delete"
> ```
>
> delete sample number 0 and sample number 1. Sample number 2 is not deleted. To delete samples 0, 1, and 2, the To property should be set to 2+1, as in
>
> ```
> TegommWav.From = 0
> TegommWav.To = 2 + 1
> TegommWav.Command = "Delete"
> ```

The next statement in the procedure

```
TegommWav.Command = "UpdateWaveBuffer"
```

issues an UpdateWaveBuffer command. This action is necessary because the user just changed the WAV file by deleting a section. As discussed earlier, whenever the user changes the WAV file, the program has to update the Wave Buffer.

The next statement is an If statement:

```
If gZooming = False Then
    gGraphSampNum1 = 0
    gGraphSampNum2 = TegommWav.Length - 1
End If
```

This If statement checks whether the user is currently in Full View mode. If the user is in Full View mode, the gGraphSampNum2 variable is updated with TegommWav.Length-1. This action is necessary because the Delete command has changed the length of the WAV file, and if the user is currently in Full View mode, gGraphSampNum2 must be updated with the new length of the WAV file. Full View mode means displaying the entire WAV file (gGraphSampNum1 is 0 and gGraphSampNum2 is TegommWav.Length-1).

The next statement

```
UpdateGraph
```

calls the `UpdateGraph()` procedure. Remember that the `UpdateGraph()` procedure displays the graph in accordance with the values of `gGraphSampNum1` and `gGraphSampNum2`.

The next statement

```
gWavFileHasChanged = True
```

raises the `gWavFileHasChanged` flag. This flag is raised because the user has just changed the WAV file by deleting a section.

The last statement in the procedure

```
cmdStop_Click
```

calls the `cmdStop_Click()` procedure. This procedure is called because if the user deletes a section of the WAV file while playback is in progress, the multimedia control stops the playback. Calling `cmdStop_Click()` ensures that the Play, Record, and Stop buttons are disabled or enabled as they should be when no playback is in progress.

The `mnuCut_Click()` Procedure

The `mnuCut_Click()` procedure is automatically executed whenever the user selects Cut from the Edit menu. This procedure first copies the current selection to the Clipboard and then deletes the current selection from the WAV file. Here is the code of the `mnuCut_Click()` procedure:

```
Sub mnuCut_Click ()

    ' Cut = Copy + Delete
    mnuCopy_Click
    mnuDelete_Click

    ' Raise the gWavFileHasChanged flag.
    gWavFileHasChanged = True

End Sub
```

As you can see, the `mnuCut_Click()` procedure is very simple. It consists of only three statements. The first statement

```
mnuCopy_Click
```

calls the `mnuCopy_Click()` procedure. Remember that the `mnuCopy_Click()` procedure copies the current selection into the Clipboard.

The next statement

```
mnuDelete_Click
```

calls the mnuDelete_Click() procedure. Recall that the mnuDelete_Click() procedure deletes the current selection from the WAV file.

The last statement

```
gWavFileHasChanged = True
```

raises the gWavFileHasChanged flag. This flag is raised because the user has just changed the WAV file by deleting a section from the file.

The mnuSilence_Click() **Procedure**

The mnuSilence_Click() procedure is automatically executed whenever the user selects Silence from the Edit menu. This procedure replaces all the samples of the current selection with values of zero volume. Here is the code of the mnuSilence_Click() procedure:

```
Sub mnuSilence_Click ()

    Dim StartPos, EndPos
    Dim Temp
    Dim I As Long

    Dim hctl As Long
    Dim Dummy As Integer

    ' Convert the selection rectangle boundaries
    ' from X coordinates to Sample coordinates.
    StartPos = X2SampleNumber(gX1)
    EndPos = X2SampleNumber(gX2)

    ' Validate the selection range.
    If StartPos > EndPos Then
       Temp = EndPos
       EndPos = StartPos
       StartPos = Temp
    End If
    If StartPos > TegommWav.Length - 1 Then
       StartPos = TegommWav.Length - 1
    End If
    If EndPos > TegommWav.Length - 1 Then
       EndPos = TegommWav.Length - 1
    End If

    ' Get the handle of the control.
    hctl = TegommWav.hctl

    ' Set mouse cursor to hourglass.
    frmWEdit.MousePointer = 11

    ' Set all the samples of the current selection
    ' with values of 0 volume (128).
    For I = StartPos To EndPos

        ' Set the sample to 128 (Zero volume).
        Dummy = tegSetByte(hctl, I, 128)
```

```
    Next I

    ' Validate the Wave Buffer.
    TegommWav.Command = "ValidateWaveBuffer"

    ' Set mouse cursor to default.
    frmWEdit.MousePointer = 0

    ' Update the graph.
    UpdateGraph

    ' Raise the gWavFileHasChanged flag.
    gWavFileHasChanged = True

    ' Simulate a click of the Stop button.
    cmdStop_Click

End Sub
```

The mnuSilence_Click() procedure sets the values of all the samples in the current selection to a value of 128 (0 volume) by using a For loop:

```
' Set all the samples of the current selection
' with values of 0 volume (128).
For I = StartPos To EndPos

    ' Set the sample to 128 (Zero volume).
    Dummy = tegSetByte(hctl, I, 128)

Next I
```

As you can see, each sample is set to a value of 128 by using the tegSetByte() function of the TegoMM.VBX control. Recall that the tegSetByte() function is declared in the general declarations section of the frmWEdit form.

The tegSetByte() function takes three parameters. The first parameter (hctl) is the handle of the multimedia control. This handle was extracted prior to entering the For loop with the statement

```
' Get the handle of the control.
hctl = TegommWav.hctl
```

The second parameter of the tegSetByte() function specifies the byte number to be set. The third parameter of the tegSetByte() function specifies the new byte value. In 8-bit WAV files a byte value of 128 corresponds to zero volume.

The first statement after the For loop is this:

```
' Validate the Wave Buffer.
TegommWav.Command = "ValidateWaveBuffer"
```

This statement validates the Wave Buffer by issuing a ValidateWaveBuffer command to the multimedia control. The ValidateWaveBuffer command must be used after using the tegSetByte() function. If you don't issue a ValidateWaveBuffer command after using the tegSetByte() function, all the changes made by the tegSetByte() function will not be effective.

> **NOTE**
>
> Use the `tegSetByte()` function to set the values of samples in 8-bit WAV files.
>
> To set the values of samples in 16-bit WAV files use the `tegSetWord()` function. The `tegSetWord()` function has the same parameters as the `tegSetByte()` function.
>
> Typically, the `tegSetByte()` and `tegSetWord()` functions are used inside a For loop to assign values to a group of samples. After the For loop terminates you need to validate the Wave Buffer by issuing a `ValidateWaveBuffer` command to the multimedia control.
>
> To read the values of samples in 8-bit WAV files you can use the `tegGetByte()` function. The `tegGetByte()` function is discussed in the next section.
>
> To read the values of samples in 16-bit WAV files you can use the `tegGetWord()` function.
>
> Using the `tegSetByte()`, `tegSetWord()`, `tegGetByte()`, and `tegGetWord()` functions is much more efficient than using the SampleValue1 and SampleValue2 properties, which were discussed earlier in this chapter.

The `mnuIncreaseVolume_Click()` Procedure

The `mnuIncreaseVolume_Click()` procedure is automatically executed whenever the user selects Increase Volume from the Edit menu. This procedure increases the values of all the samples of the current selection by 25%. Here is the code of the `mnuIncreaseVolume_Click()` procedure:

```
Sub mnuIncreaseVolume_Click ()

    Dim StartPos, EndPos
    Dim Temp
    Dim I As Long

    Dim hctl As Long
    Dim Dummy As Integer
    Dim Sample As Integer

    ' Convert the selection rectangle boundaries
    ' from X coordinates to Sample coordinates.
    StartPos = X2SampleNumber(gX1)
    EndPos = X2SampleNumber(gX2)

    ' Validate the selection range.
    If StartPos > EndPos Then
        Temp = EndPos
        EndPos = StartPos
        StartPos = Temp
    End If
    If StartPos > TegommWav.Length - 1 Then
        StartPos = TegommWav.Length - 1
    End If
    If EndPos > TegommWav.Length - 1 Then
```

```
        EndPos = TegommWav.Length - 1
    End If

    ' Get the handler of the control.
    hctl = TegommWav.hctl

    ' Set mouse cursor to hourglass.
    frmWEdit.MousePointer = 11

    ' Increase the volume of all the samples in
    ' the current selection (increase by 25%).
    For I = StartPos To EndPos

        ' Get a sample.
        Sample = tegGetByte(hctl, I)

        ' Increase the volume of the sample by 25%
        If (Sample > 128) Then
           Sample = Sample + (Sample - 128) * .25
           If Sample > 255 Then Sample = 255
        Else
           Sample = Sample - (128 - Sample) * .25
           If Sample < 0 Then Sample = 0
        End If

        ' Set the sample with the new value.
        Dummy = tegSetByte(hctl, I, Sample)

    Next I

    ' Validate the Wave Buffer.
    TegommWav.Command = "ValidateWaveBuffer"

    ' Set mouse cursor to default.
    frmWEdit.MousePointer = 0

    ' Update the graph.
    UpdateGraph

    ' Raise the gWavFileHasChanged flag.
    gWavFileHasChanged = True

    ' Simulate a click of the Stop button.
    cmdStop_Click

End Sub
```

The `mnuIncreaseVolume_Click()` procedure increases the values of all the samples in the current selection by 25% by using a `For` loop:

```
' Increase the volume of all the samples in
' the current selection (increase by 25%).
For I = StartPos To EndPos
```

```
' Get a sample.
Sample = tegGetByte(hctl, I)

' Increase the volume of the sample by 25%
If (Sample > 128) Then
    Sample = Sample + (Sample - 128) * .25
    If Sample > 255 Then Sample = 255
Else
    Sample = Sample - (128 - Sample) * .25
    If Sample < 0 Then Sample = 0
End If

' Set the sample with the new value.
Dummy = tegSetByte(hctl, I, Sample)
```

Next I

As you can see, each sample is read by using the tegGetByte() function of the TegoMM.VBX control. Recall that the tegGetByte() function is declared in the general declarations section of the frmWEdit form. After the sample is read, the volume of the sample is increased by 25% and then the tegSetByte() function is used to set the sample in the WAV file with the new value.

The tegGetByte() function takes two parameters. The first parameter (hctl) is the handle of the multimedia control. This handle was extracted prior to entering the For loop with the statement

```
' Get the handle of the control.
hctl = TegommWav.hctl
```

The second parameter of the tegGetByte() function specifies the byte number to be retrieved. The tegGetByte() function returns the value of the specified sample.

The first statement after the For loop is this:

```
' Validate the Wave Buffer.
TegommWav.Command = "ValidateWaveBuffer"
```

This statement validates the Wave Buffer by issuing a ValidateWaveBuffer command to the multimedia control. As stated earlier, the ValidateWaveBuffer command must be used after using the tegSetByte() function. If you don't issue a ValidateWaveBuffer command after using the tegSetByte() function, all the changes made by the tegSetByte() function will not be effective.

NOTE

You use the tegGetByte() function to get the values of samples in 8-bit WAV files.

To get the values of samples in 16-bit WAV files use the tegGetWord() function. The tegGetWord() function has the same parameters as the tegGetByte() function.

The mnuDecreaseVolume_Click() Procedure

The mnuDecreaseVolume_Click() procedure is automatically executed whenever the user selects Decrease Volume from the Edit menu. This procedure decreases the values of all the samples of the current selection by 25%. Here is the code of the mnuDecreaseVolume_Click() procedure:

```
Sub mnuDecreaseVolume_Click ()

    Dim StartPos, EndPos
    Dim Temp
    Dim I As Long
    Dim hctl As Long
    Dim Dummy As Integer
    Dim Sample As Integer

    ' Convert the selection rectangle boundaries
    ' from X coordinates to Sample coordinates.
    StartPos = X2SampleNumber(gX1)
    EndPos = X2SampleNumber(gX2)

    ' Validate the selection range.
    If StartPos > EndPos Then
        Temp = EndPos
        EndPos = StartPos
        StartPos = Temp
    End If
    If StartPos > TegommWav.Length - 1 Then
        StartPos = TegommWav.Length - 1
    End If
    If EndPos > TegommWav.Length - 1 Then
        EndPos = TegommWav.Length - 1
    End If

    ' Get the handler of the control.
    hctl = TegommWav.hctl

    ' Set mouse cursor to hourglass.
    frmWEdit.MousePointer = 11

    ' Decrease the volume of all the samples in
    ' the current selection (decrease by 25%).
    For I = StartPos To EndPos

        ' Get a sample.
        Sample = tegGetByte(hctl, I)

        ' Decrease the volume of the sample by 25%
        If (Sample > 128) Then
            Sample = Sample - (Sample - 128) * .25
            If Sample < 128 Then Sample = 128
        Else
            Sample = Sample + (128 - Sample) * .25
            If Sample > 128 Then Sample = 128
        End If

        ' Set the sample with the new value.
```

```
        Dummy = tegSetByte(hctl, I, Sample)

    Next I

    ' Validate the Wave Buffer.
    TegommWav.Command = "ValidateWaveBuffer"

    ' Set mouse cursor to default.
    frmWEdit.MousePointer = 0

    ' Update the graph.
    UpdateGraph

    ' Raise the gWavFileHasChanged flag.
    gWavFileHasChanged = True

    ' Simulate a click of the Stop button.
    cmdStop_Click

End Sub
```

As you can see, the code of the mnuDecreaseVolume_Click() procedure is almost identical to the code of the mnuIncreaseVolume_Click() procedure.

The mnuFile_Click() Procedure

The mnuFile_Click() procedure is automatically executed whenever the user opens the File menu. This procedure disables or enables the Save menu item of the File menu, based on the current value of the gWavFileHasChanged flag. Here is the code of the mnuFile_Click() procedure:

```
Sub mnuFile_Click ()

    ' Disable or enable the Save menu item?
    If gWavFileHasChanged = True Then
       mnuSave.Enabled = True
    Else
       mnuSave.Enabled = False
    End If

End Sub
```

As you can see, the code of the mnuFile_Click() procedure consists of one If statement. If the user has changed the WAV file (that is, gWavFileHasChanged is equal to True), the Save menu item is enabled. Otherwise, the Save menu item is disabled.

The mnuSave_Click() Procedure

The mnuSave_Click() procedure is automatically executed whenever the user selects Save from the File menu. This procedure saves the open WAV file to the disk. Here is the code of the mnuSave_Click() procedure:

```
Sub mnuSave_Click ()
```

E

```
    Dim Msg

    ' Set mouse cursor to hourglass.
    frmWEdit.MousePointer = 11

    ' Issue a Save command.
    TegommWav.Command = "Save"

    ' Set mouse cursor to default.
    frmWEdit.MousePointer = 0

    ' If Save command failed, tell the user.
    If TegommWav.Error <> 0 And TegommWav.Error <> 349 Then
        Msg = "Cannot save " + TegommWav.FileName + ". "
        Msg = Msg + "This file may be a read-only file. "
        Msg = Msg + "Check the attribute of this file in "
        Msg = Msg + "File Manager."
        MsgBox Msg, 0, "Wave Editor"
    Else
        ' Reset the gWavFileHasChanged flag.
        gWavFileHasChanged = False
    End If

End Sub
```

The first statement in the `mnuSave_Click()` procedure

```
frmWEdit.MousePointer = 11
```

sets the icon of the mouse cursor to an hourglass. This action is taken because saving the file may take a while. During this time, the hourglass indicates that the user should wait while the task is being completed.

The next statement

```
TegommWav.Command = "Save"
```

saves the WAV file to the disk by issuing a Save command to the multimedia control.

Then the statement

```
frmWEdit.MousePointer = 0
```

restores the original icon of the mouse cursor.

Finally, an `If…Else` statement is used to check whether the Save command failed:

```
If TegommWav.Error <> 0 And TegommWav.Error <> 349 Then
    Msg = "Cannot save " + TegommWav.FileName + ". "
    Msg = Msg + "This file may be a read-only file. "
    Msg = Msg + "Check the attribute of this file in "
    Msg = Msg + "File Manager."
    MsgBox Msg, 0, "Wave Editor"
Else
    ' Reset the gWavFileHasChanged flag.
    gWavFileHasChanged = False
End If
```

If the Save command failed, a message box is displayed, telling the user that the WAV file cannot be saved. If the Save command did not fail, however, the gWavFileHasChanged flag is set to False. That is, the WAV file has just been saved, so the gWavFileHasChanged flag should indicate that no changes have been made to the WAV file since the last save.

The mnuSaveAs_Click() Procedure

The mnuSaveAs_Click() procedure is automatically executed whenever the user selects Save As from the File menu. This procedure provides the user with a Save As dialog box and then saves the open WAV file with the name the user specifies. Here is the code of the mnuSaveAs_Click() procedure:

```
Sub mnuSaveAs_Click ()

Dim OriginalFileName
Dim Msg, Answer

' Set an error trap to detect the clicking
' of the Cancel key of the Save As dialog box.
On Error GoTo SaveAsError

' Fill the items of the File Type list box of
' the Open dialog box.
CMDialog1.Filter = "All Files (*.*)¦*.*¦Wave Files
                ➥ (*.wav)¦*.wav"

' Set the default File Type to Wave Files (*.wav).
CMDialog1.FilterIndex = 2

' Display the Save As dialog box.
CMDialog1.Action = 2

' Remove the error trap.
On Error GoTo 0

' If the file specified by the user exists, and its
' size is not zero, ask the user if to overwrite it.
If Dir(CMDialog1.FileName) <> "" Then
   Msg = CMDialog1.FileName + Chr(13)
   Msg=Msg+"This WAV file already exists."+Chr(13)+Chr(13)
   Msg = Msg + "Replace existing file?"
   Answer = MsgBox(Msg, MB_ICONEXCLAMATION + MB_YESNO,
                ➥ "Wave Editor")
   If Answer = IDNO Then
      Exit Sub
   End If
End If

' Set mouse cursor to hourglass.
frmWEdit.MousePointer = 11

' Store the original file name.
OriginalFileName = TegommWav.FileName

' Change the FileName of the multimedia control to
' the filename that the user selected, and issue
```

```
' a Save command.
TegommWav.FileName = CMDialog1.Filename
TegommWav.Command = "Save"

' Set mouse cursor to default.
frmWEdit.MousePointer = 0

' If Save command failed, tell the user, restore
' the original filename, and abort this procedure.
If TegommWav.Error <> 0 And TegommWav.Error <> 349 Then
    MsgBox "Cannot save " + TegommWav.FileName, 0, "ERROR"
    TegommWav.FileName = OriginalFileName
    Exit Sub
Else
    ' Reset the gWavFileHasChanged flag.
    gWavFileHasChanged = False

    ' Update the gWavNameNoPath variable.
    gWavNameNoPath = CMDialog1.Filetitle

    ' Set the title of the Window.
    SetWindowTitle

End If

' Exit the procedure.
Exit Sub

SaveAsError:
' The user clicked the Cancel button of
' the Save As dialog box.
Exit Sub

End Sub
```

The mnuSaveAs_Click() procedure is similar to the mnuSave_Click() procedure. It issues a Save command to the multimedia control to save the open WAV file to the disk. Unlike the cmdSave_Click() procedure, however, the mnuSaveAs_Click() procedure uses the common dialog box control, CMDialog1, to provide the user with a Save As dialog box. After the user specifies a filename using the Save As dialog box, the mnuSaveAs_Click() procedure sets the FileName property of the multimedia control to the filename that the user specified, and issues a Save command:

```
TegommWav.FileName = CMDialog1.Filename
TegommWav.Command = "Save"
```

The mnuSaveAs_Click() procedure also updates the title of the program's window by calling the SetWindowTitle() procedure:

```
SetWindowTitle
```

This action is necessary because the name of the open WAV file has been changed, and the program's window title should reflect this change.

The `mnuFileType_Click()` Procedure

The `mnuFileType_Click()` procedure is automatically executed whenever the user selects File Type from the File menu. This procedure displays a message box with information about the currently open WAV file. (See Figure E.32.) Here is the code of the `mnuFileType_Click()` procedure:

```
Sub mnuFileType_Click ()

    Dim Length
    Dim NumChannels
    Dim BitsPerSample
    Dim Msg

    ' Get the length, number of channels, and number
    ' of bits per sample of the WAV file.
    Length = Str(TegommWav.Length)
    NumChannels = Str(TegommWav.Channels)
    BitsPerSample = Str(TegommWav.BitsPerSample)

    ' Prepare the message.
    Msg = gWavNameNoPath
    Msg = Msg + Chr(13) + Chr(13)
    Msg = Msg + "Length: " + Length + " Samples"
    Msg = Msg + Chr(13) + Chr(13)
    Msg = Msg + "Channels: " + NumChannels
    Msg = Msg + Chr(13) + Chr(13)
    Msg = Msg + "Bits Per Sample: " + BitsPerSample

    ' Display the message.
    MsgBox Msg, MB_ICONINFORMATION, "Wave Editor"

End Sub
```

As you can see, the `mnuFileType_Click()` procedure simply displays inside a message box the FileName, Length, NumChannels, and BitsPerSample properties of the multimedia control. As discussed earlier, when the NumChannels property is 1, the WAV file is a mono WAV file. When NumChannels is 2, the WAV file is a stereo WAV file.

The `mnuZoomIn_Click()` Procedure

The `mnuZoomIn_Click()` procedure is automatically executed whenever the user selects Zoom In from the View menu. Recall that selecting Zoom In from the File menu has the same effect as clicking the Zoom In button. Therefore, the `mnuZoomIn_Click()` procedure simply calls the `cmdZoomIn_Click()` procedure:

```
Sub mnuZoomIn_Click ()

    cmdZoomIn_Click

End Sub
```

The `mnuZoomOut_Click()` **Procedure**

The `mnuZoomOut_Click()` procedure is automatically executed whenever the user selects Zoom Out from the View menu. Recall that selecting Zoom Out from the View menu has the same effect as clicking the Zoom Out button. Therefore, the `mnuZoomOut_Click()` procedure simply calls the `cmdZoomOut_Click()` procedure:

```
Sub mnuZoomOut_Click ()

    cmdZoomOut_Click

End Sub
```

The `mnuSelectAll_Click()` **Procedure**

The `mnuSelectAll_Click()` procedure is automatically executed whenever the user selects Select All from the Edit menu. This procedure displays the selection rectangle over the entire graph area. Rather than using the mouse to select the entire graph area, the user can select Select All from the Edit menu, and the selection rectangle will enclose the entire graph area. Here is the code of the `mnuSelectAll_Click()` procedure:

```
Sub mnuSelectAll_Click ()

Dim X As Single, Y As Single

' Simulate a mouse down event at the left-most point
' of the X axis.
X = linX.X1
Y = linX.Y1
Form_MouseDown 0, 0, X, Y

' Simulate a mouse move event at the right-most point
' of the X axis.
X = linX.X2
Y = linX.Y1
Form_MouseMove 0, 0, X, Y

' Simulate a mouse up event.
X = linX.X2
Y = linX.Y1
Form_MouseUp 0, 0, X, Y

End Sub
```

The first three statements of the `mnuSelectAll_Click()` procedure

```
X = linX.X1
Y = linX.Y1
Form_MouseDown 0, 0, X, Y
```

simulate a Mouse Down event. These statements have the same effect as the user pressing down the mouse button at the extreme left point on the X-axis of the graph. This simulation of a Mouse Down

event is accomplished by calling the Form_MouseDown() procedure, with the X and Y parameters specifying the coordinate of the extreme left point on the X-axis of the graph. (Recall that the X-axis is the linX line.)

The next three statements

```
X = linX.X2
Y = linX.Y1
Form_MouseMove 0, 0, X, Y
```

simulate a Mouse Move event at the extreme right point of the X-axis. These statements have the same effect as the user moving the mouse over the extreme right point on the X-axis of the graph. This simulation of a Mouse Move event is accomplished by calling the Form_MouseMove() procedure, with the X and Y parameters specifying the coordinate of the extreme right point on the X-axis of the graph.

The last three statements in the procedure

```
X = linX.X2
Y = linX.Y1
Form_MouseUp 0, 0, X, Y
```

simulate a Mouse Up event at the extreme right point of the X-axis. These statements have the same effect as the user releasing the mouse button over the extreme right point on the X-axis of the graph. This simulation of a Mouse Up event is accomplished by calling the Form_MouseUp() procedure, with the X and Y parameters specifying the coordinate of the extreme right point on the X-axis of the graph.

So the code of the mnuSelectAll_Click() procedure simulates the following sequence of events:

1. The user presses the mouse button over the extreme left point on the X-axis of the graph.
2. The user moves the mouse over the extreme right point on the X-axis of the graph.
3. The user releases the mouse button over the extreme right point on the X-axis of the graph.

This sequence of events simulates the action of the user selecting the entire graph area using the mouse.

The Form_Paint() Procedure

The Form_Paint() procedure of the frmWEdit form (the main window of the Wave Editor program) is automatically executed whenever the form needs to be repainted. When the user minimizes the form and then brings it back to the original size, for example, the form has to be repainted, so the Form_Paint() procedure is executed automatically. The code of the Form_Paint() procedure has to repaint the graph of the WAV file. Here is the code of the Form_Paint() procedure:

```
Sub Form_Paint ()
```

```
' Update the graph.
UpdateGraph

End Sub
```

As you can see, the Form_Paint() procedure simply calls the UpdateGraph() procedure:

```
UpdateGraph
```

Consequently, whenever the frmWEdit form (the Wave Editor program main window) needs to be repainted, the graph of the WAV file is drawn.

The Maximum Recording Length Menu Items

You may recall that the Wave Editor program includes a Maximum Recording Length menu that lets the user select the maximum recording length. (See Figure E.28.) When the user selects the first item in this menu, 1 Megabyte, the mnuMaxRecLen1_Click() procedure is automatically executed. Here is the code of this procedure:

```
Sub mnuMaxRecLen1_Click ()

    ' Check the mnuMaxRecLen1 menu item.
    mnuMaXRecLen1.Checked = True

    ' Un-check all the other mnuMaxReclen items.
    mnuMaxRecLen2.Checked = False
    mnuMaxRecLen3.Checked = False
    mnuMaxRecLen4.Checked = False
    mnuMaXRecLenNoLimit.Checked = False

    ' Set the gMaxRecordLength variable.
    gMaxRecordLength = 1000000

End Sub
```

As you can see, this procedure performs the following tasks:

- It checks the mnuMaxRecLen1 menu item.
- It unchecks all other menu items in the Maximum Recording Length menu.
- It sets the gMaxRecordLength variable to 1000000.

Remember that the gMaxRecordLength variable is used in the cmdRecord_Click() procedure to specify the maximum recording length.

The code that is attached to the other menu items of the Maximum Recording Length menu is similar to the code for the mnuMaxRecLen1_Click() procedure. Here is this code:

```
Sub mnuMaxRecLen2_Click ()

 ' Check the mnuMaxRecLen2 menu item.
 mnuMaxRecLen2.Checked = True

 ' Un-check all the other mnuMaxReclen items.
 mnuMaXRecLen1.Checked = False
```

```
    mnuMaXRecLen3.Checked = False
    mnuMaXRecLen4.Checked = False
    mnuMaXRecLenNoLimit.Checked = False

    ' Set the gMaxRecordLength variable.
    gMaxRecordLength = 2000000

End Sub

Sub mnuMaxRecLen3_Click ()

    ' Check the mnuMaxRecLen3 menu item.
    mnuMaXRecLen3.Checked = True

    ' Un-check all the other mnuMaxReclen items.
    mnuMaXRecLen1.Checked = False
    mnuMaXRecLen2.Checked = False
    mnuMaXRecLen4.Checked = False
    mnuMaXRecLenNoLimit.Checked = False

    ' Set the gMaxRecordLength variable.
    gMaxRecordLength = 1000000

End Sub

Sub mnuMaxRecLen4_Click ()

    ' Check the mnuMaxRecLen4 menu item.
    mnuMaXRecLen4.Checked = True

    ' Un-check all the other mnuMaxReclen items.
    mnuMaXRecLen1.Checked = False
    mnuMaXRecLen2.Checked = False
    mnuMaXRecLen3.Checked = False
    mnuMaXRecLenNoLimit.Checked = False

    ' Set the gMaxRecordLength variable.
    gMaxRecordLength = 4000000

End Sub

Sub mnuMaxRecLenNoLimit_Click ()

    Dim Answer

    ' Get confirmation from user.
    Answer = MsgBox("Are you sure you want the recording length
                 ➥ to be with no limit?", MB_YESNO +
                 ➥ MB_ICONSTOP, "Wave Editor")

    If Answer = IDYES Then

        ' Check the mnuMaxRecLenNoLimit menu item.
        mnuMaXRecLenNoLimit.Checked = True

        ' Un-check all the other mnuMaxReclen items.
        mnuMaXRecLen1.Checked = False
        mnuMaXRecLen2.Checked = False
```

```
mnuMaXRecLen3.Checked = False
mnuMaXRecLen4.Checked = False

' Set the gMaxRecordLength variable.
gMaxRecordLength = 0

End If

End Sub
```

The mnuGreen_Click() Procedure

The mnuGreen_Click() procedure is automatically executed whenever the user selects Green from the Colors menu. The Colors menu is displayed when the user selects Colors from the Options menu. (See Figure E.33.) The purpose of the mnuGreen_Click() procedure is to set the background color of the program's main window to green. Here is the code of the mnuGreen_Click() procedure:

```
Sub mnuGreen_Click ()

' Set the background color to green.
gBackgroundColor = 2
SetbackgroundColor

' Check the Green menu item.
mnuGreen.Checked = True

' Un-check the White menu item.
mnuWhite.Checked = False

' Update the graph.
UpdateGraph

End Sub
```

The first two statements of the mnuGreen_Click() procedure

```
gBackgroundColor = 2
SetbackgroundColor
```

set to green the background color of the frmWEdit form and the controls inside it. The SetBackgroundColor() procedure uses the gBackground variable to specify the background color of the form and the controls. When gBackgroundColor is set to 2, SetBackgroundColor() sets the background color of the controls to QBColor(2), which is green. The gBackgroundColor variable is also used by other procedures in the program. Whenever there is a need to clear the selection rectangle, for example, the selection rectangle is cleared by drawing a rectangle with a color of gBackgroundColor.

The next two statements

```
mnuGreen.Checked = True
mnuWhite.Checked = False
```

check the Green menu item and uncheck the White menu item.

The last statement in the procedure

```
UpdateGraph
```

calls the UpdateGraph() procedure so that the graph is displayed on the new background color.

The mnuWhite_Click() Procedure

The mnuWhite_Click() procedure is automatically executed whenever the user selects White from the Colors menu. This procedure sets the background color of the program's main window to white. Here is the code of the mnuWhite_Click() procedure:

```
Sub mnuWhite_Click ()

  ' Set the background color to white.
  gBackgroundColor = 15
  SetbackgroundColor

  ' Check the White menu item.
  mnuWhite.Checked = True

  ' Un-check the Green menu item.
  mnuGreen.Checked = False

  ' Update the graph.
  UpdateGraph

End Sub
```

As you can see, the code of the mnuWhite_Click() procedure is similar to the code of the mnuGreen_Click() procedure.

The mnuAbout_Click() Procedure

The mnuAbout_Click() procedure is automatically executed whenever the user selects About from the Help menu. This procedure simply displays an About message box. (See Figure E.36.) Here is the code of the mnuAbout_Click() procedure:

```
Sub mnuAbout_Click ()

  Dim Msg

  ' Prepare the message.
  Msg = "Wave Editor Version 1.0"
  Msg = Msg + Chr(13)
  Msg = Msg + Chr(13)
  Msg = Msg + "Copyright (C) 1990-1994 TegoSoft Inc."
  Msg = Msg + Chr(13)
  Msg = Msg + Chr(13)
  Msg = Msg + "TegoSoft Inc."
  Msg = Msg + Chr(13)
```

```
Msg = Msg + "P.O. Box 389"
Msg = Msg + Chr(13)
Msg = Msg + "Bellmore, NY 11710"
Msg = Msg + Chr(13)
Msg = Msg + Chr(13)
Msg = Msg + "Phone: (516)783-4824"

' Display the message.
MsgBox Msg, 0, "About Wave Editor"

End Sub
```

The mnuInfo_Click() Procedure

The mnuInfo_Click() procedure is automatically executed whenever the user selects Info from the Help menu. This procedure simply displays an Information message box. (See Figure E.35.) Here is the code of the mnuInfo_Click() procedure:

```
Sub mnuInfo_Click ()

Dim Msg

' Prepare the message.
Msg = Msg + "This Wave Editor was written with "
Msg = Msg + "Visual Basic for Windows, using the "
Msg = Msg + "TegoMM.VBX control. The TegoMM.VBX control "
Msg = Msg + "is an advanced multimedia control that "
Msg = Msg + "enables programmers to incorporate "
Msg = Msg + "multimedia into their programs with great "
Msg = Msg + "ease."
Msg = Msg + Chr(13) + Chr(13)
Msg = Msg + "The TegoMM.VBX control can be used to play "
Msg = Msg + "and control multimedia devices and files "
Msg = Msg + "such as:  WAV files, MIDI files, Video "
Msg = Msg + "files, and CD ROM drive (CD audio)."
Msg = Msg + Chr(13) + Chr(13)
Msg = Msg + "The TegoMM.VBX control also supports "
Msg = Msg + "playback of WAV files through the PC speaker "
Msg = Msg + "for PCs that do not have a sound card."
Msg = Msg + Chr(13) + Chr(13)
Msg = Msg + "The TegoMM.VBX control that is included "
Msg = Msg + "with the book's CD, is the limited version "
Msg = Msg + "of the control. The price of the "
Msg = Msg + "full-version TegoMM.VBX control is $29.95 "
Msg = Msg + "(plus $5.00 for shipping and handling). To "
Msg = Msg + "order the full version of the control send "
Msg = Msg + "check or money order to:"
Msg = Msg + Chr(13)
Msg = Msg + "TegoSoft Inc. Box 389 Bellmore, NY 11710"
Msg = Msg + Chr(13)
Msg = Msg + "Phone: (516)783-4824"

' Display the message.
MsgBox Msg, 0, "Information"

End Sub
```

The mnuExit_Click() Procedure

The mnuExit_Click() procedure is automatically executed whenever the user selects Exit from the File menu. This procedure terminates the program by unloading the frmWEdit form. Here is the code of the mnuExit_Click() procedure:

```
Sub mnuExit_Click ()

    Unload frmWEdit

End Sub
```

The Form_Unload() Procedure

The Form_Unload() procedure (of the frmWEdit form) is automatically executed whenever the form is unloaded, such as when the user closes the form by double-clicking the minus icon of the form. The Form_Unload() procedure is also executed after the user selects Exit from the File menu, because in the mnuExit_Click() procedure you wrote code that unloads the frmWEdit form.

The purpose of the Form_Unload() procedure is to give the user an opportunity to save the open WAV file (if the WAV file has been changed) before the form is unloaded. Here is the code of the Form_Unload() procedure:

```
Sub Form_Unload (Cancel As Integer)

 Dim Msg, Answer

 ' Before ending the program, check
 ' if the current WAV file has changed, and if
 ' it has, give the user a chance to save it.
 If gWavFileHasChanged = True Then
    Msg = gWavNameNoPath + Chr(13)
    Msg = Msg + "The WAV file has changed." + Chr(13)
    Msg = Msg + "Do you want to save current changes?"
    Answer = MsgBox(Msg, MB_ICONEXCLAMATION +
            ➥ MB_YESNOCANCEL, "Wave Editor")
    If Answer = IDYES Then
       mnuSave_Click
    End If
    If Answer = IDCANCEL Then
       Cancel = True
    End If
 End If

End Sub
```

As you can see, if the user has made changes to the WAV file (that is, gWavFileHasChanged is True) the Form_Unload() procedure displays a dialog box asking the user if the changes should be saved. If the user clicks the Yes button, the WAV file is saved. If the user clicks the No button, the WAV file is not saved. If the user clicks the Cancel button, the termination of the program is canceled by setting the Cancel parameter of the procedure to True:

```
If Answer = IDCANCEL Then
```

```
   Cancel = True
End If
```

When the Cancel parameter is set to True, the unloading of the form is canceled, and as a result the form is not unloaded.

16-bit and Stereo WAV Files

The current version of the Wave Editor program supports only 8-bit mono WAV files. When the user tries to open a WAV file that is not an 8-bit mono type, the program displays an error message box (refer to the code of the mnuOpen_Click() procedure, earlier in this appendix).

In the following sections you will learn how to enhance the Wave Editor program so that it also supports 16-bit and stereo WAV files.

To make the Wave Editor program support 16-bit and stereo WAV files, you don't have to add much code. In fact, most of the code in the current version stays as is. The only code you have to change is the code that accesses the samples.

Code for such tasks as playing the WAV file, recording sound into the WAV file, deleting samples from the WAV file, copying samples to the Clipboard, and pasting samples from the Clipboard all remains the same.

Determining the Type of WAV File

To determine the type of WAV file, you need to use the BitsPerSample and Channels properties of the multimedia control.

If the WAV file is an 8-bit type, the BitsPerSample property of the multimedia control reports 8. If the WAV file is a 16-bit type, the BitsPerSample property reports 16.

If the WAV file is a mono type, the Channels property reports 1. If the WAV file is stereo, the Channels property reports 2.

The following code shows how the BitsPerSample and Channels properties are used:

```
If TegommWav.BitsPerSample = 8 Then
   MsgBox "This is an 8-bit WAV file."
End If

If TegommWav.BitsPerSample = 16 Then
   MsgBox "This is a 16-bit WAV file."
End If

If TegommWav.Channels = 1 Then
   MsgBox "This is a mono WAV file."
End If

If TegommWav.Channels = 2 Then
   MsgBox "This is a stereo WAV file."
End If
```

Accessing Samples of 8-bit and 16-bit WAV Files

The following examples illustrate how to access samples of 8-bit and 16-bit WAV files, and how to display the values of the accessed samples as vertical lines, or bars.

Example 1 shows how to access and display a sample from an 8-bit mono WAV file. You already know how to do that because the Wave Editor program displays graphs of 8-bit mono WAV files. Example 2 shows how to access and display samples of a 16-bit WAV file.

Example 1

The following code extracts the value of sample number 500 of an 8-bit mono WAV file and draws a vertical line (bar) that corresponds to the extracted value. The line is drawn from a point whose coordinate is X,Y (where X and Y are constants).

```
TegommWav.SampleNumber = 500
Sample = TegommWav.SampleValue1 - 128
Line (X, Y)-(X, Y - Sample)
```

In this code, 128 is subtracted from the value of the sample. This subtraction is necessary because in an 8-bit mono WAV file, the midpoint value of a sample is 128. Therefore, any sample whose value is 128 is drawn as a line of zero length (because 128-128=0):

```
Line (X, Y)-(X, Y - 0)
```

Any sample whose value is larger than 128 is drawn as a vertical line above the X,Y point. For example, a sample whose value is 129 is drawn as a vertical line above the X,Y point, with a length of 1 (because 129-128=1):

```
Line (X, Y)-(X, Y - 1)
```

Any sample whose value is smaller than 128 is drawn as a vertical line below the X,Y point. For example, a sample whose value is 127 is drawn as a vertical line below the X,Y point, with a length of 1 (because 127-128=-1).

In an 8-bit WAV file, the maximum value of a sample is 255 and the minimum value is 0. The largest positive sample, therefore, is drawn as a vertical line above the X,Y point, with a length of 255-128=127. The largest negative sample is drawn as a vertical line below the X,Y point, with a length of 0-128=-128.

Example 2

The following code extracts the value of sample number 500 of a 16 bit mono WAV file and draws a vertical line (bar) that corresponds to the extracted value. The line is drawn from a point whose coordinate is X,Y (where X and Y are constants).

```
TegommWav.SampleNumber = 500
Sample = TegommWav.SampleValue1 / 250
Line (X, Y)-(X, Y - Sample)
```

In this code, the value of the sample is divided by 250. This scale-down is necessary because in a 16-bit WAV file the maximum value of a sample is 32767, and a line with a length of 32767 will not fit on the screen. Any sample whose value is 0 (the midpoint value) is drawn as a line of zero length (because 0/250=0):

```
Line (X, Y)-(X, Y - 0)
```

Any sample whose value is larger than 0 is drawn as a vertical line above the X,Y point. For example, a sample whose value is 20000 is drawn as a vertical line above the X,Y point, with a length of 80 (because 20000/250=80):

```
Line (X, Y)-(X, Y - 80)
```

Any sample whose value is smaller than 0 is drawn as a vertical line below the X,Y point. For example, a sample whose value is -3000 is drawn as a vertical line below the X,Y point, with a length of 12 (because -3000/250=-12).

Note that in a 16-bit WAV file the maximum value of a sample is 32767 and the minimum value is -32768. The largest positive sample, therefore, is drawn as a vertical line above the X,Y point, with a length of 32767/250=131. The largest negative sample is drawn as a vertical line below the X,Y point, with a length of -32768/250=-131.

> **NOTE**
>
> As stated earlier, the best way to access the samples of a WAV file is to use the sample access functions of the TegoMM.VBX control: `tegGetByte()`, `tegSetByte()`, `tegGetWord()`, and `tegSetWord()`. Using these functions is much more efficient than using the SampleValue1 and SampleValue2 properties. To see sample code that uses these functions, refer to the code of the `mnuSilence_Click()`, `mnuIncreaseVolume_Click()`, and `mnuDecreaseVolume_Click()` procedures.

Accessing Samples in a Stereo WAV File

A stereo WAV file has two channels (left and right). To access a sample in the left channel, you use the SampleValue1 property. To access a sample in the right channel, you use the SampleValue2 property.

For example, the following statements extract sample number 50 of the left channel:

```
TegommWav.SampleNumber = 50
Sample = TegommWav.SampleValue1
```

Similarly, the following statements extract sample number 50 of the right channel:

```
TegommWav.SampleNumber = 50
Sample = TegommWav.SampleValue2
```

After you extract a sample from the left or right channel of a stereo WAV file, you display it the same way you display samples of a mono WAV file. That is, a stereo WAV file can also be an 8-bit type or a 16-bit type, and depending on which type it is, you display the sample accordingly. Because a stereo WAV file has two channels, you can write a program that displays two graphs on the screen—one graph for the left channel and one graph for the right channel.

F

Video for Windows

In Chapter 4, "Creating Multimedia Programs (Part I)," and Chapter 5, "Creating Multimedia Programs (Part II)," you implemented the AllMedia program, which enables the user to play various multimedia devices and files, including AVI video files. Before you can play AVI video files your system must have the proper Video for Windows drivers. In this appendix you'll learn how to check whether your system has the AVI Video for Windows drivers installed and how to install these drivers in case they are not already installed.

Before You Can Play Video Files on Your PC. . .

Before you can play video files on your PC, you have to install special software drivers that enable your Windows system to play video files.

To see if your Windows system currently has the necessary software drivers for playing video files, complete the following steps:

❑ Start the Media Player program of Windows by double-clicking the Media Player icon. (See Figure F.1.) (The Media Player program usually resides inside the Accessories group of programs.)

Windows responds by running the Media Player program. (See Figure F.2.)

Figure F.1.
The icon of the Media Player program.

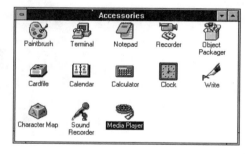

Figure F.2.
The Media Player program.

If your Windows system has the software drivers needed for playing video files, your Media Player program can play video files.

To see if your Media Player program can play video files do the following:

❑ Open the Device menu of Media Player. (See Figure F.3.)

Figure F.3.
The Media Player Device
menu.

As you can see from Figure F.3, one of the items in the Device menu is Video for Windows. If the Device menu of your Media Player program does not include this item, your Windows system does not have the software drivers necessary to play AVI video files.

The following section describes how to install the software drivers necessary for playing video files.

Installing the Video for Windows Software Drivers

If the Device menu of your Media Player program does not include the Video for Windows option, your Windows system does not have the necessary software drivers for playing video files.

To install the Video for Windows software drivers, you need to run a special Setup program that installs all the necessary video drivers. After running this Setup program, you will be able to play video files in Windows. This Setup program is included with the book's CD.

To install the Video for Windows software drivers using the Setup program that is included with the book's CD, complete the following steps:

☐ Insert a blank, formatted disk in your A: drive.

☐ Insert the book's CD into your CD-ROM drive.

☐ Copy all the files from the \LEARNVB\VIDEO directory of the book's CD into the root directory of the A: drive.

☐ Select Run from the File menu of the Program Manager and execute the A:\SETUP.EXE program.

> *Windows responds by running the SETUP program. The SETUP program initializes itself, and after a while it displays a Welcome dialog box. (See Figures F.4 and F.5.)*

Figure F.4.
The SETUP program
initializing itself.

Figure F.5.
The SETUP program's
Welcome dialog box.

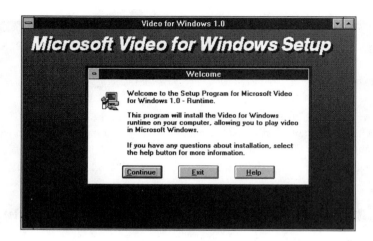

❏ Click the Continue button of the Welcome dialog box.

> *The SETUP program responds by installing all the necessary video software drivers in your*
> *Windows system. When the installation is complete, the SETUP program displays a Setup*
> *Successful dialog box. (See Figure F.6.)*

Figure F.6.
The SETUP program's
Setup Successful dialog box.

❏ Click the OK button of the Setup Successful dialog box.

Now that you have finished installing the Video for Windows software drivers, you can start play-ing video files.

The following section describes how to play a video file with the Media Player program of Win-dows. Alternatively, you can play AVI video files by using the AllMedia program, which is discussed in Chapters 4 and 5.

Playing a Video File with Media Player

Windows-compatible video files have an AVI file extension (for example, MyMovie.AVI). Just as WAV files are used in Windows to play sound, AVI files are used to play movies.

In the following steps, you will use Media Player to play an AVI file that is included on this book's CD. This AVI file is called MOVIE.AVI.

> **NOTE**
>
> The book's CD includes a sample AVI file called MOVIE.AVI. When you installed the book's CD, the MOVIE.AVI file was copied to your \LEARNVB\AVI directory.

To play the MOVIE.AVI video file with Media Player do the following:

☐ Double-click the icon of the Media Player program. (See Figure F.1.)

> *Windows responds by running the Media Player program. (See Figure F.2.)*

☐ Select Video for Windows from the Device menu of Media Player. (See Figure F.3.)

> *Media Player responds by displaying an Open dialog box. (See Figure F.7.)*

Figure F.7.
The Media Player Open dialog box.

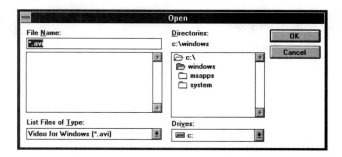

☐ Select the file C:\LEARNVB\AVI\MOVIE.AVI.

> *Media Player responds by opening the MOVIE.AVI video file and by displaying the first frame (that is, picture) of the movie.*

To start playing the movie do the following:

☐ Click the Media Player Play button (the Play button is the extreme left button).

> *Media Player responds by playing the MOVIE.AVI video file.*

To stop the playback of the file do the following:

☐ Click the Stop button (the Stop button is the second button from the left).

You can use the horizontal scroll bar of Media Player to navigate to a particular frame in the movie. For example, to start the playback from the middle of the movie, drag the thumb tab of the horizontal scroll bar to the middle of the scroll bar, and then click the Play button.

To terminate the Media Player program do the following:

☐ Select Exit from the Media Player File menu.

Creating Your Own Video Files

To create a video file yourself, you need the following hardware and software:

- A video device such as a VCR or a camcorder.
- A video capture card.
- A video capture program.

You create the video file by connecting the video device (that is, the VCR or camcorder) to the video card with cables. The video capture program processes the video that is received from the video device, and it creates the video file. (See Figure F.8.)

Figure F.8.
Creating your own video
file.

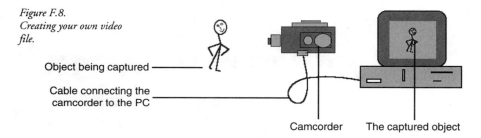

Object being captured

Cable connecting the
camcorder to the PC

Camcorder   The captured object

Index

SYMBOLS

Index

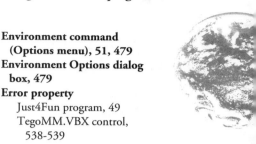

*I
n
d
e
x*

I n d e x

What's on the CD-ROM

The CD-ROM for *How to Create Real-World Applications with Visual Basic* contains

- ❏ All the source code and executable programs that are presented in the book
- ❏ Picture files (BMP files) that the programs need
- ❏ Icon files (ICO files) used by the programs
- ❏ Movie files (AVI files) used by the programs
- ❏ WAV files (sound files) used by the programs
- ❏ MIDI files (music files) used by the programs
- ❏ DDLs, VBXs, and other files that are needed for the execution of some of the EXE files
- ❏ The source code of the tutorial that teaches you how to create your own VBX files

Installing the CD-ROM

Portions of the companion CD-ROM must be installed to your hard drive. The installation program runs from within Windows. (Note: To install the files from the CD-ROM, you'll need at least 12MB of free space on your hard drive.)

1. From File Manager or Program Manager, choose **R**un from the **F**ile menu.
2. Type `<drive>INSTALL` and press Enter, where `<drive>` is the letter of the CD-ROM drive that contains the installation disc. For example, if the disc in drive D:, type `D:INSTALL` and press Enter.

Follow the on-screen instructions in the installation program. The files will be installed in the \LEARNVB directory, unless you chose a different directory during installation. Be sure to look at the README.TXT file in the root directory of the disc and the file displayed at the end of the installation process; they contain information on the files and programs that were installed.

Add to Your Sams Library Today with the Best Books for Programming, Operating Systems, and New Technologies

The easiest way to order is to pick up the phone and call

1-800-428-5331

between 9:00 a.m. and 5:00 p.m. EST.

For faster service please have your credit card available.

ISBN	Quantity	Description of Item	Unit Cost	Total Cost
0-672-30378-7		Teach Yourself Visual Basic 3.0 in 21 Days	$29.95	
0-672-30514-3		Master Visual Basic 3 (Book/CD-ROM)	$45.00	
0-672-30437-6		Secrets of the Visual Basic 3 Masters, Second Edition (Book/Disk)	$34.95	
0-672-30447-3		Teach Yourself Visual Basic for Applications in 21 Days	$29.99	
0-672-30440-6		Database Developer's Guide with Visual Basic 3 (Book/Disk)	$44.95	
0-672-30453-8		Access 2 Developer's Guide, Second Edition (Book/Disk)	$44.95	
0-672-30160-1		Multimedia Developer's Guide (Book/CD-ROM)	$49.95	
0-672-30468-6		Master Visual C++ 1.5 (Book/CD-ROM)	$49.95	
❏ 3 ½" Disk		Shipping and Handling: See information below.		
❏ 5 ¼" Disk		TOTAL		

Shipping and Handling: $4.00 for the first book, and $1.75 for each additional book. Floppy disk: add $1.75 for shipping and handling. If you need to have it NOW, we can ship product to you in 24 hours for an additional charge of approximately $18.00, and you will receive your item overnight or in two days. Overseas shipping and handling adds $2.00 per book and $8.00 for up to three disks. Prices subject to change. Call for availability and pricing information on latest editions.

201 W. 103rd Street, Indianapolis, Indiana 46290

1-800-428-5331 — Orders   1-800-835-3202 — FAX   1-800-858-7674 — Customer Service

Book ISBN 0-672-30621-2

GO AHEAD. PLUG YOURSELF INTO
MACMILLAN COMPUTER PUBLISHING.

Introducing the Macmillan Computer Publishing Forum on CompuServe®

Yes, it's true. Now, you can have CompuServe access to the same professional, friendly folks who have made computers easier for years. On the Macmillan Computer Publishing Forum, you'll find additional information on the topics covered by every Macmillan Computer Publishing imprint—including Que, Sams Publishing, New Riders Publishing, Alpha Books, Brady Books, Hayden Books, and Adobe Press. In addition, you'll be able to receive technical support and disk updates for the software produced by Que Software and Paramount Interactive, a division of the Paramount Technology Group. It's a great way to supplement the best information in the business.

WHAT CAN YOU DO ON THE MACMILLAN COMPUTER PUBLISHING FORUM?

Play an important role in the publishing process—and make our books better while you make your work easier:

- ■ Leave messages and ask questions about Macmillan Computer Publishing books and software—you're guaranteed a response within 24 hours
- ■ Download helpful tips and software to help you get the most out of your computer
- ■ Contact authors of your favorite Macmillan Computer Publishing books through electronic mail
- ■ Present your own book ideas
- ■ Keep up to date on all the latest books available from each of Macmillan Computer Publishing's exciting imprints

JOIN NOW AND GET A FREE COMPUSERVE STARTER KIT!

To receive your free CompuServe Introductory Membership, call toll-free, **1-800-848-8199** and ask for representative **#597**. The Starter Kit Includes:

- ■ Personal ID number and password
- ■ $15 credit on the system
- ■ Subscription to CompuServe Magazine

HERE'S HOW TO PLUG INTO MACMILLAN COMPUTER PUBLISHING:

Once on the CompuServe System, type any of these phrases to access the Macmillan Computer Publishing Forum:

GO MACMILLAN   **GO BRADY**
GO QUEBOOKS   **GO HAYDEN**
GO SAMS   **GO QUESOFT**
GO NEWRIDERS   **GO ALPHA**

Once you're on the CompuServe Information Service, be sure to take advantage of all of CompuServe's resources. CompuServe is home to more than 1,700 products and services—plus it has over 1.5 million members worldwide. You'll find valuable online reference materials, travel and investor services, electronic mail, weather updates, leisure-time games and hassle-free shopping (no jam-packed parking lots or crowded stores).

Seek out the hundreds of other forums that populate CompuServe. Covering diverse topics such as pet care, rock music, cooking, and political issues, you're sure to find others with the same concerns as you—and expand your knowledge at the same time.